Paralegals and Tribunal Practice and Procedure

Second Edition

Irv Ash

SCHOOL OF LEGAL AND PUBLIC ADMINISTRATION
Seneca College

Captus Press

Paralegals and Tribunal Practice and Procedure, Second Edition

© 2011 by Irv Ash and Captus Press Inc.

Captus Press Inc.
Mail: Units 14 & 15
         1600 Steeles Avenue West
         Concord, Ontario
         Canada   L4K 4M2
Telephone: (416) 736–5537
Fax: (416) 736–5793
Email: info@captus.com
Internet: http://www.captus.com

Library and Archives Canada Cataloguing in Publication

Ash, Irv
    Paralegals and tribunal practice and procedure / Irv Ash. — 2nd ed.

Includes text of Statutory Powers Procedure Act (Ontario).
    Includes bibliographical references.
ISBN 978-1-55322-238-5

1. Administrative procedure — Ontario.   2. Administrative courts — Ontario.
3. Ontario. Statutory Powers Procedure Act.   4. Administrative courts — Canada.
I. Title.

KEO891.A84 2011   342.713'0664   C2010-907743-1
KF5417.A84 2011

Canada ⋯ *We acknowledge the financial support of the Government of Canada through the Canada Book Fund for our publishing activities.*

0 9 8 7 6 5 4 3 2 1
Printed in Canada

Contents

3   Advocacy before Administrative Agencies   73

Part II
Selected Ontario Agencies

4   Social Benefits Tribunal.   85

Part III
Selected Federal Agencies

DEDICATION AND ACKNOWLEDGEMENTS

This book is dedicated to my wonderful and lovely wife Irene — for just being her.

I acknowledge everyone at Captus Press who assisted in the production of this book especially Pauline Lai. I appreciate all the help received from various people in many Ontario agencies, with contents and suggestions made, as well as various members of SOAR. Further, a nod to my colleagues at Seneca College, who were helpful to my growth as a communicator. I also wish to thank my friend, Pat Goodman, for her typing services when needed and my brother, Mel Ash.

For this new edition, I want to also acknowledge many of my students at Seneca College who used the first edition and enthusiastically pointed out out errors and typos, which have been corrected in this edition. Any still existing errors and typos in this second edition are strictly the fault of the author.

PREFACE

This book will discuss administrative law in Canada with an emphasis on selected administrative agencies, both federally and in Ontario. The author's intent is to provide aspiring and current paralegals and other interested persons with some basic concepts of administrative law. The duty to act fairly (previously the rules of natural justice), both in common law and under constitutional law, and specifically as codified under the Ontario *Statutory Powers Procedure Act* is reviewed. As well, there is a discussion of practical advocacy in administrative agency settings. The book will then explore some Ontario and federal agencies where paralegals will likely represent clients. Each agency's website will be examined for the following: (a) the enabling legislation creating and/or empowering the agency; (b) the procedures and rules governing the agency as found in rules, practice directions, forms, and policies; (c) the explanatory literature about and from the agency; (d) relevant court cases dealing with agency decisions and some agency decisions to highlight how agencies make decisions and how such decisions are viewed by the courts; and (e) some relevant forms and brochures, provided in this book as part of an appendix to each agency chapter. The examination of a number of agencies should provide readers with useful information about the agencies, as well as a template to for locating useful information about any other agency.

Part I

General Principles

1

Basic Concepts of Administrative Law

LEARNING OBJECTIVES

After reading this chapter, the reader should be able to:

- define administrative law
- differentiate between the three branches or functions of government
- elaborate on various concepts of public policy
- explain the reasons for, the types of, and the functions of agencies
- compare and contrast agencies and courts
- identify specific rules and procedures for a specific agency
- assess the relevant provisions of the *Statutory Powers Procedure Act* as they relate to the rules and procedure of Ontario agencies
- document how various sections of the *Charter of Rights and Freedoms* have been applied to agency proceedings
- illustrate and discuss principles that flow from the duty to act fairly
- distinguish between the remedies of reconsideration, appeal, and judicial review that may be available in respect of an agency proceeding
- outline various concerns in respect of appealing an agency proceeding
- summarize the various remedies available from an agency proceeding pursuant to judicial review

INTRODUCTION

In the past 30 years, the number of court cases involving administrative law has increased tremendously. The reason for the increase is tied to both the unprecedented growth of government in Canada and the definition of administrative law. The definition involves government and governmental delegates, the legal restrictions imposed on the government when implementing public policy, and the remedies available to persons "harmed" by the misuse of governmental power. This chapter will attempt, in varying detail, to deal with each component of this definition.

The courts have been given **jurisdiction**, both **inherent** and **statutory**, to oversee and remedy many governmental actions. This jurisdiction, or power, derives in common law from the *Magna Carta* in 1215 and has been strengthened over the years by various statutes and case law. Furthermore, in Canada, greater jurisdiction has been given to the courts by the constitutional documents that instituted and regulate the country, and by the federal–provincial split of jurisdictional powers. Before delving into various aspects of administrative law, it is necessary to review some aspects of government and the Canadian Constitution and to further discuss the concept of public policy and how it is legislated and enforced in the Canadian legal system.

BRANCHES OF GOVERNMENT

Canada has three branches (or functions) of government. The legislative (or parliamentary) branch includes elected Members of Parliament, both federal and provincial, and the federally appointed Senate. The major task of this branch is to introduce, debate, and institute new legislation, and to amend and/or repeal existing legislation. Once the legislation is enacted and **proclaimed in force**, it is the main duty of the executive branch (consisting of the Cabinets, both federal and provincial, and the attendant civil servants) to ensure compliance with each statute by means of governmental policy instruments (regulations and orders-in-council) that may be in force. This is achieved through the work of government ministries, departments, and agencies, as well as through boards, commissions, and tribunals. The third branch of government, the judicial branch (consisting of the persons in the legal system, i.e., judges, lawyers, and court administration staff), has basic obligations to interpret the legislation in specific cases in order to resolve disputes. If no relevant legislation is specified, the judicial branch must also determine the law to be applied. In addition to this basic obligation to interpret the legislation put before them, the courts' powers also include a review component. The courts oversee not only the appropriate exercise of substantive powers of government (constitutional law) but also the exercise of government's procedural powers (administrative law).

PUBLIC POLICY

It should be noted that almost all legislation is initiated by the governing party. By starting the legislative process, and then shepherding it to its conclusion, the governing party is putting into law parts of its governmental or public policy. This is just one facet of public policy that can be defined as a "conscious choice [of government or governmental authority] that leads to deliberate action — the passage of a law, the spending of money, an official speech or gesture, or some observable act — or inaction" (Stephen Brooks, *Public Policy in Canada: An Introduction* at 12). If it is conceded that the function of government is to govern, then any action taken by government in governing is public policy.

MECHANICS OF PUBLIC POLICY

Many different paths can be taken to achieve what the government of the day perceives as its objectives. A great deal of policy is developed internally in the caucus of the elected members of the governing party and through consultation with their advisors (sometimes their constituents) and the civil service. Policy is also derived from the party platform prior to elections; it can originate in various ways allowed by that party's internal constitution, and is developed in response to current issues. For example, policy actions can follow from senior ministers floating "trial balloons" at speaking engagements and in media interviews, from public hearings before standing committees of the legislature, or from reports from royal commissions appointed to investigate certain issues. Having determined the substance of the proposed public policy in a specific area, the government makes it governmental policy or law in a variety of ways that include (a) legislation, and (b) orders-in-council properly published in the **gazette**.

After the legislative function has been carried out, the next step is to enforce the legislation. If the legislation is regulatory, that is, it involves control of public and/or private sector operations in the "public interest", mechanisms will be found to achieve the desired ends. This is also the case for legislation that is operational in nature, such as legislation in respect of delivery of goods and/or services, review and/or advice, the use and conservation of resources, or legislation for disciplinary or other purposes.

Governments continue to enact and enforce more and more regulatory legislation. The main function of the executive branch of government is concerned with enforcing these laws. That function is often achieved by civil servants working for various ministries in the government, usually in specialized regulatory bodies. It should be noted that under constitutional law, the government can delegate its powers to legislate and enforce laws to bodies it creates. Such bodies shall, for the purposes of this chapter, be called agencies (including boards, commissions, authorities, committees, and tribunals). Although administrative law can, and does, deal with actions of Cabinet ministers and/or other elected members of government, it mostly involves judicial review and/or appeals (to be discussed below) by agencies.

AGENCIES

There are various reasons why a government would appoint an agency to deal with a specific area, including, but not limited to, the following:

1. Specific expertise can be developed and applied.
2. The magnitude and complexity of government and its attendant workload requires a shift in responsibilities from elected members to such experts.
3. It is more timely and cost efficient to use an agency to deal with recurrent matters.
4. It offers a more precise, yet flexible and timely, way to deal with specific situations than going through the more cumbersome elected bodies.
5. It is a way to distance the government from the public effect of certain decisions or actions.
6. It allows future unforeseen events to be dealt with more efficiently.

Because there are many and diverse reasons why agencies are created, there are many agencies in existence. In 1990, there were 485 government agencies in Ontario. By 1994, that number had grown to 716 (*Guide to Agencies, Boards and Commissions of the Government of Ontario* 1994 at 3. Toronto, Ont.: Queen's Printer, 1995).

There are three main types of agencies:

• Advisory — provide information to government that will assist in developing policy or the ongoing delivery of programs. Some examples of Ontario advisory agencies include the

Ontario Advisory Council on Senior Citizens and the Ontario Advisory Council for Disabled Persons.

- Operational — deliver goods and/or services necessary to implement approved government policy or programs. Operational agencies in Ontario include the Workplace Safety and Insurance Board and Criminal Injuries Compensation Board.

- Regulatory (which also include adjudicative bodies) — decision-making bodies that control public- or private-sector operations as authorized by their enabling legislation or the exercise of a licence-review function or an appeal function, with respect to both government and third-party decisions. The Canadian Radio and Telecommunications Commission (CRTC) and the Human Rights Tribunal of Ontario are examples of regulatory bodies.

Agencies may, if empowered, exercise legislative, executive, and judicial (adjudicative) functions. As will be discussed below, the legislative function includes the ability to make rules and regulations according to the procedure to be followed by the agency. The executive function includes research and advice on government policy, and its administration and enforcement. An agency may have any or all of the above-mentioned powers, which must be specifically delegated by the legislation that established the particular agency.

An agency is established by legislation enacted by the government. That **enabling legislation** will have provisions that may delegate power to the agency in order to carry out certain stated objectives. Such legislation will usually set out general procedures of the agency, such as who has the right to appear before such agency and the jurisdiction and powers of the agency. Furthermore, the agency may, under the legislation, be empowered to make rules and regulations regarding its own procedures. Finally, the legislation will authorize the staffing of the agency and determine who may be eligible to be employed there.

AGENCIES COMPARED TO COURTS — ADJUDICATIVE FUNCTION

One function of agencies can be adjudicative. Agencies may determine rights, privileges, and/or obligations of persons in relation to another person, or to a group or a society. An agency acting under such powers has been seen as having a **judicial or quasi-judicial function** that would seem to encroach on the judicial branch of government, that is, the court system.

There is considerable case law on the difference between the courts and agencies. Some agencies are similar to to courts, in that both interpret legislation and apply it to specific cases. However, there are differences in the two bodies (see Exhibit 1.1).

One of the most contentious issues in the court–agency comparison is how far the judiciary should go in recognizing agencies' obligations to make decisions based on public interest (or the collective good of society). Public interest is foreign to the courts, which have always looked to individual rights, first and foremost. This tension can be observed in the greater or lesser control that the courts have exercised over agencies during the past 50 years (discussed later in this chapter).

STEPS TO DETERMINE RULES OF AGENCIES

We shall next examine the legal restrictions imposed on agencies. To determine the specific rules and procedures, or legal restrictions, followed by a specific agency, the following should be reviewed:

1. Enabling statute creating the agency
2. Regulations pursuant to the enabling statute

EXHIBIT 1.1
A Comparison between Courts and Agencies

COURTS	AGENCIES
• interpret and apply the law	• formulate (by regulation), interpret, and apply the law
• *stare decisis* applied (inflexible)	• no *stare decisis*, although attempts to be relatively consistent (flexible)
• formal — specific rules and procedures to be followed	• more informal — there may or may not be specific rules and procedures to be followed, but more procedural latitude is allowed
• make decisions based strictly on law; no policy or public interest concerns	• make many decisions based on public policy
• no relationship with parties before them, either before or after hearing	• likely to have many relationships with parties, both before and after adjudication
• unlikely to have expertise in decision-making area	• usually have expertise in decision-making area

3. If applicable, general legislation that details rules and procedures applicable to certain agencies
4. *Canadian Charter of Rights and Freedoms* (Part I of the *Constitution Act 1982*, R.S.C. 1985, Appendix II, No. 44 (the *Charter*))
5. Rules, guidelines, and/or directives formulated by the agency
6. Rules set out in notices issued generally and/or for a particular proceeding
7. An overall common law requirement to "act fairly" and rules derived therefrom

Each of these steps will be discussed at some length to clarify how such rules and procedures are found.

Enabling Statute

As we saw above, agencies must be created by government statute that sets up an agency to advise on, operate in, and/or regulate a legislated area. Usually, such an enabling statute will detail the composition of the agency, its powers and jurisdiction, and, occasionally, rules and procedures. An agency that is set up under a specific enabling Act may also be named as the relevant agency to hear appeals of issues under different legislation. For example, the Social Benefits Tribunal (SBT) was created under section 60(1) of the *Ontario Works Act, 1997*, S.O. 1997, c. 25, Sched. A, as amended (*OWA*) which also gave it some of its powers and jurisdiction. The SBT was also given additional powers and jurisdiction under another empowering statute, the *Ontario Disability Support Program Act, 1997*, S.O. 1997, c. 25, Sched. B, as amended (*ODSPA*).

Regulations Pursuant to the Enabling Statute

Enabling statutes will have provisions that allow regulations to be made governing the rules and procedures to be applied by the agencies. Powers to develop and **promulgate** regulations are often granted to the Governor General in Council (federal Cabinet) or the Lieutenant Governor in Council (provincial Cabinet), depending on whether the enabling Act is federal or provincial. The procedures in respect of the SBT, for example, are prescribed in regulations by the Ontario Lieutenant Governor in Council. Such regulations will usually give details regarding documentation to be provided in a hearing, time limits with which there must be compliance, and other hearing procedures.

Legislation That Establishes Rules for Many Boards

Some provincial jurisdictions (currently Alberta and Ontario) have provisions that govern procedures of numerous agencies set out in one statute. In Ontario, the statute is entitled the *Statutory Powers Procedure Act*, R.S.O. 1990, c. S.22, as amended (*SPPA*). Originally enacted in the 1970s to provide "minimum rules for proceedings of certain tribunals", the *SPPA* was an attempt by the Ontario government to codify the rules and procedures that the court system had developed for administrative agencies over the years, through the common law "duty to act fairly" and its predecessor concept, the *"rules of natural justice"*. It was felt that there should be somewhat common rules and procedures for those agencies required to hold a hearing, that is, to exercise a "statutory power of decision".

It is important to note that the *SPPA* applies to all Ontario agencies exercising a statutory power of decision unless they are explicitly excluded by the provisions of the *SPPA* or another statute.

As initially conceived and enacted, the *SPPA* dealt with such matters as

1. determination of the parties to a proceeding;
2. notice provisions to advise of the case to be met and provision of time to prepare;
3. requirement of a public hearing unless there are reasons for a private hearing;
4. appropriate representation of parties at hearings, including examination and possibly cross-examination of witnesses;
5. powers of agencies to compel evidence;
6. rules regarding admissibility of evidence;
7. written decisions to be provided to all participants after the hearing; and
8. requirement of agencies to compile a record of the proceedings.

All of these matters are part of the common law "duty to act fairly", to be discussed later in this chapter.

Certain amendments were made in 1994 to the *SPPA*, under the *Statute Law Amendment Act (Government Management and Services)*, S.O. 1994, c. 27, that allow agencies that fall within the *SPPA* to have more cost-effective and efficient proceedings. Some of the amendments include (a) a general provision allowing any agency under the *SPPA* to make its own rules and procedures, and to promulgate them in the form of regulations; (b) a recognition of the value, where appropriate, of both written hearings and, especially, electronic hearings by amending the previous rules to allow such hearings; and (c) a provision permitting agencies to have pre-hearing conferences, determine more questions about admissibility of evidence, make interim orders, and have the power to review and vary a decision. More recent amendments to the *SPPA* in 1999 made certain changes, especially, but not limited to, inserting provisions for the appointment, with the consent of all the parties, of mediators, conciliators, and negotiators to facilitate resolution of a matter before a tribunal. This alternative dispute resolution system mirrors similar programs instituted in the civil court system to try to resolve matters without requiring the time, expense, and hard feelings of a court hearing. A further, more complete discussion of the *SPPA* appears in Chapter 2.

Charter of Rights and Freedoms

There are many general statements made in the *Charter* in terms of individual rights and freedoms. The judiciary has been given the power under the *Charter* to determine if a person's freedoms or rights have been infringed upon by some governmental law or action (including actions of agencies, as they are creations of governmental law). The judiciary has used various sections of the *Charter* to review the rules and procedures and, ultimately, the decisions of agencies.

Section 7 of the *Charter* states, "Everyone has the *right to life, liberty and security of the person* and the right not to be deprived thereof, except in accordance with the *principles of fundamental justice*" (italics added). Through a series of decisions, the Supreme Court of Canada (SCC) has read into those italicized words, principles of procedural fairness. Although such principles existed in the common law concept of the rules of natural justice, the *Charter* has entrenched those principles as part of the basic constitutional law of Canada.

After analyzing the decisions at the SCC, two leading authors on administrative law (Jones & de Villars, *Principles of Administrative Law* at 57–58) summarized the principles as follows:

> These [principles] include the rights to notice, and a hearing, and unbiased decision-making and all the other related, procedural rights. One must then ask whether any particular procedural right should be afforded in the specific case. Several limiting factors should be examined. First, the purpose of the impugned legislation should be considered and a balance should be struck between the demands of fairness and efficiency. The competing interests of the state and the individual must be balanced. Second, in extradition matters at least (and perhaps more generally), the Court may ask whether denying the remedy would "shock" the conscience of Canadians or violate the standards of the international community. Third, the nature of the decision-making function will be analyzed. Depending upon where the function resides [or] the continuum of administrative decision-making, a higher or lower degree of procedural fairness will be required. The closer the decision-maker is to the legislative (or policy) end of the spectrum, the lower the standard of procedural fundamental justice which is required. A higher degree of fairness is required as the decision-maker moves along the spectrum toward judicial or quasi-judicial deliberations.

Agencies have powers to force the production of documents or evidence by summons and/or subpoena, or to permit entry of premises to conduct searches by search warrants. They must comply with section 8 of the *Charter*, which states that such seizures or searches must be reasonable. Various decisions in the courts have determined that individuals must have some sort of sliding scale in their right to privacy. The reasonableness of privacy is dependent on the circumstances, such as the purposes of the search and other related factors. Furthermore, certain procedural safeguards must usually be maintained, e.g., as an impartial decision-maker authorizing such search or seizure on reasonable evidence being supplied.

Section 13 of the *Charter* states, "A witness who testifies in any proceeding has the right not to have any incriminating evidence so given used to incriminate that witness in any other proceedings, except in a prosecution for perjury or for the giving of contradictory evidence." This section is not the same as the American Fifth Amendment, which allows a person to not give any evidence that would tend to incriminate him or her. Instead, evidence given by a person may not be used to incriminate that person in a subsequent or other proceeding.

Section 14 of the *Charter* states, "A party or witness in any proceeding who does not understand or speak the language in which the proceedings are conducted or who is deaf has the right to the assistance of an interpreter." Furthermore, the interpreter must translate word for word and not summarize the information being translated. Notice that the *Charter* makes no reference as to who pays for the interpreter, making such issue open for discussion.

Rules, Guidelines, and Directives Formulated by the Agency

Some enabling statues, such as the Ontario *Workplace Safety and Insurance Act, 1997*, S.O. 1997, c. 16, Sched. A, as amended, under subsection 159(1) for the Workplace Safety and Insurance Board (WSIB) and subsection 173(1) for the Workplace Safety and Insurance Tribunal (WSIAT), give specific power to agencies to determine their own practice and procedure. Depending on the statute, the rules made by the agency, in respect of practice and procedure may have the force and effect of a regulation. The regulation, however, must be approved by the appropriate Cabinet, and the guidelines to promulgate such rules as regulations must be followed. If, however, the agency has made its rules in a non-statutory form, as described in the next paragraph, such rules must be followed if they are mandatory.

Rules Set Out in Notice Generally or for a Particular Proceeding

For reasons of flexibility, agencies usually have some latitude in determining which rules should apply generally, and in a particular proceeding, provided that the overriding concern of fairness is met. This concern is also addressed when determining whether the specific rules are mandatory (must be followed) or directory (may be followed). Although consistency in rules is preferable, it is not necessary to follow all rules if there is a risk of unfair treatment. It is recognized that in these situations agencies have the power to broadly interpret, and even change, rules as long as no party is prejudiced. On the other hand, if some or all of the parties have acted in reliance upon a specific rule, it would not be correct to amend such a rule.

Common Law Requirement to "Act Fairly" and the Rules Derived Therefrom

The steps to determine the rules of any agency discussed above should be observed through the lens of the court-developed "duty to act fairly" and its predecessor concept, the "rules of natural justice". The rules of natural justice have largely been supplanted by the duty of fairness and, therefore, are not very relevant here. The courts have used the obligation to require any decision-making body to act fairly as a means to determine a person's rights and obligations. A successful attack, by way of judicial review as discussed later, has been decried by some opponents as interference with agencies' freedom to act in determining the public interest. The reply to this position notes that the courts will only interfere where a party is treated unfairly and where the decisions have a sufficiently serious effect on the party. This suggests that the more adverse the effect on the party, the greater the duty to act fairly, as shown by an increase in the procedural protections. But in an emergency, an agency may be entitled to have more flexibility in its procedural protections, at least initially. Therefore, it can be argued that there is a sliding scale of procedural protections mandated on an agency, depending on certain factors that sometimes are recognized by the courts.

Notwithstanding any other requirements, before an agency can make a decision adverse to a person's interest, at a minimum a person should be

- told of the case to be met; and
- given an opportunity to respond.

Both "notice of the case" and "right to respond" can range, depending on the circumstances, from verbal advice to written notice to provision of documentary evidence in the former situation, and from written to electronic hearing or, most likely, oral hearing in the latter situation. These minimum requirements can be observed in rules adopted by most agencies to be fair to the parties because the courts would likely impose them anyway. However, even if no rules are prescribed for an agency to follow, the duty to act fairly will impose a number of rules on the agency as outlined in the next paragraphs.

Status

One of the most important preliminary matters to be decided by an agency is who has the status to appear before it. A person who should appear before an agency but is denied an opportunity to appear would be considered unfairly treated. The most likely person to have status as a **party to the proceeding** is a person who may be seriously affected by the outcome of the proceeding. Factors used to determine whether a person is seriously affected include the subject matter of the proceeding, the person's interest in the subject matter, and the effect that the decision might have on that interest. Using the concept of "serious effect" allows not only persons directly affected, such as a named party or the complainant in a disciplinary proceeding, to appear before it, but also members of the public who may have the status of an **intervenor**. This is especially important in an agency environment, where the public interest is so compelling and the effect of a decision might be far-reaching.

Notice

The general principle here states that, except for emergencies, advance notice advising of a proceeding where a decision may be made must be given to all persons who would be affected by the decision. Such notice should be explicit and state the time and place of the proceeding, in order that those persons affected may take action to protect their position. Whether service is verbal, written, or even by newspaper advertisement, it must be effective: the notice must reach the person and be timely enough to enable the person to adequately prepare.

Disclosure

In order for the person affected by the possible decision to have an opportunity to make appropriate submissions, the person should be informed of the case to be met. That includes disclosure of (a) all relevant information that the agency may take into account when rendering a decision, (b) the issues as presented to the agency, and (c) the penalties that could be imposed on the person. A party to a proceeding may very well be entitled to more disclosure than an intervenor. In some circumstances, only partial or even no disclosure is permissible when it involves confidential information or information that would cause harm if released. Disclosure of information must be timely and should be given as soon as reasonably possible in the circumstances.

Adjournments (or Stays)

Even where there is no provision in the enabling statute to allow it, agencies have inherent discretionary jurisdiction to adjourn proceedings to ensure fairness. An agency would likely grant a stay in the following situations: (a) a party received insufficient notice, (b) a party received late or improper disclosure, (c) a new issue is raised in the hearing, requiring time for a party to prepare, and (d) a related matter is being heard in another agency or in court. In determining whether to grant a discretionary adjournment, an agency will usually review factors such as complexity of the proceedings, previous stays, if any, interest of the persons affected, and costs of the stay. If a stay is granted, the agency will likely fix the time and place for the resumption of the proceedings.

Effective Participation (Especially the Right to Representation)

In order for a party to properly deal with a hearing, such party must be present at the hearing. That means the agency should only carry on with a hearing if all parties are present, unless it is shown that such missing party or parties had effective notice of the hearing but decided not to attend. In almost all circumstances, any person who has a right to appear in a hearing has the right to be represented by a representative who can present the case for the person. An agency may have some discretion, under its enabling Act, to allow for a representative and to take into account the ability of the parties involved to represent themselves, the nature and complexity of the proceedings (the more complex or serious the matter, the more likely that a representative will be allowed), and the possible consequences of the proceedings. If an agency denies the use of a representative, it must state its reasons for doing so. Unless the legislation requires it, the representative does not have to be a lawyer, and, in fact, almost all agencies in Ontario will allow licensed paralegals or laypersons with some specialized knowledge to represent parties in a hearing.

Public or Private (in Camera) Hearings

The general rule for most hearings, whether in court or before an agency, states that they should be public, for reasons of fairness and as a safeguard against covert actions. However, especially for hearings before an agency, there is discretion to have *in camera* hearings for national security reasons or if a person, such as a party or even a witness, could be harmed by a public hearing. In some situations, such as a hearing before the Workplace Safety and Insurance Appeals Tribunal, the hearing is private unless the parties to the hearing unanimously agree to allow the public to be present. This situation likely has to do with a possibility of embarrassment if evidence as to the worker's physical condition and health became public knowledge.

Evidence

In order to reach a decision, an agency must base all findings of fact upon the relevant evidence. On the whole, the rules of evidence, which are formal and usually strictly applied in court, are much less formal when applied by an agency. Therefore, uncertain types of evidence, such as hearsay, and unqualified "expert" evidence will likely be admitted, although in determining whether to admit the evidence the agency must also determine the relevance. Even if the evidence is admissible, the agency must also determine the evidence's weight (probative value) and its credibility. If the evidence does not have much value or is not believable, possibly because of contradictions, the agency will likely gloss over the evidence. An agency also has the right to take notice of commonly accepted facts (judicial notice) without the need for evidence to prove those facts.

Witnesses

Witnesses before an agency can give evidence in written or oral form, depending on the circumstances and the provisions of relevant legislation. Oral evidence is usually adduced by questions posed by the party calling the witness, or by members of the agency itself, who often participate in an active way, unlike most court proceedings. The difficult issue for most agencies to determine is when a party has the right to cross-examine a witness, which can be done whether the initial submission is in a written or oral form. Although certain Acts require cross-examination, an agency has discretionary power to grant it. The party must convince the agency that the party should be given the opportunity to correct or controvert any relevant and prejudicial statement made by the witness. More specifically, cross-examination will be allowed if it is the only means to reveal or test the evidence that goes to the heart of the hearing, if there is conflicting and/or contradictory evidence, and if cross-examination provides the best way to assess the credibility of the witness.

Proof and Non-suit Motions

Parties who bring an application to appear before an agency usually carry the burden of proving their case. However, the standard used to determine if the burden has been met is not the **"beyond a reasonable doubt" test** used in criminal court proceedings but, rather, the **"balance of probabilities" test** used in civil court proceedings. In making a finding of fact and the eventual decision, the agency should be reasonably satisfied that the facts occurred, which depends on such factors as the nature of the facts to be proven and the consequences that would flow from the finding of fact. Once the party with the burden or onus to prove the case has finished her/his submissions, the other party has the ability to make a motion for a non-suit (dismissal) without making any submissions. In determining whether to grant the motion, the agency must determine whether the first party made a *prima facie* case. The *prima facie* test has less of a burden of proof than the balance of probability test and is used by the agency in making its decision on the motion. It requires looking at the evidence in the light most favourable to the party who presented it. Even if the evidence is weak and not very credible, if there is any evidence at all to support the contentions of the party presenting the case, the agency should not grant a motion of non-suit.

Evidence by Compulsion

Pursuant to legislation, many agencies are granted powers to obtain relevant evidence in the following ways:

1. exercise of search and/or seizure powers;
2. use of inspection powers; and
3. use of subpoena and/or summons powers.

All of these are subject to section 8 of the *Charter.*

With respect to search and/or seizure, an authorized person is permitted to pay a surprise visit to search for and/or seize evidence. Prior authorization is given by a person, usually not a member of the agency but not necessarily a judge. Such person should not have an interest in the proceeding and should be satisfied on reasonable and probable grounds, provided under oath, that it is reasonable to grant a search and/or seizure warrant. The search should not be a general search but should be a search of a specific situation and anything relevant to it.

Inspection orders permit inspectors to view premises for spot audits and to regulate businesses as allowed under the enabling Act. The usual purpose of the inspection is to protect the public interest, and it is likely to be carried on during reasonable hours.

Documents and/or witnesses can be subpoenaed to require production and/or attendance, respectively. If there is non-compliance, contempt proceedings can be initiated before the appropriate court. If non-compliance is proven beyond a reasonable doubt, the offender can be imprisoned unless there is compliance. Certain documents cannot be compelled, most commonly those that are privileged, such as solicitor–client communications for the purposes of obtaining legal advice and Cabinet or ministerial communications where disclosure would prejudice the public interest. Summonses will be granted to compel a witness to appear if the party requesting it can show that such witness is reluctant to appear, that the evidence likely to be obtained is relevant, and that it is unlikely to be obtained by any fashion other than by a summons.

Orders and Decisions

Unless required by the appropriate legislation to be in writing, in theory, an oral final order or decision is acceptable. However, there is much case law from the SCC that requires most decisions to be in writing with reasons. The decision should be given as expeditiously as possible, and some enabling Acts even have a specific time limit for a decision to be handed down. Although it may not be required, agencies usually give reasons for the decision, especially if the decision might be raised in court on appeal or by way of judicial review (to be discussed below). The following are some of the problems that can arise if the reasons for the decision are not included:

1. Lack of reasons may undermine confidence in the agency.
2. The court will disregard the agency's expertise if it is not demonstrated by stated reasons for the decision.
3. The court can derive adverse inferences if there are no reasons to review.
4. A disturbing impression of injustice may be left with those reading the decision.
5. The parties do not know why the decision was made, or if there are any grounds for appeal or judicial review.

Further, if the enabling Act requires reasons to be given, and there are none, the decision is likely null and void. The reasons, as given, should adequately explain how the agency reached its conclusions, whether based on fact, law, or public policy.

Over and above the rules or procedures to be followed by agencies with respect to the duty to act fairly, three other principles derived originally from the rules of natural justice are important: (i) the impartiality of the decision-maker (no bias), (ii) the decision-maker's not fettering his or her discretion, and (iii) the agency's acting within its jurisdiction. If any of these principles are not followed, an application for judicial review will likely be successful.

The next three items — Bias, Improperly Fettering Discretion, and Jurisdiction — are not part of the duty to act fairly; however, the author included them here as all three, like the duty to act fairly, are derived from common law and, if there is non-compliance, will allow for the remedy of judicial review.

Bias

If, in the exercise of its powers, an agency is found to lack neutrality or impartiality and/or to have had personal interest in mind, the decision of the agency will likely be null and void. If a member of an agency is found to be biased, that member will be disqualified from hearing the case. Indicators of bias of a member of the adjudicating agency include the following:

- Pecuniary interest in the proceeding
- A friend, business associate, or relative as a party or a witness unless the connection is a past and/or distant one
- Improper conduct at the hearing, such as flippant or derogatory language, expressed feelings of hostility or antagonism, or repeated interference in the proceedings
- Private meetings with one party to the exclusion of others
- Social meetings with parties or witnesses prior to or during the hearing
- A predetermined view of the issues (although a tentative prior view is acceptable as long as there is an opening for persuasion)

It is important to remember that an appearance of bias, or a reasonable apprehension of bias (where a reasonable person would suspect that a member may be influenced by improper considerations to favour one party over another), will likely be sufficient for the court to find bias. Therefore, if a member of an agency hearing a case believes there may be a possible bias situation, it is best if the member abstains from the decision or, possibly, disqualifies or recuses her- or himself from the proceeding. Once that is done, an unbiased member or unbiased panel can be put in place. It should also be noted that certain agencies are, under statute, biased, such as labour arbitration boards with members drawn from management and labour. Please also note that not only can there be actual adjudicator bias or reasonable apprehension of adjudicator bias, there can also be actual institutional bias and reasonable apprehension of institutional bias where actual or likely bias is systemic in the agency.

Improperly Fettering Discretion

Agencies are given wide discretion in such areas as the responsibility to apply rules to each situation as it arises, as long as the agency is fair. Other areas of discretion include determining whether a specific situation is covered by the legislation, which action is warranted, and consideration of public policy applied to specific situations. An agency must observe the obligation to promote the objects of its enabling legislation. If an agency exercises its discretion arbitrarily or dishonestly, a court may rule that the agency is acting in bad faith and, therefore, that its actions are reviewable. Bad faith, however, must be proven. Discriminating against and treating a specific person differently, or making a decision based on an improper purpose or irrelevant consideration, are indicators of bad faith.

The most likely example of improper fettering of discretion is the application by an agency of *stare decisis*, or standing by precedent. Most agencies keep copies of decisions accessible, and it is quite common for appropriate and, sometimes, inappropriate prior decisions to be submitted to an agency. If the agency bases its decision solely or predominately on a prior decision without proper regard to the actual case before it, a court would likely determine that there has been improper fettering of its discretion. Although consistency is desirable, it is not an all-encompassing obligation for an agency to follow as it is in the judicial branch of government. Further, there are ways to make a decision without making it obvious that *stare decisis* was used.

Not only is it inappropriate to improperly fetter discretion, it is also wrong to not exercise discretion that is conferred on an agency. In the right circumstances, as discussed in the section on judicial review (p. 18), an agency can be compelled to exercise its discretion.

Jurisdiction

The agency can exercise the power given to it only by its enabling or empowering legislation. If it acts outside its jurisdiction, say by giving remedies it is not empowered to under the legislation, that would be outside its jurisdiction and could be challenged on judicial review. Another situation likely calling for judicial review occurs when an agency has the authority to hear a matter but refuses, which is usually referred to as "declining jurisdiction".

REMEDIES AVAILABLE IF A DECISION OF AN AGENCY IS NOT SATISFACTORY

Once an agency has made a decision, the parties should comply. There are legal mechanisms available to try to ensure compliance. However, depending on certain circumstances, especially when permitted to do so by legislation, a party may be able to have the decision

- reconsidered,
- appealed, or
- judicially reviewed.

Reconsideration involves an agency's revisiting a case, after making a decision, in order to look at it again because of a request to do so. An appeal is requested to allow an appellate body, either an appellate agency or a court, to look at the result on the merits of a case because the decision may be "wrong". An application for judicial review is made because there is some question not of the results, but of the rules and procedures used to achieve those results. To better understand options or alternatives that can be exercised, each shall be discussed in turn.

Reconsideration

Under either an enabling Act or other general legislation, such as the *SPPA*, some agencies are given the power to review or reconsider the decision made and to change it, if appropriate. An example of a reconsideration involving an agency would be the case of an applicant for some type of financial assistance benefits, who has applied for a hearing with the Social Benefits Tribunal (SBT). If the SBT has made a decision to refuse benefits, the party who was denied has the option to request reconsideration by the SBT, to appeal the decision to court, or to apply for judicial review. In choosing the appropriate option, it is important for the party to assess the reasons for his or her attempt to have the decision reversed. If the party does not like the decision, but does not have any new evidence or cannot point to errors made by the SBT, the party should not take any action. However, if he or she has evidence of errors, such as relevant evidence not considered, bias, unfair treatment by non-adherence to appropriate procedures, or mistakes of law or fact, the party should select the appropriate option. If a ground such as new evidence exists, it would be best for the party in this example to request reconsideration. This may be the best option if the expeditiousness and cost of a reconsideration overwhelmingly favour the party over either of the other options. In other words, reconsideration will happen much sooner and cost much less. The appropriate legislation will state the scope of reconsideration, if any. Note that the grounds for reconsideration of a decision of the SBT are unusually broad and not just new evidence.

Appeal

The second option available to the party in the above example would be to appeal the decision. With respect to a decision of the SBT, the appeal is made to Ontario Divisional Court. In order to determine if any appeal rights exist against the decision of any agency, either the enabling Act or other appropriate legislation must be consulted. If no appeal rights are explicitly granted in any agency's decision in the legislation, no appeal can be made. Note that the legislation could designate a court, as in the example, or another agency to hear the appeal. For example, decisions from the Workplace Safety and Insurance Board are appealed to the Workplace Safety and Insurance Appeals Tribunal. The following are important matters in respect of appeals.

Status (Who May Appeal)

As will be seen in most of the discussion of appeals, one must first and always look at the legislation to determine who can appeal. If the Act states that only a "party" may appeal or is silent on the matter, then only a party to a proceeding can appeal. However, the legislation could be broader and give status to appeal to such persons as intervenors or even some members of the general public. This can be achieved by the use of such phrases as "adversely affected", "aggrieved person", or even "interested party". The appellate body has the right to determine if the "appellant" is allowed to appeal under the words of the legislation. Although somewhat unusual because of the possible appearance of bias, some Acts allow the agency to be an appellant.

Scope of Appeal

The scope of an appeal, or the grounds upon which an appeal can be heard, is set out in the statute. Such grounds can be that the agency made errors on questions of jurisdiction, law, or fact, or some combination of such grounds. In brief, the following points are raised:

- A question of jurisdiction relates to whether the agency did not have the power to hear the case or, if initially having such power, commits some act to lose or exceed such power (Actions taken outside jurisdiction are *ultra vires* (outside the power) and may be rendered null and void.)
- A question of law relates to the interpretation and application of the law to the facts of a specific case (Although this appears to be a clear position, there has been much blurring of whether a suggested error is a question of law, fact, or jurisdiction)
- A question of fact relates to the facts as found or determined by the adjudicator, usually after the perusal of the submissions of witnesses and physical and documentary evidence

Some case law suggests it is an error of jurisdiction to make a decision where there is a total lack of evidence. Usually issues related to evidence are considered questions of fact. However, if necessary (where an appellate body wants to have the right to grant an appeal even though the Act limits appeals to questions of jurisdiction), it has been decided in some cases to call it an error of jurisdiction. The question of alleged errors and their categorization is even more important for judicial review and shall be discussed further below.

Type of Appeal

Depending on the statute, the appellate body could hear the appeal in a number of ways:

- A hearing *de novo* (a new hearing), where the appellate body would act as a new adjudicator and rehear the matter without any reference to the decision appealed (The parties would be able to submit any and all evidence to support their positions.)
- A new hearing where the appellate body has the right to look at and, even, refer somewhat to the decision appealed from
- A review of a record of the agency that arrived at the decision, without oral hearing of arguments by the party or parties, regarding errors made by the agency that appear on the record (This method is most often used in appeals from a court decision.)

Furthermore, the error must be appealable pursuant to the statute granting the appeal rights. In this way of appeal, the agency is required to produce a record that will usually include the following documents: (a) specific decision under appeal, (b) any interlocutory or interim orders, (c) the reasons for the decision, (d) the notice for the original adjudication from which the decision arose, (e) all documentary evidence, and (f) the transcript of the proceedings, if any. The first means of appeal is the broadest and, in effect, puts the appellate body in the position of a body hearing the matter for the first time.

The method of appeal will have a direct relationship to the powers of the appellate body to make a decision. If hearing *de novo* is the type required by statute, the appellate body's decision will replace that of the original agency decision-maker. However, other modes of appeal, especially by reviews of the record, will likely mean a return to the agency for a new hearing, although before a new adjudicator or panel. To ensure that the new adjudicator does not make the same mistakes, the appellate body may be able to provide directions along with the order for a new hearing.

General Concerns Regarding Appeals

Items such as notice of appeal, leave to appeal (where required), and stay of an agency decision during the process of appeal are all detailed in the enabling Act or other relevant legislation. Normally, rules about the time to file and where to file an appeal are strictly enforced. There is, however, the ability in most circumstances to exercise discretion to extend the time where it would be fair to do so. If leave to appeal is required, a *prima facie* case must be made by the possible appellant of the substance of the arguments supporting the requested appeal. The general position on stays (or holding in abeyance) is that an application for a stay before the appellate body must be granted if the decision has been appealed. Normally, the agency's decision is effective immediately, even if an appeal has been launched; but the appellate body, if granted such power, can order a stay until the decision is made on the appeal.

Two further points should be made about appeals and how they relate to applications for judicial review. First, it is usually better, if the grounds allow it, to launch an appeal rather than make application for judicial review. The powers of the appellate body to possibly hear the case anew and consider the merits of the decision are almost always wider than the reviewing court's power. Second, if the application for judicial review is made while appeal rights exist but have not been explored, the court will almost invariably refuse to hear the application until all appeal rights have been exhausted.

Judicial Review

The third way that a decision of an agency can be challenged is by an application for judicial review. Such application was formerly by the mechanism of a prerogative writ. This method is still available, but other mechanisms now exist to provide similar review. This method shall be considered in detail, including (i) specific remedies available (i.e., prerogative writs, statutory applications, and remedies under private law), (ii) the grounds for the types of review, (iii) privative clauses (statutory provisions to try to limit or even prevent review), and (iv) other specific concerns.

Prerogative Writs

Prerogative writs are mechanisms developed over the centuries by English common law to control arbitrary government action. Initially, they were orders issued by the Crown to oversee and direct the actions of its underlings. Over time, issuance of these writs was transferred to superior courts and became part of their inherent jurisdiction to supervise governmental decisions.

As these writs can be granted on a discretionary basis (similar to equitable remedies), there are certain situations where the court will usually refuse to grant this remedy. As previously discussed, if there is another valid remedy available, such as appeal, the court will likely not grant the application. Another reason to exercise the discretion not to grant a writ is that the grant would be ineffective because it would be academic or useless. Other situations where the writ may be refused relate to the actions of the party who objects and brings the application:

1. If the party has waived or acquiesced knowingly in the agency's error;
2. If the party has taken too long to seek this remedy (*laches*); or

3. If the party has, by his or her conduct, such as bad faith, become disentitled to review (**clean hands doctrine**).

Generally, the court requires that the applicant for a writ be a person who has a sufficient interest in the proceeding. The application is brought against an agency who, depending on circumstances, may be able to participate actively in the court review or may only be a neutral friend to the court.

The five prerogative writs still in use, to varying degrees, are *certiorari*, prohibition, *mandamus*, *quo warranto*, and *habeas corpus*.

CERTIORARI

This writ allows the court to quash (basically, stop or nullify) a final decision of an agency on certain grounds, usually errors of jurisdiction made by the agency. Originally part of the superior court's inherent jurisdiction to supervise inferior courts, it was extended over the years to include certain supervisory powers over agencies. It can be applied only after the agency has made the improper decision, and not before that time. Historically, *certiorari* was available if an agency acted judicially or quasi-judicially; however, more recent cases have decided that it can also be used to quash decisions of agencies acting administratively. Limitations to the use of this writ include its non-applicability to legislative decisions or delegated legislation or the Crown itself (except for certain situations). However, it does apply to public bodies whose power is granted by legislation.

PROHIBITION

Prohibition is essentially the same as *certiorari* in terms of its history and limitations, except that it can be applied for at any stage prior to the making of the final decision. It is used, therefore, to try to prevent something from being done before the ultimate order or award is made.

MANDAMUS

An application for mandamus, if granted, will result in an order by the court to compel an agency to perform a statutory duty where the agency has refused to do its duty. If the power an agency is refusing to exercise is discretionary, *mandamus* would likely ensue — but only to require such agency to exercise the discretion, not to dictate the way it must be exercised. In order to use this writ the following circumstances must exist:

- The applicant must have status to apply; in this situation, there must be a public duty to act owed by an agency to the applicant.
- An explicit demand has been made to the agency that it must act, and there has been a refusal to do so.
- As with all prerogative writs, it does not apply against the Crown or its agents when not acting under a statutory duty.

QUO WARRANTO

Rarely applied for, this writ, if granted, will state that a person has the right to hold a public office. It is of little relevance to agency proceedings.

HABEAS CORPUS

This writ, which is centuries old, is used to quash an illegal detention of the applicant. Only the detained persons or someone acting on their behalf can make application. The grounds for granting the writ relate to errors of law or jurisdiction.

Statutory Applications in the Nature of Judicial Review
PROVINCIAL (ONTARIO AND ALBERTA)

Most provinces have legislation to provide potential applicants an alternative to requesting one of the prerogative writs against provincial agencies. In fact, some of the provinces, including Ontario, have, in effect, abolished some of the prerogative writs. The Ontario statute that accomplishes that task is the *Judicial Review Procedure Act*, R.S.O. 1990, c. J.1, as amended (*JRPA*), specifically section 7, which turns applications for *mandamus*, prohibition, and *certiorari* into applications under the *JRPA*. The intent of the legislation was to make such applications a summary proceeding with fairly consistent procedures to be heard by the Ontario Divisional Court. Under section 2(1)1, an application is made by way of an originating notice to request an order in the nature of *mandamus*, prohibition, and *certiorari*. That provision means that all the laws developed under those three specified remedies are still important. Section 2(1)2 of the *JRPA* also puts into summary form two kinds of private law remedies (discussed below) historically available to applicants. Under that section, the applicant can request a declaration or an injunction, or both remedies, in relation to the exercise or purported exercise of a statutory power of decision. "Statutory power of decision" is defined as the power conferred on an agency by a statute to make a decision affecting the rights, duties, or powers of any person, or the eligibility of a person to receive a licence or benefit. Note that the application in replacement of the three prerogative writs is not restricted to the exercise of statutory power. Detailed rules of procedure with respect to the *JRPA* are set out in the Ontario *Rules of Civil Procedure*. Also note that the definition of "party" includes some groups that are not persons at law and, therefore, likely did not previously have standing to bring an application for a prerogative writ. Alberta has very similar legislation to the Ontario legislation discussed in this paragraph.

FEDERAL

In making application for any of the prerogative writs against an agency under federal jurisdiction, the *Federal Court Act*, R.S.C. 1985, c F-7, as amended (*FCA*), states that the Federal Court — Trial Division has exclusive jurisdiction over all such applications. An exception to this provision provides that the Federal Court of Appeal has the exclusive jurisdictions over applications in 15 specified federal agencies. The application for judicial review, so called, is made pursuant to the rules and procedures of section 18.1 of the *FCA*. As in the *JRPA*, such applications are meant to be heard in a summary fashion. The section also gives extensive powers to the court to order all the types of relief that could be granted under the prerogative writs, if any of the enumerated errors exist. When the *FCA* was first enacted, certain wordings allowed for an application for judicial review only if the agency was acting in a judicial or quasi-judicial manner. This led to many cases where the issue was not whether there was an error that could be reviewed, but whether the agency was exercising a judicial or quasi-judicial jurisdiction. Recognizing this problem, the legislators amended the *FCA*, effective in 1992, to remove the distinction between judicial and quasi-judicial jurisdiction.

Remedies under Private Law

Relief may also exist pursuant to common law and/or equitable remedies awarded through an ordinary lawsuit. Specifically, one could simply sue the agency in tort, likely for some form of negligence, although some intentional torts could also support the action. In this situation, the claimant alleges that an agency has either committed an intentionally improper conduct that interferes with that person (intentional tort), or is careless in performing some action that causes damage to the person to whom such agency owes a duty of care (negligence). In order for an action in tort to succeed, the conduct complained of must be illegal or *ultra vires*. A review of the case law indicates that the court will likely find agencies liable if the elements of the specific tort can be proven. However, the courts have also recognized the need for flexibility for agencies to effectively function. It should also be noted that, historically, there was a limit to the parties one could sue: In the past, "Crown immunity" had basically prevented a person from bringing a tort action against the Crown in an official capacity. Federal and provincial legislation has effectively brought Crown immunity to an end — although strict time limits have been imposed to restrict the right of action. There is much more material to be discussed about tortious actions that can be brought against agencies, but that is outside the scope of this chapter; however, the relief that can be granted in consequence of a successful action in tort are discussed below.

DECLARATORY RELIEF

This discretionary relief (also known as declaratory judgment or declaration) is a non-coercive judgment of the court setting out the legal positions of the parties and/or the law applicable to them. Although not binding since there is no legal way to enforce such a judgment, declarations have become an accepted way for a person to have a court determine whether an agency had the power to take certain actions. It is also a very flexible remedy, with few technical requirements to be followed, and can be used in a number of ways. The courts have normally issued declarations against agencies as part of their supervisory function with respect to the legality of certain governmental actions. Remember that a declaration can be obtained in summary fashion under the *FCA* and, with limitations, as an exercise of statutory power under the *JRPA*.

INJUNCTION

An injunction is a discretionary equitable remedy by which the court can order a party to act or refrain from acting in a certain way, and if there is non-compliance a party would be liable for contempt of court. There are two main types of injunctions, both of which have been used against agencies after a successful tort action. One type is a mandatory injunction, similar to *mandamus*, to compel an agency to act in a lawful manner. The other type is a prohibitory injunction, similar to prohibition, to restrain an agency that acts, or even threatens to act, in an illegal fashion.

Furthermore, injunctions are available on an interim basis, without a full-blown trial and, possibly, without initial notice to the other side. An interim injunction will enjoin an agency until such time as the cause of action is tried and, possibly, a permanent injunction is granted. Standing to bring an action for an injunction, along with Crown immunity issues, must be addressed before an injunction can be successfully obtained. Also, in a similar way to declaratory relief, injunction relief can be granted under both the *FCA*, for federal agencies, and under the *JRPA*, for Ontario agencies.

DAMAGES

In any successful action for tort, the court has the obligation to award the common law remedy of damages to compensate the victim for certain types of loss or injury suffered as result of the tort. Once the amount (or quantum) of damages is proven on the balance of probabilities to the court's satisfaction, the court will order the **tortfeasor** to pay such damages. Not only will the innocent party be compensated for losses suffered through no fault of such party, but liability for damages may act as deterrence to the wrongdoer. The potential for deterrence can clearly be seen in the ability of the court to award punitive or exemplary damages in circumstances where an agency has acted maliciously. These principles dealing with damages have been accepted where a tort action has been successful against an agency. One issue still open for resolution is whether a purely economic loss is compensable. As in the other two private remedies examined above, items such as standing and Crown immunity may be relevant. There is no provision for a summary award of damages under either the *FCA* or the *JRPA*.

Although in some jurisdictions it is possible to apply for one or more prerogative writs, to apply for statutory judicial review, and to commence a private law action for one or more of the private law remedies, most persons will likely make application only under the appropriate statute. Application is made in a summary fashion and is, therefore, less costly and more expedient and provides grounds, in most circumstances, at least as broad as the other remedies. Although a discussion of grounds for judicial review can be overwhelming, the following are some concepts to remember.

Grounds for Judicial Review

As previously mentioned, the grounds for most appeals of agency decisions usually relate to the merits or the result of the decision by questioning the findings of fact by the adjudicator. Typically, the grounds for judicial review relate to how the result was achieved and are likely determined by looking for jurisdictional or legal errors. It is possible that a resourceful court can make what appears to be a possible question of fact into a question of law; however, the grounds for judicial review tend to be very narrow. A vast amount of case law exists on the sole issue of whether an alleged error of an agency is reviewable, but an analysis of the law is beyond the scope of this chapter. However, certain principles can be canvassed.

The major focus of determining proper grounds for judicial review revolves around the statutory power of an agency to take a particular action. Usually the court must determine if the statutory power exists, or, if it does exist, whether an agency has either exceeded or has somehow lost its statutory power. This is a search to discover the jurisdiction of the agency. It can also be classified as a question of law because if an agency took an action without the statutory power or the jurisdiction to do so, such action would be declared illegal. Determining jurisdiction often requires the reviewing court to interpret appropriate legislation to determine exactly what an agency's jurisdiction is.

As an agency is a creation of its enabling Act and other relevant legislation, understanding the words of all of such legislation is usually the first step the court takes to determine whether an agency has acquired the appropriate jurisdiction. Other initial issues may include whether there has been compliance with all preliminary matters, such as proper notice. Any or all of these issues may be examined in order for the court to determine if the agency has acquired jurisdiction.

If the jurisdiction is properly acquired, an agency's actions can still be reviewed if it exceeds or loses its jurisdiction. Broadly speaking, an agency can exceed or lose jurisdiction in three ways: (i) abuse of discretion, (ii) no compliance with the duty to be fair, and (iii) bias. (Refer to material detailed earlier, pp. 10–15, in this chapter for a more comprehensive discussion.) Certain concepts regarding each of the three ways jurisdiction can be lost are discussed below.

Abuse of discretion can include the following actions: (i) exercising a discretionary power in bad faith for improper or irrelevant considerations; (ii) making a decision with no evidence whatsoever or by ignoring relevant information; (iii) using discretion to obtain an improper result because it is discriminatory or unreasonable, or it is made due to a misunderstanding of the law; and (iv) improperly fettering discretion. Notice how an evidentiary problem, which is normally a question of fact, can become an abuse of discretion issue. A reviewing court can find that because there is no evidence to support the exercise of discretion, an agency can lose its jurisdiction; therefore, the decision is reviewable.

The origins of procedural fairness, or the duty of any agency to be fair to parties before it, are derived from the rules of natural justice. These rules of natural justice, developed over the centuries to try to ensure that a party was treated fairly, were initially reserved for agencies acting in a judicial or quasi-judicial manner. The need to characterize the function of an agency was all-important because if an agency was acting in a legislative or executive manner, the rules of natural justice were likely not applicable. However, in most but not all situations, it is no longer relevant to characterize function since an agency is required to act fairly in most of its functions. The determination of whether an agency has acted fairly is based upon whether the rules following the duty to act fairly, as stated earlier in this chapter, have been followed. Such rules of natural justice are basically that any such rule must be dependent on fairness to the persons involved in the proceeding.

The loss of jurisdiction due to the bias of an agency is also derived from the duty to be fair. Various types of bias by agencies are discussed elsewhere in this chapter. It is important to note the problem of whether bias should be judged by the strict objective test used in courts or by a more subjective standard for agencies need to consider public policy in their decision making. Such public policy obligations may make an agency's actions appear biased to a party. Many agency members have criticized the courts in going too far to make agency proceedings appear like court proceedings. Different considerations often apply for agencies and courts.

A further ground for review, specifically for an application for an order of, or in the nature of, *certiorari*, is an error on the face of the record. These are errors of law and not jurisdictional errors that are clear from looking at the record of the proceeding. They allow the court to quash a decision of an agency. An example of an error of law is an agency's incorrectly interpreting and/or applying a statutory provision other than its own enabling legislation. Numerous recent cases have tried to place limitations on which errors of law, on the face of the record, are quashable by positing tests to be followed. These tests arose to try to deal with "privative clauses", discussed below. The most important test suggests that errors of law that are "patently unreasonable" are errors of jurisdiction and, therefore, reviewable even with a privative clause. This test has been used, and possibly misused, in numerous court decisions to try to determine the ambit of judicial review by way of *certiorari*. Such cases have made it difficult to state a consistent principle to be applied, other than that the test is important in this area as a way around a privative clause.

Privative Clauses

A privative clause is a statutory provision intended to prevent, or at least limit, the right of the judiciary to hear appeals or judicial review applications. The legislature's intent in using such a clause stems from a concern that the courts have intervened too readily and in areas better left to an agency's expertise and streamlined procedure. No matter what the specific wording of a privative clause is, it will not prevent a court from reviewing an agency's action based on a jurisdictional error. Therefore, a privative clause will only be of use where there is an error of law on the face of the record. The three common general types of privative clauses in use are as follows:

1. A final and binding clause, or similar wording, that means there is no appeal of an agency's decision but that still allows the court to determine whether any jurisdictional errors exist if the decision is patently unreasonable.
2. An exclusive jurisdiction clause to the effect that only an agency has exclusive jurisdiction to determine certain matters. This clause has the same basic effect as in item 1.
3. A clause that prevents any application for any prerogative writ or declaration. Again, this clause has the same basic effect as item 1.

There has been much discussion about whether an agency's decision should be reviewable by the courts and, if so, what the appropriate limits are, if any, to such review. This is yet another issue that threatens to go unanswered in the near, and possibly distant, future, although the 2008 SCC case of *Dunsmuir v. New Brunswick*, 2008 SCC 9 (the *Dunsmuir* case) has addressed some of the issues by positing a two-part test regarding the standard of review. If the decision is clearly based upon the agency's expertise, the standard is whether the decision was based on *reasonableness*, thereby having the court defer to such expertise. If, on the other hand, the agency made a decision not in its expertise, such as statutory interpretation, the decision must be *correct*. There are still other concerns that are usually considered under judicial review.

Other Concerns in Judicial Review

There are always time limits, invariably short, within which to apply for judicial review. Such time limits often are strictly enforced, although there is usually some discretion, based on fairness, to extend the time. The time limit is usually found in the enabling legislation or any rules pursuant to it. A stay of an agency decision is not automatically in place upon making an application for judicial review. It must be specifically and separately applied for to the appropriate court, which must be convinced of the efficacy of granting a stay. The hearing is a review, not a new hearing, which is why the record, as discussed previously, is so important. This is an absolute necessity where the review application is based on an error of fact on the record. Problems occur in this area where the agency does not have much in the way of transcripts. Usually the successful party in an application for judicial review will have costs awarded in his or her favour.

POSSIBLE TRENDS IN ADMINISTRATIVE LAW IN CANADA

There is a fair amount of tension between those who believe that agencies should have comparative freedom from the courts and those who want agencies to follow rules and procedures as overseen by courts. On the one hand, there is the obligation by agencies to follow and even develop public policy, which is or may be foreign to the court's perspective of individual rights. On the other hand, there is the court's traditional role to ensure justice is done and seen to be done. There is a need for the expertise and cost-effectiveness of agencies, but should these be at the expense of fairness to a specific person? There have been relatively recent examples of methods to try to find new ways to resolve issues even before they get to an agency hearing, let alone to court. One example is the use of mediation in some situations before the WSIB. There have been attempts to have a different forum for review than the court, as in the use in a number of provinces of an ombudsperson. This governmental, yet independent, official has the power to scrutinize governmental abuses affecting members of the public. Such investigation includes not only how the result was achieved, but the merits of the result. In England, a Council of Tribunals was created to review and approve all rules and procedures adopted by agencies. This comprehensive and considered approach to ensure fair rules may result in less need for parties to appear before the court to argue an unfair rule. However, even if some or all of the steps discussed in this paragraph are taken, cases will still be forthcoming. There are just too many concerns still debated to foresee an early end to the tensions.

CHAPTER SUMMARY

In this chapter, the reader discovered a definition of administrative law that led into a discussion of the three branches of government. After a summary review of public policy, the essential characteristics of agencies were introduced. Specifically, agencies are seen as creations of government that, if empowered to do so, can exercise many of the same functions of any or all of the three branches of government. Various types of agencies and a comparison between agencies and the courts were discussed.

After the concept and uses of agencies were explored, there was a lengthy discussion of the ways to determine what specific rules and procedures are applicable to a specific agency. This discussion included an exploration of such factors in the Ontario *Statutory Powers Proce-*

dure Act; sections 7, 8, 13, and 14 of the *Charter of Rights and Freedoms*; and the "duty to act fairly". The duty to act fairly was first defined and then broken down into some of its component parts to allow the reader to discover how the common law provides at least some procedural protections to parties involved in an agency proceeding. Other common law principles of no bias and no fettering the discretion and the jurisdiction of the decision-maker were also introduced.

Remedies available if there is a complaint or concern regarding an agency proceeding were then discussed. The remedies are (a) reconsideration by the same agency, (b) appeal to another agency or to court or both, or (c) judicial review by the courts. Substantial details regarding the requirements, procedure, scope, and type of appeal were discussed. Also reviewed were the remedies available under judicial review: (a) prerogative writs; (b) statutory applications, both federally and in Ontario; and (c) private law remedies of tort, declaratory relief, injunction, and damages.

Finally, there was a discussion of possible future trends in administrative law in Canada.

GLOSSARY OF NEW TERMS AND KEY CONCEPTS

balance of probabilities test   The standard used by the trier of fact in a civil proceeding (the judge or the jury, where appropriate) to determine whether the plaintiff or the defendant has won the case. If the evidence is more in favour of one party, even if just barely, then that party should be awarded the decision in the case.

beyond a reasonable doubt test   The standard used by the trier of fact in a criminal proceeding (judge or the jury, where appropriate) to determine whether the accused is found guilty or not guilty. If there is any reasonable doubt that the accused did not commit the offence charged, there must be a finding of not guilty.

clean hands doctrine   A principle of the law of equity that requires someone seeking to invoke an equitable rule to have conducted himself or herself fairly and honourably in the events leading up to and during the proceeding, and in the proceeding itself.

enabling legislation (act, statute)   A law that permits a person (which for most purposes includes an individual, a corporation, and an agency) to do something that, prior to the law, the person was not permitted to do.

gazette   The name of a publication issued by both the federal and provincial governments in Canada on a regular basis, containing official notices and announcements, and in which regulations made under the authority of a statute are first published.

judicial or quasi-judicial (function, manner, jurisdiction)   The authority or power of a court or a body similar to a court (that is, a body with the power to decide a person's rights) to decide matters before it. The rules of natural justice were historically applied to these bodies as well as to court proceedings. These bodies were different from agencies, whose decisions applying administrative jurisdiction were not subject to the rules of natural justice.

inherent jurisdiction (also statutory jurisdiction)   A power or right that is vested in an authority (agency or court) intrinsically (*statutory jurisdiction* is a power or right that is vested in an authority derived from legislation).

intervenor   A person who is given status to participate in a proceeding even though the person is not a party to the proceeding.

proclaimed in force   A bill does not come into force (or become a statute) automatically when it is passed; it must first be proclaimed in force, that is, officially recognized as a statute.

promulgate   To publish a law.

stare decisis   Latin, "following precedent"; a legal doctrine that says that if a prior case is decided in a higher court in the same jurisdiction and on similar facts, then that prior case decision must be followed by subsequent courts.

tortfeasor   A person who commits a tort (a civil wrong excluding an action in contract).

ultra vires   Latin, "outside (or beyond) the power"; an action or a statute that is determined by the courts to be outside the powers assigned to the legislature that enacted it.

REVIEW QUESTIONS

1. What are the three branches of government in Canada?
2. Describe how public policy becomes law in Canada.
3. Where would you find how an agency was created, and the powers granted to it?
4. Discuss at least five reasons an agency may be created.
5. Detail the three types of agencies that can exist.
6. Set out five differences between an agency and a court.
7. What are the seven steps to determine which rules and procedures apply to a specific agency?
8. How does the *Statutory Powers Procedure Act* determine rules and procedures to be applied to an Ontario agency?
9. Discuss how four sections of the *Charter of Rights and Freedoms* are used to imply rules to be used in an agency proceeding.
10. What are the two main components or principles that are derived from the "duty to act fairly"?
11. List and explain the three remedies available if there is a problem or concern arising from an agency proceeding.
12. Set out three types of appeal, and the scope of each.
13. What are the remedies available when it is determined that judicial review will be allowed?
14. Discuss the grounds that must exist before judicial review may be awarded.
15. What is a privative clause, and how is it used to avoid judicial review?
16. List and discuss three methods in which public policy is derived or developed.
17. In order for notice to meet the requirement of the duty to act fairly, how may it be given in order to achieve its ends?
18. What is the usual burden of proof used by agencies to determine whether a case has been proven?
19. How does an agency deal with "hearsay" evidence before it at a hearing?
20. List three ways in which most agencies can obtain evidence by compulsion.
21. List three types of relief available if a person successfully sues an agency under tort law.

DISCUSSION QUESTIONS

1. Agencies are a better way to determine a person's rights than are the courts. Discuss.
2. If an agency is meant to deal with matters in an expeditious and cost-effective manner and if the expertise is developed in the agency, is it worthwhile or even appropriate to allow a court to interfere with an agency's decision?
3. Have the various statutory and common law protections imposed on an agency's proceedings placed enough or too many rules on an agency's proceedings?

4. Should there be so many remedies available to a person who is concerned with an agency proceeding?
5. What changes would you make in Canadian administrative law? Why?
6. Why do the philosophies of some incoming governments lead to an expansion of the number and powers of agencies, and some lead to a contraction of the numbers and powers of agencies?
7. Discuss the current and future effects of the *Charter of Rights and Freedom* on agencies.
8. List four indicators of bias in an agency and/or an adjudicating member.

SUGGESTED READINGS

Blake, Sara. *Administrative Law in Canada*, 2d ed. (Toronto, Ont.: Butterworths, 1997).

Brooks, Stephen. *Public Policy in Canada: An Introduction*, 3d ed. (Toronto, Ont.: Oxford University Press, 1998).

Finkelstein, Neil, & Brian M. Rogers (eds.), *Recent Developments in Administrative Law* (Toronto, Ont.: Carswell, 1987).

Jones, David & Anne de Villars. *Principles of Administrative Law*, 2d ed. (Toronto, Ont.: Carswell, 1994).

Law Society of Upper Canada. *Administrative Law: Principles, Practice and Pluralism* (Scarborough, Ont.: Carswell, 1993).

———. *Recent Developments in Administrative Law* (Toronto, Ont.: Department of Continuing Legal Education, 1995).

Macaulay, Robert W., & James L.H. Sprague, *Practice and Procedure before Administrative Tribunals* (Toronto, Ont.: Carswell, 1994).

Moskoff, Franklin R., ed. *Administrative Tribunals: A Practice Handbook for Legal Counsel* (Aurora, Ont.: Canada Law Book Inc., 1989).

WEBSITES

University of Toronto Law Library with Administrative Law links: <http://www.law-lib.utoronto.ca/resources/topic/admin.htm>

York University Law Library with Administrative Law links: <http://www.info.library.yorku.ca/depts/law/linksadm.htm>

The Canadian Legal Network website providing links to other sites: <http://canlaw.net/administrative.htm>

University of Montreal Faculty of Law site with many links to statutes, cases, etc.: <http://www.lexum.umontreal.ca/index-en.html>

2

The *Statutory Powers Procedure Act* in General

LEARNING OBJECTIVES

After reading this chapter, the reader should be able to:

- elaborate on the principle of statute annotation
- appreciate how minimum standards of acting fairly are imposed by statute on most Ontario agencies
- summarize key provisions of the *SPPA*
- identify how cases and/or decisions assist in the interpretation of statutory provisions
- illustrate and discuss how minimum standards of the duty to act fairly are applied in Ontario agencies
- distinguish between lawyers, licensed paralegals, and lay representatives as dealt with under the *SPPA*
- document the importance of public hearings in administrative law and the exceptions to this principle under Ontario law
- explain the importance of costs in relation to Ontario agencies

INTRODUCTION

The Ontario statute, the *Statutory Powers Procedure Act*, R.S.O. 1990, c. S.22, as amended (*SPPA*), can be called a statute of general application as it applies to most Ontario agencies. As noted in the previous chapter, this statute was to set out "minimum" rules of fair procedure that should apply to tribunals (as defined under the Act) and is basically a codification, as extended, of the case law developed under the rules of natural justice, more currently called the duty to act fairly. See the previous chapter for a brief discussion of the history of the *SPPA*, both in its original form and after the major amendments to it made in 1994 and 1999.

This chapter will examine specific and important provisions of the *SPPA* and, where appropriate, briefly discuss court cases and/or agency decisions that have examined such specific sections of the Act (called "annotating"). It is hoped that upon reviewing this chapter, the reader will have a better idea of the relevance of the *SPPA*, either directly or indirectly, to Ontario agencies and how procedures need to be followed to make sure a person has a fair hearing.

THE *SPPA* CLAUSES

Section 1 — Interpretation

Subsection (1) has definitions of 10 words or phrases, and three are important to the reader:

> "representative" means a person authorized under the *Law Society Act* to represent a person in a proceeding (this is the definition, in addition to ss. 10 and 23(3) of the *SPPA*, that allows those licensed by the Law Society of Upper Canada, including lawyers and paralegals to represent a person before a tribunal);

> "statutory power of decision" means the power to make a decision, given by or under a statute, affecting a person's legal rights, powers, privileges, immunities, duties or liabilities or the eligibility of a person to receive or continue a benefit or licence (this broad definition is needed to differentiate those agencies who have a statutory power of decision and therefore to whom the *SPPA* may apply under s. 3 and those agencies which do not exercise a statutory power of decision and to whom the *SPPA* does not apply);

> "tribunal" means one or more persons upon which a statutory power of decision is conferred by or under a statute (even agencies not specifically named as a tribunal would be covered by the definition and are referred to as such under the *SPPA* as long as it exercises a statutory power of decision).

Also defined are various types of hearings.

The definition of "statutory power of decision" was examined in the Ontario Divisional Court (Div. Ct.) case of *Lerew v. St Lawrence College of Applied Arts and Technology*, [2005] O.J. No. 1436, 196 O.A.C. 363, 138 A.C.W.S. (3d) 591 (the *Lerew* case) involving an application for judicial review of a decision of a student appeals committee. The court, in deciding whether the procedural fairness provisions of the *SPPA* applied, looked at whether that Act was applicable and to do so looked at the definition of "statutory power of decision". The court looked at the definition in subsection 1(1) and the applicability provision in subsection 3(1) and stated that the "[c]ommittee here does not exercise a statutory power of decision, as it is not exercising a specific power or right conferred by statute to make a decision".

Subsection (2) extends the meaning of the word "person" as used in the Act.

Section 2 — Liberal Construction of the Act and Rules

The *SPPA* and any rules made under sections 17.1(4) and 25.1 are to be "liberally construed to secure the just, most expeditious and cost-effective determination of every proceeding on its merits". This gives authority to the tribunal to interpret the provisions of the Act or the rules made pursuant to it in a broad fashion to achieve a just, fast, and inexpensive result.

Section 3 — Application of the Act

Subsection (1) states that the *SPPA* applies to a proceeding by a tribunal in the exercise of a statutory power of decision where the tribunal is required by or under a statute or otherwise by law to hold or afford parties to a proceeding an opportunity for a hearing before making a decision subject to subsection (2). This means that any tribunal making a decision affecting a person's rights that has to give the parties the opportunity for a hearing is bound by this Act, except where subsection (2) applies or where the enabling legislation states that the *SPPA* does not apply.

Subsection (2) sets out specific situations where the *SPPA* does not apply, including the various Ontario courts and situations where specific other rules and procedures apply, such as the coroner, arbitrators, and those persons who investigate and make a report that is not determinative of the final decision.

The Div. Ct. case of *Harrison v. Orillia Soldiers' Memorial Hospital*, [2006] O.J. No. 3973, 56 Admin. L.R. (4th) 198, 153 A.C.W.S. (3d) 993 (the *Harrison* case) examined subsections 3(1) and 3(2) to determine if the decision of the hospital board to revoke privileges fell within the applicability provision of the *SPPA*. The court determined that under subsection 3(1), for the Act to be applicable, the tribunal was required by or under legislation or "otherwise by law" to hold a hearing. Specifically it stated as follows:

> While the Board owes a duty of procedural fairness to a physician when it decides to revoke or suspend an appointment, a full and formal hearing is not required at common law. The fact that the Hospital, in its by-laws, chose to provide certain procedural safeguards for the affected individual does not trigger the full application of the *SPPA* to its proceedings.

Section 4 — Waiver

Subsection (1) states that any procedural requirement of the *SPPA* or other legislation applying to "a proceeding may be waived with the consent of the parties and the tribunal". Subsection (2) allows for a waiver of rules made under the *SPPA*, also by consent. These provisions allow for the waiver of any procedural requirements or rules as long as all the parties and the tribunal consent, thereby allowing for flexibility, if needed, and not enforcing rules by rote.

Section 4.1 — Disposition without Hearing

Unless the enabling legislation requires a hearing, the tribunal can make a decision without a hearing if the parties consent. This provides flexibility where all agree a hearing is not needed.

Section 4.2 — Panels Related to Certain Matters

Subsection (1) allows the chair of a tribunal to assign one or more members to a panel to hear and determine a procedural or interlocutory matter. The Div. Ct. case of *Lennon v. Ontario (Superintendent of Financial Services)* (2007), 87 O.R. 736, 231 O.A.C. 83, 161 A.C.W.S. (3d) 805 (the *Lennon* case) examined subsection 4.2(1) in relation to an appeal of an FST decision.

The court declined to interfere with the Superintendent of Financial Services' decision of consenting to the merger of two pension plans. The appeal alleged that the FST denied procedural fairness to the appellants in a number of ways, including the specific situation set out in the court's decision:

> The appellant objected to these affidavits being filed without requiring the affiants to testify in person. This issue was raised in a pre-hearing conference with the Tribunal Chair, who afforded all sides an opportunity to be heard. The appellant did not object to this pre-hearing procedure at the time, before the full panel of the Tribunal, or before us. The appellant does not challenge the jurisdiction of a single member of the Tribunal to make this ruling prior to the hearing." (Such procedure is authorized by s. 4.2(1) of the *SPPA*.)

In assigning members to such a panel, subsection (2) states that the chair shall take into consideration any requirement imposed by other applicable legislation "that the tribunal be representative of specific interests".

Section 4.2.1 — Panel of One

Subsection (1) allows the chair of a tribunal to decide that a panel of one can hear a proceeding unless there is a statutory requirement of more than one person on the panel, and subsection (2) permits a panel of less than what is statutorily required if all the parties consent. The intent is to spread a fixed number of adjudicators over more hearings if possible and if needed.

Section 4.3 — Expiry of Term

If the term of office of a tribunal member participating in a hearing where the decision is not yet given expires, the term shall be deemed to continue for the purpose of participating in the decision. As one of the requirements of the duty to act fairly is that the person who heard the case should make the decision, this provision tries to remove the impediment of an expiring term to such principle.

The Sup. Ct. J. case of *Conway v. Darby* (2008), 174 A.C.W.S. (3d) 353 (the *Darby* case) discussed section 4.3 in respect of a submission made to the effect that the adjudicator who heard the original matter was no longer a member of the Consent and Capacity Board and, therefore, could not hear new submissions regarding costs. The appeal on that matter, however, was withdrawn since the adjudicator could hear the new matter, as stated in the case:

> Mr. Nemetz, the Board member who initially heard the matter, was no longer a member of the Board so the costs of the initial hearing would be wasted as a hearing *de novo* would be required. Respondent's counsel advised that Mr. Nemetz would be able to continue the hearing pursuant to section 4.3 of the *Statutory Powers Procedure Act*, R.S.O. 1990, c. S.22.

Section 4.4 — Incapacity of Member

Subsection (1) states that if a tribunal member, "who has participated in a hearing, becomes unable, for any reason, to complete the hearing or to participate in the decision, the remaining member or members may complete the hearing and give a decision" subject to subsection (2), which says that subsection (1) does not apply if other legislation deals with the issue. Section 4.4 allows a hearing to proceed even if one member of a panel of adjudicators cannot continue due to incapacity.

Section 4.5 — Decision Not to Process
Commencement of Proceeding

Subsection (1) permits the tribunal or its administrative staff to decide not to process the documents relating to the commencement of a proceeding if (i) the documents are incomplete or are received after the time required to commence has elapsed, or the fee required is not paid, or there is some other technical defect, and (ii) the decision not to process is made in compliance with subsection (3), which requires the tribunal to make rules under section 25.1 respecting the making of such decision. As well, any of the grounds for refusing to process and the requirement for the processing to be resumed must be set out in the notice prescribed in subsection (2). The intent here is to allow the tribunal or its staff to not process documents if there are defects, on the conditons that there are rules in place and there is some possibility for the party to correct such defects.

Section 4.6 — Dismissal of Proceeding without Hearing

Subsection (1) states that, subject to the requirements of giving notice and considering submissions under subsection (5) and the rules covering early dismissal of a proceeding under section 25.1 containing the items set out in subsection (6),

> a tribunal may dismiss a proceeding without a hearing if
> (a) the proceeding is frivolous, vexatious or is commenced in bad faith;
> (b) the proceeding relates to matters that are outside the jurisdiction of the tribunal; or
> (c) some aspect of the statutory requirements for bringing the proceeding has not been met.

This provision is intended to prevent abuses of the process and to have matters that should not be heard by the tribunal dismissed early on in the process without wasting undue time and money.

The arbitration decision under the Financial Services Commission of Ontario auspices in *Luskin v. Personal Insurance Co. of Canada*, 2007 FSCO A06-001216 (the *Luskin* decision), involved whether the arbitration should be dismissed based on the non-performance of obligations imposed on the insured and his counsel in pre-hearings, as well as their non-attendance at pre-hearings. The arbitrator dismissed the arbitration with the following explanation:

> It is unusual to dismiss an arbitration prior to a full hearing on the merits, absent the consent of both parties to a dismissal. There are, however, rare instances when the circumstances suggest that a matter should not be forced to proceed through the system to a formal arbitration hearing, such as when the outcome is a foregone conclusion and there is absolutely no possibility of success.
>
> The easy, uncontroversial route to take is to let this arbitration proceed, unopposed, to the final hearing, with the opposing party accumulating costs all the way. In this matter, I think such an approach is inappropriate, a waste of resources, and potentially unfair to both parties.
>
> On the face of it, it would be a travesty of justice and waste of resources if there was no way to terminate an arbitration in circumstances where there was no possibility of success at a hearing. Certainly, if a party bringing the arbitration is unwilling to participate in the process, and providing instructions to counsel, let alone appearing for pre-hearings, motions, and hearings as required, such would likely be the case.
>
> An early dismissal of an arbitration relies on more than just an interpretation of the general principles of the arbitration system. At least three potential bases for an early decision dismissing an arbitration are found in the *Statutory Powers Procedure Act* (*SPPA*), a law which applies to all arbitrations.

The arbitrator then made reference to sections 4.6(1), 4.6(2), and 7(1) and then examined the word "vexatious" as used in subsection 4.6(1)(a), which relates to an abuse of process or bringing "the administration of justice and the arbitration system into disrepute".

Subsection (2) requires that before there is an early dismissal under subsection (1), the tribunal shall give notice, complying with subsection (3), of its intent to dismiss to all parties if the proceeding is being dismissed on grounds of matters that are outside the jurisdiction of the tribunal or to the party commencing the proceeding for any other grounds. Written submissions by a party who receives a notice of early dismissal may be made in accordance with subsection (4), which must be considered by the tribunal under subsection (5).

Section 4.7 — Classifying Proceedings

> A tribunal may make rules under section 25.1 classifying the types of proceedings that come before it and setting guidelines as to the procedural steps or processes (such as preliminary motions, pre-hearing conferences, alternative dispute resolution mechanisms, expedited hearings) that apply to each type of proceeding and the circumstances in which other procedures may apply.

This is one of a number of sections that gives a tribunal authority to deal with certain matters if the tribunal makes such rules under section 25.1.

Section 4.8 — Alternative Dispute Resolution

Subsection (1) mandates the tribunal to direct parties in a proceeding to participate in an alternative dispute resolution (ADR) mechanism (defined in subsection (2) as including "mediation, conciliation, negotiation or any other means of facilitating the resolution of issues in dispute") for resolving the whole or an issue in a proceeding if the tribunal has made rules to that effect (and containing procedural guidelines as outlined in subsection (3)), under section 25.1, and if all parties consent to participating in it. As in the court system, there is a move toward resolving disputes in agencies by ADR. The rules of the tribunal made under section 25.1 can also require mandatory ADR in all or specific circumstances pursuant to subsection (4). Note also that subsection (5) states that the rules may provide that the person appointed to conduct the ADR be independent of the tribunal or a member of the tribunal; but if a member is so appointed, then such member cannot subsequently hear the matter unless the parties consent.

Section 4.9 — Person Conducting ADR Not Compellable and Notes Kept May Not Be Used As Evidence

Subsection (1) states that no person appointed to do the ADR "shall be compelled to give testimony or produce documents in a proceeding before the tribunal or in a civil proceeding with respect to matters that come to his or her knowledge in the course of exercising his or her duties under this or any other Act" and no notes or records kept by such person are admissible in a civil proceeding under subsection (2). This is to ensure that the parties participating know that anything said in the ADR process cannot be used in a subsequent proceeding and, therefore, the parties may be more forthcoming.

Section 5 — Parties

> The parties to a proceeding shall be the persons specified as parties by or under the statute under which the proceeding arises or, if not so specified, persons entitled by law to be parties to the proceeding.

If the enabling legislation does not specify who the parties are, such determination would be done in accordance with case law.

The Div. Ct. case of *McFadyen v. Ontario (Mining and Lands Commission)*, [2007] O.J. No. 4875, 232 O.A.C. 239, 162 A.C.W.S. (3d) 873 (the *McFadyen* case) involved an application for judicial review of an order of the Mining and Lands Commissioner, partly on the basis that the applicants submitted that they were not added as parties to the proceedings that led to the order. The court examined section 5 of the *SPPA* regarding who are parties to a matter before a tribunal. In looking at the facts, the court stated that the Commissioner allowed the applicants to make a submission and file affidavit material supporting their request to be added as parties and had an oral hearing. The court held that the Commissioner applied the correct approach in determining party status:

> The tribunal is not restricted to the test that is applicable to court proceedings, but may consider other matters, including the subject-matter of the decision-making power, the nature of the issue to be decided at the hearing and the object of the governing legislation.

Section 5.1 — Written Hearings

Written hearings, as defined in subsection 1(1), may be held if the tribunal's rules made under section 25.1 deal with it. The tribunal shall not hold a written hearing if a party satisfies the tribunal that there is good reason for not doing so under subsection (2), but this does not apply under subsection (2.1) if the hearing is dealing with procedural matters. In other words, if the rules allow written hearings, they can be used for procedural matters and for any other matter unless a party shows there are good reasons not to use a written hearing. Note also that subsection (3) states, "[i]n a written hearing, all the parties are entitled to receive every document that the tribunal receives in the proceeding."

An example of the use of a written hearing is illustrated in the Human Rights Tribunal of Ontario's (HRTO) decision of *Domingues v. Fortino*, 2007 HRTO 7 (CanLII) (the *Domingues* decision). The HRTO first noted the power of the Tribunal to hold a written hearing under section 5.1 of the *SPPA* and then cited a previous decision:

> In *Sanford v. Koop*, 2005 HRTO 28 (CanLII), the Tribunal held that it had the authority to hold a written hearing in appropriate circumstances. While not purporting to enumerate all cases where a written hearing would be appropriate, the Tribunal specifically found that where a respondent chooses not to participate in the Tribunal's legal processes and the Commission or Complainant requests a written hearing, it would be rare for the Tribunal to schedule an oral hearing (*Sanford*, *supra*, at paras. 19 and 21).

In *Sanford*, the HRTO also discussed, at paragraphs 30 and 31 of its decision, the nature of evidence that would normally be required at a written hearing:

> Again, case law suggests that mere pleadings will not be sufficient to establish an evidentiary basis for findings of fact and remedial orders, where a hearing is required to be held (*Re City of Windsor*, *supra*). The Tribunal finds however that affidavits or statutory declarations by persons who would otherwise have provided *viva voce* evidence had the hearing been held as an oral hearing would be a proper form of evidence. These could contain statements based on personal knowledge, or information and belief (as long as

the basis for the information and belief was set out in the affidavit). Also, business records and medical reports which would normally be admissible before the Tribunal without the necessity of calling the maker of the document, would generally be admitted. The Tribunal would retain the power to question an affiant, or rule or place conditions upon the admissibility of a document.

The Tribunal notes that it is always to be open to parties to make submissions as to the appropriate form of evidence in a written hearing in a particular case. The comments above set out what the Tribunal considers appropriate in the normal course, and in circumstances where a respondent chooses not to participate in a hearing.

Section 5.2 — Electronic Hearings

Electronic hearings, as defined in subsection 1(1), may be held if the tribunal's rules made under section 25.1 deal with it. The tribunal shall not hold an electronic hearing if a party satisfies the tribunal that it is likely to cause the party significant prejudice under subsection (2), but this does not apply under subsection (3) if the hearing is dealing with procedural matters. In other words, if the rules allow electronic hearings, they can be used for procedural matters and for any other matter unless a party shows it is likely to cause the party significant prejudice. Note also that subsection (4) states, "[in an] electronic hearing, all the parties and the members of the tribunal participating in the hearing must be able to hear one another and any witnesses throughout the hearing." The electronic set up must allow all persons involved to hear each other, which, in theory, allows both telephone conference calls and video-conferencing.

Section 5.2.1 — Combination of Hearings

> A tribunal may, in a proceeding, hold any combination of written, electronic and oral hearings.

Section 5.3 — Pre-hearing Conferences

Subsection (1) mandates that, subject to any other applicable legislation pursuant to subsection (1.1), if pre-hearing conferences are covered in rules made pursuant to section 25.1, tribunals may direct the parties to participate in a pre-hearing conference to consider the following:

(a) the settlement of any or all of the issues;
(b) the simplification of the issues;
(c) facts or evidence that may be agreed upon;
(d) the dates by which any steps in the proceeding are to be taken or begun;
(e) the estimated duration of the hearing; and
(f) any other matter that may assist in the just and most expeditious disposition of the proceeding.

The subsection allows for a broad type of pre-hearing conference, which can be used to achieve multiple purposes and are aimed at making the ultimate resolution of the matter faster and cheaper to obtain. In the Ontario Municipal Board (OMB) decision of *Re the City of Burlington Official Plan Amendment No. 3* (2006), 54 O.M.B.R. 340, 2006 CLB 13469 (the *Burlington* decision), a motion was brought to determine the validity of an order made by the OMB in a pre-hearing procedure. The OMB dismissed the motion referring to, *inter alia*, powers given to it to deal with such situations, including section 5.3 of the *SPPA*:

[S]ection 5.3(1) of the *SPPA* ... permits the Board, in the context of pre-hearing conferences, to make orders that may "assist in the just and most expeditious disposition of the proceeding".

Under subsection (2), the chair can designate anyone, even a member of the tribunal, to preside over the pre-hearing conference and such member so designated may make orders considered necessary or advisable with respect to the conduct of the proceeding pursuant to subsection (3). However, if such member presides at the pre-hearing in which the parties attempt to settle issues, that member cannot also preside at the hearing unless the parties consent under subsection (4). This disqualification is to attempt to have the adjudicator not hear matters before the hearing that might affect the decision. Please note subsection (5) may allow for pre-hearing conferences to be done electronically, which are done by many agencies.

Section 5.4 — Disclosure

Subsection (1) mandates that, subject to any other applicable legislation pursuant to subsection (1.1), if there are rules in this area made pursuant to section 25.1,

> the tribunal may, at any stage of the proceeding before all hearings are complete, make orders for,
> (a) the exchange of documents;
> (b) the oral or written examination of a party;
> (c) the exchange of witness statements and reports of expert witnesses;
> (d) the provision of particulars;
> (e) any other form of disclosure.

This provision allows disclosure in agencies, which may not be as formal or detailed as in the court system but is absolutely essential for fair hearings. Note that subsection (2) states that subsection (1) does not authorize the disclosure of privileged information.

The Div. Ct. case of *York Region District School Board v. Ontario College of Teachers* (2007), 154 A.C.W.S. (3d) 804, 2007 CLB 8617, 56 Admin. L.R. (4th) 313, 221 O.A.C. 55 (the *York Region* case), deals with an application for the judicial review of a decision made by the Discipline Committee of the Ontario College of Teachers (the Discipline Committee). The application was based on solicitor–client privilege and inadvertent disclosure of documents. In the case, the judge noted the relevant section of the *SPPA*:

> Section 5.4(2) of the *Statutory Powers Procedure Act* makes an order for disclosure subject to the same exception for privileged information.

Section 6 — Notice of Hearing

Subsection (1) states that the "parties to a proceeding shall be given reasonable notice of the hearing by the tribunal" and such notice, pursuant to subsection (2), shall include a reference to the statutory authority under which the hearing will be held. The purpose of the provision is to ensure the parties have sufficient time and explanation of the hearing in order to properly prepare for it. Specific details of what is to be included in a notice of oral hearing, written hearing, and electronic hearing are enumerated in subsections (3), (4), and (5), respectively. These subsections provide a guide for the tribunal as to the minimum contents of the notice depending on the format of hearing involved.

Toronto Transit Commission v. A.T.U., Local 113 (2007), 164 A.C.W.S. (3d) 810, 2007 CLB 13690, [2007] OLRBREP.SEPT/OCT 982, 233 O.A.C. 14 (the *TTC* case) is a Div. Ct. case that involves an application for judicial review of two decisions of the Ontario Labour Relations Board (the OLRB). The application was litigated on the basis of a telephone conference call setting up a hearing with limitations on the presentation of evidence. The court summarized the situation as follows:

> [The appellant] took the position that the Board had exceeded its jurisdiction by conducting the hearings as "expedited hearings"; the first, on short notice and without the Union's participation; and the second, with unfairly limited presentation time. As a result, it complained it had not been afforded full opportunity to present evidence and make submissions. This was alleged to be a natural justice denial of procedural fairness and required the setting aside of both orders.

One of the arguments raised was that section 6 of the *SPPA* "also requires a notice of hearing, sets out the content of the notice and gives the parties a similar right to demonstrate that significant prejudice will likely be caused by an electronic hearing". The court held that section 6 of the *SPPA* as well as the Rules of Procedure of the OLRB and its enabling legislation allowed the OLRB to act as it did, and therefore there was no denial of natural justice.

Section 7 — Effect of Non-attendance at Hearing After Due Notice

Where notice of an oral hearing under subsection (1), a written hearing under subsection (2), or an electronic hearing under subsection (3) is given to a party and that party does not attend the oral hearing, does not participate in the written hearing or act under subsection 6(4)(b), or does not participate in the electronic hearing or act under subsection 6(5)(c), the tribunal may proceed in the absence or without the participation of that party and that party is not entitled to any further notice in the proceeding. The intent of this provision is to allow the hearing to proceed even if a party is absent or not participating, as long as proper notice has been given and, therefore, making the process fair to all parties.

In the appeal order of *McCormack v. Aviva Canada Inc.* (2008), Appeal P06-00024 (the *McCormack* decision), conducted under the auspices of the Financial Services Commission of Ontario (FSCO), the FSCO dismissed the appeal of the representative of the insured of the arbitration order, which required that representative to personally pay expenses of the insurance company.

In examining the matter, the Director's Delegate discussed the ramifications of section 7:

> You seem to suggest that, since Mr. McCormack has not responded, he can be noted in default and your appeal can succeed automatically. However, that is not how matters proceed at tribunals. The *Statutory Powers Procedure Act*, R.S.O. 1990, c. S.22, only provides that, where a party does not attend at a hearing despite receiving notice, "the tribunal may proceed in the absence of the party and the party is not entitled to any further notice in the proceeding." [s. 7(1)]
>
> You must still proceed with the appeal if you wish to reverse the arbitrator's decision. As for Mr. Isabella seeking arbitration expenses after he asked for a withdrawal without expenses, I remind you that the same expenses provisions — that a representative may be liable for advancing a frivolous or vexatious claim — apply on appeal as at arbitration.

Section 8 — Where Character of the Party Is At Issue

> Where the good character, propriety of conduct or competence of a party is an issue in a proceeding, the party is entitled to be furnished prior to the hearing with reasonable information of any allegations with respect thereto.

This provision gives the party notice and information of such issue, allowing for better preparation.

In the Div. Ct. case of *Yar v. College of Physicians and Surgeons of Ontario* (2009), 174 A.C.W.S. (3d) 1199, 2009 CLB 1240 (the *Yar* case), Dr. Yar appealed the finding of professional misconduct by a panel of the Discipline Committee of the College of Physicians and Surgeons of Ontario (the Discipline Committee). In determining the appeal, the court looked at the adequacy of notice given to the person subjected to disciplinary proceedings:

> Adequacy of notice is a fundamental principle inherent in the duty of procedural fairness in disciplinary proceedings. This has been codified in section 8 of the *Statutory Powers Procedure Act*, R.S.O. 1990, c. S.22 which provides the notice requirements in the context of a disciplinary proceeding.

Section 9 — Public and Private Hearings and Maintenance of Order

Oral hearings are to be public under subsection (1) except

> where the tribunal is of the opinion that,
> (a) matters involving public security may be disclosed; or
> (b) intimate financial or personal matters or other matters may be disclosed at the hearing of such a nature, having regard to the circumstances, that the desirability of avoiding disclosure thereof in the interests of any person affected or in the public interest outweighs the desirability of adhering to the principle that hearings be open to the public,
> in which case the tribunal may hold the hearing in the absence of the public.

Similarly, members of the public are to have reasonable access to the documents submitted in a written hearing under subsection (1.1) unless, in the opinion of the tribunal, the two grounds in subsection (1) apply; electronic hearings are to be open to the public under subsection (1.2) unless, in the opinion of the tribunal, the grounds in subsection (1) apply or it is not practical to do so. Although the public should be invited to attend any hearing, there has to be a balance between the rights of public security and the rights of privacy of persons not to have intimate financial or personal matters widely known. Subsection (2) authorizes the tribunal to make such orders and give such directions as it considers necessary for the maintenance of order at the hearing and if such order or direction is disobeyed, the tribunal may call for the assistance of any peace officer to enforce such order or direction, taking such action as necessary. This allows the tribunal to obtain assistance to maintain order, which may not be initially available unlike a court.

The Div. Ct. case of *Lifford Wine Agencies Ltd. v. Ontario (Alcohol and Gaming Commission)*, [2003] O.J. No. 4972, 179 O.A.C. 76, 127 A.C.W.S. (3d) 1 (the *Lifford Wine* case) involved a hearing before the Alcohol and Gaming Commission of Ontario, ordered to be held *in camera*. The court made the following statement regarding open hearings:

> Section 9(1) of the *Statutory Powers Procedure Act* and the common law both strongly favour open hearings, particularly when involving a hearing before a public body such as in this case. There are strong public policy reasons for this. A quote from the judgment of Doherty J.A. in *Her Majesty the Queen v. Toronto Star Newspapers et al.*, [2003] O.J. No. 4006:
>
> > [4] "A publication ban should only be ordered when:
> > (a) such an order is necessary in order to prevent a serious risk to the proper administration of justice because reasonably alternative measures will not prevent the risk, and
> > (b) the salutary effects of the publication ban outweigh the deleterious effects on the rights and interests of the parties and the public, including the effects on the right to free expression, the right of the accused to a fair and public trial, and the efficacy of the administration of justice."

That quote deals with a publication ban, however the same practical test applies in the instant case.

Section 9.1 — Proceedings Involving Similar Questions

Unless the *Consolidated Hearings Act*, as set out in subsection (2), applies or the provisions of subsections (3) or (4) applies, subsection (1) states that

If "two or more proceedings before a tribunal involve the same or similar questions of fact, law or policy, the tribunal may,
  (a) combine the proceedings or any part of them, with the consent of the parties;
  (b) hear the proceedings at the same time, with the consent of the parties;
  (c) hear the proceedings one immediately after the other; or
  (d) stay one or more of the proceedings until after the determination of another one of them.

It is hoped that similar matters can be dealt with more expeditiously and hopefully more economically by giving the tribunal various alternative mechanisms to deal with them. The Ontario Municipal Board's 2007 joint decision (No. 0489) in *Lee-Mar Investments Ltd. v. Toronto (City)*, File No. LC060012 and *Maple Leaf Firelog Products Company v. Toronto (City)*, File No. LC060026 (jointly called the *Lee-Mar/Maple Leaf* decision), is an example of such a consolidation. Furthermore, under subsection (5), if "the parties to the second-named proceeding consent, the tribunal may treat evidence that is admitted in a proceeding as if it were also admitted in another proceeding that is heard at the same time" under subsection 9.1(1)(b).

Section 10 — Right to Representation

A party to a proceeding may be represented by a representative.

This section along with the definition of representative in subsection 1(1) and the details of subsection 23(3) allows paralegals licensed by the Law Society of Upper Canada to represent persons at an agency without being excluded by the tribunal on the grounds of incompetence: See *Romanchook v. Garda Ontario*, [2009] HRTO 1077, an interim decision of the HRTO where this matter was discussed (the *Romanchook* decision).

The Federal Court of Appeal, in the case of *Law Society of Upper Canada v. Canada (Minister of Citizenship and Immigration)* (2008), 295 D.L.R. (4th) 488, 2008 CLB 5684, 168 A.C.W.S. (3d) 152, 2008 FCA 243, 72 Imm. L.R. (3d) 26, 383 N.R. 200 (the *LSUC* case), looked at representation by non-lawyers in different jurisdictions in Canada:

Representation by non-lawyers is a common feature of administrative adjudication: see, for example, Ontario's general administrative procedural code, the *Statutory Powers Procedure Act*, R.S.O. 1990, c. S.22, section 10.

Section 10.1 — Examination of Witnesses

A party to a proceeding may, at an oral or electronic hearing,
  (a) call and examine witnesses and present evidence and submissions; and
  (b) conduct cross-examinations of witnesses at the hearing reasonably required for a full and fair disclosure of all matters relevant to the issues in the proceeding.

This provision allows a party to adduce evidence and question the other side's evidence to ideally permit the fairest hearing possible.

The Sup. Ct. J. case of *Conway v. Ontario* (2008), 172 A.C.W.S. (3d) 503, 2008 CLB 12281 (the *Conway* case), involves an appeal of a decision of the Consent and Capacity Board on various grounds, including that the appellant was not permitted to cross-examine a witness. In looking at such ground, the court stated the following:

> Section 10.1(b) of the *Statutory Powers Procedure Act*, R.S.O. 1990, c. S.22, provides that a party to a proceeding may conduct cross-examinations of witnesses "reasonably required for a full and fair disclosure of all matters relevant to the issues in the proceeding."

Section 11 — Rights of Witnesses to Representation

Under subsection (1), a witness at an oral or electronic hearing is entitled to be advised by a representative as to his or her rights. Such representative can take no other part in the hearing except with leave of the tribunal. Further pursuant to subsection (2) where the hearing is closed to the public, the witness's representative is not entitled to be present except when that witness is giving evidence. Under this provision, witnesses are entitled to independent advice as needed.

Section 12 — Summonses

Subsections (1)–(3.1) in this section relate to (i) the ability of the tribunal to issue summonses to require any person, including parties, to give evidence under oath/affirmation and to produce documents and things in evidence; (ii) the form and service of summons; and (iii) fees and allowances allowed for such summons. Subsections (4)–(7) detail the ability of a judge of the Superior Court of Justice to issue a bench warrant against a person based upon proving certain facts under subsections (5)–(7). Such warrant is to be in prescribed form and is directed to any police officer for apprehension of the person to be brought before the tribunal in accordance with subsection (4.1). If there is a concern that a witness will not appear, the mechanism of asking for a summons, which ultimately leads to the issuance of a bench warrant, may ensure the appearance where possible and is also useful as the hearing will likely be adjourned pending the appearance of such witness. Without the service of a summons, it is unlikely that the tribunal will adjourn the hearing pending the arrival of the recalcitrant witness.

In the arbitration pre-hearing decision in *Kuan v. Kingsway General Insurance Co.* (2008), FSCO A07-002341 (the *Kuan* decision), conducted under the auspices of the FSCO, there was an order for production of documents. The arbitrator of the case justified its decision with a reference to the *SPPA*:

> Section 12(1) of the *Statutory Powers Procedure Act*, R.S.O. 1990, c. S.22 ("*SPPA*") also grants extensive powers to tribunals, including arbitrators, to order the production of relevant evidence in matters before them.

Section 13 — Contempt Proceedings

Subsection (1) states that if a person, without lawful excuse, does not do required acts as set out in clauses (a) and (b), or if a person does any other thing in court that would be considered contempt of court, "the tribunal may, of its own motion or on the motion of a party to the proceeding, state a case to the divisional court setting out the facts and that court may inquire into the matter and, after hearing any witnesses who may be produced against or on behalf of that person and after hearing any statement that may be offered in defence, punish or take steps for the punishment of that person in like manner as if he or she had been guilty of contempt of the court" provided that subsection (1) also applies to a person doing the acts set out in subsection (2). Although tribunals do not have the court's inherent jurisdiction to directly manage its process up to and including putting the offender into custody, they can use this section to have a court take whatever steps are necessary to manage the hearing against unlawful disruptions.

In the case of *Petsinis v. Escalhorda*, [2000] O.J. No. 3324, [2000] O.T.C. 570, 99 A.C.W.S. (3d) 486 (the *Petsinis* case), the Superior Court of Justice dealt with an application for leave to appeal a contempt order arising out of a proceeding under the *Tenant Protection Act*. In looking at the issue of contempt, the court noted that the *SPPA* "does not authorize a tribunal to make a finding of contempt itself. It simply allows the tribunal to state a case to the divisional court for it to make a finding of contempt."

Section 14 — Protection for Witnesses

Subsection (1) protects witnesses giving evidence in two ways as follows:

> A witness at an oral or electronic hearing shall be deemed to have objected to answer any question asked him or her upon the ground that the answer may tend to criminate him or her or may tend to establish his or her liability to civil proceedings at the instance of the Crown, or of any person, and no answer given by a witness at a hearing shall be used or be receivable in evidence against the witness in any trial or other proceeding against him or her thereafter taking place, other than a prosecution for perjury in giving such evidence.

Although Canadian law does not give a right not to answer questions on the basis that the answers would tend to incriminate them, the protection in this section, similar to evidence in a court setting, means evidence given is not admissible in any other proceeding taking place after except for prosecution for perjury.

Section 14 was discussed in the Ontario Municipal Board decision of *Kimvar Enterprises Inc. v. Simcoe (County)* (2007), 57 O.M.B.R. 493, 2007 CLB 13145, 37 M.P.L.R. (4th) 294 (the *Kimvar* decision). The case involves a motion to adjourn. One of the grounds for the motion is expressed below:

> The Moving Parties submit that Kimvar has launched a number of lawsuits against members of the IDA and related individuals. Accordingly, their ability to make their case before the Board is impaired as key witnesses find themselves intimidated to publicly oppose the development.

In looking at the submission, the OMB stated the following:

> The Board finds that the existence of these lawsuits cannot possibly be a basis for an adjournment. As Mr. Miller submitted, intimidation is a defined tort and it is simply not enough to come before the Board and say I am afraid to give evidence because I will get sued. The Board is subject to the requirements of the *Statutory Powers Procedure Act*, R.S.O. 1990, c. S.22 (SPPA). Witnesses who appear before the Board are subject to the protection set out in section 14 of the SPPA.

Section 15 — Evidence

Subsection (1) states that the tribunal may admit as evidence, whether sworn or admissible in court, any oral testimony, document, or thing "relevant to the subject-matter of the proceeding and may act on such evidence, but the tribunal may exclude anything unduly repetitious". Subsections (2) and (3) set out the specific situations where evidence is inadmissible at a hearing: (i) evidence considered privilege under the law (ss. (2)(a)), (ii) evidence designated as inadmissible by the enabling or other statute (ss. (2)(b)), and (iii) oral testimony, documents, or things for which the extent or purpose of its use as evidence is expressly limited by an Act (ss. (3)). Instead of the extensive rules of evidence with the countless exceptions used in court, tribunals are allowed to admit any evidence, with certain exceptions, that is relevant and not unduly repetitious. Copies of a document or other thing may be admitted as evidence if the tribunal is satisfied as to its authenticity under subsection (4) and copies of documents certified by a member of the tribunal are admissible as evidence in a proceeding in which the document is admissible as evidence of the document under subsection (6). Subsection (5) allows, if the tribunal gives leave and authorizes it, for a photocopy of the document to be filed as evidence. The original document can either be released or photocopied and certified by a member of the tribunal to be given instead.

The Div. Ct. case of *Ontario Racing Commission v. Hudon* (2008), 173 A.C.W.S. (3d) 666, 2008 CLB 14037 (the *Ontario Racing* case), looked at the admissibility of evidence in dealing with an application for judicial review. The court made the following observations:

> The wording of s. 15(1) is permissive. It grants a tribunal the discretion to accept or reject evidence that is not admissible in a court. Depending on the circumstances, a tribunal may reasonably decide that evidence inadmissible at common law should not be admitted before it.

Section 15.1 — Use of Previously Admitted Evidence

Previously admitted evidence, as defined in subsection (2), means evidence admitted in other court or tribunal proceeding before may be treated as evidence admitted by the tribunal in its proceeding if the parties consent (ss. (1)). This power of allowing the use of previously admitted evidence, pursuant to subsection (3), is in addition to the power of the tribunal to admit evidence under section 15. With the parties' consent, this additional power to admit evidence allows the tribuanl to circumvent the formal rules regarding admitting evidence, leading to a faster and less costly proceeding.

An example of a decision that discussed the use of previously admitted evidence can be found in *F.(D.) v. Wawanesa Insurance Co.* (2006), FSCO A05-000779 (the *F.(D.)* decision), an arbitration pre-hearing decision conducted under the auspices of the FSCO. The arbitrator of the case was requested to order that the insurer pay for the transcript of the evidence of a previous arbitration between the parties. The arbitrator ruled against the request because section 15.1 requires the consent of both parties to the use of previously admitted evidence and the insurer did not consent in this case. In other words, there was no jurisdiction for the arbitrator in this case to order it.

Section 15.2 — Witness Panels

> A tribunal may receive evidence from panels of witnesses composed of two or more persons, if the parties have first had an opportunity to make submissions in that regard.

If such situation occurs, this power should reduce the time needed for the proceeding as a panel can give the evidence at the same time instead of calling separate witnesses.

Section 16 — Notice of Facts and Opinions

This section allows the tribunal, in making its decision, to take notice of facts judicially noticed and "notice of any generally recognized scientific or technical facts, information or opinions within its scientific or specialized knowledge". This power allows for a faster hearing as this information can be taken notice of without the need for a party to adduce evidence to prove it. The adjudicator who takes notice in this way should state what was taken notice of in the decision so the parties are aware of it.

Section 16.1 — Interim Decisions and Orders

A tribunal may make interim decisions and orders under subsection (1) that may impose conditions on them per subsection (2) and may not need to be accompanied by reasons under subsection (3). There are many situations where the tribunal hears an issue, often raised by motion, which must be decided prior to hearing the whole matter and the power given to a tribunal under this section allows tribunals to make decisions on such preliminary or specific matters.

The Div. Ct. case of *Franklin v. College of Physicians and Surgeons of Ontario* (2007), 161 A.C.W.S. (3d) 496, 2007 CLB 9849, 230 O.A.C. 206 (the *Franklin* case), looked at the specific issue of awarding costs on the interim order of an adjournment, which was brought before the court on judicial review. The court stated the following on the issue:

> The Discipline Committee has no jurisdiction to order costs as a condition of an interim decision to adjourn a hearing, pursuant to s. 16.1(2) of the *Statutory Powers Procedure Act*, R.S.O. 1990, c. S.22.
>
> There are numerous decisions of this and other courts holding that express statutory authority is required for an administrative tribunal to order costs (see, for example, *Birnbaum v. Institute of Chartered Accountants of Ontario*, [1991] O.J. No. 330 (Div. Ct.) at 3; *Persaud v. Society of Management Accountants of Ontario* (1997), 144 D.L.R. (4th) 375 (Div. Ct.) at 384).
>
> The cases relied on by the College suggesting a power to award costs deal with this issue in *obiter* (see *Howatt v. College of Physicians and Surgeons of Ontario*, [2003] O.J. No. 138 (Div. Ct.) at paragraph 32 and *Re Morgan v. Association of Ontario Land Surveyors* (1980), 28 O.R. (2d) 19 (Div. Ct.) at 22).

Section 16.2 — Time Frames

> A tribunal shall establish guidelines setting out the usual time frame for completing proceedings that come before the tribunal and for completing the procedural steps within those proceedings.

This power allows tribunals to set up guidelines and time frames to ensure that matters proceed at a proper pace.

Section 17 — Decisions; Interest

Subsection (1) states that a decision must be given as follows:

> A tribunal shall give its final decision and order, if any, in any proceeding in writing and shall give reasons in writing therefor if requested by a party.

Although this provision is permissive, due to case law, tribunals will give reasons for almost any decision. In the Div. Ct. case of *Ontario (Alcohol and Gaming Commission Registrar) v. Arena Entertainment Inc.* (2008), 167 A.C.W.S. (3d) 131, 2008 CLB 4390, 235 O.A.C. 195 (the *Arena* case), the court looked at the issue of giving reasons:

> Section 17(1) of the *Statutory Powers Procedure Act*, R.S.O. 1990, c. S.22, requires the Board to give its final decision and order in writing and give reasons in writing therefor.
>
> The purpose of providing adequate reasons is to explain to the parties the basis of the decision and to permit appellate courts to properly review the decision. The appellant is correct that reasons must reflect consideration of the main relevant factors and must reveal the reasoning process (see *Gray v. Ontario (Disability Support Program, Director)* (2002), 59 O.R. (3d) 364 (Ont. C.A.) at page 374 citing *VIA Rail Canada Inc. v. Canada (National Transportation Agency)* (2001), 193 D.L.R. (4th) 357 (F.C.A.) citing *Baker v. Canada (Minister of Citizenship and Immigration)*, [1999] 2 S.C.R. 817 and *Northwestern Utilities et al v. Edmonton (City)*, [1978] 1 S.C.R. 684).

Subsection (2) allows the tribunal to award interest as follows:

> A tribunal that makes an order for the payment of money shall set out in the order the principal sum, and if interest is payable, the rate of interest and the date from which it is to be calculated.

This power gives tribunals the power to award interest where appropriate and not necessarily on a fixed scale subject to the enabling legislation and its rules and practice directions.

Section 17.1 — Costs

Pursuant to subsection (2), if "the conduct or course of conduct of a party has been unreasonable, frivolous or vexatious or a party has acted in bad faith" and the tribunal has made rules under subsection (4) with respect to ordering costs, the circumstances to which costs may be ordered and the amount of costs or the manner in which the cost is to be determined, the tribunal under subsection (1) may order a party to pay all or part of another party's costs in a proceeding. The section imports the Canadian court's power to award cost in the Agency setting to effectively punish those parties that act in a reprehensible manner. Note that under subsection (5), subsections 25.1(3)–(6) apply to rules made under subsection (4). Subsections (6)–(9) are continuance and transition provisions dealing with situations that could occur after the institution of the amendments allowing the awarding of costs enacted in 2006.

In the case of *Ontario (Environmental Protection Act, Director) v. Becker Milk Co.*, [2005] O.J. No. 4514 (the *Becker Milk* case), the Superior Court of Justice dealt with an appeal by the Director from an order of the Environmental Review Tribunal (ERT) awarding costs of an appeal to the respondents on the grounds that the ERT had no jurisdiction to award costs. The position of the ERT was that it had jurisdiction pursuant to section 17.1 of the *SPPA* as it made rules pursuant to section 25.1 of the *SPPA* dealing with costs as follows and stated the finding of the court thereafter:

> COSTS
> 73. In a proceeding in which the Tribunal has statutory authority to award costs, parties are required to make every effort to negotiate a costs settlement. Applications for a costs award can be submitted to the Tribunal only when a negotiated settlement cannot be reached. Negotiated settlements do not require Tribunal review or approval.
> 74. A costs application may be filed with the Tribunal at any time prior to the conclusion of the Hearing, or no later than within 30 days from the date of the issuance of the decision and reasons therefor, or final order.

> It is evident from a reading of these rules that they do not meet the requirements of section 17.1(2)(b) of the *SPPA*. Accordingly, it is our respectful view that the rules of the Tribunal were insufficient to enable the Tribunal to acquire authority to award costs pursuant to section 17.1(2)(b) of the *SPPA*.

> Although the Tribunal has adopted Guidelines on Costs Awards in addition to guidelines on various other matters, guidelines are not rules and do not serve to substitute for the rules required by section 17.1(2)(b) of the *SPPA*. The distinction between rules and guidelines is recognized by section 27 of the *SPPA* which reads as follows:

> > Rules, etc., available to public
> > 27. A tribunal shall make any rules or guidelines established under this or any other Act available for examination by the public. 1999, c. 12, Sched. B, s. 16(9).

> Nor has the Tribunal provided, as in the previous version of its rules, that its rules require compliance with the guidelines, thereby perhaps effectively incorporating the guidelines into the rules.

In the decision *Kimvar Enterprises Inc.* (Kimvar) *v. Nextnine Limited et al.* (Nextnine) (2009), OMB PL050290, the OMB was asked to award Kimvar costs of approximately $3,200,000 against various losing parties of the OMB proceeding known as the "the Big Bay Point" hearing. These costs were sought on a partial indemnity basis for legal and consulting costs incurred by and on behalf of Kimvar and others. To determine the result, the OMB determined the following issues:

> The application requires determination of whether the conduct of Nextnine and Gilberts during the Big Bay Point proceeding warrants an award of costs. When distilled, three main issues emerge from Kimvar's application. First, can the Board, as a matter of law, award costs against Gilberts, the law firm that represented Nextnine during the hearing. Second, was the conduct of Nextnine (and Gilberts, if the answer to the first issue is yes) unreasonable, frivolous or vexatious or in bad faith such that an award of costs should be made in favour of Kimvar. Third, should an award of costs be denied on the basis that Kimvar's application has been brought for improper purposes and, as a matter of public policy, should costs be awarded in any event. Prior to responding to the issues, a brief summary of the applicable law is set out below.

The Board first states that the statutory jurisdiction to award costs is found in both s. 97(1) of the *Ontario Municipal Board Act* and s. 17.1 of the *SPPA* provided that the tribunal has made rules to allow for the awarding of costs. In this case the rules exists in Rules 102–104 which make awarding of costs against a party dependant on the party's conduct being "unreasonable, frivolous or vexatious or if the party acted in bad faith."

The OMB found that the conduct complained of against Nextnine should not attract costs.

In looking at the issue regarding an award of costs against the law firm representing Nextnine, the following was found:

> Section 97(2) of the OMB Act does not specify "by whom" or "to whom" costs are to be paid. The Board is given discretion. By analogy to section 131 of the CJA a reasonable interpretation is that it means "by which parties"; however, there is no direction from the court in this regard. Nevertheless, the Board's Rules are clear on costs. The Board has stated clearly that where one party believes that another party has acted unreasonably or there is bad faith, that party can ask for costs. The Board is the master of its own practice and procedure. The Board has made a policy choice that in the event costs are at issue, it is for a party to seek costs against another party. The Board rejects the argument that because the Board's Rules do not preclude costs being sought against counsel resort must be had to the Rules of Civil Procedure. The opposite is true. The Rules are structured to provide clear direction on costs and need not be augmented.
>
> Finally, Kimvar argued that if costs cannot be awarded against a non-party (e.g. legal counsel), the Board would lose its ability to control its own process. The Board disagrees and there is no reason to believe that unreasonable conduct will escape scrutiny. First, parties will always remain liable for conduct that attracts an award of costs and each case is considered on its own merits. The Board notes that distinguishing improper conduct as between a party and its counsel is in any event not always easy. Kimvar was clear at the outset that it could not actually know the degree of responsibility for improper conduct before and at the hearing, which should respectively be borne by Nextnine and Gilberts. Second, under the SPPA any tribunal, including the Board, can prevent abuses of process. The standard is high (see *Volfson v. Royal & Sun Alliance Insurance Co. of Canada*, 2005 CarswellOnt 5232 (Ont.Div.Ct.)). Abuse of process was not the foundation of the claim against Gilberts.

Finally, the OMB looked at the issue of whether the application for costs had been brought for improper purposes. For example, if the cost claim was brought for the purpose of silencing public opposition, it constitutes an improper purpose. The OMB found that if an award of costs is made in this situation, it would create a "chilling effect" and discourage public participation in its process.

The resulting finding of the OMB clarified the awarding of costs in OMB hearings and also dealt with the concept of "strategic lawsuit against public participation (SLAPP)" as follows:

> The decision in this matter is intended to reinforce and reiterate the Board's practice that costs are not awarded lightly nor are they awarded routinely. Awards of costs are rare, especially proportionate to the number of cases decided by the Board. Potential parties and the public should not be fearful of participating in Board proceedings, a sentiment that has been expressed in decision after decision. Costs should never be used as a threat or a reason to dissuade public participation. The Board has the statutory jurisdiction to award costs for the purpose of controlling its process. Costs before the Board have never been intended to follow "the cause" nor are they intended in any way to indemnify a successful party. Each application for costs is decided on its own merit, based on an assessment of conduct.

Section 18 — Notice of Decision

Subsection 1 states that the "tribunal shall send each party who participated in the proceeding, or the party's representative, a copy of its final decision or order, including the reasons if any have been given", by regular lettermail (with deemed delivery by such method per subsection (2)), by electronic or telephone transmission (with deemed delivery by such method per subsection (3)) and by some other method that allows proof of receipt if the tribunal's rules made under section 25.1 deal with the matter (with deemed delivery by such method per subsection (4)). This section gives the tribunal flexibility in sending out the decision as well as stating the deemed delivery of it, which will set the clock in terms of the time line to take the next step, if any. The specified deemed delivery days, as set out in subsections (2)–(4), do not apply under subsection (5) if "a party that acts in good faith does not, through absence, accident, illness or other cause beyond the party's control, receive the copy until a later date than the deemed date of delivery".

The appeal of the criminal case, *R. v. Devgan* (2007), 226 C.C.C. (3d) 312, 2007 CLB 23, 76 W.C.B. (2d) 122, 53 C.R. (6th) 104 (the *Devgan* case), heard in the Superior Court of Justice, dealt with the issue of the notice of the decision. The court had to determine the impact of section 18 on the case before it, and it stated the following:

> The notice requirement in s. 18 of the *SPPA* requires a "tribunal" to send each party who participated in a proceeding, a copy of its final decision or order.

The case then discussed whether the particular Registrar had a "statutory power of decision" as defined by section 1, and found no such power.

Section 19 — Enforcement of Orders

Subsection (1) states as follows: "A certified copy of a tribunal's decision or order in a proceeding may be filed in the Superior Court of Justice by the tribunal or by a party and on filing shall be deemed to be an order of that court and is enforceable as such." Under subsection (2) a party who files an order under this section shall notify the tribunal within 10 days after filing. Subsection (3) states the sheriff shall enforce the order as if it were an execution issued by the Superior Court of Justice upon the receipt of a certified copy of such order for the payment of money.

The arbitration decision of *Peters v. Aviva Canada Inc.* (2007), FSCO A05-000196 and A05-000197 (the *Peters* decision), conducted under the auspices of the FSCO, is an example of a decision that discussed the enforcement of orders. In the case, the arbitrator made an order regarding the expenses and interest awarded in winning the arbitration. The arbitrator made the following finding:

> While the alternative might be to apply the post-judgement interest provisions of the *Courts of Justice Act*, these provisions relate specifically to court judgements, not arbitral orders. While section 19(1) of the *Statutory Powers Procedure Act* provides for a certified copy of a tribunal's decision or order in a proceeding to be filed in the Superior Court of Justice, the result is that such an order is enforceable as an order of the Superior Court, not that the provisions of the *Courts of Justice Act* are imported *holus bolus* into the administrative forum.

Section 20 — Record of Proceeding

> A tribunal shall compile a record of any proceeding in which a hearing has been held which shall include,
> (a) any application, complaint, reference or other document, if any, by which the proceeding was commenced;
> (b) the notice of any hearing;
> (c) any interlocutory orders made by the tribunal;
> (d) all documentary evidence filed with the tribunal, subject to any limitation expressly imposed by any other Act on the extent to or the purposes for which any such documents may be used in evidence in any proceeding;
> (e) the transcript, if any, of the oral evidence given at the hearing; and
> (f) the decision of the tribunal and the reasons therefor, where reasons have been given.

This section sets out what is to be contained in a record of a tribunal's proceeding. Note that a transcript of the hearing is only included if it exists, and most tribunals do not have transcripts produced.

Section 21 — Adjournments

This section allows a hearing to be adjourned by a tribunal on its own motion or where it is shown to the tribunal's satisfaction "that the adjournment is required to permit an adequate hearing to be held", recognizing the need for adjournments where necessary.

Section 21.1 — Correction of Errors

This section allows for clear minor errors to be corrected by the tribunal as follows:

> A tribunal may at any time correct a typographical error, error of calculation or similar error made in its decision or order.

In the appeal order of *Ramalingam v. State Farm Mutual Automobile Insurance Co.* (2008), Appeal P05-00026 (the *Ramalingam* decision), conducted under the auspices of the FSCO, the appeal involved an arbitration order regarding expenses. In examining the matter, the Director's Delegate discussed the use of section 21.1 as follows:

> I note, however, that subsequent to Arbitrator Feldman's decision, the arbitration expense order and other portions of the *Dwumaah* decision were amended on December 6, 2007 as a calculation error in accordance with Rule 65.5 of the *Code* and section 21.1 of the *Statutory Powers Procedure Act*, R.S.O. 1990, c. S.22.

Section 21.2 — Power of Review

The power of review or reconsideration, as it is more commonly called, is given to the tribunal under subsection (1) as follows:

> A tribunal may, if it considers it advisable and if its rules made under section 25.1 deal with the matter, review all or part of its own decision or order, and may confirm, vary, suspend or cancel the decision or order

provided the review shall take place within a reasonable time after the decision or order is made under subsection (2). Further to subsection (3), if there is a conflict between to power to review in this section and any other Act, such Act prevails. This mechanism, if used in the right situation, is faster and cheaper than appeal or judicial review.

In the Ontario Labour Relations Board decision of *6377289 Canada Inc. v. Tang* (2007), 57 Employment Practices Branch File No. 48001421, Docket No. 3373-06-ES (the *Tang* decision), section 21.2 was discussed. The case involved a reconsideration of a decision. Although the issue whether to grant reconsideration is specific to its enabling legislation, it is useful to see what factors are to be taken into account when deciding whether to reconsider:

> The Board's power to reconsider decisions under the *Employment Standards Act, 2000*, S.O. 2000, c. 41, as amended (the "Act") arises from section 21.2(1) of the *Statutory Powers Procedure Act*. The test applied by the Board is the same as it applies to requests for reconsideration under the *Labour Relations Act*. In order to provide parties before the Board with a substantial degree of certainty, the Board generally treats its decisions as final. Thus, the Board will not permit a party to attempt to reargue its case under the guise of a request for reconsideration. The Board will not normally reconsider a decision unless:
>
> (a) A party wishes to make representations or objections not already considered by the Board that it had no opportunity to raise previously;
> (b) A party wishes to adduce evidence which could not previously have been obtained with reasonable diligence and which would be practically conclusive of the issue or make a substantial difference to the outcome of the case; or
> (c) The request raises significant and important issues of Board policy which the Board is convinced were decided wrongly in the first instance.
>
> The Board may also consider such factors as the motives for the request for reconsideration in light of a party's conduct, and the resulting prejudice to another party if the case is reopened. See generally *Cineplex Odeon Corp.*, [1996] OLRB Rep. Nov./Dec. 922 and the cases cited therein.

Section 22 — Administration of Oaths

> A member of a tribunal has power to administer oaths and affirmations for the purpose of any of its proceedings and the tribunal may require evidence before it is to be given under oath or affirmation.

It is fairly common for most tribunals currently to give an affirmation rather than an oath as an oath may require a number of holy books to be available depending on the belief of the person so swearing, which may not be easily available, especially if the hearing is in a temporary location.

Section 23 — Powers re Control of Proceedings

Subsection (1) gives the tribunal broad powers, as it considers proper, to prevent abuse of its process by making such orders or giving such directions, including the power to reasonably limit further examination or cross-examination of a witness where what was done was sufficient to disclose fully and fairly all matters relevant per subsection (2). In addition to the contempt powers set out in section 13, tribunals should have a sufficient arsenal of powers to prevent abuse of the process. Subsection (3) is important to someone acting on behalf of another and is supposed to give the tribunal some authority to exclude those incompetent to work in the process as follows:

> A tribunal may exclude from a hearing anyone, other than a person licensed under the *Law Society Act*, appearing on behalf of a party or as an adviser to a witness if it finds that such person is not competent properly to represent or to advise the party or witness, or does not understand and comply at the hearing with the duties and responsibilities of an advocate or adviser.

The OMB decision of *Re Mississauga (City) Official Plan Amendment No. 25* (2008), 59 O.M.B.R. 80, 2008 CLB 3906, discussed subsection 23(3) as it relates to "lay" representation. The case involved the competence of a party's representative and discussed licensed paralegals and also "lay" representatives. The OMB laid out the issue and the facts as follows:

> The City challenges Mr. Dell's competence to represent the appellants before this tribunal. The basis of the challenge is that Mr. Dell, in appearing on behalf of other persons, would be tantamount to providing unauthorized legal services.
>
> The challenge arises from the recent amendments to a number of statutes, including the *Law Society Act*, R.S.O. 1990, c. L.8, which has the effect of setting forth a more rigorous regime dealing with the question of the provision of paralegal services. Motivated by the protection of the public, the provision of legal services in some areas of the law under the Act is limited or prohibited depending whether the persons are holders of licences, exempted by Statute or exempted by By-law.
>
> The City argued that pursuant to Section 1(5) of the *Law Society Act*, if a person engages in conduct that involves the application of legal principles, and judgements, he will be providing legal services. Section 1(6) of the Act provides for an expansive definition and in subparagraph 3 of this subsection, the meaning of "provision of service" is to include representation of a person in a proceeding before an Adjudicative Body. "Adjudicative Body" is defined to include a tribunal established under an Act of Parliament or the Legislature of the Province of Ontario.
>
> Based on what was presented, it seems that if a person is to represent someone before the Board in matters requiring the application of legal principles and making legal judgements, he may fall within the ambit of providing legal services.

The OMB then considers specifically subsection 23(3):

> Lay representations before the Board is a feature of life that has been flourishing since its inception. The instances where difficulties arise are few and far between. For this Board, it is not a problem and certainly not a problem in need of a solution. Whether representatives are legal, lay or combined, the Board has always been able to conduct our hearings in a manner befitting a tribunal functioning under the *Statutory Powers Procedure Act*, R.S.O. 1990, c. S.22, and complying with the rules of natural justice. These include cases where there are multi-parties with multifarious concerns and poly-technical issues. The Municipal Bar, to its credit, has never taken on an officious air or elitist stance towards unrepresented parties or lay representatives. Over the decades, our adjudication has evolved to a stage where coexistence with lay representatives or unrepresented parties is a norm rather than an exception. To upset this delicate but seamlessly workable balance, the Board would require far more persuasive arguments than what have been presented by Mr. Minkowski.
>
> What Mr. Minkowski has not done, whether by design or inadvertence, is to refer to and engage in an in-depth analysis in relation to Section 23(3) of the *Statutory Powers Procedure Act*, R.S.O. 1990, c. S.22.

After quoting subsection 23(3), the OMB asked the following questions and makes a finding:

> Does this provision suggest that the Board has some discretion to allow persons with competence that are neither licensed nor exempted from the *Law Society Act* to represent others at our hearings? If the Board is obligated *ab initio*, as suggested by the City to exclude representatives other than those persons authorized under the *Law Society Act*, why does this provision seem to provide an escape? Does this provision not point to a direction that is overlooked: namely, the administrative tribunals can use the yardstick of competence as the test whether a lay representative, other than those authorized, can appear? Does representation of hearings inevitably require the application of legal principles and legal judgements? If not, does it not make sense for this Board at least, to deal with matters on a case-by-case basis, or does the *Law Society Act* mandate a different approach?
>
> These and some other ramifications are required to be addressed and addressed fully before the Board would make a *carte blanche* prohibition.
>
> The City has not presented any evidence indicating that Mr. Dell is not competent to represent others. Nor has it turned to the relevant provision as indicated above and make a fulsome submission in this regard. Additionally, the Board has misgivings whether Mr. Dell is appreciative whether he might be in an exempted category.
>
> Accordingly, the Board will not exclude Mr. Dell from representing others for reasons enumerated above.

This decision notes that lawyers and licensed paralegals are to be treated in the same fashion under subsection 23(3). Also see the *Romanchook* decision cited in Section 10 above. Note that before an amendment in 2006, this provision would allow a tribunal to exclude an incompetent paralegal; but as the amendment classifies a paralegal licensed by the LSUC as a representative, such exclusion cannot occur. However, it is possible that someone could make a complaint to the LSUC about a particular paralegal.

Section 24 — Notice

Subsection (1) allows the tribunal, where it is of the opinion that it is impractical to give notice of the hearing or the decision itself to all or any of the parties individually, to give notice to such parties either by public advertisement or by otherwise as the tribunal directs, and a notice of the decision, under subsection (2) "shall inform the parties of the place where copies of the decision and the reasons therefor, if reasons were given, may be obtained". This again gives flexibility to the agency when sending out the notice of a hearing or the actual decision where needed.

Section 25 — Appeal Operates As a Stay, Exception

Subsection (1) says that an appeal from a decision of a tribunal to a court or other appellate body, other than an application for judicial review or proceedings under subsection 2(1) of the *Judicial Review Procedure Act*, which is deemed not an appeal under subsection (2), operates as a stay in the matter unless another piece of legislation that applies to the proceeding expressly provides to the contrary, or the tribunal, or the court, or other appellate body orders otherwise. This provision, when applicable, obviates the need to request a stay and therefore lessens paperwork.

In the appeal order of *I.(N.) v. Allstate Insurance Co. of Canada* (2008), Appeal P07-00024 (the *N.I.* decision), conducted under the auspices of the FSCO, the appeal requesting a stay of an arbitration order was dismissed. The Director's Delegate first quoted section 25 and then stated the following:

Subsection 283(6) of the *Insurance Act*, R.S.O. 1990, c. I.8 (as amended) expressly provides that an appeal does not stay the order of an arbitrator, unless the Director decides otherwise. As stated by Delegate McMahon in *Guardian Insurance Company of Canada and Armstrong*, (FSCO P00-00037, July 20, 2000), a stay from an order of an arbitrator at the Financial Services Commission of Ontario ("FSCO") is the exception, rather than the rule.

As noted in prior cases, the stay as an exception on appeal also differs from the *Ontario Rules of Civil Procedure*, R.R.O. 1990, Regulation 194, which provide, at Rule 63.01(1), that the delivery of a notice of appeal from an interlocutory or final order stays, until the disposition of the appeal, any provision of the order for the payment of money, except a provision that awards support or enforces a support order.

Given that arbitration orders, in significant measure, reimburse expenditures arising from a motor vehicle accident or replace lost income, services or possessions, the same considerations regarding support orders exist, including the need for timely payment. Further, subsection 283(6) of the *Insurance Act* is consistent with subsection 283(1) (which limits appeals of the order of an arbitrator to a question of law), both provisions showing deference to arbitration decisions.

Delegate McMahon, in determining whether a stay should be granted in *Armstrong*, adopted Delegate Richardson's criteria in *Canadian Home Assurance Company and Scavuzzo* (OIC P-000626, May 18, 1992), namely:

1. the *bona fides* of the appeal;
2. the substance of the grounds for appeal; and,
3. the hardship to the respective parties if the stay is granted or refused.

Section 25.0.1 — Control of Process

The section again gives the tribunal the power to control its process as it states as follows:

> A tribunal has the power to determine its own procedures and practices and may for that purpose,
> (a) make orders with respect to the procedures and practices that apply in any particular proceeding; and
> (b) establish rules under section 25.1.

Many agencies make their own rules pursuant to section 25.1, to take advantage of the extra powers available under this statute and/or make appropriate practice directions.

The Div. Ct. case of *Ontario Kraft Canada Inc. v. Menkes Lakeshore Ltd.* (2007), 159 A.C.W.S. (3d) 7, 2007 CLB 5197, 228 O.A.C. 1, 56 O.M.B.R. 391, 37 M.P.L.R. (4th) 42 (the *Ontario Kraft* case), looked at the issue of the control of the process:

> Under the *Statutory Powers Procedure Act*, R.S.O. 1990, c. S.22 (SPPA), s. 25.0.1, the Board, as an administrative tribunal exercising a statutory power of authority, maintains absolute jurisdiction and control over its own procedure.

Section 25.1 — Rules

As noted in many sections above, a tribunal can make its own rules governing the practice and procedure before it, pursuant to subsection (1), which may be of general or particular application under subsection (2). The rules shall be consistent with the *SPPA* and with other applicable Acts under subsection (3) and, as required by subsection (4), are to be made available by the tribunal to the public in English and French. The power to make such rules is in addition to any other power to adopt rules granted under any other legislation (ss. (6)). The rules made under this section are not regulations according to subsection (5).

See *Becker Milk* case under section 17.1, above.

Section 26 — Regulations

This section allows for the making of regulations for a specific purpose as follows:

> The Lieutenant Governor in Council may make regulations prescribing forms for the purpose of section 12.

Section 27 — Rules, etc., Available to the Public

> A tribunal shall make any rules or guidelines established under this or any other Act available for examination by the public.

As a result of the mandate, the rules are currently easily available by downloading them from an agency's website.

See *Becker Milk* case under section 17.1, above.

Section 28 — Substantial Compliance

This provides for less strict formality by allowing for substantial compliance as follows:

> Substantial compliance with requirements respecting the content of forms, notices or documents under this Act or any rule made under this or any other Act is sufficient.

Section 32 — Conflict

This provision is meant to make this statute prevail over other legislation if there is a conflict, unless the other legislation expressly stated that its provisions and regulations override those in the *SPPA*:

> Unless it is expressly provided in any other Act that its provisions and regulations, rules or by-laws made under it apply despite anything in this Act, the provisions of this Act prevail over the provisions of such other Act and over regulations, rules or by-laws made under such other Act which conflict therewith.

CHAPTER SUMMARY

This chapter examined most of the sections of the *SPPA* through excerpts of the Act, with explanation of their significance where warranted. Further, if possible, a case or a decision that discussed the provision was also cited and reviewed to assist the reader to better understand the importance of various provisions of the legislation, which provides the "minimum rules of fair procedures" applicable to most Ontario agencies. The cases and decisions reviewed in this chapter also throw light on how specific Ontario agencies, including some agencies discussed in succeeding chapters, discuss this important legislation.

REVIEW QUESTIONS

1. What is an annotated statute?
2. What is a "statutory power" of decision, and why is it important in Ontario administrative law?
3. In what situations does the *SPPA* apply to Ontario agencies, and in what situation does it not apply?

4. What circumstance will allow the term of a tribunal member to continue past expiry?
5. In what circumstances can a matter before a tribunal be dismissed without a hearing under both statute and case law?
6. What requirements and benefits are imposed upon an Ontario tribunal wishing to allow the parties to use Alternative Dispute Resolution?
7. How are the parties to a matter before an Ontario agency determined?
8. What are the various formats of hearing allowed by the *SPPA*, and how can an Ontario agency allow the parties to choose a particular format?
9. What are the requirements for each type of format of hearing?
10. What can occur if a party does not attend a hearing of which such party received proper notice?
11. What provisions of the *SPPA* allow an Ontario agency to control its own process?
12. When is evidence admissible in a hearing of an Ontario agency?
13. Are written reasons for a decision by an Ontario agency required, and if so, when?
14. What is reconsideration, and when can it be utilized?
15. Do the rules of an Ontario agency have to be available to the public, and if so, how are they made available?

DISCUSSION QUESTIONS

1. Due to the 2006 amendments to legislation allowing licensed paralegals to act for parties before Ontario agencies, is there now a distinction between lawyers and licensed paralegals on one side and lay representatives on the other? If so, is this appropriate or should the consumer have greater choices to obtain representation?

2. In the Canadian system of law, one of the factors used in the court system to encourage settlement is the award of costs to the winning side from approximately one-third to a virtual indemnity of the winner's expenses to be paid by the losing side. It seems that this concept is starting to appear in agency hearings. Is this a good turn of events, considering that agencies were historically meant to be cheaper, faster, and more efficient than the courts?

Appendix 2.1
The *Statutory Powers Procedure Act*
R.S.O. 1990, C. S.22

INTERPRETATION

1.(1) In this Act,

"electronic hearing" means a hearing held by conference telephone or some other form of electronic technology allowing persons to hear one another;

"hearing" means a hearing in any proceeding;

"licence" includes any permit, certificate, approval, registration or similar form of permission required by law;

"municipality" has the same meaning as in the *Municipal Affairs Act*;

"oral hearing" means a hearing at which the parties or their representatives attend before the tribunal in person;

"proceeding" means a proceeding to which this Act applies;

"representative" means, in respect of a proceeding to which this Act applies, a person authorized under the *Law Society Act* to represent a person in that proceeding;

"statutory power of decision" means a power or right, conferred by or under a statute, to make a decision deciding or prescribing,

  (a) the legal rights, powers, privileges, immunities, duties or liabilities of any person or party, or

  (b) the eligibility of any person or party to receive, or to the continuation of, a benefit or licence, whether the person is legally entitled thereto or not;

"tribunal" means one or more persons, whether or not incorporated and however described, upon which a statutory power of decision is conferred by or under a statute;

"written hearing" means a hearing held by means of the exchange of documents, whether in written form or by electronic means.

Meaning of "person" extended

    (2) A municipality, an unincorporated association of employers, a trade union or council of trade unions who may be a party to a proceeding in the exercise of a statutory power of decision under the statute conferring the power shall be deemed to be a person for the purpose of any provision of this Act or of any rule made under this Act that applies to parties.

LIBERAL CONSTRUCTION OF ACT AND RULES

2. This Act, and any rule made by a tribunal under subsection 17.1(4) or section 25.1, shall be liberally construed to secure the just, most expeditious and cost-effective determination of every proceeding on its merits.

APPLICATION OF ACT

3.(1) Subject to subsection (2), this Act applies to a proceeding by a tribunal in the exercise of a statutory power of decision conferred by or under an Act of the Legislature, where the tribunal is required by or under such Act or otherwise by law to hold or to afford to the parties to the proceeding an opportunity for a hearing before making a decision.

Where Act does not apply

(2) This Act does not apply to a proceeding,

(a) before the Assembly or any committee of the Assembly;
(b) in or before,
  (i) the Court of Appeal,
  (ii) the Superior Court of Justice,
  (iii) the Ontario Court of Justice,
  (iv) the Family Court of the Superior Court of Justice,
  (v) the Small Claims Court, or
  (vi) a justice of the peace;
(c) to which the Rules of Civil Procedure apply;
(d) before an arbitrator to which the *Arbitrations Act* or the *Labour Relations Act* applies;
(e) at a coroner's inquest;
(f) of a commission appointed under the *Public Inquiries Act*;
(g) of one or more persons required to make an investigation and to make a report, with or without recommendations, where the report is for the information or advice of the person to whom it is made and does not in any way legally bind or limit that person in any decision he or she may have power to make; or
(h) of a tribunal empowered to make regulations, rules or by-laws in so far as its power to make regulations, rules or by-laws is concerned.

WAIVER

Waiver of procedural requirement

4.(1) Any procedural requirement of this Act, or of another Act or a regulation that applies to a proceeding, may be waived with the consent of the parties and the tribunal.

Same, rules

(2) Any provision of a tribunal's rules made under section 25.1 may be waived in accordance with the rules.

DISPOSITION WITHOUT HEARING

4.1 If the parties consent, a proceeding may be disposed of by a decision of the tribunal given without a hearing, unless another Act or a regulation that applies to the proceeding provides otherwise.

PANELS, CERTAIN MATTERS

4.2(1) A procedural or interlocutory matter in a proceeding may be heard and determined by a panel consisting of one or more members of the tribunal, as assigned by the chair of the tribunal.

Assignments

(2) In assigning members of the tribunal to a panel, the chair shall take into consideration any requirement imposed by another Act or a regulation that applies to the proceeding that the tribunal be representative of specific interests.

Decision of panel

(3) The decision of a majority of the members of a panel, or their unanimous decision in the case of a two-member panel, is the tribunal's decision.

PANEL OF ONE, REDUCED PANEL

Panel of one

4.2.1(1) The chair of a tribunal may decide that a proceeding be heard by a panel of one person and assign the person to hear the proceeding unless there is a statutory requirement in another Act that the proceeding be heard by a panel of more than one person.

Reduction in number of panel members

(2) Where there is a statutory requirement in another Act that a proceeding be heard by a panel of a specified number of persons, the chair of the tribunal may assign to the panel one person or any lesser number of persons than the number specified in the other Act if all parties to the proceeding consent.

EXPIRY OF TERM

4.3 If the term of office of a member of a tribunal who has participated in a hearing expires before a decision is given, the term shall be deemed to continue, but only for the purpose of participating in the decision and for no other purpose.

INCAPACITY OF MEMBER

4.4(1) If a member of a tribunal who has participated in a hearing becomes unable, for any reason, to complete the hearing or to participate in the decision, the remaining member or members may complete the hearing and give a decision.

Other Acts and regulations

(2) Subsection (1) does not apply if another Act or a regulation specifically deals with the issue of what takes place in the circumstances described in subsection (1).

DECISION NOT TO PROCESS COMMENCEMENT OF PROCEEDING

4.5(1) Subject to subsection (3), upon receiving documents relating to the commencement of a proceeding, a tribunal or its administrative staff may decide not to process the documents relating to the commencement of the proceeding if,

(a) the documents are incomplete;
(b) the documents are received after the time required for commencing the proceeding has elapsed;
(c) the fee required for commencing the proceeding is not paid; or
(d) there is some other technical defect in the commencement of the proceeding.

Notice

(2) A tribunal or its administrative staff shall give the party who commences a proceeding notice of its decision under subsection (1) and shall set out in the notice the reasons for the decision and the requirements for resuming the processing of the documents.

Rules under s. 25.1

(3) A tribunal or its administrative staff shall not make a decision under subsection (1) unless the tribunal has made rules under section 25.1 respecting the making of such decisions and those rules shall set out,

(a) any of the grounds referred to in subsection (1) upon which the tribunal or its administrative staff may decide not to process the documents relating to the commencement of a proceeding; and
(b) the requirements for the processing of the documents to be resumed.

Continuance of provisions in other statutes

(4) Despite section 32, nothing in this section shall prevent a tribunal or its administrative staff from deciding not to process documents relating to the commencement of a proceeding on grounds that differ from those referred to in subsection (1) or without complying with subsection (2) or (3) if the tribunal or its staff does so in accordance with the provisions of an Act that are in force on the day this section comes into force.

DISMISSAL OF PROCEEDING WITHOUT HEARING

4.6(1) Subject to subsections (5) and (6), a tribunal may dismiss a proceeding without a hearing if,

(a) the proceeding is frivolous, vexatious or is commenced in bad faith;

(b) the proceeding relates to matters that are outside the jurisdiction of the tribunal; or

(c) some aspect of the statutory requirements for bringing the proceeding has not been met.

Notice

(2) Before dismissing a proceeding under this section, a tribunal shall give notice of its intention to dismiss the proceeding to,

(a) all parties to the proceeding if the proceeding is being dismissed for reasons referred to in clause (1)(b); or

(b) the party who commences the proceeding if the proceeding is being dismissed for any other reason.

Same

(3) The notice of intention to dismiss a proceeding shall set out the reasons for the dismissal and inform the parties of their right to make written submissions to the tribunal with respect to the dismissal within the time specified in the notice.

Right to make submissions

(4) A party who receives a notice under subsection (2) may make written submissions to the tribunal with respect to the dismissal within the time specified in the notice.

Dismissal

(5) A tribunal shall not dismiss a proceeding under this section until it has given notice under subsection (2) and considered any submissions made under subsection (4).

Rules

(6) A tribunal shall not dismiss a proceeding under this section unless it has made rules under section 25.1 respecting the early dismissal of proceedings and those rules shall include,

(a) any of the grounds referred to in subsection (1) upon which a proceeding may be dismissed;

(b) the right of the parties who are entitled to receive notice under subsection (2) to make submissions with respect to the dismissal; and

(c) the time within which the submissions must be made.

Continuance of provisions in other statutes

(7) Despite section 32, nothing in this section shall prevent a tribunal from dismissing a proceeding on grounds other than those referred to in subsection (1) or without complying with subsections (2) to (6) if the tribunal dismisses the proceeding in accordance with the provisions of an Act that are in force on the day this section comes into force.

CLASSIFYING PROCEEDINGS

4.7 A tribunal may make rules under section 25.1 classifying the types of proceedings that come before it and setting guidelines as to the procedural steps or processes (such as preliminary motions, pre-hearing conferences, alternative dispute resolution mechanisms, expedited hearings) that apply to each type of proceeding and the circumstances in which other procedures may apply.

ALTERNATIVE DISPUTE RESOLUTION

4.8(1) A tribunal may direct the parties to a proceeding to participate in an alternative dispute resolution mechanism for the purposes of resolving the proceeding or an issue arising in the proceeding if,

(a) it has made rules under section 25.1 respecting the use of alternative dispute resolution mechanisms; and

(b) all parties consent to participating in the alternative dispute resolution mechanism.

Definition

(2) In this section,

"alternative dispute resolution mechanism" includes mediation, conciliation, negotiation or any other means of facilitating the resolution of issues in dispute.

Rules

(3) A rule under section 25.1 respecting the use of alternative dispute resolution mechanisms shall include procedural guidelines to deal with the following:

1. The circumstances in which a settlement achieved by means of an alternative dispute resolution mechanism must be reviewed and approved by the tribunal.
2. Any requirement, statutory or otherwise, that there be an order by the tribunal.

Mandatory alternative dispute resolution

(4) A rule under subsection (3) may provide that participation in an alternative dispute resolution mechanism is mandatory or that it is mandatory in certain specified circumstances.

Person appointed to mediate, etc.

(5) A rule under subsection (3) may provide that a person appointed to mediate, conciliate, negotiate or help resolve a matter by means of an alternative dispute resolution mechanism be a member of the tribunal or a person independent of the tribunal. However, a member of the tribunal who is so appointed with respect to a matter in a proceeding shall not subsequently hear the matter if it comes before the tribunal unless the parties consent.

Continuance of provisions in other statutes

(6) Despite section 32, nothing in this section shall prevent a tribunal from directing parties to a proceeding to participate in an alternative dispute resolution mechanism even though the requirements of subsections (1) to (5) have not been met if the tribunal does so in accordance with the provisions of an Act that are in force on the day this section comes into force.

MEDIATORS, ETC.: NOT COMPELLABLE, NOTES NOT EVIDENCE

Mediators, etc., not compellable

4.9(1) No person employed as a mediator, conciliator or negotiator or otherwise appointed to facilitate the resolution of a matter before a tribunal by means of an alternative dispute resolution mechanism shall be compelled to give testimony or produce documents in a proceeding before the tribunal or in a civil proceeding with respect to matters that come to his or her knowledge in the course of exercising his or her duties under this or any other Act.

Evidence in civil proceedings

(2) No notes or records kept by a mediator, conciliator or negotiator or by any other person appointed to facilitate the resolution of a matter before a tribunal by means of an alternative dispute resolution mechanism under this or any other Act are admissible in a civil proceeding.

PARTIES

5. The parties to a proceeding shall be the persons specified as parties by or under the statute under which the proceeding arises or, if not so specified, persons entitled by law to be parties to the proceeding.

WRITTEN HEARINGS

5.1(1) A tribunal whose rules made under section 25.1 deal with written hearings may hold a written hearing in a proceeding.

Exception

(2) The tribunal shall not hold a written hearing if a party satisfies the tribunal that there is good reason for not doing so.

Same

(2.1) Subsection (2) does not apply if the only purpose of the hearing is to deal with procedural matters.

Documents

(3) In a written hearing, all the parties are entitled to receive every document that the tribunal receives in the proceeding.

ELECTRONIC HEARINGS

5.2(1) A tribunal whose rules made under section 25.1 deal with electronic hearings may hold an electronic hearing in a proceeding.

Exception

(2) The tribunal shall not hold an electronic hearing if a party satisfies the tribunal that holding an electronic rather than an oral hearing is likely to cause the party significant prejudice.

Same

(3) Subsection (2) does not apply if the only purpose of the hearing is to deal with procedural matters.

Participants to be able to hear one another

(4) In an electronic hearing, all the parties and the members of the tribunal participating in the hearing must be able to hear one another and any witnesses throughout the hearing.

DIFFERENT KINDS OF HEARINGS IN ONE PROCEEDING

5.2.1 A tribunal may, in a proceeding, hold any combination of written, electronic and oral hearings.

PRE-HEARING CONFERENCES

5.3(1) If the tribunal's rules made under section 25.1 deal with pre-hearing conferences, the tribunal may direct the parties to participate in a pre-hearing conference to consider,

(a) the settlement of any or all of the issues;

(b) the simplification of the issues;

(c) facts or evidence that may be agreed upon;

(d) the dates by which any steps in the proceeding are to be taken or begun;

(e) the estimated duration of the hearing; and

(f) any other matter that may assist in the just and most expeditious disposition of the proceeding.

Other Acts and regulations

(1.1) The tribunal's power to direct the parties to participate in a pre-hearing conference is subject to any other Act or regulation that applies to the proceeding.

Who presides

(2) The chair of the tribunal may designate a member of the tribunal or any other person to preside at the pre-hearing conference.

Orders

(3) A member who presides at a pre-hearing conference may make such orders as he or she considers necessary or advisable with respect to the conduct of the proceeding, including adding parties.

Disqualification

(4) A member who presides at a pre-hearing conference at which the parties attempt to settle issues shall not preside at the hearing of the proceeding unless the parties consent.

Application of s. 5.2

(5) Section 5.2 applies to a pre-hearing conference, with necessary modifications.

DISCLOSURE

5.4(1) If the tribunal's rules made under section 25.1 deal with disclosure, the tribunal may, at any stage of the proceeding before all hearings are complete, make orders for,

(a) the exchange of documents;

(b) the oral or written examination of a party;

(c) the exchange of witness statements and reports of expert witnesses;

(d) the provision of particulars;

(e) any other form of disclosure.

Other Acts and regulations

(1.1) The tribunal's power to make orders for disclosure is subject to any other Act or regulation that applies to the proceeding.

Exception, privileged information

(2) Subsection (1) does not authorize the making of an order requiring disclosure of privileged information.

NOTICE OF HEARING

6.(1) The parties to a proceeding shall be given reasonable notice of the hearing by the tribunal.

Statutory authority

(2) A notice of a hearing shall include a reference to the statutory authority under which the hearing will be held.

Oral hearing

(3) A notice of an oral hearing shall include,

(a) a statement of the time, place and purpose of the hearing; and

(b) a statement that if the party notified does not attend at the hearing, the tribunal may proceed in the party's absence and the party will not be entitled to any further notice in the proceeding.

Written hearing

(4) A notice of a written hearing shall include,

(a) a statement of the date and purpose of the hearing, and details about the manner in which the hearing will be held;

(b) a statement that the hearing shall not be held as a written hearing if the party satisfies the tribunal that there is good reason for not holding a written hearing (in which case the tribunal is required to hold it as an electronic or oral hearing) and an indication of the procedure to be followed for that purpose;

(c) a statement that if the party notified neither acts under clause (b) nor participates in the hearing in accordance with the notice, the tribunal may proceed without the party's participation and the party will not be entitled to any further notice in the proceeding.

Electronic hearing

(5) A notice of an electronic hearing shall include,

(a) a statement of the time and purpose of the hearing, and details about the manner in which the hearing will be held;

(b) a statement that the only purpose of the hearing is to deal with procedural matters, if that is the case;

(c) if clause (b) does not apply, a statement that the party notified may, by satisfying the tribunal that holding the hearing as an electronic hearing is likely to cause the party significant prejudice, require the tribunal to hold the hearing as an oral hearing, and an indication of the procedure to be followed for that purpose; and

(d) a statement that if the party notified neither acts under clause (c), if applicable, nor participates in the hearing in accordance with the notice, the tribunal may proceed without the party's participation and the party will not be entitled to any further notice in the proceeding.

EFFECT OF NON-ATTENDANCE AT HEARING AFTER DUE NOTICE

7.(1) Where notice of an oral hearing has been given to a party to a proceeding in accordance with this Act and the party does not attend at the hearing, the tribunal may proceed in the absence of the party and the party is not entitled to any further notice in the proceeding.

Same, written hearings

(2) Where notice of a written hearing has been given to a party to a proceeding in accordance with this Act and the party neither acts under clause 6(4)(b) nor participates in the hearing in accordance with the notice, the tribunal may proceed without the party's participation and the party is not entitled to any further notice in the proceeding.

Same, electronic hearings

(3) Where notice of an electronic hearing has been given to a party to a proceeding in accordance with this Act and the party neither acts under clause 6(5)(c), if appli-

cable, nor participates in the hearing in accordance with the notice, the tribunal may proceed without the party's participation and the party is not entitled to any further notice in the proceeding.

WHERE CHARACTER, ETC., OF A PARTY IS IN ISSUE

8. Where the good character, propriety of conduct or competence of a party is an issue in a proceeding, the party is entitled to be furnished prior to the hearing with reasonable information of any allegations with respect thereto.

HEARINGS TO BE PUBLIC; MAINTENANCE OF ORDER

Hearings to be public, exceptions

9.(1) An oral hearing shall be open to the public except where the tribunal is of the opinion that,

(a) matters involving public security may be disclosed; or

(b) intimate financial or personal matters or other matters may be disclosed at the hearing of such a nature, having regard to the circumstances, that the desirability of avoiding disclosure thereof in the interests of any person affected or in the public interest outweighs the desirability of adhering to the principle that hearings be open to the public,

in which case the tribunal may hold the hearing in the absence of the public.

Written hearings

(1.1) In a written hearing, members of the public are entitled to reasonable access to the documents submitted, unless the tribunal is of the opinion that clause (1)(a) or (b) applies.

Electronic hearings

(1.2) An electronic hearing shall be open to the public unless the tribunal is of the opinion that,

(a) it is not practical to hold the hearing in a manner that is open to the public; or

(b) clause (1)(a) or (b) applies.

Maintenance of order at hearings

(2) A tribunal may make such orders or give such directions at an oral or electronic hearing as it considers necessary for the maintenance of order at the hearing, and, if any person disobeys or fails to comply with any such order or direction, the tribunal or a member thereof may call for the assistance of any peace officer to enforce the order or direction, and every peace officer so called upon shall take such action as is necessary to enforce the order or direction and may use such force as is reasonably required for that purpose.

PROCEEDINGS INVOLVING SIMILAR QUESTIONS

9.1(1) If two or more proceedings before a tribunal involve the same or similar questions of fact, law or policy, the tribunal may,

(a) combine the proceedings or any part of them, with the consent of the parties;

(b) hear the proceedings at the same time, with the consent of the parties;

(c) hear the proceedings one immediately after the other; or

(d) stay one or more of the proceedings until after the determination of another one of them.

Exception

(2) Subsection (1) does not apply to proceedings to which the *Consolidated Hearings Act* applies.

Same

(3) Clauses (1)(a) and (b) do not apply to a proceeding if,

(a) any other Act or regulation that applies to the proceeding requires that it be heard in private;

(b) the tribunal is of the opinion that clause 9(1)(a) or (b) applies to the proceeding.

Conflict, consent requirements

(4) The consent requirements of clauses (1)(a) and (b) do not apply if another Act or a regulation that applies to the proceedings allows the tribunal to combine them or hear them at the same time without the consent of the parties.

Use of same evidence

(5) If the parties to the second-named proceeding consent, the tribunal may treat evidence that is admitted in a proceeding as if it were also admitted in another proceeding that is heard at the same time under clause (1)(b).

RIGHT TO REPRESENTATION

10. A party to a proceeding may be represented by a representative.

EXAMINATION OF WITNESSES

10.1 A party to a proceeding may, at an oral or electronic hearing,

(a) call and examine witnesses and present evidence and submissions; and

(b) conduct cross-examinations of witnesses at the hearing reasonably required for a full and fair disclosure of all matters relevant to the issues in the proceeding.

RIGHTS OF WITNESSES TO REPRESENTATION

11.(1) A witness at an oral or electronic hearing is entitled to be advised by a representative as to his or her rights, but such representative may take no other part in the hearing without leave of the tribunal.

Idem

(2) Where an oral hearing is closed to the public, the witness's representative is not entitled to be present except when that witness is giving evidence.

SUMMONSES

12.(1) A tribunal may require any person, including a party, by summons,

(a) to give evidence on oath or affirmation at an oral or electronic hearing; and

(b) to produce in evidence at an oral or electronic hearing documents and things specified by the tribunal,

relevant to the subject-matter of the proceeding and admissible at a hearing.

Form and service of summons

(2) A summons issued under subsection (1) shall be in the prescribed form (in English or French) and,

(a) where the tribunal consists of one person, shall be signed by him or her;
(b) where the tribunal consists of more than one person, shall be signed by the chair of the tribunal or in such other manner as documents on behalf of the tribunal may be signed under the statute constituting the tribunal.

Same

(3) The summons shall be served personally on the person summoned.

Fees and allowances

(3.1) The person summoned is entitled to receive the same fees or allowances for attending at or otherwise participating in the hearing as are paid to a person summoned to attend before the Superior Court of Justice.

Bench warrant

(4) A judge of the Superior Court of Justice may issue a warrant against a person if the judge is satisfied that,

(a) a summons was served on the person under this section;
(b) the person has failed to attend or to remain in attendance at the hearing (in the case of an oral hearing) or has failed otherwise to participate in the hearing (in the case of an electronic hearing) in accordance with the summons; and
(c) the person's attendance or participation is material to the ends of justice.

Same

(4.1) The warrant shall be in the prescribed form (in English or French), directed to any police officer, and shall require the person to be apprehended anywhere within Ontario, brought before the tribunal forthwith and,

(a) detained in custody as the judge may order until the person's presence as a witness is no longer required; or
(b) in the judge's discretion, released on a recognizance, with or without sureties, conditioned for attendance or participation to give evidence.

Proof of service

(5) Service of a summons may be proved by affidavit in an application to have a warrant issued under subsection (4).

Certificate of facts

(6) Where an application to have a warrant issued is made on behalf of a tribunal, the person constituting the tribunal or, if the tribunal consists of more than one person, the chair of the tribunal may certify to the judge the facts relied on to establish that the attendance or other participation of the person summoned is material to the ends of justice, and the judge may accept the certificate as proof of the facts.

Same

(7) Where the application is made by a party to the proceeding, the facts relied on to establish that the attendance or other participation of the person is material to the ends of justice may be proved by the party's affidavit.

CONTEMPT PROCEEDINGS

13.(1) Where any person without lawful excuse,

(a) on being duly summoned under section 12 as a witness at a hearing makes default in attending at the hearing; or
(b) being in attendance as a witness at an oral hearing or otherwise participating as a witness at an electronic hearing, refuses to take an oath or to make an affirmation legally required by the tribunal to be taken or made, or to produce any document

or thing in his or her power or control legally required by the tribunal to be produced by him or her or to answer any question to which the tribunal may legally require an answer; or

(c) does any other thing that would, if the tribunal had been a court of law having power to commit for contempt, have been contempt of that court,

the tribunal may, of its own motion or on the motion of a party to the proceeding, state a case to the Divisional Court setting out the facts and that court may inquire into the matter and, after hearing any witnesses who may be produced against or on behalf of that person and after hearing any statement that may be offered in defence, punish or take steps for the punishment of that person in like manner as if he or she had been guilty of contempt of the court.

Same

(2) Subsection (1) also applies to a person who,

(a) having objected under clause 6(4)(b) to a hearing being held as a written hearing, fails without lawful excuse to participate in the oral or electronic hearing of the matter; or

(b) being a party, fails without lawful excuse to attend a pre-hearing conference when so directed by the tribunal.

PROTECTION FOR WITNESSES

14.(1) A witness at an oral or electronic hearing shall be deemed to have objected to answer any question asked him or her upon the ground that the answer may tend to criminate him or her or may tend to establish his or her liability to civil proceedings at the instance of the Crown, or of any person, and no answer given by a witness at a hearing shall be used or be receivable in evidence against the witness in any trial or other proceeding against him or her thereafter taking place, other than a prosecution for perjury in giving such evidence.

(2) Repealed.

EVIDENCE

What is admissible in evidence at a hearing

15.(1) Subject to subsections (2) and (3), a tribunal may admit as evidence at a hearing, whether or not given or proven under oath or affirmation or admissible as evidence in a court,

(a) any oral testimony; and

(b) any document or other thing,

relevant to the subject-matter of the proceeding and may act on such evidence, but the tribunal may exclude anything unduly repetitious.

What is inadmissible in evidence at a hearing

(2) Nothing is admissible in evidence at a hearing,

(a) that would be inadmissible in a court by reason of any privilege under the law of evidence; or

(b) that is inadmissible by the statute under which the proceeding arises or any other statute.

Conflicts

(3) Nothing in subsection (1) overrides the provisions of any Act expressly limiting the extent to or purposes for which any oral testimony, documents or things may be admitted or used in evidence in any proceeding.

Copies

(4) Where a tribunal is satisfied as to its authenticity, a copy of a document or other thing may be admitted as evidence at a hearing.

Photocopies

(5) Where a document has been filed in evidence at a hearing, the tribunal may, or the person producing it or entitled to it may with the leave of the tribunal, cause the document to be photocopied and the tribunal may authorize the photocopy to be filed in evidence in the place of the document filed and release the document filed, or may furnish to the person producing it or the person entitled to it a photocopy of the document filed certified by a member of the tribunal.

Certified copy admissible in evidence

(6) A document purporting to be a copy of a document filed in evidence at a hearing, certified to be a copy thereof by a member of the tribunal, is admissible in evidence in proceedings in which the document is admissible as evidence of the document.

USE OF PREVIOUSLY ADMITTED EVIDENCE

15.1(1) The tribunal may treat previously admitted evidence as if it had been admitted in a proceeding before the tribunal, if the parties to the proceeding consent.

Definition

(2) In subsection (1),

"previously admitted evidence" means evidence that was admitted, before the hearing of the proceeding referred to in that subsection, in any other proceeding before a court or tribunal, whether in or outside Ontario.

Additional power

(3) This power conferred by this section is in addition to the tribunal's power to admit evidence under section 15.

WITNESS PANELS

15.2 A tribunal may receive evidence from panels of witnesses composed of two or more persons, if the parties have first had an opportunity to make submissions in that regard.

NOTICE OF FACTS AND OPINIONS

16. A tribunal may, in making its decision in any proceeding,

(a) take notice of facts that may be judicially noticed; and
(b) take notice of any generally recognized scientific or technical facts, information or opinions within its scientific or specialized knowledge.

INTERIM DECISIONS AND ORDERS

16.1(1) A tribunal may make interim decisions and orders.

Conditions

(2) A tribunal may impose conditions on an interim decision or order.

Reasons

(3) An interim decision or order need not be accompanied by reasons.

TIME FRAMES

16.2 A tribunal shall establish guidelines setting out the usual time frame for completing proceedings that come before the tribunal and for completing the procedural steps within those proceedings.

DECISION; INTEREST

Decision

17.(1) A tribunal shall give its final decision and order, if any, in any proceeding in writing and shall give reasons in writing therefor if requested by a party.

Interest

(2) A tribunal that makes an order for the payment of money shall set out in the order the principal sum, and if interest is payable, the rate of interest and the date from which it is to be calculated.

COSTS

17.1(1) Subject to subsection (2), a tribunal may, in the circumstances set out in rules made under subsection (4), order a party to pay all or part of another party's costs in a proceeding.

Exception

(2) A tribunal shall not make an order to pay costs under this section unless,

(a)   the conduct or course of conduct of a party has been unreasonable, frivolous or vexatious or a party has acted in bad faith; and

(b)   the tribunal has made rules under subsection (4).

Amount of costs

(3) The amount of the costs ordered under this section shall be determined in accordance with the rules made under subsection (4).

Rules

(4) A tribunal may make rules with respect to,

(a)   the ordering of costs;

(b)   the circumstances in which costs may be ordered; and

(c)   the amount of costs or the manner in which the amount of costs is to be determined.

Same

(5) Subsections 25.1(3), (4), (5) and (6) apply with respect to rules made under subsection (4).

Continuance of provisions in other statutes

(6) Despite section 32, nothing in this section shall prevent a tribunal from ordering a party to pay all or part of another party's costs in a proceeding in circumstances other than those set out in, and without complying with, subsections (1) to (3) if the tribunal makes the order in accordance with the provisions of an Act that are in force on February 14, 2000.

Transition

(7) This section, as it read on the day before the effective date, continues to apply to proceedings commenced before the effective date.

Same

(8) Rules that are made under section 25.1 before the effective date and comply with subsection (4) are deemed to be rules made under subsection (4) until the earlier of the following days:

1. The first anniversary of the effective date.
2. The day on which the tribunal makes rules under subsection (4).

Definition

(9) In subsections (7) and (8),

"effective date" means the day on which section 21 of Schedule B to the *Good Government Act, 2006* comes into force.

NOTICE OF DECISION

18.(1) The tribunal shall send each party who participated in the proceeding, or the party's representative, a copy of its final decision or order, including the reasons if any have been given,

(a) by regular lettermail;
(b) by electronic transmission;
(c) by telephone transmission of a facsimile; or
(d) by some other method that allows proof of receipt, if the tribunal's rules made under section 25.1 deal with the matter.

Use of mail

(2) If the copy is sent by regular lettermail, it shall be sent to the most recent addresses known to the tribunal and shall be deemed to be received by the party on the fifth day after the day it is mailed.

Use of electronic or telephone transmission

(3) If the copy is sent by electronic transmission or by telephone transmission of a facsimile, it shall be deemed to be received on the day after it was sent, unless that day is a holiday, in which case the copy shall be deemed to be received on the next day that is not a holiday.

Use of other method

(4) If the copy is sent by a method referred to in clause (1)(d), the tribunal's rules made under section 25.1 govern its deemed day of receipt.

Failure to receive copy

(5) If a party that acts in good faith does not, through absence, accident, illness or other cause beyond the party's control, receive the copy until a later date than the deemed day of receipt, subsection (2), (3) or (4), as the case may be, does not apply.

ENFORCEMENT OF ORDERS

19.(1) A certified copy of a tribunal's decision or order in a proceeding may be filed in the Superior Court of Justice by the tribunal or by a party and on filing shall be deemed to be an order of that court and is enforceable as such.

Notice of filing

(2) A party who files an order under subsection (1) shall notify the tribunal within 10 days after the filing.

Order for payment of money

(3) On receiving a certified copy of a tribunal's order for the payment of money, the sheriff shall enforce the order as if it were an execution issued by the Superior Court of Justice.

RECORD OF PROCEEDING

20. A tribunal shall compile a record of any proceeding in which a hearing has been held which shall include,

(a) any application, complaint, reference or other document, if any, by which the proceeding was commenced;

(b) the notice of any hearing;

(c) any interlocutory orders made by the tribunal;

(d) all documentary evidence filed with the tribunal, subject to any limitation expressly imposed by any other Act on the extent to or the purposes for which any such documents may be used in evidence in any proceeding;

(e) the transcript, if any, of the oral evidence given at the hearing; and

(f) the decision of the tribunal and the reasons therefor, where reasons have been given.

ADJOURNMENTS

21. A hearing may be adjourned from time to time by a tribunal of its own motion or where it is shown to the satisfaction of the tribunal that the adjournment is required to permit an adequate hearing to be held.

CORRECTION OF ERRORS

21.1 A tribunal may at any time correct a typographical error, error of calculation or similar error made in its decision or order.

POWER TO REVIEW

21.2(1) A tribunal may, if it considers it advisable and if its rules made under section 25.1 deal with the matter, review all or part of its own decision or order, and may confirm, vary, suspend or cancel the decision or order.

Time for review

(2) The review shall take place within a reasonable time after the decision or order is made.

Conflict

(3) In the event of a conflict between this section and any other Act, the other Act prevails.

ADMINISTRATION OF OATHS

22. A member of a tribunal has power to administer oaths and affirmations for the purpose of any of its proceedings and the tribunal may require evidence before it to be given under oath or affirmation.

POWERS RE CONTROL OF PROCEEDINGS

Abuse of processes

23.(1) A tribunal may make such orders or give such directions in proceedings before it as it considers proper to prevent abuse of its processes.

Limitation on examination

(2) A tribunal may reasonably limit further examination or cross-examination of a witness where it is satisfied that the examination or cross-examination has been sufficient to disclose fully and fairly all matters relevant to the issues in the proceeding.

Exclusion of representatives

(3) A tribunal may exclude from a hearing anyone, other than a person licensed under the *Law Society Act*, appearing on behalf of a party or as an adviser to a witness if it finds that such person is not competent properly to represent or to advise the party or witness, or does not understand and comply at the hearing with the duties and responsibilities of an advocate or adviser.

NOTICE, ETC.

24.(1) Where a tribunal is of the opinion that because the parties to any proceeding before it are so numerous or for any other reason, it is impracticable,

(a) to give notice of the hearing; or
(b) to send its decision and the material mentioned in section 18,

to all or any of the parties individually, the tribunal may, instead of doing so, cause reasonable notice of the hearing or of its decision to be given to such parties by public advertisement or otherwise as the tribunal may direct.

Contents of notice

(2) A notice of a decision given by a tribunal under clause (1)(b) shall inform the parties of the place where copies of the decision and the reasons therefor, if reasons were given, may be obtained.

APPEAL OPERATES AS STAY, EXCEPTION

25.(1) An appeal from a decision of a tribunal to a court or other appellate body operates as a stay in the matter unless,

(a) another Act or a regulation that applies to the proceeding expressly provides to the contrary; or
(b) the tribunal or the court or other appellate body orders otherwise.

Idem

(2) An application for judicial review under the *Judicial Review Procedure Act*, or the bringing of proceedings specified in subsection 2(1) of that Act is not an appeal within the meaning of subsection (1).

CONTROL OF PROCESS

25.0.1 A tribunal has the power to determine its own procedures and practices and may for that purpose,

(a) make orders with respect to the procedures and practices that apply in any particular proceeding; and
(b) establish rules under section 25.1.

RULES

25.1(1) A tribunal may make rules governing the practice and procedure before it.

Application

(2) The rules may be of general or particular application.

Consistency with Acts

(3) The rules shall be consistent with this Act and with the other Acts to which they relate.

Public access

(4) The tribunal shall make the rules available to the public in English and in French.

Legislation Act, 2006, Part III

(5) Rules adopted under this section are not regulations as defined in Part III (Regulations) of the *Legislation Act, 2006.*

Additional power

(6) The power conferred by this section is in addition to any power to adopt rules that the tribunal may have under another Act.

REGULATIONS

26. The Lieutenant Governor in Council may make regulations prescribing forms for the purpose of section 12.

RULES, ETC., AVAILABLE TO PUBLIC

27. A tribunal shall make any rules or guidelines established under this or any other Act available for examination by the public.

SUBSTANTIAL COMPLIANCE

28. Substantial compliance with requirements respecting the content of forms, notices or documents under this Act or any rule made under this or any other Act is sufficient.

29.–31. Repealed.

CONFLICT

32. Unless it is expressly provided in any other Act that its provisions and regulations, rules or by-laws made under it apply despite anything in this Act, the provisions of this Act prevail over the provisions of such other Act and over regulations, rules or by-laws made under such other Act which conflict therewith.

33., 34. Repealed.

FORMS 1, 2 Repealed.

3

Advocacy before Administrative Agencies

LEARNING OBJECTIVES

After reading this chapter, the reader should be able to:

- appreciate the importance of good advocacy to the legal system and the parties involved
- elaborate on key principles in being a good advocate
- distinguish between being a good advocate in court versus being a good advocate in an agency setting, if applicable
- detail the various ways a good advocate prepares for a hearing
- compare and contrast tips suggested in appearing before the Assessment Review Board versus appearing before the Human Rights Tribunal of Ontario
- differentiate between introducing evidence in an agency hearing versus a court trial
- understand the importance of updating legal knowledge in being a good advocate
- detail the need for appropriate behaviour when dealing with an agency in order to achieve the best result for a client
- demonstrate the key concepts of good advocacy

INTRODUCTION

In order to provide the best service possible to a client involved in a matter before an administrative agency, an Ontario paralegal has "a duty to provide legal services and discharge all responsibilities to clients, tribunals, the public and other licensees honourably and with integrity" (R. 1.03(a) of the *Paralegal Rules of Conduct*), meaning that although the paralegal must be zealous in representing the client's position and interests, the representative must do so within the *Paralegal Rules of Conduct* as published by the Law Society of Upper Canada.

Advocacy before administrative agencies is much like advocacy before the courts and requires similar preparation and strategies. In practice, however, some subtle differences that need to be observed. The bottom line, nevertheless, is that being a good advocate in any setting requires thorough preparation of the client's case by looking through the lens of the setting in which you are appearing. Rather than the author jotting down points to remember in order to become an effective advocate, the reader would be best served by hearing directly from decision-makers as to what techniques are best used when advocating for a client before an administrative agency. The author requested a list of hints or do's and don'ts from an educational committee of an agency, a current and a former vice-chair of an agency, and a current justice of the peace. These hints are set out below with little editing so that the reader has direct advice, unfiltered by the author. Although there is a fair amount of duplication, that duplication should indicate important commonalities and stress that such advice is very useful to the reader.

TIPS FOR PARTIES APPEARING BEFORE THE ASSESSMENT REVIEW BOARD

Offered by the ARB Members' Education Committee
Rick Stephenson (Chair of the Board),
Susan Mather (Vice-Chair and Chair of the Education Committee),
Marcie Bourassa and Bob Butterworth (Vice-Chairs),
Bernie Cowan, Joe Wyger, Don Whitehurst, Janet Walker, Sandra Driesel, and
Peter Andrews (Members)

1. Know the relevant legislation and regulations — review relevant Board decisions.

2. Be familiar with Board Rules of Practice and Procedure (available on the Board's website).

3. Check the ARB's website for other helpful information.

4. Learn about the ARB's process. Proceedings can vary among tribunals.

5. Provide disclosure in advance. Send copies of your exhibits to the other parties in advance of the hearing date (often required by the rules) even if not required, and ask for copies of their material.

6. Meet with other parties in advance of the hearing date.
   (a) Settlements are encouraged.
   (b) If you are unable to resolve by settlement, try to narrow issues.
   (c) An agreed statement of facts and/or description of the property saves everyone a lot of time and effort and reduces the risk.

7. Check the meeting location in advance and arrive early for the hearing. The board meets in municipalities across Ontario; some locations are difficult to find. Hearings generally proceed on a "first come, first served" basis.

8. Turn cell phones off.

9. Address the tribunal, not the other parties.

10. Be sure the adjudicator's note-taking is finished before moving on to your next point. Most board meetings are not recorded. Members rely heavily upon their note-taking.

11. Have extra copies of exhibits available.

12. Advise your client that exhibits remain with the board for at least six months and are returned only upon request.

13. Be courteous and always respectful, not argumentative.

14. Be brief, but keep in mind you only have one opportunity to present your case.

15. Focus your oral arguments and evidence.

16. Remember that case law is not evidence. It should be held for final submissions.

17. When submitting written briefs, highlight the important passages and direct the board to those passages during the hearing. Never assume that the board will read passages after a hearing. Direct the adjudicator to key points in your written material.

18. Be aware that photos on cell phones and video equipment cannot be received as exhibits.

TEN TIPS FOR ADVOCACY BEFORE TRIBUNALS
Courtesy of David A. Wright,
Acting Chair, Human Rights Tribunal of Ontario

1. **Learn About the Tribunal**
   Be sure to know as much as possible about the tribunal you will be appearing before. If you have not done so before, start by reading the relevant legislation, the tribunal rules, and some of its case law. Learn about the tribunal's culture by talking to colleagues and tribunal staff. Remember that tribunals' approaches to dispute resolution are often different from each other and from those of the courts.

2. **Be Prepared**
   Start your preparation well in advance of the hearing to avoid making last-minute requests or amendments. Know the facts and your theory of the case throughout the litigation process. Make any preliminary or interim requests as soon as possible. Remember that mediation requires preparation, too!

3. **Listen To and Educate Your Client**
   Listen to your client's full story; do not be too quick to dismiss aspects of what he or she tells you as irrelevant. Understand your client's point of view and concerns — remember you are there to represent his or her interests. Tell your client what to expect at the hearing or mediation, and give him or her a realistic assessment of the possible end result prior to the outcome.

4. **Have a Mediation Strategy**

   Think about various possible options for settlement, and about how the other side will approach the issues and what their concerns are. Explore your client's bottom line before the mediation commences.

5. **Write Carefully**

   Well-written letters and submissions are of the utmost importance. Write in a short, clear, and straightforward manner. Use plain language, not "legalese".

6. **Focus Your Oral and Written Arguments**

   Be sure you have fully thought out how your facts relate to the statute, rules, and any relevant cases. Explain this to the decision maker in a concise manner. Use summaries and introductions, and explain the structure of your arguments at the outset.

7. **Make Concessions When Appropriate**

   It is rarely better, from a strategic point of view, to make an argument that will almost certainly lose than to concede. Being fair to the other side helps give the tribunal confidence in you. Making appropriate agreements with the other side before the hearing will save time, effort, and possibly your client's money.

8. **Look at the Issues from the Adjudicator's Perspective**

   Remember that you have to convince the adjudicator, who has different concerns from your client's. These include making the right decision, being consistent with other tribunal members, having the hearing run smoothly and efficiently, being fair to all parties and getting to the heart of the issues in dispute. The adjudicator is always thinking about how he or she will write the decision.

9. **Listen Carefully to the Adjudicator's Questions**

   Adjudicators generally ask questions to understand or test your position, not to trip you up or throw you off your game plan. Questions show what is concerning the adjudicator. When you answer them, consider carefully why the adjudicator is asking them and how you can allay his or her concerns.

10. **Be Courteous**

    Always treat the tribunal and the opposing party or representative with respect and courtesy. Being aggressive or impolite will not help your client.

DOs AND DON'Ts FOR PARALEGALS APPEARING BEFORE ADMINISTRATIVE AGENCIES

Courtesy of Her Worship Mary A. Ross Hendriks,
Justice of the Peace, Toronto Region, Ontario Court of Justice
(formerly Vice-chair, Human Rights Tribunal of Ontario)

Please be mindful of the fact that the *Statutory Powers Procedure Act* (*SPPA*) applies to most hearings conducted by Ontario boards. This has some real significance to you as a representative. First, the *SPPA* empowers boards to create their own Rules of Practice. Please ensure that you are aware of the latest rules and forms used by the boards before which you appear, since they are often amended every few years to keep pace with change. You can find these rules and forms on various board websites. You must use these rules and forms. Please be mindful of any deadlines set within these rules, so that you are able to map out a schedule for your pre-hearing preparations.

The *SPPA* also allows for a real relaxation of the rules of evidence. Sections 2 and 15 of the *SPPA* allow virtually anything to be admitted and permit the adjudicator to decide what weight, if any, to give it. That being the case, while documents that would normally be hearsay may be admitted into evidence, you have merely proven to the tribunal that a document exists, not the truth of its contents. The rules of evidence apply in criminal proceedings and in provincial offence cases. You should read a few leading textbooks on evidence, even in the administrative context, to understand fully how these rules apply or are modified by the *SPPA*, since this is critical knowledge for you as representatives.

Adjudicators find it very helpful if representatives provide them with a bound book of case law upon which they rely, which should include a cover page that sets out each case, its citation, and a cross-reference to the tab in the brief. The cover page should set out the title of proceeding, and your name and Law Society number in the bottom right-hand corner. It is also very helpful to provide adjudicators with a copy of your final submissions in a written form, even if you make final submissions orally. A cover page should also be included here, with the title of proceeding, the words "Final Submissions", and your name and Law Society number in the bottom right-hand corner. It is very professional to do this, and it helps supplement the notes that the adjudicators make for themselves.

Most board hearings are not recorded officially, unlike court proceedings, and so it is impossible to order a transcript. If your case is of extremely grave importance, please discuss with your client whether you are able to hire an official court reporter to prepare transcripts, which will be an official record of the proceeding. Determine this prior to the commencement of the hearing, and then approach the Registrar of the board to seek the adjudicator's permission to create an official record. As a matter of courtesy, you should offer to share copies of this record with all participants and the adjudicator. You may be able to do some cost-sharing with the opposing side, but the board will not contribute to the cost of these transcripts, which may be very high. The notes of an adjudicator or a member of the bench are normally held at common law to be beyond production, so if you cannot have an official record created, then it is up to you to bring a colleague with you to make detailed notes while you present your case. Your colleague may use pen and paper or a laptop to do so. If you are short-staffed, you may need to make your own notes.

In terms of expert witnesses, most boards have rules that deal with the amount of notice required for the opposing side. Typically, representatives provide the opposing side with a "willsay" of what the expert will say in evidence, and a copy of his or her résumé. Experts must be qualified by the board before they begin testifying. Please ensure that you are aware of how to qualify an expert witness, and how an expert's qualifications may be challenged by the other side.

Once you know who will be adjudicating your case, you may wish to read some of their prior decisions in cases related to your case. You should also read the decisions of their colleagues in related matters, particularly recent ones. You can access <www.canlii.org> from any computer (although that site only has decisions of selected boards) and obtain case law for free, and then note them up online. You may also enter the adjudicator's name, to read his or her decisions. In order to prepare fully, I urge you to obtain a private publisher's annotated copy of the statute that you are using (if it exists), read all the key cases listed, and note them up. The results of your legal research will help you craft your key arguments in advance and provide the analysis you will need for your final submissions.

Many legal publications, including *The Law Times* and the *Lawyers Weekly*, for example, are available on a subscription basis. I urge you to subscribe to a broadly based publication in newspaper format, which is relatively inexpensive, plus any specialized law journals or periodicals in the areas in which you practise so that you are able to keep up with changes to the law. If this is a financial burden, please regularly visit law and government libraries, such as the excellent one on labour, pay equity and human rights law housed with the Ontario Labour Relations Board (on different floors), and avail yourself of the journals and periodicals there. In addition, please attend continuing legal education lectures offered by a number of providers on a regular basis in order to increase your knowledge base. If you miss a lecture, you may be able to purchase it on CD or watch a re-broadcast of it. The practitioners who speak at these lectures and who provide papers spend a great deal of time and energy preparing, and their materials may help you see issues in a new light.

Finally, encourage your clients to avail themselves of any mediation opportunities that may be provided by the board for free, or even arrange for the services of a privately appointed mediator, chosen by both representatives. Mediation is an excellent tool and, for most cases, is a more efficient way of dealing with litigious matters. If your client's case is not a leading case that is going to change the law, then a confidential mediation session is something that should be pursued.

ANALYSIS OF HINTS AND LISTS

All the points listed and discussed above should be taken to heart by the practitioner, but there are three points that should be stressed, as follows.

- Preparation is essential to the advocate and takes many forms. Understanding your client's case and the law applicable to it as well as the other side's positions, being familiar with the evidence likely to be adduced and the witnesses that will be called, and knowing the procedures to be followed in the proceedings before the agency are just some of the items that need work. As noted above, being knowledgeable about the appropriate legislation and rules of the specific agency will go a long way in preparing to represent your client.

- Closely related to preparation is the necessity to update your knowledge of the appropriate law, including the enabling legislation and any other relevant statutes and regulations. These can change constantly (especially regulations) and you will not engender confidence with the adjudicator if you reference items no longer in force. Updating your knowledge of the case law (i.e., court judgments) relevant to the agency and your matter, is important as a Court of Appeal decision you may be relying on may have been overturned at the Supreme Court of Canada in the meantime. Alternatively, a new decision at variance or in support of what you believe is an important case may have occurred. You should also update your knowledge of decisions of the agency, as key points in your matter may have recently been determined that may have an impact on your matter. Although agencies are not bound by *stare decisis*, they do try to be consistent, if possible, so having the latest decisions will be useful to the advocate.

- Being courteous may seem to be a small point, but it can have huge impact on the confidence the adjudicator has in the representative. As well, it can also affect one's reputation, especially if the representative is discourteous to the adjudicator, to the other side, or to witnesses, not to mention how it might impact on the adjudicator in hearing the case and making a decision. After all, the adjudicator is human.

Numerous pages of this book could be filled with advice on how to be a great advocate; however, it is probably best to read a variety of the large number of texts written on advocacy as well as to observe good advocates in person. Most important, though, is one's use of such information to practise good advocacy in your matters. With experience, a representative will improve; and by following the hints above and desiring to be excellent in the work that is entailed, the representative will quickly become a reliable, trustworthy, and effective advocate.

CHAPTER SUMMARY

This chapter provided a review of tips offered by three "inside" sources of good advocacy skills needed to best present a client's case. It was felt that persons on the front lines hearing advocates would provide the best practical advice in how to succeed. By setting out each source's tips or comments in full, it is hoped that the reader can compare and contrast and, by dint of repetition, focus on the key concepts of good advocacy.

REVIEW QUESTIONS

1. What tip(s) are mentioned in all three sources quoted in the chapter?
2. What should a good advocate do before a hearing?
3. What should a good advocate do during a hearing?
4. What should a good advocate do after a hearing?
5. How can an advocate enhance her/his reputation with (a) the client, (b) the agency, and (c) her/his peers?
6. List five actions that would be viewed as bad advocacy.

EXERCISE

After reviewing the chapter, demonstrate good advocacy skills in presenting an argument before an adjudicator (a student posing) based upon the *Barker v. Famous Players, A Division of Viacom Canada Inc.*, 2004 HRTO 10 interim decision (the *Barker* decision), specifically the issue of reprisal discussed in that decision and briefed in Chapter 6.

SUGGESTED READINGS

Adair, Geoffrey. *On Trial: Advocacy Skills Law and Practice* (Markham, Ont.: Lexis, Nexis Butterworths, 2004).

Blatt, Arlene, & JoAnn Kurtz. *Advocacy for Paralegals* (Toronto, Ont.: Emond Montgomery Publications Limited, 2009).

Cromwell, Thomas (compiled by). *Effective Written Advocacy* (Aurora, Ont.: Canada Law Book, a division of The Cartwright Group Ltd., 2008).

Finlay, Brian, & Cromwell, Thomas. *Witness Preparation Manual*, 2d ed. (Aurora, Ont.: Canada Law Book Inc., 1999).

Noble, Cinnie, L. Leslie Dizgan, & D. Paul Emond. *Mediation Advocacy: Effective Client Representation in Mediation Process* (Toronto, Ont.: Emond Montgomery Publications Limited, 1998).

Salhany, Roger. *Cross-Examination: The Art of the Advocate*, 3d ed. (Markham, Ont.: Lexis, Nexis Butterworths, 2006).

White, Robert. *The Art of Trial* (Aurora, Ont.: Canada Law Book Inc., 1993).

Steusser, Lee. *An Advocacy Primer*, 3d ed. (Toronto, Ont.: Carswell, 2005).

Sopinka, John, Donald Houston, & Melanie Sopinka. *The Trial of an Action*, 2d ed. (Toronto, Ont.: Butterworths, 1998).

Part II

Selected Ontario Agencies

How to Deal with Selected Ontario Agencies

This part of the text discusses selected Ontario tribunals, boards, and commissions under the following topics:

- Overview and background
- Enabling legislation, including statute(s) and any appropriate regulation(s)
- Relevant regulation(s), if any (in addition to those discussed in enabling legislation)
- Tribunal procedures:
    - Rules
    - Practice directions
    - Forms
- Policies
- Explanatory literature from the Tribunal
- Relevant cases and/or decisions

Selected tribunals and boards applicable to paralegals representing clients at those agencies will be discussed. The objective of Part II is to provide guidelines for paralegals who represent a client in these Ontario tribunals. The material included and discussed will primarily be drawn from individual tribunal's own website, which will be referenced extensively, as well as from the websites of the appropriate government departments that deal with these tribunals. Ontario tribunals that fall under the *Statutory Powers Procedure Act* (*SPPA*), in whole or in part, will be noted in the section dealing with tribunal procedures. The cases and decisions mentioned in the Relevant Cases and/or Decisions section can be found on the tribunal's website or from research into cases and decisions online or at most law libraries. Although paralegals are not lawyers, to be a good advocate and to best represent a client, it is necessary for them to find, understand, and use appropriate cases and/or decisions in their work. Further research over and above that supplied in this book must always be done by the paralegal in preparing to appear before any tribunal.

The review of websites and the research for this edition of the book were done in Fall 2010. Since the law constantly changes, paralegals should continue to verify information provided here to ensure its currency and validity. By applying a systematic review of the website of a tribunal that is not explored in this book, paralegals can learn the practice and procedure of any tribunal before which they may appear.

4

Social Benefits Tribunal

LEARNING OBJECTIVES

After reading this chapter, the reader should be able to:

- understand how to research any Ontario agency by exploring its website for important information needed to understand the agency's practices and procedures and how a paralegal would properly represent a client before such agency by doing so with the Social Benefits Tribunal (SBT)
- document the background of the SBT
- detail and explain the provisions of the enabling legislation relevant to the SBT
- elaborate on various concepts of public policy relevant to the SBT
- state whether any regulations made under the enabling legislation is relevant to the SBT and, if so, to discuss such provisions
- compare and prioritize the various sources of practice and procedure of the SBT
- identify the specific rules and procedures for the SBT and how they would be applied in a proceeding before, during, and after a hearing of the SBT
- review and explain the procedures and practices of the SBT by way of a flow chart and key forms and documents available on the SBT website
- assess whether the relevant provisions of the *Statutory Powers Procedure Act* apply to the SBT
- outline the various explanatory literature available on the SBT website to assist the paralegal to understand the SBT and better represent the client
- appreciate the need to find decisions and/or cases in order to understand and argue the law before the SBT
- illustrate and discuss principles that flow from the various cases and decisions as they relate to the SBT

INTRODUCTION

The Social Benefits Tribunal (SBT) is an Ontario adjudicative agency created and given power by legislation to hear appeals from decisions made by persons working in or through the Ontario Ministry of Community and Social Services regarding social assistance, as set out on the SBT website: <www.sbt.gov.on.ca>.

OVERVIEW AND BACKGROUND

Basic social assistance is provided in Ontario by or through the Ministry of Community and Social Services to those in immediate financial need either due to lack of, or insufficiency in, employment or due to disabilities, and it also supports children with severe disabilities. Before the creation of the SBT, its predecessor, the Social Assistance Review Board (SARB), considered appeals regarding social assistance under the *Family Benefits Act* and other statutes. As of the summer of 2010, SARB's few final appeals were being wrapped up; when that process is complete, it will likely cease to exist.

ENABLING LEGISLATION

The SBT was created on June 1, 1998, under subsection 60(1) of the *Ontario Works Act, 1997*, S.O. 1997, c. 25, Sched. A, as amended (the *OWA*), which also gave the SBT some of its powers and jurisdiction. The SBT was also given additional powers and jurisdiction under another empowering statute, the *Ontario Disability Support Program Act, 1997*, S.O. 1997, c. 25, Sched. B, as amended (the *ODSPA*). The sections of both Acts and the relevant regulations related to the SBT are set out below.

OWA and O. Reg. 134/98

Assistance under OWA

This statute was enacted to establish a program to, among other things, provide "temporary financial assistance to those in need while they satisfy obligations to become and stay employed" (ss. 1(b)) by providing both employment assistance (s. 4) and basic financial assistance (s. 5) to those persons who satisfy all conditions of eligibility under the Act and the regulations made under it (ss. 7(1)). The delivery of financial assistance is delegated to delivery agents by the Minister of Community and Social Services (ss. 38.(1)). Pursuant to subsection 39(1), there are 47 Consolidated Municipal Service Managers at the municipal level (in Northern Ontario, they are called District Social Services Administration Boards) and 109 First Nations delivery agents (as detailed in the ministry website: <www.mcss.gov.on.ca/mcss/english/pillars/programs/ow.htm>).

Decision of the Administrator and Internal Review

Every delivery agent appoints an administrator to oversee the administration under the Act (s. 43) and who, among other things, determines eligibility for employment assistance and basic financial assistance (s. 44). Once an administrator makes a decision regarding the eligibility for and the amount, if any, of assistance, "such administrator shall give notice to the applicant or recipient of a decision that may be appealed and the notice shall advise the applicant or recipient that he or she may request an internal review of the decision" (s. 24). The formalities and contents of the notice of decision are set out in O. Reg. 134/98, s. 67. According to subsection 26(1) of the Act, any decision by an administrator regarding eligibility for, or the amount of, basic financial assistance may be appealed to the SBT, other than decisions set out in subsection 26(2) of the Act and section 68 of O. Reg. 134/98. **Before the appeal to the SBT of a decision can be commenced, there must be a request to do an internal review (s. 27(1)).** An internal review occurs when the applicant or recipient requests that the administrator consider the decision and whether or not to change it. The specifics about timing for the request for an internal review are set out in section 27 of the *OWA* and section 69 of O. Reg. 134/98. An internal review must be completed within 10 days of the request to do it and must be done by someone who did not make the original decision (s. 70 of O. Reg. 134/98). Details regarding delivery of and the contents of the internal review are given in section 71 of O. Reg. 134/98. Under subsection 27(4) of the *OWA*, the *SPPA* does not apply to the internal review.

Appeal to the SBT

The specifics of appeal to the SBT are detailed in section 28 of the *OWA* and sections 72–79 of O. Reg. 134/98. The date to request an appeal is 30 days from the date the decision is final. (That time can be extended by the SBT under subsection 28(2) of the *OWA*.) The appeal shall commence no later than one year from the date of the decision and shall be done with a notice of appeal form approved by the Minister (s. 72 of O. Reg. 134/98). The notice of appeal shall set out the reasons for requesting the appeal (ss. 28(1)). The parties to the hearing before the SBT are the "administrator, the applicant or recipient who requested the hearing, and any other persons specified by the Tribunal" (ss. 28(4)), and the Director can be added to the proceeding by the SBT if requested by the Director (ss. 28(5)). A spouse can also be added as a party in a specific circumstance, but such spouse cannot launch an appeal of that determination (ss. 28(6–7)).

Upon receipt of the notice of appeal, the SBT shall send a copy of the notice to any other parties in the proceeding (O. Reg. 134/98, ss. 73(1)). Subsection 28(8) allows the administrator and the Director to make written submissions in place of, or in addition to, appearing at a hearing. The submissions, however, must be filed with the SBT within 30 days after the administrator has received a copy of the notice of appeal and shall then be provided to all other parties (O. Reg. 134/98, ss. 73(2–3)). Under subsection 28(10) of the *OWA*, the "parties to a hearing shall be given an opportunity before the hearing to examine any written or documentary evidence that a party proposes to introduce at the hearing". The SBT is required under section 74 of O. Reg. 134/98 to send within 60 days of receipt of the notice of appeal, the notice of hearing, including whether it is to be an oral hearing (in which case to include date, place, and time of hearing) or "paper" (written), and the dates that the parties are to provide written submissions and documentary evidence to the SBT. **The SBT is required to give the parties at least 30 days' notice of the hearing. Under subsection 28(11) of the *OWA*, the onus lies on the appellant to satisfy the SBT that the decision of the administrator is wrong.** Some of the procedures for the conduct of an oral hearing before the SBT include the following:

- The appellant shall present his or her case first at oral hearing of an appeal before the SBT, unless the administrator agrees otherwise.

- The SBT shall ensure that the evidence at an oral hearing of an appeal is recorded by notes taken by an SBT member participating in the hearing or by a method from which a transcript can be produced.

These are set out in section 76 of O. Reg. 134/98 and should be referred to if there is an oral hearing of the appeal.

Interim Assistance

After the request for an appeal but before the SBT can make a decision, the SBT, under section 30 of the *OWA*, can direct the administrator to provide interim assistance "to an applicant or recipient if the Tribunal is satisfied that the person will suffer financial hardship during the period needed for the Tribunal to complete its review and give notice of its decision" up to a maximum as set out in section 77 of O. Reg. 134/98. The *SPPA* does not apply to any proceeding of the SBT regarding interim assistance (ss. 30(3)).

Decision of the SBT

Within 60 days after it last receives evidence or submissions on the appeal (O. Reg. 134/98, ss. 78(1)), the SBT must deliver a written decision to the parties. Under section 31 of the *OWA*, the SBT's orders include (a) denying the appeal, (b) granting the appeal, (c) granting the appeal in part, or (d) referring the matter back to the administrator for reconsideration with any directions the SBT considers proper. Furthermore, the SBT decision must include reasons and takes effect when it is made and, if it is appealed, continues in effect until a decision of the Divisional Court is made on appeal. Appeals can be denied if the proceedings fall within the circumstances listed in section 34 of the *OWA*. The SBT's findings of fact shall be based exclusively on evidence admissible and facts of which notice may be taken under sections 15, 15.1, 15.2, and 16 of the *SPPA*, and the decision shall include the principal findings of fact and its conclusions based on those findings (ss. 78(2–3)). Note that under section 33 of the *OWA*, the SBT "shall refuse to hear an appeal if it determines the appeal to be frivolous or vexatious".

Reconsideration of SBT Decision

Section 79 of O. Reg. 134/98 details the ability to ask the SBT to reconsider its decision on the appeal, including the timelines and other procedural matters.

Appeal of SBT Decision

There is no privative clause preventing an appeal of an SBT decision: subsection 36(1) of the *OWA* states that the "Director and any party to a hearing may appeal the Tribunal's decision to the Divisional Court on a question of law". Currently, the *Law Society Act* and the Paralegal Rules of Conduct do not allow paralegals to appear in Divisional Court, so we will skip the review of the procedures of the SBT under the *OWA* and its O. Reg. 134/98 and continue with a review of the appropriate sections of the enabling legislation for further information. However, if you are faced with a decision that should be appealed, note that under section 81 of O. Reg134/98, the appeal **must** be commenced by filing a notice of appeal with Divisional Court, usually within 30 days after receiving the decision of the SBT.

General Jurisdictional and Procedural Matters of the SBT

General provisions regarding the SBT are contained in Part IV of the *OWA*, specifically, sections 60–67. Section 64 envisions either one adjudicator or a panel made up of one presiding member and the rest of the panel. Sittings for hearings can occur anywhere in Ontario "and in the manner and at the times the Tribunal considers most convenient for the proper discharge and speedy dispatch of its business" (ss. 65(1)); alternately, the SBT may hold a paper hearing (ss. 65(2)). **Notwithstanding the *SPPA*, all hearings before the SBT are private (ss. 66(1)).** Also under subsection 66(2), no members hearing the matter shall have had any prior dealings with the matter or *ex parte* communication with any parties except as allowed under the subsection 66(3), where hearing members seek legal advice or have discussion with other members of the Tribunal. Pursuant to subsection 66(4), only the member who was present throughout the hearing and heard the evidence and argument of the parties can make a decision of that Tribunal hearing. A request can be made under subsection 66(5) to the SBT, and if it believes that there will be financial hardship to a party or witness attending the hearing, it may pay such party or witness travelling and living expenses, as necessary, to enable such attendance at the hearing. There are specific restrictions on the jurisdiction of the SBT to make a decision or to inquire into specific situations as set out in section 67.

ODSPA and O. Reg. 222/98

Assistance under ODSPA

The *ODSPA*, among other things, "provides income and employment support to eligible persons with disabilities" (ss. 1(a)). Under subsection 10(1), an application for income support shall be made to the Director of the Ontario Disability Support Program (the Director), using a form as required by the Director and containing information required by section 14 of O. Reg. 222/98.

Decision of the Director and Internal Review

The Director oversees the administration under the Act (ss. 37(1)) and, among other things, determines eligibility for income support (s. 38). Once the Director makes a decision regarding the eligibility for and the amount, if any, of income support, the "Director shall give notice to the applicant or recipient of a decision that may be appealed and the notice shall advise the applicant or recipient that he or she may request an internal review of the decision" (s. 19). The formalities and contents of the notice of decision are set out in O. Reg. 222/98, s. 56. According to subsection 21(1) of the *ODSPA*, any decision by the Director regarding eligibility for, or the amount of, income support may be appealed to the SBT other than decisions set out in subsection 21(2), decisions regarding employment support (ss. 21(3)), and those in section 57 of O. Reg. 222/98. **Before the appeal to the SBT of a decision can be commenced, there must be a request to do an internal review (ss. 22(1)).** An internal review occurs when the applicant or recipient requests that the Director consider whether or not to change the decision. The specifics about timing for the request for an internal review are set out in section 22 of the *ODSPA* and section 58 of O. Reg. 222/98. An internal review must be completed within 10 days of the request to do it and must be done by someone who did not make the original decision (O. Reg. 222/98, s. 59). Details regarding delivery and contents of the internal review are detailed in section 60 of O. Reg. 222/98. Under subsection 22(4) of the *ODSPA*, the *SPPA* does not apply to the internal review.

Appeal to the SBT

The specifics of appeal to the SBT are detailed in section 23 of the *ODSPA* and sections 61–65 of O. Reg. 222/98. The date to request an appeal is 30 days from the date the decision is final (although that time can be extended under subsection 23(2) of the *ODSPA*). The appeal shall commence no later than one year from the date of the decision and shall be done using a notice of appeal form approved by the Minister (O. Reg. 222/98, s. 61). The notice of appeal shall set out the reasons for requesting the appeal (ss. 23(1)). The parties to the hearing before the SBT are the "Director, the applicant or recipient who requested the hearing and any other persons specified by the Tribunal" (ss. 23(4)). A spouse can also be added as a party in a specific circumstance, but such spouse cannot launch an appeal of that determination (ss. 23(5–6)). Upon receipt of the notice of appeal, the SBT shall send a copy of the notice to any other parties in the proceeding (O. Reg. 222/98, ss. 62(1)). Subsection 23(7) allows the Director to "make written submissions in place of or in addition to appearing at a hearing" to be filed with the SBT within 30 days after the Director has received a copy of the notice of appeal and submissions shall then be provided to all other parties (O. Reg. 222/98, ss. 62(2–3)). Under subsection 23(9) of the *ODSPA*, the parties to a hearing are entitled to examine, before the hearing, any written or documentary evidence that a party proposes to introduce at the hearing. The SBT is required under section 63 of O. Reg. 222/98 to send within 60 days of receipt of the notice of appeal, the notice of hearing, including whether it will be an oral hearing (in which case to include date, place, and time of hearing) or paper (written) hearing, and the dates by which the parties are to provide written submissions and documentary evidence to the SBT. The SBT is required to give the parties at least 30 days notice of the hearing. **Under subsection 23(10) of the *ODSPA*, the onus lies on the appellant to satisfy the SBT that the decision of the Director is wrong.** Some of the procedures for the conduct of an oral hearing before the SBT include the following:

- The appellant shall present his or her case first on an oral hearing of an appeal before the SBT, unless the Director agrees otherwise.
- The SBT shall ensure that the evidence at an oral hearing of an appeal is recorded by notes taken by an SBT member participating in the hearing or by a method from which a transcript can be produced.

These are set out in section 65 of O. Reg. 222/98 and should be referred to if there is an oral hearing of the appeal.

Interim Assistance

After the request for an appeal but before the SBT can make a decision, the SBT, under section 25 of the *ODSPA*, can direct the Director to provide interim assistance, up to a maximum as set out in section 66 of O. Reg. 222/98, to a recipient if the SBT is convinced that the person will suffer financial hardship during the period that the SBT needed to complete its review and give notice of its decision. The *SPPA* does not apply to any proceeding of the SBT regarding interim assistance (ss. 25(3)).

Decision of the SBT

Within 60 days after it last receives evidence or submissions on the appeal (O. Reg. 222/98, ss. 67(1)), the SBT must deliver a written decision to the parties. Under section 26 of the *ODSPA*, the SBT can (a) deny the appeal; (b) grant the appeal; (c) grant the appeal in part; or (d) refer the matter back to the Director for reconsideration, with any directions the SBT considers proper. Further, such decision must include reasons and takes effect when it is made and, if it is appealed, continues in effect until a decision of the Divisional Court is made on appeal. Appeals can also be denied if the proceedings fall within the circumstances listed in section 29 of the *ODSPA*. The SBT's findings of fact shall be based exclusively on evidence admissible and facts of which notice may be taken under sections 15, 15.1, 15.2, and 16 of the *SPPA*, and the decision shall include the principal findings of fact and its conclusions based on those findings (ss. 67(2–3)). It is also important to note that, under section 28 of the *ODSPA*, the SBT "shall refuse to hear an appeal if it determines the appeal to be frivolous or vexatious".

Reconsideration of SBT Decision

Section 68 of O. Reg. 222/98 details the ability to ask the SBT to reconsider its decision on the appeal, including the timelines and other procedural matters.

Appeal of SBT Decision

There is no privative clause preventing an appeal of the decision of the SBT: subsection 31(1) of the *ODSPA* states that the "[a]ny party to a hearing may appeal the Tribunal's decision to the Divisional Court on a question of law". Currently the *Law Society Act* and the Paralegal Rules of Conduct do not allow paralegals to appear in Divisional Court, so we will not review the procedures of the SBT under the *ODSPA* and its O. Reg. 222/98, but we will continue to review the appropriate sections of both Act and regulation for further information. However, if you are faced with a decision that should be appealed, note that under section 70 of O. Reg. 222/98, the appeal *must* be commenced by filing a notice of appeal with Divisional Court, usually within 30 days after receiving the SBT's decision.

General Jurisdictional and Procedural Matters of the SBT

General provisions regarding the SBT are contained in Part IV of the *OWA* — specifically, sections 60–67. As those general sections of the *OWA* set out features of the SBT, the *ODSPA*, which gives the SBT jurisdiction to hear appeals under its statute, takes the SBT as it finds it and therefore those general provisions still apply to the SBT. The review of those general sections of the *OWA*, above, would be useful even if your case were under the *ODSPA*.

RELEVANT REGULATIONS

The review of the regulations relevant to the procedures of the SBT was done in the review of the enabling legislation above.

PROCEDURES OF TRIBUNAL

The SBT does not have rules detailing the procedures of the tribunal but, rather, uses the procedures set out by the enabling legislation discussed above, as well as "Practice Directions" published on the SBT website. "Policy Directives", as listed at the end of this chapter and published on the Ministry of Community and Social Services website (<www.mcss.gov.on.ca/mcss/english/pillars/social/ow-directives/ow_policy_directives.htm> and <www.mcss.gov.on.ca/mcss/english/pillars/social/odsp-is-directivesODSP_incomesupport.htm>), are not binding on the SBT, as it is stated on the Ministry's website that in any conflict between the Policy Directives and the Practice Directions, the Practice Directions would rule. However, it might be useful to understand the Ministry's position on the items listed there. Following is a discussion of each.

PRACTICE DIRECTIONS OF SBT

The Practice Directions are not rules of the SBT specifically but, rather, are the intended guidelines for the procedures that the SBT would like everyone to follow when appearing before the SBT. As there are no specific rules promulgated by either the SBT or anyone else entitled to do so, the Practice Directions, and applicable provisions of the *SPPA* and provisions of the enabling legislation as discussed above, provide guidance to all persons dealing with the SBT. Set out below are summaries, including quoted provisions of the Practice Directions, but the reader should review the whole text to obtain complete information on each.

Practice Direction 1 — Interim Assistance

This direction discusses the ability of the SBT to award interim assistance while waiting for the hearing and the decision, if the SBT feels that the appellant will face financial hardship during such time. If the appellant loses at the hearing, any interim assistance will be an overpayment and subject to recovery. When assessing applications for interim assistance, the SBT must consider legislation as well as relevant court decisions. The determination of interim assistance is a separate decision-making process from the appeal, and the success or failure of an interim assistance application has no bearing on the end result of the appeal. The appellant must complete, as fully as possible, the tribunal's "Application for Interim Assistance", which is section 4 of the Appeal Form (to be discussed below). A party who objects to an interim assistance decision shall write to the Chair of the Social Benefits Tribunal, setting out detailed reasons why that decision should be reversed or amended, with a copy of the letter to the other party. The reasons for objecting will be assessed by the Tribunal and a written response will be sent to both parties as quickly as possible.

Practice Direction 2 — Reconsideration Requests

With the power of discretion, the SBT is able to discourage unnecessary requests and still allow for reconsideration hearings where a serious error or omission has occurred. In exercising its discretion to grant reconsideration hearings, the SBT needs to strike a balance between preserving the finality of Tribunal decisions and the need to address substantive problems in the tribunal's decisions with the need for a further appeal to court or judicial review. A request to reconsider a decision must be made in writing using the prescribed form "Application for Reconsideration" (to be discussed below) and must be signed by the applicant. The SBT will take into account the following factors when deciding whether to grant a reconsideration hearing:

- Has the tribunal acted outside its jurisdictions?
- Has the tribunal violated the rules of natural justice or procedural fairness?
- Has the tribunal made a serious error of law?
- Could the new evidence that would have had a material effect on the decision have been obtained by reasonable diligence for the original hearing? (This includes evidence that has come into existence after the original hearing.)
- Is there any other substantial ground relevant to the decision?

The SBT will send a Notice of Hearing providing the date, time, and place of the reconsideration hearing, if it is granted. Any member of the SBT can be assigned to hear the reconsideration other than the member who made the original decision unless it is a limited reconsideration.

Practice Direction 3 — Rules for Electronic Hearings

Noting that electronic hearings can be held pursuant to the *SPPA*, the direction allows the SBT to have telephone hearings if all the parties and the Tribunal members who participate in the hearing are able to hear one another and any witnesses throughout the hearing. Further, it is noted that a telephone hearing of the SBT is private and confidential; thus, the parties are required to make arrangements to ensure the privacy and confidentiality of the hearing are maintained at their premises. A telephone hearing can be used for procedural issues and any other matter unless a party objects and the SBT is convinced that such a hearing is likely to cause significant prejudice to that party. Factors that the SBT may consider in determining whether a telephone hearing should be held include the following:

- The nature of the appeal and whether it is suitable to hear the matter by telephone
- The type of evidence that may be required for the hearing and whether credibility is an issue
- The ability to conduct a fair and private hearing
- The number of persons that may be involved in the hearing, including parties, counsel, and witnesses
- The need to expedite certain types of appeals
- Convenience to the parties
- A party's request for a telephone hearing and the reasons for the request
- Estimated duration of the hearing
- The cost and efficiency of conducting a hearing by telephone
- Special circumstances, such as the unavailability of an interpreter

The contents of a notice of a telephone hearing and the ability of and the procedures for a party to object to it, unless it is of a procedural issue, if such hearing would likely cause the party significant prejudice are discussed.

Practice Direction 4 — Rescheduling of Hearings and Adjournments

The SBT wants a hearing to occur at the date, time, and place already set unless it agrees to change it. The fact that a legal representative cannot attend an already scheduled hearing is not necessarily grounds to change the date. A request to change a date should be made as soon as it is known that there is a problem. Although the SBT will likely change a date only for exceptional circumstances, it can change the hearing date on its own motion to accommodate internal issues.

The SBT will give the parties at least 30 days' notice of the hearing date unless the parties give written consent to have a hearing at an earlier date. If a party requests a rescheduled date, it must be in writing and given to both the SBT and the other party, including reasons why a new date is required and a daytime telephone number to discuss the request. The most important factor the SBT will consider when there is a request to change the hearing date is whether the change is necessary to ensure a fair and timely hearing. Other factors considered include the existence of any previous changes, whether the request was made at the earliest opportunity, whether the party made reasonable efforts to avoid the need for a new date, whether anyone would be prejudiced if the request was granted or denied, or whether there is a serious personal emergency or compassionate factor. An adjournment request can also be made at the commencement of the hearing, but the party requesting should be prepared to start the hearing if the request is refused.

Usually, the SBT will reschedule if all parties consent.

Practice Direction 5 — Early Resolution Program

This program, although not mandatory, as it is on consent, allows the parties to use "Early Resolution Opportunities" (ERO, and also known as Early Resolution Program or ERP) to use a variety of alternative dispute resolution processes to resolve appeals prior to the formal tribunal hearing. The program will allow the SBT to identify and implement early opportunities to resolve cases, making the tribunal fair and efficient and thereby reducing backlogs and costs. In the event that the ERO did not fully resolve the issues, it will narrow and clarify issues to make eventual hearings more timely and focused.

ERO is a private and confidential process that includes "in-person or telephone pre-hearing conferences, in-person or telephone settlement discussions, negotiations, conciliations and mediations". An ERO session will *not* be rescheduled. A Notice of Early Resolution Opportunity Session will be sent to the parties after the filing of the appeal. What is to be included in such a notice is detailed in section 5.2 of Practice Direction 5. The reasons a party would participate in such a session are discussed in section 6.1 of Practice Direction 5. Written submissions may be filed with the SBT and the other parties at least five days before the session. If a party objects to the session or fails to attend, the session will not proceed and the appeal will continue. The possible outcomes of the session are discussed in section 10.1 of Practice Direction 5.

Practice Tips — Early Resolution Program
The Early Resolution Pilot Program (ERP) is meant to be flexible, and these tips, while not legally binding or enforceable, are meant to provide practical suggestions to participants involved in the ERP. It is critical that all parties have the authority to resolve the appeal at the time of the session. The parties should exercise "good faith participation", meaning being available to participate and being fully prepared. Early disclosure and exchange of documents should take place as soon as possible but certainly before the session begins.

Practice Direction 6 — Procedure for Human Rights Issues or Challenges
In the "What's New" Web page of the SBT website at the time of this edition's review (Summer 2010), under the heading, "No Two-Stage Procedure for Appeals Involving Human Rights Code Challenges to Section 5(2) of ODSP Act", reference is made to the April 20, 2009 case where the "Divisional Court upheld the Social Benefits Tribunal's November 30, 2006 decision and agreed that s. 5(2) of the ODSP Act was contrary to the *Human Rights Code* and should not be applied — see *Director, ODSP v. Tranchemontagne and Werbeski*" and therefore *Human Rights Code* challenges to s. 5(2) do not have to use the two-stage procedure set out immediately below as set out in the new Practice Direction 6 effective February 1, 2010. The Web page further states:

> The Tribunal has made a minor addition to Practice Direction 6 by adding s. 10.7 to indicate that the Tribunal may contact the parties to facilitate settlement discussions and determine whether a Stage 2 hearing is necessary when the Appellant has made a *Human Rights Code* challenge.

The 2006 Supreme Court of Canada decision of *Tranchemontagne v. Ontario (Director, Disability Support Program)* (the SCC case of *Tranchemontagne*, which shall be discussed in more detail in a later section in this chapter) states that the SBT has jurisdiction, which it cannot decline, to consider challenges to its enabling legislation (in this case, "human rights issue or challenge" under the provisions of the Ontario *Human Rights Code*). The SBT, following the case, instituted a procedure to deal with human rights issues and challenges. A procedure was put in place to ensure the SBT will receive sufficient notice of appeals that raise human rights issues so that the issues can be dealt with in an efficient and effective manner, while maintaining a fair appeal process.

The first step for a party raising a human rights issue or challenge is to file a written notice with the SBT containing particulars of the challenge, the section(s) of the *Ontario Human Rights Code* (*Code*) relied upon, the desired remedy, and contact particulars of the party's representative. The SBT will send the written notice to the other parties within 10 days of receipt. A party who wishes to reply to such written notice must notify the SBT and send a copy of its intent to the Ministry of Community and Social Services, the Attorney General of the Province of Ontario, and the other parties within 15 days of receiving the written notice forwarded by the SBT. Where a party does not send a written notice of its intention to reply in the proper time, the SBT will assume that such party will not be participating in the human rights issue or challenge. The SBT will address the human rights challenge or issue only after the main issue on the appeal has been heard if it is raised pursuant to these procedures. If the appeal of the main issue is granted, the human rights issue or challenge will not be dealt with, and the SBT shall notify all parties of that fact. But if the SBT denies the appeal on the main issue, within 60 days after delivering its written decision denying the appeal on the main issue, it shall send a written notice that a second hearing to consider the human rights issue or challenge will be scheduled. Any reconsideration requests will be processed and ruled upon before proceeding with the second hearing. If all parties, by written notice sent to the SBT, agree to proceed directly to the human rights issue or challenge raised without holding a hearing on the appeal of the main issue, then all parties shall further file with the SBT an "Agreed Statement of Facts" dealing with the main appeal.

The SBT also reserves the right to deal with human rights issues or challenges not done in accordance with these procedures in unusual or exceptional circumstances. Parties appearing before the SBT on a human rights issue or challenge must comply with disclosure requirements required by the enabling legislation of the SBT. However, written submissions and evidence from the parties in respect of the human rights issue or challenge will not be required until the SBT hears that issue. The disclosure requirement may be waived by the SBT if a party does not have legal representation for the purposes of the hearing dealing with the human rights issue or challenge. Where appropriate, the SBT can set out disclosure timelines, other than what is set out here, in consultation with the parties to the hearing. Other disclosure procedures in this situation are detailed in sections 9.4 to 9.9 of Practice Direction 6. Also, Practice Direction 8, discussed below, deals with pre-hearing conferences that can be held in relation to a human rights issue or challenge.

If the SBT determines that, after receipt of a party's notice, the human rights issue or challenge is frivolous or vexatious, it may refuse to hear it, after notifying the party who raised it. As such, the other procedures set out here do not apply.

If a party does not follow the required procedure in raising a human rights issue or the challenge is without reasonable cause, the party will not be entitled to raise the human rights issue or challenge, except in an unusual or exceptional circumstance.

Practice Direction 7 — Recording Proceedings
Practice Direction 7 is currently not applicable.

Practice Direction 8 — Pre-Hearing Conferences
The procedure used by the SBT for scheduling and conducting pre-hearing conferences is set out in Practice Direction 8. Pre-hearing conferences can be held at the request of a party or at the direction of the SBT (unless there are special or unusual circumstances to dispense). A pre-hearing conference request by a party must be made in writing, with reasons set out, and within 10 days of the filing of the appeal. Where an appeal raises a human rights issue or challenge, a pre-hearing conference is mandatory, and all parties must attend to discuss procedural

matters prior to the hearing. For the purposes of this Practice Direction, a pre-hearing conference is a meeting with all the parties conducted by a SBT member by way of one or a combination of telephone, videoconferencing, oral in-person session, or in writing. The purposes of the pre-hearing conferences are those set out in the provisions of the *SPPA*, and evidence is not to be presented. Once a pre-hearing conference is requested or directed, a Notice of Pre-Hearing Conference will be sent, as soon as practicable, to the parties, setting out the format(s) of the conference and its date, place, and time. Details about the choice of format are discussed in sections 8.4 to 8.6 and the matters that can be dealt with in the pre-hearing conference are set out in section 9.1 of Practice Direction 8. The various outcomes of the pre-hearing conference are detailed in sections 10.1 to 10.5 of Practice Direction 8.

POLICY DIRECTIVES

Policy Directives appear on the Ontario Ministry of Community and Social Services website: <www.mcss.gov.on.ca>. The directives provide background non-binding information on the topics listed below.

Policy Directives Regarding *OWA* and the *ODSPA*

Policy directives related to both the *OWA* and the *ODSPA* appear on the Ontario Ministry of Community and Special Services website, <www.mcss.gov.on.ca>, and can provide background on various relevant topics involving the SBT, such as the ones set out immediately below, but these directives are not legally binding.

Policy Directives Regarding the *OWA*

Section 10 — Appeals

(a) Section 10.1 — Overview of appeals
Provides an overview of various appeals and the obligations imposed on parties.
(b) Section 10.2 — Notice and internal review process
Outlines basic elements and features of an internal review process.
(c) Section 10.3 — Recovery of interim assistance
Outlines how to calculate an overpayment in interim assistance to determine the amount to recover.

Policy Directives Regarding the *ODSPA* — Income Support Directives

13.1. Notice of Decision and Internal Review Process
Sets out the requirement for written notice of decisions and the Internal Review process.

13.2. Appeals
Outlines processes, rules and responsibilities when dealing with appeals to the SBT and for subsequent appeals to Divisional Court.

13.3. Recovery of Interim Assistance
Outlines how to calculate an overpayment in interim assistance to determine the amount to recover.

FORMS[1]

1. Appeal Form

This form must be used to appeal a decision under the enabling legislation of the SBT. **The form is set out in the Appendix to this chapter but it is important to check for the most current form on the SBT website, as changes can often occur.** A discussion of aspects of the appeal form appears in the "FAQ's/AppealForms" Web page of the SBT website. Once completed, the appeal form can be faxed, mailed, or delivered to the offices of the SBT at the location or number specified on the website. The timeline for filing the appeal form is stated as being after the decision to cancel, reduce, or put on hold your assistance within 30 days after either you have requested and received an internal review decision or after 10 days of requesting but not having received an internal review decision. If you do not file within the timelines, you must state the reasons for the late filing.

2. Application for Reconsideration

Either party can request a reconsideration using the application set out in the Appendix, by providing the reasons why the request should be granted and filing with the SBT within 30 days after receiving the decision of the SBT. A discussion of aspects of the appeal form appears in the "FAQ's/Reconsideration" section of the SBT website. A reconsideration is a fresh hearing of the appeal, and the party requesting will receive a letter from the SBT within 60 days after it receives the Application for Reconsideration stating whether or not a reconsideration hearing will be granted.

POLICIES

1. Ministry Policies

See Policy Directives of Ministry of Community and Social Services, discussed in page 96.

2. Policies of the SBT

There is one named policy of the SBT as announced on the "What's New" Web page as follows: "We are pleased to provide the Customer Service Policy of the Social Benefits Tribunal, which can be found under the title Practice Directions. This policy incorporates the standards set out in the Accessibility Standards for Customer Service passed under the *Accessibility for Ontarians with Disabilities Act, 2005*. The Policy reflects the core principles of dignity, independence, integration and equal opportunity for access to and use of services at the Tribunal." If appropriate to the reader, review the policy on the website.

There also is "Member Conduct Complaint Procedure" on the website. The Member Conduct Complaint Procedure states that any person can complain about a member's conduct, either in a specific hearing or general conduct outside of a hearing, by following the procedures set out therein. It makes note that all members must comply with the "Rules of Conduct and Conflict of Interest Guidelines for the Social Benefits Tribunal and the Social Assistance Review Board" and after a complaint in writing is made, the Chair of the SBT will determine the investigation and remedial action warranted in each individual case balancing the integrity and fairness of the hearing and the independence of the adjudicator.

---

[1] Forms discussed in this section can be found in the Appendix to this chapter.

EXPLANATORY LITERATURE FROM THE SBT

1. Appeal Your Decision to the Social Benefits Tribunal[2]

This is a brochure, as set out in the Appendix to this chapter, that explains to lay people how to appeal the decision made by the administrator or Director, as the case may be, to the SBT. Legal representatives can peruse the brochure, but they need to understand the procedures in more detail, as discussed.

2. Annual Report, 2008–2009

The SBT furnishes to the public, by way of posting it on its website, an annual report discussing important matters that arose in the fiscal year in its heading. The 2008–2009 annual report was on the website at the time of review for this edition (Fall 2010) and therefore it shall be discussed to give the reader an idea of what normally appears.

The chair's message commences the report discussing important events in the life of the SBT over that year's period including detailing the number of appeals in the year and the reasons why, as well as new initiatives undertaken by the Tribunal.

Next, the membership, with biographical sketches, of the SBT is detailed.

Recognizing that the enabling legislation allows for both appeals and judicial review of the decisions of the SBT to Divisional Court (Div. Ct.) and be further appealed to the Ontario Court of Appeal (Ont. C.A.) and the Supreme Court of Canada (SCC), important decisions of those courts related to the SBT are then discussed. Although such cases can be researched, it is a handy tool to look at important cases which will affect the decisions of the SBT. The first case discussed is the *Sheldrick* case, a 2008 decision of the Ont. C.A. in which the court had to determine if the SBT erred in applying the "person with a disability" test in respect of the appellant. The Ont. C.A. held that the SBT had not erred and the Div. Ct. should not have ruled that it did. The court stated that the SBT "had provided full and adequate reasons for why the medical opinion evidence, when viewed in the context of all the evidence before it, including the evidence of activities of daily living and the Appellant's own testimony, was not determinative of the 'substantial impairment' requirement."

The *Tranchemontagne* case is a 2009 case of the Div. Ct. dealt with an appeal of the SBT mandated by the SCC decision that the SBT had to determine the validity of s. 5(2) of the *ODSPA* and whether it violated the *Ontario Human Rights Code*. The Div. Ct. upheld the ruling of the SBT that the section did in fact violate the *Code*. The *Jemiolo* case, a 2009 Div. Ct. judgment, looked at whether medical report evidence to determine if the claimant was sufficiently disabled as to be classified as a person with a disability, which was dated some months after the Director's decision, could be used in the determination. The court held that evidence after the Director's decision could be used in a re-application, but it cannot be used to change the Director's decision unless it relates to the person's condition prior to the Director's decision. In the *Bigras* and *Daigle* case, a 2008 Div. Ct. judgment, the court looked at reduced special diet allowances made to the appellants due to amendments to the law in 2005. The court upheld the SBT decision to reduce the allowances as the previous award was not vested in the appellants and therefore they had to re-apply under the amended regulation. The last case discussed is the *Billotte* case, a 2009 decision of the Div. Ct. which looked at "whether or not the Appellant's attendance in an adult day-treatment program constituted "reasonably required medical treatment" within the meaning of section 44(1) of the Regulation." The SBT determined that the attendance did constitute reasonably required medical treatment, but the

---

[2] Included in the Appendix to this chapter.

court held that the SBT erred in law as the attendance in the day treatment program could not be viewed as medical treatment.

The next part of the Annual Report 2008–2009 deals with important decisions of the SBT. Because decisions of the SBT are private, no names are used and therefore each is referenced by the issue dealt with and not the name of the appellant. The first is a SBT decision ruling that a Sponsor lacks status to appeal to the SBT regarding recovery of social assistance paid to sponsored immigrant while a valid sponsorship agreement in force, as only a person who received social assistance can appeal due to the statute. The next area reviewed by the SBT related to the determination of whether a child of school age was part of the appellant's benefit unit in terms of attending school and making satisfactory progress with studies. The Administrator looked at an entire academic year's report card and decided that there was no satisfactory progress. The SBT stated that the entire period of time the child was in the benefit period and "also concluded that "satisfactory progress" needed to be considered in the context of this particular child's learning challenges." Another area discussed how to view "Special Diet Allowance — What is the Effect of the Physician Confirming Overlapping Medical Conditions on the Schedule 1" especially in light of a Ministry Q & A Memo which stated that certain overlapping items should be excluded. The SBT held that the Memo was a guideline only and had no force of law and that they should be guided by the Regulation only. The next area discussed involved a situation where an application for social assistance under the *OWA* was made by an applicant with a spouse and dependants residing in another country. The administrator required the spouse to verify the application, but the SBT held that the spouse is only involved if the spouse is part of the benefit unit which, in fact, was not yet the case. The next matter dealt with a request for reconsideration of a 2002 SBT decision on the basis that the change in law due to a SCC case and Practice Decision 6 allowed for a Human Rights challenge which the SBT denied in its 2002 decision. The SBT held that there is one year limitation to ask for a reconsideration and it was five years past such timeline. Further, changes in law do not allow a party to "re-litigate" a matter already heard as the matter is *res judicata*. The final area reviewed was whether the War Veterans Allowance was income and would be used to disqualify from *ODSPA* or were exempt as it was an award for pain and suffering. The SBT found that such payments were for pain and suffering. Both the evidence adduced and the fact that the payments were tax exempt gave credence to the position that the payment was for pain and suffering.

The final part of the Annual Report 2008–2009 are 16 statistical tables related to appeals to the SBT categorized in different ways.

3. Full Text of SBT Decision: 9910-07541R and 0005-04579

The final item on the website (posted in Spring 2008 but removed sometime later and still removed as of the review for this edition in the summer of 2010) to give legal representatives some insight into the thinking of the SBT is a full text, but anonymized, of an important decision of the SBT. As the hearings and therefore the decisions of the SBT are private, it is difficult to review decisions, but at least one decision is discussed in full. See Exhibit 4.1 herein, a brief done by the author to summarize the decision. **Although this decision is no longer posted the author has decided to still leave the decision in the text as a "brief of a decision of the SBT."**

4. FAQs

The pages on the website discussed above have been posted to address concerns that a lay person may have in respect of various issues related to the SBT. A legal representative can peruse the pages to get a simplified discussion of various areas but should only rely on the

EXHIBIT 4.1
A Sample SBT Decision Brief

DECISION BRIEF
of the SBT

PARTIES: T and W (the "Appellants")
Director, Ontario Disabilities Support Program (the "Respondent")

WHERE FOUND:

SBT WEBSITE — WHAT'S NEW — SELECTED DECISIONS: 9910-07541R AND 0005-04579

BACKGROUND:

This matter arose as two separate applications by the Appellants to the Respondent for support pursuant to the *ODSPA* as being persons with a disability. The Appellants were denied benefits, and after a request for internal review the Appellants were denied again. The Appellants then appealed to the SBT. The SBT ruled that the Appellants' appeals were dismissed due to subsection 5(2), which states that a person is not eligible for income support if the disability is alcoholism. The SBT also stated it did not have jurisdiction to consider the applicability of subsection 5(2) pursuant to the *Ontario Human Rights Code* (the *Code*). The Appellants' appeals were joined and taken to the Divisional Court, which agreed with the SBT that it had no jurisdiction to consider the *Code* and dismissed the appeal. After leave to appeal was granted, the Court of Appeal held that the SBT had the power to declare a provision of the *ODSPA* inapplicable due to its discriminatory nature but that the SBT was not the most appropriate forum for which a *Code* issue could be decided and therefore dismissed the appeal. The Appellants then appealed to the Supreme Court of Canada (the "SCC"). The SCC, by majority decision, allowed the appeal and stated, "The case will be remitted to the SBT so that it can rule on the applicability of s. 5(2) of the *ODSPA*." This hearing before the SBT was the remitted matter: applicability of subsection 5(2) of the *ODSPA*.

ISSUES:

1. "In the original decision rendered by the Tribunal regarding whether or not the Appellants qualified for income support as persons with a disability, did the Tribunal determine that the Appellants met the test for a person with a disability set out in subsection 4(1) of the *ODSPA*?"
2. "Were the rights of the Appellants guaranteed by section 1 of the *Code* infringed when the Director of the ODSP found the Appellants ineligible for ODSP income support as a result of the application of subsection 5(2) of the *ODSPA*?"

DECISION:

For reasons set out in the decision, the appeal was granted. First, the original decisions of the SBT determined that both Appellants were persons with a disability and therefore qualified for income support under the *ODSPA*. Second, subsection 5(2) of the *ODSPA* contravenes section 1 of the *Code* and should not be applied to the Appellants and provided they are otherwise eligible, they are eligible to receive income support.

REASONS:

After dealing with some preliminary issues, the SBT reviewed the appropriate legislative provisions and then looked at the original decisions to determine, in the first case, that it found the Appellant W. was a person with a disability under subsection 4(1) of the *ODSPA*. In respect of Appellant T., although there was no explicit statement of the finding of a person with a disability, the finding was implicit in the reasons in the decision especially the extensive review concerning the jurisdiction of the SBT in relation to the *Code*. This issue had to be

Continues....

Exhibit 4.1 continued

resolved in this way to address issue 2 as there would be no need to look at the *Code* in relation to the application of subsection 5(2) of the *ODSPA* without such a finding. The SBT quoted, with approval, the three-part test used in the SCC case of *Law v. Canada (Minister of Employment and Immigration)*, [1999] S.C.R. 497 (the "*Law* case") as follows:

> First, does the impugned law (a) draw a formal distinction between the claimant and others on the basis of one or more personal characteristics, or (b) fail to take into account the claimants already disadvantaged position within Canadian society resulting in substantially different treatment between the claimant and others on the basis of one or more personal characteristics? If so, there is a differential treatment for the purposes of s. 15(1). Second, was the claimant subject to different treatment on the basis of one or more of the enumerated analogous grounds? And third, does the differential treatment discriminate in a subjective sense, bringing into play the <u>purpose</u> of s. 15(1) of the *Charter* in remedying such ills as prejudice, stereotyping, and historical disadvantage? The second and third inquiries are concerned with whether the differential treatment constitutes discrimination in the substantive sense intended by s. 15(1).

Even though the *Law* case looked at the equality provisions of the *Charter*, the SBT held that the test used in it was applicable to *Code* cases, relying on the Ontario Court of Appeal case of *Ontario Human Rights Commission v. Ontario*, 19 O.R. 387. Furthermore, applying the reasoning of the Alberta Queen's Bench in *Gwinner v. Alberta (Human Resources and Employment)*, [2002] A.J. No. 1045, the SBT held that it was not necessary to apply the third part of the test used in the *Law* case here or in many human rights cases. After applying the first two parts of the test used in the *Law* case, the SBT found that the Appellants have "established a distinction ... made based on an enumerated ground set out in the *Code*; denial of a service based on disability. As such, the Appellants have established substantive inequality under the first two steps in the *Law* case. Accordingly, the Appellants do not have to establish a violation to human dignity." The rest of the decision applies the test used in the *Law* case including the third part using the contextual approach set out in the *Law* case even though the SBT found it was not necessary to do so to find "that the Appellants have been discriminated against not just because of their addiction but because of how they became addicted (as discussed in the SCC cases of *Law Society of British Columbia v. Andrews*, [1989] 1 S.C.R. 143 and *Brooks v. Canada Safeway Ltd.*, [1989] 1 S.C.R. 1219). Subsection 5(2) of the *ODSPA* accords different treatment to the Appellants on the basis of *how* they became disabled rather than on the basis of disability."

enabling legislation, the Practice Directions, and the *SPPA* to fully understand the procedures of the SBT.

RELEVANT CASES AND/OR DECISIONS

The cases and decisions discussed next are not meant to be exhaustive and are only those found in the spring of 2008. They should not be relied upon as legal opinion but are, rather, the author's viewpoint. An update of cases and decisions and the reader's own research and briefing must be done in any event.

Sixteen cases of the Ontario Court of Appeal (C.A.) and Divisional Court (Div. Ct.) and before one judge of the Superior Court of Justice (Sup. Ct. J.) are reviewed and discussed. The Supreme Court of Canada (SCC) case of *Tranchemontagne v. Ontario (Director, Disability Support Program)* (the SCC case of *Tranchemontagne*) is briefed due to its importance. The cases shall be discussed in chronological order, with the oldest one first.

Guy v. Northumberland (County) Administrator, Ontario Works

Guy v. Northumberland (County) Administrator, Ontario Works, [2001] O.J. No. 2166, 201 D.L.R. (4th) 752, 147 O.A.C. 261, 105 A.C.W.S. (3d) 1165 (the *Guy* case), is a 2001 Div. Ct. case, which relates to the cancellation of social benefits to an applicant and her two minor sons under the *OWA* and which was upheld by the SBT. The reason the administrator cancelled the social benefits was due to the fact that the trust funds beneficially owned by the two sons, which were considered assets, were not disclosed by the applicant. Although the *OWA* did not define "assets", there was a policy directive that defined the term to include a beneficial interest in assets held in trust that can be readily converted to cash. In looking at the evidence before it, the SBT held that the beneficial interest was an asset and was liquid and accessible and confirmed the decision of the administrator. The court held that the "standard of review for decisions of the Social Benefits Tribunal and its predecessor, the Social Assistance Review Board, is one of correctness". The court then stated that the SBT was looking at the assets. "It is clear from the decision of the Tribunal reviewed above that the concepts of liquidity and accessibility continue to play an important role in the Tribunal's attempt to define assets. In my view, the Tribunal's approach is correct. To do otherwise would make a mockery of the legislation." However, the court had to determine whether the SBT was correct in finding the trust funds accessible. After looking at previous cases on point, the court looked at the terms of the trust and the intention of the testator. The court found that the funds were not accessible by the two sons and held that the SBT erred and that the trust funds were to be excluded as assets for the purposes of determining eligibility.

Ontario (Director, Disability Support Program) v. Eluck

Ontario (Director, Disability Support Program) v. Eluck, [2001] O.J. No. 3764, 151 O.A.C. 369, 109 A.C.W.S. (3d) 172 (the *Eluck* case), is a 2001 Div. Ct. decision on whether the Director of the Disability Support Program "had authority to cancel, rather than suspend Mr. Eluck's income support in circumstances where he was incarcerated for a period in excess of one month". Eluck had been receiving social assistance as he was categorized as a "permanently unemployable person". The Director, upon learning that Eluck was in jail for five months, cancelled his assistance. "Mr. Eluck appealed that decision to the Social Benefits Tribunal, which determined that while the Director was correct in finding that the Appellant was ineligible for benefits while he was incarcerated, the Director had no authority to cancel Mr. Eluck's benefits due to his incarceration. The Tribunal found that Mr. Eluck remained eligible for benefits as a person with a disability and that his benefits were simply suspended for the period of his incarceration, and not cancelled." The Director appealed the decision of the SBT on the basis of a question of law. After looking at various sections of the enabling legislation, the court held that the *ODSPA* "is social welfare legislation that confers benefits and ought to be interpreted in a broad and generous manner, with any ambiguities resolved in favour of the benefit claimant". Furthermore, the court held that "the argument of the Director strains both the intent and the wording of the Act and the Regulation. Specifically, the Act permits the 'suspension' of income and that is specifically what sections 9, 26(2) and 35 of the Regulation comprehend. To accept the argument of the Director would mean that in every case of 'suspension' there would be an automatic 'cancellation', which would betray the specific power mandated by the Act." The decision of the SBT was, therefore, upheld.

McLaughlin v. Ontario (Director, Disability Support Program)

In *McLaughlin v. Ontario (Director, Disability Support Program)*, [2002] O.J. No. 1740 (the *McLaughlin* case), a 2002 Div. Ct. decision, the applicant appealed the decision of the Disability Support Program Director to the SBT that he did not suffer from substantial physical impairment. The SBT applied the test of "substantial physical impairment" under subsection 4(1)(a) of the *ODSPA* and agreed with the Director. The appellant submitted that the SBT had applied the wrong test, but the court held that the reasons for the decision demonstrate that the SBT applied the proper test. As to the argument that the SBT erred "by imputing the substantial-restriction-of-daily-activities concept of subsection 4(1)(b) into its 'substantial impairment' consideration", if that was an error, the court held that that was in applying the law to the facts, which is a matter of mixed fact and law and not appealable as only questions of law are appealable.

Gray v. Ontario (Director, Disability Support Program)

The 2002 Ont. C.A. case of *Gray v. Ontario (Director, Disability Support Program)*, [2002] O.J. No. 1531 (the *Gray* case), deals with "the important issue of the appropriate determination of substantial impairment within the meaning of s. 4(1) of the *ODSPA*". The court starts with the proposition that "as social welfare legislation, any ambiguity in the interpretation of the *ODSPA* should be resolved in the claimant's favour". The discussion then examined the phrase "person with a disability" and the word "substantial" as follows:

> Compared with its predecessor and with similar federal legislation, it would appear that the current definition of "person with a disability" in the *ODSPA* was intended to encompass a broader segment of society and to provide assistance to persons with significant but not severe long-term functional barriers.
>
> With respect to the interpretation of the word "substantial" in s. 4(1)(a) of the *ODSPA*, I am of the view that the word should be given a flexible meaning related to the varying circumstances of each individual case in a manner consistent with the purposes of the Act.
>
> Although we are dealing with a social assistance scheme as contrasted with the interpretation of legislation related to insurance, I believe that a useful analogy may be drawn from the exception provided in s. 266 of the *Insurance Act*, R.S.O. 1990, c. I.8. In this provision, personal injury litigation arising from automobile accidents is prohibited except for persons with "permanent serious impairment of an important bodily function". In *Meyer v. Bright* (1993), 15 O.R. (3d) 129 (C.A.), this court has interpreted this provision as follows at p. 142:
>
> > An impairment of an important bodily function which is serious to one person may not necessarily be a serious one for someone else. The task of the court in each case will be to decide whether the impairment is serious to the particular injured person who is before the court. In performing that task the question will always be the detrimental effect which the impairment has upon the life of the particular injured person. It is impossible for this court to lay down general guidelines of the concept of seriousness in all cases. Each case must be decided upon its own facts.

The judgment then focuses on the SBT's decision against the appellant in terms of the evidence as found by the tribunal and whether the tribunal drew from previous cases as well as the enabling legislation, that is, "[t]he Tribunal's decision shall include the principal findings of fact and its conclusions based on those findings" (O. Reg. 222/98, ss. 67(3)). In looking at the SBT's decision, the court found the following:

> It is simply unclear what relevant evidence the Tribunal accepted and what it rejected. It is my view that the Tribunal has not fulfilled its responsibilities pursuant to

section 67(3) of the *ODSPA* to set out the principal findings of fact and its conclusions based on those findings.

There is little or no explanation of the reasoning process that led the Tribunal to conclude that "the Appellant is not a person with a disability within the meaning of section 4(1) of the *Ontario Disability Support Program Act*". It was incumbent upon the Tribunal to make findings of fact concerning the appellant's testimony and the reports prepared by her doctor.

The Tribunal also appears to have asked itself the wrong question when it stated that "according to her testimony (the appellant) is able to cope on a day-to-day basis". The issue is, of course, not whether the appellant "can cope on a day-to-day basis" but whether she can function in the workplace, function in the community, or attend to her personal care. Both the appellant and her physician stated that she could not, and I repeat that the Tribunal emphasized that the appellant was a credible witness.

Both the errors made by the SBT as set out in the quoted passages above allowed the court to state that there was a question of law and an error. However, the judgment stated, "in light of s. 31(5) of the *ODSPA*, we are constrained in the relief we may grant. Thus, the matter is referred back to the Tribunal for reconsideration in accordance with the direction that this court is satisfied that the appellant is 'a person with a disability within s. 4(1) of the *Ontario Disability Support Program Act*'".

Gioris v. Ontario (Director, Disability Support Program)

Gioris v. Ontario (Director, Disability Support Program), [2002] O.J. No. 2416, 161 O.A.C. 277 (the *Gioris* case), was a 2002 Div. Ct. decision that dealt with judicial review. The appellant had a hearing before the SBT, where he raised numerous alleged instances of breaches of the rules of natural justice. The court broke down his arguments into five issues as follows:

1. Did the Tribunal breach its duty to proceed fairly and follow the principle of *audi alteram partem* when it expelled the applicant from the hearing?
2. Did the Tribunal make an error of law and exceed its jurisdiction by not accepting his actual childcare expenses as "necessary"?
3. Did the Tribunal make a reviewable error by failing to take notice of a final decision of the Social Assistance Review Board?
4. After inviting the Applicant to make submissions on tape-recording the hearing, did the Tribunal deal unfairly with the Applicant by refusing to hear his submissions at the beginning of the next day?
5. Did the Tribunal exceed its jurisdiction and deny the Applicant fairness by failing to provide 30 full days' notice of the hearing date as required by the regulations?

The court focused on issues 1, 4, and 5 in its decision and stated, with respect to the appellant being "expelled" from the hearing, that the SBT has the right to control its own process, and the actions of the appellant were such that the SBT could properly exclude him and not be in breach of the rules of natural justice, especially as the appellant suffered no prejudice. In terms of issue 4, the court held that the SBT was not required to tape-record its hearings under its enabling legislation and that the SBT was exercising its discretion not to tape the hearings. With respect to the short notice (in this case 27 days, instead of the mandated 30 days for the 13th and 14th appeals, which raised the same issues as the first 12 appeals) the court held that it "was an efficient and sensible solution that created no unfairness to the applicant". Finally, the court made its last finding that the appellant "has not shown any breach of the rules of natural justice [by the SBT]. If he had shown such a breach, we would have exercised our discretion to refuse him a re-hearing as we are all of the view that there was no miscarriage of justice".

Thomas v. Ontario (Director, Disability Support Program)

In *Thomas v. Ontario (Director, Disability Support Program)*, [2004] O.J. No. 2702, 131 A.C.W.S. (3d) 1175 (the *Thomas* case), a 2004 Div. Ct. decision, the appellant appealed the SBT decision on the basis that key evidence was not addressed in the reasons of the Tribunal in this case. The court held that the SBT "was obligated to address this evidence and make findings of fact" and sent the case back to the SBT for a new hearing before a differently constituted tribunal.

Sandiford v. Ontario (Director, Disability Support Program)

The issue of "person with a disability" was the focus of *Sandiford v. Ontario (Director, Disability Support Program)*, [2005] O.J. No. 858, 195 O.A.C. 143, A.C.W.S. (3d) 857 (the *Sandiford* case), a 2005 Div. Ct. decision. After reviewing the matter to date and the procedural elements to be followed due to the enabling legislation, the court focused on the evidence given at the SBT and the SBT's decision in finding that the appellant did not have a substantial physical or mental impairment as required by subsection 4(1) of the *ODSPA*. The court held that the SBT erred in concluding that the evidence did not constitute verification of the appellant's condition. Quoting relevant passages of the *Gray* case, the court held that the word "substantial" had a flexible meaning and the "Tribunal must then evaluate the whole of the evidence to assess whether the statutory test is met", which the SBT did not do. Further, the court held that the SBT erred in drawing an adverse inference from the fact that a nurse practitioner completed the required "Activities of Daily Living Report" on the ground that she was not a person involved in the appellant's treatment. "The nurse practitioner had known the appellant for two years. In light of demands made upon physicians' time and the shortage of general practitioners, resort to other persons with prescribed qualifications is not unreasonable. The nurse practitioner was authorized by the regulations to complete the form." Finally, the court held that there was an error in applying the test for substantial impairment. Based on the errors, the court granted the appeal pursuant to subsection 31(5)(b) of the *ODSPA*, rather than referring it back to the tribunal, as there was urgency in the matter and the court could apply the test on the basis of the written medical evidence alone.

Rea v. Simcoe (County Administrator, Social Services Department)

Rea v. Simcoe (County Administrator, Social Services Department), [2005] O.J. No. 5543, 79 O.R. (3rd) 583, 205 O.A.C. 297, 144 A.C.W.S. (3d) 758 (the *Rea* case), is a 2005 Ont. C.A. decision regarding the effect of not providing information relating to changes in the appellant's circumstances in accordance with section 7 of the *OWA* and section 14 of O. Reg. 134/98. After looking at sections 14(1) and 35 of O. Reg. 134/98, the court held that the requirement of providing updated information was central to the entire scheme of the *OWA* and therefore when the appellant's assistance was terminated, so was her dependent daughter's.

Dowswell v. Ontario (Disability Support Program, Director)

Dowswell v. Ontario (Disability Support Program, Director), [2006] O.J. No. 973, 265 D.L.R. (4th) 511, 208 O.A.C. 200, 146 A.C.W.S. (3d) 739 (the *Dowswell* case), is a 2006 Div. Ct. case that deals with the determination of the benefit unit and what should properly occur when there is a separation in the benefit unit in terms of retroactive payments. The court held that there was a question of law raised by the SBT's decision and the standard for review as per the *Gray* case is correctness. As the Director knew of the parties' separation at the time of awarding retroactive benefits, it was not correct in law to provide a windfall to the non-separated spouse of the appellant's disability benefit. The court therefore held that the appellant should receive an equal share of the retroactive payment.

Crane v. Ontario (Director, Disability Support Program)

In *Crane v. Ontario (Director, Disability Support Program)*, [2006] O.J. No. 4564, 83 O.R. (3rd) 321, 278 D.L.R. (4th) 374, 217 O.A.C. 61, 153 A.C.W.S. (3d) 236 (the *Crane* case), a 2006 Ont. C.A. case, the key issue again was the definition of the term "person with a disability" as defined by subsection 4(1) of the *ODSPA*. After all the required proceedings had been utilized, an appeal went to the Divisional Court on the basis that the SBT erred in law in its interpretation of subsection 4(1) and also in its findings of the facts of "three years continuous part-time employment". A majority of the Divisional Court held that the SBT incorrectly interpreted subsection 4(1) and also made a palpable and overriding error. The Court of Appeal did not agree with the Divisional Court on its interpretation of subsection 4(1) and, rather, agreed with the interpretation by the SBT:

> In summary, s. 4(1) of the *ODSPA* presents three questions — substantial impairment, substantial restriction in certain activities, and verification. These are separate questions that require separate analysis and answers. The onus is on the claimant to establish all three factors. Accordingly, if the Tribunal concludes that the claimant has failed to establish one of the factors, it need not deal with the other factors. Finally, in some cases (but not all) there can be an overlap in the evidence relevant to the factors in paragraphs (a) and (b) of s. 4(1). That is because although the concept of impairment is anchored in medicine, the determination of whether an impairment is substantial will require consideration of the whole person, including a person's ability to function in the domains of personal care, community and workplace.
>
> The Divisional Court conflated or collapsed the analysis required under s. 4(1)(a) and (b) into a single inquiry. It erred in so doing.
>
> The Tribunal, on the other hand, framed its analysis in a proper fashion. With respect to s. 4(1)(a), it focused on the medical evidence relating to Ms. Crane's impairment, including the report and extensive clinical notes of the family doctor, and reports by a rheumatologist and a psychiatrist.

The Court of Appeal, however, did find, as the majority of the Divisional Court found, that the SBT made an error in its critical finding of fact that Ms. Crane worked continuously for three years part-time when the evidence showed it was only fourth months:

> In my view, the majority was correct to conclude that this misapprehension of the evidence amounted to a palpable and overriding error. The Tribunal made the same error twice, so there can be no suggestion that the error was merely a typographical error. The error relates to a crucial part of the evidence, namely, Ms. Crane's work history. The error is a substantial one — there is a large difference between four months and three years continuous part-time work. Finally, as McMurtry C.J.O. emphasized in *Gray*, the *ODSPA* is remedial legislation. It follows from these points that Ms. Crane is entitled to have her claim assessed on the basis of an accurate understanding by the Tribunal of the crucial aspects of her current situation, including her employment history.

A new hearing before a different member of the SBT was ordered.

Omar v. Ontario (Director, Disability Support Program)

The issue of the alleged conflict between two sections of the regulation made under the *ODSPA* was the focus of the 2007 Div. Ct. decision, *Omar v. Ontario (Director, Disability Support Program)*, [2007] O.J. No. 1216, 156, A.C.W.S. (3d) 509 (the *Omar* case). After ruling that there was no conflict between subsection 47(7) and subsection 64(1)(a) of O. Reg. 222/98 and therefore there was no ability for the SBT to hear new evidence of the appellant's condition in the period following the Director's decision, the court directed that the SBT conduct a hearing in accordance with the regulations and that new evidence after the date of the Director's decision would have to be heard on a re-application for support.

Lloyd v. Ontario (Director, Disability Support Program)

In *Lloyd v. Ontario (Director, Disability Support Program)*, [2007] O.J. No. 1452, 217 O.A.C. 385, 156 A.C.W.S. (3d) 1202 (the *Lloyd* case), a 2007 Div. Ct. case, the issue of "person with a disability" under subsection 4(1) of the *ODSPA* was explored again. In this case, both the Director and the SBT held that the appellant was not a person with a disability as her chronic pain was not substantial impairment based on the evidence. The court found that the SBT "erred in law by applying the wrong test in that it assessed the appellant's condition on her good days when she had a higher level of physical activity as opposed to assessing her condition during her recurrent bad days".

The court found the SBT also "failed to make findings respecting the frequency and unpredictability of bad days in its analysis of whether the appellant had a substantial impairment". Based on these errors, the court referred the matter back to the SBT for a fresh hearing before a different panel.

Wareham v. Ontario (Minister of Community and Social Services)

In the 2008 Sup. Ct. J. decision, *Wareham v. Ontario (Minister of Community and Social Services)*, [2008] O.J. No. 166 (the *Wareham* case), the court dealt with a motion to strike a statement of claim in a class action law suit making various claims against the administration of the *ODSPA*. Although the case does not deal with the SBT, it is useful in looking at the enabling legislation.

In striking out the claims, except for the claim under section 7 of the *Canadian Charter of Rights and Freedoms*, the court set out a useful summary of the substantive rules and procedures of the *ODSPA*, given as follows:

> The provisions of the *ODSPA* and of Regulation 222/98 (the "Regulation") made pursuant to it are complex and elaborate. Among other things, they provide for decisions to be made to grant, or refuse, support by a Director of the ODSP appointed by the Minister, the manner in which applications are to be made, the information they must contain, the persons who are to make determinations of disability, internal reviews of contested decisions, appeals to the Social Benefits Tribunal established under the OW, and appeals on questions of law to the Divisional Court. There are also extensive provisions for the recovery of amounts paid to persons who were not eligible, and overpayments, and for periodic reviews of determinations of disability. Time limits are imposed for completing applications, for requests for internal reviews and for various steps involved in appeals to the Tribunal and requests for it to reconsider its decisions. There are also stipulated times within which internal reviews of the Director's decisions, and decisions of the Tribunal, must be completed. There is, however, no time limit for the Director's initial decision on an application.
>
> The provisions for evaluating an applicant's assets and budgetary requirements and the calculation and payment of income support and other benefits are particularly elaborate and extend over more than 20 pages of the Regulation. Despite — or, perhaps, because of — the evident minute attention to detail that is reflected in the legislation, the Regulation and the more than 80 policy directives issued by the Ministry of Community and Social Services, the plaintiffs' claim that the Crown has created and maintained an unnecessarily time-consuming and inefficient application process. They rely, in particular, on their plea that the overwhelming majority of applicants experience a

delay of between six months to one year before receiving an initial response to their application.

The application process is in two parts. Financial eligibility must first be determined by applying through an OW, or an ODSPA, office. If a favourable determination is made, the applicant will be provided with a disability determination package ("DDP") which must be completed and returned to the disability adjudication unit within 90 days. The DDP consists of a number of forms which include a health status report and an "Activities of Daily Living Index" that must be completed by a prescribed health care professional. The disability adjudication unit includes persons appointed by the Director under section 4(2) of the *ODSPA* to make determinations of disability.

The court then set out the position of the plaintiffs as follows:

The plaintiffs claim that the delays, and other alleged deficiencies of the ODSP, have resulted from the Crown's negligence; impaired the mental and physical health of class members and violated their human dignity and self-worth; discriminated against them on the basis of their disability; violated their right to security of the person; breached a fiduciary duty owed to them; and resulted in the Crown's unjust enrichment.

SPPA

Smith v. Ontario (Director, Disability Support Program)

Smith v. Ontario (Director, Disability Support Program), [2008] O.J. No. 302 (the *Smith* case), is a 2008 Div. Ct. decision. Here, the appellant appealed the decision of the Director, and thereafter the SBT, on the question of his entitlement to a retroactive payment for special diet allowance, which was denied in both instances. His grounds for appealing the decision of the SBT were stated as follows:

(a) the Tribunal erred by fundamentally misapprehending the facts;

(b) the Tribunal erred in law by failing to interpret the applicable Regulation retroactively; and

(c) the Tribunal failed to comply with rules of natural justice by basing its decision on a lack of corroborative evidence without giving him notice that such evidence would be required.

After stating that the test used by the court to determine questions of law is one of correctness, the court said the first ground was not valid because it is not a question of law and the reasons given for the decision demonstrate that the SBT was alive to the evidence presented before it. With respect to the second ground, the court held that whether the regulation was retroactive or not, the evidence did not indicate that the appellant was entitled to the retroactive payment. As it was considered by the SBT, the SBT did not err in law. With respect to the ground of judicial review due to breaches in the rules of natural justice, in basing the decision on the failure of the appellant to provide corroborative evidence, the court held that since such evidence would clearly be necessary, no notice that the evidence would be required is necessary. "He has not been prejudiced in any way by the lack of notice."

Oliveira v. Ontario (Director, Disability Support Program)

Oliveira v. Ontario (Director, Disability Support Program), [2008] O.J. No. 622, 2008 ONCA 123 (the *Oliveira* case), is a recent Ont. C.A. case, which had to determine the effect of joint custody, where the spouses had custody of their three young children on an alternating week basis, on income support to the head of the benefit unit for the dependent children. The Director found that the appellant was entitled to only one-half of the income support payments. The SBT agreed that one-half of the payments for basic needs component was appropriate, but for shelter allowance and benefits, such as drug and dental coverage, the SBT found that full payments were appropriate. The appellant appealed the SBT finding that reducing income support to reflect one-half of basic needs was a question of law on the basis that there is no authority under the enabling legislation for the SBT to award one-half of basic needs. The court agreed with the Divisional Court, which first heard the appeal, that the appeal should be dismissed and, after looking at relevant cases, especially the SCC case of *Tranchemontagne*, determined that a tribunal can interpret legislation by going beyond it in the right circumstances. Specifically, the court stated the following:

> Furthermore, administrative bodies empowered to decide questions of law "may presumptively go beyond the bounds of their enabling statute and decide issues of common law or statutory interpretation that arise in the course of a case properly before them, subject to judicial review on the appropriate standard". See *Tranchemontagne v. Ontario (Director, Disability Support Program)*, [2006] 1 S.C.R. 513 at para. 24, *per* Bastarache J., upholding this court's decision on the issue of whether the Tribunal had jurisdiction to consider the Ontario *Human Rights Code*, R.S.O. 1990, c. H.19. Bastarache J. noted at para. 26, "[t]he presumption that a tribunal can go beyond its enabling statute ... exists because it is undesirable for a tribunal to limit itself to some of the law while shutting its eyes to the rest of the law."

Using that concept, the court found the following:

> In situations where a recipient of income support is a co-resident, is incarcerated or in hospital, the amount of income support paid is proportionately reduced. See O. Reg. 222/98, ss. 17, 35, 36. Thus, the intention of the legislation is to account for the realities of a given situation. The appellant submits, however, that the prescribed deductions are the only ones permitted by the Act and Regulation, and the Tribunal had no choice but to order payment of 100 per cent of basic needs throughout the year.
>
> I disagree with this view. Where the legislation in question does not expressly confer a power, gaps in legislation may be filled when doing so is necessary to the operation of the legislative scheme.

As the original legislation did not envision joint custody, the court held that a tribunal had the jurisdiction to make the order it did, and as there is a basis for the order, there was no error in law. The two other submissions of the appellant, that the finding ignored the evidence and that such a finding breached the *Ontario Human Rights Code*, were quickly held not applicable in the facts of the case and the appeal was dismissed.

Bongard v. Ontario (Director, Disability Support Program)

Bongard v. Ontario (Director, Disability Support Program), [2008] O.J. No. 1461 (the *Bongard* case), the final case to be discussed here, is a 2008 decision of the Divisional Court. *Bongard* dealt with the definition of spouse under subsection 1(1)(a) of O. Reg. 222/98 under the *ODSPA*. The issue was whether a statutory declaration signed by the appellant and Ms. Bernier is a mutual declaration as required by the definition of spouse in the Regulation and whether the SBT erred in law by so finding. The court held as follows:

> The Tribunal found on the basis of the signed form and all the circumstances that the requirements of s. 1(1)(a) of the regulation had been satisfied. We are not persuaded that the Tribunal made an error of law. It was open to the Tribunal to take into account the surrounding circumstances to determine whether the statement made in the signed form constituted a declaration by both the appellant and Ms. Bernier.
>
> We are also satisfied that the Tribunal's reasons are adequate, as they make findings of fact, took into account competing arguments and explained how the decision was arrived at.

The court therefore dismissed the appeal.

TRANCHEMONTAGNE: A CASE BRIEF

The SCC case of *Tranchemontagne* has changed the SBT's procedure as mentioned in Practice Direction 6, discussed above. A detailed discussion of the case is presented, in a case brief, below.

PARTIES: T and W (the "Appellants")
Director, Ontario Disabilities Support Program (the "Respondent")
CHRC, OHRC, The SBT and others (the "Intervenors")

CASE CITATIONS: [2006] S.C.J. No. 14, [2006] A.C.S. No. 14, 2006 SCC 14, 2006 CSC 14, [2006] 1 S.C.R. 513, [2006] 1 R.C.S. 513, 266 D.L.R. (4th) 287, 347 N.R. 144, J.E. 2006-879, 210 O.A.C. 267, 42 Admin. L.R. (4th) 104, 2006 CarswellOnt 2350, 147 A.C.W.S. (3d) 326, EYB 2006-104056, 56 C.H.R.R. D/1

BACKGROUND (FACTS)

This matter arose as two separate applications by the Appellants to the Respondent for support pursuant to the *ODSPA* as being a person with a disability. The Respondent denied benefits, and after a request for internal review the Respondent denied again. The Appellants then appealed to the SBT. The SBT dismissed the Appellants' appeals due to subsection 5(2), which states that a person is not eligible for income support if the disability is alcoholism. The SBT also stated it did not have jurisdiction to consider the applicability of subsection 5(2) pursuant to the *Ontario Human Rights Code* (the *Code*). The Appellants' appeals were joined and taken to the Divisional Court, which agreed with the SBT that it had no jurisdiction to consider the *Code* and dismissed the appeal. After leave to appeal was granted, the Court of Appeal held that the SBT had the power to declare a provision of the *ODSPA* inapplicable due to its discriminatory nature but that the SBT was not the most appropriate forum for which a *Code* issue could be decided and therefore dismissed the appeal. The Appellants then appealed to the Supreme Court of Canada.

ISSUES

A majority of the court (a 4–3 split among the judges) determined there were two main issues in the case:

1. Does the SBT have the jurisdiction to consider the *Code* in rendering its decisions?
2. If the answer to the first question is "yes", should the SBT have declined to exercise its jurisdiction in the present cases?

DECISION

For reasons set out in the majority decision, the appeal was allowed. The case was remitted to the SBT so that it could rule on the applicability of subsection 5(2) of the *ODSPA*.

REASONS

To answer the jurisdiction issue, the majority first looked at relevant sections of both enabling statutes, specifically sections 1, 4, 5, 29(3) and 31(1) of the *ODSPA* and sections 1 and 67(2) of the *OWA*, as well as the Preamble and sections 1 and 47(1) and (2) of the *Code*. The majority looked at the legislative intent and scheme of both the *ODSPA* and the *OWA* and then noted that the jurisdiction of the SBT involves questions of law. The majority held the SBT had power to examine to go beyond its enabling statute:

> The presumption that a tribunal can go beyond its enabling statute — unlike the presumption that a tribunal can pronounce on constitutional validity — exists because it is undesirable for a tribunal to limit itself to some of the law while shutting its eyes to the rest of the law. The law is not so easily compartmentalized that all relevant sources on

a given issue can be found in the provisions of a tribunal's enabling statute. Accordingly, to limit the tribunal's ability to consider the whole law is to increase the probability that a tribunal will come to a misinformed conclusion. In turn, misinformed conclusions lead to inefficient appeals or, more unfortunately, the denial of justice.

The majority then addressed the argument that the wording of subsection 67(2) of the *OWA* does not give the SBT the jurisdiction to look at subsection 5(2):

> That section provides that the SBT cannot determine the constitutional validity of a provision or regulation and cannot determine the legislative authority for making a regulation. ...
>
> The *Code* emanates from the Ontario legislature. As I will elaborate below, it is one thing to preclude a statutory tribunal from *invalidating* legislation enacted by the legislature that created it. It is completely different to preclude that body from *applying* legislation enacted by that legislature in order to resolve apparent conflicts between statutes. The former power — an act of defying legislative intent — is one that is clearly more offensive to the legislature; it should not be surprising, therefore, when the legislature eliminates it. Yet the latter power represents nothing more than an instantiation of legislative intent — a legislative intent, I should note, that includes the primacy of the *Code* and the concurrent jurisdiction of administrative bodies to apply it.
>
> Thus the argument based on s. 67(2) is defeated because the legislature could not possibly have intended that the *Code* be denied application by analogy to the Constitution. While it clearly prohibited the SBT from considering the constitutional validity of laws and regulations, it equally clearly chose not to invoke the same prohibition with respect to the *Code*.

The majority then looked at section 47 of the *Code* and stated the following:

> The importance of the *Code* is not merely an assertion of this Court. The Ontario legislature has seen fit to bind itself and all its agents through the *Code*: s. 47(1). Further, it has given the *Code* primacy over all other legislative enactments: s. 47(2). As a result of this primacy clause, where provisions of the *Code* conflict with provisions in another provincial law, it is the provisions of the *Code* that are to apply.

The majority then differentiated between the effect of the primacy provisions in the *Code* versus section 52 of the *Canadian Charter of Rights and Freedoms* and stated the following in answering the first issue:

> I therefore conclude that the SBT has jurisdiction to consider the *Code*. The *ODSPA* and *OWA* confirm that the SBT can decide questions of law. It follows that the SBT is presumed to have the jurisdiction to consider the whole law. More specifically, when it decides whether an applicant is eligible for income support, the SBT is presumed able to consider any legal source that might influence its decision on eligibility. In the present appeal, the *Code* is one such source.
>
> There is no indication that the legislature has sought to rebut this presumption. To the contrary, the legislature has announced the primacy of the *Code* and has given itself clear directions for how this primacy can be eliminated in particular circumstances. The legislature has indeed prohibited the SBT from considering the constitutional validity of enactments, or the *vires* of regulations, but it did nothing to suggest that the SBT could not consider the *Code*. I cannot impute to the legislature the intention that the SBT ignore the *Code* when the legislature did not even follow its own instructions for yielding this result.
>
> The *ODSPA* and *OWA* do evince a legislative intent to prevent the SBT from looking behind the statutory and regulatory scheme enacted by the legislature and its delegated actors. However, consideration of the *Code* is not analogous. Far from being used to look behind the legislative scheme, the *Code* forms part of the legislative scheme. It would be contrary to legislative intention to demand that the SBT ignore it.

In discussing the second issue about whether the SBT should have declined jurisdiction, the majority stated that once the SBT had the jurisdiction to hear the case, it could decline jurisdiction to look at the *Code* issue if the legislature gave it the power to so decline. After looking at the enabling legislation again, as well as how the legislature gave power to both the OHRC and the courts to decline jurisdiction, the majority stated the following:

> Since the SBT has not been granted the authority to decline jurisdiction, it cannot avoid considering the *Code* issues in the appellants' appeals. This is sufficient to decide the appeal.

In *obiter dicta* the court then looked at reasons why the SBT should look at *Code* issues and the judge writing for the majority stated the following at the end of his decision:

> I conclude that the SBT is a highly appropriate forum in which to argue the applicability of s. 5(2) of the *ODSPA* under the *Code*. In general, encouraging administrative tribunals to exercise their jurisdiction to decide human rights issues fulfills the laudable goal of bringing justice closer to the people. But more crucial for the purposes of the present appeal is the fact that the legislature did not grant the SBT the power to defer to another forum when it is properly seized of an issue. Absent such authority, the SBT could not decline to deal with the *Code* issue on the basis that a more appropriate forum existed.

The minority decision also looked at the enabling legislation and the *Code* and determined that the SBT cannot invalidate a provision of the enabling legislation, which defines its mandate and therefore lacked jurisdiction.

REVIEW QUESTIONS

1. What is the enabling legislation for the SBT?
2. Where would you find the practices and procedures of the SBT?
3. Pursuant to the enabling legislation, how does the *SPPA* apply to the SBT?
4. What does the privative clause of the enabling legislation related to the SBT prevent and allow and under what circumstances?
5. What practices and procedures of the SBT deal with the procedures before the SBT in dealing with human rights issues? Briefly summarize such procedures.
6. What practices and procedures gives discretion and flexibility to the SBT in applying the SBT Rules?
7. What forms are important with the SBT, and how are they utilized?
8. What is the appropriate procedure to have a motion dealt with by the SBT?
9. What jurisdiction is the SBT given to reconsider a decision under the various procedures and practices of the SBT?
10. How do the various procedures of the SBT deal with Alternative Dispute Resolution?

EXERCISE

Based upon the facts of the *Tranchemontagne* case briefed in the chapter, fill out form(s) to institute this matter currently before the SBT.

Appendix 4.1
Overview of Procedural Stages of a Matter Before the SBT

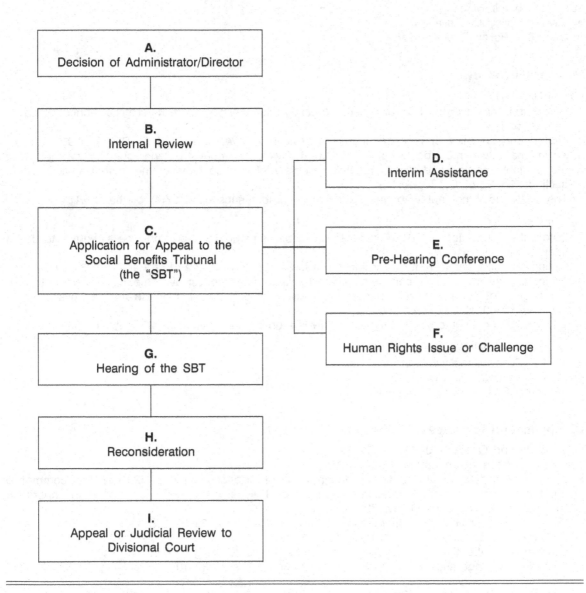

SUMMARY

A. Decision of Administrator/Director

If decision by

(a) Administrator
  - *OWA*, s. 44 — Eligibility and amount of basic financial assistance;
  - *OWA*, s. 24 — Notice of decision to applicant;
  - O. Reg. 134/98, s. 67 — Formalities of contents of the notice of decision

(b) Director
  • *ODSPA*, s. 38 — Eligibility and amount of income support;
  • *ODSPA*, s. 19 — Notice of decision to applicant;
  • O. Reg. 222/98, s. 56 — Formalities of contents of the notice of decision

Look at the following:
• *OWA* — Policy Directive 33.0
• *ODSPA* — Policy Directive 13A

B. Internal Review

OWA, ss. 27(1)
• Before the appeal to the SBT of a decision can be commenced, there must be a request to do an internal review;
• Timing and specifics of request for internal review in *OWA*, s. 27 and O. Reg. 134/98, s. 69;
• An internal review must be completed within 10 days of the request by someone who did not make the original decision and details regarding delivery of and contents of the internal review are in sections 70–71 of O. Reg. 134/98;
• The *SPPA* does not apply to an internal review under subsection 27(4) of the *OWA*.

ODSPA, ss. 22(1)
• Before the appeal to the SBT of a decision can be commenced, there must be a request to do an internal review;
• Timing and specifics of request for internal review in *ODSPA*, s. 22 and O. Reg. 222/98, s. 58;
• An internal review must be completed within 10 days of the request by someone who did not make the original decision and details regarding delivery of and contents of the internal review are in sections 59–60 of O. REG. 222/98;
• The *SPPA* does not apply to an internal review under subsection. 22(4) of the *ODSPA*.

Look at the following:
• *OWA* — Policy Directive 33.0
• *ODSPA* — Policy Directive 13A
• FAQs on SBT website — Internal Review

C. Application for Appeal to the SBT

OWA, s. 28 and O. Reg. 134/98, ss. 72–79
• Detail specifics of an appeal to the SBT;
• 30 days from date decision is final although it can be extended (*OWA*, ss. 28(1,2)) and commence no later than one year from decision date and appeal requested by notice of appeal form approved by minister (O. Reg. 134/98, s. 72);
• Notice of appeal shall set out reasons for appeal (*OWA*, ss. 28(1));
• Parties to appeal set out in *OWA*, ss. 28(4,7);
• Upon receipt, the SBT sends copy of notice to parties (O. Reg. 138/98, ss. 73(1));
• Format of hearings and disclosure discussed under *OWA*, ss. 28(8–10) and O. Reg. 134/98, ss. 73–74;
• Under subsection 28(11) of *OWA*, the onus is on the appellant to satisfy the SBT on the appeal that the decision of the administrator is wrong;
• According to subsection 26(1) of *OWA*, any decision by an administrator regarding eligibility for or the amount of basic financial assistance may be appealed to the SBT other than decisions set out in subsection 26(2) and section 68 of O. Reg. 134/98;
• Under section 33 of the *OWA*, the SBT "shall refuse to hear an appeal if it determines the appeal to be frivolous or vexatious".

ODSPA, s. 23 and O. Reg. 222/98, ss. 61–65
• Detail specifics of an appeal to the SBT;
• 30 days from date decision is final although it can be extended (*ODSPA*, ss. 23(1,2)) and commence no later than one year from decision date and appeal requested by notice of appeal form approved by minister (O. Reg. 222/98, s. 61);

- Notice of appeal shall set out reasons for appeal (*ODSPA*, ss. 23(1));
- Parties to appeal set out in *ODSPA*, ss. 23(4,6);
- Upon receipt, the SBT sends copy of notice to parties (O. Reg. 222/98, ss. 62(1));
- Format of hearings and disclosure discussed under *OWA*, ss. 28(7–9) and O. Reg. 222/98, ss. 62–63;
- Under subsection 23(10) of *ODSPA*, the onus is on the appellant to satisfy the SBT on the appeal that the decision of the director is wrong;
- According to subsection 21(1) of *ODSPA*, any decision by a director regarding eligibility for, or the amount of, income support may be appealed to the SBT other than decisions set out in subsection 21(3) and section 57 of O. Reg. 222/98;
- Under section 28 of the *ODSPA*, the SBT "shall refuse to hear an appeal if it determines the appeal to be frivolous or vexatious".

Look at the following:
- *OWA* — Policy Directive 32.0
- *OWA* — Policy Directive 33.0
- *ODSPA* — Policy Directive 13A
- *ODSPA* — Policy Directive 13B
- FAQs on the SBT website — Appeal Forms
- SBT website — Forms — Appeal Form

D. Interim Assistance

OWA, s. 30: After the request for an appeal, but before the SBT can make a decision, the SBT can direct the administrator to provide interim assistance "to an applicant or recipient if the tribunal is satisfied that the person will suffer financial hardship during the period needed for the tribunal to complete its review and give notice of its decision" up to a maximum as set out in section 77 of O. Reg. 134/98.

The *SPPA* does not apply to any proceeding of the SBT regarding interim assistance (ss. 30(3)).

ODSPA, s. 25: After the request for an appeal, but before the SBT can make a decision, the SBT can direct the director to provide interim assistance "to an applicant or recipient if the tribunal is satisfied that the person will suffer financial hardship during the period needed for the tribunal to complete its review and give notice of its decision" up to a maximum as set out in section 66 of O. Reg. 222/98.

The *SPPA* does not apply to any proceeding of the SBT regarding interim assistance (s. 25(3)).

Look at the following:
- *OWA* — Policy Directive 35.0
- *ODSPA* — Policy Directive 13C
- FAQs ON SBT website — Interim Assistance
- SBT website — Forms — Appeal Form
- SBT website — Practice Direction 1 — Interim Assistance

E. PRE-HEARING CONFERENCE

The enabling legislation of the SBT does not have provisions dealing with pre-hearing conferences, so the procedures come from the *SPPA*, as interpreted by the SBT and set out in Practice Direction 8:

> While pre-hearing conferences can be held at the request of a party, in writing setting out the reasons for the request within 10 days of the filing of the appeal, or at the direction of the SBT (unless there are special or unusual circumstances to dispense), where an appeal raises a human rights issue or challenge, parties must attend a pre-hearing conference to discuss procedural matters prior to the hearing. For the purposes of this Practice Direction, a pre-hearing conference is a meeting with all the parties conducted by a member of the SBT by way of one or a combination of telephone, videoconferencing, oral in-person session, or in writing. The purposes of the pre-hearing conferences are those set out in the provisions of the *SPPA* and evidence is not to be presented. Once a pre-hearing conference is requested or directed, a 'notice of pre-hearing conference' shall be sent, as soon as practicable, to the parties setting out the format(s) of the conference and its date place and time. Details about the choice of for-

mat are discussed in ss. 8.4 to 8.6 and the matters that can be dealt with in the pre-hearing conference are set out in s. 9.1 of Practice Direction 8. The various outcomes of the pre-hearing conference are detailed in ss. 10.1 to 10.5 of Practice Direction 8.

Look at the following:
• SBT website — Practice Direction 8 — Pre-hearing Conferences

F. Human Rights Issue Or Challenge

The enabling legislation of the SBT does not have provisions dealing with human rights issue or challenges, so the procedures have been derived based upon the 2006 SCC case of *Tranchemontagne v. Ontario (Director, Disability Support Program)* as interpreted by the SBT and set out in Practice Direction 6.

To raise human rights issue or challenge, written notice is given to the SBT containing particulars of the challenge, the section(s) of the *Ontario Human Rights Code* (*Code*) relied upon, the desired remedy and contact particulars of the party's representative. The SBT will send a letter to the party raising the *Code* challenge, acknowledging the appeal and requesting particulars regarding the *Code* challenge, which will be provided to the SBT within 30 days of receiving the SBT letter in accordance with section 6.3.

The SBT will send the written notice and the particulars to the other parties within 10 days of receipt. A party who wishes to reply to such written notice must notify the SBT, with a copy of the intent to the Ministry of Community and Social Services, the Attorney General of the Province of Ontario and the other parties, of the intention to reply within 10 days of receiving the written notice forwarded by the SBT. Where a party does not send a written notice of the party's intention to reply in the proper time, the SBT will assume that such party will not be participating in such human rights issue or challenge raised.

Generally, the SBT will hold pre-hearing conference in accordance with sections 9.1 to 9.5. The SBT will only address the human rights challenge or issue after the main issue on the appeal has been heard and must be the issue raised pursuant to these procedures. If the appeal of the main issue is granted, the human rights issue or challenge will not be dealt with and the SBT shall notify all parties of that fact. If the SBT denies the appeal on the main issue, it shall send a written notice, within 60 days after delivering its written decision denying the appeal on the main issue, that a second hearing to consider the human rights issue or challenge will be scheduled. Any reconsideration requests will be processed and ruled upon before proceeding with the second hearing. The SBT also reserves the right to deal with a human rights issue or challenge not done in accordance with these procedures in unusual or exceptional circumstances. Parties appearing before the SBT on a human rights issue or challenge must comply with disclosure requirements required by the enabling legislation of the SBT. If the SBT determines that, after receipt of a party's notice, the human rights issue or challenge is frivolous or vexatious, it may refuse to hear it after notifying the party who raised it and the other procedures set out here do not apply. If a party does not follow the required procedure in raising a human rights issue or the challenge is without reasonable cause, the party will not be entitled to raise the human rights issue or challenge, except in unusual or exceptional circumstance.

Look at the following:
• SBT website — Practice Direction 6 — Procedure for human rights issue or challenge

G. Hearing of the SBT

The procedures in respect of the actual hearing before the SBT are set out in the provisions of the *SPPA* and as set out in the website of the SBT. Following are specifics that occur after the appeal.

OWA
• Within 60 days after it last receives evidence or submissions on the appeal (O. Reg. 134/98, ss. 78(1)), the SBT must deliver to the parties a written decision to, under section 31 of the *OWA*,
 (a) deny the appeal,
 (b) grant the appeal,
 (c) grant the appeal in part, or

(d) refer the matter back to the administrator for reconsideration in accordance with any directions the SBT considers proper.

Such decision must include reasons for the decision and takes effect when it is made and, if it is appealed, continues in effect until a decision of the Divisional Court is made on appeal. Appeals can also be denied if the proceedings fall within the circumstances listed in section 34 of the *OWA*. The SBT's findings of fact shall be based exclusively on evidence admissible and facts of which notice may be taken under sections 15, 15.1, 15.2 and 16 of the *SPPA* and the decision shall include the principal findings of fact and its conclusions based on those findings (ss. 78(2–3)).

ODSPA
- Within 60 days after it last receives evidence or submissions on the appeal (O. Reg. 222/98, ss. 67(1)), the SBT must deliver to the parties a written decision to, under section 26 of the *ODSPA*
  (a) deny the appeal,
  (b) grant the appeal,
  (c) grant the appeal in part, or
  (d) refer the matter back to the director for reconsideration in accordance with any directions the SBT considers proper.

Such decision must include reasons for the decision, which takes effect when it is made and, if it is appealed, continues in effect until a decision of the Divisional Court is made on appeal. Appeals can also be denied if the proceedings fall within the circumstances listed in section 29 of the *ODSPA*. The SBT's findings of fact shall be based exclusively on evidence admissible and facts of which notice may be taken under sections 15, 15.1, 15.2 and 16 of the *SPPA* and the decision shall include the principal findings of fact and its conclusions based on those findings (ss. 67(2–3)).

Look at the following:
- *OWA* — Policy Directive 34.0
- *ODSPA* — Policy Directive 13B
- FAQs on the SBT website — Hearings
- FAQs on the SBT website — Decisions
- The SBT website — Brochures — Appeal your decision to the SBT

H. Reconsideration

OWA: Section 79 of O. Reg. 134/98 details the ability to ask the SBT to reconsider its decision on the appeal, including the timelines and other procedural matters.

ODSPA: Section 68 of O. Reg. 222/98 details the ability to ask the SBT to reconsider its decision on the appeal, including the timelines and other procedural matters.

Look at the following:
- FAQs on the SBT website — Reconsideration
- SBT website — Forms — Application for Reconsideration Form
- SBT website — Practice Direction 2 — Reconsideration Requests

I. Appeal or Judicial Review to Divisional Court

The procedures in respect of appeals and judicial review of the decision of the SBT are set out in the provisions of the *SPPA* and the *Judicial Review Procedure Act* and as set out in the website of the SBT. Following are specifics that occur after the decision of the SBT is sent to the parties:

- *OWA* — There is no privative clause preventing an appeal of the decision of the SBT: subsection 36(1) of the *OWA* states that the "director and any party to a hearing may appeal the tribunal's decision to the divisional court on a question of law". The procedures of the SBT under the *OWA* section 36 and its O. Reg. 134/98 have further information.

- *ODSPA* — There is no privative clause preventing an appeal of the decision of the SBT: subsection 31(1) of the *ODSPA* states that the "director and any party to a hearing may appeal the tribunal's decision to the divisional court on a question of law". The procedures of the SBT under the *ODSPA*, s. 31 and its O. Reg. 222/98 have further information.

Look at the following:
- *OWA* — Policy Directive 34.0
- *ODSPA* — Policy Directive 13B
- FAQs on the SBT website — Divisional Court Appeals

Appendix 4.2
The Appeal Form[1]

Social
Benefits
Tribunal
Ontario

Appeal Form

Questions?

Toronto:
(416) 326-0978

Outside Toronto:
1-800-753-3895

Fax:
(416) 326-5135

Mail to:
Registrar
Social Benefits Tribunal
1075 Bay Street, 7th Floor
Toronto ON
M5S 2B1

Please attach copies of the following to this form:

• the original **Notice of Decision**

• your **request for an internal review** and

• the **Internal review decision** (if you received one).

Disponible en français.

Before you can appeal to the Tribunal, you must request an internal review by the office that made the original decision.

1. General Information

☐ Mr ☐ Mrs ☐ Ms ☐ Miss

Last Name _____

First Name _____

Address _____

_____ Apartment_____

City _____ Postal Code _____

Telephone ( ) _____

• When were you born?

_____ / _____ / _____
Day / Month /Year

• Which ☐ Ontario Works or ☐ Ontario Disability office do you deal with?

Office name _____

Office address _____

Case worker's name _____

Case worker's telephone ( ) _____

2. Internal Review

• What is the date of your Notice of Decision?

_____ / _____ / _____
Day / Month /Year

• When did you make your request for an internal review?

_____ / _____ / _____
Day / Month /Year

• Did you receive an internal review decision?

☐ Yes

☐ No

Office Use Only

File number _____

Date post-marked _____

---

[1] Source: SBT website <www.sbt.gov.on.ca>

Important: If you do not attend your hearing and fail to provide a reasonable explanation for you absence, your appeal will be denied. In addition, you will not be allowed to appeal a subsequent decision on the same issue for two years.

The Social Benefits Tribunal does not have the authority to review all social assistance decisions. We will advise you in writing of the reasons if your appeal cannot be heard.

You must file your appeal within 30 days of the end of the internal review period. If you do not do so, you must explain why you were late filing. The Tribunal may extend the time for filing this appeal, if it is satisfied that there is a reasonable explanation for the delay.

3. Your Reasons for Appealing

- What are you appealing?

  ☐ Ontario Works

  ☐ Ontario Disability Support Program (disability, seniors or children with severe disabilities).

- Why are you appealing? Check **all** the boxes that apply to you.

  ☐ I was refused assistance.
  ☐ My assistance has been reduced.
  ☐ I have an overpayment.
  ☐ The amount of my assistance is wrong.

  ☐ My assistance has been cancelled.
  ☐ My assistance is on hold.
  ☐ They say I am not disabled.

- What is the effective date of the decision you are appealing?

  _____ / _____ / _____
  Day   / Month   /Year

- You **must** explain **what** you disagree with in the original decision and **why**. Use the space below and attach additional pages if necessary.

  _____

_____
_____
_____
_____
_____
_____
_____
_____
_____

- Will you need any of the following services at the hearing?

  ☐ Interpreter: Language _____   Dialect _____

  ☐ Sign language interpreter   ☐ Wheelchair access

Signature _____ Date _____

The Social Benefits Tribunal collects the personal information requested on this form under the *Ontario Works Act, 1997* or the *Ontario Disability Support Program Act, 1997*. It will be used for the purpose of conducting the appeal and will be shared with the respondent. If you have any questions, please contact the FIPP representative at the Tribunal at 1-800-753-3895.

This completes the appeal section. If you are experiencing financial hardship, see section 4 on Interim assistance.

Interim assistance is financial help you may be eligible to receive while waiting for your appeal to be concluded.

The Tribunal may order that you receive interim assistance if you will experience financial hardship as a result of the original decision made by your local office. To assess your request for interim assistance, the Tribunal requires detailed financial information.

You will be notified in writing of the Tribunal's decision regarding interim assistance.

Note: If you lose your appeal, your interim assistance shall be assessed as an overpayment.

4. Application for Interim Assistance

- Describe your household. How many people, including yourself, have you applied on behalf of?

  _____ adults   _____ children

- Check the box beside those sentences that best describe [your] situation.
  - ☐ I am looking for work.
  - ☐ I am in an employment assistance program.
  - ☐ I am attending school   ☐ full-time   ☐ part-time
    ☐ high school   ☐ college   ☐ university   ☐ other.
  - ☐ I am under 18 and cannot live at home.
  - ☐ I am working, but earn less than the Ontario Works entitlement.

- Are you receiving any money at all?   ☐ Yes   ☐ No

- If you live with your spouse/same-sex partner, is he/she receiving any money?
  ☐ Yes   ☐ No

- If you or your spouse/same-sex partner are receiving money, please provide details of your household income below. Include the amount you receive, when you last received it and how often you receive this income.

Type of Income	Amount	Date Last Received	Weekly, Monthly, or Other (Specify)
Example: Income A	**$ 100.00**	**June 1**	**Monthly**
Earnings from a job	$		
Vacation pay	$		
Ontario Works (OW)	$		
Ontario Disability Support Program (ODSP)	$		
Workplace Safety & Insurance Benefits (WSIB)	$		
Employment Insurance	$		
Canada Pension Plan	$		
Disability insurance (other than CPP, WSIB)	$		
Support payments	$		
Trust fund income	$		
Ontario Student Assistance Plan (OSAP)	$		
Rental/boarder income	$		
Borrowed money	$		
Foreign Pension	$		
Self-employment earnings	$		
Other	$		
	$		

- Will you be receiving any money next month that you have not already listed?
  ☐ Yes   What type? _____   Amount $ _____
  ☐ No

- Provide the details below of the assets you or any member of your household have.
  Bank accounts (personal and business) $_____
  Stocks, bonds, GICs $_____
  RSPs $_____
  Land or property other than your home $_____
  Other (specify) $_____

- How much money do you pay each month for:
  Rent $_____
  Mortgage $_____
  Property taxes $_____
  Room and board $_____
  Heat $_____
  Electricity $_____
  Water $_____
  Food $_____
  Other (specify) $_____

- Are you behind in any of your payments or unable to pay these expenses?
  ☐ Yes   What expenses have you been late paying or unable to pay? _____
  ☐ No

- Have you received an eviction notice or notice that your electricity or other service will be shut off?
  ☐ Yes   Provide details _____
  ☐ No

- Please provide any additional information that you feel the Tribunal should know regarding your financial circumstances.

_____

_____

_____

_____

_____

_____

_____

_____

_____

_____

Signature _____   Date _____

The Social Benefits Tribunal collects the personal information requested on this form under the *Ontario Works Act, 1997* or the *Ontario Disability Support Program Act, 1997*. It will be used in determining interim assistance. If you have any questions, please contact the FIPP representative at the Tribunal at 1-800-753-3895.

Appendix 4.3
Application for Reconsideration[2]

SOCIAL BENEFITS TRIBUNAL
Ontario

Application for Reconsideration

Questions?
Toronto:
(416) 326-0978

Outside Toronto:
1-800-753-3895

Fax:
(416) 326-5135

Mail to:
Registrar
Social Benefits Tribunal
1075 Bay Street, 7ᵗʰ Floor
Toronto ON
M5S 2B1

Office Use Only

File number _____

Date post-marked _____

The Reconsideration Process

You have thirty (30) days after receiving the appeal decision to submit your application for reconsideration.

The Tribunal will advise you within sixty (60) days of receiving your request whether or not it will grant a reconsideration hearing.

Disponible en français.

(10/98)

1. General Information

This application is to be used when you request the Social Benefits Tribunal to reconsider a decision made on an appeal. Please complete all of the following sections. For more information on the reconsideration process, please see the side panels.

- Are you the appellant ☐ or the respondent ☐ ?

- The file number on the appeal decision is

- The date of the appeal decision is _____ / _____ / _____
  Day

2. Information about the Appellant

Mr ☐   Mrs ☐   Ms ☐   Miss ☐

LAST NAME _____

FIRST NAME _____

ADDRESS _____

APARTMENT _____ TELEPHONE ( ) _____

CITY _____ POSTAL CODE _____

- Appellant's date of birth is _____ / _____ / _____
  Day   / Month   / Year

3. Information about the Respondent

- The Respondent is an ☐ Ontario Works office or ☐ Ontario Disability office.

OFFICE NAME _____

OFFICE ADDRESS _____

CITY _____ POSTAL CODE _____

TELEPHONE ( ) _____

CONTACT _____

---

[2] Source: SBT website <www.sbt.gov.on.ca>

4. Request for Reconsideration

- Why should the Tribunal grant your request for a reconsideration hearing. Please give your reasons below. Attach additional pages if necessary.

_____
_____
_____
_____
_____
_____
_____
_____
_____
_____
_____
_____
_____
_____
_____
_____
_____
_____
_____

You must send a copy of this application for reconsideration to those people who were parties to the original appeal decision.

Other parties may, within fifteen (15) days of receiving copies of this application for reconsideration, file a written submission with the Tribunal in response to this application.

If you have any questions about the collection of this information, please contact the Tribunal at 1-800-753-3895.

5. Notice of Service

- Were there other parties to the original hearing other than the appellant and respondent?　　No ☐　　　Yes ☐　Please provide the name(s):

_____

- I have served a copy of this application on the other parties by:
  ☐ prepaid regular post to the last known address,
  ☐ delivering it personally,
  ☐ sending a facsimile (fax).

Signature _____　Date _____

Name (please print) _____

Appendix 4.4
How to Appeal Your Decision to the SBT[3]

 **Social
Benefits
Tribunal**

Ontario

How to

Appeal Your

Decision

to the

Social

Benefits

Tribunal

If you disagree with a decision that affects the amount of or your eligibility for social assistance, you may ask the Social Benefits Tribunal to hold a hearing where you can present your case.

The Tribunal is an independent, quasi-judicial body that hears appeals concerning social assistance, as set out in the Ontario Works Act, 1997 *and the* Ontario Disability Support Program Act, 1997.

CONTACTING THE TRIBUNAL

MAIL: Social Benefits Tribunal
1075 Bay Street, 7th Floor
Toronto ON M5S 2B1

TELEPHONE: Toronto and area: 416-326-0978
Toll-free: 1-800-753-3895
TTY: 416-325-3408
TTY (toll free): 1-800-268-7095
TTY (Ottawa): 613-566-2235

FAX: 416-326-5135

WEBSITE: www.sbt.gov.on.ca

Computer terminals are available at the Tribunal office to access our website only.

FORMS

Appeal Forms are available at the Tribunal office and on our website, at all Ontario Works (OW) and Ontario Disability Support Program (ODSP) offices and community legal clinics.

BEFORE YOU FILE AN APPEAL

Before you may file an appeal with the Tribunal, you **must** request an internal review from the office that made the original decision concerning your social assistance. If you do not request an internal review, you may not appeal a decision to the Tribunal.

You have 10 days from the date you receive the original decision to request an internal review. Your request must be in writing.

The Social Benefits Tribunal does not conduct internal reviews.

FILING AN APPEAL

You may appeal to the Tribunal if you disagree with a decision that affects the amount of or your eligibility for social assistance, **and when**

---

[3] Source: SBT website <www.sbt.gov.on.ca>

1. you have requested and received an internal review decision, **or**

2. you have requested but not received an internal review decision within 10 days of your request.

From the date of either (1) or (2) above, you have 30 days to file an appeal. You must use the Social Benefits Tribunal Appeal Form (see the section entitled Forms for availability).

If you do not file your appeal within this period, you will have to explain why you are filing late and the Tribunal will decide at the appeal hearing whether or not to proceed with your appeal.

INTERIM ASSISTANCE

Interim assistance is financial aid you may be eligible to receive while waiting for your hearing. To qualify, you must be experiencing financial hardship. It is helpful to provide detailed financial information and documents to support your claim, for example, proof of arrears in rent, an eviction notice or unpaid bills. To apply, complete section 4 of the Appeal Form.

The Tribunal notifies you in writing whether or not you have qualified. If interim assistance is ordered, your local office issues your cheques. **The Social Benefits Tribunal does not issue cheques.**

Receiving interim assistance does not affect the outcome of your appeal. However, if you lose your appeal, you may have to repay your interim assistance.

LAWYERS AND REPRESENTATIVES (LEGAL AND NON-LEGAL)

It is not necessary to have someone represent you at the hearing, but if you prefer representation, find a lawyer or other representative *as soon as possible*. **Hearings will not be rescheduled because of delays in seeking assistance.**

Anyone over the age of 18, who is not a witness in your case, may act as your representative. You must advise the Tribunal in writing of the name of your representative.

Before the Tribunal can speak with your lawyer or other representative, you must give us written authorization. Until we receive your authorization, we may communicate only with you about your appeal.

The pamphlet *Where to Get Help with Your Appeal* available at the Tribunal office or on our website, will give you more information about representation.

AFTER YOU FILE AN APPEAL

The Tribunal processes your appeal and schedules your hearing. Prior to your hearing, you will receive the following:

1. An acknowledgement letter stating

   ▪ your Appeal File Number. This number appears on all our correspondence to you. Use it on all your documents and letters to us and have it ready when calling the Tribunal;

   ▪ the name and telephone number of your Client Service Representative (CSR) who is the person assigned to manage your case. Direct your questions about your appeal to your CSR. Call your CSR's direct line or call the Tribunal's main switchboard and follow the recorded instructions; and

   ▪ the pamphlet Where to Get Help with Your Appeal.

2. A letter about **interim assistance**, if you applied for it, telling you whether or not you have qualified.

3. A **Notice of Hearing** telling you where and when your hearing will be held.

SUBMISSION FROM YOUR LOCAL OFFICE

The Tribunal asks for a submission from the office that made the original decision which you are appealing. This submission gives the reasons why the local office made its decision.

If a submission is written, you have the right to receive a copy of it. At the hearing, you will have an opportunity to provide evidence to show why you think the decision is wrong.

YOUR DOCUMENTS

Use any documents you think will help you present your case. File copies of your documents with the Tribunal and with the office that made the original decision at least 20 days before the date of your hearing. You may deliver them in person, by mail or fax. Documents not received by this deadline may or may not be used at the hearing.

You are responsible for getting the documents you want to use at your appeal. If you need additional documents from your OW or ODSP office, from your doctor or others, you may authorize your lawyer or other representative to help you.

KEEPING YOUR FILE UP TO DATE

It is important that you keep your file up to date. Notify your CSR by telephone or in writing when your address or telephone number changes or when your personal or financial circumstances change. Also notify your local office of any changes.

Use your Appeal File Number and indicate your OW or ODSP office on your letters.

WITHDRAWING YOUR APPEAL

Notify your CSR immediately if you decide to withdraw your appeal for any reason. Also notify the office that made the original decision if you withdraw your appeal.

Have your Appeal File Number ready when you call.

THE HEARING

It is important that you appear for your hearing on the date and at the time you have been given in your Notice of Hearing. If you do not appear, the hearing may go ahead as scheduled and you will not have a chance to present your case. If you fail to appear and do not have a reasonable explanation, you will almost certainly lose your appeal.

PLACE

The Tribunal holds hearings across Ontario. Your hearing may be in your community or in a neighbouring community. If you think you will have trouble getting to the hearing, contact your CSR as soon as you receive your Notice of Hearing.

TIME

Hearings are scheduled for one and a half hours, longer in some cases. To ensure that you have enough time for your hearing, let your CSR know if you are bringing a witness or if there are other reasons why you may need more time. It is your responsibility to be on time for your hearing.

INTERPRETERS

If your first language is neither English nor French and you need an interpreter, fill out the appropriate section on the Appeal Form or notify your CSR well in advance of your hearing. It is important that you identify your dialect so that the Tribunal can ensure that an accredited interpreter is present at your hearing.

SPECIAL NEEDS

If you require special equipment, services or assistance, contact your CSR well in advance of the hearing, if possible, so that arrangements can be made.

WHO MAY ATTEND A HEARING ?

- The Presiding Tribunal Member(s)

- You, the appellant

- Respondent(s) from the office that made the original decision

- Any witnesses

- Any lawyers and legal or non-legal representatives.

The Presiding Tribunal Member makes the final decision about who can sit in your hearing.

PRESENTING THE CASE

A Tribunal hearing is not a formal court proceeding. The Presiding Tribunal Member introduces those attending and briefly explains how the hearing will proceed.

Both parties have an opportunity to present their cases.

You will be asked to promise to tell the truth and may be required to answer questions. You will be allowed to ask questions of the other side.

THE DECISION

The Tribunal does not give its decision at the hearing. The Presiding Tribunal Member reviews the evidence after the hearing and issues a written decision. A copy of the decision will be mailed to you.

RECONSIDERATION HEARING

Either party may request a reconsideration of the Tribunal's decision by submitting an Application for Reconsideration, with reasons, to the Tribunal, within 30 days of receiving the Tribunal's decision.

COURT APPEALS

You may appeal the Tribunal's decision to the Divisional Court on questions of law. You may wish to get legal assistance to do this.

If you have any comments or suggestions about the operations of the Tribunal, please send them in writing to the Tribunal office.

Additional information about the Social Benefits Tribunal is available on our website at www.sbt.gov.on.ca.

The information presented here is for general guidance and convenience; it is not meant to be a final interpretation of the legislation.

Disponible en français.

IMPORTANT NOTICE

MEDICAL REPORTS

The law regarding filing medical documents in relation to a hearing has changed.

If you are appealing a denial or cancellation of benefits under ODSP because the Director decided that you are not a person with a disability, and you have additional medical documents for the hearing, the documents must be submitted to the Disability Adjudication Unit and the Tribunal as soon as possible and no later than **30 days** before the date of your hearing.

5

Assessment Review Board

LEARNING OBJECTIVES

After reading this chapter, the reader should be able to:

- understand how to research any Ontario agency by exploring its website to find the important information needed to understand the agency's practices and procedures and how a paralegal would properly represent a client before such agency by doing so with the Assessment Review Board (ARB)
- document the background of the ARB
- detail and explain the provisions of the enabling legislation relevant to the ARB
- elaborate on various concepts of public policy relevant to the ARB
- state whether any regulations made under the enabling legislation are relevant to the ARB and if so, to discuss such provisions
- compare and prioritize the various sources of practice and procedure of the ARB
- identify the specific rules and procedures for the ARB and how they would be applied in a proceeding before, during, and after a hearing of the ARB
- review and explain the procedures and practices of the ARB by way of a flow chart and key forms and documents available on the ARB website
- assess whether the relevant provisions of the *Statutory Powers Procedure Act* apply to the ARB
- outline the various explanatory literature available on the ARB website to assist the paralegal to understand the ARB and better represent the client
- appreciate the need to find decisions and/or cases in order to understand and argue the law before the ARB
- illustrate and discuss principles that flow from the various cases and decisions as they relate to the ARB

INTRODUCTION

The Assessment Review Board (ARB) (www.arb.gov.on.ca) is an Ontario statutorily created adjudicative agency. Its key function is to hear complaints from people who believe properties are incorrectly assessed or classified in respect of municipal taxes. The ARB also deals with other complaints, such as school support designation and some property tax appeals. The ARB holds hearings across Ontario.

Readers should note that on the "Welcome to the Assessment Review Board (ARB)" Web page, a video prepared by the ARB shows a sample hearing to provide people with an idea of what to expect.

The ARB website is accessed through the website for the Environmental and Land Tribunals of Ontario (www.elto.gov.on.ca). On the "Welcome to ELTO" page of that website, the Executive Chair of the ELTO states as follows:

> ELTO was formally designated as Ontario's first cluster of tribunals under the *Adjudicative Tribunals Accountability, Governance and Appointments Act 2009*, on April 7, 2010. I believe the decision by the Government to group these five important tribunals reflects a recognition of the key role each plays resolving disputes, within the applicable legislative framework, to support strong, healthy communities and achieve outcomes that are in the public interest, and of the potential to better fulfill that role by bringing the tribunals together.

A brief description of how this cluster formed is set out the ARB Annual Report 2008–2009:

> In September 2006, the Ontario government appointed an Agency Cluster Facilitator to work with five tribunals in the municipal, environment and land-use planning sectors to find ways to improve services through cross-agency coordination of operations, administration and dispute resolution. The five tribunals included in the cluster were: the Assessment Review Board (ARB), the Board of Negotiation (BON), the Conservation Review Board (CRB), the Environmental Review Tribunal (ERT) and the Ontario Municipal Board (OMB).

The reader who wishes to understand the procedures and practices of the ARB from this date forward should not only explore the ARB website but also the ELTO website, although at the time of review for this edition in the fall of 2010, nothing of procedural substance related to the ARB is posted on the site.

OVERVIEW AND BACKGROUND

The 2006–2007 Annual Report for the ARB provides a succinct history and overview of the ARB and assessment in Ontario as follows:

> Property assessments have been conducted in what is now Ontario since 1793. In 1970, the province assumed the role of assessing property from municipalities and replaced the Courts of Revision with the Assessment Review Court (ARC). ARC was renamed the Assessment Review Board in 1983.
>
> With the enactment of the *Fair Municipal Finance Act, 1997*, the ARB became the province's sole adjudicative tribunal for property assessment complaints. The legislation reduced duplication and ensured that the Board was the final tribunal of appeal for such complaints. Prior to 1998, ARB decisions could be appealed to the Ontario Municipal Board (OMB).
>
> In 1998, an amendment to the *Assessment Review Board Act* gave the ARB the capacity to dismiss frivolous complaints. Decisions by the Board are final and binding,

subject only to appeal to Divisional Court on questions of law when the Court grants leave to appeal. The Board also exercises the power to review its decisions.

The Board's jurisdiction and its authority are defined by the *Assessment Review Board Act*, the *Assessment Act*, the *Municipal Act, 2001*, the *City of Toronto Act, 2006*, the *Education Act* and the *Statutory Powers Procedure Act*.

Each of the statutes mentioned in the last sentence of the paragraphs quoted have either been reviewed in the previous chapter on the *SPPA* or are discussed in the relevant sections later in this chapter.

There are four major participants in the property assessment system of Ontario:

1. The provincial government, through the Ministry of Finance, sets the laws regarding property assessment.
2. Municipalities are responsible for setting tax rates and collecting property taxes.
3. The Municipal Property Assessment Corporation (MPAC) assesses and classifies all properties in Ontario.
4. The Assessment Review Board (ARB) hears complaints filed by property owners if there is a dispute between a property owner and MPAC.

MPAC is a statutory, non-profit corporation created under the *Municipal Property Assessment Corporation Act, 1997*, and managed by a board composed largely of municipal representatives. It conducts property assessments throughout the province as well as assessment updates and other non-relevant activities.

During the fiscal year of April 1, 2007, to March 31, 2008, the ARB received approximately 87,000 complaints and resolved over 61,000 of them.

ENABLING LEGISLATION

The jurisdiction and authority of the ARB are defined by the following legislation:

(i) The *Assessment Review Board Act*, R.S.O. 1990, c. A.32, as amended (*ARBA*), establishes the ARB and also sets out a few procedural rules.
(ii) The *Assessment Act*, R.S.O. 1990, c. A.31, as amended.
(iii) The *Municipal Act, 2001*, S.O. 2001, c. 25, as amended.
(iv) The *Education Act*, R.S.O. 1990, c. E.2, as amended.
(v) The *City of Toronto Act, 2006*, S.O. 2006, c. 11, Sched. A, as amended, gives jurisdiction to the ARB.
(vi) The *Provincial Land Tax Act, 2006* S.O. 2006, c. 33, Sched. Z.2, as amended.
(vii) The *Statutory Powers Procedure Act* (*SPPA*), which is a statute of general application, imposes minimum rules of procedure and ties the ARB Rules that have been published into the procedure.

All the legislation, except the *Statutory Powers Procedure Act*, which is discussed in Chapter 2 are examined as each relates to the ARB.

The *ARBA*

The *ARBA* replaced the previous statute in 1990 and continued the ARB (s. 2). Under section 3, the Lieutenant Governor in Council (the Ontario Cabinet) appoints the chair and vice-chairs and other members of the ARB. Only one member of the ARB is sufficient to constitute a quorum, and therefore there only has to be one member to adjudicate a hearing with all the jurisdiction and powers of the ARB (s. 5). Pursuant to section 6, a chair or vice-chair has power to assign, change, and prescribe duties to the members to various sittings of the ARB. The oath required to be taken by every member before entering her/his duties is set out in section 7. Under section 8.1, the ARB may set and charge fees, subject to the approval of the Attorney General, for proceedings under the *Assessment Act* and the *Municipal Act*, for furnishing copies of forms, notices, or documents filed with or issued by the ARB for other services provided by the ARB. Different kinds of complaints, applications, and appeals can be treated differently in fee setting, which is made available to the public usually by regulation (e.g., O. Reg. 290/07 sets out fees for some applications under the *City of Toronto Act*). The ARB can also waive or refund all or part of a fee charged in the appropriate circumstances. Further to section 8.2, the ARB may, on its own or at the motion of any party, dismiss a complaint or an appeal brought before it, without holding a hearing as the ARB considers appropriate, on any of the following three grounds:

1. The ARB is of the opinion that the proceeding is frivolous or vexatious, is commenced in bad faith, or is commenced only for the purpose of delay.
2. The ARB is of the opinion that the reasons set out in the complaint or appeal do not disclose any apparent statutory ground on which it can make a decision.
3. The complainant or appellant has not responded to the ARB's request for further information within the time the ARB specified.

Before dismissing an appeal or complaint under any of these grounds, the ARB shall notify the appellant or complainant and give such person the opportunity to respond.

Pursuant to section 9, effective January 1, 2009, the chair of the ARB shall determine where the board sits to hear and decide all complaints relating to assessments. Finally, under section 12, the municipality where sittings of the ARB are held is required to provide a suitable room and other necessary accommodation for the ARB.

The *Assessment Act*

Definitions and Purpose

The ARB is defined as being the ARB under subsection 1(1) of the *ARBA*, which means that the *Assessment Act* does not create the ARB but only gives it jurisdiction. The Minister of Finance, under subsection 2(2), is given the authority to make regulations, which include resolving issues as to whether land is in the farm property class or managed forests property class or whether land is conservation land (ss. 2(d.3) and (d.4), which are related to procedures to be used by the ARB); as of the time of this writing, no such regulations exist. (As always, the reader should keep up-to-date with the legislation if involved with the ARB or any tribunal.) The purpose of the *Assessment Act* is to set up a system to assess land value so that municipal (or realty) taxes can be determined. The assessment depends on such factors as the current value of the land (ss. 19(1)), the classification of the real property (s. 7), and the support of a specific type of school board (s. 16). The assessment is done by MPAC (as defined in ss. 1(1)) using factors and procedures set out under the assessment legislation and includes classes of land exempt from taxation in order to produce an annual assessment roll within the time period set out in section 36 for each municipality and in accordance with section 14 for each locality and non-municipal territory.

School Support Designation

MPAC is also required under section 16 to provide an annual school support list. Under subsection 16(3), "[a]ny person may apply in a form approved by the Minister [of Finance] to the assessment corporation to have his or her name included or altered in the assessment roll as a supporter of a type of school board under the *Education Act*". A refusal by MPAC will require it to "inform the applicant in writing that the application is refused, that the school support of the applicant as designated on the list prepared under [s. 16(9)] will be confirmed on the notice of assessment to which the applicant is entitled under section 31 and that the applicant may, upon receipt of the notice of assessment, appeal the school support designation as confirmed by [MPAC] to the Assessment Review Board under section 40". Note also subsection 16(10) states the following:

> Where an application under this section has been received by [MPAC] before the day fixed for the return of the roll but has not been considered by the corporation until after the delivery of the notice of assessment provided for in section 31, [MPAC] shall, if [it] refuses the application, inform the applicant in writing that the inclusion or amendment requested in the application is refused and that an appeal may be taken by appealing to the Assessment Review Board the applicant's school support designation as shown on the notice of assessment delivered under section 31 but, where [MPAC] approves the application, the corporation shall deliver to the applicant an amended notice of assessment.

Change of Information

If there is a change in the information required but not reflected in the last assessment roll, MPAC shall deliver, in accordance with section 31 and in a form approved by the Minister of Finance, a notice of assessment with information required by subsection 31(1) to every person affected by such change. The notice of assessment shall be accompanied by an information notice and delivered by a certain date and in a certain manner, all in accordance with section 31.

Appeal under s. 36

The assessment roll is returned by MPAC to the municipality clerk (or similar person for non-municipal lands) on the date set out in subsection 36(2), although the date to return can be extended by MPAC under subsections 36(2) and (3). The timeline for the ARB to hear appeals, including complaints under section 33 (omitted assessments) and section 34 (supplementary assessments), for that assessment roll is set out in subsection 36(5) as being as soon as practicable after the return of the assessment roll. The last revised assessment roll is accomplished as set out in section 37; however, subsection 37(5) states that "[n]othing in this section deprives a person of a right of appeal provided for in this Act, which may be exercised and the appeal proceeded with in accordance with this Act, despite the fact that the assessment roll has become the last revised assessment roll".

Reconsideration by MPAC

Section 39.1 details the ability of a person who received, or would be entitled to receive, a notice of assessment to request MPAC "to reconsider any matter relating to the assessment or classification of the property, including any matter that could form the basis of an appeal under subsection 40(1) or an application under s. 46, no later than March 31 of the taxation year in respect of which the request is made" or as extended by the ARB. Note that if the request for reconsideration relates to a change of corrections under section 35, the time to request is just 90 days from the mailing date of the notice of correction. The reconsideration request must be made within the time limits as set out in subsections 39.1(2) and (3) and must give the basis for the person's request and all the relevant facts (ss. 39.1(4)) that will be considered by MPAC (ss. 39.1(5)). Regulations regarding disclosure by both MPAC and the person requesting reconsideration can be made by the Minister of Finance (ss. 39.1(6)), but as of the time of writing, none has been published. Under subsection 39.1(7), MPAC shall mail to the requesting party the results of the reconsideration by either September 30 of the taxation year or November 30 of the taxation year if such extension is agreed upon. However, if the request for reconsideration relates to a notice of correction, the date to get the results is 180 days after the request is made (ss. 39.1(8)). In the case that MPAC and the requestor can settle, MPAC shall give notice of settlement to either the municipality clerk or the Minister of Finance as required (ss. 39.1(9)). The municipality or the Minister can object to the settlement under subsection 39.1(11), but the appeal must be made (i) to the ARB within 90 days after receiving notice of settlement, and (ii) on the basis that section 40 applies — the assessment roll had been changed to reflect the settlement.

Appeal under s. 40

Specific details of an appeal to the ARB are covered under the various subsections of section 40. Under subsection (1)(a), any person may appeal to the ARB on the following bases:

(i) the current value of the person's land or another person's land is incorrect,

(ii) the person or another person was wrongly placed on or omitted from the assessment roll,

(iii) the person or another person was wrongly placed on or omitted from the roll in respect of school support,

(iv) the classification of the person's land or another person's land is incorrect, or

(v) for land, portions of which are in different classes of real property, the determination of the share of the value of the land that is attributable to each class is incorrect.

Another basis for appeal can be any ground that the Minister of Finance may prescribe, but as of the date of this writing, there is no regulation prescribing another basis. **Note that if a timely request for reconsideration is not made in respect of certain classes of property as set out in subsection 40(3), no appeal may be brought to the ARB**, except where there are extenuating circumstances as determined by the ARB (ss. 40(4)). There are further end dates to appeal to the ARB, depending on specific circumstances as set out in subsections 40(5) to (8). Where the appellant is a person other than the person who was assessed, procedures are stated under subsection 40(9). Pursuant to subsection 40(10), upon receipt of an appeal, the ARB shall immediately send a copy to MPAC. The parties to the appeal are MPAC, the appellant(s) and the person whose assessment is the subject of the appeal, and the municipality in which the land is located, or the Minister of Finance if it is non-municipal land (ss. 40(11)). The ARB shall give at least 24 days' notice to all the parties to the hearing before the date of the hearing (ss. 40(12)). Regulations regarding disclosure by the parties to the appeal can be made by the Minister of Finance (ss. 40(13)), but none has been published to date; however, R. 56 of the ARB Rules of Practice and Procedure, to be discussed below, does discuss discovery.

The mechanisms for adding a party to the appeal are discussed in subsection 40(14) and the person whose property is the subject to the appeal is given the opportunity to make the closing statement at the hearing under subsection 40(15). Where the valuation is the ground for appeal, a recent amendment states that MPAC has the burden to prove the correctness of the current value (ss. 40(17)). However, if the appellant refuses (i) to give MPAC a reasonable opportunity to inspect the property under section 10 or (ii) to comply with a request for information and documentation under section 11, the burden of proving the correctness of the current value shall rest with the appellant (ss. 40(18)). It is possible that even if MPAC does not meet the burden, the ARB may have little choice but to confirm if the complainant fails to provide determinative evidence. Pursuant to subsection 40(19), after hearing the evidence and the submissions of the parties, the ARB shall determine the matter.

Once the decision has been made, the ARB shall immediately forward its decision to the municipality clerk under subsection 40(20) or the Minister of Finance under subsection 40(21) as the case may be, and such person "shall alter the assessment roll in accordance with the decisions of the [ARB] from which no further appeal is taken, indicate on the roll that the alteration has been made and complete the roll by totalling the amounts of the assessments in the roll and inserting the total". Subsection 40(22) states that the ARB, "as to all matters within its jurisdiction under this section, has authority to hear and determine all questions of law or of fact and a decision of the Board under this section is final and binding unless it is appealed under section 43.1". Some specific situations are dealt with in subsections 40(23) to (28).

Palpable Errors in Assessment Roll

The ARB is given authority, where there are palpable errors in the assessment roll, to correct the roll if no alteration in assessed values or classification of land is involved and, if there is such an alteration, to extend the time for bringing appeals and direct MPAC to be the appellant (s. 40.1).

Assessment Roll as Evidence

A certified copy of the assessment roll as evidence in a hearing is discussed in section 42 as follows:

> The following documents may be received in evidence by a court or tribunal, without proof of the signature of the person certifying the document and without production of the original of which the document purports to be a copy:
>
> 1. A document that is a copy of all or part of the assessment roll for a municipality, certified by the clerk of the municipality to be a true copy of it.
> 2. A document that is a copy of all or part of the assessment roll for non-municipal territory, certified by the Minister to be a true copy of it.

Stating a Case

Under section 43, the ARB may, upon application of any person or on its own motion, and upon such security (i.e., money to be put up) as it determines is necessary, "state a case in writing for the opinion of the Divisional Court upon any question that, in the opinion of the [ARB], is a question of law", and the Divisional Court shall hear and determine such stated case. This provision is used in very limited circumstances, and, if used, all the parties have to agree to pay their own costs and to indemnify the ARB.

Leave to Appeal to Divisional Court

Under section 43.1, an appeal from the ARB on a question of law lies upon the leave of appeal to the Divisional Court, and an application for leave to appeal shall be made within 30 days of the mailing of the decision by the ARB.

Powers of the ARB

Pursuant to subsection 44(1),

> Upon an appeal on any ground against an assessment, the [ARB] or court, as the case may be, may reopen the whole question of the assessment so that omissions from, or

errors in the assessment roll may be corrected, and the amount for which the assessment should be made, and the person or persons who should be assessed therefor may be placed upon the roll, and if necessary the assessment roll, even if returned as finally revised, may be opened so as to make it correct in accordance with the findings made on appeal.

Also under subsection 44(3),

in determining the value at which any land shall be assessed, the [ARB] shall,
(a) determine the current value of the land; and
(b) have reference to the value at which similar lands in the vicinity are assessed and adjust the assessment of the land to make it equitable with that of similar lands in the vicinity if such an adjustment would result in a reduction of the assessment of the land.

Further Powers of the ARB

The powers of the ARB in respect of an appeal are stated in section 45:

Upon an appeal with respect to an assessment, the Assessment Review Board may review the assessment and, for the purpose of the review, has all the powers and functions of the assessment corporation in making an assessment, determination or decision under this Act, and any assessment, determination or decision made on review by the Assessment Review Board shall be deemed to be an assessment, determination or decision of the assessment corporation and has the same force and effect.

Applications to the Superior Court of Justice

Applications to the Superior Court of Justice for certain situations are discussed in section 46 but note subsection 46(6) which states, "Despite the fact that a question of the assessment of any person is pending before the Assessment Review Board, the judgment of the Superior Court of Justice or the Divisional Court shall be given effect to and is binding upon the Board." In other words, the decision of the Divisional Court will bind the ARB.

Limitation on Defences

Section 49 is the last section that involves ARB:

No matter that could have been raised by way of appeal to the [ARB] or in a proceeding with respect to an assessment in a court within the times limited for bringing the appeal or proceeding under this Act shall be raised by way of defence in any proceeding brought by or on behalf of a municipality or, in the case of land in non-municipal territory, by the Minister.

The *Municipal Act*

All the situations involving the ARB under the *City of Toronto Act* are covered under the *Municipal Act*, which deals with the municipalities generally, thus including the municipality of Toronto.

Taxes on Eligible Property — Comparables

The first provision is section 331, which deals with taxes on eligible property to be taxed at the same level as comparable properties (ss. 331(1)). The four steps the municipality is to use to determine the municipal and school taxes for eligible properties are set out in subsection 331(2) and in accordance with section 329. Under subsection 331(6), MPAC "shall identify six comparable properties with respect to an eligible property for the purposes of this section or, if there are fewer than six comparable properties, as many comparable properties as there are" and provide immediately the list of comparable properties to the municipality (ss. 331(8)) so that the city can determine the taxes in accordance with the section.

Pursuant to subsection 331(9), the municipality shall mail to the owner of each eligible property the list of the comparable properties and the determination made under the section with respect to that eligible property within 60 days after the date the list is received by the municipality. The owner is then given the right to complain to the ARB as stated in subsection 331(11):

> The owner of an eligible property or the local municipality may, within 90 days of the mailing of information under subsection (9), complain to the Assessment Review Board in writing concerning the properties on the list and request that up to six alternative properties be used as comparable properties for the purposes of this section.

There is also a mechanism for the owner to complain to the ARB where MPAC could not provide a list of comparable properties under subsections 331(10) and (12). A complaint to the ARB under either scenario is to be treated in accordance with subsection 331(13) as a complaint under section 40 of the *Assessment Act*. Appeals of decisions from the ARB to Divisional Court on questions of law (ss. 331(14)) are dealt with under section 43.1 of the *Assessment Act*. The authority granted to the ARB pursuant to subsection 331(15) is to either identify up to six comparable properties from among the comparable properties (situated in the same municipality as the subject property) proposed by the complainant or by MPAC, or to determine that there are no comparable properties. Once the ARB has made its decision, the municipality under subsection 331(18) shall determine the taxes for municipal and school purposes in accordance with the decision.

Dividing Land into Parcels and Apportioning Taxes

Section 356 involves decisions made by a municipal council in dividing land into parcels (ss. (1)(a)) and apportioning the taxes on application of either the municipal treasurer or the owner of the land (ss. (1)(b)). Within 14 days of the municipal council making its decision, pursuant to subsection (5), it shall give a notice to the applicant and/or owner of the decision and state the last date to appeal the decision; within 35 days after the decision, the applicant and/or owner may appeal the municipal council's decision with respect to the apportionment of taxes to the ARB (ss. (6)) by filing a notice of appeal with the registrar of the ARB. Under subsection (7), upon giving notice to the appellant and/or owner and the municipal treasurer, the ARB shall hear the appeal and apportion the taxes under subsection (1)(b). Since the municipality is also given the power under subsection (8) to pass a by-law to delegate the authority to make the determination to apportion taxes directly rather than going through the municipal council, in such case a certified copy of such by-law shall be forwarded to the registrar of the ARB and MPAC, as well as a copy of every application to which the by-law applies in accordance with subsection (9). **If you are dealing with a municipality under section 356, check to see if the municipality has passed the requisite by-law to determine if you should proceed to the municipal council or directly to the ARB. Note, the decision of the ARB with respect to subsection (1)(b) as well as municipal council's decision with respect to subsections (1)(a) and (c) are final (ss. 356(10)), which means that this is a privative clause.** Copies of the decisions by the ARB and municipal council are to be forwarded to the municipal treasurer and MPAC under subsection (11), and pursuant to subsection (12), the municipal treasurer shall immediately adjust the tax roll in accordance to the decisions made.

Cancellation, Reduction, or Refund of Taxes — s. 357 and s. 334

The ARB also reviews decisions that involve cancellation, reduction, or refund of taxes set out in subsection 357(1) including subsection (d.1), where the applicant is unable to pay taxes due to sickness or extreme poverty. On or before February 28 of the year following the year in which the application is made (ss. (3)) or other deadline per subsection (4), on application to and filed with the municipal treasurer by the owner of the land or another interested person as set out in subsection (2), the municipality can cancel, reduce, or refund taxes on eight circumstances detailed in subsection (1). Municipal council can have a meeting, make its decision under subsection (5), give notice of its decision under subsection (6) and allow the applicant to appeal the decision to the ARB under subsection (7). It can also delegate the power to make a decision to the ARB by by-law under subsection (11). If a by-law is passed, a certified copy of such by-law shall be forwarded by municipal council to the registrar of the ARB and MPAC as well as a copy of every application to which the by-law applies in accordance with subsection (12). **If you are dealing with a municipality under section 357, check to see if the municipality has passed the requisite by-law to determine if you should proceed to municipal council or directly to the ARB. Note that the decision of the ARB is final (ss. (17)), which means that this is a privative clause.** Copies of the decisions by the ARB and municipal council are to be forwarded to MPAC under subsection (18). Furthermore, note that under section 334 an application to the municipal treasurer for cancellation, reduction, or refund of taxes levied *with respect to the year in which the application is made* may be made by a person who was overcharged by reason of a gross or manifest error that is a clerical error — the transposition of figures, a typographical error, or similar type of error in the calculation of taxes, using the same procedure as set out in section 357.

Cancellation, Reduction, or Refund of Taxes — s. 358

On the other hand, taxes that were overcharged *in one or both of the two years preceding the year in which the application is made* and the overcharge was caused by a gross or manifest error in the preparation of the assessment roll that is clerical or factual in nature, including the transposition of figures, typographical errors or similar errors, but not an error in judgment in assessing the property, are dealt with in section 358 rather than section 357. The application to the municipal treasurer to cancel, reduce, or refund the taxes can be made only pursuant to subsection (2) by the owner of the land or another interested person as set out in subsection 357(2). The timing to bring the application is set out in subsections (3) and (4), subject to a further restriction of no application if the circumstance of subsections (5) exists. Under subsection (6), the municipal treasurer is to send a copy of the application to MPAC and the registrar of the ARB. Municipal council can either have a hearing to decide the application pursuant to subsection (9) or pass a by-law delegating power to the ARB to hear the application directly under subsection (12).

Increase of Taxes — s. 359 and s. 337

Section 359 allows for an application to be made by the municipal treasurer for the municipality to increase taxes levied on land in the year the application is made to the extent of any undercharge caused by a gross or manifest error that is a clerical or factual error, including the transposition of figures, a typographical or similar error, but not an error in judgment in assessing the land. The deadline for the application is set out in subsection (2.1), and the application cannot be made if the circumstance set out in subsection (2) occurs. Municipal council can either have a hearing to decide the application pursuant to subsection (3) or pass a by-law delegating power to the ARB to hear the application directly under subsection (8). **If you are dealing with a municipality under section 359, check to see if the municipality has passed the**

requisite by-law to determine if you should proceed to municipal council or directly to the ARB. If there is no by-law, the municipal council holds a meeting on the application, gives notice of its decision under subsection (4), and allows the affected land owner to appeal the decision to the ARB under subsection (5).

Where a person is undercharged taxes as set out in section 337, the procedure detailed in section 359 applies. **The decision of the ARB is final (ss. (11)), which means that this is a privative clause.** Also note that if there is a calculation error as described in subsection 359.1(1), the municipal council will hold a meeting under subsection (2) and an appeal can be made pursuant to subsection (4) to the ARB in accordance with subsections 359(5) to (7).

Rebates on Taxes Due to Vacant Portions of Property — s. 364

Section 364 deals with the procedure involving rebates on taxes to owners of properties, in any of the commercial or industrial classes defined in subsection 308(1), that have vacant portions, and that procedure ultimately can involve the ARB. Applications can be made for a rebate if the tax rebate program meets the six requirements enumerated in subsection (2). Within 120 days after the municipality mails to the applicant its determination of the rebate (ss. (14)), the applicant can make written complaint to the ARB. The applicant can also file a complaint with the ARB if the municipality fails to make a determination 120 days after receiving the application (ss. (15)). The ARB shall determine the amount of the rebate under subsection (16). **Note that subsection (18) allows an appeal of the ARB decision on a question of law to the Divisional Court, and, therefore, there is no complete privative clause.**

If the municipality determines that a rebate, or any portion of the rebate, made under subsection (22), has been paid in error, the municipality, subject to the time limit set out in subsection (23), may notify the owner of the property on which the rebate was made the amount of the overpayment. Upon so doing, the overpaid amount shall have priority lien status and shall be added to the tax roll. The owner of the property who was sent a notice of overpayment of the rebate has the right under subsection (24) to make written complaint to the ARB that the rebate was properly payable.

The *City of Toronto Act*

The *City of Toronto Act* is derived from the *Municipal Act*; therefore, both are very similar, as the reader will discover when reviewing both.

Purpose

One of the purposes of the *City of Toronto Act* is to determine the appropriate levels of spending and taxation for the City of Toronto. In order to help with such determination, the legislation gives the right to complain or appeal many situations that establish the assessment roll and thereby help to decide the appropriate levels of municipal taxation. The forum for such complaints and appeals is often the ARB. The following are various provisions of the legislation that give authority or jurisdiction to the ARB.

Taxes on Eligible Property — Comparables

The first provision is section 294, which deals with taxes on eligible property to be taxed at the same level as comparable properties (ss. 294(1)). The four steps the City is to use to determine municipal and school taxes for eligible properties are set out in subsection 294(2) and in accordance with section 291. To ensure a fair tax level, MPAC is required to provide a list of *six* comparable properties with respect to an eligible property, or as many as there are if fewer than six are available (ss. 294(6)), to the City as soon as practicable (ss. 294(8)) so that the

City can determine the taxes in accordance with the section. Pursuant to subsection 294(9), the City shall mail to the owner of each eligible property the list of the comparable properties and the determination made under the section with respect to that eligible property within 60 days after the date the list is received by the City. The owner is then given the right to complain to the ARB as stated in subsection 294(11):

> The owner of an eligible property or the City may, within 90 days of the mailing of information under subsection (9), complain to the Assessment Review Board in writing concerning the properties on the list and request that up to six alternative properties be used as comparable properties for the purposes of this section.

There is also a mechanism for the owner to complain to the ARB where MPAC could not provide a list of comparable properties under subsections 294(10) and (12). A complaint to the ARB under either scenario is to be treated in accordance with subsection 294(13) as a complaint under section 40 of the *Assessment Act*, and under section 43.1 of the *Assessment Act* for appeals of ARB decisions to Divisional Court on questions of law (ss. 294(14)). The authority granted to the ARB pursuant to subsection 295(15) is either to identify up to six comparable properties (in the City or Municipality of Toronto) from among the comparable properties proposed by the complainant or MPAC or to determine that there are no comparable properties. Once the ARB has made its decision, the City under subsection 294(18) shall determine the taxes for municipal and school purposes in accordance with the decision.

Dividing Land into Parcels and Apportioning Taxes

Section 322 involves city council dividing land into parcels (ss. (3)) and apportioning the taxes on application of either the city treasurer or the owner of the land (ss. (1)). Within 14 days of city council making its decision, city council, pursuant to subsection (4), shall give a notice to the applicant and/or owner of the decision and state the last date to appeal the decision. Within 35 days after the decision, the applicant and/or owner may appeal to the ARB city council's decision with respect to the apportionment of taxes (ss. (5)) by filing a notice of appeal with the registrar of the ARB. Under subsection (6), upon giving notice to the appellant and/or owner and the city treasurer, the ARB shall hear the appeal and apportion the taxes under subsection (1)(b).

Under subsection (7), the City is also given the power to pass a by-law to delegate the authority to make the determination to apportion taxes directly rather than going through city council, and in that case a certified copy of such by-law shall be forwarded to the registrar of the ARB and MPAC, as well as a copy of every application to which the by-law applies in accordance with subsection (8). **There is such a by-law passed at the time of this writing, and the reader should look at it in detail if faced with this situation. Note that the decision of the ARB with respect to subsection (1)(b), as well as city council's decision with respect to subsections (1)(a) and (c) are final (ss. (9)), which means that this is a privative clause.** Copies of the decisions by the ARB and city council are to be forwarded to the city treasurer and MPAC under subsection (10), and the city treasurer shall immediately adjust the tax roll in accordance to the decisions, pursuant to subsection (11).

Cancellation, Reduction, or Refund of Taxes — s. 323 and s. 297

Another situation that involves cancellation, reduction, or refund in taxes is set out in section 323 for the reasons described in subsection 323(1), including subsection (e) due to sickness or extreme poverty. On or before February 28 of the year following the year in which the application is made (ss. (3)) or other deadline per subsection (4), on application to and filed with the city treasurer by the owner of the land or another interested person (ss. (2)), the City can cancel, reduce, or refund taxes in accordance with the eight circumstances detailed in subsection (1). City council can either have a meeting, make its decision under subsection (5), give notice of its decision under subsection (6), and allow the applicant to appeal the decision to the ARB under subsection (6), or delegate the power to make a decision to the ARB by by-law under subsection (11). In accordance with subsection (12), if a by-law is passed, a certified copy of such by-law shall be forwarded by city council to the registrar of the ARB and MPAC, as well as a copy of every application to which the by-law applies. **There is such a by-law passed at the time of this writing and the reader should look at it in detail if faced with this situation. Note that the decision of the ARB is final (ss. (17)), which means that this is a privative clause.** Copies of the decisions by the ARB and city council are to be forwarded to MPAC under subsection (18). Note that under section 297, a person who was overcharged by reason of a gross or manifest error that is clerical, including the transposition of figures, a typographical error or similar type of error, in the calculation of taxes can make an application to the city treasurer for cancellation, reduction, or refund of taxes that were levied *in the year in which the application is made*, using the same procedure as set out in section 323.

Cancellation, Reduction, or Refund of Taxes — s. 325

For overcharges in taxes that occurred *in one or both of the two years preceding the year in which the application is made*, and that were caused by a gross or manifest error in the preparation of the assessment roll that was clerical or factual in nature, including the transposition of figures, a typographical error or similar errors, but not an error in judgment in assessing the property, they are dealt with in section 325 rather than section 323. The application to the city treasurer to cancel, reduce, or refund the taxes can be made only, pursuant to subsection (2), by the owner of the land or another interested person as set out in subsection 323(2). The timing to bring the application is set out in subsections (3) and (4), subject to a further restriction of no application if the circumstance of subsection (5) exists. Under subsection (6), the city treasurer is to send a copy of the application to MPAC and the registrar of the ARB. City council can either have a hearing to decide the application, pursuant to subsection (9), or pass a by-law delegating power to the ARB to hear the application directly, under subsection (11). **The decision of the ARB is final (ss. (14)), which means that this is a privative clause.**

Increase of Taxes — s. 326 and s. 300

Section 326 allows for an application to be made by the city treasurer for the City to increase taxes levied on land in the year in which the application is made to the extent of any undercharge caused by a gross or manifest error that is clerical or factual, including the transposition of figures, a typographical error or similar error, but not an error in judgment in assessing the land. The deadline for the application is set out in subsection (3) and no application can be made if the circumstance set out in subsection (2) occurs. City council can either have a hearing to decide the application, pursuant to subsection (4), or pass a by-law delegating power to the ARB to hear the application directly, under subsection (9). If there is no by-law, city council shall hold a meeting on the application, give notice of its decision, under subsection (5), and allow the applicant to appeal the decision to the ARB, under subsection (6). Where a person is undercharged taxes, as set out in section 300, the procedure detailed in section 326 applies. **The decision of the ARB is final (ss. (12)), which means that this is a privative clause.**

Rebates on Taxes Due to Vacant Portions of Property — s. 331

Section 331 deals with rebates on taxes to owners of properties that are in any of the commercial or industrial classes defined in subsection 275(1) that have vacant portions. Applications can be made for a rebate if the tax rebate program meets the six requirements enumerated in subsection (2), and once the City determines the amount of the rebate, under subsection (14), the applicant can appeal within 120 days after the City mails to the applicant the determination of the rebate. If the City fails to make a determination after 120 days after receipt of the application, under subsection (15), the applicant can make written complaint to the ARB. The ARB, under subsection (16), shall determine the amount of the rebate. **Note that under subsection (17), an appeal lies on a question of law to the Divisional Court from the decision of the ARB and, therefore, there is no complete privative clause.** Subject to the time limit set out in subsection (23), subsection (22) allows the City to rectify errors in the payment of a rebate made under section 331 by notifying the owner of the property of which the rebate was made the overpaid amount. Upon so doing, the overpaid amount will have priority lien status and will be added to the tax roll. The property owner who was sent the notice of overpayment of the rebate has the right under subsection (24) to make written complaint to the ARB that the rebate was properly payable. Section 40 of the *Assessment Act* applies to the complaints made under section 331 of the *City of Toronto Act* except that MPAC is not a party to the complaint.

The *Education Act*

As noted earlier, subsection 16(3) of the *Assessment Act* states that any person can apply in a form approved by the Minister of Finance to MPAC to have his or her name included or altered in the assessment roll as a specific kind of school supporter under the *Education Act*. Subsections 16(9) and (10) then allow that person to make a complaint to the ARB about MPAC's decision. Similar provision is included in section 236, which allows a person, on application to MPAC under s. 16 of the *Assessment Act*, to have their name included or altered on the assessment roll as a supporter of a specific type of school boards prescribed under s. 257.4. It is in this way that the *Education Act* is connected to the ARB.

The *Provincial Land Tax Act*

This Act also gives jurisdiction to the ARB, to deal with appeals to it on the issue of an annual tax levied pursuant to section 2 as "in the amount determined under section 5 on land that is included in the tax roll for non-municipal territory and that, under the *Assessment Act*, is liable to assessment and taxation". The powers of the ARB in this situation are set out in sections 8 and 9.

RELEVANT REGULATIONS

The review of regulations relevant to the procedures of the ARB (currently only some fees) was done along with the review of the enabling legislation above.

PROCEDURES OF BOARD

The ARB has "RULES OF PRACTICE AND PROCEDURE" (the "ARB Rules") effective April 1, 2009, on its website on the Web page "Legislation and ARB Rules", downloadable on Adobe. As noted in the ARB Rules, they were made under section 25.1 of the *SPPA*, which as noted in a previous chapter, allows an agency to make its own rules. It contains 152 rules. There are comments for some of the rules *"which further explain or provide examples. The [ARB] Rules also have headings, for easier reading. Neither the headings nor the comments are part of the [ARB] Rules".* **Please note because of the leeway given by the ARB Rules to the**

ARB not to follow them, the ARB Rules may not be as specific and binding as they appear to be at first glance but should still be followed unless the ARB advises differently. There are a number of forms appearing in various areas of the ARB website. The ARB Rules and the forms shall be discussed in summary fashion and in varying detail below, but the reader should only rely on her/his own reading and interpretation of both rather than relying on the author's. Please note that the procedures in the enabling legislation also are applicable as is the *SPPA* where noted in the ARB Rules.

RULES

General (Rs. 1–5)
The ARB Rules are applicable to all proceedings before the ARB but the attachments to the ARB Rules are for convenience and should be updated (R. 1). There are definitions of 30 words or terms used in the ARB Rules (R. 2). Those definitions must be referenced when looking at the ARB Rules to fully understand their meaning. The ARB Rules are to be liberally interpreted to ensure the just, most expeditious, and least expensive determination of every proceeding on its merits (R. 3). If the ARB Rules do not cover a procedure, the ARB may do what is necessary and permitted by law to decide a matter (R. 4). Substantial compliance of requirements in respect of content of forms, notices, and documents under ARB Rules or any Act is sufficient (R. 5).

Relief from Rules (Rs. 6–7)
The parties must consent before the ARB can permit exceptions from the procedural requirements contained in legislation (R. 6). The ARB may allow exceptions to the ARB Rules, or grant other relief it considers appropriate, to ensure real questions in issue are determined in a just manner (R. 7).

Non-compliance (Rs. 8–10)
If a party or a participant refuses or fails without reasonable excuse to follow the ARB Rules, etc., the ARB may, after giving the defaulting person an opportunity to cure the default and after considering issues of prejudice and abuse of process, make orders set out therein, including dismissing the matter (Rs. 8 and 9) provided that if an applicant, without reasonable excuse, does not attend at a hearing, the ARB, where it considers appropriate, can dismiss the matter summarily (R. 10).

Representatives (Rs. 11–13)
A party may attend in person or by a representative and if the representative is not licensed by the LSUC must obtain a written authorization to so act, which the ARB may request at any time (R. 11). Notice to a representative is deemed to be given to the client (R. 12). Pursuant to R. 13, where a party or representative is in a hearing event, such person may be both advocate and witness in the direct hearing stream unless otherwise ordered by the ARB. In the case-managed stream, such person may be both advocate and witness unless the ARB orders otherwise, and the representative is not a lawyer appearing as counsel. If the representative is appearing in both roles, notice must be given to the other parties at least 21 days prior to the hearing event.

Time (Rs. 14–17)

Unless otherwise stated, time under the ARB Rules or in an ARB order is computed under the applicable law (R. 14). The ARB may extend or reduce any time required in the ARB Rules or an ARB order with any terms and conditions either by motion or on its own initiative (R. 15). If written consent is given by all those to be served, time for delivery of a document may be extended or reduced (R. 16). The ARB will not proceed with a hearing at the time for commencement for at least 10 minutes after for an electronic hearing and at least 30 minutes after for an in-person hearing (R. 17).

Extension of Time for Request for Reconsideration (R. 18)

The ARB may extend the time for filing a request for reconsideration with MPAC, if in its view, the circumstances set out in the request by the appellant provide sufficient reasons.

Initiating Procedures (Rs. 19–21)

Unless any statutes or the ARB Rules provide or the ARB directs otherwise, an appeal may be commenced by letter or an Appeal Form containing the requirements listed in R. 19, including the appropriate fee, unless the ARB directs otherwise (R. 21). Notwithstanding rule 19, persons filing appeals for many persons and/or many properties must file them in accordance with the directions of the ARB with specific provisions applying to third party complaints under the *Provincial Land Tax Act, 2006*, the *Municipal Act, 2001*, and the *City of Toronto Act, 2006* (R. 20).

Screening of Appeals (Rs. 22–29)

Administrative screening, that is the ARB staff stop processing an appeal because the information submitted is not complete until the technical defect is corrected, shall be conducted by the ARB on the six factors set out in R. 22. If the information submitted is not complete, the ARB will stop processing the appeal and will only continue processing once considered complete by the ARB's established requirements (R. 23). Before rejecting an incomplete application, the ARB will notify the party and provide an opportunity to respond within the time set out in the notification (R. 24) unless the request for information is dispensed with under R. 25. Once an incomplete appeal is amended, the amended appeal and further materials shall be provided to the other parties and the ARB (R. 26). If the appeal was corrected within the stated time, the appeal will be deemed properly filed on the day it was initially received (R. 27). A member of the ARB may screen matters and may dismiss them without holding a hearing event if any of the four circumstances set out in R. 28 exist. The ARB will notify the appellant and will provide the appellant opportunity to respond within the time stated in the notification before dismissing any appeal (R. 29).

Late Appeals (R. 30)

Late appeals may be considered by the ARB if the applicant provides the ARB with an affidavit satisfying the ARB of the circumstances set out in clause (a), states that the notice under the appropriate legislation was not received by a certain date, and, as set out in clause (b), the affidavit states the date that the appellant or representative became aware of the matter being appealed.

Notice (Rs. 31–32)

Notices under the ARB Rules or an ARB order are to be in writing unless otherwise directed by ARB (R. 31), and an affidavit must be filed at the beginning of the proceeding to prove that notice was properly given (R. 32).

Special Notices

Notice of Higher Assessment and/or Higher Tax Rate Property Class (Rs. 33–34)

The requirements for notice where a party requests a change in property class to a class with a higher tax rate or an assessment that would result in a higher assessment than that fixed by the MPAC are set out in Rs. 33 and 34.

Notice to Shift Burden of Proof (Reverse Onus) (R. 35)

If MPAC requests that the ARB make a finding to shift the burden of proof over to the appellant as to the correctness of the current value of land under the *Assessment Act*, it must give written notice of it to all the other parties and file the notice with the ARB at least 21 days prior to the hearing.

Notice of Issue Estoppel (R. 36)

If a party intends to raise issue estoppel at a hearing, it must give written notice to the other parties at least 21 days prior to such hearing.

Service (Rs. 37–41)

The six methods of service of notice or a document by one party on another party or person are set out in R. 37 and shall be sent to the persons set out in R. 38. The proof of service requirements are set out in R. 39. Any document served by fax or e-mail after 5:00 p.m. is deemed to have been served on the next business day (R. 40), and if a document is more than 12 pages long, including cover page, it cannot be served by fax unless the person receiving it has given advance permission (R. 41).

Documents, Disclosure Exhibits, Filing (Rs. 42–55)

Documents served on parties and/or filed with the ARB can only be amended in accordance with R. 42, including motions made under R. 43 and the power of the ARB under R. 44. In addition to all other requirements, two copies of each document must be filed with the ARB at the hearing unless there is an ARB direction otherwise (R. 45). In respect of the case-managed stream, certain statements as set out in R. 46 must be filed with the ARB at the time of filing the Certificate of Readiness or, if waived, at least 14 days prior to the hearing. In addition to any requirements of the ARB Rules, the ARB may direct the parties to exchange and file documents and submissions at any time upon a party's request or on its own initiative (R. 47). The time limits for disclosure of documentary evidence intended to be presented at a hearing are set out in R. 48, and if such disclosure does not occur, the ARB may refuse to accept the documents at the hearing. The timelines and requirements in the case-managed stream for expert reports and calling of an expert witness without a report are stated in R. 49 as are the requirements of reply report under R. 50 and a supplemental report in R. 51. One copy of all written arguments must be provided to each panel member and to each party under R. 52. Unless the ARB order provides otherwise, a person may examine any document filed with the

ARB or visual evidence and make copies pursuant to R. 53. The ARB may order that any document filed be treated as confidential (R. 54). Upon request of the person filing it, the ARB may return the exhibit, but only 120 days after the ARB decision is issued or mailed (R. 55).

Discovery (R. 56)

The ARB may grant an order for discovery in manner as set out in clauses (a) to (g) of R. 56 where a party has requested by notice of motion, together with an affidavit detailing the efforts to obtain the desired information, why the information is needed and the fact that the information has been refused or no answer received.

Motions (Rs. 57–64)

A notice of motion, if oral or electronic, requires that a hearing date be obtained and must be submitted with an affidavit setting out a brief statement of the facts by the person swearing the affidavit (R. 57). Unless the ARB agrees to a lesser time, the notice of motion and all supporting documents must be served by the moving party at least 10 days before the oral or telephone conference call or such other times as set out in R. 58 and must also provide an affidavit of such service. A responding party must serve a notice of response if the party intends to do any of the two things mentioned in R. 59. Unless the ARB agrees to a lesser time, the notice of response must be served by the moving party on all parties at least two days before the hearing of the motion as set out in R. 60 and must also provide an affidavit of such service on or before the hearing. Both the moving and responding parties can submit oral evidence at the hearing of the motion during an oral or electronic hearing if permission is requested from the ARB upon filing the motion or response (R. 62). A motion can be made at an oral hearing only if the need for it arises out of events in the hearing, and the procedures for the motion shall be ordered by the presiding member; but generally, if a moving party knows that a motion will be made, it should be served in accordance with R. 57, and the party should request that ARB reduce the time required for service (R. 63). Any person, other than the applicant and any person made a party by statute, who wishes to take part in a proceeding either as a party or a participant must comply with R. 64.

Settlement before ARB Proceedings (Rs. 65–66)

Where the parties reach a settlement before any hearing is held, the ARB may hold a brief hearing into the terms of the settlement, and, if there is compliance with the statutes, the ARB may issue a decision approving it. Further, the parties must either appear at an in-person hearing or submit Minutes of Settlement to the ARB (R. 65). The form and contents of the Minutes of Settlement are set out in R. 66.

Withdrawal of Appeals (Rs. 67–68)

An applicant may, by notice of withdrawal to the ARB and other parties, withdraw the applicant's appeal as set out in clause (a), with leave of the ARB under the jurisdiction granted to it under R. 68, and in clause (b), as of right until the hearing is commenced only, of R. 67.

Compelling Attendance of Witness by Summons (Rs. 69–70)

A party who wishes to require a witness in Ontario to attend an oral or electronic hearing may serve a summons on such person and shall obtain such summons for the ARB by complying with the requirements of and the different situations set out in R. 69. A summons must be personally delivered on the witness together with attendance money at least five days before the time of attendance (R. 70).

Language of Proceedings (Rs. 71–76)

Either English or French — or partly in both or, where requested, sign language interpretation — are the languages the ARB can use to conduct proceedings (R. 71). If a person wants a hearing in whole or in part in French or using sign language interpretation, at least 25 days before the hearing he or she must notify the ARB (R. 72). If a person requires interpretation services in any language other than those set out in R. 71 in order to participate in a hearing or for a witness called by such person, the person must provide a qualified interpreter at the person's expense (R. 73). Under R. 74, a French language or bilingual proceeding shall by presided over by a member or panel who are bilingual. If considered by the ARB as necessary for the fair determination of the matter, written evidence or submissions provided in either English or French could be ordered to be provided by the person in the other language translated by a qualified translator at that person's expense (R. 75). Written decisions and decisions of the ARB for French language or bilingual proceedings will be issued in English and French (R. 76).

Streaming (Rs. 77–83)

In the comments prior to R. 77, there is a discussion of the two types of streams — the direct hearing stream and the case-managed stream — along with what generally happens in each stream and the factors used by the ARB in choosing the appropriate stream.

A matter can be scheduled by the ARB into (a) the direct hearing stream or (b) the case-managed stream (R. 77). If there is a request for reconsideration, an appeal will be put in the direct hearing stream (R. 78). A change of the hearing stream can occur either by a party making a written request with reasons and copied to the other parties no later than 30 days before the issuance of the first Notice of Hearing or by the ARB at any time on its own motion if it considers it appropriate to do so (R. 79). Where the ARB considers that two or more matters are related in ways as set out in R. 80, it may take the actions under the rule. When two or more proceedings are consolidated, the procedures set out in R. 81 occur. When two or more proceedings are heard together but not consolidated, the procedures set out in R. 82 occur. The ARB can separate consolidated proceedings or matters heard together at any time for the reasons set out in R. 83.

Direct Hearing Stream Procedures (Rs. 84–85)

A limited number of pre-hearing conferences may be held in the direct hearing stream without transfer of the appeal into the other stream (note only the ARB by order can transfer an appeal to the other stream) and pre-conference rules apply in accordance with R. 84. A party who requests a pre-hearing conference must do so in accordance with R. 85.

Case-Managed Stream Procedures (Rs. 86–87)

The parties, prior to the pre-hearing conference, must follow one of the three sets of procedures, depending on the circumstances listed in R. 86. The purpose and the outcome of the first pre-hearing conference is set out in R. 87.

Form of Statements (Rs. 88–92)

The content of the Statements of Issues and Responses shall at minimum contain the information set out in R. 88, depending on the issue in question as set out in the rule. The ARB, under R. 89, requires written notification by letter that such statements have been served. Hearings requiring MPAC, the appellant, or the respondent to show cause can occur on the basis of the situations set out in R. 90. At subsequent pre-hearing conferences, the ARB may inquire of the parties what is required of productions and discoveries for the matter to proceed expeditiously and may make an order to that effect under R. 91. The scheduling of subsequent pre-hearing conferences shall occur pursuant to R. 92.

Certificates of Readiness and Objection (Rs. 93–96)

In the case-managed stream, each party shall file with the ARB the appropriate Certificate of Readiness and Certificate of Objection in accordance with R. 93. Upon receipt of a Certificate of Objection or a motion for an extension of time, the ARB shall schedule a pre-hearing conference to deal with the objection or motion and thereafter may issue an order declaring that the matter may proceed (R. 94). No hearing for the purposes of finally resolving an appeal in the case-managed stream shall be scheduled except in accordance with R. 95. Where the parties have not filed their Certificates of Readiness within six months of the issuance of a procedural order and the file appears inactive, the ARB may on its own motion hold a pre-hearing to determine the status of the matter (R. 96).

Adjournments (Rs. 97–101)

Under R. 97, hearing event dates are fixed unless the ARB agrees to an adjournment. If all parties consent, a written request for an adjournment must be given to the ARB as set out in R. 98; however, the ARB may require the parties to attend to argue in person, and the ARB will determine if it shall grant the adjournment. If there is an objection by one party to the adjournment, the requesting party must bring a motion at least 10 days before the hearing event date; but if the adjournment request is fewer than the 10 days before, the requesting party must give notice and motion materials to the ARB and the other parties. If, however, the ARB refuses, the request can be made at the beginning of the hearing event (R. 99). Upon being informed of unavoidable emergencies as set out in R. 100, the ARB will grant last-minute adjournments. Upon the adjournment request, the ARB may order anything set out in R. 101.

Pre-hearing Conferences (Rs. 102–109)

At the request of a party or on its own initiative, the ARB may direct the parties to take part in a pre-hearing conference, which can include all or one of (a) settlement conferences, (b) motions, and (c) preliminary hearing matters in order to accomplish any of the items listed in R. 102. If a party fails to attend the pre-hearing conference in person or by authorized representative, the ARB may proceed without that party and even dismiss the appeal (R. 103). If a party requests to have or to convert a hearing event to such a pre-hearing conference, that party must comply with the provisions of R. 104. Under R. 105, the ARB member presiding may conduct and convert from one of (a) settlement conferences, (b) procedural discussions, and (c) preliminary hearing matters to another with the consent of the parties. The ARB may state in the notice of pre-hearing that the parties be prepared for any or all three. If the ARB is satisfied that a party objects to the same member's presiding at a preliminary portion of a pre-hearing conference after presiding over an ADR event at the pre-hearing, the ARB may set a later date for the preliminary hearing before another member (R. 106). The member conducting the pre-hearing conference may issue any order as set out in R. 107, and such member is bound by the procedural order resulting from the pre-hearing conference unless the member has good reason to vary the order (R. 108). The ARB may convene a status pre-hearing conference at any time under R. 109.

Alternative Dispute Resolution (Rs. 110–119)

Under R. 110, the ARB may direct, on its own accord or at the request of the parties, the parties to take place in an ADR event, which may be oral or electronic and at short notice, even by telephone. The person presiding may make use of any appropriate dispute resolution process to help the parties resolve the issues, provided the parties can, by written advice to the ARB, suggest the most appropriate method. The person presiding will explain the process to be used in accordance with R. 111. If, during the ADR event, the parties do not settle all the issues in dispute, the presiding person may assist the parties in arriving at a statement of agreed facts and remaining issues in an ADR report, which shall be used in accordance with R. 112. Unless otherwise ordered, at least three days before the ADR event date, the parties shall prepare and produce, to the ARB and to the other parties, disclosure as required by R. 113. The procedures and authority granted in respect of an ADR event are set out in R. 114. Unless all parties consent, as detailed in Rs. 115 and 116, an ARB member may not preside at a hearing of issues not resolved at the ADR event that she/he presided. All documents created for or anything said in an ADR event, or any offer to settle, are confidential and cannot be introduced in that or any subsequent proceeding without both the approval of the ARB and the consent of the person who created the document or made the statement. Notes of the presiding person at the ADR event are confidential and that person is not a competent or compellable witness, all in accordance with R. 117. A proposed settlement must satisfy the requirements under the legislation under which the proceeding arises. If the ARB is not satisfied that the proposed settlement does so, it will hold a hearing to hear evidence on that issue in accordance with R. 118. Further to R. 119, when setting hearing dates, the ARB may give priority to matters that have been the subject of an ADR event.

Methods of Holding Hearing Events (Rs. 120–130)

The ARB can hold hearing events or any part of a hearing event orally (in person), electronically, or in written form in accordance with the *SPPA* and the ARB Rules.

Electronic Hearings (Rs. 120–125)

The ARB may hold a hearing event by teleconference or videoconference or other automated means to determine matters as set out in R. 120. In deciding whether to hold a hearing event by automated means, the ARB may consider relevant factors as set out in R. 121. If a party objects to an electronic hearing, it must do so pursuant to R. 122, but if the ARB, in looking at the objection, finds that an electronic hearing will not cause significant prejudice, it may confirm that it will hold the electronic hearing on the original date (R. 123). The ARB may direct the arrangements for the electronic hearing to protect the integrity of the hearing process as set out in R. 124. The requirement for participants in a videoconference hearing is set out in R. 125.

Written Hearings (Rs. 126–130)

The ARB may hold a hearing, in whole or in part, in writing unless a party objects and satisfies the ARB there is good reason for not doing so under R. 126. In determining whether to hold a written hearing, the ARB may look at any relevant factors, such as those as set out in R. 127. If a party objects to an electronic hearing, it must do so pursuant to R. 128. If a written hearing is to be held, the parties are to exchange documents, including the affidavit or something similar required under R. 130, in accordance with the provisions of R. 129.

Conduct of Proceedings (Rs. 131–139)

All hearings shall be open to the public except for determinations as set out in R. 131. Unless the ARB Rules or the appropriate legislation provides differently, the ARB may fix the procedure at a hearing event (R. 132). At the start of the hearing, the ARB will confirm the name of the applicant and the parties **must** confirm the information set out in R. 133 for each property and assessment that is the subject of the hearing. If a party is absent from the hearing event, such party cannot have any part of the event re-opened or recommenced without leave of the ARB under R. 134. Photographic, audio, and video recording of open hearings will be permitted only on the conditions that the ARB considers appropriate (R. 135). A person who wishes to record a proceeding must ask authorization to do so in the manner provided under R. 136, and in considering the request the ARB shall consider such issues as are set out in that rule. If the ARB does approve recording, it shall do so on the conditions set out in R. 137. The recording permitted by the ARB shall be subject to the conditions set out in R. 138. The ARB can withdraw permission to record on the grounds set out in R. 139.

Written Reasons for Decision (R. 140)

A party who requires written reasons for an ARB decision must make such request at the conclusion of the hearing or in writing within 14 days of the end of the hearing, and a party intending to ask for a review of the ARB decision must request written reasons.

Board Decisions (R. 141)

The ARB Registrar will issue a written decision, unless the ARB directs otherwise, and the decision is effective on the date it is released, unless stated otherwise.

Correcting Minor Errors (Rs. 142–144)

Any minor errors in a decision or order, such as those as set out in R. 142, may be corrected by the ARB at any time and without prior notice to the parties, and there is no fee if a party requests this type of correction. But, under R. 143, if a party requests a change that the ARB considers substantive, the ARB will treat such request for review under R. 146. Under R. 144, until the issuance of the decision, no party shall, without notice to and the consent of all other parties to the hearing, undertake communications directly with the presiding member in respect of the hearing following the end of the hearing.

Rehearing (R. 145)

The ARB may order that a matter be reheard if a Notice of Hearing was not issued or a party failed to attend a scheduled hearing because of circumstances outside the control of a party.

Review of a Board Decision/Order (Rs. 146–152)

Under R. 146, the ARB may review all or part of a decision, may confirm, vary, suspend, or cancel the decision and may order a rehearing before a different member. Further, under R. 147, the ARB may consider a request to review a decision if **the party requesting the review has requested written reasons for the decision** and if the information and materials required by R. 148 are provided to the ARB. Also, **note that a request for review does not**

automatically stay the effect of the original decision unless requested and the ARB makes such order. A written request for review shall be made to the Chair of the ARB within 30 days of the issue of the decision of the ARB and shall include the items set out in R. 148. Only if the reasons in the request to review a Board decision convincingly argued that the ARB made an error listed in R. 149 will the ARB hear a motion to review a decision or grant a rehearing without a motion. The ARB will refuse the review motion if any of the procedural situations set out in R. 150 occurs. Various procedures to be followed on the review request are set out in R. 151 and on the motion for review in R. 152.

PRACTICE DIRECTIONS

Practice Direction #1 effective April 1, 2009, is a provision allowing for a transition to new ARB Rules, which are also effective the same date, advising how hearings in the process should be dealt, and stating the following for new appeals: "All appeals for the 2009 and subsequent years will be scheduled into the Direct Hearing Stream or the Case Managed Stream in accordance with the Board's Streaming Strategy — 2009 and Beyond."

FORMS

In order to discuss the forms provided on both the ARB and MPAC websites that are relevant to the reader, it is necessary to discuss them in context. As various forms are largely duplicated, only the first of the connected forms will be discussed in detail, plus a brief description of the related forms. As always, the reader should review all forms necessary to properly comply with the procedures for the particular complaint made under the fact situation and the appropriate legislation.

Request for Assessment Reconsideration by MPAC

> After each reassessment, MPAC sends property owners a Property Assessment Notice that shows the current value of the property as of the valuation date. After property owners have received their Property Assessment Notices, they may request that MPAC reconsider the assessed value of their property, if they believe it is incorrect. The procedure for requesting this reconsideration is described on the Property Assessment Notice itself.

How MPAC does assessments is summarily described in the document entitled "Resolving Assessment Concerns". The form to be used in requesting reconsideration of MPAC assessment is Request for Reconsideration; both are available on MPAC's website. (See Appendix to this chapter for a Request for Reconsideration by MPAC.)

If MPAC agrees to change the assessment as a result of the reconsideration, there is no charge for such reconsideration and also no need to file an appeal with the ARB. However, if MPAC does not agree to change the assessment before the cut-off date for filing complaints with the ARB, an appeal may be filed with the ARB along with the applicable filing fee set out on the ARB Web page entitled "Appeal Process". The Web page discusses the procedure that leads to the appeal stage, how to file appeal forms, and how to request a filing fee refund in three specific instances, using a "Notice of Withdrawal of Complaint, Application or Appeal (R. 38.1) Form", accessible on that page. A series of useful definitions can also be found on the ARB website.

The appeal forms used to get a matter before the ARB are dependent on the legislation and the sections of the legislation. The appeal forms for various legislation are accessible online through the Web page entitled "Filing an Appeal".

Appeal under the Assessment Act

The appeal form for annual (s. 40), omitted (s. 33), and supplementary (s. 34) assessment is included in the Appendix to this chapter along with instructions for filling each out.

The deadline for filing an Annual Assessment appeal is March 31 of the year following the tax year and 90 days from the notice date for other types of assessment. **Note that the section 49 Complaint Form is used only for that year's assessment and for the following four reasons:**

* Value or classification of the property is incorrect.
* Person is wrongly placed on or left off the assessment roll.
* Person is wrongly placed on or left off the assessment roll, regarding school support.
* Where land is divided into different property classes, the allocation of the land into each class is incorrect.

Appeal under the Municipal Act

The appeal forms, which also include instructions and a summary of how to prepare for a hearing event, are accessible on the ARB's website under the Web page entitled "Municipal Act Appeals". The forms for appeal under the *Municipal Act* are as follows:

* Application/Appeal — Apportionment — s. 356 (included in the Appendix to this chapter)
* Complaint — Comparables — s. 331
* Application/Appeal — Sickness or Poverty — s. 357
* Complaint — Vacant Unit Rebate — s. 364
* Application/Appeal — Cancel, Reduce, Refund — ss. 357, 358, 359
* Application/Appeal — Limitation of Taxes — ss. 334, 337

Check with the municipality where the assessment is in dispute to determine if, pursuant to the appropriate section of the *Municipal Act*, a by-law was passed that delegated responsibility to hear the matter directly to the ARB. If such by-law exists, the form is an application; if there is no such by-law, the form is an appeal to the ARB after an unfavourable ruling by the municipal council.

Appeal under the City of Toronto Act, 2006

As the *City of Toronto Act, 2006* has many of the same provisions of the *Municipal Act*, the forms used under both are nearly identical. Set out below are the names of the forms used for assessment disputes in Toronto and found on the Web page "City of Toronto Act Appeals":

* Application/Appeal — Apportionment — s. 322 (See Appendix to this chapter)
* Complaint — Comparables — s. 294
* Application/Appeal — Sickness or Poverty — s. 323
* Complaint — Vacant Unit Rebate — s. 331
* Application/Appeal — Cancel, Reduce, Refund — ss. 323, 325, 326
* Application/Appeal — Limitation of Taxes — ss. 297, 300

Check with the City of Toronto to determine if, pursuant to the appropriate section of the *City of Toronto Act, 2006*, a by-law was passed that delegated responsibility to hear the matter directly to the ARB. If such by-law exists, the form is an application; if there is no such by-law, the form is an appeal to the ARB after an unfavourable ruling by the Toronto council.

A narrative summary of the procedure — from complaint, application, appeal stage to decision — appears on the ARB Web page entitled "Appeal Process". Although useful, reliance should be placed on the relevant sections of the enabling legislation and the ARB Rules for the precise and exact requirements and timelines.

Similarly, a narrative summary of the procedure from the decision stage to possible appeals appears on the Web page entitled "Decisions". Again, although useful, reliance should be placed on the relevant sections of the enabling legislation and the ARB Rules for the precise and exact requirements and timelines.

POLICIES

Due to the *Ontarians with Disabilities Act, 2001* (ODA) and the *Accessibility for Ontarians with Disabilities Act, 2005* (AODA), the cluster of tribunals under ELTO, including the ARB, have instituted an Accessibility Policy. The reader should review the Accessibility Policy if needed. There are "Vision Mission Values" statements for MPAC on its website, which is relevant in dealing with MPAC in the following areas: (i) the initial assessment, (ii) a request for reconsideration, and (iii) as an opposing party before the ARB.

EXPLANATORY LITERATURE FROM THE BOARD

The ARB website provides various useful online literature to assist the reader with the ARB's process.

1. "Filing an Assessment Appeal" brochure explains in layman's terms the procedure of filing various complaints with the ARB. (See Appendix to this chapter).

2. On the Web page entitled "Hearing Process" is a pamphlet "Preparing for your hearing" which explains the procedure of hearings before the ARB in layman's terms. (See Appendix to this chapter).

3. On the Web page entitled "Municipal Act Appeals" are an "Information Sheet" which explains in layman's terms appeals under the *Municipal Act* and a sheet of "FAQ" that lists commonly asked questions and answers regarding such appeals.

4. On the Web page entitled "City of Toronto Appeals" are an "Information Sheet" which explains in layman's terms appeals under the *City of Toronto Act* and a sheet of "FAQ" that lists commonly asked questions and answers regarding such appeals.

5. On the Web page entitled "Annual Reports" are the Annual Reports for each of the years 1999–2000 to 2008–2009. The Annual Reports contain that year's chair's message, the ARB overview, operations for that year, financials for the ARB and a listing including original appointment date of the members of the ARB.

6. On the Web page entitled "Filing an Appeal" is Information Sheet #3 discussing what one needs to know in filing an appeal with the ARB. (See Appendix to this chapter).

7. There are electronic services available on the website to determine when a matter is being heard and its status upon providing certain information on the site.

RELEVANT CASES AND/OR DECISIONS

The cases and decisions discussed below are not meant to be exhaustive and are only those found in the spring of 2008. They should not be relied upon as legal opinion but are, rather, the author's viewpoint. The reader must continue to update and research cases and decisions, and briefing by the reader should be done in any event.

Fourteen recent matters, including cases from the Ontario Court of Appeal (C.A.), the Divisional Court (Div. Ct.), and before one judge of the Superior Court of Justice (Sup. Ct. J.), as well as decisions of the ARB, are discussed in chronological order with the oldest one first (unless the case is one in a series, in which case the discussion will begin with the lowest level court to the highest). The selection is intended to give the reader a sampling of how these cases and decisions have been decided and their relevance to the ARB. Not every case discussed is a ground-setting decision; however, the review should give the reader some idea of how the ARB and the courts have dealt with various procedural and substantive issues in the first decade of the 21st century.

Ambler v. Municipal Property Assessment Corp., Region No. 7

In the ARB decision of *Ambler v. Municipal Property Assessment Corp., Region No. 7*, [2005] O.A.R.B.D. No. 643, File No. 44733, Hearing No. 106795, Complaint Nos. 1661382, 1688295, 1734038, 1734061 (the *Ambler* ARB decision), the issue was whether the subject property should be classified entirely in the Industrial Property class or whether a portion of it should be classified in the Commercial Property class. Based on the facts and the legislation, specifically, subsection 5(2)(b) of O. Reg. 282/98, the ARB held that the classification should be entirely in the Industrial Property class. Leave to appeal the *Ambler* ARB decision was moved in *Ambler v. Municipal Property Assessment Corp., Region No. 7*, [2006] O.J. No. 2124, 24 M.P.L.R. (4th) 95, 148 A.C.W.S. (3d) 520, 2006 CarswellOnt 3258 (the *Ambler* leave case). In this 2006 motion hearing, the Superior Court of Justice looked at the facts and detailed what happened at the ARB hearing (more than what is discussed in the *Ambler* ARB decision). The judge held that in order for leave to appeal to be granted generally, the moving party must satisfy the court with the following:

(a) there is some reason to doubt the correctness of the Board's decision; and
(b) the point of law is of sufficient importance to merit the attention of the Divisional Court.

Municipal Property Assessment Corp. v. Minto Developments Inc., [2002] O.A.R.B.D. No. 253 leave to appeal to Div. Ct. granted, [2003] O.J. No. 404 (QL).

Ontario Property Assessment Corp. v. Praxair Canada Inc., [2001] O.A.R.B.D. No. 110, leave to appeal to Divisional Court granted, [2001] O.J. No. 2200 (Div. Ct.) (QL).

1098478 Ontario Ltd. v. Ontario Property Assessment Corp. Region No. 11, [1999] O.A.R.B.D. No 129 (2001), leave to appeal to Div. Ct. granted, [2000] O.J. No. 2050 (QL).

Based on the submissions of both parties, the court held that there was doubt of the correctness of the ARB decision on the following:

(a) [The ARB] dwelt on a section 5 analysis before dealing with the section 6 analysis [of O. Reg. 282/98]. In my view that ought to have been reversed and a different decision may have been made.
(b) [The ARB] treated the two lessees as being one corporation. This is contrary to well established law on the subject. The fact that the companies had the same directors and officers, does not necessarily clothe them with the same commercial interest.

The judge was also satisfied that the case dealt with important issues sufficient to warrant granting leave as the legislation was, at that time, relatively recent and should have Div. Ct. jurisprudence. The *Ambler* ARB decision was appealed and heard at the Divisional Court in 2007: *Ambler v. Municipal Property Assessment Corp., Region No. 7*, [2007] O.J. No. 1672, 224 O.A.C. 54, 157 A.C.W.S. (3d) 18 (the *Ambler* Div. Ct. case). The court held that the ARB "erred in law in failing to interpret and apply s. 6(1) of O. Reg. 282/98 under the *Assessment Act*, R.S.O. 1990, c. A.31, to determine whether the portion of the building used by Swish fell within that provision". After reviewing the findings of fact of the ARB that Swish had no involvement in manufacturing, the court found the following:

> Given the Board's findings of fact, the Board erred in holding that the entire property fell within the industrial property class. Had the Board given proper consideration to the language of s. 6(1), the Board should have concluded that the portion of the property used by Swish fell within the commercial property class.

Based on this finding, the court allowed the appeal and, instead of referring the matter back to the ARB, used its power under section 44 of the *Assessment Act* to order the Swish portion of the property to be classified under the Commercial Property class.

Chong v. Municipal Property Assessment Corp., Region No. 14

Chong v. Municipal Property Assessment Corp., Region No. 14, [2005] O.A.R.B.D. No. 337, File No. 39783, Hearing No. 102993, Complaint Nos. 1716292, 1736933 (the *Chong* ARB decision) dealt with the issue of how nuisance factors on property, such as a hydrant, a watermain valve, a sewer grate at the bottom of the driveway, and a school sign on the other side of the driveway affect the value of the property, and whether an adjustment should be made in the assessment. The ARB heard evidence from both parties about comparable properties as the property value was assessed using the Sales Comparison Approach. The presiding member of the ARB also looked at the definition of "current value" as well as subsection 19(1) and subsection 44(2) of the *Assessment Act* and held that subsection 19(1), which states that assessment is based on current value, is paramount to subsection 44(2), which looks at values of similar properties. Based on that finding, the ARB concluded "that there is no better evidence of current value of a property than actual evidence of what a willing buyer paid to a willing seller for the subject property or comparable properties in the required time frame". After looking at comparable properties sold during the relevant period of time, the ARB confirmed the MPAC assessment:

> In this case, the Board looked for evidence to support the complainant's position that a series of nuisance factors negatively affect the value of his property. The Board must be persuaded that the nuisance has resulted in a loss of market value. However, it found none. The Board relies on the sales of similar properties in order to arrive at a value for a property that did not sell in the base year of 2003 or shoulder years of 2002 and 2004. The Board finds that the evidence does not support a finding that the assessment of the subject property is incorrect. The evidence of sales suggests the property is correctly assessed.

The homeowner made a motion for leave to appeal in *Chong v. Municipal Property Assessment Corp., Region No. 14*, [2006] O.J. No. 2126, 148 A.C.W.S. (3d) 514, to the Superior Court of Justice (the *Chong* leave case). An interesting preliminary matter was raised in the motion regarding whether the homeowner who initially brought an application for judicial review of the *Chong* ARB decision, could then bring the motion for leave to appeal well after the 30-day requirement in the legislation. The application for judicial review failed for the following reason:

> The full panel of the Divisional Court dismissed his application for judicial review on the basis that a statutory appeal route was available, and in the absence of exceptional circumstances, the full panel did not have discretion to hear this application.

Even though it could be argued that the homeowner should be estopped from bringing the motion for leave to appeal after his application for a judicial review failed, the judge found there was no prejudice that would accrue to the respondents should the motion be allowed to proceed and be heard. The homeowner stated that the ARB "in arriving at its decision, broke laws, abused its statutory powers and ignored his concerns. He itemized a number of specific complaints in support of his position". The court noted that there can only be an appeal of the ARB decision on a question of law pursuant to section 43.1 of the *Assessment Act*:

> There is a 2-pronged test for granting leave to appeal being, first, whether there is some reason to doubt the correctness of the decision of the Board and, second, whether the decision involves a point of law of sufficient importance to merit the attention of the Divisional Court. (*Mullabrack Inc. v. Ontario Property Assessment Corp., Region No. 16*, [2001] O.J. No. 1047 (Div. Ct.).)

The court held that the test for granting leave had not been met as the motion does not raise a question of law.

> The Board is required to determine the correct current value after hearing the evidence and submissions of the parties. The reasons demonstrate that the Board heard the parties and that there was evidence upon which the Board could make its decision. In any event, the determination of the correctness of the current value is a question of fact. There is no appeal from factual determinations.

Arguments raised regarding bias of the presiding member of the ARB and an OMB decision not being followed were insufficient to support the motion as was the refusal of the ARB not to allow a recording of the hearing:

> There is no statutory or common-law requirement that the Board arrange to record the proceedings before it. Rule 105 of the Board's rules provides for the recording and transcription of the Board's proceedings. With leave of the Board, any party may arrange for a qualified verbatim reporter to attend at the parties own expense for the purpose of recording all testimony. Chong did not arrange for a qualified verbatim reporter to attend at his expense, notwithstanding his stated intention that he wanted the proceedings recorded. He did not request leave from the Board to arrange for such a reporter to attend at his own expense.

Further allegations of negligence by the assessor and MPAC were considered without foundation. The motion was therefore dismissed.

Thousand Island Tax/Duty Free Store Ltd. v. Municipal Property Assessment Corp.

Thousand Island Tax/Duty Free Store Ltd. v. Municipal Property Assessment Corp., [2006] O.J. No. 924, 28 M.P.L.R. (4th) 92, 208 O.A.C. 78, 146 A.C.W.S. (3d) 588, 2006 CarswellOnt 1406 (the *Thousand Island* case) is a 2006 Div. Ct. case involving a stated case put to the court by the ARB under section 43 of the *Assessment Act* and is discussed here as an example of the practice of stating a case allowed by the legislation. The ARB is given the power under the legislation to frame questions of law for the court to answer and based upon the decision of the court to deal with complaints or applications/appeals before it. In this case, the ARB posed two questions to the court:

1. Does the use of the direct capitalization of income methodology (the "income method") in valuing duty free stores result in the valuation of the properties in question contrary to the general provisions of the Act which mandate only the valuation of real property as defined in sections 1 and 3 of the *Assessment Act*?

2. If the answer to (a) is yes, do ss. 3(2) and (3) of the *Assessment Act* preclude the use of the income method of valuation and mandate in its place the use of the depreciated replacement cost plus land methodology or any other specific method of valuation for duty free stores located on the land of a bridge or tunnel authority at an international crossing?

The court answered "no" to the first question, and therefore it did not answer the second question. In arriving at the decision, the court determined that the issue before it "is whether revenue solely attributable to the use of the bridge or tunnel can be considered in the assessment of the duty free stores". In looking at the relevant legislation, the court stated that there was no general provision directing the assessor to use any particular methodology in determining current value and, therefore, the appropriate method to determine current value is a question of fact for the ARB, pursuant to *Municipal Property Assessment Corporation v. Inmet Mining Corp.*, [2002] O.J. No. 3540 (Div. Ct.) at para. 14. The court held that the income approach taken by MPAC in respect of the facts was not appropriate.

UniRoyal Goodrich Holdings Inc. v. Municipal Property Assessment Corp., Region No. 21

UniRoyal Goodrich Holdings Inc. v. Municipal Property Assessment Corp., Region No. 21, [2006] O.A.R.B.D. No. 130, File No. 44880, Hearing No. 103266, Complaint Nos. 10911, 31291, 1196216, 1332431, 1413211, 1413212, 1413213, 1413214, 1426705, 1426706 (the *UniRoyal* ARB decision) focused on sections 33, 34, and 40 complaints under the *Assessment Act*. The issue before the ARB was the determination of the classification of certain warehouses and structures located on the specific property. The structures were classified as "Large Industrial Property" and the complainant wanted to change the classification to "Commercial Property" due to a change in O. Reg. 282/98 under sections 5, 6, and 14.

The ARB heard expert witnesses from both parties on the uses of the warehouses and the classifications under the regulation, as well as having a site visit of the structures. The ARB stated that inherent in the change to the regulation "is the issue of separation of any warehouse facilities vis-à-vis the manufacturing areas". The ARB found as a fact that the warehouses are separated from each other and from the manufacturing areas by a series of firewalls and then stated the following:

> The Board finds that because of the firewalls and the independent support walls that support the roofs of each of the warehouses and the manufacturing facility, each warehouse is a separate independent building from the other. This finding is supported by two definitions the Board was made aware of, the definition of "building" contained in the Ontario Building Code and the dictionary definition of "building". Subsection 5(2) of the Classification Reg., as amended, introduces the word "building" into the classification analysis but nowhere in the *Assessment Act* or supporting Regulations is there any attempt to define the word "building". The Board, therefore, adopts both the Ontario Building Code and the dictionary definition as a guideline in defining "building".

The ARB then continued with the following:

> The Board must also address the issue of "minimal linkage". The Board heard evidence from both sides on the issue of linkage as it relates to the openings in the fire doors and the transfer of tires from the manufacturing plant to the warehouse area. The Board does not consider the linkage to be even minimal, given the fact that the fire

> doors are part of the firewall and an independent structure that separates three of the four warehouse areas and the manufacturing plant from each other. Based upon all of the evidence, the Board is satisfied that the four warehouses may possibly comply with the requirements set out in section 5 of the Classification Reg., and may be eligible to be classified in the Commercial Property Class.
>
> To complete the determination of the proper classification, the Board must individually look at each separate area and determine if all of the requirements of section 5 have been met.

The ARB then looked at each warehouse in question in relation to the evidence relating to each and found that warehouses #3 and #4 were separate buildings, did not contain manufacturing, and therefore fit within the "Commercial Property Class". The ARB found warehouses #1 and #2 were one building, and although the "whitewall protectorant application" was not a manufacturing process, the "nailguard operation" was and therefore would be classified as "Large Industrial Property Class".

In this case, the ARB only made a determination of the property tax classes that apply to the warehouses for the years under complaint. The Board was advised at the hearing by the parties that they had reached an agreement on the current value of the property and the apportionment of the current value between the buildings and structures. The Board was aware that "Minutes of Settlement with respect to the total current value for each complaint and the apportionment of the value between the buildings and structures for each complaint either had or would be executed." The apportionments were received from the parties and attached to the decision as Schedule "A".

MPAC made a motion for leave to appeal to the Superior Court of Justice in *UniRoyal Goodrich Holdings Inc. v. Municipal Property Assessment Corp., Region No. 21*, [2007] O.J. No. 1233, 156 A.C.W.S. (3d) 517 (the *UniRoyal* leave case). The grounds for the appeal were that the ARB erred in classifying warehouses #3 and #4 and the firewalls in the Commercial Property Class. The court started with the test for a leave case:

> The test on a motion for leave to appeal is twofold: is there good reason to doubt the correctness of the tribunal's decision and is there a question of law of sufficient importance to merit the attention of the Divisional Court (*1098748 Ontario Ltd. v. Ontario Property Assessment Corporation, Region No. 11*, [2000] O.J. No. 2050 (Div. Ct.) at para. 22).

The judge looked at the evidence before the ARB and the interpretation of subsection 5(2) and said the determination was based largely on a finding of fact and that the conclusion made by the presiding member was correct. As to the submission that the reasons of the ARB were inadequate, the court held that "the reasons are adequate and meet the requirements in *Gray v. Director of the Ontario Disability Support Program* (2002), 59 O.R. (3d) 364 (Ont. C.A.) (the *Gray* case). They deal with the issues, make appropriate findings of fact and explain the result". The court also stated that the ARB, in the classification of the firewalls, while not specifically requested by the parties and although the ARB may have erred in not giving notice before dealing with the issue, was not doubted in the correctness of the classification. The motion was therefore dismissed.

Toronto (City) v. 28 Goldene Way

In the ARB decision of *Toronto (City) v. 28 Goldene Way*, [2007] O.A.R.B.D. No. 640, File No. 59346A, Hearing No. 130586, Application No. 1785420 (the *Goldene* decision), an application was made to the ARB under subsection 356(1) of the *Municipal Act* to apportion unpaid taxes for a tax year. The issues before the ARB were as follows:

1. Are there unpaid taxes for taxation year 2002 on the land which had roll number 1904-094-240-00200-0000 ("parent roll number")?
2. If there are unpaid taxes for taxation year 2002 on the parent roll number, should they be apportioned among the twenty-two subject parcels created out of the parent roll number ("child roll numbers"), in proportion to their relative value when the assessment roll for taxation year 2002 was returned, or in any other manner?

In this particular situation, the City of Toronto, through a by-law, delegated power to hear application in respect of apportionment claims under section 356 to the ARB to hear such a complaint, which is why this is an application and not an appeal to the ARB. The ARB found that there were unpaid taxes by the builder and that the builder defaulted in paying the taxes when selling various homes to the subsequent owners. The ARB recognized that the word "may" in subsection 359(1) means that the power to apportion the taxes is discretionary. In noting the problems in collecting the unpaid taxes from the builder and expressing sympathy to the subsequent owners, the ARB held "that it would be better to avoid the unpleasantness, uncertainties, delays and expense of such Court proceedings, by apportioning the unpaid taxes equitably among the 22 child roll numbers in proportion to their relative values as determined by MPAC".

Vadala v. Municipal Property Assessment Corp., Region No. 26

In *Vadala v. Municipal Property Assessment Corp., Region No. 26*, [2007] O.A.R.B.D. No. 727, File No. DM 195, Hearing No. 135021, Complaint Nos. 1699881, 1699882 (the *Vadala* decision), a motion for review was made under R. 114 of the ARB Rules, alleging that the ARB had acted outside its jurisdiction in the original decision. The *Vadala* decision is noted here as an example of a request for the ARB to reconsider its decision. The problem, which led to the request to review, hinged on whether the municipality, Lambton Shores, or the County of Lambton properly brought the complaint to the ARB. Although the property owners complained, two panels of the ARB increased the taxes and allowed the complainant to make the complaint. The ARB ruling on the motion for review denied the motion because, in working through the chain of events, it found that the county properly made the complaint (ratifying the actions of a delegate) and, therefore, that there was no issue of the ARB acting outside its jurisdiction in allowing the complaint to proceed.

Franklin Sandblasting and Painting Ltd. v. Municipal Property Assessment Corp., Region No. 25

In the ARB decision of *Franklin Sandblasting and Painting Ltd. v. Municipal Property Assessment Corp., Region No. 25*, [2007] O.A.R.B.D. No. 766, File No. 64051, Hearing No. 137218, Appeal No. 1713321 (the *Franklin Sandblasting* decision), the applicant made an appeal under section 357 of the *Municipal Act* regarding reduction of taxes. The property in question contained a structure with an office and a shop, of which 50% was destroyed by fire. The applicant rented other premises during the seven months that it took to rebuild and made application to city council to reduce the taxes. City council reduced the taxes for a lesser amount than was requested on the basis that the property being assessed at current value should be reduced but should not be zero as contended. The ARB justified its decision in denying the appeal in the following statement: "Taxes are calculated based on current value and it makes sense to the Board that any reduction and refund should be calculated based upon the change to the current value."

Rudell v. Municipal Property Assessment Corp., Region No. 25

In *Rudell v. Municipal Property Assessment Corp., Region No. 25*, [2007] O.A.R.B.D. No. 776, File No. 64303A, Hearing No. 138407 (the *Rudell* decision), complaints were made to the ARB regarding the proper assessment of nine properties on the Bruce peninsula. MPAC produced a list of comparable properties for the ARB to look at and determine current value under sections 19 and 44 of the *Assessment Act*. The complainants used two ads in two newspapers as their comparable properties sold. The ARB stated the following finding:

> The Board does not agree with Mr. Rudell and Mr. Ross that the sale of the nine lots by the Town of South Bruce Peninsula to the current owners in July 2006 established the current value of the properties. The Board does not consider these municipal sales as valid indicators of current value.
>
> The Board finds that the one-day advertisement in the Toronto Star and two days advertisement in the Owen Sound Sun Times offered limited exposure to the market. Even with the municipal website advertising the properties, the Board finds that the properties were not exposed to the market for a reasonable amount of time.
>
> The Board is satisfied that the nine sales were sold under special circumstances. The Board finds that the sale prices paid for the nine lots are not comparable to any other evidenced sales or evidenced assessments in the vicinity.
>
> The onus is on the complainant to prove that the assessed values are incorrect. No evidence has been provided to show any other properties in the vicinity, other than the nine municipal sales, that have sold or that are assessed as low as the 2006 sales prices, four of which are being appealed in this hearing.
>
> The Board finds that there is no evidence before it to suggest that a correction to the current value is required for the four appealed properties. Similar properties in the vicinity are all assessed at $20,500.

The complaints were dismissed and the assessed values confirmed.

Municipal Property Assessment Corp. v. Cisco Systems Co.

In *Municipal Property Assessment Corp. v. Cisco Systems Co.*, [2008] O.J. No. 295, 42 M.P.L.R. (4th) 315, 233 O.A.C. 187, 164 A.C.W.S. (3d) 567, 2008 CarswellOnt 371 (the *Cisco* case), MPAC appealed to the court on questions of law set out in a consent order granting leave to appeal a decision of the ARB as follows:

> (i) Did the Board err in law in its interpretation of the meaning of the words "parcel" in the *Assessment Act* and in O. Reg. 282/98?
>
> (ii) Did the Board err in law in holding that two separate improved lots, on a registered plan of subdivision can be combined as 'a single parcel' with a single roll number for purposes of s. 14 of O. Reg. 282/98?

The court looked at the facts of the subject properties and the classification given by the ARB as a "Large Industrial Property Class" based on its interpretation of sections 6 and 14 of O. Reg. 282/98 as well as the use of the word "parcel" in section 14 of the *Assessment Act*.

The court found that Ottawa is the only municipality in Ontario where the tax rate for "Large Industrial Property Class" is lower than the "Industrial Property Class"; and the court believed that triggered the proceedings of the case. Since tax rates are set by the municipality, the court concluded that the tax rate is neutral when considering an assessable classification. The judge further answered the question whether the ARB had erred in law as follows:

> The [ARB] recognizes that the concept of occupation is an integral and important factor as to what constitutes a "parcel". From Section 14 of the *Act*, elements referable to the word "parcel" include a whole subdivision or a portion thereof or the whole or portion of a building in "separate occupation". From the regulation "parcel or a portion of a

parcel of land" is used, with occupation to be by a single occupant and with square footage to exceed 125,000 square feet. The elements of single occupation and square footage are essential elements to determine the classification of a parcel or a portion of a parcel.

The court found that the decision of the ARB was correct and therefore did not err in law and the appeal was dismissed.

St. George and St. Rueiss Coptic Orthodox Church v. Toronto (City)

The *St. George and St. Rueiss Coptic Orthodox Church v. Toronto (City)*, [2008] O.J. No. 1046 (the *St. George Church* case) is a leave to appeal case before the Superior Court of Justice. An application was made to the ARB pursuant to section 357 of the *Assessment Act*, requesting an exemption due to land being used in connection with "a place of worship". The ARB did not find the land exempt and also refused a request for a review. The focus of the court's decision was on the ARB's refusal to review. The request to review, made under ARB Rule 62.02(4)(b), included a statutory declaration, which was considered and discussed in refusing the request. The court found the following:

> For purposes of this motion, it is important to focus on the decision to refuse the Request for Review, rather than on the decision of the Original Board. That is often easier said than done because the decision to refuse the Request for Review derives from the Original Board decision. In this case, the Chair of the ARB made a fresh finding of fact and law on the point in issue in the application for leave.
>
> The threshold for finding that there is good reason to doubt the correctness of the decision to refuse the Request for Review is low. I need not conclude that the decision is wrong or even probably wrong.
>
> I am satisfied that there is good reason to doubt the correctness of the decision dated June 20, 2007 because of the absence in the decision of a reference to "land used in connection with" a place of worship. The focus on "place of worship" alone may be found to be an error of mixed fact and law. To the extent that that finding encompasses a question of law, that criterion has been met.

Based on the above finding, the court held that leave was granted to determine if the ARB in its decision to refuse the request for review "erred in law in finding that the land used by a Church for storage of Church property and for Church youth programs cannot be 'used in connection with' a 'place of worship' pursuant to s. 3(1)3(i) of the *Assessment Act*".

REVIEW QUESTIONS

1. What is the enabling legislation for the ARB?
2. Where would you find the practices and procedures of the ARB?
3. How does the *SPPA* apply to the ARB?
4. What do the privative clauses of the enabling legislation prevent and allow, and under what circumstances?
5. What is a stated case as discussed in the enabling legislation?
6. What rule(s) gives discretion and flexibility to the ARB in applying the ARB Rules?
7. What rule(s) deal with disclosure, and what is the result of insufficient disclosure?
8. What rule(s) deal with motions, and what is the appropriate procedure to have a motion dealt with by the ARB?
9. What is the difference between reconsideration before MPAC and a review of an ARB decision, and how is each accomplished?

10. What jurisdiction is the ARB given to reconsider a decision under the various procedures and practices of the ARB?
11. How do the various procedures and practices of the ARB deal with the ability to appear on behalf of a party before the ARB?
12. How do the various procedures and practices of the enabling legislation deal with appeals under each such statute?

EXERCISE

Based upon the facts of the *UniRoyal* ARB case discussed in the chapter, fill out appropriate form(s) to institute this matter currently before the ARB.

Appendix 5.1
Overview of Procedural Stages of a Matter Before the ARB

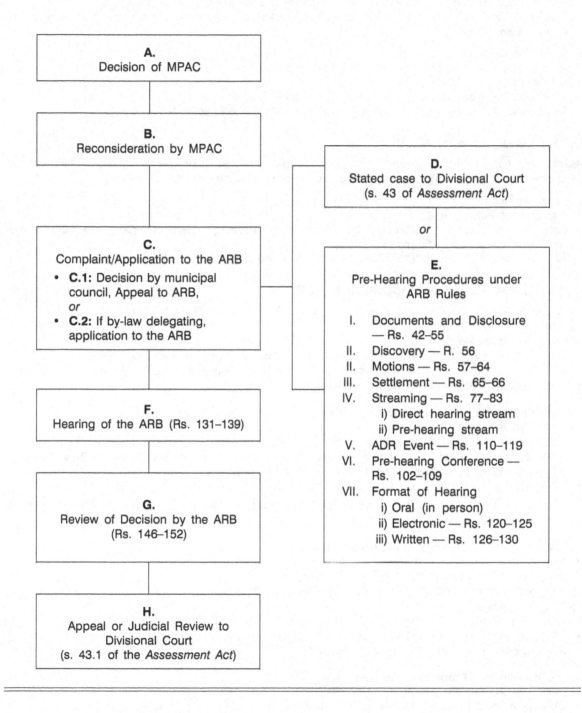

SUMMARY

A. Decision of MPAC

If decision by MPAC
- Send Notice of Assessment under section 31 of the *Assessment Act*
- Notice of Assessment to include school support designation under the *Education Act* and section 16 of the *Assessment Act*

Look at the following:
- *Assessment Act*, ss. 31, 36, 16
- *Education Act*, s. 257.6
- ARB website Web pages "MPAC" and "Complaint Process"
- MPAC website, Web page "Property Owners — "Assessment Notices"

B. Reconsideration by MPAC

Assessment Act, s. 39.1 — Ability of person to request MPAC to reconsider any matter relating to the assessment or classification of property under time limits under the section

Look at the following:
- *Assessment Act*, s. 39.1
- Request for Reconsideration on MPAC website — Property Owners — "Concerns about Your Assessed Value" and "Forms"
- ARB website Web page "Complaint Process" — Filing a Complaint with the ARB

C. Complaint, Application/Appeal to the ARB

Assessment Act, s. 33 (Omitted assessment) or s. 34 (Supplementary Assessment)
— Complaint to ARB
Look at the following:
- ARB website Web page "Complaint Process" — Filing a Complaint with the ARB
- ARB website Web page "Complaint Types" — Complaint Forms for section 33 and section 34
- ARB website Web page "Filing a Complaint"

Assessment Act, s. 40 — Complaint to ARB
Look at the following:
- ARB website Web page "Complaint Process" — How to File a Complaint pamphlet
- ARB website Web page "Complaint Types" — Complaint Forms for section 40 — **Only available when complaints can be made under appropriate timeline.**
- ARB website Web page "Filing a Complaint"

Due to similarities in the legislation, the documents used for complaints, applications, and appeals are similar for the *Municipal Act* and *City of Toronto Act*.

Taxes on Eligible Property — Apportionment
- *Municipal Act*, s. 356 and *City of Toronto Act*, s. 322
- If no by-law, appeal from council to the ARB
- If by-law exists, application to ARB — Privative Clause

Look at the following:
- ARB website Web page "Municipal Act appeals" — Form "ARB M1"
- ARB website Web page "City of Toronto appeals" — Form "ARB COTA1"
- ARB website Web page "Filing a Complaint"

Taxes on Eligible Property — Comparables
- *Municipal Act*, s. 331 and *City of Toronto Act*, s. 294
- Complaint to the ARB — Appeal to Divisional Court

Look at the following
- ARB website Web page "Municipal Act appeals" — Form "ARB M2"
- ARB website Web page "City of Toronto appeals" — Form "ARB COTA2"
- ARB website Web page "Filing a Complaint"

Cancel, Reduce, Refund — Sickness or Poverty
* *Municipal Act*, s. 357 and *City of Toronto Act*, s. 323
* If no by-law, appeal from council to the ARB
* If by-law exists, application to ARB — Privative Clause

Look at the following:
* ARB website Web page "Municipal Act appeals" — Form "ARB M3"
* ARB website Web page "City of Toronto appeals" — Form "ARB COTA3"
* ARB website Web page "filing a Complaint"

Increase in Taxes — Vacant Unit Rebate
* *Municipal Act*, s. 364 and *City of Toronto Act*, s. 331
* Complaint to the ARB — Appeal to Divisional Court

Look at the following:
* ARB website Web page "Municipal Act appeals" — Form "ARB M4"
* ARB website Web page "City of Toronto appeals" — Form "ARB COTA4"
* ARB website Web page "Filing a Complaint"

Cancel, Reduce, Refund
* *Municipal Act*, ss. 357–359 and *City of Toronto Act*, ss. 323, 325, 326
* If no by-law, appeal from council to the ARB
* If by-law exists, application to ARB — Privative Clause

Look at the following:
* ARB website Web page "Municipal Act appeals" — Form "ARB M5"
* ARB website Web page "City of Toronto appeals" — Form "ARB COTA5"
* ARB website Web page "Filing a Complaint"

Limitation of Taxes
* *Municipal Act*, ss. 334, 337 and *City of Toronto Act*, ss. 297, 300
* If no by-law, appeal from council to the ARB
* If by-law exists, application to ARB — Privative Clause

Look at the following:
* ARB website Web page "Municipal Act appeals" — Form "ARB M6"
* ARB website Web page "City of Toronto appeals" — Form "ARB COTA6"
* ARB website Web page "Filing a Complaint"

For *Municipal Act* Forms look at
* ARB website Web page "Municipal Act appeals" — "Frequently Asked Questions" and "Municipal Act pamphlet"

For *City of Toronto Act* Forms look at
* ARB website Web page "City of Toronto Act appeals" — "Frequently Asked Questions" and "City of Toronto Act pamphlet"

For both
* ARB website Web page "Complaint Process" — How to File a Complaint Pamphlet

All forms can be obtained indirectly through ARB website Web page "File a Complaint".

There are also services available on ARB website, Web pages "E Calendar" and "E Status".

D. Stated Case to Divisional Court

Assessment Act, s. 43 — the ARB may, upon application of any person or on its own motion, and upon such security as it determines is necessary, "state a case in writing for the opinion of the Divisional Court upon any question that, in the opinion of the [ARB], is a question of law" and the Divisional Court shall hear and determine such stated case.

Look at the *Assessment Act*, s. 43

E. Pre-hearing Procedures under ARB Rules

    I. Documents and Disclosure — Rs. 42–55

    II. Discovery — R. 56

    III. Motions — Rs. 57–64

    IV. Settlement — Rs. 65–66

    V. Streaming — Rs. 77–83

        i) Direct Hearing Stream

        ii) Pre-hearing stream

    VI. ADR Event — Rs. 110–119

    VII. Pre-hearing Conference — Rs. 102–109

    VIII. Format of Hearing

        i) Oral (in person)

        ii) Electronic — Rs. 120–125

        iii) Written — Rs. 126–130

Look at the following:
ARB website — Web pages "Legislation and ARB Rules" — Rules of Practice and Procedure and "Hearing Process"

F. Hearing of the ARB

- *ARBA*
- ARB Rules

Look at the following:
- ARB website — Web pages "Legislation and ARB Rules" — Rules of Practice and Procedure and "Hearing Process"
- ARB website Web pages "Complaint Process" — Filing a Complaint with the ARB and "Hearing Process" — How to Prepare for Your Hearing pamphlet

G. Review of the Decision by ARB

- ARB Rules — Rs. 146–152

Look at the following:
ARB website Web pages — "Decisions" and "Legislation and ARB Rules" — Rules of Practice and Procedure

H. Appeal or Judicial Review to Divisional Court

The procedures in respect of appeals and judicial review of the decision of the ARB are set out in the provisions of the *SPPA* and the *Judicial Review Procedure Act* and as set out in the website of the ARB. Following are specifics that occur after the decision of the ARB is sent to the parties: *Assessment Act*, s. 43.1

Look at the following:
ARB website Web pages — "Decisions" and "Legislation and ARB Rules" — Rules of Practice and Procedure

Appendix 5.2
Request for Reconsideration by MPAC[1]

mpac MUNICIPAL PROPERTY ASSESSMENT CORPORATION

Request for Reconsideration

| 2009 |

Section 1: About your property

Roll number

| | - | | - | | - | | - | | - | |

Property address

Municipality

Owner 1 (Last Name, First Name)	Owner 2 (Last Name, First Name)

Home phone number	Alternate phone number	Email Address

If we should send follow-up information somewhere other than the property address, please indicate below:

Mailing Address

What is your property's value on January 1, 2008 as shown on your Property Assessment Notice 2008? | $ |

Section 2: Reasons for reconsidering your property's assessed value

Please provide specific reasons as to why you would like us to review your assessment, as required under Section 39.1 of the Assessment Act. Use a second sheet of paper if necessary.

Section 3: Supporting documentation

☐ Sale information for this property and other similar properties

☐ Other documents, such as the municipal zoning records or health unit reports

☐ Assessed value of similar properties

☐ Photos of this property or other properties

Section 4 – Signature of owner

X	Date (dd/mm/yyyy)

You may send the completed form in any one of several ways. If completed online, just follow the instructions.

by email to: enquiry@mpac.ca
by fax to: 1 866 297-6703
by mail to: Municipal Property Assessment Corporation (MPAC), PO Box 9808, Toronto, ON, M1S 5T9

---

[1] Source: MPAC website <http://www.mpac.ca/>

Request for Reconsideration

Page 2

Section 5: Representative information

If you would like someone else to act for you while we reconsider the value of your property, please complete this Section by indicating their name below and providing a Letter of Authorization. You may also use the Representative Authorization Form available on our website at www.mpac.ca or by calling us at 1 866 296-6722.

Name representative (Last name, first name)	LSUC License Number	Telephone

A representative may act on behalf of a property owner. There have been recent changes to the *Law Society Act* with respect to the requirements of who can act as a representative for a property owner. If you are not the owner of the property, you must also supply a Letter of Authorization endorsed by the property owner stating that you are representing the owner in this matter. Persons approved by the Law Society of Upper Canada to practice law or provide legal services in Ontario do not require Letters of Authorization.

The Municipal Property Assessment Corporation (MPAC) is responsible for accurately classifying and valuing all properties in Ontario. If you feel that your property assessment is not a reasonable reflection of your property's value and/or classification as of January 1, 2008, you can ask us to review them by completing this form using a black, bold pen and sending it to us. You do not have to pay for this review. Your privacy is protected under the *Municipal Freedom of Information and Protection of Privacy Act.*

Our review of your property's value will be completed within 10 to 12 weeks. If we need more information from you or more time to complete the review, we will contact you. When the review is complete, we will send you a letter to give you the results of the review. The deadline to submit a Request for Reconsideration for the 2009 tax year is March 31, 2009.

You can review the value of properties in your area by way of free reports available through **AboutMyProperty**™ at www.mpac.ca . These may assist you in determining if your assessment is reasonable for your neighbourhood.

If you need any help in completing this form, please call our Customer Contact Centre at 1 866 296-6722 or for the hearing impaired, call 1 877 TTY-MPAC.

How MPAC Reviews your Assessed Value

When we review your property's assessed value, we look at the information you provide with your request and the information we have in our files including:

- Details of your property such as the size of your lot;
- The size, type, condition and age of any buildings that may be on the property; and
- Depreciation, nuisances or any other factors that could have an impact on the current value of your property.

We also compare your property's assessed value with sales and values of similar properties in the area.
We will contact you for further information if required. When the review is completed, we will notify you of the results in writing.

How To File An Appeal With The ARB

You may also file an Appeal with the Assessment Review Board (ARB), an independent tribunal of the Ontario Ministry of the Attorney General. There are specific application forms and fees involved. As this is now an Appeal, owners of residential, farm or managed forest properties must first receive a decision from MPAC regarding a Request for Reconsideration. The deadline to file an Appeal with the ARB is 90 days from the date of MPAC's written decision.

You can find more information including forms, fees and how to file an Appeal online at the ARB web site at www.arb.gov.on.ca or by calling toll free 1 800 263-3237 or 416 314-6900.

Appendix 5.3
Instructions and Form for Complaint under s. 34 or s. 33[2]

 ARB Assessment Appeal Form Instructions

Assessment Review Board, 655 Bay Street, Suite 1500, Toronto, Ontario M5G 1E5 **Phone:** (416) 314-6900 or 1-800-263-3237
Fax: (416) 314-3717 or 1-877-849-2066 **Website:** www.arb.gov.on.ca **E-mail:** assessment.review.board@ontario.ca

The Assessment Review Board's (ARB) appeal process has changed for 2009. Please read all information carefully. Refer to your Property Assessment Notice from the Municipal Property Assessment Corporation (MPAC) and/or your Request for Reconsideration (RFR) decision when filling out the ARB appeal form.

Questions about your assessment should be directed to MPAC at 1-866-296-6722. MPAC prepares and sends out assessment notices. The ARB and MPAC are two separate organizations.

Filing deadlines
If your property or a portion of it is classified as **residential, farm, managed forest or conservation land:**
   1. You *MUST* file a Request for Reconsideration (RFR) with MPAC or the Program Administrator first.
   2. You *MUST* receive a RFR decision *before* filing an appeal with the ARB. If you think the RFR is wrong, you may then file an appeal with the ARB.
   3. Your deadline to file with the ARB is 90 days from the mailing date on the RFR decision.

If your property is in **any other property class:**
   1. You may file a RFR with MPAC **or** appeal directly with the ARB.
   2. If you think the RFR decision is wrong, you may then file an appeal with the ARB. Your deadline to file with the ARB is 90 days from the mailing date on the RFR decision.
   3. If you file directly with the ARB, your deadline to file is March 31, 2009, for annual assessment appeals, or 90 days from the notice date for other types of assessments.

Note: If you are filing for the 2008 tax year, your deadline to file with the ARB is on your assessment notice.

Part 1: Appeal Information

Your Property Assessment Notice from MPAC tells you the type of assessment you have been sent and the tax years for your assessment. The effective date of taxation only applies to supplementary, omitted and correction of factual error assessments.

Part 2: Property Information and Classification

In this section, provide the 19-digit roll number (see MPAC assessment notice) assigned to the property and the property address. Check the box indicating the classification of your property. Your property classification determines the process of your appeal. See the information on filing deadlines at the top of this page for details on the process.

Part 3: Appellant information

Identify who you are, where you live and how to contact you. Please notify the Assessment Review Board, in writing, of any changes in your address or telephone number.
   •   If you are not the property owner, also complete Part 5 of the appeal form.
   •   If you have chosen someone else to act on your behalf with regard to this appeal, also complete Part 6 of the appeal form.
   •   Sign your name where indicated.
   •   Choose the language you would like to communicate in by checking the box beside English or French.

Part 4: Reason(s) for Appeal

Check **only** the reason(s) that apply to your appeal. If your reason is not listed, fill it in under 'other.' For more information about property assessment appeals and property classification, see the Assessment Act and Ontario Regulation 282/98.

Part 5: Third Party Appeal Information (Complete if you are NOT the owner of the property)

If you are **not** the owner of the property, fill in the name and address of the property owner. As a non-owner, you must appeal the assessment directly to the ARB and may not file a RFR with MPAC. You must send a copy of the appeal form to the owner by the filing deadline. If the property owner is not sent a copy, the ARB may not consider your appeal to be valid. Please write in the date you sent the property owner a copy of the appeal form.

---

[2] Source: ARB Website <http://www.arb.gov.on.ca/english/home.html>

Part 6: Representative Authorization

Representatives who are not licensed by the Law Society must confirm that they have written authorization. If you are the appellant filling out this form, complete this section, sign it and provide a copy to your representative. If you are the representative filling out this form, complete this section and make sure you have written authorization - signed by the appellant - to act on his or her behalf. Check the box indicating that written authorization has been provided.

Note: Anyone in Ontario providing legal services requires a licence, unless the person is not captured by the Law Society Act or is exempt by a Law Society by-law. By-law 4 exempts persons who are not in the business of providing legal services and occasionally provide assistance to a friend or relative for no fee. For information on licensing please refer to the Law Society of Upper Canada's website www.lsuc.ca or call 416-947-3315 or 1-800-668-7380.

Part 7: Special Property Class Tax Rates (farms, managed forests and conservation lands)

Property owners of these special property classes must file a Request for Reconsideration (RFR) with the appropriate agency. If you believe the value or classification is wrong you must file a RFR with MPAC first. If you believe your property is eligible for special class tax programs, you must file a RFR with the Program Administrator first. After you receive a RFR decision, you may appeal that decision to the ARB.

Farm Property Class Tax Rate Program
Eligible farmlands may be classed in the Farm Property Class and taxed at 25 per cent of the municipal residential rate. For information about the farm property class tax rate program or the process of filing a RFR, contact the Ontario Ministry of Agriculture, Food and Rural Affairs at 1-800-469-2285.

Managed Forest Tax Incentive Program
Eligible properties may be classed in the Managed Forest Property Class and taxed at 25 per cent of the municipal residential rate. For information about the managed forest tax incentive program or the process of filing a RFR, please contact the Ontario Forestry Association at 1-800-387-0790 or the Ontario Woodlot Association at 1-888-791-1103.

Conservation Land Tax Incentive Program
Eligible properties may be classed in the Conservation Land Property Class and that portion of the property will be 100 per cent tax exempt. For information about the conservation land tax incentive program or the process of filing a RFR, please contact the Ministry of Natural Resources at 1-800-268-8959.

Part 8: How to File an Appeal

Use only ONE of the following options:

E File:	Fax to:	Mail or deliver to:
www.arb.gov.on.ca	416-645-1819 or 1-866-297-1822 (toll free)	Assessment Review Board, 655 Bay Street
*Note: there is a $10 discount if you E File	***The Board does not confirm receipt of faxes. Keep the transmission report from your fax.**	Suite 1500 Toronto, Ontario M5G 1E5

If you are unsure whether you filed correctly and file more than once, please mark any additional submissions COPY to avoid duplicate charges. You will receive an acknowledgement letter by mail once your appeal has been processed, followed by a Notice of Hearing, once your hearing has been scheduled.

The ARB complies with the Accessibility for Ontarians with Disabilities Act, 2005. Please contact the ARB if you have any questions about accessibility.

Part 9: Required Filing Fee

Residential, farm, managed forest or conservation land properties.................................$75* for each roll number
All other property classes..$150* for each roll number
*Note: there is a $10 discount if you E File

Fill in the amount of the **total fee submitted** in the space provided. Please pay in Canadian funds. *E Filed or faxed appeals* can be paid by VISA, MasterCard or American Express. *Mailed appeals* can be paid by cheque or money order, payable to the **Minister of Finance**. Write the roll number on the front of the cheque or money order. **Do not mail cash.** If a financial institution returns your cheque, an administration fee of $35 will apply. *If you are filing in person,* you can pay by cash, cheque, money order, debit card or credit card. **There are no refunds of the filing fee.**

Fee payment information is confidential and will not be placed on file.

Contact the Assessment Review Board at 416-314-6900 or toll free at 1-800-263-3237 or online at **www.arb.gov.on.ca**.

ARB Assessment Appeal Form

Assessment Review Board, 655 Bay Street, Suite 1500, Toronto, Ontario M5G 1E5
Phone: (416) 314-6900 or 1-800-263-3237 **Fax:** (416) 314-3717 or 1-877-849-2066
Website: www.arb.gov.on.ca **E-mail:** assessment.review.board@ontario.ca

| Appeal # |
| Receipt # |
| Date Stamp |
| *For office use only* |

IMPORTANT: Read below
1. Refer to your **Property Assessment Notice** from MPAC before filling out this form.
2. See form instructions for an explanation of appeal deadlines and how to fill out this form.
3. Issues of **tax exemption** can **only** be addressed by the **Superior Court of Justice**.
4. The ARB complies with the Accessibility for Ontarians with Disabilities Act, 2005. Please contact the ARB if you have any questions about accessibility.

If your property or a portion of it is residential, farm, managed forest or conservation land, you *must* file a RFR and receive a RFR decision *before* filing an appeal with the ARB.

Part 1: Appeal Information (Check your Notice of Assessment from MPAC)

I received this type of assessment: ☐ Annual ☐ Supplementary ☐ Omitted ☐ Correction of Factual Error

Tax year: _____ Effective date of taxation: (D/M/Y) _____/_____/_____ Appeal deadline: (D/M/Y) ____/____/_____

Provide the mailing date of your RFR decision: (D/M/Y) _____/_____/_____

Part 2: Property Information and Classification

Roll number: ☐☐☐☐☐ - ☐☐☐ - ☐☐☐☐☐ - ☐☐☐☐☐ - ☐☐☐☐   19-digit number on Property Assessment Notice

Street Address: _____ Municipality: _____

☐ Residential, farm, managed forest or conservation lands - You MUST file a RFR first.
☐ All other property classes - You may file directly with the ARB without a RFR, OR you may file a RFR.

Part 3: Appellant Information (Address changes must be made in writing to the ARB.)

Last name: _____ First name: _____

Company (if any): _____ Mailing address: _____

City: _____ Province: _____ Postal code: _____ Country (if not Canada): _____

Home #: _____ Business/other #: _____ Fax #: _____

E-mail address: _____ Appellant signature: _____
Are you the owner of this property? ☐ yes ☐ no **If no, fill out Part 5 of this form** (and the rest of form.)
Do you have a representative? ☐ yes ☐ no **If yes, fill out Part 6 of this form** (and the rest of form.)
I would like to communicate with the ARB in ☐ English **or** ☐ French

Part 4: Reason(s) for Appeal (Check ONLY the reasons that apply.)

The property assessment value from MPAC is:
☐ Too high   ☐ Too low

☐ The property is a farm, managed forest or conservation land
(see Part 7 to fill in the reasons for this appeal and complete the rest of form.)

☐ The property is incorrectly classified

☐ Other: _____

Part 5: Third Party Appeal Information (Complete if you are NOT the owner of the property.)

*Note: As a non-owner, you must appeal the assessment to the ARB. You cannot file a RFR. The appeal deadline is March 31, 2009 for annual assessments, or 90 days from the notice date for other types of assessments. You must also send a copy of this appeal form to the property owner before the deadline.
Name of property owner: _____

Mailing address of above: _____

☐   Yes, I delivered/mailed a copy of this appeal form to the property owner on (D/M/Y): _____/_____/_____

ARB Assessment Appeal Form, continued   *(Please copy the roll number from page 1)*

Roll Number: ☐☐☐☐☐ — ☐☐☐ — ☐☐☐ — ☐☐☐☐ — ☐☐☐☐

Part 6: Representative Authorization (Only fill out this section if you have representation.)

Company name: _____ Name of representative: _____

Mailing address: _____ Apt/Suite/Unit#: _____ City: _____

Province: _____ Postal code: _____ Business/other telephone #: _____

Home telephone #: _____ Fax #: _____ E-mail address: _____

Representatives who are not licensed by the Law Society of Upper Canada must confirm that they have written authorization by checking the box below.

☐ *I certify that I have written authorization from the appellant to act as a representative with respect to this appeal on his or her behalf and I understand that I may be asked to produce this authorization at any time.*

Note: Anyone in Ontario providing legal services requires a licence, unless the person is not captured by the Law Society Act or is exempt by a Law Society by-law. By-law 4 exempts persons who are not in the business of providing legal services and occasionally provide assistance to a friend or relative for no fee. For information on licensing please refer to the Law Society of Upper Canada's website www.lsuc.ca or call 416-947-3315 or 1-800-668-7380.

Part 7: Special Property Class Tax Rates (This section is for farms, managed forests and conservation lands.)

☐ **I believe the property is eligible for a special property class tax rate** *(See appeal form instructions for further information on property class tax rate programs. You must first file a RFR with the appropriate agency and receive a RFR decision before you can file your appeal with the ARB.)*

Farms

Is your property (or a portion of it) currently classified as a farm?   ☐ yes   ☐ no
I believe this classification is: ☐ correct   ☐ incorrect
I believe the value assigned to the property is: ☐ too high   ☐ too low
☐ **I wish to request eligibility for the Farm Property Class Tax Rate Program**

Managed forests

Is your property (or a portion of it) currently classified as a managed forest?   ☐ yes   ☐ no
I believe this classification is: ☐ correct   ☐ incorrect
I believe the value assigned to the property is: ☐ too high   ☐ too low

☐ **I wish to request eligibility for the Managed Forest Tax Incentive Program**
Provide your Managed Forest Plan Number: _____
I believe the amount of managed forest should be: ☐ increased   ☐ decreased   ☐ remain the same

Conservation lands

Is your property (or a portion of it) classified as conservation land?   ☐ yes   ☐ no
I believe this classification is: ☐ correct   ☐ incorrect
I believe the value assigned to the property is: ☐ too low   ☐ too high

☐ **I wish to request eligibility for the Conservation Land Tax Incentive Program**
How many acres are currently classified as conservation land? _____
Should the amount of conservation land be: ☐ increased   ☐ decreased   ☐ remain the same

Personal information requested on this form is collected under section 40 of the Assessment Act. After an appeal is filed, all information relating to this appeal may become available to the public. For additional information, please contact an ARB public inquiry assistant at (416) 314-6900 or toll-free at 1-800-263-3237. The Assessment Act is available at www.arb.gov.on.ca.

ARB Assessment Appeal Form, continued (Please copy the roll number from page 1)

Roll Number: [ ][ ][ ][ ] — [ ][ ][ ] — [ ][ ][ ] — [ ][ ][ ][ ] — [ ][ ][ ][ ]

Part 8: How to File an Appeal

File your appeal using only ONE of the following options:

Internet: www.arb.gov.on.ca - Use the E File service - credit card required
*There is $10 discount if you E File

Mail: Assessment Review Board, 655 Bay Street, Suite 1500, Toronto, Ontario M5G 1E5

Fax: (416) 645-1819 or 1-866-297-1822 (toll free) (For appeals ONLY)
Due to the volume of faxes received, the ARB is unable to confirm receipt of faxes – please print the transmission report from your fax machine.

In person: 655 Bay Street, Suite 1500 (Bay Street, north of Dundas)

For additional information, call (416) 314-6900, (toll free) 1-800-263-3237 or visit our website: www.arb.gov.on.ca.
Please file your appeal only ONCE. If you are unsure that your filing attempt was successful and resubmit, please mark any other submissions COPY to avoid duplicate charges.

Part 9: Required Filing Fee

Residential, farm, managed forest and conservation land properties......................$75* for each Roll Number
All other property classes...$150* for each Roll Number
***There is $10 discount if you E File**

Total fee submitted: $_____ by: ☐ Cheque   ☐ Money Order OR

Credit card: ☐ Visa   ☐ MasterCard   ☐ American Express

Credit card #: _____ Expiry date: _____/_____
                                                                                                                    month   year

Cardholder's name: _____

Cardholder's signature: _____

Note: The information you fill in under this section is confidential. It will only be used to process your appeal and will not be placed on file.

- If you are **not** paying by credit card, the filing fee must be received by cheque or money order, in Canadian funds, payable to the **Minister of Finance.** Please note the applicable roll number(s) on the front of the cheque or money order. **Do not send cash by mail.**
- If a financial institution returns your cheque, or if you cancel or stop payment, an administrative fee of $35 will apply.
- You will receive an **Acknowledgement Letter** once your appeal is processed.
- There are no refunds of the filing fee.

For office use only:

Fee Received: $_____   ☐ Cash   ☐ Cheque   ☐ Money order   ☐ Credit card

Verified by: _____

Appendix 5.4
Application/Appeal — Apportionment, s. 356[3]

Environment and Land Tribunals Ontario
Assessment Review Board, 655 Bay Street, Suite 1500, Toronto, Ontario M5G 1E5
Phone: (416) 212-6349 or 1-866-448-2248 **Fax:** (416) 314-3717 or 1-877-849-2066
Website: www.elto.gov.on.ca

MUNICIPAL ACT APPLICATION/APPEAL – APPORTIONMENT

Form and Instructions for filing a *Municipal Act, 2001* application/appeal with the Assessment Review Board and information on how to prepare for your hearing event.

Please note: This form is for Municipal Act applications/appeals – Apportionment only. Do not use this form to file assessment complaints (sections 33, 34 or 40 of the *Assessment Act*). Do not use this form for any other applications, appeals and/or complaints under the *Municipal Act, 2001*. Different forms are available to file the other applications, appeals and complaints. Issues of tax exemption can only be addressed by the Superior Court of Justice.

Before Filing: Please contact the municipality where the property is located for information regarding the tax account and the application/appeal process. The ARB can only accept applications under section 356.(1)(b) where the municipality has passed a by-law that gives the ARB the same authority as municipal council to decide on Municipal Act applications. Before filing with the ARB, please ensure that the municipality has passed such a by-law.

Required Filing Fee: $25.00 for each roll number. Your application/appeal will not be accepted without the required filing fee.

Filing Deadline: Filing deadlines are established by legislation and cannot be waived by the ARB. Filing deadlines depend on the type of application or appeal you are making.

Important: Please attach to your appeal a copy of the supporting document requested in Part 2 of the appeal form. The ARB cannot determine if your appeal has been filed on time without the supporting document.

Accessibility: We are committed to providing services as set out in the Accessibility for Ontarians with Disabilities Act, 2005. If you have any accessibility needs, please contact our Accessibility Coordinator as soon as possible.

These descriptions are summarized – please refer to the *Municipal Act, 2001*.		
SECTION NUMBER AND APPLICATION/APPEAL REASON		**FILING DEADLINE**
356.(1)(b)	To apportion taxes where land is assessed in a block. Filing for multiple taxation years is considered one application with one filing fee.	No deadline.
356.(6)	Appeal a decision that the municipal council made on an application under section 356.(1)(b).	File within 35 days after Council makes its decision.

Instructions for filing a *Municipal Act, 2001* application/appeal with the Assessment Review Board

---

Part 1: Property Information

Please refer to your municipal property tax bill or property assessment notice when completing this section.

Roll Number: The roll number is a 19-digit number assigned to each property. Please ensure that this number is accurately recorded on each page of the application/appeal form.

Street Address and Property Description: Enter the municipal address of the property for which you are filing a Municipal Act application/appeal.

Municipality: Note the city, town or village in which the property is located.

Preferred Language: Check the appropriate box indicating your language preference for receiving ARB services, including hearings, notices and other public information materials.

ARB-M1 – Rev.02.19.2010   Page 1 of 3

---

[3] Source: ARB website <http://www.arb.gov.on.ca/english/home.html>

Part 2: Application/Appeal Information

Application/Appeal Reason:
Check the appropriate box to indicate the reason for your application/appeal. Check only one box. Continue moving to the right along the same row to complete the application/appeal. Application can be made under 356.(1)(b) for multiple taxation years.

The ARB can only accept applications under section 356.(1)(b) where the municipality has passed a by-law that gives the ARB the same authority as municipal council to decide on Municipal Act applications. Before filing with the ARB, please ensure that the municipality has passed such a by-law.

Taxation Year:
Write in the taxation year(s) that are the subject of your application(s)/appeal.

Supporting Documents:
Supporting documents are required by the Assessment Review Board to determine if your Municipal Act appeal has been filed within legislated deadlines. Check the appropriate box to indicate you have attached a copy of the supporting document to the appeal form.

If you do not have your supporting document, do not wait to file the appeal. **Filing deadlines are established by legislation and cannot be waived.** If you do not submit the required document with your appeal, the ARB will send you an Acknowledgement Letter requesting a copy of the required document.

Filing Deadline:
This is the last day a Municipal Act application/appeal can be filed with the Assessment Review Board. **Filing deadlines are established by legislation and cannot be waived.** Filing deadlines are not the same for all section numbers. It is important that you file your Municipal Act appeal by the deadline indicated for the section number. It will not be accepted after the deadline has passed.

MPAC's Statement of Relative Value:
Check the appropriate box to indicate if you have received a Statement of Relative Value produced by the Municipal Property Assessment Corporation (MPAC). If you have received the Statement of Relative Value, you must enclose a copy of the statement with your application/appeal form.

If you do not have a Statement of Relative Value, please record the name, mailing address and roll number for each of the current owners. The ARB requires this information as the legislation requires that the Board send Notices of Hearing to all parties.

Additional Pages:
If you require more room, please attach additional page(s) and check the box on the bottom line to indicate you have attached additional page(s).

Part 3: Applicant/Appellant Information

Representative:
Check the appropriate box to indicate if you have a representative to act on your behalf with regard to this application/appeal. If you have a representative, please complete Parts 3 and 4 of the form.

Owner:
Check the appropriate box to indicate if you are the owner of the property.

Contact Information:
Provide your contact information including name, address and telephone number(s).

You must notify the Assessment Review Board in writing of any change of address or telephone number.

Personal information requested on this form is collected under the various sections of the *Municipal Act, 2001*. After an application/appeal is filed, all information relating to this application may become available to the public. For additional information, please contact an ARB Public Inquiry Assistant at (416) 212-6349 or toll-free at 1-866-448-2248. The *Municipal Act, 2001* is available at www.elto.gov.on.ca.

Part 4: Representative Authorization

If you have chosen someone to act on your behalf, please provide their name, address, telephone number, fax number and e-mail address. You will need to sign this section and provide your representative with a copy of the form. If you provided a letter or another form of written authorization for your representative, please make sure the representative checked the box in this section confirming he or she received your written authorization.

Part 5: How to File an Application/Appeal

You can file your application/appeal in a number of ways. Please choose only ONE of the following filing options:

Mail it to: Assessment Review Board, 655 Bay Street, Suite 1500, Toronto, Ontario M5G 1E5

Fax it to: (416) 314-3717 or 1-877-849-2066 (toll free) (For faxing applications, appeals and complaints only.)

Deliver it in person to: 655 Bay Street, 15th Floor. (East side of Bay Street, north of Dundas)

Please file only ONCE. If you are unsure that your filing attempt was successful and resubmit, please mark any other submissions COPY to avoid duplicate charges.

You will receive an Acknowledgement Letter by mail once your application/appeal has been received by the ARB followed by a Notice of Hearing once your hearing has been scheduled.

Please note: Once you have filed your Municipal Act application/appeal, any additional correspondence with the ARB should be copied to all parties.

Part 6: Required Filing Fee

" **If you are faxing your Municipal Act application/appeal**, payment must be made by VISA, MasterCard or American Express, in Canadian funds. Please include your credit card number, expiry date, cardholder's name and the cardholder's signature.

" **If you are mailing your Municipal Act application/appeal**, payment can be made by credit card, cheque or money order, in Canadian funds, payable to the **Minister of Finance**. Please note the applicable roll number(s) on the front of the cheque or money order. **Please do not mail cash.** Please note that if a financial institution returns your cheque, an administration fee of $35 will apply.

" **If you are delivering your Municipal Act application/appeal in person**, payment can be made by cash, cheque, money order, debit card or credit card.

The filing fee is non-refundable. You will receive an **Acknowledgement Letter** in the mail once your application/appeal has been received, followed by a **Notice of Hearing** when your hearing has been scheduled. **The information you fill in under Required Filing Fee is confidential. It will only be used to process your application/appeal and will not be placed on file.**

How to Prepare for Your Hearing Event

1. Gather the information you require to support your case, including:
   " your initial application to the municipal council and any decision of the municipal council (if you are appealing a decision of municipal council);
   " your property tax bill;
   " any factual information, including documents that you require to support your case.

2. Contact the municipality to discuss your case.

3. Consider how you will present your case to the Board.
   " Decide which documents you will provide to the Board at the hearing.
      " Bring photocopies to the hearing of any documents you would like the Board to consider in support of your case. We suggest three copies of each document: one for the Board, one for the municipality, and one for you.
   " Decide whether you will require any witnesses other than yourself to give evidence at the hearing.
      " Contact your witnesses once you receive the Notice of Hearing to inform them of the hearing date, time and location.
      " If necessary, you can obtain a Summons to Witness from the Board's Registrar.
   " Consider whether there is any need for parties to exchange documents prior to the hearing.
      " Request from the municipality copies of any documents they will be relying on to support their position.
      " Prior to the hearing, consider providing the municipality with copies of the documents that you will be relying on at the hearing.

At this point, please remove the instructions (pages 1, 2 & 3) from the following application/appeal form and keep the information on how prepare for your hearing event.

MUNICIPAL ACT APPLICATION/APPEAL – APPORTIONMENT

Environment and Land Tribunals Ontario
Assessment Review Board, 655 Bay Street, Suite 1500, Toronto, Ontario M5G 1E5
Phone: (416) 212-6349 or 1-866-448-2248 **Fax:** (416) 314-3717 or 1-877-849-2066
Website: www.elto.gov.on.ca

Application/appeal #
Receipt #
Date Stamp
For office use only

Please note: This form is for Municipal Act applications/appeals – Apportionments only. Do not use this form to file assessment appeals (sections 33, 34 or 40 of the *Assessment Act*). Do not use this form for any other applications, appeals and/or complaints under the *Municipal Act, 2001.* Different forms are available to file the other applications, appeals and complaints. Issues of tax exemption can only be addressed by the Superior Court of Justice.

Before Filing: Please contact the municipality where the property is located for information regarding the tax account and the application/appeal process. The ARB can only accept applications under section 356.(1)(b) where the municipality has passed a by-law that gives the ARB the same authority as municipal council to decide on Municipal Act applications/appeals. Before filing with the ARB, please ensure that the municipality has passed such a by-law.

Required Filing Fee: $25.00 for each roll number. Your application/appeal will not be accepted without the required filing fee.

Filing Deadline: Filing deadlines are established by legislation and cannot be waived by the ARB. Filing deadlines depend on the type of application or appeal you are making. Please see Part 2 for the filing deadline.

Important: Please attach to this appeal form a copy of the supporting document requested in Part 2. The ARB cannot determine if your appeal has been filed on time without the supporting document.

Accessibility: We are committed to providing services as set out in the Accessibility for Ontarians with Disabilities Act, 2005. If you have any accessibility needs, please contact our Accessibility Coordinator as soon as possible.

Part 1: Property Information (Please print clearly)

Roll number: ☐☐☐☐ - ☐☐☐☐ - ☐☐☐☐☐ - ☐☐☐☐☐ - ☐☐☐☐

PLEASE copy this roll number in the space provided at the top of every page of this form

Street address: _____

Municipality: _____

Please choose preferred language: ☐ English   ☐ French

Part 2: Application/Appeal Information

These descriptions are summarized – please refer to the *Municipal Act, 2001.*			
PLEASE CHECK ONLY ONE REASON FOR YOUR APPLICATION/APPEAL	TAX YEAR(S) YOU ARE APPEALING	SUPPORTING DOCUMENT(S) YOU MUST ATTACH TO THIS APPLICATION/APPEAL FORM	FILING DEADLINE
☐ **Application: section 356.(1)(b)** To apportion taxes where land is assessed in a block. Filing for multiple taxation years is considered one application with one filing fee. ☐ The municipality has passed a by-law delegating these applications to the ARB. If not, apply to the municipality instead.	_____ _____ _____ _____ _____	None	No deadline

OR

☐ **Appeal: section 356.(6)** Appeal a decision that the municipal council made about your application under section 356.(1)(b).	_____	Attach a copy of the decision you received from the municipality. ☐ I have attached a copy.	File within 35 days after council makes its decision.

AND (Continue to next page to complete the Application/Appeal Information section.)

Roll Number: ☐☐☐☐☐ – ☐☐☐ – ☐☐☐ – ☐☐☐☐☐ – ☐☐☐☐

Part 2: Application/Appeal Information - Continued

Complete this section for applications under section 356.(1)(b) and appeals under section 356.(6).

I have received MPAC's Statement of Relative Value (check the correct answer below).

☐ Yes **If yes, you must enclose a copy of the statement with this application/appeal.**

☐ No   **If no, you must include the names, mailing addresses and roll numbers of the new parcel owners (current owners).**

Owner's Name	Owner's Mailing Address	New Parcel Roll Number

If you require more room, please attach additional page(s). If you have attached additional pages, please check here. ☐

Roll Number: ☐☐☐☐–☐☐☐–☐☐☐–☐☐☐☐☐–☐☐☐☐

Part 3: Applicant/Appellant Information

Do you have a representative? ☐ Yes ☐ No **If yes, complete Parts 3 & 4.**

Are you the owner of the property? ☐ Yes ☐ No

Last name: _____ First name: _____

Company name (if applicable): _____

Mailing address: _____
           Street address   Apt/Suite/Unit#   City

           Province   Country (if not Canada)   Postal Code

Business/other telephone #: _____ Home telephone #: _____

Fax #: _____ E-mail address: _____

Applicant/appellant signature: _____

      Please note: You must notify the Assessment Review Board in writing of any change of address or telephone number.

> **Personal Information requested on this form is collected under the various sections of the *Municipal Act, 2001*.** After an application/appeal is filed, all information relating to this application/appeal may become available to the public. For additional information, please contact an ARB Public Inquiry Assistant at (416) 212-6349 or toll free at 1-866-448-2248. The *Municipal Act, 2001* is available at www.elto.gov.on.ca.

Part 4: Representative Authorization

I hereby authorize the named company and/or individual(s) to represent me:

Company name: _____

Last name: _____ First name: _____

Mailing address: _____
           Street address   Apt/Suite/Unit#   City

           Province   Country (if not Canada)   Postal Code

Telephone #: _____ Fax #: _____

E-mail address: _____

Applicant/appellant signature: _____

Representatives who are NOT legal counsel **must** *confirm that they have* **written authorization** *by checking the box below.*

☐ I certify that I have written authorization from the complainant to act as a representative with respect to this complaint on his or her behalf and I understand that I may be asked to produce this authorization at any time.

> **Note:** Anyone in Ontario providing legal services requires a licence, unless the group or individual is not captured by the Law Society Act or is exempt by a Law Society by-law. By-law 4 exempts persons who are not in the business of providing legal services and occasionally provide assistance to a friend or relative for no fee. For information on licensing please refer to the Law Society of Upper Canada's website www.lsuc.ca or call 416-947-3315 or 1-800-668-7380.

Roll Number: ☐☐☐☐ — ☐☐☐ — ☐☐☐ — ☐☐☐☐☐ — ☐☐☐☐

Part 5: How to File an Application/Appeal

File your application/appeal using only ONE of the following options:

Mail it to: Assessment Review Board, 655 Bay Street, Suite 1500, Toronto, Ontario M5G 1E5

Fax it to: (416) 314-3717 or 1-877-849-2066 (toll free) (For faxing applications, appeals and complaints only.)

Deliver it in person to: 655 Bay Street, 15th Floor. (East side of Bay Street, north of Dundas)

For additional information, call (416) 212-6349, (toll free) 1-866-448-2248 or visit our website: www.elto.gov.on.ca.

Please file your application/appeal only ONCE. If you are unsure that your filing attempt was successful and resubmit, please mark any other submissions COPY to avoid duplicate charges.

Part 6: Required Filing Fee

Total fee submitted: $_____   by: ☐ Cheque   ☐ Money Order   OR

Credit card: ☐ Visa   ☐ MasterCard   ☐ American Express

Credit card #: _____   Expiry date: _____ / _____
                                                                      month   year

Cardholder's name: _____

Cardholder's signature: _____

- If you are not paying by credit card, the filing fee must be received by cheque or money order, in Canadian funds, payable to the **Minister of Finance**. Please note the applicable roll number(s) on the front of the cheque or money order. **Please do not send cash by mail**.
- If you are paying by VISA, MasterCard or American Express, **the Board will accept a faxed application/appeal with the full credit card information requested above**.
- **Please note that if a financial institution returns your cheque, an administrative fee of $35 will apply. The fee is non-refundable.**
- You will receive an **Acknowledgement Letter** followed by a **Notice of Hearing**.

The information you fill in under Required Filing Fee is confidential.
It will only be used to process your application/appeal and will not be placed on file.

For office use only:

Fee Received: $_____   ____ Cash   ____ Cheque   ____ Money order   ____ Credit card

Verified by: _____

Appendix 5.5
Application/Appeal — Apportionment, s. 322[4]

Environment and Land Tribunals Ontario
Assessment Review Board, 655 Bay Street, Suite 1500, Toronto, Ontario M5G 1E5
Phone: (416) 212-6349 or 1-866-448-2248 **Fax:** (416) 314-3717 or 1-877-849-2066
Website: www.elto.gov.on.ca
Ontario

CITY OF TORONTO ACT APPLICATION/APPEAL – APPORTIONMENT

Form and Instructions for filing a City of Toronto Act, 2006 application/appeal with the Assessment Review Board and information on how to prepare for your hearing event.

Please note: This form is for City of Toronto Act, 2006 applications/appeals – Apportionment only. Do not use this form to file assessment complaints (sections 33, 34 or 40 of the Assessment Act). Do not use this form for any other applications, appeals and/or complaints under the City of Toronto Act, 2006 or the Municipal Act, 2001. Different forms are available to file the other applications, appeals and complaints. Issues of tax exemption can only be addressed by the Superior Court of Justice.

Before Filing: Please contact the City for information regarding the tax account and the application/appeal process. The ARB can only accept applications under section 322.(1)(b) where the City has passed a by-law that gives the ARB the same authority as municipal council to decide on City of Toronto Act, 2006 applications. Before filing with the ARB, please ensure that the municipality has passed such a by-law.

Required Filing Fee: $25.00 for each roll number. Your application/appeal will not be accepted without the required filing fee.

Filing Deadline: Filing deadlines are established by legislation and cannot be waived by the ARB. Filing deadlines depend on the type of application or appeal you are making.

Important: Please attach to your appeal a copy of the supporting document requested in Part 2 of the appeal form. The ARB cannot determine if your appeal has been filed on time without the supporting document.

Accessibility: We are committed to providing services as set out in the Accessibility for Ontarians with Disabilities Act, 2005. If you have any accessibility needs, please contact our Accessibility Coordinator as soon as possible.

These descriptions are summarized – please refer to the City of Toronto Act, 2006.	
SECTION NUMBER AND APPLICATION/APPEAL REASON	**FILING DEADLINE**
322.(1)(b) To apportion taxes where land is assessed in a block. Note: Filing for multiple taxation years is considered one application with one filing fee.	No deadline.
322.(5) Appeal a decision that the municipal council made on an application under section 322.(1)(b).	File within 35 days after council makes its decision.

Instructions for filing a City of Toronto Act, 2006 application/appeal with the Assessment Review Board

Part 1: Property Information

Please refer to your municipal property tax bill or property assessment notice when completing this section.

Roll Number: The roll number is a 19-digit number assigned to each property. Please ensure that this number is accurately recorded on each page of the application/appeal form.

Street Address and Property Description: Enter the address of the property for which you are filing a City of Toronto Act, 2006 application/appeal.

Preferred Language: Check the appropriate box indicating your language preference for receiving ARB services, including hearings, notices and other public information materials.

---

[4] Source: ARB website <http://www.arb.gov.on.ca/english/home.html>

Part 2: Application/Appeal Information

Application/Appeal Reason:

Check the appropriate box to indicate the reason for your application/appeal. Check only one box. Continue moving to the right along the same row to complete the application/appeal. Application can be made under 322.(1)(b) for multiple taxation years.

Taxation Year:

Write in the taxation year(s) that are the subject of your application(s)/appeal.

Supporting Documents:

Supporting documents are required by the Assessment Review Board to determine if your City of Toronto Act, 2006 appeal has been filed within legislated deadlines. Check the appropriate box to indicate you have attached a copy of the supporting document to the appeal form.

If you do not have a copy of your supporting document, do not wait to file the appeal. **Filing deadlines are established by legislation and cannot be waived.** If you do not submit the required document with your appeal, the ARB will send you an Acknowledgement Letter requesting a copy of the required document.

Filing Deadline:

This is the last day a City of Toronto Act, 2006 application/appeal can be filed with the Assessment Review Board. **Filing deadlines are established by legislation and cannot be waived.** Filing deadlines are not the same for all section numbers. It is important that you file your City of Toronto Act, 2006 application/appeal by the deadline indicated for the section number. It will not be accepted after the deadline has passed.

MPAC's Statement of Relative Value:

Check the appropriate box to indicate if you have received a Statement of Relative Value produced by the Municipal Property Assessment Corporation (MPAC). If you have received the Statement of Relative Value, you must enclose a copy of the statement with your application/appeal form.

If you do not have a Statement of Relative Value, please record the name, mailing address and roll number for each of the current owners. The ARB requires this information as the legislation requires that the Board send Notices of Hearing to all parties.

Additional Pages:

If you require more room, please attach additional page(s) and check the box on the bottom line to indicate you have attached additional page(s).

Part 3: Applicant/Appellant Information

Representative:

Check the appropriate box to indicate if you have a representative to act on your behalf with regard to this application/appeal. If you have a representative, please complete Parts 3 and 4 of the form.

Owner:

Check the appropriate box to indicate if you are the owner of the property.

Contact Information:

Provide your contact information including name, address and telephone number(s).

Please note: You must notify the Assessment Review Board in writing of any change of address or telephone number.

Personal information requested on this form is collected under the various sections of the City of Toronto Act, 2006. After an application/appeal is filed, all information relating to this application may become available to the public. For additional information, please contact an ARB Public Inquiry Assistant at (416) 212-6349 or toll free at 1-866-448-2248. The City of Toronto Act, 2006 is available at www.elto.gov.on.ca.

Part 4: Representative Authorization

If you have chosen someone to act on your behalf, please provide their name, address, telephone number, fax number and e-mail address. You will need to sign this section and provide your representative with a copy of the form. If you provided a letter or another form of written authorization for your representative, please make sure the representative checked the box in this section confirming he or she received your written authorization.

Part 5: How to File an Application/Appeal

You can file your application/appeal in a number of ways. Please choose only ONE of the following filing options:

Mail it to: Assessment Review Board, 655 Bay Street, Suite 1500, Toronto, Ontario M5G 1E5

Fax it to: (416) 314-3717 or 1-877-849-2066 (toll free) (For faxing applications, appeals and complaints only.)

Deliver it in person to: 655 Bay Street, 15th Floor. (East side of Bay Street, north of Dundas)

Please file only ONCE. If you are unsure that your filing attempt was successful and resubmit, please mark any other submissions COPY to avoid duplicate charges.

You will receive an Acknowledgement Letter by mail once your application/appeal has been received by the ARB followed by a Notice of Hearing once your hearing has been scheduled.

Please note: Once you have filed your City of Toronto Act, 2006 application/appeal, any additional correspondence with the ARB should be copied to all parties.

Part 6: Required Filing Fee

- **If you are faxing your City of Toronto Act, 2006 application/appeal**, payment must be made by VISA, MasterCard or American Express, in Canadian funds. Please include your credit card number, expiry date, cardholder's name and the cardholder's signature.

- **If you are mailing your City of Toronto Act, 2006 application/appeal**, payment can be made by credit card, cheque or money order, in Canadian funds, payable to the **Minister of Finance**. Please note the applicable roll number(s) on the front of the cheque or money order. **Please do not mail cash.** Please note that if a financial institution returns your cheque, an administration fee of $35 will apply.

- **If you are delivering your City of Toronto Act, 2006 application/appeal in person**, payment can be made by cash, cheque, money order, debit card or credit card.

The filing fee is non-refundable. You will receive an **Acknowledgement Letter** in the mail once your application/appeal has been received, followed by a **Notice of Hearing** when your hearing has been scheduled.

The information you fill in under Required Filing Fee is confidential. It will only be used to process your application/appeal and will not be placed on file.

> For further information, please contact the Assessment Review Board at 416-212-6349,
> toll free at 1-866-448-2248 or online at **www.elto.gov.on.ca**.

How to Prepare for Your Hearing Event

1. Gather the information you require to support your case, including:
   - your initial application to the municipal council and any decision of the municipal council (if you are appealing a decision of municipal council);
   - your property tax bill;
   - any factual information, including documents that you require to support your case.

2. Contact the municipality to discuss your case.

3. Consider how you will present your case to the Board.
   - Decide which documents you will provide to the Board at the hearing.
     - Bring photocopies to the hearing of any documents you would like the Board to consider in support of your case. We suggest three copies of each document: one for the Board, one for the municipality and one for you.
   - Decide whether you will require any witnesses other than yourself to give evidence at the hearing.
     - Contact your witnesses once you receive the Notice of Hearing to inform them of the hearing date, time and location.
     - If necessary, you can obtain a Summons to Witness from the Board's Registrar.
   - Consider whether there is any need for parties to exchange documents prior to the hearing.
     - Request from the municipality copies of any documents they will be relying on to support their position.
     - Prior to the hearing, consider providing the municipality with copies of the documents that you will be relying on at the hearing.

At this point, please remove the instructions (pages 1, 2 & 3) from the following application/appeal form and keep the information on how to prepare for your hearing event.

CITY OF TORONTO ACT APPLICATION/APPEAL – APPORTIONMENT

Environment and Land Tribunals Ontario
Assessment Review Board 655 Bay Street, Suite 1500, Toronto, Ontario M5G 1E5
Phone: (416) 212-6349 or 1-866-448-2248 **Fax:** (416) 314-3717 or 1-877-849-2066
Website: www.elto.gov.on.ca

Application/appeal #
Receipt #
Date Stamp
For office use only

Please note: This form is for City of Toronto Act, 2006 applications/appeals – Apportionment only. Do not use this form to file assessment complaints (sections 33, 34 or 40 of the Assessment Act). Do not use this form for any other applications, appeals and/or complaints under the City of Toronto Act, 2006 or the Municipal Act, 2001. Different forms are available to file the other applications, appeals and complaints. Issues of tax exemption can only be addressed by the Superior Court of Justice.

Before Filing: Please contact the City for information regarding the tax account and the application/appeal process. The Assessment Review Board (ARB) can only accept applications under section 322.(1)(b) where the municipality has passed a by-law that gives the ARB the same authority as municipal council to decide on City of Toronto Act, 2006 applications. Before filing with the ARB, please ensure that the municipality has passed such a by-law.

Required Filing Fee: $25.00 for each roll number. Your application/appeal will not be accepted without the required filing fee.

Filing Deadline: Filing deadlines are established by legislation and cannot be waived by the ARB. Filing deadlines depend on the type of application or appeal you are making. Please see Part 2 for the filing deadline.

Important: Please attach to this appeal form a copy of the supporting document requested in Part 2. The ARB cannot determine if your appeal has been filed on time without the supporting document.

Accessibility: We are committed to providing services as set out in the Accessibility for Ontarians with Disabilities Act, 2005. If you have any accessibility needs, please contact our Accessibility Coordinator as soon as possible

Part 1: Property Information (Please print clearly)

Roll number: ☐☐☐☐ — ☐☐☐ — ☐☐☐☐☐ — ☐☐☐☐☐ — ☐☐☐☐

PLEASE copy this roll number in the space provided at the top of every page of this form

Street address: _____

Municipality: **City of Toronto**

Please choose preferred language: ☐ English ☐ French

Part 2: Application/Appeal Information

These descriptions are summarized – please refer to the City of Toronto Act, 2006.			
PLEASE CHECK ONLY ONE REASON FOR YOUR APPLICATION/APPEAL	**TAX YEAR(S) YOU ARE APPEALING**	**SUPPORTING DOCUMENT(S) YOU MUST ATTACH TO THIS APPLICATION/APPEAL FORM**	**FILING DEADLINE**
☐ **Application: section 322.(1)(b)** To apportion taxes where land is assessed in a block. Note: Filing for multiple taxation years is considered one application with one filing fee. ☐ The municipality has passed a by-law delegating these applications to the ARB. If not, apply to the municipality instead.	_____ _____ _____ _____ _____	None	No deadline

OR

☐ **Appeal: section 322.(5)** Appeal a decision that the municipal council made on an application under section 322.(1)(b).	_____	Attach a copy of the decision you received from the municipality. ☐ I have attached a copy.	File within 35 days after council makes its decision.

Continue to next page to complete the Application/Appeal Information section.

Roll Number: ☐☐☐☐☐ — ☐☐☐ — ☐☐☐ — ☐☐☐☐☐ — ☐☐☐☐

Part 2: Application/Appeal Information - Continued

Complete this section for applications under section 322.(1)(b) and appeals under section 322.(5).

I have received MPAC's Statement of Relative Value (check the correct answer below).

☐ Yes **If yes, you must enclose a copy of the statement with this application/appeal.**

☐ No **If no, you must include the names, mailing addresses and roll numbers of the new parcel owners (current owners).**

Owner's Name	Owner's Mailing Address	New Parcel Roll Number

If you require more room, please attach additional page(s). If you have attached additional pages, please check here. ☐

Roll Number: ☐☐☐☐☐ – ☐☐☐ – ☐☐☐ – ☐☐☐☐☐ – ☐☐☐☐

Part 3: Applicant/Appellant Information

Do you have a representative? ☐ Yes ☐ No **If yes, complete Parts 3 & 4.**

Are you the owner of the property? ☐ Yes ☐ No

Last name: _____ First name: _____

Company name (if applicable): _____

Mailing address: _____

Street address	Apt/Suite/Unit#	City

Province	Country (if not Canada)	Postal Code

Business/other telephone #: _____ Home telephone #: _____

Fax #: _____ E-mail address: _____

Applicant/appellant signature: _____

   Please note: You must notify the Assessment Review Board in writing of any change of address or telephone number.

> Personal information requested on this form is collected under the various sections of the City of Toronto Act, 2006. After an application/appeal is filed, all information relating to this application/appeal may become available to the public. For additional information, please contact an ARB Public Inquiry Assistant at (416) 212-6349 or toll free at 1-866-448-2248. The City of Toronto Act, 2006 is available at www.elto.gov.on.ca.

Part 4: Representative Authorization

I hereby authorize the named company and/or individual(s) to represent me:

Company name: _____

Last name: _____ First name: _____

Mailing address: _____

Street address	Apt/Suite/Unit#	City

Province	Country (if not Canada)	Postal Code

Telephone #: _____ Fax #: _____

E-mail address: _____

Applicant/appellant signature: _____

Representatives who are NOT legal counsel **must** *confirm that they have* **written authorization** *by checking the box below.*

☐ I certify that I have written authorization from the complainant to act as a representative with respect to this complaint on his or her behalf and I understand that I may be asked to produce this authorization at any time.

> Note: Anyone in Ontario providing legal services requires a licence, unless the group or individual is not captured by the Law Society Act or is exempt by a Law Society by-law. By-law 4 exempts persons who are not in the business of providing legal services and occasionally provide assistance to a friend or relative for no fee. For information on licensing please refer to the Law Society of Upper Canada's website www.lsuc.ca or call 416-947-3315 or 1-800-668-7380.

Roll Number: ☐☐☐☐ — ☐☐☐ — ☐☐☐ — ☐☐☐☐☐ — ☐☐☐☐

Part 5: How to File an Application/Appeal

File your application/appeal using only ONE of the following options:

Mail it to: Assessment Review Board, 655 Bay Street, Suite 1500, Toronto, Ontario M5G 1E5

Fax it to: (416) 314-3717 or 1-877-849-2066 (toll free) (For faxing applications, appeals and complaints only.)

Deliver it in person to: 655 Bay Street, 15th Floor. (East side of Bay Street, north of Dundas)

For additional information, call (416) 212-6349, (toll free) 1-866-448-2248 or visit our website: www.elto.gov.on.ca.

Please file your application/appeal only ONCE. If you are unsure that your filing attempt was successful and resubmit, please mark any other submissions COPY to avoid duplicate charges.

Part 6: Required Filing Fee

Total fee submitted: $_____   by: ☐ Cheque   ☐ Money Order   OR

Credit card: ☐ Visa   ☐ MasterCard   ☐ American Express

Credit card #: _____   Expiry date: _____/_____
                                                                         month   year

Cardholder's name: _____

Cardholder's signature: _____

- If you are **not** paying by credit card, the filing fee must be received by cheque or money order, in Canadian funds, payable to the **Minister of Finance**. Please note the applicable roll number(s) on the front of the cheque or money order. **Please do not send cash by mail.**
- If you are paying by VISA, MasterCard or American Express, **the Board will accept a faxed application/appeal with the full credit card information requested above.**
- **Please note that if a financial institution returns your cheque, an administrative fee of $35 will apply.**
- **The fee is non-refundable.**
- You will receive an **Acknowledgement Letter** followed by a **Notice of Hearing.**

> **The information you fill in under Required Filing Fee is confidential.**
> **It will only be used to process your application/appeal and will not be placed on file.**

For office use only:

Fee Received: $_____   ____ Cash   ____ Cheque   ____ Money order   ____ Credit card

Verified by: _____

Appendix 5.6
Filing a Complaint with the ARB[5]

Ontario

Assessment
Review
Board

Filing a property
assessment appeal with
the ARB

2009 Taxation year

Read this brochure if:

* **You want to file an
  appeal against your
  property assessment**
* **You would like to know
  more about the ARB's
  appeal process**
* **You would like general
  information about the
  ARB**

The process for filing an appeal with the
Assessment Review Board (ARB) has
changed. Review the steps below to help you
with the process.

Step 1

a. Check your assessment notice from the
   Municipal Property Assessment Corporation
   (MPAC).

b. If your property is classified as
   **residential, farm, managed forest or
   conservation land:**
   i.   You must file a Request for
        Reconsideration (RFR) with MPAC or
        the Program Administrator first.
   ii. You will receive a decision on the RFR
        and if you disagree with that decision,
        you may file an appeal with the ARB.
   iii. Your deadline to file with the ARB is 90
        days from the mailing date of the RFR
        decision.

c. If your property is classified as **any other
   property class:**
   i.   You may file either a RFR with MPAC or
        an appeal directly with the ARB.
   ii. If you file a RFR and do not agree with
        MPAC's decision, you may then file an
        appeal with the ARB. Your deadline to
        file with the ARB is 90 days from the
        mailing date of RFR decision.
   iii. If you file directly with the ARB, your
        deadline to file with the ARB is March
        31, 2009 for annual assessment
        appeals, or 90 days from the notice
        date for other types of assessments.

Filing a property assessment appeal with the ARB

---

5 Source: ARB website <http://www.arb.gov.on.ca/english/home.html>

What happens after filing?

- You will receive a letter from the Board confirming your appeal was received.

- You will receive a Notice of Hearing in the mail once your hearing date has been scheduled. It will tell you the date, place and time of your hearing.

- See the pamphlet, "Preparing for your hearing at the ARB," for more information on how to get ready for your hearing.

What does the ARB do?

In a court-like setting, the Board **resolves disputes** about property assessments.

The Board **holds hearings** about property assessments. In most cases, it is up to MPAC to prove that its assessment is right. However, if you disagree with MPAC's assessment, you should have evidence with you at the hearing to support your arguments. The municipality is also invited to the hearing and may participate.

The Board **makes decisions** based on the evidence presented at the hearing and the law.

The Board also deals with very specific property tax appeals under the Municipal Act and the City of Toronto Act. Contact your municipality or the Board for more information on these appeals.

What does MPAC do?

MPAC assesses and classifies properties in Ontario. They prepare and mail out property assessment notices.

If you have any questions about your assessment notice or believe your assessment is wrong **contact MPAC first.**

Filing with MPAC is different than filing with the Board. Contact MPAC at 1-866-296-6722 to find out more about their process.

> **MPAC and the ARB are two separate organizations.**

What's the cost for filing an appeal?

- $75 for residential, farm, managed forest or conservation land properties
- $150 for all other property classes

*Get a $10 discount if you E File!

Is the fee refundable?

There are no refunds of the filling fee.

Can the ARB lower my property taxes?

If the Board changes your assessment, your municipality should update your taxes. Municipalities are responsible for setting your tax rate. Contact your municipality with questions about your property taxes.

What is the deadline to file my appeal?

See steps 1 (b) and (c) for your appeal deadline.

Who can I speak to if I have a question?

The Board's Public Inquiry Office is available during regular business hours to answer your questions about ARB processes. Call (416) 314-6900 or toll free 1-800-263-3237. You may also e-mail the Board at assessment.review.board@ontario.ca or check the Board's website, www.arb.gov.on.ca. Contact MPAC if you have questions about your assessment.

Useful terms and phrases

Assessment Act: The Assessment Act is the law that governs how properties are assessed in Ontario. The Board must follow the Assessment Act when it makes decisions about a property's assessed value or classification. To view the act visit www.e-laws.gov.on.ca.

Current value: Property assessments are based on their "current value." Current value is the amount a willing buyer would pay a willing seller in an "arm's length" transaction on the valuation date.

Property assessment: A property assessment is MPAC's valuation of the land, buildings and improvements on a property on the valuation date. A property's assessment value is used to determine how much property tax an owner will pay to the municipality each year. However, the assessment value is not the only factor that determines property taxes.

Roll number: This is the 19-digit number assigned to every property for identification purposes. This number will appear on your assessment notice from MPAC.

Valuation date: This is the date that the property's value is determined. The valuation date for the 2009 taxation year is January 1, 2008.

Step 2

Fill out an ARB Assessment Appeal Form. The forms are available from:

- ○ The Board's website (www.arb.gov.on.ca)
- ○ The Board's office in Toronto
- ○ MPAC's offices
- ○ City Tax offices

or

E File directly through the Board's website www.arb.gov.on.ca and receive a $10 discount!

Step 3

File your appeal:

- ■ **Online:** www.arb.gov.on.ca (Choose the E File option and receive a $10 discount)
- ■ **By fax:** (416) 645 1819 or 1-866-297-1822
- ■ **By mail:** Assessment Review Board 655 Bay Street, Suite 1500 Toronto, ON M5G 1E5
- ■ **In person:** 655 Bay Street (just north of Dundas Street) 15th Floor, Toronto.

The information contained in this pamphlet is not intended as a substitute for legal or other advice. In providing this information, the **Assessment Review Board** (ARB) assumes no responsibility for any errors or omissions in this pamphlet, and shall not be liable for any reliance placed on the information in this pamphlet.

For additional information, including the ARB's Rules of Practice and Procedure, see **www.arb.gov.on.ca** or call **(416) 314-6900 or 1-800-263-3237.**

Ontario

The **Assessment Review Board (ARB)** is an independent adjudicative tribunal established under statute by the Province of Ontario that hears appeals filed by property owners who believe there is an error in the assessed value or classification of a property. The ARB, which operates under a variety of legislation including the Assessment Act, also deals with some property tax appeals.

Produced by:
Assessment Review Board
655 Bay Street, Suite 1500
Toronto, Ontario M5G 1E5
Phone: (416) 314-6900 or 1-800-263-3237
Fax: 416-314-3717 or 1-877-849-2066
E-mail:
Assessment.Review.Board@ontario.ca
Website: www.arb.gov.on.ca

ISSN: 1708-6825
ISBN 978-1-4249-7858-8

Assessment Review Board

Appendix 5.7
Preparing For Your Hearing with the ARB[6]

The **Assessment Review Board** (ARB) is an independent adjudicative tribunal established under statute by the Province of Ontario that hears complaints filed by property owners who believe there is an error in the assessed value or classification of a property. The ARB, which operates under a variety of legislation including the *Assessment Act*, also deals with complaints on matters such as school support designation and municipal tax appeals.

Produced by:

Assessment Review Board
655 Bay Street, Suite 1500
Toronto, ON M5G 1E5
Phone: (416) 314-6900 *or* **1-800-263-3237**
Fax: (416) (416) 314-3717 *or* **1-877-849-2066**
E-mail:
Assessment.Review.Board@jus.gov.on.ca
Website: www.arb.gov.on.ca

ISSN 1708-6787
ISBN 0-7794-9115-7
© The Queen's Printer for Ontario, 2005

Assessment

Review

Board

Preparing for Your
Hearing at the ARB

The information contained in this pamphlet is not intended as a substitute for legal or other advice, and in providing this information, the Assessment Review Board (ARB) assumes no responsibility for any errors or omissions in this pamphlet, and shall not be liable for any reliance placed on the information in this pamphlet. Additional information, including the ARB's Rules of Practice and Procedure, is available at www.arb.gov.on.ca, or by calling (416) 314-6900 or 1-800-263-3237.

---

[6] Source: ARB website <http://www.arb.gov.on.ca/english/home.html>

What happens after I file a Complaint with the ARB?

After the ARB has received and processed your complaint, you will receive an acknowledgment letter. Once the complaint is scheduled for a hearing, the complainant and all other parties will receive a Notice of Hearing with the date, time and location of the hearing. This notice is usually sent 14 days before the hearing. For more information on how to file a complaint, please see the "Filing a Complaint with the ARB " pamphlet or click on the "Complaint Process" link on the ARB website, **www.arb.gov.on.ca.**

What is the status of my complaint?

You may check the current status of your complaint on our website by using the E-Status link. You will need your 19-digit property roll number to use this service.

What is a pre-hearing conference?

A pre-hearing is a preliminary meeting that is held to clarify complex issues before the hearing takes place. In most cases, residential property complaints do not require pre-hearings. But at the request of a party or on its own initiative, the Board may direct the parties to participate in a pre-hearing conference.

Where will my hearing be held?

The Notice of Hearing will indicate the place, day and time of the hearing. You can also find this information on our website by using the E-Status link. Hearings are usually held in the municipality where the property is located. It is important to arrive on time since most complaints are heard on a first come, first served basis.

What should I bring to the hearing?

A hearing is your opportunity to explain to the ARB why you think your property assessment is wrong. Your evidence, and the evidence presented by other parties, will be considered by the ARB when making a decision.

You may want to bring the following information to your hearing:

- ☐ Detailed information, such as location, lot size, square footage, number of rooms, number of stories and building age, on the property named in your complaint;
- ☐ Detailed information, as above, on comparable properties in the vicinity of your property;
- ☐ Sales information on the property and comparable properties;
- ☐ Assessed values of the property and comparable properties;
- ☐ Photographs of the property and comparable properties; and
- ☐ Three extra copies (in addition to your own set of documents) of all documents and evidence you intend to introduce, for the ARB's records, the MPAC assessor and the municipal representative.

IMPORTANT: If current sales information is not available the ARB may consider sales figures from other years.

Where can I find the information I need for the hearing?

- At your local MPAC assessment office and/or MPAC's website, **www.mpac.ca**;
- Your municipal office (town hall or city hall);

- Land registry offices, which contain the sales history of all properties in the area.

What happens at a hearing?

Hearings follow a standard format, described as follows:

ARB Member's opening remarks

At the beginning of the hearing day, the ARB Member will explain how the hearing will proceed. Generally, complaints are heard on a first come, first served basis.

The hearing process

- MPAC will describe the property in question and explain how the assessment was determined;
- You will be given a chance to explain why you think the assessment is wrong by presenting evidence;
- MPAC may question you and/or any witnesses;
- MPAC will present evidence supporting the current assessment;
- You may question MPAC about that evidence.

Note: *In some cases, the municipality or another interested party may participate in the hearing. In these cases, the other party will be given the same opportunity to present and question evidence and/or witnesses.*

Closing statements

- This is your chance to summarize your case. Your closing statement should summarize all of your evidence, the assessor's evidence, your dispute with the assessor's evidence and why you think the assessment is wrong:
- MPAC will also give its closing statements.

When does the ARB make a decision?

At the end of your hearing, the ARB member may give an oral decision. ARB decisions are sent to the complainant, MPAC and the municipality usually within 6-8 weeks following the hearing. If you would like a detailed account of how the decision was made, you may request written reasons either at the hearing or in writing within 14 days of the hearing.

In cases where the Member wants to consider the evidence further, he or she will reserve the decision until a later date. If the Member reserves the decision, written reasons will be prepared without a formal request. It may take longer to issue a decision involving written reasons.

What if I disagree with the Board's decision?

If you do not agree with an ARB decision, you may, within 30 days of the release of the written reasons, ask the ARB to review the decision. For the ARB to consider reviewing the decision you need to:

- Ask for **written reasons** for the decision within **14 days of your hearing date;**
- Submit an **affidavit** outlining the reasons for the request for review;
- Submit a **$125 filing fee** by cheque or money order made payable to the Minister of Finance.

If you believe there is an error of law in the ARB's decision, you have 30 days from the release of the decision to file a **Leave to Appeal** through the Divisional Court, a branch of the Superior Court of Justice.

If you believe the ARB has acted outside its jurisdiction, you may file an application for a Judicial Review. There is no specific time limit to file this type of application.

Do I have to attend my hearing?

You are responsible for attending your hearing unless you authorize a lawyer or representative to appear in your place. If you do not attend your hearing, the ARB may dismiss your complaint.

What if I want to change the hearing date?

To request a change in hearing date please notify the ARB, in writing, by letter, fax or e-mail as soon as possible. Make sure to include your name, property address, roll number and the reason why you want to change the hearing date. The ARB does not always approve this request, particularly when it is made on short notice. Interested parties will be advised in writing of the Assessment Review Board's decision on your request.

Please note: *You are not guaranteed a new hearing date. The ARB will review your request and advise you as soon as possible if the request has been granted.*

What if I miss my hearing?

If you miss your hearing and would like the ARB to schedule another hearing for your complaint, you must write to the Chair of the ARB explaining why you missed your hearing.

Useful terms and phrases

Affidavit: This is a legal document that contains evidence provided in writing and made under oath or affirmation. An affidavit must be sworn or affirmed before a commissioner of oaths, notary public, treasurer or clerk of a municipality, municipal councillor or lawyer.

Adjournment: This means to postpone (a hearing) to another date.

Arms-Length Transaction: This is a transaction that is negotiated by unrelated parties, each acting in their own self-interest.

Current Value: This is, generally, the amount a willing buyer would pay a willing seller for a property in an arm's-length transaction.

Leave to Appeal: A decision of the Board may be appealed to the Superior Court of Justice only on a question of law (see section 43.1 of the *Assessment Act*). To initiate this process, the complainant must apply to the Court and seek leave to appeal. Parties should consult legal counsel to explore this option.

Valuation Date: This is the date when your property value is determined. For example, the valuation date for the 2006 taxation year is January 1, 2005.

Written reasons: These set out an explanation of the Member's decision. Only prepared if party requests reasons, or Member reserves decision.

Appendix 5.8
Municipal Act Appeals and FAQ[7]

 Environment and Land Tribunals Ontario
Assessment Review Board   **Information Sheet 3**

Here's what you need to know about filing your assessment appeal with the ARB

Step 1 – Know your filing deadline
a. Check your assessment notice from the Municipal Property Assessment Corporation (MPAC).
b. If your property, or a part of it, is **residential, farm, managed forest or conservation lands:**
    i. You **must** file a Request for Reconsideration (RFR) with MPAC first and receive their response. If you disagree with MPAC's response, you may file an appeal with the Board.
    ii. Your deadline to file with the Board is 90 days from the mailing date on the letter of response from MPAC.
c. If your property is **commercial, industrial or multi-residential**:
    i. You may file either an RFR with MPAC **or** an appeal directly with the Board.
    ii. If you file a RFR and do not agree with MPAC's decision, you may then file an appeal with the Board. Your deadline to file with the Board is 90 days from the mailing date of MPAC's decision.
    iii. If you file directly with the Board, your deadline to file is shown on your MPAC notice.

Note: MPAC's process is free. The Board requires a filing fee.

Step 2 – Know how to file
a. You can **E File** using the Board's website **www.arb.gov.on.ca** and receive a $10 discount!

b. You can fill out **paper** appeal forms available:
- On the Board's website, www.arb.gov.on.ca
- At the Board's office in Toronto
- At some MPAC offices
- At some city tax offices
- By calling the Board

Step 3 – Know how to send us your appeal form (if not E Filing)
- **By fax:**
  Local: (416) 314-3717 or toll-free: 1-877-849-2066
- **By mail:**
  Assessment Review Board
  655 Bay Street, Suite 1500
  Toronto, ON M5G 1E5
- **In person:**
  655 Bay Street (just north of Dundas Street) 15th Floor, Toronto

Step 4 – Know what happens next
- You will receive a letter from the Board confirming your appeal was received.
- Notice of your hearing will be sent to you before the hearing date telling you the date, place and time of your hearing.
- See the information sheet "Preparing for your hearing at the ARB," for more information on how to get ready for your hearing.

---

[7] Source: ARB website <http://www.arb.gov.on.ca/english/home.html>

Frequently asked questions

What does the Board do?

In a court-like setting, the Board **hears appeals**, **holds hearings** and **makes decisions** about property assessments. If you disagree with your property assessment from MPAC, you may file an appeal and have a hearing at the Board. The hearing is your chance to explain why you disagree with MPAC's assessment. Sometimes, your municipality may also participate in the hearing.

The Board also deals with very specific property tax appeals under the Municipal Act, the City of Toronto Act and the Provincial Land Tax Act. Contact your municipality or the Board for more information on these types of appeals.

What is the Municipal Property Assessment Corporation (MPAC)?

MPAC assesses and classifies properties in Ontario. They prepare and mail out property assessment notices. If you have any questions about your assessment notice or believe your assessment is wrong **contact MPAC first.** MPAC is a completely different organization than the Board. Contact MPAC at 1-866-296-6722 to find out more about its process.

What's the cost for filing an appeal?

- *$75 for a residential, farm managed forest property
- *$150 for multi-residential, commercial, or industrial property

*Receive a $10 discount when you E File!

Can I get a refund of the filing fee?

There are **no refunds** of the filing fee, even if you settle with MPAC before your hearing.

Can the Board lower my property taxes?

If the Board changes your assessment, your municipality should update your taxes. Municipalities are responsible for setting your tax rate. Contact your municipality with questions about the amount of your property taxes.

Can I file an appeal even if my assessment is the same as last year's?

You can file an appeal for this tax year as long as it is before the deadline.

What is the deadline to file my appeal?

The deadline to file your appeal should be on your notice from MPAC or on the response from MPAC on your RFR. If you are unsure of the deadline, please contact the Board.

Are the hearing venues accessible?

We are committed to providing services as set out in the Accessibility for Ontarians with Disabilities Act, 2005. If you have any accessibility needs, please contact our Accessibility Coordinator as soon as possible.

Who can I speak to if I have a question?

The Board's Public Inquiry Office is available during regular business hours to answer your questions about ARB processes. Call (416) 314-6900 or toll free 1-800-263-3237. You may also e-mail the Board at **assessment.review.board@ontario.ca** or check the Board's website. Contact MPAC if you have questions about your assessment.

The **Environment and Land Tribunals Ontario (ELTO)** includes the Assessment Review Board, Board of Negotiation, Conservation Review Board, Environmental Review Tribunal, Ontario Municipal Board, Niagara Escarpment Hearing Office and the Office of Consolidated Hearings. The Tribunals operate under specific legislative requirements and share resources and best practices. The Assessment Review Board hears appeals from persons who believe there is an error in the assessed value or classification of a property and also deals with some types of property tax appeals under the Municipal Act and City of Toronto Act. For more information contact us at:

Environment and Land Tribunals Ontario
655 Bay Street, Suite 1500, Toronto, ON M5G 1E5
Telephone: (416) 212-6349 or toll free: 1-866-448-2248
Website: www.elto.gov.on.ca

ISBN 0-7794-5789-X / © Queen's printer for Ontario, 2008

Disponible en français: Voici que vous devez savoir au sujet du remboursement de vos dépenses

6

Human Rights Tribunal of Ontario

LEARNING OBJECTIVES

After reading this chapter, the reader should be able to:

- research any Ontario agency by exploring its website to find the important information needed to understand the agency's practices and procedures and how a paralegal would properly represent a client before such agency by doing so with the Human Rights Tribunal of Ontario (HRTO)
- document the background of the HRTO
- detail and explain the provisions of the enabling legislation relevant to the HRTO
- elaborate on various concepts of public policy relevant to the HRTO and the Human Rights Legal Support Centre
- state whether any regulations made under the enabling legislation are relevant to the HRTO and, if so, to discuss such provisions
- compare and prioritize the various sources of practice and procedure of the HRTO
- identify the specific rules and procedures for the HRTO and how they would be applied in a proceeding before, during, and after a hearing of the HRTO
- review and explain the procedures and practices of the HRTO by way of a flow chart and key forms and documents available on the HRTO website
- assess whether the relevant provisions of the *Statutory Powers Procedure Act* apply to the HRTO
- outline the various explanatory literature available on the HRTO website to assist the paralegal to understand the HRTO and better represent the client
- appreciate the need to find decisions and/or cases in order to understand and argue the law before the HRTO
- illustrate and discuss principles that flow from the various cases and decisions as they relate to the HRTO

INTRODUCTION

The Human Rights Tribunal of Ontario (HRTO) is an independent, adjudicative body. As of June 30, 2008, an individual who wants to make a discrimination claim will file an application at the HRTO. The HRTO, in addition to the courts and other Ontario tribunals, has jurisdiction to exercise the powers conferred under the Ontario *Human Rights Code*, R.S.O. 1990, c. H.19, as amended (*Code*), to be the decision-making body for all applications claiming a violation of human rights under the *Code*.

OVERVIEW AND BACKGROUND

On June 30, 2008, the scheme of making applications in respect of alleged breaches of the *Code* was changed from a system where complaints were made to the Human Rights Commission of Ontario (HRCO), which would investigate and then refer some complaints to the HRTO, to a system where any person could make application directly to the HRTO. Although there are transition provisions dealing with matters in the system that are still with the HRCO, the intent is for a person to start the process with the HRTO. The HRTO Rules and its Forms, Practice Directions and Policies have all changed effective June 30, 2008, to accommodate the change. On the home page of the HRTO website, the Chair of the HRTO notes that a major reason for the change is the fact that under the previous system "the enforcement procedures can be extremely time consuming and costly for the parties" and that the new system may change that. The home page also has links to two explanatory documents downloadable in MS Word and Adobe pdf formats: "The New Human Rights System and the Human Rights Tribunal of Ontario" and "What's New — Details about our facilities, recruitment, new rules and procedures, policies and transition cases". The first document talks about what has changed, including the amended *Code*, which establishes the new Human Rights Legal Support Centre that provides advice, support, and representation for applicants, while the HRCO continues to play its important public interest function. The second document discusses changes intended to occur as part of the transition phase.

The Human Rights Legal Support Centre has its own website and anyone making application to the HRTO should study its content. The Centre is supposed to provide "services rang[ing] from legal assistance in filing an application at the HRTO to legal representation on human rights applications". It may provide opportunities for employment for paralegals and may also become a legal resource for persons claiming discrimination under the *Code*.

A notice dated August 9, 2010 was inserted on the "What's New" Web page as follows:

> In December 2009, the *Adjudicative Tribunals Accountability, Governance and Appointments Act, 2009* received Royal Assent. The Act allows government to cluster tribunals and agencies with common stakeholders and related issues in order to improve public services.
>
> The clustering initiative promotes the best use of resources through cross-agency cooperation and coordination of operations and administration. It will also enhance consistency in tribunal practices, procedures and decision making.

This is likely the beginning of a cluster similar to the cluster of tribunals formed including the ARB as set out in Chapter 5. The reader should check back on the HRTO website from time to time to see how the formation of the cluster may affect, if at all, the practices and procedures of the HRTO.

On Friday June 11, 2010, the Ontario Bar Association, Continuing Legal Education department held a seminar (one of a series of annual seminars) entitled "Ontario's Human Rights System: Keeping on Top of Key Developments" which this writer attended. At the seminar, presenters such as the acting chair of the HRTO, David Wright spoke. Many of the presenters produced papers upon which their talks were based and the binder for such papers should be available from the Ontario Bar Association. Specifically, Mr. Wright provided figures for the number of hearings in the last year and such figures will appear in the 2008/09 Annual Report to be posted on the website.

ENABLING LEGISLATION

The jurisdiction and authority of the HRTO are defined by the *Code* (which creates the HRTO and sets out a few procedural rules), while the *Statutory Powers Procedure Act* is a statute of general application, which imposes minimum rules of procedure and ties the HRTO Rules that have been published into the process. Set out below is a discussion of the *Code*. In matters before the HRTO, other sections of the relevant enabling legislation are discussed and possibly interpreted; however, those sections are outside the purview of this book, other than as discussed in the selected decisions and cases in this chapter.

The *Code*

A broad overview of the *Code* is set out in the Applicant's Guide found on the "New Applications" Web page of the HRTO website as follows:

> The Ontario *Human Rights Code* is a provincial law that recognizes the dignity and worth of every person. The *Code* gives every person the right to equal treatment and equal opportunities in five areas (known as social areas):
>
> - Employment
> - Housing
> - Goods, Services and Facilities
> - Contracts
> - Membership in trade and vocational associations (such as unions)
>
> The *Code* protects the people of Ontario from being discriminated against or harassed on any of the following grounds:
>
> 1. Race
> 2. Colour
> 3. Ancestry
> 4. Place of origin
> 5. Citizenship
> 6. Ethnic origin
> 7. Disability
> 8. Creed
> 9. Sex, including sexual harassment, pregnancy, and gender identity
> 10. Sexual orientation
> 11. Family status
> 12. Marital status
> 13. Age
> 14. Receipt of public assistance [**Note:** This ground applies **only** to claims about housing.]
> 15. Record of offences [**Note:** This ground applies **only** to claims about employment.]

[*Note that numbers were substituted for the bullet points made in the original document for ease of reference.*]

> The *Code* also has sections that prohibit the following:

- Discrimination because a person has a relationship, association, or other dealing with a person or persons who are identified by one of the grounds listed above. This falls under Association.
- Reprisal or threats of reprisal because a person has claimed rights or taken part in a proceeding under the *Code*.
- Reprisal or threats of reprisal because a person has refused to infringe on another's rights.
- Sexual solicitation or advances by a person who is in a position to give or deny a benefit.
- Reprisal or threats of reprisal for rejecting a sexual solicitation.

Keeping the Overview quoted above in mind, we shall look at specific provisions of the *Code*, especially those provisions relevant to the HRTO.

Preamble

The *Code*, in its preamble, states "it is public policy in Ontario to recognize the dignity and worth of every person and to provide for equal rights and opportunities without discrimination that is contrary to law". The *Code* is the mechanism used to achieve such public policy.

Services

As stated in section 1, every person has a right to equal treatment with respect to services, goods, and facilities, without discrimination. See the first 13 grounds listed in the Overview discussed above.

Accommodation

Pursuant to subsection 2(1), every person has a right to equal treatment with respect to the occupancy of accommodation, without discrimination (see the first 14 grounds listed in the Overview discussed above). Under O. Reg. 290/98, landlords are entitled to request credit references and rental history information from a prospective tenant and use such information in selecting or refusing the tenant and not be in breach of the *Code*. Note that accommodation rights also include the freedom from harassment by the landlord or agent of the landlord or by an occupant of the same building because of the 14 grounds under subsection 2(2). Further, persons aged 16 or 17 who have withdrawn from parental control have accommodation rights and cannot be discriminated against even though they are aged less than 18 as per section 4. To emphasize the point, subsection 7(1) states that every person has the right to freedom from harassment because of his/her sex when obtaining accommodation.

Contracts

Under section 3, every person having legal capacity has a right to contract on equal terms without discrimination (see the first 13 grounds listed earlier).

Employment

Section 5(1) states that every person has a right to equal treatment with respect to employment without discrimination (see the grounds listed earlier, except #14, which applies only to accommodation). Freedom from harassment in the workplace on any of the 14 grounds is also guaranteed under subsection 5(2). To emphasize the point, subsection 7(2) states that every person has the right to freedom from harassment in the workplace because of his/her sex.

Vocational Associations

Pursuant to section 6, every person has a right to equal treatment with respect to membership in any trade union, trade or occupational association or self-governing profession without discrimination on any of the first 13 grounds listed in the Overview.

Sexual Solicitation

Freedom from unwelcome sexual solicitation or advances from a person "in a position to confer, grant or deny a benefit or advancement to" the complainant is set out in subsection 7(3)(a).

Reprisals and Infringement

These concepts are addressed in subsection 7(3)(b) and sections 8 and 9, respectively.

Definitions

Under the definitions in sections 10 and 46, various words and terms are defined.

Defences

The defence of reasonable and *bona fide* requirement, qualification, or factor is to exempt a claim of discrimination under sections 11 and 17 of the *Code*.

Special Program

Under section 14, exemption from discrimination is conferred on, and a right under the *Code* is not infringed, if a special program is designed to relieve hardship or economic disadvantage, or to assist disadvantaged persons or groups to achieve or attempt to achieve equal opportunity or that is likely to contribute to the elimination of the infringement of rights". Note that, under subsection 14(10), the HRTO can find that a special program meets the requirements of section 14, even if the HRCO did not designate it as such.

Special Employment

Specific situations in employment are not an infringement on the right to equal treatment with respect to employment if such situations fit within section 24. Any tribunal including the HRTO and the courts when looking at reasonable accommodation of employment situations and the factors involved in accommodating and determining undue hardship shall look at subsections 24(2) and 24(3), respectively.

Discrimination in Employment under Government Contracts

Government contracts are to be in accordance with the *Code* under section 26, and it is a condition of the contract that it does so. If the HRTO finds a breach of condition, "the breach of condition is sufficient grounds for cancellation of the contract, grant, contribution, loan or guarantee and refusal to enter into any further contract with or make any further grant, contribution, loan or guarantee to the same person".

Policies by the HRCO

The HRCO may publish policies to provide guidance in the applications of Parts I and II pursuant to section 30.

Inquiries and Search Warrants

Under section 31, the HRCO may conduct an inquiry for the purpose of carrying out its functions prescribed by this Act if the Commission believes it is in the public interest to do so. The rest of the section sets out what happens on an inquiry and the powers of the HRCO. In conducting the inquiry, the HRCO can authorize a person to apply to a justice of the peace for a search warrant under section 31.1, and pursuant to section 31.2, evidence obtained on an inquiry under section 31 or section 31.1 may be used as evidence in a proceeding before the HRTO.

Part IV — The HRTO

The continuation, make-up, remuneration, and similar items regarding the HRTO are set out in section 32.

Applications to the HRTO

Although applications to the HRTO are supposed to be made within one year of the alleged infringing incident under both subsections 34(1) and (8), the HRTO can extend, by subsection 34(2), the time if it "is satisfied that the delay was incurred in good faith and no substantial prejudice will result to any person affected by the delay". The application to the HRTO shall be in the form approved by it per subsection 34(3). Applications on behalf of another can be made pursuant to subsection 34(5) and such person making application can participate in the proceeding in accordance with the HRTO Rules. Under subsection 34(11), a person cannot make an application to the HRTO if

(a) a civil proceeding has been commenced in a court in which the person is seeking an order under section 46.1 with respect to the alleged infringement and the proceeding has not been finally determined or withdrawn; or

(b) a court has finally determined the issue of whether the right has been infringed or the matter has been settled

but final determination only occurs under s. 34(12) after the time for appealing expires and there is no appeal.

Applications by the HRCO

Section 36 states that the HRCO can make application to the HRTO for an order under section 45.3 if it is of the opinion that (a) it is in the public interest to do so and (b) such order could provide the appropriate remedy. Under subsection 36(3), an application by the HRCO does not affect the right of a person to make application under section 34, and applications made under sections 34 and 35 in respect of the same matter shall be dealt with in the same proceeding unless the HRTO determines otherwise (ss. 36(4)).

Parties

The rules for what persons are parties to an application to the HRTO under sections 34 and 35 are set out in section 36.

Intervention by the HRCO

As set out in section 37, the HRCO can intervene in such role as the HRTO sees fit, having regard to the role and mandate of the HRCO, or as a party.

Powers of the HRTO

Section 39 states that the HRTO "has the jurisdiction to exercise the powers conferred on it by or under this Act and to determine all questions of fact or law that arise in any application before it". Further, under section 40, the HRTO "shall dispose of applications made under this Part by adopting the procedures and practices provided for in its rules or otherwise available to the Tribunal which, in its opinion, offer the best opportunity for a fair, just and expeditious resolution of the merits of the applications" and the rules and the procedures shall be liberally construed to allow the HRTO to so adopt (s. 41).

The SPPA and the HRTO Rules

Under section 42, the provisions of the *SPPA* apply to a proceeding before the HRTO unless there is a conflict with the HRTO Rules or the enabling legislation, and in such conflict the HRTO rules or the enabling legislation shall prevail. The HRTO may make rules pursuant to subsection 43(1) and it has done so (see the HRTO Rules discussed below). Note that subsection 43(2) states that the HRTO Rules require that a matter in the jurisdiction of the HRTO cannot be disposed of "without affording the parties an opportunity to make oral submissions in accordance with the rules", and final disposition of any matter requires written reasons. Other items, which may be included in the HRTO Rules, are enumerated in subsection 43(3). The rules to apply to proceedings generally or that could apply to a specific proceeding or a type of proceeding under subsection 43(4) and any rules made by the HRTO shall only be made after holding public consultation (ss. 43(7)). The failure of the HRTO to follow its rules and practices under subsection 43(8) "is not a ground for setting aside a decision of the [HRTO] on an application for judicial review or any other form of relief, unless the failure or the exercise of a discretion caused a substantial wrong which affected the final disposition of the matter". Finally, subsection 43(9) allows the HRTO to draw an adverse inference if a situation as set out in that provision occurs.

HRTO Inquiry

Section 44 is similar to section 31 in that an inquiry can be ordered upon request of a party to the application, in this case by the HRTO, rather than the HRCO, if the HRTO is satisfied that

(a) an inquiry is required in order to obtain evidence;
(b) the evidence obtained may assist in achieving a fair, just and expeditious resolution of the merits of the application; and
(c) it is appropriate to do so in the circumstances.

The inquiry details, including searching without warrant, powers of the inquiry, and the obligation on the person doing the inquiry to prepare a report and submit it to the HRTO, are all set out in section 44.

Deferral and Dismissal of an Application

The HRTO can defer an application in accordance with its rules under section 45 and may dismiss an application, also in accordance with its rules, if it is of the opinion under section 45.1 that "another proceeding has appropriately dealt with the substance of the application."

Orders of the HRTO on Applications under s. 34

If the HRTO is of the opinion that a party to an application has infringed upon another party's rights under Part I, the HRTO has the authority to make one or more orders, even if not requested, to pay compensation, restitution, or any other act (including future acts) required that, in the opinion of the HRTO, promotes compliance with the *Code*, all as set out in section 45.2.

Orders of the HRTO on Applications under s. 35

If the HRTO is of the opinion that a party to an application has infringed upon a right under Part I, the HRTO has the authority to make any orders to do any act (including future practices) required, which, in the opinion of the HRTO, promotes compliance with the *Code*, all as set out in section 45.3.

Matters Referred to the HRCO

The HRTO can refer any matters arising out of a proceeding to the HRCO if, in its opinion, they are matters of public interest or otherwise of interest to the HRCO, but the HRCO has the discretion to deal with such matters so referred, all under section 45.4.

HRCO Policies Considered by the HRTO

Under section 45.5, the HRTO may consider HRCO policies approved under section 30, but it shall consider such policies if a party to the proceeding or an intervenor request that it do so.

Stated Case to Divisional Court

In any proceeding where the HRCO was a party or an intervenor, as well as where the HRTO makes a final decision or order and the HRCO believes that the decision or order is not consistent with a policy under section 30, it may apply to the HRTO to have the HRTO state a case to the Divisional Court (ss. 45.6(1)). The details of a stated case, including but not limited to the parties to it, and submissions by the HRTO are set out further in subsections of section 45.6.

Reconsideration by the HRTO

Any party to a proceeding before the HRTO may request that the HRTO reconsider its decision in accordance with the HRTO rules (ss. 45.7(1)). The HRTO can also reconsider its decision upon its own motion (ss. 45.7(2)). Note that, pursuant to subsection 45.6(7) with respect to a stated case, there is a time limit imposed for a reconsideration — within 30 days of receipt of the decision of the Divisional Court. Within that time limit, any party to the stated case proceeding may apply to the Tribunal for a reconsideration of the original HRTO decision or order in accordance with section 45.7.

Decisions of the HRTO are Final Except ...

Note that, in theory, there is a privative clause in section 45.8: "Subject to section 45.6 of this Act [stated case], section 21.1 of the *Statutory Powers Procedure Act* [correction of errors] and the Tribunal rules [which generally does not allow appeals to court], a decision of the Tribunal is final and not subject to appeal and shall not be altered or set aside in an application for judicial review or in any other proceeding unless the decision is patently unreasonable." This privative clause would not prevent judicial review.

Settlements

Settlements between the parties are discussed in section 45.9, and the procedures if there is a contravention of the settlement are detailed in the subsections of the section.

Part IV.1 — Human Rights Legal Support Centre

The Human Rights Legal Support Centre is set up in section 45.11 as a corporation without share capital.

The objects of it are as follows:

(a) to establish and administer a cost-effective and efficient system for providing support services, including legal services, respecting applications to the Tribunal under Part IV;

(b) to establish policies and priorities for the provision of support services based on its financial resources.

The services to be provided by the Human Rights Legal Support Centre are as follows:

1. Advice and assistance, legal and otherwise, respecting the infringement of rights under Part I.
2. Legal services in relation to,
    i. the making of applications to the Tribunal under Part IV,
    ii. proceedings before the Tribunal under Part IV,
    iii. applications for judicial review arising from Tribunal proceedings,
    iv. stated case proceedings,
    v. the enforcement of Tribunal orders.
3. Such other services as may be prescribed by regulation.

General Provisions

Under certain sections of the *Code*, as set out in section 46.2 or an order of the HRTO, anyone who is guilty of an offence is, on conviction, liable to a fine to a maximum of $25,000. The *Code* prevails over any other legislation, as stated in subsection 47(2): "Where a provision in an Act or regulation purports to require or authorize conduct that is a contravention of Part I, this Act applies and prevails unless the Act or regulation specifically provides that it is to apply despite this Act." Finally, the transitional provisions of Part VI are applicable to situations as therein stated and should be examined if a situation comes within the parameters of those provisions.

RELEVANT REGULATIONS

The review of the regulations relevant to the procedures of the HRTO (currently O. Reg. 290/98 discussed above and R.R.O. 1990, Reg. 642, as amended, regarding the form of search warrants) was done above in the review of the enabling legislation.

PROCEDURES OF TRIBUNAL

The HRTO has "Rules of Procedure — Applications under the *Human Rights Code* Part IV" (the "HRTO Rules") effective July 1, 2010, on its Web page "New Applications" on the Web link "Rules of Procedure Governing Part IV Applications", downloadable in both Word and Adobe. As noted in the HRTO Rules preamble, they were made under "the authority to make rules to govern its practices and procedures", under the *Code* that is section 42, which also states that the provisions of the *SPPA* apply to HRTO proceedings unless there is a conflict with the HRTO Rules, in which case the Rules prevail. It contains 27 main rules and a referenced list of forms. There are a number of forms both listed in the HRTO Rules and appearing in various areas of the HRTO website. **The HRTO Rules and the forms shall be discussed in summary fashion and in varying detail below, but the reader should rely only on her/his reading and interpretation of both rather than on the author.** Please note that the procedures in the enabling legislation also are applicable, as are the *SPPA* and the *Code* where noted in the HRTO Rules.

RULES

General Rules (R. 1)

Rule 1.1 states that the HRTO Rules apply to all applications under Part IV of the *Code* and "will be liberally interpreted and applied by [HRTO] to facilitate an accessible process and to ensure the fair, just and expeditious resolution of the merits of the matters before it". Practice directions (which currently exist), may be issued by the Chair of the HRTO under R. 1.2. The forms, established by the HRTO, are not part of the HRTO Rules (R. 1.3). Thirteen words or phrases are defined in R. 1.4. Numerous powers of the HRTO are listed in Rs. 1.5–1.7. Various methods, depending on the situation, to calculate time are set out in Rs. 1.8–1.10. Specific methods of communication with the HRTO, including the entitlement to do so in French and English, are detailed in Rs. 1.11–1.13. Rule 1.14 allows that persons "may be self-represented, represented by a person licensed by the Law Society of Upper Canada or by a person authorized to provide legal services in accordance with the *Law Society Act* and its regulations and by-laws." Some of the contents of documents to be filed with the HRTO, except Forms 1–3, and how the filing is to occur are set out in Rs. 1.16–1.17. Situations when documents are deemed to be filed are listed in R. 1.19. The need to use a statement of delivery form to verify the delivery of all documents on the parties except forms 1–3 is required by R. 1.20. When and how such statement is to be filed is set out in R. 1.23. Various methods of delivery of documents are enumerated in R. 1.21 and the deeming of when delivered by R. 1.22.

Accommodation of *Human Rights Code*-Related Needs (R. 2)

Please note the first sentence of R. 2.1:

> Parties, representatives and witnesses are entitled to accommodation of *Code*-related needs by the Tribunal and should notify the Registrar as soon as possible if accommodation is required.

Tribunal Proceedings (R. 3)

The obtaining of a witness summons and how it is to be delivered are set out in Rs. 3.1–3.2. Documents obtained in the proceedings can only be used in the proceeding pursuant to R. 3.3. The HRTO can set dates for the proceedings with or without consultation of the parties (R. 3.4). Rule 3.5 states that the HRTO "may conduct hearings in person, in writing, by telephone, or by other electronic means, as it considers appropriate. However, no Application that is within the jurisdiction of the [HRTO] will be finally disposed of without affording the parties an opportunity to make oral submissions in accordance with these Rules". Under R. 3.7, the HRTO does not normally record or transcribe its proceedings, but if a recording does exist, it does not form part of the record in a judicial review situation. Proceedings can be in English,

French or bilingual, and if requested in ASL or QSL or interpretation into any other language if there is notification of the Registrar as soon as possible (Rs. 3.8–3.9). Unless the HRTO determines otherwise, all proceedings are to be open to the public under R. 3.10, although the HRTO may make an order to protect the confidentiality of personal or sensitive information (R. 3.11). Rule 3.12 requires that all written decisions of the HRTO be available to the public. The consequences of a party's not attending a hearing, when notified of it, are spelled out in R. 3.13. Rule 3.14 deals with who can file, as well as how and when to file, a request to intervene.

Notice of Constitutional Question (R. 4)

Rule 4.1 states the following:

> Where a party intends to question the constitutional validity or applicability of any law, regulation, by-law or rule or where a party claims a remedy under s. 24(1) of the *Charter of Rights and Freedoms*, in relation to an act or omission of the Government of Canada or the Government of Ontario, a Notice of Constitutional Question must be delivered to the Attorneys General of Canada and Ontario and all other parties and filed with the Tribunal as soon as the circumstances requiring the notice become known and, in any event, at least (fifteen) 15 days before the question is to be argued.

Non-compliance with the Rules (R. 5)

Pursuant to R. 5.1, where a party does not comply with the HRTO Rules, the HRTO can grant relief from such failure on terms the HRTO considers appropriate. The HRTO can also vary or waive the applicability of the HRTO Rules as it considers appropriate under R. 5.2. The HRTO can do any of the enumerated acts in R. 5.5 if a respondent does not respond to a delivered application. Where a party seeks to present evidence or make submissions with respect to fact or issue not raised in any documents required under the HRTO Rules, the HRTO "may refuse to allow the party to present evidence or make submissions about the fact or issue unless satisfied that there would be no substantial prejudice and no undue delay to the proceedings" (R. 5.7).

Applications: ss. 34(1) and 34(5) of the *Code* (R. 6)

Rule 6.1 requires that applications under subsection 34(1) and (5) must be filed in completed Form 1 or Form 4, respectively. The required contents of Form 1 and 4 are detailed in R. 6.2. Applications not fully completed as determined by the HRTO may be sent back and may be re-submitted under R. 6.4. An application accepted by the HRTO shall be dealt with pursuant to R. 6.6. An application under subsection 34(5) shall, under R. 6.8, be filed with the signed consent of the person on whose behalf the application is brought.

Applications with Request to Defer Consideration (R. 7)

According to R. 7.1, an application under R. 6.1 can be made at the same time with a request to the HRTO to defer consideration of the application, in accordance with R. 14, if there are other legal proceedings dealing with the same subject matter. Such request of deferral must contain the material set out in R. 7.3.

Response to Applications under ss. 34(1) and 34(5) of the *Code* (R. 8)

Rule 8.1 states as follows: "To respond to an Application under subsection 34(1) or subsection 34(5) of the *Code*, a Respondent must file a complete Response in Form 2 not later than 35 days after a copy of the Application was sent to the Respondent by the [HRTO]." The response must contain the material set out in R. 8.2 and if not complete, may be sent back and re-submitted under R. 8.3. A response accepted by the HRTO will be sent by the HRTO to the persons listed in R. 8.4.

Reply (R. 9)

Form 3 must be used to reply to a response (R. 9.1) and deal only with new matters raised in the response (R. 9.2). The delivery and filing of the reply is set out in R. 9.3.

Withdrawal of an Application (R. 10)

Except where the withdrawal forms part of a settlement, the applicant must deliver a completed Form 9 to the persons listed in R. 10.1. Rule 10.3 states the following: "Where a Respondent or other person or organization receiving notice under Rule 10.1 wishes to respond to a Request to Withdraw, the response must be in Form 11, Response to Request, and must be filed no later than two days after the Request to Withdraw was delivered" and delivered to any other person who received Form 9 before it is filed with the HRTO (R. 10.4).

Request to Intervene (R. 11)

Rule 11.1 states: "The [HRTO] may allow a person or organization to intervene in any case at any time on such terms as the [HRTO] may determine. The [HRTO] will determine the extent to which an intervenor will be permitted to participate in a proceeding" and such intervention must be made by Form 5 (R. 11.2) and must comply with R. 11.3. Under R. 11.4, party who wishes to respond to Form 5 must do so by Form 11. Intervention by the HRCO, with or without the consent of the applicant, can be accomplished in accordance with Rs. 11.6–11.13.

Commission Applications under s. 35 of the *Code* (R. 12)

Commission Applications under section 35 of the *Code* must be by Form 7, a response to it by Form 8, and followed by a case conference that will be convened as set out in Rs. 12.1–12.5.

Dismissal of an Application Outside the HRTO's Jurisdiction (R. 13)

Rule 13.1 says the HRTO "may, on its own initiative or at the request of a Respondent, filed under Rule 19, dismiss part or all of an Application that is outside [its] jurisdiction". If the HRTO believes that it is outside its jurisdiction, it shall issue a Notice of Intention to Dismiss the Application in accordance with R. 13.2, and the HRTO shall deal with a dismissal under Rs. 13.3–13.5.

Deferral of an Application by the HRTO (R. 14)

According to R. 14.1, the HRTO "may defer consideration of an Application, on such terms as it may determine, on its own initiative, at the request of an Applicant under Rule 7, or at the request of any party" but, before deferring, give the parties notice of such intention as well as the opportunity to make submissions under R. 14.2. Under R. 14.5, the HRTO "may, on its own motion, require a deferred Application to proceed in appropriate circumstances".

Mediation (R. 15)

At any time after the application is filed, mediation assistance may be offered by the HRTO or requested by a party (R. 15.1). The parties and their representatives must sign a confidentiality agreement before mediation starts (R. 15.2), and the HRTO may direct that a person with the authority to settle be present (R. 15.3). Everything disclosed in a mediation is confidential and can only be raised before the HRTO or in another proceeding in accordance with R. 15.4. Rule 15.6 states the following about settlement:

> Where the terms of any settlement are in writing and signed by the parties the parties may request that the [HRTO] dispose of the matter in accordance with their agreement by filing a confirmation of settlement using Form 25 (Settlement). Parties may also ask the [HRTO] to issue a consent order in accordance with s. 45.9 of the *Code*. A completed Form 25 must be filed within ten (10) days of the date of the agreement.

Mediation-Adjudication with the Agreement of the Parties (R. 15A)

By written and signed mediation-adjudication agreement under R. 15A.2, the parties can agree that the HRTO member hearing the Application may act as mediator who can then continue to hear the matter as adjudicator (R. 15A.1).

Disclosure of Documents (R. 16)

No later than 21 days after the HRTO sends a confirmation of a hearing to the parties, each party must deliver to the other party documents as detailed in R. 16.1, and a statement of delivery verifying such delivery must be filed. As set out in R. 16.2, unless otherwise ordered by the HRTO, at or before 45 days prior to the first scheduled day of hearing, each party must deliver to the other party documents he or she relies upon. In addition to filing a statement of delivery verifying such delivery, each party must also file such documents to the HRTO under R. 16.3. Readers should note R. 16.4: "**No party may rely on or present any document not included on a document list and provided to other parties in accordance with Rule 16.1 and 16.2, and filed with the [HRTO] under Rule 16.3, except with the permission of the [HRTO].**"

Disclosure of Witnesses (R. 17)

Rules 17.1–17.4 require a witness list — including information detailed in Rs. 17.1–17.2 and, in the case of expert witnesses, the information under R. 17.3 — to be delivered and filed in the same manner as R. 16.1. **If it is not so filed and delivered, or if a witness is not in the delivered and filed material, the witness may not be presented at the hearing except with the permission of the HRTO under R. 17.4.**

Case Assessment (R. 18)

Rule 18.1 states that the HRTO "may prepare and send the parties a Case Assessment Direction where it considers it appropriate. The Case Assessment Direction may address any matter that, in the opinion of the [HRTO], will facilitate the fair, just and expeditious resolution of the Application and may include directions made in accordance with any of its powers in Rules 1.6 and 1.7 and the parties must be prepared to respond to any issues identified in such direction under R. 18.2".

Request for an Order During Proceedings (R. 19)

Rule 19 involves what are normally called motions (whether prior to or in the hearing) but are referred to in the rule as "requests for an order during proceedings". The request can be made at any time during a proceeding by oral submission or in writing (R. 19.1). The written request, made by Form 10, is to be delivered and filed in accordance with R. 19.2, and must contain the enumerated items in R. 19.4. The response to the written request, made by Form 11, is to be delivered and filed in accordance with R. 19.5, and must contain the enumerated items in R. 19.6. Rule 19.7 states that the HRTO "will determine whether a Request for Order will be heard in writing, in person, or electronically and, where necessary, will set a date for the hearing of the Request".

Summary Hearings (R. 19A)

Rule 19A.1 states as follows: "The [HRTO] may hold a summary hearing, on its own initiative or at the request of a party, on the question of whether an Application should be dismissed in whole or in part on the basis that there is no reasonable prospect that the Application or part of the Application will succeed" and in such hearing Rs. 16 and 17 do not apply, although the HRTO may give directions on procedures prior to the summary hearing (R. 19A.2). Under R 19A.3, where a party requests that an Application be dismissed under R. 19A, Form 26 shall be delivered in accordance with such rule.

HRTO-Ordered Inquiries (R. 20)

Rule 20.1 states that a party may request an Order from the HRTO to appoint a person to conduct an inquiry under section 44(1) of the *Code*. A Request for a Tribunal-Ordered Inquiry must be made in Form 12, delivered to the other parties, and filed with the HRTO. The Request must be made promptly after the party becomes aware of the need for an inquiry. The contents of Form 12 are set out in R. 20.2. The response to the request is by Form 13 and is to be delivered and filed under R. 20.3; it must contain complete submissions in support of the party's position under R. 20.4. Rule 20.6 states the "person conducting an inquiry will prepare a written report and submit it to the [HRTO] and the parties in accordance with the terms of reference established by the [HRTO]" and that written report can only be evidence in the proceeding if any of the elements of R. 20.7 are met.

Expedited Proceedings (R. 21)

It is stated in R. 21.1 that an applicant may request the HRTO to deal with an Application on an expeditious manner based on circumstances that require urgent resolution to the disputed issues. A Request to Expedite an Application must be made in Form 14 and filed with the Application in accordance with Rules 6.1 or 24.1 and meet the requirements of R. 21.2. A response to a request to expedite must be by Form 15 and must comply with R. 21.3.

Where the Substance of an Application Has Been Dealt with in Another Proceeding (R. 22)

The HRTO can dismiss an application if it has been appropriately dealt with in another proceeding, provided the parties can make oral submissions before the dismissal (Rs. 22.1–22.2).

Interim Remedies (R. 23)

An applicant, under R. 23.1, may request the HRTO to order an interim remedy in an Application by submitting a Form 16 (Request for Interim Remedy). Request for Interim Remedy must include the items set out in R. 23.3. The HRTO may grant the interim remedy if the requirements of R. 23.2 are met. A response to the request for an interim remedy must be in Form 17 and must comply with R. 23.4 and include the requirements set out in R. 23.5.

Contravention of Settlements (R. 24)

An application alleging contravention of a settlement must be by Form 18 (R. 24.1) and must comply with Rule 24.2. A response to the application alleging contravention must be by Form 19 and comply with R. 24.3.

Request to Amend Clerical Errors (R. 25)

A party may request, within 30 days from the date of a decision or order, or at any time by the HRTO, correction of typographical or similar error in the decision or order, and the same panel shall consider such request, unless the Chair determines otherwise (Rs. 25.1–25.2).

Request for Reconsideration (R. 26)

Please note that under R. 26.1, any **"party may request reconsideration of a final decision of the Tribunal within (thirty) 30 days from the date of the decision"** and such request shall be by Form 20 (R. 26.2) and contain the information required by R. 26.3. (Note that some flexibility regarding the 30 days deadline is provided in R. 26.5.1, which states, "A Request for Reconsideration made more than 30 days following the Decision will not be granted unless the Tribunal determines that the delay was incurred in good faith and no substantial prejudice will result to any person affected by the delay.") A party who is served with Form 20 responds only if directed to do so by the HRTO by Form 21 in accordance with R. 26.4. The HRTO will grant the request for reconsideration only if it is satisfied that one of the elements of R. 26.5 exists and will provide the parties an opportunity to make submissions (R. 26.6), which, unless determined otherwise by the HRTO, shall be by written submissions (R. 26.7). The power given to the HRTO when it decides to reconsider its decision is set out in R. 26.8. The HRTO can also reconsider its decision on its own initiative (R. 26.9), and it will determine the procedure for such reconsideration (R. 26.10).

Stated Case to Divisional Court (R. 27)

Rule 27.1 states that where the HRTO "has made a final decision or order in a proceeding in which the Commission was a party or intervenor, the Commission may, under section 45.6 of the *Code*, apply to the [HRTO] to have the [HRTO] state a case to the Divisional Court" and such application shall be by Form 22 in accordance with R. 27.2. The rest of Rule 27 (Rs. 27.3–27.6) relates to (i) parties both in support and in opposition to the HRCO's application, and (ii) the fact that the application is in and of itself a stay to a final decision or order unless otherwise ordered by the HRTO or the court.

List of Forms Referred to in the Rules

Form	Title	Rule
1	Application	6
2	Response	8
3	Reply	9
4	Application Filed on Behalf of Another Person	6
5	Request to Intervene	11
6	Notice of Commission Intervention (with Consent)	11
7	Application by Commission	12
8	Response to Commission Application	12
9	Request to Withdraw	10
10	Request for Order During Proceedings	19
11	Response to a Request for Order During Proceedings	19
12	Request for Tribunal-ordered Inquiry	20
13	Response to Request for Tribunal-ordered Inquiry	20
14	Request to Expedite Proceeding	21
15	Response to Request to Expedite Proceeding	21
16	Request for Interim Remedy	23
17	Response to Request for Interim Remedy	23
18	Application for Contravention of Settlement	24
19	Response to Application for Contravention of Settlement	24
20	Request for Reconsideration	26
21	Response to Request for Reconsideration	26
22	Commission Application to Request Stated Case	27
23	Statement of Delivery	1.23
24	Summons to Witness	3.1
25	Settlement	15
26	Request for Summary Hearing	19A

PRACTICE DIRECTIONS

Practice directions may be issued by the Chair of the HRTO under the HRTO Rules (R. 1.2). For applications to the HRTO after June 30, 2008, five practice directions in place as of the time of writing were found on the "New Applications" Web page, by use of the Web link "Practice Directions". All these practice directions govern Part IV applications under the *Human Rights Code*.

Practice Direction on Requests for Language Interpretation

This Practice Direction states the following:

> Where a party requires language interpretation or sign language interpretation services in order to participate fully in a hearing (including a Case Resolution Conference), or mediation, and makes a request that the HRTO provide such services, the HRTO will provide for interpretation services to be available to the requesting party at the hearing and/or in the mediation conference.
>
> Requests for language interpretation or sign language interpretation services must be made to the Registrar as soon as possible and well in advance of a scheduled hearing or mediation.

Practice Direction on Reconsideration

The applicability of this Practice Direction is set out in the following:

> Decisions of the HRTO are final and are not subject to appeal. However, parties may request that the HRTO reconsider a final decision it has made. Reconsideration is a discretionary remedy; there is no right to have a decision reconsidered by the HRTO. Generally, the HRTO will only reconsider a decision where it finds that there are compelling and extraordinary circumstances for doing so and where these circumstances outweigh the public interest in finality of orders and decisions.

Note that in "every case where a request is made to reconsider a decision, the HRTO must decide whether it is advisable to do so in the circumstances. If the HRTO decides it is advisable to grant a request for reconsideration, it must then decide whether the previous decision should be changed and, if so, how it should be changed". The HRTO makes its decision whether or not to grant a request for reconsideration based on the facts of the situation and on the criteria set out in the HRTO Rules (R. 26.5). Some examples for both granting and not granting the request are set out in the Practice Direction.

The procedure for the request for reconsideration is set out in the Practice Direction and the HRTO Rules. Please note that in "most cases the member who heard the original matter will be assigned to determine the reconsideration request".

Practice Direction on Recording Hearings

This Practice Direction states that, while it may allow it in its discretion, the HRTO does not normally record or transcribe its proceedings although the HRTO "will record the hearings when it is necessary to accommodate *Code*-related needs of the panel, a party or a representative who would otherwise be unable to participate in the hearing". With the consent of the HRTO, the parties "may record hearings using their own equipment and transcribe those recordings at their own expense" but such recordings do not form the record of the proceedings on appeal or judicial review.

The HRTO "may permit a party to have a court reporter record the hearing at the party's expense", resulting in an official transcript. Copies shall be to given to the other parties, and the HRTO and will normally be part of the record and will form part of the record of the proceedings on appeal or judicial review.

Practice Direction on Hearings in Regional Centres

To make its hearings and mediations accessible, the HRTO will hold hearings in the various regional centres: Toronto, Kingston, London, North Bay, Ottawa, Sarnia, Sault Ste. Marie, Sudbury, Timmins, Thunder Bay, and Windsor, and any other location to accommodate the parties and the witnesses. Any request to change the location should be in writing and made to the Registrar as soon as possible.

Practice Direction on Applications on Behalf of Another Person

This Practice Direction recognizes that some persons lack legal capacity to file a human rights application on their own behalf for reasons such as mental incapacity or being a minor. It then states that under subsection 34(1) of the *Code*, applications can be made on behalf of a minor by a "Next Friend" and on behalf of a person with mental incapacity by, depending on circumstances, either a "Litigation Guardian" or by a "Substitute Decision-Maker".

Further, applications "on behalf of another person may be filed under section 34(5) of the [*Code*] if the other person would be permitted to bring their own Application under the [*Code*] and consents to the application".

Such person who brings an application on behalf of another person is expected to take the necessary or required steps of any applicant in proceedings before the HRTO.

Practice Direction on Electronic Filing by Licensed Representatives

Applications (Form 1) and Responses (Form 2) must be signed by the applicant or respondent except where they are filed electronically, by email or as a Smart Form, by the licensed representative (lawyer or licensed paralegal) of the applicant or respondent. By so filing, the representative undertakes that she/he has the authorization to represent the client, the client has reviewed the document, and has confirmed the declaration set out in the Practice Direction in such form(s).

Practice Direction on Communicating with the Human Rights Tribunal of Ontario

This Practice Direction sets out general information as to how the approach to communicating with the HRTO for both parties and representatives and with each other. Also discussed is how the HRTO will communicate its decisions. All written communications with the HRTO should be through the Registrar. Procedures for e-mail communication are set out. Finally it is noted that "[c]ommunications that are unduly lengthy, repetitive or disrespectful of any other participant or the Tribunal may be rejected."

Practice Direction on Hearings before the Human Rights Tribunal of Ontario

This Practice Direction provides information on how hearings, in general, as well as Case Resolution Conferences, and hearings in the Transitional Applications stream may be conducted, but not to the conduct of summary hearings, which has its own Practice Direction set out below. It is noted that the "HRTO is committed to a process that is accessible; fair, just and expeditious; responsive to the parties that appear before the HRTO; appropriate to the nature of the particular case; and, able to determine the merits of an application, considering the facts and the relevant legal principles." To achieve this, the HRTO adopts a flexible approach to hearings, taking into account the above core values. The principal objective of the process is always fair and timely, and the outcome must be based on the facts, the law, and the merits of the application.

A human rights application will proceed to a hearing if the parties to the application do not agree to mediation or the mediation fails to produce a settlement. The HRTO will send the parties a Notice of the hearing. The procedures thereafter should follow what is stated in the Practice Direction until closer to the hearing date when an HRTO adjudicator will decide whether to issue a Case Assessment Direction to assist the parties to prepare for the hearing after reviewing the documents and witness statements in the file. Some cases's Case Assessment Direction preparation may involve a case conference call with the parties. A Case Assessment Direction may deal with items that are set out in the Practice Direction.

A hearing or Case Resolution Conference before the HRTO is a legal proceeding. The parties are expected to attend prepared and to present their case through evidence (witnesses and documents) and submissions. The role and powers of the adjudicator are then discussed.

Practice Direction on Naming Respondents

(Note: The information in this document relating to naming respondents applies only to applications filed under section 34 or 35 of Part IV of the Ontario *Human Rights Code*.) "Individual respondents", "organizational respondents", and "government respondents" are discussed as it is necessary to correctly identify each respondent in an application before the HRTO. The HRTO does not hear applications involve matters that fall under federal jurisdiction. Example of such works and undertakings are listed in the practice direction.

Practice Direction on Requests to Expedite an Application and Requests for an Interim Remedy

(Note: The information in this document relating to Requests to Expedite and Requests for an Interim Remedy applies to new applications filed under section 34 or 35 of Part IV of the Ontario *Human Rights Code*.)

The HRTO's Rules allow an applicant to request that their application be dealt with in an expedited manner. However, only in *exceptional circumstances* will the HRTO expedite an application and give it priority over other applications:

> In its decisions, the HRTO has refused to grant requests to expedite unless the circumstances are truly urgent, requiring the resolution of the human rights dispute in a particularly rapid manner as compared with the time required to complete the HRTO's regular process (*Weerawardane v. 2152458 Ontario Ltd.*, 2008 HRTO 53 (CanLII)) or where refusal to expedite will render the remedy for the alleged human rights breach moot or unavailable (*Ebrahimi v. Durham District School Board*, 2009 HRTO 1062 (CanLII)).
>
> Except in the rarest of circumstances and without a compelling explanation, an applicant who has not filed the application promptly after identifying the alleged human rights breach will not be given the priority for HRTO resources of an expedited proceeding *Kwan v. Hospital for Sick Children*, 2009 HRTO 621 (CanLII)).

Upon a decision to order an expedited proceeding, the HRTO will determine the changes that are necessary to its processes for that particular case. Changes to the processes may include abridgement of response, reply, and disclosure timelines and, where the parties consent to mediate, scheduling rapid mediation dates and/or setting early hearing dates.

The HRTO may also exercise its powers under the *Human Rights Code* and Rule 1.7 to direct the hearing process to ensure a resolution be made expeditiously. The HRTO reviews requests to expedite and may shorten the times for filing the Response to Request to Expedite (Form 15) in urgent circumstances.

The procedure for requesting an expedited procedure is set out in the Practice Direction, including Form 14, and possibly other forms to be filled out, and the contents thereof. Note that Form 14 "**must also include one or more declarations signed by persons with direct first-hand knowledge detailing all of the facts upon which the applicant relies in support of the Request to Expedite**." Information on declarations can be found in "What is a Declaration?" section on the Web page.

A party to an application can seek interim remedy, but the party must prove that the request meets all elements of the Rule, as clearly stated in the Tribunal's decision in *TA v. 60 Montclair*, 2009 HRTO 369 (CanLII). The Tribunal's decision to grant an interim remedy is based on whether the interim remedy is "necessary to facilitate and ensure the Tribunal is able to award a complete, appropriate and effective remedy at the end of a hearing, should a violation of the *Code* be found".

Declarations signed by persons with direct first-hand knowledge detailing all of the facts are also required to support the Request for an Interim Remedy.

Practice Direction on Scheduling of Hearings and Mediations, Rescheduling Requests, and Requests for Adjournments

This Practice Direction discusses approaches to balancing competing interests in scheduling and rescheduling mediation and hearings, as well as dealing with requests for adjournments. Note that the information in this Practice Direction also applies to s. 53(5) hearings and s. 53(3) Case Resolution Conferences in the Transitional Applications stream, and all references to "hearings" also apply to Case Resolution Conferences.

Practice Direction on Summary Hearing Requests

Using the approach set out in this Practice Direction, a party can request a summary hearing "on the question of whether the application should be dismissed in whole or in part on the basis that there is no reasonable prospect that the application will succeed". The HRTO can also initiate a summary hearing on such or other issues. The procedures before, during, and after the summary hearing are set out in the Practice Direction as well.

The information in this direction applies *only* to applications filed under section 34 or 35 of Part IV of the Ontario *Human Rights Code*. Summary hearings are not available for Transition Applications related to human rights complaints filed with the Human Rights Commission before June 30, 2008.

FORMS

For applications to the HRTO after June 30, 2008, 26 forms were in place as of the time of writing. They were found on the "New Applications" Web page, by use of the Web link "Forms" and consist of links to both downloadable MS Word and Adobe pdf versions of the same 26 forms listed at the end of the HRTO Rules plus Form 25 for settlement.

Form 1 — Application under Part IV of the *Human Rights Code*

This form is the general application under section 34 of the *Code* and consists of two pages of instruction and 10 pages of forms to be filled out. (See Appendix to the chapter for a copy of the form.)

Supplemental Forms

Depending on which of the five areas of discrimination alleged, in addition to Form 1, one of the Supplemental Forms also needs to be filled out and filed.

- Form 1-A — Employment
- Form 1-B — Housing
- Form 1-C — Goods, Services or Facilities
- Form 1-D — Contracts
- Form 1-E — Membership in a Vocational Association

Form 2 — Response

This form is a response to a Form 1 application. (See Appendix to this chapter for this form.)

The other 24 forms, as listed in the table shown at the end of the HRTO Rules, should be downloaded and completed as necessary.

POLICIES

There are four policies of the HRTO on its website as of the date of writing, downloadable in both MS Word and Adobe pdf formats and accessed by the Web link "Policies" on "The Law and Policies" Web page.

Policy on Accessibility and Accommodation

This policy is predicated on three guiding principles in making all HRTO services accessible:

- Services should be provided in a manner that respects the dignity and independence of members of the public.
- Services should be provided in a manner that fosters physical and functional access to the [HRTO]'s processes and promotes the inclusion, and full participation of members of the public.
- All persons should be given equal opportunity to obtain, use and benefit from the Tribunal's services. Where required, individualized accommodation will be provided, short of undue hardship.

The HRTO "will promote equal access for all individuals including parties, witnesses and representatives, to fully participate in its processes, short of undue hardship". This policy applies to all the HRTO's public offices and all HRTO staff and members.

Requests for accommodation will be considered on an individualized basis and are to be made to the Registrar. The policy also discusses the services and facilities of the HRTO available to accommodate those that need such accommodation.

Policy on Representation before the HRTO

Due to the importance of the policy to the readers of this book, the policy is set out in full in the Appendix to this chapter.

Policy on Public Complaints

This policy sets out how complaints about the HRTO's "services and/or conduct of an adjudicator or staff person are to be made and resolved" and details important information about making a complaint when the HRTO will not deal with the complaint and how a complaint is made.

EXPLANATORY LITERATURE FROM THE TRIBUNAL

Other than the documents already discussed, there are four guides that explain the Forms and processes of the new procedures before the HRTO on the Web page entitled "New Applications": "Applicant's Guide", Respondent's Guide", "Plain Language Guide", and "Guide to Preparing for a Hearing Before the HRTO" (all downloadable in MS Word and Adobe pdf formats). The reader may want to refer to the three guides to gain further insight into the procedures; however, a clear understanding of the HRTO Rules will probably benefit the reader more.

Formerly access directly on the website to decisions of the HRTO, but now there is a link to "HRTO Decisions on CanLII", which allows free access to many previous decisions of the HRTO.

RELEVANT CASES AND/OR DECISIONS

The cases and decisions discussed below are not meant to be exhaustive and are only those found in July of 2008. The discussion reflects only the author's viewpoint and should not be regarded as legal opinion. Readers should continue to update and research on new cases and decisions, and briefing must be done in all circumstances.

Thirteen matters, including cases before the Divisional Court (Div. Ct.) and before one judge of the Superior Court of Justice (Sup. Ct. J.), as well as decisions of the HRTO, shall be discussed in chronological order, with the oldest one first (unless the case is one in a series, which will be discussed starting with the lowest court) to give the reader a sampling of how these cases and decisions have been decided and their relevance to the HRTO. Not every case discussed is a ground-setting decision; however, the review should give the reader some idea of how the HRTO and the courts have dealt with various procedural and substantive issues in the first decade of the 21st century.

Barker v. Famous Players, A Division of Viacom Canada Inc.

Barker v. Famous Players, A Division of Viacom Canada Inc., 2004 HRTO 10 (the *Barker* decision), is an interim decision, which is set out in a decision brief form, partly as an example of decision briefing for the reader.

PARTIES: Ontario Human Rights Commission (the "Commission")
Nancy Barker, Scott Simser and Gary Malkowski (the "Complainants")
Famous Players, A Division of Viacom Canada Inc. (the "Respondent")

WHERE FOUND: URL: http://www.canlii.org/en/on/onhrt/doc/2004/2004hrto10/2004hrto10.html

BACKGROUND (FACTS)

This matter arose as complaints made to the Commission by the Complainants, alleging that their rights to equal treatment with respect to services, goods, and facilities without discrimination as required by the *Ontario Human Rights Code* (*Code*) has been infringed by the Respondent; that is, by failing to provide captioning services in its movie theatres.

Motions, brought on consent, to combine the three matters and with respect to adjournment of the hearing dates scheduled for August 2004 were both granted. The motion brought by the Respondent to further postpone its disclosure obligations was granted based upon certain factual findings not relevant to this brief. The motion regarding Mr. Simser's amending his complaint to add a new allegation of reprisal was heard and ruled on in this decision. Mr. Simser submitted that a reprisal occurred based upon an e-mail sent by the public affairs department of the Respondent on February 21, 2003, which stated in part as follows: "Essentially the complainant is demanding we immediately install Rear Window Captioning on ALL of our 845 screens across Canada."

ISSUES

1. What is the meaning of reprisal as set out in section 8 of the *Code*?
2. Is the e-mail sent by the department of the Respondent, on its face, sufficient to give rise to the appearance of reprisal within the meaning of section 8 of the *Code* subject to any natural justice concerns?
3. If the second issue is answered in the affirmative, can Mr. Simser amend his Complaint to include the allegation of reprisal?

DECISION

For reasons set out in the decision where the adjudicator discussed the meaning of reprisal and found that the e-mail did not give rise to the appearance of reprisal, Mr. Simser's motion to amend the Complaint to include the allegation of reprisal was dismissed.

REASONS

The word "reprisal" is set out in section 8 of the *Code* in relation to a person being able to make a claim and enforce his or her rights under the *Code* without "reprisal". The adjudicator refers to the following judgments and decisions to help her interpret the meaning of reprisal as used in section 8: The Ont. C.A. case of *Entrop v. Imperial Oil Ltd. (No. 7)* (2000), 37 C.H.R.R. D/481 (the *Entrop* case), agreed with the predecessor board to the HRTO that reprisal is a deliberate, wilful, and reckless action in retaliation for the complainant filing the complaint. The Divisional Court judgment in *Jones v. Amway of Canada Ltd.* (2002), 159 O.A.C. 331 (the *Jones* case), agreed with the adjudicator of the predecessor board's decision with the statement that "[a]lthough it is clear that in human rights law generally there is no need to prove an intent to discriminate, we have great difficulty appreciating how there can be a breach of section 8 without an intent to perpetrate the prohibited conduct".

The adjudicator agrees with the above and the decision of *Ketola v. Alue Propane Inc. (No. 1)* (2002), 44 C.H.R.R. D/20 (the *Ketola* decision). She states the following:

> The Tribunal believes that the right set out in section 8 stands apart from the other provisions within Part I of the *Code* for which intent is not required, because ... its purpose is to protect the assertion of human rights from collateral attack that would otherwise "gut" the *Code* and render it ineffectual.

Based upon the need for, at least, the appearance of the intent to retaliate and upon reviewing the facts, finding that the e-mail is not a reprisal but an attempt to lobby, the adjudicator finds insufficient facts to support the argument that there is a triable issue with respect to reprisal. Based upon that reasoning of no triable issue, as well as the fact it would be against natural justice to require the Respondent to expend time and expense necessary to answer this new allegation, the adjudicator dismisses the motion.

McEwan v. Commercial Bakeries Corp.

In *McEwan v. Commercial Bakeries Corp.*, [2004] O.H.R.T.D. No. 13, 2004 HRTO 13, File No. HR-0568-03 (the *McEwan* decision), an HRTO decision, the issues were related to preliminary motions for disclosure of certain medical records and witness statements made by the respondent. The complainant stated that his medical condition caused a disability and the treatment by his employer in not accommodating him infringed on his right to equal treatment with respect to employment without discrimination. The adjudicator in determining that some records should be disclosed, and not others, at this time first noted the duty to disclose and the relevance of medical records in matters before the courts and tribunals:

> Everyone owes a general duty to give evidence relevant to the matters in issue, so that the truth may be ascertained: *M.(A.) v. Ryan*, [1997] 1 S.C.R. 157. Moreover, at common law, the test for production is arguable relevance.
>
> Unlike the civil courts that follow the *Rules of Civil Procedure*, the Tribunal is not bound by any particular rule that mandates the production of medical records. Thus, while the courts must comply with *Rule* 31.10, and the case law that follows it, the Tribunal only looks to these sources for guidance where relevant.

After looking at the justification for the production of medical records in civil litigation matters, the adjudicator said the following about situations such as the one before her:

> In comparison, individuals who are found to be disabled within the meaning of the *Code* are seeking accommodation of their disabilities, rather than financial recovery for the causation of them. For the most part, since causation is not normally in issue, less medical information is required for human rights cases dealing with disability than for per-

sonal injury cases. However, where the existence of the disability is itself very much in issue, the Tribunal must engage in a balancing exercise.

Taking into account the case law in the matter, the adjudicator noted the balancing act that must be done in situations such as the one before her:

> As a matter of natural justice and fairness, the Tribunal must balance the general duty to require production of all relevant material in disability cases, where the disability itself is in dispute, so that Respondents have sufficient opportunity to advance their case, versus the invasion of the Complainant's privacy vis-à-vis his confidential conversations and private records with his physicians and psychological counsellors.

Finding that the medical records more than met the test of arguable relevance, the adjudicator ordered that those records be disclosed, but witness statements and lists should not be disclosed at that time when the respondent does not even know what witnesses would be called.

Modi v. Paradise Fine Foods Ltd.

Modi v. Paradise Fine Foods Ltd., [2005] O.H.R.T.D. No. 225, 2005 HRTO 25, File No. HR-0569-03 (the *Modi* decision) dealt with the issue of the admissibility of character evidence in an HRTO hearing. In this situation, the complainant alleged that the respondent was acting in a discriminatory manner in serving the complainant. The respondent's defence was that he was not at the store when the alleged incident occurred. He wanted to call witnesses who would give evidence as to how he generally comported himself in the store. The adjudicator had to determine whether the respondent could call such witnesses and, after determining such evidence to be "character" evidence, stated the legal position regarding admissibility as follows:

> Character evidence is generally inadmissible in civil proceedings in Canada, and the [HRTO] (and its predecessor, the Ontario Board of Inquiry (Human Rights Code)) has applied that principle: *Rubio v. A-Voz Portuguese Canadian Newspaper Ltd.*, [1997] O.H.R.B.I.D. No. 10; *Chacko v. Transpharm Canada Inc. (c.o.b. Toronto Institute of Pharmaceutical Technology)*, [2001] O.H.R.B.I.D. No. 11. In contrast, similar fact evidence is more readily admissible. Classification of the nature of the relevant evidence therefore tends to be critical.
>
> In Chacko, M.A. McKellar states the situation simply and usefully:
>
> > [11] The propositions underlying the so-called "similar fact rule" may be briefly stated. Generally speaking, evidence going to a party's character or reputation is not relevant and not admissible. In some circumstances, however, evidence that the party whose behaviour is now impugned has previously acted in a manner similar to that currently alleged is admissible. Whether such evidence is admissible is a discretionary decision, requiring the probative value of the evidence to be assessed against its prejudicial effect.

As the respondent in this situation stated that he was not there, the evidence from the witnesses would be character evidence and not admissible.

Smith v. Ontario (Human Rights Commission)

Smith v. Ontario (Human Rights Commission), [2005] O.J. No. 377, 195 O.A.C. 323, 38 C.C.E.L. (3d) 135, 136 A.C.W.S. (3d) 1106 (the *Smith* case), is a 2005 Div. Ct. case dealing with an appeal of an HRTO decision, which was set out in the *Code* (which currently has no right to appeal a decision of the HRTO). The HRTO found that the complainant's race was not a factor in the decision to terminate employment, and therefore he was not entitled to compensation for lost wages, and that the poisoned workplace that existed was not wilful or reckless and therefore the complainant was not entitled to compensation for mental anguish. As there is no longer the right to appeal HRTO decisions under the *Code*, the case finding the standard of review is currently irrelevant to HRTO decisions. However, the case does state the law with respect to poisoned work environments in general and to the situation in the case:

> Where termination occurs within a poisoned work environment, a proper consideration of whether the termination was discriminatory requires that it be examined in the context of the poisoned work environment. See *Naraine v. Ford Motor Co. of Canada (No. 4)* (1996), 27 C.H.R.R. D/230 (Ont. Bd. Inq.) upheld [1999] O.J. No. 2530, 34 C.H.R.R. D/405 (Ont. Div. Ct.); *Moffatt v. Kinark Child and Family Services*, [1998] O.H.R.B.I.D. No. 19.
>
> On this record, a finding that race was a factor is not only available, but in our view would have been made if the Tribunal had not assessed the evidence with a view to determining the existence of racial motivation, but had assessed the evidence to determine whether race was a factor in the termination.
>
> We are all of the view that the appeal should be allowed and the decision of the Tribunal that race was not a factor is set aside.

Boodhram v. 2009158 Ontario Ltd. (c.o.b. A Buck or Two #324)

Boodhram v. 2009158 Ontario Ltd. (c.o.b. A Buck or Two #324), [2005] O.H.R.T.D. No. 54, 2005 HRTO 54, File No. HR-0976-05 (the *Boodhram* decision) is interesting because of its finding of the law with respect to an award for general damages for a breach of rights under the *Code*. In this case, the HRTO had a written hearing for which the Respondents did not file submissions although they were properly served. The adjudicator found the uncontradicted evidence showed discrimination in employment on a ground of disability, namely an injury on the job for which the complainant was terminated, and then had to determine the appropriate compensation. In determining the general damages to award in the situation, the HRTO made the following statement:

> [The HRTO] and the Courts have recognized that there is an intrinsic value to the rights set out in the *Code* and a breach of those rights will merit the award of general damages. Jurisprudence also recognizes that general damage awards should not be set so low as to trivialize a breach of human rights. See: *Shelter Corp. v. Ontario (Human Rights Commission)* (2001), 39 C.H.R.R. D/111 (Div. Ct.) at paras. 43 and 44; *Gohm v. Domtar Inc. (No. 4)* (1990), 12 C.H.R.R. D/161 at paras. 126–127 (Ont. Bd. of Inq.).
>
> The Commission provided a number of cases in which general damage awards were made and which set out the criteria to be used in assessing the quantum of general damages. In the present case there was a single incident of discriminatory conduct and the behaviour of the Respondents does not appear to have been with particular malicious intent. Also, there was no evidence presented of mental anguish or distress, and the Commission did not seek damages in that regard. However, Ms. Boodhram's rights under the Code were violated and she is entitled to an award of general damages which recognizes the significance of those rights. Considering the facts of this case and the facts in the authorities provided by the Commissions, the Tribunal finds that the $5,000 sought is reasonable and appropriate. See: *Ontario (Human Rights Comm.) v. Ontario (Ministry of Health) (No. 2)* (1995), 24 C.H.R.R. D/250 (Ont. Bd. of Inq.) (total award of $7,000 for general damages); *Arias v. Desai* (2003), 45 C.H.R.R. D/308 (H.R.T.O.) (total general damages of $25,000); *Ketola v. Value Propane Inc. (No. 2)* (2002), 44 C.H.R.R. D/37 (Ont. Bd. of Inq.) (total general damages of $20,000); *deSousa v. Gauthier* (2002), 43 C.H.R.R. D/128 (Ont. Bd. of Inq.) (total award of $25,000 for general damages and mental anguish); *Baylis-Flannery v. DeWilde (No.2)* (2003), 48 C.H.R.R. D/197 (H.R.T.O.) (total general damages of $35,000).

[Note that the remedial provisions under the *Code* have been changed as of June 30, 2008.]

York Advertising Ltd. v. Ontario (Human Rights Commission)

York Advertising Ltd. v. Ontario (Human Rights Commission), [2005] O.J. No. 1808, 197 O.A.C. 185, 197 O.A.C. 185, 139 A.C.W.S. (3d) 108, 55 C.H.R.R. D/308 (the *York* case) is a 2005 Div. Ct. case dealing with judicial review of a decision of the HRTO. The facts of the case are set out in the following paragraphs:

> This proceeding arises out of a complaint filed by the respondent, Jane Doe (her pseud-onym was substituted by the Tribunal for her proper surname), with the respondent, Ontario Human Rights Commission ("the Commission") in which she alleged that the applicants and the respondent, Hetherington, had infringed her right to equal treatment with respect to employment without discrimination based on her gender and her right to freedom from harassment in the workplace based on her gender. York was her employer and Murphy was York's data processing manager. Hetherington was formerly employed by York, but during the time frame covered by the complaints he provided services to York as an independent contractor through his company, the respondent Richland Marketing Inc. ("Richland").
>
> At the Commission's invitation, York and Murphy agreed to mediate Doe's com-plaint. As a result of that mediation, York, Murphy and Doe entered into minutes of settlement which included a provision for a payment by York and Murphy to Doe. The minutes provided that the settlement was in full settlement of all claims by Doe against York and Murphy and recited that Doe had already executed a full and final release. The minutes also recited that the settlement did not constitute an admission by York and Murphy of any violation of the *Human Rights Code*, R.S.O. 1990, c. H.19 ("the *Code*").
>
> That settlement was then approved by the Commission and thereby became final.

The HRCO referred Doe's complaint against Hetherington to the HRTO and the decision made as a result thereof made findings against York, Richland, and Murphy, who then made application for judicial review of the decision as the HRTO "made various adverse findings of fact against York and Murphy and concluded that they too had violated various sections of the" *Code*. The court upheld the application for judicial review:

> The making of the adverse findings and conclusions against the applicants in the circum-stances of this case constituted a violation of natural justice and due process.
>
> It is the applicants' position that it was not open to the Tribunal to expand its authority to inquire into issues beyond those referred to it by the Commission, namely, issues involving only Doe and Hetherington and that, by doing so, it exceeded its statu-tory jurisdiction. The Commission supports this position and the Tribunal opposes it. It is my view that the applicants' position is correct. The Tribunal's adverse findings and conclusions against the applicants reveal the over-reach by the Tribunal beyond what had been referred to it by the Commission in violation of the limits of its authority as set out in sections 36(1) and 39(1). By making findings and conclusions of wrongdoing against the applicants the Tribunal was, in effect, adjudicating a complaint that had not been referred to it by the Commission.

The court provides the following to clarify its position:

> In the circumstances of this case, the applicants were entitled to assume that, once the terms of the settlement reached had been fully finalized, they could safely disengage themselves entirely from the complaints process without fear of being in jeopardy of being the subject of adverse findings and conclusions by the Tribunal. It would be incomprehensible, and contrary to law, that a statutory procedure for the resolution of human rights complaints in Ontario could lead to findings of wrongdoing against a party who had been released from the complaints process through a settlement, and who had no formal notice of the hearing, was not a party to it, and did not participate.

Metcalfe v. Papa Joe's Pizza & Chicken Inc.

Metcalfe v. Papa Joe's Pizza & Chicken Inc., [2005] O.H.R.T.D. No.46, 2005 HRTO 46 File No. HR-0595-04 and HR-0596-04 (the *Metcalfe* HRTO decision) involved an alleged discrimination based on sex and family status and the reprisal as the aftermath of a police investigation into the alleged sex discrimination. Believing the evidence of the complainants, the HRTO awarded damages in compensation, as well as of a number of public interest remedies.

Papa Joe's Pizza v. Ontario (Human Rights Commission)

Papa Joe's Pizza v. Ontario (Human Rights Commission), [2007] O.J. No. 2499, 225 O.A.C. 256, 59 C.C.E.L. (3d) 98, 158 A.C.W.S. (3d) 794, 2007 CarswellOnt. 4054 (the *Papa Joe's* case) is a 2007 Div. Ct. case appealing the *Metcalfe* HRTO decision. In deciding the case, the court held that the following three issues had to be decided:

1. Did the tribunal err in admitting similar fact evidence?
2. Did the reasons meet the minimum standard required to support the findings that Mr. Toufighjou violated the human rights of Ms. Metcalfe and Mr. Hoogerdijk?
3. Did the reasons meet the minimum standard required to support the compensations awards and public interest orders?

The court throughout the decision decried the lack of reasons given in the *Metcalfe* HRTO decision:

> The reasons for the decision are sparse and, from the perspective of appellate review, leave a lot to be desired. The issue is whether those reasons are so inadequate and insufficient that they constitute a denial of natural justice based on procedural fairness. The duty to provide meaningful reasons is important.

In respect of the first issue regarding similar fact evidence, the court said the following:

> Similar fact evidence in a case such as this is by its nature prejudicial. The issue is whether its probative value outweighs that prejudice. Though s. 15 of the *Statutory Powers Procedure Act*, R.S.O. 1990, c. S.22 relaxes the rules of evidence somewhat, caution is required.
>
> Factors to consider in ruling on the admissibility of similar fact evidence in this case include:
> (a) whether the evidence put forward does indeed involve similar facts;
> (b) whether the evidence is put forward simply to cast doubt on Mr. Toufighjou's character, or to imply or establish his propensity or predisposition towards committing such acts (in which case it should not be admitted); and
> (c) whether the introduction of the evidence will confuse the issues by requiring the tribunal to engage in collateral issues beyond the subject matter of the complaint.

The court held that the similar fact evidence could be used in this case and was used properly for the following reasons:

> The similar fact evidence went beyond mere propensity to commit a particular act or acts, or evidence of bad character. From the outset, this case was clearly a credibility contest between Ms. Metcalfe and Mr. Toufighjou. It is evident the tribunal member concluded the similar fact evidence would have probative value if it could assist him in determining credibility. ...
>
> The tribunal member was cognizant of the correct legal test for the admission of the similar fact evidence, had the discretion to admit it, and reasonably exercised that discretion.

As to the issue of the whether the reasons met the minimum standard required to support the finding, the court said they did:

> Once the tribunal member accepts the evidence of Ms. Metcalfe as truthful, it becomes the "clear and cogent" evidence required to support the findings against Mr. Toufighjou because there is no credible evidence to the contrary.

With respect of the reasons meeting the minimum standards required for the damages and public interest remedies ordered, the court said the reasons did not meet the minimum standard and then went on to modify the awards based on the reasons in the judgment.

Stephens v. Lynx Industries Inc.

Stephens v. Lynx Industries Inc., [2006] O.H.R.T.D. No. 33, 2006 HRTO 31. 58 C.H.R.R. D/274, File No. HR-0589-04 and HR-0590-04 (the *Stephens* decision) is a useful HRTO decision for its discussion as to when a tribunal can re-open or reconsider a decision. This case is not as relevant to the HRTO now because the HRTO Rules expressly give the HRTO authority to re-open a decision; it was significant at the time this case was before the tribunal when there was no equivalent rule. The HRCO made a motion to Divisional Court to ask the HRTO to re-open its decision where it awarded costs to the respondents and also named specific persons of the HRCO within the award. The HRCO said persons of the HRCO should not be specifically named. The court stated the three issues it had to determine in this case:

> The first deals with whether the Tribunal is *functus officio* at common law in this case. In particular, the questions to be addressed in relation to this issue are whether the Tribunal has the power to re-open its own hearings and, if so, whether this is a case in which this power should be exercised. The second is whether the Tribunal has jurisdiction to entertain this motion or whether the fact that the Commission has appealed to the Divisional Court prevents the Tribunal from all further actions in relation to this matter by virtue of the *Statutory Powers Procedure Act*, R.S.O. 1990, c. 22 (SPPA) ss. 25(1). The third is the discrete issue of whether the names of the Commission staff should be suppressed in this case.

The concept of *functus officio* was discussed first because the concept would prevent an agency from re-opening its decision as it has completed its hearing and no longer has jurisdiction unless an exception to the doctrine exists, as stated by the court:

> The common law doctrine of functus officio maintains that a final decision of a decision-making body cannot be re-opened except for very limited and exceptional reasons (*In re Nazaire Co.* (1879), 12 Ch.D. 88, *Paper Machinery Ltd. v. J.O. Ross Engineering Corp.*, [1934] S.C.R. 186). Originally created for the courts, the doctrine has extended to apply to administrative tribunals as well (*Chandler v. Alberta Association of Architects*, [1989] 2 S.C.R. 848; *Grier v. Metro International Trucks Ltd.* (1996), 28 O.R. (3d) 67 (Div. Ct) (Grier). In the case of administrative tribunals, four exceptions to the *functus* doctrine justifying the re-opening of a decision can be discerned from the jurisprudence. These are situations in which:
> (a) the power to re-open has been conferred on the tribunal by legislation (see e.g. *Grillas v. Minister of Manpower and Immigration*, [1972] S.C.R. 577)
> (b) the tribunal has failed to dispose of an issue which is fairly raised by the proceedings and of which the tribunal is empowered by its enabling statute to dispose (see e.g. *Chandler, supra*)
> (c) the tribunal has made a clerical error or error in expressing its manifest intention (see *In re Nazaire Co.* (1879), 12 Ch.D. 88, *Paper Machinery Ltd. v. J.O. Ross Engineering Corp.*, [1934] S.C.R. 186)

(d) the tribunal has made an error that renders its decision a nullity such as "a denial of natural justice which vitiate[s] the whole proceedings" (see *Chandler* at para. 25, *Ridge v. Baldwin*, [1964] A.C. 40 (H.L.)) or "a misapprehension of an important fact lying at the heart of the litigation" (*Grier, supra*) which may stem from its reliance on factual errors made by the parties (see e.g. *Grier, supra*; *Kingston (City) v. Ontario (Mining & Lands Commissioner)* (1977), 18 O.R. (2d) 166 (Div. Ct.)) (*Kingston*)).

As the HRTO, at that time, had no authority to re-open its case, either under its enabling legislation or its rules, the court had to find a denial of natural justice under the fourth exception to order the HRTO to re-open its decision. Based upon a finding of insufficient time for the HRCO to prepare for the issue of costs, the court found a denial of natural justice and granted the motion subject to the appeal that the HRCO filed on the decision to the court.

Chornyj v. Trus Joist, a Division of Weyerhaeuser

Chornyj v. Trus Joist, a Division of Weyerhaeuser, 2006 HRTO 10, 49 C.C.E.L. (3d) 293, 2006 CarswellOnt. 2782, 56 C.H.H.R. D/96, File No. HR-0977-05 (the *Chornyj* HRTO decision) is an HRTO interim decision in which the respondents brought three motions, the key ones asking for either a dismissal or limiting of the complaint based upon an overview of the situation:

> This is a complaint brought under the *Human Rights Code*, R.S.O. 1990, c. H.19, as amended ("the *Code*"), alleging an infringement of sections 5(1) and 9. The Complaint was filed on or about May 29, 2003, and was referred to the Human Rights Tribunal of Ontario ("the Tribunal") on June 16, 2005. The case involves a challenge to a pre-employment drug testing policy and an allegation that a job offer made to the Complainant was improperly withdrawn as a result of a positive drug test.

In this matter, the complainant was hired for a job subject to drug testing and when the drug test was positive for marijuana, the job offer was revoked whereupon the complainant made a complaint of discrimination based upon a perceived disability. The HRTO found that the issues to be decided were as follows:

> 1. Does the Tribunal lack jurisdiction to deal with this Complaint and as a result, should the Complaint be dismissed without a hearing on the merits?
> 2. Should the Tribunal restrict the scope of the hearing to only the marijuana elements of the Respondent's pre-employment drug testing policy?

In looking at the first issue, the adjudicator set out the general legal principles regarding a motion to dismiss a case:

> In considering a motion to dismiss a case without a hearing, or to strike pleadings, or to otherwise narrow the inquiry into a complaint, it is important to bear in mind certain fundamental and well established principles of human rights law. Human rights tribunals and the Courts have long recognized the special "quasi-constitutional" status of human rights legislation. The *Code* must be interpreted and applied in a large, liberal and purposive manner. The approach to human rights adjudication should never be overly legalistic and technical, but rather should enhance accessibility and ensure that determinations are made on the true merits of the case. As the Court said in *Action Travail des Femmes v. Canadian National Railway Co.*, [1987] 1 S.C.R. 1114, "[w]e should not search for ways and means to minimize those rights and to enfeeble their proper impact (at 1134). (See also: *Ontario Human Rights Commission et al. v. Simpsons-Sears Ltd. (O'Malley)*, [1985] 2 S.C.R. 536, at 546–547; *Toneguzzo v. Kimberly Clark*, [2005] O.H.R.T.D. No. 45, 2005 HRTO 45.)
> It has been said that for a Respondent to succeed in having a complaint dismissed without a hearing, it must be "plain and obvious" that the complaint will fail. The Hon-

ourable Mr. Justice Peter Cory, sitting as a panel of this Tribunal noted that the usual standard applied in civil proceedings for dismissal without a hearing, ought to be even more rigorous in human rights cases:

> A stringent test must be met if this motion is to succeed. That is to say, it must be "plain and obvious" that the *Coroners Act* is consistent with the *Code* and the Complainants are certain to fail (see *Odhavji Estate v. Woodhouse*, [2003] 3 S.C.R. 263 at para. 15). It is indeed appropriate that this stringent test be applied to proceedings taken pursuant to the *Human Rights Code* which are frequently taken by individuals seeking to have their basic rights recognized and enforced ... (*Braithwaite v. Ontario (Chief Coroner)*, [2005] O.H.R.T.D. No. 31, 2005 HRTO 31 at para. 13)

He went on to say that the form and sufficiency of pleadings in a human rights case should not be scrutinized in the same manner as in civil proceedings. Rather, "complainants should simply be required to meet standards of basic fairness" (See: *Braithwaite*, *supra* at para 14. See also: *Toneguzzo, supra*).

The HRTO applied the legal principles and held that "[e]mployment is a social area covered by the *Code*. Disability (which includes perceived disability) is a ground of discrimination covered by the *Code*. The subject matter of the Complaint falls within the jurisdiction of the *Code* and the Tribunal". The adjudicator then stated that the alleged ground of discrimination deserved to be heard and not dismissed without a hearing. The adjudicator, in passing, stated what normally happens in a human rights case (at that time):

> In a typical human rights case, the Commission and the complainant will lead evidence to establish a *prima facie* case of discrimination. The onus then shifts to the respondent to provide a non-discriminatory explanation for its actions. The onus then shifts back to the Commission and complainant to prove that the explanation is pretextual, that the real reason for the impugned action was tainted by discrimination (See: *O'Malley, supra*).

Based on all of the above, the HRTO dismissed the motion.

Weyerhaeuser Co. (c.o.b. Trus Joist) v. Ontario (Human Rights Commission)

Weyerhaeuser Co. (c.o.b. Trus Joist) v. Ontario (Human Rights Commission), [2007] O.J. No. 640, 279 D.L.R. (4th) 480, 221 O.A.C. 245, [2007] CLLC para. 230–012, 156 A.C.W.S. (3d) 187 (the *Weyerhaeuser* case) is a 2007 Div. Ct. case dealing with judicial review of the *Chornyj* HRTO decision. After recounting the facts and background of the case, the Divisional Court determined the standard of review to be applied in a HRTO decision, even an interim decision, as follows:

> The Ontario Court of Appeal in *Entrop v. Imperial Oil Ltd.* (2000), 50 O.R. (3d) 18 at paras. 42–43 (C.A.) [*Entrop*] outlined the applicable standards of review with respect to an appeal from a final decision of a Board of Inquiry (now the Tribunal). On a question of law the standard is correctness. On findings of fact and questions of mixed fact and law the standard is reasonableness *simpliciter*.
>
> In this case, however, there is no final decision. Rather, this is an application to judicially review an interim decision of the Tribunal. The *Code* does not provide a right of appeal from an interim decision of the Tribunal. In my opinion, this does not change the standards of review described in *Entrop, supra*. In *Dr. Q. v. College of Physicians and Surgeons of British Columbia*, [2003] 1 S.C.R. 226 at para. 27, the Supreme Court held that "silence [regarding a right of appeal] is neutral and does not imply a high standard of scrutiny". It follows that silence also does not imply a lower standard of scrutiny.

The standard of review in this case turns on the nature of the question before the Tribunal. I agree that Chornyj was not claiming he had a *Code*-protected right to lie. Chornyj claimed he was subject to discrimination in employment because of his recreational marijuana use. The alleged grounds of discrimination were disability and/or perceived disability. Therefore, there were two distinct issues before the Tribunal.

The first issue was whether a person who engages in recreational marijuana use can maintain a claim of discrimination on the ground of disability where that person admits he is not disabled by his marijuana use. This is a question of law subject to the correctness standard of review. The second issue was whether Weyerhaeuser's Standard is *prima facie* discriminatory on the ground of perceived disability because in effect it treated Chornyj as if he were disabled by drug dependency. This is a question of mixed fact and law subject to the reasonableness *simpliciter* standard of review.

The court then looked at the adjudicator's view of the matter depending on a perceived disability:

> In *Quebec (Commission des droits de la personne et des droits de la jeunesse) v. Montreal (City); Quebec (Commission des droits de la personne et des droits de la jeunesse) v. Boisbriand (City)*, [2000] 1 S.C.R. 665 at para. 71 [*Boisbriand*], the Supreme Court concluded there is a subjective component of discrimination that protects individuals from discrimination on the ground of perceived disability.
>
> The more difficult question is how a claimant can prove another party (for example, a prospective employer) "perceives" the claimant as having a disability. In *Boisbriand*, *supra* at paras. 76–84, the Supreme Court said that a multidimensional analysis is required. This approach was adopted by the Alberta Court of Queen's Bench in *Alberta (Human Rights and Citizenship Commission) v. Kellogg Brown & Root (Canada) Co.*, [2006] A.J. No. 583 at para. 89 (Q.B.) [*Kellogg*]. As *Kellogg* is similar in many respects to the case at bar it is instructive to examine it in more detail.
>
> *Kellogg* involved a claim of discrimination by one Mr. Chiasson, a recreational marijuana user, who was terminated shortly after he began work with Kellogg, Root and Brown (Canada) Company ("KBR") because of a positive result in a pre-employment drug test. Under KBR's drug testing policy, the offer of employment was conditional on Chiasson's pre-employment drug test being negative. To assess whether Chiasson was subject to discrimination on the ground of perceived disability, S.L. Martin J. looked to evidence of actual subjective belief of Chiasson's drug dependency on the part of KBR and its employees, as well as the consequences of a positive drug test in KBR's drug testing policy.
>
> S.L. Martin J. found there was evidence that KBR representatives and some of its employees subjectively believed Chiasson was drug dependent. Her Honour also found that the harsh consequence of a positive drug test prescribed by the drug testing policy (automatic dismissal) also indicated that KBR subjectively believed any person testing positive on a pre-employment drug test was a substance abuser. Taken together, she concluded Chiasson's dismissal was *prima facie* discriminatory on the ground of perceived disability: *Kellogg*, *supra* at paras. 90–94.
>
> Applying the *Kellogg* analysis to this case, I conclude the Tribunal erred in finding that Chornyj had a tenable claim of discrimination on the ground of perceived disability, and therefore it was unreasonable that the Tribunal refused to dismiss his complaint.

Because a failed drug test did not mean, under the Weyerhaeuser's Standard, that an employee was automatically fired but in reality many other steps would be taken to assist the employee, there was no tenable basis and it was plain and obvious that the complainant could not succeed with the claim of discrimination based upon a perceived disability. As the HRTO had no reasonable ground to refuse the motion to dismiss, the application for judicial review was granted and prohibition was ordered preventing the HRTO from hearing the matter.

Incorporated Synod of the Diocese of Toronto v. Ontario (Human Rights Commission)

Incorporated Synod of the Diocese of Toronto v. Ontario (Human Rights Commission), [2008] O.J. No. 1692 (the *Diocese* case) is a 2008 Div. Ct. case dealing with a judicial review application where the "applicants seek an order quashing the decision of the Commission referring the subject matter of the complaint to the Human Rights Tribunal of Ontario ('the Tribunal') and an order prohibiting the Tribunal from holding a hearing with respect to the complaint". This case involved the jurisdiction of the HRTO to hear the matter for two reasons:

(1) the relationship between the Incorporated Synod of the Diocese of Toronto ("the Diocese") and the complainant is not a "service" within the meaning of s. 1 of the *Ontario Human Rights Code* ("the *Code*"); and

(2) by virtue of the amendment of the complaint, the content of the investigating officer's case analysis, and concessions made by counsel for the Commission on this application, the "subject matter" of the complaint as referred to the Tribunal by the Commission has ceased to exist and there is nothing upon which the Tribunal can proceed.

Under the current legislation, the HRCO does not usually investigate and refer matters to the HRTO; this case, however, has an interesting discussion on what matters should be heard before the HRTO:

> In our view, there is a clear jurisdictional issue raised as to whether the relationship between the Diocese and its postulants can be characterized as a "service" within the meaning of s. 1 of the *Code*. This is not a pure question of law. A proper analysis of the issue can only be done on a factual record establishing, for example, the nature of the relationship between the Diocese and those it accepts as postulants, the mutual obligations and expectations between them, what is provided to the postulants by the Diocese, the basis upon which things are provided to postulants, and the like. Those factual determinations are best made by the Tribunal, which would have the advantage of hearing live evidence on these issues if it thought it advisable. Also, the Tribunal has special expertise on issues of interpreting its home statute and the reviewing court would benefit from that opinion.
>
> We are therefore of the view, that the preliminary jurisdictional issue is best decided in the first instance by the Tribunal. There is considerable jurisprudence supporting leaving such issues to be determined by the Tribunal except in the rarest of cases where it can be said that a proceeding before the Tribunal is "fatally flawed": *Re Roosma and Ford Motor Co.* (1988), 66 O.R. (2d) 18 (Div. Ct.); *Ontario College of Art v. Ontario (Human Rights Commission)* (1993), 11 O.R. (3d) 798 (Div. Ct.); *Ressel v. Board of Directors of Chiropractic*, [1990] O.J. No. 1715 (Div. Ct.). This is not one of those rare situations that would warrant the intervention of this Court at this stage.

In this particular case, the court held that applications would be dismissed as the HRTO had jurisdiction to hear the matter.

Smith v. Menzies Chrysler Inc.

Smith v. Menzies Chrysler Inc., [2008] O.H.R.T.D. No.35, 2008 HRTO 37 File No. HR-1368-07 (the *Smith* HRTO interim decision) is an HRTO interim decision that dealt with four motions:

(a) a request for the adjudicator to recuse herself due to apprehension of bias,

(b) request to examine the complainant's counsel,

(c) a request for an order to stay or dismiss the complaint because to proceed would constitute an abuse of process, and

(d) a request to examine the complainant.

The matter arose when the William David Smith, the complainant, filed a complaint with the Ontario Human Rights Commission on December 14, 2006, alleging discrimination, harassment, and reprisal in employment on the basis of sex and sexual orientation. Further, in "March 2007, the complainant commenced a civil action in the Ontario Superior Court of Justice against the corporate respondent and personal respondent Graham alleging wrongful dismissal, infliction of mental harm, negligence, assault and conspiracy."

Dealing with each motion separately, there was a request for the adjudicator to recuse herself because of the situation that occurred at the initial conference call where one of the counsel for one of the respondents made a humorous comment in terms of an allegation upon which the adjudicator requested counsel to refrain from this type of humour. The allegation was that this action could be a reasonable apprehension of bias. The adjudicator stated the law in this area and the fact it did not exist in these facts as follows:

> As I noted in my oral ruling, the threshold test for reasonable apprehension of bias promulgated by de Grandpré J. in *Committee for Justice and Liberty v. National Energy Board*, [1978] 1 S.C.R. 369 is a high standard. The apprehension of bias must be both *reasonable* and *serious*, *supra* at 395. The test, at 394, is as follows:
>
>> [T]he apprehension of bias must be a reasonable one, held by reasonable and right minded persons, applying themselves to the question and obtaining thereon the required information ... [T]hat test is "what would an informed person, viewing the matter realistically and practically — and having thought the matter through — conclude. Would he think it is more likely than not that the [decision-maker], whether consciously or unconsciously, would not decide fairly. The only concern articulated by the respondents as the basis for an apprehension of bias was my single request to Mr. Mack during the Initial Conference Call. Specifically, I asked Mr. Mack, to refrain from joking about the allegations in the case. I note that Mr. Mack acceded to my request and no further discussion regarding this matter occurred.
>
>> Upon considering the above-noted test in the context of the exchange between Mr. Mack and myself, I concluded that the circumstances of the Initial Conference Call did not give rise to a reasonable apprehension of bias. I held that a reasonable person, viewing the matter realistically and having thought the matter through, would not perceive my direction to Mr. Mack reflected a lack of neutrality about the current dismissal motion or a predisposition towards the merits of the complaint. I concluded the alleged "disfavour" did not meet the threshold necessary to support disqualification for a reasonable apprehension of bias. Accordingly, the motion to recuse for apprehension of bias was dismissed.
>
>> I add that, in certain circumstances like this case, a simple request by an adjudicator to counsel to refrain from a particular line of humour is consistent with the Vice-Chair's responsibilities to foster an atmosphere conducive to a judicial process and respectful of, and sensitive to, the human rights issues that come before the Tribunal. Although Tribunal hearings can be less formal and legalistic, particularly with respect to rules of evidence, so as to promote accessibility, flexibility and expeditiousness, a relaxed tone to the proceedings does not diminish the seriousness of the rights, responsibilities and defences provided under the *Code*. A human rights hearing is a legal proceeding and it is critical that all parties, including counsel or representatives, maintain a level of decorum fitting the quasi-judicial nature of the process and necessary for the orderly administration of the Tribunal hearing.

In terms of the request to examine the complainant's counsel due to the "unusual" strategy of having instituted both a human rights complaint and a civil action, the HRTO held that the law of solicitor–client privilege trumps the request:

> In *Pritchard v. Ontario (Human Rights Commission)*, [2004] 1 S.C.R. 809 at para. 16, Major J., on behalf of the Supreme Court of Canada, described solicitor–client privilege

as "all-encompassing" and held that it applies to a broad range of communications between lawyer and client "... as long as the communication falls within the usual and ordinary scope of the professional relationship". The Court confirmed that solicitor–client privilege is "nearly absolute" and that "exceptions to it will be rare", at para. 18.

The respondents seek to examine complainant's counsel in order to explore Mr. McKeever's alleged pattern of pursuing both human rights and civil claims. The respondents have proffered no other purpose or rationale for a line of examination that will necessarily intrude upon solicitor–client privilege. I find the contention that Mr. McKeever routinely advises his clients to seek human rights and civil recourse does not address the question of whether the continuance of this proceeding would amount to an abuse of the Tribunal's process, and consequently does not justify an incursion into areas sedulously protected by solicitor–client privilege. I further note that sections 5.4(2) and 15(2)(a) of the *Statutory Powers Procedure Act*, R.S.O. 1990, c. S.22 (*SPPA*), bar an order for disclosure or admission of privileged information."

With regard to the motion to stay or dismiss the complaint based upon abuse of process, the adjudicator dealt with all the foundations of such alleged abuse and dismissed each one. Regarding abuse of process due to duplicative proceedings, the adjudicator noted the human rights complaint and the civil action involved different parties, different legal issues and different remedies and then noted the case law in the area:

> I note that since 2003 there have been competing lines of authority with respect to these issues and all parties referred to various decisions which either mentioned or distinguished *McKelvey* [*McKelvey v. D'Ercole* (2003), 32 C.C.E.L. (3d) 119 (Ont. S.C.J.)]. I further note the outcome in the 2005 decision of *Schmidt v. Elko Properties Ltd.*, *supra*. In that case, the employer defendant was unsuccessful in seeking a stay of a wrongful dismissal action pending determination of the plaintiff's human rights complaint. Leave to appeal was denied by Justice Hambly of the Superior Court, who commented, at para. 9, that "... the absolute statement of Justice Echlin in *McKelvey*, *supra*, that an employee cannot pursue a claim before the Human Rights Commission and a civil action based on the same facts goes too far. It is not supported by the case law".
>
> Lastly, although the respondents' submissions raised but did not squarely address the doctrine of *res judicata* and issue estoppel, I have considered the general concepts in arriving at this decision, and in particular the analysis of the principles in *Ford Motor Co. of Canada v. Ontario (Human Rights Commission)*, [2001] O.J. No. 4937 (Ont. C.A.), and the authorities cited therein. I find the first branch of the doctrine of *res judicata*, known as issue estoppel, is not applicable to the case at hand. The present situation does not satisfy the three criteria explained in *Ford Motor Co.*, *supra*, at para. 63: (i) the civil lawsuit is still in its early stages and there is no final decision; (ii) the parties are not the same; and (iii) nor are the issues and questions to be determined by this Tribunal the same.
>
> In the circumstances of this case, I do not find the pursuit of both a human rights complaint and civil action amount to an abuse of process. The respondents' "duplication" argument fails to recognize that Clark Menzies, Mark Lyons and the Commission are not parties in the civil proceeding and that there are distinct interests, issues and remedies that are pertinent to each of these participants and specific to the human rights process. I echo the suggestion of other decision-makers that the parties can prevent relitigation and double recovery by ensuring the second judicial body is fully informed about any findings and awards made by the first, see *Farris v. Stanbach Ontario Inc.*, [2004] O.J. No. 1227 (Sup. Ct. J.) and *Schmidt*, *supra*.

The arguments suggesting abuse of process due to undue prejudice and bad faith were also addressed and found wanting.

As to the final motion of examining the complainant, the HRTO held that such examination should be part of the hearing itself.

REVIEW QUESTIONS

1. What is the enabling legislation for the HRTO?
2. Where would you find the practices and procedures of the HRTO?
3. List five grounds (or groups) protected under the *Code* from being discriminated against or harassed.
4. Pursuant to the *Code*, how does the SPPA apply to the HRTO?
5. What does the privative clause of the *Code* related to the HRTO prevent and allow and under what circumstances?
6. What is a stated case as discussed in the *Code* and the HRTO Rules?
7. What Rule(s) gives discretion and flexibility to the HRTO in applying the HRTO Rules?
8. What Rules deal with Form 1, Form 2, and Form 3?
9. What Rule(s) deal with disclosure and what is the result of insufficient disclosure?
10. What Rule(s) deal with motions and what is the appropriate procedure to have a motion dealt with by the HRTO?
11. What jurisdiction is the HRTO given to reconsider a decision under the various procedures and practices of the HRTO?
12. How do the various procedures and practices of the HRTO deal with the ability to appear on behalf of a party before the HRTO?
13. How do the various procedures and practices of the HRTO deal with giving access to persons before the HRTO and dealing with their needs?

EXERCISE

Based upon the facts of the *Barker* case briefed in the chapter, fill out the form(s) to institute this matter currently before the HRTO.

Appendix 6.1
Overview of Procedural Stages of a Matter Before the HRTO

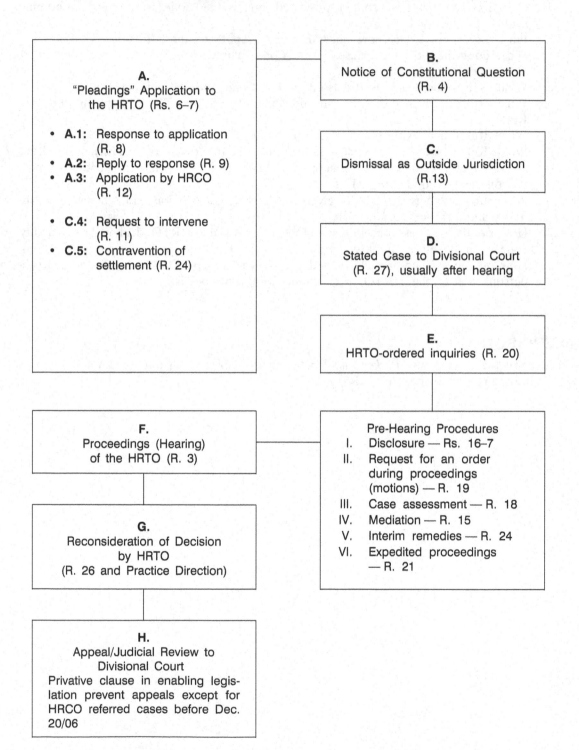

A.
"Pleadings" Application to the HRTO (Rs. 6–7)

- **A.1:** Response to application (R. 8)
- **A.2:** Reply to response (R. 9)
- **A.3:** Application by HRCO (R. 12)

- **C.4:** Request to intervene (R. 11)
- **C.5:** Contravention of settlement (R. 24)

B.
Notice of Constitutional Question (R. 4)

C.
Dismissal as Outside Jurisdiction (R.13)

D.
Stated Case to Divisional Court (R. 27), usually after hearing

E.
HRTO-ordered inquiries (R. 20)

F.
Proceedings (Hearing) of the HRTO (R. 3)

Pre-Hearing Procedures
I.   Disclosure — Rs. 16–7
II. Request for an order during proceedings (motions) — R. 19
III. Case assessment — R. 18
IV. Mediation — R. 15
V.   Interim remedies — R. 24
VI. Expedited proceedings — R. 21

G.
Reconsideration of Decision by HRTO (R. 26 and Practice Direction)

H.
Appeal/Judicial Review to Divisional Court
Privative clause in enabling legislation prevent appeals except for HRCO referred cases before Dec. 20/06

Appendix 6.2
Form 1: Application under s. 34 of the *Code*[1]

Ontario

Human Rights Tribunal of Ontario

Application under Section 34 of the Human Rights Code (Form 1)

(Disponible en français)

www.hrto.ca

How to Apply to the Human Rights Tribunal of Ontario

Before you start:

1. Read the questions and answers below to find out if the Human Rights Tribunal of Ontario (the Tribunal) has the ability to deal with your Application.

2. Download and read the **Applicant's Guide** from the Tribunal's website www.hrto.ca. If you need a paper copy or accessible format, contact us:

   Human Rights Tribunal of Ontario
   655 Bay Street, 14th floor
   Toronto, Ontario
   M7A 2A3

   Phone: 416-326-1312   Toll-free: 1-866-598-0322
   Fax: 416-326-2199   Toll-free: 1-866-355-6099
   TTY: 416-326-2027   Toll-free: 1-866-607-1240
   Email: hrto.registrar@ontario.ca
   Website: www.hrto.ca

   The Tribunal has other guides and practice directions to help all parties to an application understand the process. Download copies from the Tribunal's website at www.hrto.ca or contact us.

3. Complete each section of this Application form. As you fill out each section, refer to the instructions in the **Applicant's Guide.**

Getting help with your Application

For free legal assistance with the application process, contact the **Human Rights Legal Support Centre.** Website: www.hrlsc.on.ca. Mail: 180 Dundas Street West, 8th Floor, Toronto, Ontario M7A 0A1. Phone: 416-314-6266. Toll-free: 1-866-625-5179. Fax: 416-314-6202; Toll-free fax: 1-866-625-5180. TTY: 416-314-6651. Toll-free TTY: 1-866-612-8627.

Questions About Filing an Application with the Tribunal

The following questions and answers are provided for general information. They should not be taken as legal advice or a determination of how the Tribunal will decide any particular application. For legal advice and assistance, contact the **Human Rights Legal Support Centre.**

Who can file an Application with the Tribunal?

You can file an application if you believe you experienced discrimination or harassment in one of the five areas covered by the Ontario *Human Rights Code* (the *Code*). The *Code* lists a number of grounds for claiming discrimination and harassment. To find out if you have grounds for your complaint under the *Code*, read the **Applicant's Guide.**

What is the time limit for filing an Application?

You can file an application up to one year after you experienced discrimination or harassment. If there was a series of events, you can file up to one year after the last event. In some cases, the Tribunal may extend this time.

The discrimination happened outside Ontario. Can I still apply?

In most cases, no. To find out about exceptions, contact the **Human Rights Legal Support Centre.**

---

[1] Source: HRTO website <http://www.hrto.ca/>

Ontario

Human Rights Tribunal of Ontario

Application under Section 34 of the Human Rights Code (Form 1)

My complaint is against a federal government department, agency, or a federally regulated business or service. Should I apply to the Tribunal?

No. Contact the Canadian Human Rights Commission. Website: www.chrc-ccdp.ca. Mail: 344 Slater Street, 8th Floor, Ottawa, Ontario K1A 1E1. Phone: (613) 995-1151. Toll-free: 1-888-214-1090. TTY: 1-888-643-3304. Fax: (613) 996-9661.

Should I use this form if I am applying because a previous human rights settlement has been breached?

No. If you settled a previous human rights application and the respondent did not comply with the settlement agreement, use the special application called **Application for Contravention of Settlement, Form 18**. For a paper copy, contact the Tribunal.

Can I file this Application if I am dealing with or have dealt with these facts or issues in another proceeding?

The *Code* has special rules depending on what the other proceeding is and at what stage the other proceeding is at. **Read the Applicant's Guide and get legal advice, if:**

1. You are currently involved in, or were previously involved in a civil court action based on the same facts and asked for a human rights remedy; or

2. You have ever filed a complaint with the Ontario Human Rights Commission based on the same subject matter; or

3. You are currently involved in, or were previously involved in another proceeding (for example, union grievance) based on the same facts.

How do I file an application on behalf of another person?

To file an application on behalf of another person, you must complete and file this Application (Form 1) as well as an Application on Behalf of Another Person (Form 4). When completing this Application, you must check the box in Question 1 that indicates you are filing an Application on Behalf of Another Person (Form 4). You must provide your name and contact information in Question 1.

The completed Form 4 can be attached to your Application or sent to the Tribunal separately by mail, fax or email. If sent separately, it must be sent within **five (5) days** following the filing of your Application.

For more information on applications on behalf of another person, please see the Tribunal's Practice Direction.

Note: If you are a lawyer or other legal representative assisting an applicant with their Application do not use the Application on Behalf of Another Person (Form 4) to provide your details. A lawyer's or other legal representative's details should be provided in section 3, "Representative Contact Information," of this Application (Form 1).

Learn more

To find out more about human rights in Ontario, visit www.ohrc.on.ca or phone 1-800-387-9080.

Ontario

Human Rights Tribunal of Ontario

Application under Section 34 of the Human Rights Code (Form 1)

Instructions: Complete all parts of this form, using the **Applicant's Guide** for help. If your form is not complete, the Tribunal may return it to you. This will slow down the application process. If you are filling this out on paper, please print and ensure that the information you include is legible. At the end of this form, you will be required to read and agree to a declaration that the information in your Application is complete and accurate (if you are a lawyer or legal representative assisting an applicant with this Form 1, please see the **Practice Direction On Electronic Filing of Applications and Responses By Licensed Representatives**).

Contact Information for the Applicant

1. Personal Contact Information

☐ Check here if you are filing an Application on Behalf of Another Person. **Note:** you must *also* complete a Form 4.

Please give us your personal contact information. This information will be shared with the respondent(s) and all correspondence from the Tribunal and the respondent(s) will go here. **If you do not want the Tribunal to share this contact information, you should complete section 2, below, but you must still provide your personal contact information for the Tribunal's records.**

First (or Given) Name	Middle Name	Last (or Family) Name

Street #	Street Name	Apt/Suite

City/Town	Province	Postal Code	Email

Daytime Phone	Cell Phone	Fax	TTY

What is the best way to send information to you?
(if you check email, you are consenting to the delivery of documents by email)   ☐ Mail   ☐ Email ☐ Fax

2. Alternative Contact Information

If you want the Tribunal and respondent(s) to contact you through another person, you must provide contact information for that person below. You should fill this section out if it will be difficult for the Tribunal to reach you at the address above or if you want the Tribunal to keep your contact information private. **If you complete this section, all of your correspondence will be sent to you in care of your Alternative Contact.**

First (or Given) Name	Middle Name	Last (or Family) Name

Street #	Street Name	Apt/Suite

City/Town	Province	Postal Code	Email

Daytime Phone	Cell Phone	Fax	TTY

Ontario

Human Rights Tribunal of Ontario

Application under Section 34 of the Human Rights Code (Form 1)

What is the best way to send information to you at your alternative contact?
(if you check email, you are consenting to the delivery of documents by email)   ☐ Mail   ☐ Email ☐ Fax

3. Representative Contact Information

Complete this Section only if you are authorizing a lawyer or other Representative to act for you.

☐ I authorize the organization and/or person named below to represent me.

First (or Given) Name	Last (or Family) Name

Organization (if applicable):

Street #	Street Name	Apt/Suite

City/Town	Province	Postal Code	Email

Daytime Phone	Cell Phone	Fax	TTY

LSUC No. (if applicable):

What is the best way to send information to your representative?
(if you check email, you are consenting to the delivery of documents by email)   ☐ Mail   ☐ Email ☐ Fax

4. Respondent Contact Information

Provide the name and contact information for any respondent against which you are filing this Application. If there is more than one respondent and you are filling this out on paper, please attach a separate sheet of paper with the information for each respondent. Number each page.

a) Organization Respondent

Name the organization you believe discriminated against you. You should also indicate the contact person from the organization to whom correspondence can be addressed.

Full Name of Organization	

Name of Contact Person from the Organization

First (or Given) Name	Last (or Family) Name	Title

Street #	Street Name	Apt/Suite

City/Town	Province	Postal Code	Email

Daytime Phone	Cell Phone	Fax	TTY

Ontario

Human Rights Tribunal of Ontario

Application under Section 34 of the Human Rights Code (Form 1)

b) Individual Respondent

If you believe that an individual should be a respondent, provide their name and contact information below. Prior to naming individuals, you should consult the Tribunal's **Practice Direction on Naming Respondents** available on our website at www.hrto.ca.

First (or Given) Name	Middle	Last (or Family Name)

Street #	Street Name	Apt/Suite

City/Town	Province	Postal Code	Email

Daytime Phone	Cell Phone	Fax	TTY

Grounds of Discrimination

5. Grounds Claimed

The Ontario *Human Rights Code* lists the following grounds of discrimination or harassment. Put an "X" in the box beside each ground that you believe applies to your Application. You can check more than one box.

- ☐ Race
- ☐ Colour
- ☐ Ancestry
- ☐ Place of Origin
- ☐ Citizenship
- ☐ Ethnic Origin
- ☐ Disability
- ☐ Creed
- ☐ Sex, Including Sexual Harassment, Pregnancy, And Gender Identity
- ☐ Sexual Solicitation or Advances
- ☐ Sexual Orientation
- ☐ Family Status
- ☐ Marital Status
- ☐ Age
- ☐ Receipt of public assistance (Note: This ground applies only to claims about Housing)
- ☐ Record of offences (Note: This ground applies only to claims about Employment)
- ☐ Association with a Person Identified by a Ground Listed Above
- ☐ Reprisal or Threat of Reprisal

Ontario

Human Rights Tribunal of Ontario

Application under Section 34 of the Human Rights Code (Form 1)
Areas of Discrimination under the Code

6. Area of Alleged Discrimination

The Ontario *Human Rights Code* prohibits discrimination in five areas. Put an "X" in the box beside the area where you believe you have experienced discrimination (choose one). See **Applicant's Guide** for more information on each area.

☒ Employment (Complete and attach Form 1-A)

☐ Housing (Complete and attach Form 1-B)

☐ Goods, Services, and Facilities (Complete and attach Form 1-C)

☐ Contracts (Complete and attach Form 1-D)

☐ Membership in a Vocational Association (Complete and attach Form 1-E)

Does your Application involve discrimination in any other areas? ☒ Yes   ☐ No

Put an "X" in the box beside any other areas where you believe you experienced discrimination:

☐ Employment ☐ Housing ☐ Goods, Services, and Facilities ☐ Contracts ☐ Membership in a Vocational Association

Facts that Support Your Application

7. Location and Date (See Applicant's Guide)

Please answer the following questions.

a) Did these events happen in Ontario?	☐ Yes	☐ No
b) In what city/town?		
c) What was the date of the last event? (dd/mm/yyyy)		
d) If you are applying more than one year from the last event, please explain why:		

8. What Happened

In the space below, describe each event you believe was discriminatory. Add more pages if you need to. Number each page.

> For each event, be sure to say:
> · **What** happened
> · **Who** was involved
> · **When** it happened (day, month, year)
> · **Where** it happened

Be as complete and accurate as possible. Be sure to give details of every incident of discrimination you want to raise in the hearing.

Ontario

Human Rights Tribunal of Ontario

Application under Section 34 of the Human Rights Code (Form 1)

The Effect On You

9. How the Events You Described Affected You

Tell us how the events you described affected you (e.g. were there financial, social, emotional or mental health, or other effects)? Add more pages if you need to. Number each page.

The Remedy

10. The Remedy You are Asking for (See Applicant's Guide)

Put an "X" in the box beside each type of remedy you are asking that the Tribunal order. Explain why you want it in the space below.

☐ **Monetary Compensation**   **Enter the Total Amount $_____**

Explain below how you calculated this amount:

☐ **Non-monetary Remedy – Explain below:**

☐ **Remedy for Future Compliance (Public Interest Remedy) – Explain below:**

Mediation

11. Choosing Mediation to Resolve your Application

Mediation is one of the ways the Tribunal tries to resolve disputes. It is a less formal process than a hearing. Mediation can only happen if both parties agree to it. A Tribunal Member will be assigned to mediate your Application. The Member will meet with you to talk about your Application. The Member will also meet with the respondent(s) and will try to work out a solution that both sides can accept. If mediation does not settle all the issues, a hearing will still take place and a different Member will be assigned to hear the case. Mediation is confidential.

Do you agree to try mediation?   ☐ **Yes**

Other Legal Proceedings

12. Civil Court Action (see Applicant's Guide)

Note: If you answer "Yes" to any of these questions, you must send a copy of the statement of claim that started the court action.

a) Has there been a court action based on the same facts as this Application?	☐ **Yes (Answer 12b)** ☐ **No (Go to 13)**

01/07/2010

Ontario

Human Rights Tribunal of Ontario

Application under Section 34 of the Human Rights Code (Form 1)

b)	Did you ask the court for a remedy based on the discrimination?	☐ Yes (Answer 12c)	☐ No (Answer 12g)
c)	Is the court action still going on?	☐ Yes (Answer 13)	☐ No (Answer 12d)
d)	Was the court action settled?	☐ Yes (Answer 13)	☐ No (Answer 12e)
e)	Has the court action been decided?	☐ Yes (Answer 13)	☐ No (Answer 12f)
f)	Was the court action withdrawn?	☐ Yes (Answer 13)	☐ No (Answer 12g)
g)	If the court action does not ask for a remedy based on the discrimination, are you asking the Tribunal to defer (postpone) your Application until the court action is completed?	☐ Yes	☐ No

13. Complaint Filed with the Ontario Human Rights Commission (see Applicant's Guide)

Note: If you answer "Yes", you must attach a copy of the complaint.

Have you ever filed a complaint with the Commission based on the same facts as this Application?	☐ Yes	☐ No

14. Other Proceeding - in Progress (see Applicant's Guide)

Note: If you answer "Yes" to Question "14a", you must attach a copy of the document that started the other proceeding.

a)	Are the facts of this Application part of another proceeding that is still in progress?	☐ Yes (Answer 14b)	☐ No (Go to 15)

b) Describe the other proceeding:

☐ A union grievance	Name of union:	
☐ A claim before another board, tribunal or agency	Name of board, tribunal, or agency:	
☐ Other	Explain what the other proceeding is:	

c) Are you asking the Tribunal to defer (postpone) your Application until the other proceeding is completed?	☐ Yes	☐ No

15. Other Proceeding - Completed (see Applicant's Guide)

Note: If you answer "Yes" to Question "15a", you must attach a copy of the document that started the other proceeding and a copy of the decision from the other proceeding.

a)	Were the facts of this Application part of some other proceeding that is now completed?	☐ Yes (Answer 15b)	☐ No (Go to 16)

b) Describe the other proceeding:

Ontario

Human Rights Tribunal of Ontario

Application under Section 34 of the Human Rights Code (Form 1)

☐ A union grievance	Name of union:
☐ A claim before another board, tribunal or agency	Name of board, tribunal, or agency:
☐ Other	Explain what the other proceeding is:

c) Explain why you believe the other proceeding did not appropriately deal with the substance of this Application.

Documents that Support this Application

16. Important Documents You Have

If <u>you</u> have documents that are important to your Application, <u>list</u> them here. List only the most important. Indicate whether the document is privileged. **See the Applicant's Guide.**
Note: You are <u>not</u> required to send copies of these documents at this time. However, if you decide to attach copies of the documents you list below to your Application they <u>will</u> be sent to the other parties to the Application along with your Application.

Document Name	Why It Is Important To My Application

17. Important Documents the Respondent(s) Have

If you believe the <u>respondent(s)</u> have documents that you do not have that are important to your Application, list them here. List only the most important.

Document Name	Why It Is Important To My Application	Name of Respondent Who Has It

Ontario

Human Rights Tribunal of Ontario

Application under Section 34 of the Human Rights Code (Form 1)

18. Important Documents Another Person or Organization Has

If you believe another person or organization has documents that you do not have that are important to your Application, list them here. List only the most important.

Document name	Why it is important to my Application	Name of Person or Organization Who Has It

Confidential List of Witnesses

19. Witnesses

Please list the witnesses that you intend to rely on in the hearing. **Note:** The Tribunal will not send this list to the respondent(s). **See the Applicant's Guide.**

Name of Witness	Why This Witness Is Important To My Application

Other Important Information

20. Other Important Information the Tribunal Should Know

Is there any other important information you would like to share with the Tribunal?

Ontario

Human Rights Tribunal of Ontario

Application under Section 34 of the Human Rights Code (Form 1)
Checklist of Required Documents

21. Area of Discrimination from Question 6

Attach a form for each area you checked in Question 6

- ☐ Employment (Form 1-A)
- ☐ Housing (Form 1-B)
- ☐ Good, Services, and Facilities (Form 1-C)
- ☐ Contracts (Form 1-D)
- ☐ Membership in Vocational Association (Form 1-E)

22. Other Documents, from Question 12 to 15

Confirm whether you are sending the Tribunal any of the following documents:

- ☐ A copy of a statement of claim (from Question 12)
- ☐ A copy of a complaint filed with the Ontario Human Rights Commission (from Question 13)
- ☐ A copy of a document that started another proceeding based on these facts (from Question 14 or 15)
- ☐ A copy of a decision from another proceeding based on these facts (from Question 15)

23. Declaration and Signature

Instructions: Do not sign your Application until you are sure that you understand what you are declaring here.

Declaration:

To the best of my knowledge, the information in my Application is complete and accurate.

I understand that information about my Application can become public at a hearing, in a written decision, or in other ways determined by Tribunal policies.

I understand that the Tribunal must provide a copy of my Application to the Ontario Human Rights Commission on request.

I understand that the Tribunal may be required to release information requested under the Freedom of Information and Protection of Privacy Act (FIPPA).

‾‾‾‾‾‾
Name

‾‾‾‾‾‾‾‾‾‾‾‾‾‾‾‾‾‾‾‾‾   ‾‾‾‾‾‾‾‾
Applicant's Signature   **Date** (dd/mm/yyyy)

☐ Please check this box if you are filing your Application electronically. This represents your signature. You <u>must</u> fill out the date, above.

Ontario

Human Rights Tribunal of Ontario

Application under Section 34 of the Human Rights Code (Form 1)

Accommodation Required

If you require accommodation of *Code*-related needs please contact the Registrar at:

Email: HRTO.Registrar@ontario.ca
Phone: 416-326-1519   Toll-free: 1-866-598-0322
Fax: 416-326-2199   Toll-free: 1-866-355-6099
TTY: 416-326-2027   Toll-free: 1-866-607-1240

Where to Send your Application

Note: Only file your Application <u>once</u>. If the Tribunal receives this Application more than once, it will only accept the first Application form received.

Send your completed Application form and any attachments to:

Human Rights Tribunal of Ontario
655 Bay Street, 14th floor
Toronto, Ontario
M7A 2A3

Fax:416-326-2199 Toll-free: 1-866-355-6099
Email: HRTO.Registrar@ontario.ca

Appendix 6.3
Form 2: Response to an Application under s. 34 of the *Code*[2]

Ontario

Human Rights Tribunal of Ontario

Response to an Application under Section 34 of the *Human Rights Code* (Form 2)

(Disponible en français)

www.hrto.ca

How to Respond to an Application Where You Are Named as a Respondent

Use this form if you have been named as a respondent in a human rights application under section 34 of the *Human Rights Code*.

If you fail to respond to the Application, you may be deemed to have accepted all of the allegations in the Application, and the Tribunal may proceed without further notice to you.

Before you start:

1. Read the questions and answers below.

2. Download and read the **Respondent's Guide** from the Tribunal's website **www.hrto.ca**. If you need a paper copy or accessible format contact us at:

   Human Rights Tribunal of Ontario
   655 Bay Street, 14th floor
   Toronto, Ontario
   M7A 2A3

   Phone: 416-326-1312 Toll-free: 1-866-598-0322
   Fax: 416-326-2199 Toll-free: 1-866-355-6099
   TTY: 416-326-2027 Toll-free: 1-866-607-1240
   Email: hrto.registrar@ontario.ca
   Website: www.hrto.ca

   The Tribunal has other guides and practice directions to help all parties to an application understand the process. Download copies from the Tribunal's website or contact us.

3. Complete each section of the Response form that applies to you. As you fill out each section, refer to the instructions in the **Respondent's Guide**.

Questions about Responding to an Application

The following questions and answers are provided for general information. They should not be taken as legal advice or a determination of how the Tribunal will decide any particular application.

What happens if I fail to complete a Response form?

You may be deemed to have accepted all the allegations. The Tribunal may deal with the Application without any further notice to you.

What is the time limit for responding?

Respondents must file a completed Response form no later than **thirty-five (35) days** after the Tribunal sends them a copy of the Application. The cover letter from the Tribunal gives you the exact date.

Are there defences to discrimination under the Human Rights Code?

Yes, there are some defences and exemptions in the *Code*. Please see the **Respondent's Guide**. If you believe one of these applies, please explain how when you fill out the Response form.

01/07/2010   Form 2 – Page 1 of 12

---

[2] Source: HRTO Website <http://www.hrto.ca/>

Ontario

Human Rights Tribunal of Ontario

Response to an Application under Section 34 of the *Human Rights Code* (Form 2)

Can the Tribunal deal with an application where the facts and issues have been dealt with or are being dealt with in another proceeding?

The *Code* has special rules depending on what the other proceeding is and at what stage the other proceeding is at. Read the **Respondent's Guide** and get legal advice if:

1. You are currently involved in, or were previously involved in a civil action based on the same facts and the applicant asked for a human rights remedy; **or**
2. A complaint was ever filed with the Ontario Human Rights Commission based on the same subject matter; **or**
3. You are currently involved in, or were previously involved in another proceeding (for example, a union grievance) based on the same facts.

You must file a Response even if you believe that the Tribunal should defer the Application or that the Application is outside the jurisdiction of the Tribunal, except where you allege the issues in dispute fall within exclusive federal jurisdiction.

Learn more

To find out more about human rights in Ontario, visit www.ohrc.on.ca or phone 1-800-387-9080.

Ontario

Human Rights Tribunal of Ontario

Response to an Application under Section 34 of the *Human Rights Code* (Form 2)

Note: Complete all parts of this form, using the **Respondent's Guide** for help. If your form is not complete, the Tribunal may return it to you. If you are filling this out on paper, please print and ensure that the information you provide is legible. At the end of this form, you will be required to read and agree to a declaration that the information in your Response is complete and accurate (if you are a lawyer or legal representative assisting a respondent with this Form 2, please see the **Practice Direction On Electronic Filing of Applications and Responses By Licensed Representatives**).

Respondents must file a completed Response form no later than **thirty-five (35) days** after the Tribunal sends them a copy of the Application. The cover letter from the Tribunal gives you the exact date.

Tribunal File Number	

Contact Information for the Respondent

1. Respondent Contact Information – Organization

Contact information for a responding organization, such as a corporation, association, or group. Please complete both this section and Question 3.

Full Name of Organization	

Organization Type:	☐ Corporation
	☐ Partnership
	☐ Sole proprietorship
	☐ Unincorporated business/organization
	☐ Other (specify): ____

Name of the person within this organization who is authorized to negotiate and bind the organization with respect to this Application:

First (or Given) Name	Last (or Family) Name	Title

Street #	Street Name	Apt/Suite

City/Town	Province	Postal Code	Email

Daytime Phone	Cell Phone	Fax	TTY

What is the best way to send information to you?

(If you check email, you are consenting to the delivery of documents by email)   ☐ Mail   ☐ Email   ☐ Fax

Ontario

Human Rights Tribunal of Ontario

Response to an Application under Section 34 of the *Human Rights Code* (Form 2)

2. Respondent Contact Information – Individual

If you have been named as an individual respondent, please complete this section and then go to Question 3.

First (or Given) Name	Middle Name	Last (or Family) Name

Street #	Street Name	Apt/Suite

City/Town	Province	Postal Code	Email

Daytime Phone	Cell Phone	Fax	TTY

What is the best way to send information to you?

(if you check email, you are consenting to the delivery of documents by email)

☉ Mail   ☐ Email   ☐ Fax

3. Representative Contact Information

Complete this Section only if you are authorizing a lawyer or other Representative to act for you.

☐ I authorize the organization and/or person named below to represent me.

First (or Given) Name	Last (or Family) Name

Organization (if applicable):

Street #	Street Name	Apt/Suite

City/Town	Province	Postal Code	Email

Daytime Phone	Cell Phone	Fax	TTY

LSUC No. (if applicable):

What is the best way to send information to your representative?

(if you check email, you are consenting to the delivery of documents by email)

☐ Mail   ☐ Email   ☐ Fax

Contact Information- Additional Respondent(s) and Affected Person(s)

Please complete this section if you believe another person or organization should be named as a respondent or given notice as an affected person.

Ontario

Human Rights Tribunal of Ontario

Response to an Application under Section 34 of the *Human Rights Code* (Form 2)

4. Contact Information - Additional Respondent

If there is another organization or person who is not already named as a respondent on the Application form and who you believe should be named as a respondent, provide their contact information here. See the Tribunal's **Practice Direction on Naming Respondents** for more information on how to correctly name a potential respondent.

If you are providing contact information for more than one organization or person you believe should be named as an additional respondent, and you are filling this out on paper, attach another sheet of paper with the full contact information for each additional respondent. Number each page.

Organization (if applicable):

First (or Given) Name	Last (or Family) Name		

Street #	Street Name		Apt/Suite

City/Town	Province	Postal Code	Email

Daytime Phone	Cell Phone	Fax	TTY

5. Contact Information – Affected Person

If there is any other organization (such as a union or occupational association responsible for collective bargaining) or person who is not already named as an affected person on the Application form and who might be affected by this Application to the Tribunal, provide their contact information here.

If you are providing contact information for more than one affected person, and you are filling this out on paper, attach another sheet of paper with the full contact information for each affected person. Number each page.

Organization (if applicable):

First (or Given) Name	Last (or Family) Name		

Street #	Street Name		Apt/Suite

City/Town	Province	Postal Code	Email

Daytime Phone	Cell Phone	Fax	TTY

Ontario

Human Rights Tribunal of Ontario

Response to an Application under Section 34 of the *Human Rights Code* (Form 2)
Request for Early Dismissal of the Application

6. Request for Dismissal without Full Response

Complete this section only if you are requesting that the Tribunal dismiss the Application because one of the four situations below applies. Put an "X" in the box that applies. Please see the **Respondent's Guide**.

I request that the Tribunal dismiss this Application because:

☐ A claim based on the same facts has been filed in civil court, requesting a remedy based on the alleged human rights violation. (Attach a copy of the statement of claim and the court decision, if any. Include all your submissions in support of your request to dismiss the Application on this basis. The Tribunal may decide your request based only on your submissions.)

☐ A complaint was filed with the Ontario Human Rights Commission based on the same, or substantially the same, facts as this Application. (Attach a copy of the complaint and the decision, if any. Include all your submissions in support of your request to dismiss the Application on this basis. The Tribunal may decide your request based only on your submissions.)

☐ The applicant signed a full and final release with respect to the same matter. (Attach a copy of the release. Include all your submissions in support of your request to dismiss the Application on this basis. The Tribunal may decide your request based only on your submissions.)

☐ The issues in dispute in the Application are within exclusive federal jurisdiction. (Include all your submissions in support of your request to dismiss the Application on this basis. The Tribunal may decide your request based only on your submissions.)

Note: If you put an "X" in any of the boxes above, go to Question 20. Except in these four situations, or as otherwise directed by the Tribunal, requests to dismiss an Application will not be considered without a complete response.

7. Request for Dismissal under s. 45.1 of the Code with Full Response

Complete this section only if you are requesting that the Tribunal dismiss the Application because another proceeding has in whole or in part appropriately dealt with the substance of the Application. Put an "X" below if you are making this request. Please see the **Respondent's Guide**.

a)	☐ I request that the Tribunal dismiss the Application because another proceeding has in whole or in part appropriately dealt with the substance of the Application. (Attach a copy of the decision)
b)	Please name the other proceeding: _____
c)	Explain why you believe the other proceeding has in whole or in part appropriately dealt with the substance of the Application. _____

Note: You must complete the entire Response form and attach a copy of the document that started the proceeding and a copy of the decision.

Ontario

Human Rights Tribunal of Ontario

Response to an Application under Section 34 of the *Human Rights Code* (Form 2)
Request to Defer the Application

8. Request to Defer

Complete this section only if the facts of the Application are part of another proceeding that is still in progress.

a) Describe the other proceeding:

☐ A union grievance	Name of union:
☐ A claim before another board, tribunal or agency	Name of board, tribunal, or agency:
☐ Other	Explain what the other proceeding is:
b) Are you asking the Tribunal to defer (postpone) the Application until the other proceeding is completed? (Attach a copy of the document that started the other proceeding)	☐ Yes ☐ No

Responding to the Allegations in the Application

9. Responding to the Allegations

Please summarize the facts and defences that support your Response to this Application. See the **Respondent's Guide**.

> **Please include as part of your Response:**
> - any submissions you make that the Application is outside the Tribunal's jurisdiction;
> - what allegations in the Application you agree with;
> - what allegations in the Application you disagree with;
> - any additional facts that you intend to rely on; and
> - any defences that you intend to rely on.

If you are filling this out on paper and need more space, please add more pages. Number each page.

10. Exemptions

Complete this section only if you are relying on one of the exemptions found in the *Code*. (See the **Respondent's Guide**)

a) What exemption in the *Code* do you believe applies to this Application?

b) Please explain why you believe the exemption applies:

11. Knowledge of the Events

Ontario

Human Rights Tribunal of Ontario

Response to an Application under Section 34 of the *Human Rights Code* (Form 2)

a) When and how did you first become aware of the events described in the Application?

b) How did you respond and what was the outcome?

12. Disability and Employment

Complete this section only if the applicant alleges that they experienced discrimination in employment on the ground of disability. (See **Respondent's Guide**)

a) Did you know about the applicant's particular needs before seeing the Application?	☐ Yes ☐ No

b) What are the requirements (essential job duties) of the position in question?

c) Do you have a written policy, job description or other documentation that describes the requirements of the job?	☐ Yes ☐ No
d) Was the applicant unable to perform the requirements of the job because of their disability?	☐ Yes ☐ No (Go to 13)

e) If you answered "Yes" to 12d, what have you done to try to meet the particular needs of the applicant so that they could do the job? Explain why you believe you met your duty to accommodate. If you are filling this out on paper and you need more space, please add more pages. Number each page.

Note: If you said "Yes" to Question 12c, you must attach a copy of the policy, job description or other document that describes the requirements of the job.

Questions About Internal Human Rights Policies

13. Internal Human Rights Policies

Complete this section only if the respondent is an organization. Please see the **Respondent's Guide**.

a) Do you have a policy related to the type of discrimination alleged in the Application?	☐ Yes ☐ No
b) Do you have a complaint process to deal with discrimination and harassment?	☐ Yes ☐ No (Go to 14)
c) Did the applicant make a complaint under the internal complaint process about the facts in this Application?	☐ Yes ☐ No (Go to 14)
d) Describe how the organization responded and what was the outcome of the complaint process?	

Note: You must attach a copy of the policy, complaint process, or the document that started the complaint, and the decision, if any.

Ontario

Human Rights Tribunal of Ontario

Response to an Application under Section 34 of the *Human Rights Code* (Form 2)
Mediation

14. Choosing Mediation to Resolve the Application

Mediation is one of the ways the Tribunal tries to resolve disputes. It is a less formal process than a hearing. Mediation can only happen if both parties agree to it. A Tribunal Member will be assigned to mediate the Application. The Member will meet with you to talk about your Response. The Member will also meet with the applicant and will try to work out a solution that both sides can accept. If mediation does not settle all the issues, a hearing will still take place and a different Member will be assigned to hear the case. Mediation is confidential.

Do you agree to try mediation? ☐ **Yes**

Documents that Support your Response

15. Important Documents You Have

If you have documents that are important to your Response, list them here. List only the most important. Indicate whether the document is privileged. See the **Respondent's Guide**.

Note: You are not required to send copies of your documents at this time. However, if you decide to attach copies of the documents you list below to your Response they will be sent to the other parties to the Application along with your Response.

Document Name	Why It Is Important To My Response

16. Important Documents the Applicant Has

If you believe the applicant has documents that are important to your Response, that you do not have, list them here. List only the most important.

Document Name	Why It Is Important To My Response

17. Important Documents Another Person or Organization Has

If you believe another person or organization has documents that are important to your Response, that you do not

Ontario

Human Rights Tribunal of Ontario

Response to an Application under Section 34 of the *Human Rights Code* (Form 2)

have, list them here. List only the most important.

Document Name	Why It Is Important To My Response	Name of Person or Organization Who Has It

Confidential List of Witnesses

18. Witnesses

Please list the witnesses that you intend to rely on in the hearing. **Note:** The Tribunal will not send this list to the applicant. See the **Respondent's Guide**.

Name of Witness	Why This Witness Is Important To My Response

Other Important Information

19. Other Important Information the Tribunal Should Know

Is there any other important information you would like to share with the Tribunal?

Checklist of Required Documents

20. Documents from Questions 6 to 13

Put an "X" in the box beside the documents that you are <u>required</u> to send with your Response. Put the Tribunal file number on each document.

☐ Copy of a statement of claim and the Court decision, if any (from Question 6)

Ontario

Human Rights Tribunal of Ontario

Response to an Application under Section 34 of the *Human Rights Code* (Form 2)

- ☐ Copy of a complaint filed with the Ontario Human Rights Commission and decision, if any (from Question 6)
- ☐ Copy of a full and final release that the applicant signed dealing with same matter (from Question 6)
- ☐ Submissions in support of a Request for Dismissal without Full Response (under Question 6)
- ☐ Copy of a decision from another type of proceeding that appropriately dealt with the substance of the Application (from Question 7)
- ☐ Copy of a document that started another type of proceeding based on the same facts (from Questions 7 & 8)
- ☐ Copy of the policy, job description or other document that describes the requirements of the job (from Question 12)
- ☐ Copy of your organization's policy on discrimination or harassment relevant to this Application (from Question 13)
- ☐ Copy of your organization's complaints process relevant to this Application (from Question 13)
- ☐ Copy of the applicant's internal complaint (from Question 13)
- ☐ Copy of the decision from the internal complaint process (from Question 13)

21. Declaration and Signature

Instructions: Do not sign your Response until you are sure that you understand what you are declaring here.

Declaration:

To the best of my knowledge, the information in my Response is complete and accurate.

I understand that information about my Response can become public at a hearing, in a written decision, or in other ways determined by Tribunal policies.

I understand that the Tribunal must provide a copy of my Response to the Ontario Human Rights Commission on request.

I understand that the Tribunal may be required to release information requested under the Freedom of Information and Protection of Privacy Act (FIPPA).

_____
Name

_____
Respondent's Signature

_____
Date (dd/mm/yyyy)

☐ Please check this box if you are filing your response electronically. This represents your signature. You <u>must</u> fill out the date, above.

Accommodation Required

If you require accommodation of *Code* related needs please contact the Registrar at HRTO.Registrar@ontario.ca or

Phone: 416-326-1312   Toll-free: 1-866-598-0322
Fax: 416-326-2199   Toll-free: 1-866-355-6099
TTY: 416-326-2027   Toll-free: 1-866-607-1240

Where to Send your Response

Ontario

Human Rights Tribunal of Ontario

Response to an Application under Section 34 of the *Human Rights Code* (Form 2)

Note: Only file your Response <u>once</u>. If the Tribunal receives this Response more than once, it will only accept the first Response Form received.

Send your completed Response Form and any attachments to:

Human Rights Tribunal of Ontario
655 Bay Street , 14th Floor
Toronto, Ontario
M7A 2A3

Fax: 416-326-2199   Toll-free: 1-866-355-6099
Email: HRTO.Registrar@ontario.ca

Appendix 6.4
Policy on Representation before the Tribunal[3]

Ontario

Human Rights Tribunal of Ontario

Policy on Representation before the HRTO

A party or witness before the Human Rights Tribunal of Ontario (HRTO) may be self-represented or represented by a lawyer or paralegal licensed by the Law Society of Upper Canada (LSUC).

A party or witness may be represented by an unlicensed person if that person falls within a category the LSUC has exempted from its licensing requirements. The current exemptions permit an unpaid friend or family member, an employee or volunteer from a trade union, and students, volunteers and employees of Legal Aid clinics, among others, to act as a representative. The LSUC's website contains a complete list of the approved exemptions.

A person who is not licensed, whose license is suspended or who is not in a exempted category will not be permitted to act as a representative in an HRTO proceeding.

A licensed representative must provide her/his LSUC license number to the HRTO. The HRTO may ask an unlicensed representative to identify the LSUC category to which he or she belongs.

The HRTO may exclude a representative from a hearing where necessary to prevent an abuse of its processes or, in the case of unlicensed representatives, where the Tribunal finds the representative is not competent to properly represent or to advise the party or witness, or does not understand and comply at the hearing with the duties and responsibilities of an advocate or adviser.

Representatives must treat each other and the Tribunal with courtesy and respect. Both licensed and unlicensed representatives are expected to know and follow the HRTO's Rules and any directions or orders made during the proceeding. Acting on the client's behalf and instructions, a representative is responsible for all communications with the HRTO and the other parties and for preparing and presenting the client's case to the HRTO.

The HRTO will do its best to accommodate a representative's schedule when setting hearing and mediation dates. Representatives retained after hearing or mediation dates are set must be available on those dates. Adjournments to accommodate a new representative's schedule or preparation needs will only be granted in exceptional circumstances.

---

[3] Source: HRTO website <http://www.hrto.ca/>

7

Financial Services Tribunal

LEARNING OBJECTIVES

After reading this chapter, the reader should be able to:

- understand how to research any Ontario agency by exploring its website to find the important information needed to understand the agency's practices and procedures and how a paralegal would properly represent a client before such agency by doing so with the Financial Services Tribunal (FST)
- document the background of the FST
- detail and explain the provisions of the enabling legislation relevant to the FST
- elaborate on various concepts of public policy relevant to the FST
- state whether any regulations made under the enabling legislation are relevant to the FST and, if so, discuss such provisions
- compare and prioritize the various sources of practice and procedure of the FST
- identify the specific rules and procedures for the FST and how they would be applied in a proceeding before, during, and after a hearing of the FST
- review and explain the procedures and practices of the FST by way of a flow chart and key forms and documents available on the FST website
- assess whether the relevant provisions of the *Statutory Powers Procedure Act* apply to the FST
- outline the various explanatory literature available on the FST website to assist the paralegal to understand the FST and better represent the client
- appreciate the need to find decisions and/or cases in order to understand and argue the law before the FST
- illustrate and discuss principles that flow from the various cases and decisions as they relate to the FST

INTRODUCTION

The Financial Services Tribunal (FST) is an independent, adjudicative body composed of 9 to 15 members, including the Chair and two Vice-Chairs. The FST hears appeals from decisions and reviews proposed decisions of the Superintendent of the Financial Services Commission of Ontario (FSCO). The FST has exclusive jurisdiction to exercise the powers conferred under the *Financial Services Commission of Ontario Act, 1997*, S.O. 1997, c. 28, as amended (the *FSCO Act*). Other Acts that also confer powers on, or assign duties to, the FST are as follows:

* *Pension Benefits Act*
* *Insurance Act*
* *Mortgage Brokerages, Lenders and Administrators Act, 2006*
* *Loans and Trust Corporations Act*
* *Credit Unions and Caisses Populaires Act, 1994*
* *Co-operative Corporations Act*

In addition, the FST has exclusive jurisdiction to determine all questions of fact or law that arise in the proceedings before it and has authority to make rules for the practice and procedure to be observed in the proceeding before it. The FST can also order a party before it to pay the costs of the FST or the other party of the proceeding.

OVERVIEW AND BACKGROUND

The FST is part of FSCO and a brief history and overview of both can be found on the FSCO website (www.fsco.gov.on.ca):

> The Financial Services Commission of Ontario (FSCO) was created on July 1, 1998, as an arm's-length agency of the [Ontario] Ministry of Finance. FSCO integrates the operations of the former Ontario Insurance Commission, Pension Commission of Ontario, and Deposit Institutions Division of the Ministry of Finance. FSCO comprises three key parts: the Commission; the [FST]; and the Superintendent and Staff.
>
> As of March 1, 2008, FSCO regulated or registered 394 insurance companies, 7,755 pension plans, 207 credit unions and *caisses populaires*, 55 loan and trust companies, 1,290 mortgage brokers, 1,610 co-operative corporations, as well as approximately 39,700 insurance agents, 4,040 corporate insurance agencies and 1,145 insurance adjusters.

As stated under its mandate, "FSCO provides regulatory services that protect financial services consumers and pension plan beneficiaries, and support a healthy and competitive financial services industry."

There is information about the financial services industry regulated by FSCO on its website and information on how the FST deals with matters before it from such regulated industries on the FST website (www.fstontario.ca). Both websites will be examined in this chapter but the reader should, in addition, review the appropriate parts of each website as required.

ENABLING LEGISLATION

The jurisdiction and authority of the FST, as mentioned earlier, are defined by several Acts:

* The *FSCO Act* (which creates the FST and sets out a few procedural rules)
* The *Pension Benefits Act*, R.S.O. 1990, c. P.8, as amended (*PBA*)
* The *Insurance Act*, R.S.O. 1990, c. I.8, as amended
* The *Mortgage Brokerages, Lenders and Administrators Act, 2006*, S.O. 2006, c. 29, as amended (*MBLAA*)

- The *Loan and Trust Corporations Act*, R.S.O. 1990, c. L.25, as amended (*LTA*)
- The *Credit Unions and Caisses Populaires Act, 1994*, S.O. 1994, c. 11, as amended (*CUCPA*)
- The *Co-operative Corporations Act*, R.S.O. 1990, c. C.35, as amended (*CCA*)

All of these Acts give jurisdiction to the FST, while the *Statutory Powers Procedure Act*, a statute of general application, imposes minimum rules of procedure and, therefore, ties the FST Rules that have been published into the procedure the FST follows. Set out below is a discussion of all the above legislation, except the *Statutory Powers Procedure Act*, as to how each relates to the FST. In matters before the FST, other sections of this relevant enabling legislation are discussed and possibly interpreted; however, these sections are outside the purview of this book and are only discussed in the decisions and cases included in this chapter.

The *FSCO Act*

The *FSCO Act* created both FSCO and the FST. The FST is under FSCO as a regulatory and adjudicative body to regulate many of the provincially controlled parts of the financial services industry in Ontario. Under the Act, there is no regulation specifically relevant to the FST.

Definitions and Purposes

Under the definitions in section 1, various terms are defined, including the following:

- "Commission" means FSCO.
- "Regulated sector" means those persons covered by the enabling legislation mentioned earlier.
- "Superintendent" means the superintendent of FSCO.
- "Tribunal" means the FST.

The purposes of FSCO are set out in section 3 as follows:

- to provide regulatory services that protect the public interest and enhance public confidence in the regulated sectors;
- to make recommendations to the Minister on matters affecting the regulated sectors;
- to provide the resources necessary for the proper functioning of the Tribunal.

Creation of the FST

The FST is established under subsection 6(1), and the Lieutenant Governor in Council (the Ontario Cabinet), under subsection 6(4), shall appoint as members of the FST, to the extent practicable, persons who have experience and expertise in the regulated sectors. A matter before the FST shall be heard by one or more members appointed by the chair of the FST (ss. 7(1)), who takes into consideration the experience and expertise required to enable the panel to decide the issues raised in the matter before it (ss. 7(2)).

Conflict of Interest Guidelines

Pursuant to subsection 9(1), FSCO shall establish conflict of interest guidelines that the employees and members of FSCO and the members of the FST must comply with. Such guidelines are in place for the FST and shall be discussed later.

Not Required to Testify

Note that under subsection 10(2), the Superintendent, the Director, or members of the FST shall be exempted from testifying in a civil proceeding, in a proceeding before the Superintendent or the Tribunal, or in any other tribunal proceedings for information the person obtained in his or her duties under this Act or other Acts. No employee or person engaged by the Superintendent, Commission, and the FST shall be required to testify, except with the consent of the Superintendent (s. 10(3)).

Statements of Priorities and Policy Statements and Annual Reports

FSCO is required under subsection 11(1) to produce annually a statement of proposed priorities for the fiscal year, which is published on the FSCO website on the Web page "FSCO Statement of Priorities". As set out in subsection 12(1), the Minister of Finance may make policy statements related to FSCO, and the FST shall make decisions in accordance with these policy statements (ss. 12(3)). A number of policy statements with respect to pension policy can be found on the FSCO website. Annual reports are filed by FSCO (ss. 15(1)). Currently, Annual Reports between 1999–2000 and 2005–2006 are available on the FSCO website.

Certificates Issued by the FST

The following is stated in subsection 18(1) with regard to certifying documents:

> The Tribunal may issue a certificate,
> (a) stating that a copy of, or extract from, a document or thing in the custody of the Tribunal is a true copy of, or extract from, the document or thing;
> (b) stating the date when a document was served on, delivered to or filed with the Tribunal; or
> (c) stating the date when the Tribunal received or issued a document or notification.

Any official documents of the FST, including certificates that purport to be signed by the FST, shall be received in evidence as proof of the facts stated without proving the signature or position of the person who signed it, in absence of evidence to the contrary (ss. 19(1)).

Proceedings before the FST

The jurisdiction of the FST is broad and includes those set out in section 20:

> The Tribunal has exclusive jurisdiction to,
> (a) exercise the powers conferred on it under this Act and every other Act that confers powers on or assigns duties to it; and
> (b) determine all questions of fact or law that arise in any proceeding before it under any Act mentioned in clause (a).

The FST makes decisions by orders, including conditions set out in the orders as well as interim orders (ss. 21(1)–(3)). **Generally, there is a privative clause, subsection 21(4), which states that all orders of the FST are final and conclusive for all purposes unless the Act under which the FST made the order provides for an appeal.** Section 22 sets out certain procedural rules for the FST (to be discussed in detail later under the FST Rules):

> For a proceeding before the Tribunal, the Tribunal may,
> (a) make rules for the practice and procedure to be observed;
> (b) determine what constitutes adequate public notice;
> (c) before or during the proceeding, conduct any inquiry or inspection that the Tribunal considers necessary; or
> (d) in determining any matter, consider any relevant information obtained by the Tribunal in addition to evidence given at the proceeding, if the Tribunal first informs the parties to the proceeding of the additional information and gives them an opportunity to explain or refute it.

Under subsections 23(1)–(2), the FST has the same power as the Superior Court of Justice in civil trial actions to summons and enforce attendance of witnesses, compel them to give evidence, including evidence by affidavit, and to produce documents, etc. Under section 24, the FST can order the other side to pay costs, including FST costs, as specified, all in accordance with the FST Rules.

Fees, Forms, and Regulations

Under subsection 27(1), FSCO, subject to the approval of the Minister of Finance, can set fees and require such fees to be paid. Also, the Superintendent can require the use of forms, and the parties using them must complete the forms as necessary (ss. 27(2)–(3)). Under section 28, the Lieutenant Governor in Council may make regulations.

The *Pension Benefits Act*

The *PBA* gives the FST jurisdiction to deal with matters originally proposed or refused by the Superintendent of FSCO under the PBA. There is no regulation under the Act specifically relevant to the FST.

Definition

"Tribunal" is defined in subsection 1(1) as the FST.

Superintendent Refusing or Proposing

The Superintendent is required to serve notice in the issues that it is given jurisdiction to deal with:

- Section 89(1): Proposes to (a) refuse to register a pension plan, or (b) refuse an amendment, or (c) revoke a registration.

- Section 89(2): Proposes to make or refuse to make an order in relation to
    - repayment of money transferred out of a pension fund (ss. 42(9));
    - repayment of money paid to purchase a pension, deferred pension, or ancillary benefit (ss. 43(5));
    - return of assets transferred to a pension fund of successor employer (ss. 80(6));
    - return of assets transferred to a new pension fund (ss. 81(6));
    - the Guarantee Fund, which applies to a pension plan (s. 83);
    - administration of a pension plan in contravention of the Act or regulation (s. 87);
    - preparation of a report (s. 88).

- Section 89(3): Proposes to make or refuse an order requiring an administrator to accept an employee as a member of a class of employees for whom a pension plan is established or maintained.

- Section 89(3.1): Proposes to give or refuse consent, pursuant to subsection 78(1), to an application that is filed in accordance with subsection 78(2) and is for the payment of a surplus to the employer.

- Section 89(3.2): Proposes to consent or refuses to consent, pursuant to subsection 78(4), to an application that is filed in accordance with subsection 78(4) and is for a return of an excess amount.

- Section 89(4): Proposes to refuse to give an approval or consent, or proposes to attach terms and conditions to an approval or consent under the PBA or the regulations, other than a consent referred to in subsection 89(3.1) or (3.2).

- Section 89(5): Proposes to make an order requiring the windup of a pension plan or declaring a pension plan wound up.

In addition to serving notice to the appropriate parties as listed in the subsections above, the Superintendent in any of the situations described in subsections 89(1)–(5) must give written reasons along with the notice.

Hearing by the FST

Under subsection 89(6), the notices the Superintendent gives or are required to be sent in any of the situations in subsections 89(1)–(5) must state that the person on whom the notice is served is entitled to a hearing by the FST if that person delivers to the FST, within 30 days after service of the notice, notice in writing requiring a hearing. If the person who is served the notice does not require a hearing before the FST, the Superintendent may carry out the proposal stated in the notice (ss. 89(7)); but where a hearing is required, the FST, pursuant to subsection 89(8), shall set a time for and hold a hearing. The parties to a hearing are set out in subsection 89(11). **There is no privative clause in respect of section 89 hearings, as stated in subsection 91(1): "A party to a proceeding before the Tribunal under section 89 may appeal to the Divisional Court from the decision or order of the Tribunal."**

Power of the FST

The FST has the following powers in any of its hearings:

> At or after the hearing, the Tribunal by order may direct the Superintendent to carry out or to refrain from carrying out the proposal and to take such action as the Tribunal considers the Superintendent ought to take in accordance with this Act and the regulations, and for such purposes, the Tribunal may substitute its opinion for that of the Superintendent. (s. 89(9))

The *Insurance Act*

This Act has numerous provisions related to the FST in terms of jurisdiction and other matters. There are a number of Regulations relevant to substantive concerns under the Act, but the O. Reg. 403/96, the Statutory Accident Benefits Schedule (SABS), in particular, has historically been very important in matters before the FST relevant to paralegals. Even with the 2008 change in the regulation of paralegals in this area from FSCO and an overall regulation of paralegals in all areas by the LSUC, the SABS remains important.

Definition

"Tribunal" is defined in subsection 1(1) as the FST.

Appeal of Superintendent's Decision

Sections 15–22 deal with decisions made by the Superintendent by order, how such orders can be made, and the power of the Superintendent in those situations, including the power to reconsider the order. Section 17 deals with appeals to the FST by persons affected by the Superintendent's orders, if an appeal is provided for under the Act (ss. 17(1)). Under subsection 17(2), to appeal, a written notice of appeal must be made within a specified time period after the Superintendent's decision:

> [N]otice of appeal shall be in writing and shall be served on the Superintendent and filed with the Tribunal within 30 days after the date of the Superintendent's decision or within such other time period that this Act specifies.

The ability of the FST to hold a hearing and who the parties are on appeal are dealt with in subsections 17(3) and (4). Pursuant to subsection 17(5), on hearing the appeal, the FST may, by order, confirm, vary, or rescind the decision. The FST may also substitute its decision for that of the Superintendent. Also note that filing the notice of appeal does not automatically stay the order, but the FST has the power to stay it until it disposes of the matter (ss. 17(6)).

Reference Hearings

Section 19 deals with reference hearings. Under subsection 19(1), if the Lieutenant Governor in Council feels that a public hearing is necessary for a certain insurance issue, he or she may ask the Tribunal to examine and report on any question related to that issue. Subsection 19(2) allows the FST to determine who the parties are to such a hearing.

Exclusive Jurisdiction

Under subsection 20(2), anybody, including the FST, conducting proceedings under this Act, has exclusive jurisdiction to exercise the powers the Act conferred upon him or her and to determine all questions of fact or law arising in the proceeding before him or her. **Unless an appeal is provided under the Act, his or her decision is final and conclusive for all purposes.**

Service of Documents

Unless otherwise provided in the FST Rules, service of documents in an FST proceeding that may result in an order or decision affecting the rights or obligations of a person licensed under this Act may be made in accordance with methods provided under section 33.

Situations Allowing Appeal to the FST from a Decision, etc., of the Superintendent

In any of the situations identified below, the decision, etc., of the Superintendent may be appealed to the FST with no further details specified regarding the appeal (likely subsection 20(2) applies and the decision of the FST is final). Look at the sections below for more information when dealing with a matter on the Superintendent's decision, etc.:

- Section 28 — application for a licence
- Section 55 — form term, conditions on licence
- Section 66 — require an insurer to deposit securities
- Section 110 — prohibition order on variable life insurance contract
- Section 117 — prohibition order on issuing or using form of insurance policy
- Section 121.23 — determination of affiliation
- Section 382 — issuance of licence for exchange or approval of change
- Section 389.1 — divestment order
- Section 393 — licensing of agents
- Section 426 — approval or rejection of transfer of contracts to another insurer
- Section 435.1 — approval of substantial investment

- Section 435.13 — divestment order to insurer
- Section 437.13 — order designating a person to be a related party

Disciplinary Actions against Insurers

Under section 58, the Superintendent can make a report dealing with negative findings against an insurer with the intention of cancelling or suspending the insurer's licence or taking possession or control of the insurer's assets. Written notice, with a copy of the report may be given to the insurer (s. 58(2)). Within 15 days after receiving the notice, the insurer may request in writing that the Tribunal hold a hearing before the Superintendent takes any action described in the notice (s. 58(3)). If a request is made in such time, the FST shall hold a hearing (s. 58(4)). Under subsections 58(6) and (7), the Superintendent can protect the public's interest by making an interim order until the final determination of the hearing. Pursuant to subsection 58(8), if the FST finds certain circumstances exist, it may cancel or suspend the insurer's licence or order the Superintendent to take control of the insurer's assets. The insurer may appeal to the Divisional Court any FST order that directs the Superintendent to take control of its assets within 30 days after a copy of the order is delivered to an officer of the insurer (s. 63).

Grounds to Decline to Issue or Terminate, etc., an Insurance Contract, etc.

Under subsection 238(2), an insurer intending to decline to issue, terminate, or refuse to renew a contract, or refuse to provide or continue a coverage or endorsement must file with the Superintendent the grounds for such action. If the Superintendent notifies the insurer that such grounds are prohibited (ss. 238(4)–(5)), the insurer has 15 days, after receiving notice, to appeal the decision to the FST (ss. 238(6) and (9)). In receipt of the request within the time allowed, the FST shall hold a hearing (s. 238(10)). At the hearing if the FST finds that the ground or the manner in which it applies falls within subsection 238(4), the FST can forbid the insurer from using the ground or from using it in a specified manner (s. 238(12)).

Suspension or Revocation of Licence of the Exchange

Pursuant to subsections 390(1) and (2), the Superintendent can give written notice, together with a report, to a licensed exchange or its attorney, stating its intention to suspend or revoke the licence of the exchange. Within 15 days after receiving the notice, the exchange or its attorney may request in writing that the FST hold a hearing before the Superintendent takes any action described in the notice (s. 58(3)). The FST shall hold a hearing if the request is made within the time allowed (s. 58(4)). Under subsection 390(6), the FST, at a hearing, if it agrees with the Superintendent's report, may suspend or revoke the licence of the exchange.

Application for Risk Classification System and Rates for Automotive Insurance under ss. 412, 412.1, 413, 413.1, 415, 416, and 417

Application by an insurer for a risk classification system and rates for automotive insurance under section 410 is approved unless the Superintendent, within 60 days, or later if extended, by written notice notifies the applicant of the non-approval. The Superintendent shall refuse the application if any of the situations in 412(6) exists.

Within 15 days after receiving the notice by the Superintendent not to approve the application, the applicant may appeal the decision in writing to the FST (s. 412.1(1)). Pursuant to subsection 412.1(2), if the appeal is made within the time period allowed, the FST shall hold a hearing at which it may (i) approve or refuse to approve the application, (ii) vary the risk classification system or the rates, and (iii) impose on the approval conditions or restrictions that the FST considers appropriate in the circumstances.

The ability for the FST to ask for additional information and the criteria to be applied in the hearing are both set out in subsections 412.1(3)–(4). Other non-approvals to risk classification systems and rates by the Superintendent that may trigger appeals to the FST if notice is given within 15 days are detailed in the following provisions:

- Section 413
- Section 413.1
- Section 415
- Section 416
- Section 417

Report on an Unfair or Deceptive Practice

Section 441(1) allows the Superintendent to make a report on a person that the Superintendent believes has committed or is committing an unfair or deceptive act or practice, or has pursued or is pursuing any course of conduct that might reasonably be expected to result in a state of affairs that would constitute an unfair or deceptive act or practice. Written notice, with a copy of the report, may be given to the person stating the Superintendent's intention to order actions set out in subsection 441(2). Within 15 days after receiving the notice, the person may request in writing that the Tribunal hold a hearing before the Superintendent takes action (s. 441(3)). The FST shall hold a hearing if a request is made in such time (ss. 441(5)). The Superintendent can make an interim order to protect the public under subsection 441(4). Look at subsection 441(8) for the power of the FST to make an order.

Statutory Accident Benefits Schedule (SABS)

This area used to be very relevant to paralegals and their regulation by FSCO. There were also a few decisions emanating from the FST and some follow-up case law from the courts that were important. However, changes in various legislation ended all filing requirements, restrictions, and FSCO's oversight for the SABS representatives under the *Insurance Act*, effective May 1, 2008. As noted in Bulletin No. A-04/08 on the FSCO website, "On or after May 1, 2008, only individuals who are licensed to provide legal services or who are exempt from licensing requirements under the [LSUC] By-Laws, can represent claimants in the dispute resolution process at FSCO." Even though the FST is no longer involved, other than for complaints arising prior to May 1, 2008, because this area can be an area of practice for paralegals licensed by the LSUC, a brief discussion is provided here, and readers interested in the SABS representation should review the appropriate provisions of the legislation.

Under subsection 268(1) of the *Insurance Act*, all valid motor vehicle liability policies provide statutory accident benefits stated in the SABS:

> [Every] contract evidenced by a motor vehicle liability policy, including every such contract in force when the *Statutory Accident Benefits Schedule* is made or amended, shall be deemed to provide for the statutory accident benefits set out in the *Schedule* and any amendments to the *Schedule*, subject to the terms, conditions, provisions, exclusions and limits set out in that *Schedule*.

In accordance with subsection 268(3), the insurer is liable to pay the benefits under the SABS.

The current SABS (O. Reg. 403/96) details benefits available for an automobile liability policy defined under the *Insurance Act*:

- Income replacement benefit — Part II
- Non-earner benefit — Part III
- Caregiver benefit — Part IV
- Medical, rehabilitation, and attendant care benefits and case manager services — Part V
- Payment of other expenses — Part VI
- Death and funeral benefit — Part VII
- Optional benefits — Part VIII

The procedures for claiming benefits are detailed in Part X of the regulation.

Effective September 1, 2010, O. Reg. 34/10 comes into force, replacing O. Reg. 403/96 for any matters arising from and after such date. The O. Reg. 34/10 has many of the same provisions as the previous SABS, including to following:

- Income replacement, non-earner and caregiver benefits — Part II
- Medical, rehabilitation, and attendant care benefits (which include case manager services) — Part III
- Payment of other expenses — Part IV
- Death and funeral benefits — Part V
- Optional benefits — Part VI

The procedures for claiming benefits are detailed in Part VII of the regulation.

Note: To determine the current law, the reader should closely examine such regulation.

Representation is very restrictive in the motor accident claim process, as stated in subsection 398(1):

> ... no person shall, on the person's own behalf or on behalf of another person, directly or indirectly,
> (a) solicit the right to negotiate, or negotiate or attempt to negotiate, for compensation, the settlement of a claim for loss or damage arising out of a motor vehicle accident resulting from bodily injury to or death of any person or damage to property on behalf of a claimant; or
> (b) hold himself, herself or itself out as an adjuster, investigator, consultant or otherwise as an adviser, on behalf of any person having a claim against an insured or an insurer for which indemnity is provided by a motor vehicle liability policy, including a claim for Statutory Accident Benefits.

Only lawyers acting in the usual course of the practice of law are allowed in the process. However, the SABS can be handled by a licensed paralegal, as stated in section 18 of the regulation, *Automobile Insurance*, R.R.O. 1990, O. Reg. 664:

> A person who is authorized to provide legal services in Ontario pursuant to the *Law Society Act* is exempt from subsection 398(1) of the *Insurance Act* in respect of a claim for benefits under the Statutory Accident Benefits Schedule.

In other words, even supervised staff at law firms will require a licence from the LSUC to represent claimants in the dispute resolution process at FSCO.

The *Mortgage Brokerages, Lenders and Administrators Act, 2006*

The *MBLAA* was proclaimed into force on July 1, 2008, and its predecessor was repealed at the same time. There is no regulation under the Act specifically relevant to the FST. As this legislation is so new, there are no decisions or cases on it yet. It is unclear at this time if there will be a need for paralegals to represent clients before the FST with respect to this legislation; therefore, a brief review is in order.

Definition

"Tribunal" is defined in subsection 1(1) as the FST.

Licences

There are four types of Licences under this Act:

(a) brokerages for persons or entities other than an individual (s. 7);
(b) mortgage brokers for individuals (s. 8);
(c) mortgage agents for individuals (s. 9);
(d) mortgage administrators for persons (s. 10).

All four licences are subject to conditions that may be imposed by the Superintendent or by the Tribunal.

Superintendent's Proposal to Deal with Licences

The Superintendent can propose to deal with licences in any of the following situations set out in subsection 21(1):

1. Refuse to issue a licence.
2. Issue a licence and, without the applicant's consent, impose conditions.
3. Amend a licence without the licensee's consent.
4. Refuse to renew a mortgage broker's or agent's licence.
5. Renew a mortgage broker's or agent's licence and, without the applicant's consent, amend the conditions to which the licence is subject.
6. Suspend a licence without the licensee's consent, except by an interim order authorized by subsection 18(3) or 19(3).
7. Revoke a licence without the licensee's consent.
8. Refuse to allow the surrender of a licence.
9. Allow the surrender of a licence and, without the applicant's consent, impose conditions concerning its surrender.

However, pursuant to subsection 21(2), the Superintendent must issue a written notice, with reasons for the proposal made under subsection 21(1), to the applicant or licencee, along with a notification that the applicant or licencee can request a hearing by the Tribunal about the proposal. Information about the process for requesting the hearing should also be included in the notification. If a hearing is not requested, the Superintendent may carry out the proposal (s. 21(7)).

Under subsection 21(3), if a hearing is requested within 15 days after the applicant or licencee received the Superintendent's notice, the FST shall hold a hearing. The FST may, by order, (a) direct the Superintendent to carry out the proposal, with or without changes; (b) substitute its opinion for that of the Superintendent; and (c) impose conditions it considers appropriate in the circumstances (s. 21(4)). An order of the FST takes effect immediately, but if it is appealed under subsection 21(5), the FST may grant a stay until the appeal is determined (s. 21(6)).

No Privative Clause

There is no privative clause in respect of section 21 hearings, as indicated in subsection 21(5): "A party to a hearing before the Tribunal may appeal to the Divisional Court from the decision or order of the Tribunal."

Further Superintendent Proposals and Orders

The Superintendent must comply with the provisions of the section when making proposals or orders under the following sections:

(i) proposal made under section 35 (dealing with compliance under requirements of the Act);

(ii) proposal made under section 39 (regarding general administrative penalties);

(iii) order made under section 36 (freezing assets, trust funds, etc.);

(iv) order made under section 40 (applying summary administrative penalties).

Except orders made under section 36, the affected party can request a hearing by the FST. The party must appeal within 15 days of receipt of the proposal or order. For FST appeals of orders made under section 36, the provisions of subsections 36(15) and (16) are to be followed. Details regarding the hearings in all four situations are set out in the appropriate sections and should be reviewed if a matter under any of those sections is encountered.

The *Loan and Trust Corporations Act*

There are currently no decisions on the *LTA*. As it is unclear if there will be a need for paralegals to represent clients before the FST with respect to this legislation, a brief review is in order.

Definition

"Tribunal" is defined in subsection 1(1) as the FST.

Hearing before the FST

The Superintendent pursuant to section 192 may make, cease, or perform orders, and there may be a hearing before the Superintendent to consider the order. Under subsection 193(1), the following may occur:

> A party to a hearing before the Superintendent under section 192 may, within 15 days after receiving the Superintendent's decision, appeal the decision to the Tribunal by serving a notice in writing of the appeal on the Superintendent and filing the notice with the Tribunal.

Evidence shall be presented at the hearing, which at the discretion of the FST may be heard in private or in public (s. 197). The FST shall, under subsection 193(2), confirm, vary, or revoke the Superintendent's order. The Superintendent is entitled, by section 194, to attend and be represented by counsel at the hearing before the FST. Finally, under section 196, "[o]ral evidence taken before the Superintendent or the Tribunal may be recorded and, if recorded, copies of a transcript of it shall be furnished upon request on the same terms and for the same fees as in the Superior Court of Justice."

The *Credit Unions and Caisses Populaires Act, 1994*

There are currently no decisions on the *CUCPA*. As it is unclear whether there will be a need for paralegals to represent clients before the FST with respect to this legislation, a brief comment is in order.

Definition

"Tribunal" is defined in subsection 1(1) as the FST.

There are amendments that have been published but were not yet in force at the time of writing.

The *Co-operative Corporations Act*

There are currently no decisions on the *CCA*. As it is unclear if there will be a need for paralegals to represent clients before the FST with respect to this legislation, a brief comment is in order.

Definition

"Tribunal" is not defined in subsection 1(1) but "Superintendent" is, as meaning the superintendent of FSCO. As the Superintendent can delegate his or her powers, under subsection 5(3) of the *FSCO Act*, to anyone employed by FSCO, the FST can obtain jurisdiction under the *CCA*.

RELEVANT REGULATIONS

The review of the regulations relevant to the procedures of the FST (currently only dealing with some fees) was done above in the review of the enabling legislation.

PROCEDURES OF TRIBUNAL

The FST has "Rules of Practice and Procedure for Proceedings before the Financial Services Tribunal" (the FST Rules) effective August 1, 2004, on its website on the Web link "Rules for Hearings before Tribunals", also downloadable in Adobe pdf format.

As noted in the FST Rules (R. 1.02), the rules were made under and were subject to the *SPPA*, which, as noted in a previous chapter, allows an agency to make its own rules, as well as the *FSCO Act*. The FST Rules contain 51 main rules and two appendices. There are a number of forms attached to the FST Rules and appearing in various areas of the FST and FSCO websites. **The FST Rules and the forms shall be discussed in summary fashion and in varying detail below, but the reader should rely only on her/his reading and interpretation of both.** Please note that the procedures in the enabling legislation also are applicable, as are the *SPPA* and the *FSCO Act*, where noted in the FST Rules.

RULES

Part I: General (Rs. 1–7)

R. 1 deals with the application and interpretation of rules. It states that the FST Rules apply to all proceedings of the FST, subject to Practice Directions issued under R. 2.04 and 47.01 (R. 1.01). Rule 1.02 allows the FST to amend the rules, subject to requirements of *FSCO Act* and the *SPPA*. Rule 1.03 requires that the Rules be broadly interpreted to produce the quickest, most just, and cheapest determination of issues.

General authority of the FST is covered in R. 2, including the right for the FST to do whatever is necessary if procedures are not covered in the Rules (2.01), that a defect in form or a technical breach will not make invalid the proceeding or anything produced or resulted from it (R. 2.03), and that the FST may issue Practice Directions as it deems appropriate (R. 2.04).

Definitions are set out in R. 3, methods to calculate time in R. 4, the ability of the FST to extend or abridge time periods in R. 5, and the ability of a person to use French language services in R. 6. Note that R. 7 deals with Constitutional questions. For example, filing and serving notice of the intention to raise the issue with the Attorney General of both Ontario and Canada 15 days before the question is heard by the FST under R. 7.01, and the content of such notice in R. 7.02.

Part II: Filing and Service of Documents (Rs. 8–11)

Under R. 8, Filing Documents, filing is defined as effective delivery and the receipt by the Registrar of the FST (R. 8.01). All documents are to be filed in quadruplicate (R. 8.02) and can be filed by the methods set out in R. 8.03. Documents will be date-stamped and are deemed to be filed as of that date (R. 8.04). Also note R. 8.08, which states that a party shall immediately serve all other parties with a copy of all documents filed with the FST, subject to the rule regarding confidential documents.

Service is dealt with in R. 9 with three key rules: R. 9.02 (as to methods of service), R. 9.03 (regarding other types of service where an oral or electronic hearing is in progress), and R. 9.06 (which sets out the date of effective service depending on how the service is accomplished).

All documents filed or served are subject to confidentiality under the *Freedom of Information and Protection of Privacy Act*, and documents filed with respect to a settlement conference shall be placed on the public record (R. 10.01). Confidential documents are discussed in R. 11, where the procedures for a motion by a party, or an interested person, for a document or part thereof to be held confidential are set out in R. 11.01–11.05. The FST in hearing the motion has the authority to make such order as set out in R. 11.06, keeping in mind the criteria for private hearings set out in R. 28.02 (R. 11.07). The portion of a hearing dealing with a document ordered by the FST to be held confidential shall be held in private.

Part III: Orders (Rs. 12–14)

Under R. 12, orders can be made by the FST (R. 12.01), a copy of which with written reasons is to be delivered by the Registrar to the parties (R. 12.02), with the FST having the right to correct any errors, typographical or similar, in the order, etc. (R. 12.03).

With respect to procedural orders, the steps are set out under R. 13. The FST can make or amend any procedural orders at any time (R. 13.01) and waive any or part of any FST Rules (R. 13.02). FST procedural orders override any FST Rule if found to be inconsistent (R. 13.04). Also note R. 13.05, which allows waiver of any procedural requirements in the enabling legislation or the *SPPA*, with the consent of the parties and the FST. Details about the procedures regarding motions, including timing of, content of, and the authority of the FST to make orders in respect of motions are covered in R. 14

Part IV: Pre-hearing Procedures (Rs. 15–20)

Rule 15 deals with the commencement of proceedings and states in R. 15.01 that a proceeding is initiated by a written Request for Hearing (Form 1) or by a written Notice of Appeal (Form 2), with details about filing, service, and time to do so set out in R. 15.02 and R. 15.03, respectively. Pre-hearing conferences are covered in R. 16. **The various purposes for holding pre-hearing conferences are set out in R. 16.01.** Provided in R. 16.02 are the formats of the pre-hearing conference. Issuance of a pre-hearing conference memorandum, with specific contents, by the FST is required in accordance with R. 16.04. How the contents of memorandum is to be used and the fact that the member who conducted the pre-hearing conference should not, unless the parties agree by written consent, sit on the hearing panel are set out in R. 16.05 and R. 16.06, respectively.

Service of written notice of a pre-hearing conference and the contents thereof are set out in R. 17. Rule 18 deals with settlement conferences including format (R. 18.02), required participation of the parties (R. 18.04), adjournments (R. 18.05), related procedures (R. 18.06), and disclosure without prejudice (R. 18.07). Rule 19 talks about the uses of interrogatories and the ability of the FST to issue directions about them. The responses to interrogatories, the filing of a notice of motion to the FST to deal with unsatisfying responses, and the use of them at a hearing are detailed in the various subrules of R. 20.

Part V: Hearings (Rs. 21–30)

Hearing formats, as set out in R. 21.01, are oral, written, or electronic. Hearings combining two or more formats are also permissible. The notice of hearing is discussed under R. 22 and the content of it is specifically examined (R. 22.03). The specifics of the extra content of a notice of an oral hearing and an electronic hearing are set out in R. 23.01 and R. 24.01, respectively. Details regarding electronic hearings are spelled out in R. 25, including the relevant factors the FST should consider when having an electronic hearing (R. 25.01) and the procedure for a party objecting to the holding of an electronic hearing (Rs. 25.02–25.04).

The specifics of the extra content of a notice of a written hearing are set out in R. 26.01. Details regarding written hearings are spelled out in R. 27, including the procedure for a party objecting to the holding of a written hearing (Rs. 27.02–27.04). Hearings in the absence of the public are the subject of R. 28. The general rule regarding open hearings, depending on the format, are spelled out in R. 28.01, and reasons the FST should examine in ordering a hearing in the absence of the public are set out in R. 28.02. Rule 29 deals with the recording of a hearing and transcripts. A party can, at its own expense, arrange for a court reporter to record all or any part of a proceeding with the leave of the FST (R. 29.01), but no person shall make a visual or audio recording of a proceeding unless authorized by the FST (R. 29.04). The FST can adjourn a hearing on conditions it considers just under R. 30.01.

Part VI: Evidence and Witnesses (Rs. 31–36)

Rule 31 deals with disclosure and the production of documents. The disclosure of evidence and documents as well as a list of documents the party is refusing to disclose and the reasons thereof are set out in R. 31.01. The procedure for a notice of motion when a party has refused to produce a relevant document is set out in Rs. 31.02–31.03. Privilege is protected under R. 31.04 and the continuous disclosure obligation is stated in R. 31.05. The details and the time for furnishing disclosure of allegations of misconduct of a party whose good character, proper conduct, or competency is an issue are stated in R. 32.01.

Written evidence is the subject of R. 33, including the time for service of written evidence relied upon (R. 33.01) and the format the FST can direct the evidence to be submitted (Rs. 33.02–33.03). Rule 34 discusses reports of experts, including time for the service of such report (R. 34.01), time for receiving party to serve its expert's report, given insufficient time (R. 34.02), and how the FST may deal with such expert reports (R. 34.03).

Witnesses are dealt with in R. 35, including how evidence is to be given (Rs. 35.01 and 35.05), time for service of the witness's name and the witness statement on the other party (R. 35.02), time for service of witness name and statement by the receiving party if there is insufficient time given (R. 35.03), and directions the FST may give witnesses regarding the evidence to be given (R. 35.06). Details regarding summonses to witnesses are stated in R. 36, including forms to be used. Form 3(a) or Form 3(b) in Appendix A are to be sent to the Registrar (R. 36.01), who may sign it (R. 36.02), and personal service along with attendance fee set are out in Appendix B (R. 36.03).

Part VII: Summary Dismissal (R. 37)

If a party has missed a required deadline or is taking an undue amount of time before taking the next step, the FST, through the Registrar, may give such party notice of intention to dismiss the proceeding without hearing if proper steps are not taken with the time required (R. 37.01). The FST, if it is of the opinion that the proceeding meets the criteria set out in R. 37.02, must give notice of the intention to dismiss the proceeding, as required by the same rule. In either notice of intention to dismiss, made under Rs. 37.01 and 37.02, the party entitled to notice has the right to make written submissions under R. 37.03. The procedures for the FST to consider the written submissions and the power of the FST to deal with dismissal are discussed in Rs. 37.04 and 37.05.

Part VIII: Parties and Participation (Rs. 38–41)

Rule 38 details issues related to party status, including filing and serving the Application for Party Status (Form 4 in Appendix A), as required by R. 38.01, and the procedure for the FST in determining whether to make an order to grant a person party status (Rs. 39.02–39.04). The FST has the right to restrict or impose conditions on the participation of a person who was granted party status under Rs. 39.01 and 39.02. Where a party is acting in a representative capacity, that party has the same rights and responsibilities of a party acting in a purely personal or non-representative capacity (R. 40.01). Withdrawal is discussed in R. 41. The time when the requestor or appellant in a proceeding can withdraw is dealt with in R. 41.01, and the time for the responding party to do so, in R. 41.02. Requests for costs against the party who withdraws or discontinues may be done in accordance with R. 41.04.

Part XI: Appeal from Decision or Order of the Superintendent (Rs. 42–43)

The parties on an appeal from the Superintendent's decision or order to the FST are defined in R. 42.01. The appeal process is detailed in R. 43, including the record for the appeal (R. 43.01) and the evidence to be used in the appeal before the FST (Rs. 43.02–43.03).

Part X: Costs (Rs. 44–47)

Rule 44 deals with the costs of the parties, including the ability for a party to ask for costs (R. 44.02) and the amount and payment of the costs (R. 44.03). The criteria for the FST to consider in determining an award of costs is enumerated in R. 45.01. The FST can also order that a party, subject to an order, pays the costs of the FST (as defined in R. 46.02) under R. 46.01, using the criteria enumerated in R. 46.04. Rule 47.01 allows the FST to issue a Practice Direction with respect to costs, detailing general costs assessment policies.

Part XI: Review of Orders (Rs. 48–51)

A review of any interim or final order can be carried out at the request of a party (R. 48.01) or the initiation of the panel or member of the FST (R. 48.02). The procedure in requesting a review is elaborated on in R. 49, including the time periods (Rs. 49.01–49.02) and the contents for the request for review (R. 49.04). Rule 50 discusses the decision on the request for review, especially the circumstances listed in R. 50.01 that can be considered by the panel or member of the FST in deciding whether to review. The procedures for conducting a review are set out in R. 51.

Appendices
The appendices to the FST Rules on the website are as follows:

- **Appendix A: Forms**
  - Request for Hearing
  - Notice of Appeal
  - Summons to Witness (Oral Hearing)
  - Summons to Witness (Electronic Hearing)
  - Application for Party Status

- **Appendix B: Attendance Fees for Witnesses**

PRACTICE DIRECTIONS
As noted in R. 1.01 of the FST Rules, the FST Rules apply to all proceedings of the FST, subject to Practice Directions issued under R. 2.04 (dealing with any Practice Direction) and R. 47.01 (a Practice Direction regarding costs, which has been issued and will be discussed below), including the Practice Direction regarding Financial Hardship Proceedings (which also has been issued and will be discussed below). Note that provisions of the Practice Directions will override the FST Rules if there is a conflict with a rule. Set out in the following are summaries, including quoted provisions of the Practice Directions. The reader should review the whole text to obtain complete information on each direction.

Practice Direction on Cost Awards
This Practice Direction is meant to supplement and clarify the principles that the FST will use when making cost awards, which are outlined in some detail in Rs. 44–47 of the FST Rules. The FST will not normally consider an award of costs unless one of the parties requests it, and it will consider such requests on a case-by-case basis. The general position in awarding costs is expressed in the following quote:

> A party will not be subject to costs only because it has lost a hearing. The [FST] is more likely to make a cost award against a party if it has engaged in conduct which is clearly unreasonable, frivolous, or vexatious. The [FST] is less likely to make a cost award against a party that has been reasonable, cooperative, and helpful to the [FST].

Examples of conduct of a party that the FST would likely consider to be (a) unreasonable, frivolous, or vexatious versus (b) reasonable, cooperative, and helpful to the FST are enumerated in clauses a. and b. of paragraph 2 of the Practice Direction.

There are situations where the FST may order a party to pay the costs of the FST. The circumstances in which the FST will make such an order must be particularly extraordinary or highly unusual. Examples of such circumstances are set out in paragraph 3 of the Practice Direction.

As stated in paragraph 4, the FST will not make any order awarding payment of costs unless a party has requested an order with costs and the party against whom the order is requested is given a reasonable opportunity to make oral or written submissions to the FST as the FST may direct.

Finally, paragraph 5 states that awards of costs will bear interest in the same manner as awards of costs under section 129 of the *Courts of Justice Act*, unless the FST provides otherwise.

Practice Direction Regarding Financial Hardship Proceedings

The applicability of this Practice Direction is set out in the following paragraph:

> This Practice Direction applies to proceedings before the Tribunal pursuant to subsection 89(6) of the *Pension Benefits Act* regarding a Notice of Proposal by the Superintendent to refuse to consent to an application to withdraw money from a locked-in retirement account, life income fund or locked-in retirement income fund based on financial hardship. Any such proceeding shall be referred to as a 'Financial Hardship Proceeding'.

It should also be noted that unless the FST orders otherwise, Rs. 8.08, 9, 11, 15 to 29, and 31 to 47 do not apply to a Financial Hardship Proceeding.

After defining "Applicant", this Practice Direction details the various procedures to be followed in a Financial Hardship Proceeding: commencement of proceedings, the deadline to make the request along with copies of various documents, the Superintendent's response, and the Applicant's reply and deadlines to file, the right of the FST to get further information, the Applicant's ability to withdraw, and some contents and publishing of the FST order. It also states the fact that the proceeding will be conducted in a written hearing format unless agreed otherwise. Note that all personal and financial information in the documents in this proceeding shall be held in confidence.

Practice Direction Pertaining to Proceedings Brought Under the *MBLAA*

This Practice Direction applies to expected modifications to some of the FST Rules strictly in proceedings under subsections 21(3), 35(4), or 39(5) of the *MBLAA*. Due to the recent proclamation of the Act, the number of hearings before the FST is likely to surge due to the licensing requirement (ss. 7–12) and the licensing process (ss. 13–22) of the legislation.

With respect to pre-hearing procedures, the process is initiated by the "Request for Hearing" (in Form 1). In most situations there will be no pre-hearing conferences, but if one is directed by the FST it shall usually be done by teleconference.

Unless the FST directs otherwise, hearings shall be oral and in Toronto before a panel of one. The hearings shall be scheduled by the Registrar and for a half-day, and usually no adjournment will be granted.

With respect to evidence and witnesses, the deadline for disclosure and production of various documents, reports, and statements under Rs. 31–5 is 14 days before the hearing, and the party who wishes to file documentary evidence at the hearing shall have four copies available at the hearing.

The Practice Direction in Respect of Court Reporting

This Practice Direction refers to R. 29.01 of the FST Rules, allowing a party to arrange at its expense a court reporter to record a proceeding with the leave of the FST. But note that, as a general practice, the FST will order and pay for the services of a court reporter for all hearings where evidence includes testimony of witnesses. The parties are then able to obtain copies of the transcript at their own expense, pursuant to Rs. 29.02–29.04.

FORMS

The FST forms are provided on the FST website and can be accessed by a link in FSCO's website. The forms are discussed in context that is relevant to readers. As always, the reader should review all forms necessary to properly comply with the procedures for the particular matter in dispute under the fact situation and the appropriate legislation.

Forms for Hearings before the FST

* Form 1: Request of Hearing
  This form is used to request a hearing in respect of a proposed or intended decision of the Superintendent and is downloadable at the FST website. (A copy of this form is included in the Appendix to this chapter.)

* Form 2: Notice of Appeal
  This form is used to appeal a decision or order of the Superintendent and is downloadable at the FST website. (A copy of this form is included in the Appendix to this chapter.)

* Form 3(a): Summons for a witness at oral hearing.

* Form 3(b): Summons for a witness at an electronic hearing.

* Form 4: Application for Party Status
  This form is used for anyone requesting to be granted party status under R. 38 of the FST Rules. (A copy of this form is included in the Appendix to this chapter.)

Forms for Financial Hardship Proceedings

All forms are downloadable on the FST Forms Web page and relate to the forms needed under the Practice Direction for the financial hardship proceedings.

* Form 1.1: Request for Hearing (Instructions Form 1.1 regarding Financial Hardship Proceedings is included in the Appendix to this chapter.)
* Form 1.2: Superintendent's Response
* Form 1.3: Applicant's Response (Note that the form is entitled "Applicant's Reply", which is what the form is called in the Practice Direction)

There are many more forms available on the FSCO website, which will not be discussed here as they are not specifically relevant to the FST, but the reader may want to peruse the "Forms" page of that website as matters before the Superintendent are instituted with forms appearing there.

POLICIES

There are no policies of the FST on its website. There is a "Conflict of Interest Guidelines" Web page, which sets out guidelines for members of the FST to follow in certain possible conflict of interest situations and what a member should do when facing a possible conflict of interest situation.

EXPLANATORY LITERATURE FROM THE TRIBUNAL

The FST website offers many resources, and some of the more relevant ones are discussed here.

1. On the Web page entitled "FST Decisions", there are alphabetically listed FST decisions in the following areas:
   - Financial Hardship Decisions
   - Loan & Trust Decisions
   - Insurance Decisions
     - *Insurance Act* Section Index
   - Mortgage Decisions
     - *Mortgage Brokers Act* Section Index
     - *Mortgage Brokerages, Lenders and Administrators Act* Section Index
   - Paralegal/SABS Representative Decisions
     - *Insurance Act* Section Index
   - Pension Decisions
     - *Pension Benefits Act* Section Index

   Note that many, but not all, of the FST decisions are available in Adobe pdf format for free.

   There is also a link, on the same Web page, to "FSCO's Summaries of FST and PCO Decisions", which provides summaries prepared by FSCO on a number of FST or PCO (FST's predecessor, Pension Commission of Ontario) decisions, usually with a link to the full decision. As stated on each summary and in the review of "Relevant Cases and/or Decisions" prepared by the author in this book, the reader should not rely on the summaries and reviews but should read the full text and determine for herself/himself the law flowing through each decision.

2. On the Web page entitled "Frequently Asked Questions (FAQ's)", there is a commentary that explains in layman's terms the procedure of hearings with respect to the FST.

3. There is an electronic service available on the website on the "Hearing Schedule" Web page to determine when a matter is being heard and its status under the name of the matter.

RELEVANT CASES AND/OR DECISIONS

The cases and decisions discussed below are not meant to be exhaustive and are only those found in the spring of 2008. The cases and decisions included here should not be relied upon as legal opinion but, rather, as the author's viewpoint. Readers must continue to update cases and decisions and conduct their own research, and briefing must be done in any event.

Eleven matters, including cases from the Divisional Court (Div. Ct.) and before one judge of the Superior Court of Justice (Sup. Ct. J.) and decisions of the FST, shall be discussed in chronological order with the oldest one first (unless the case is one in a series, in which case the cases will be discussed from the lowest court to the highest court). The selection is aimed at giving the reader a sampling of how these cases and decisions have been decided and their relevance to the FST. Not every case discussed is a ground-setting decision. However, the review of these cases and decisions should give the reader some idea of how the FST and the courts have dealt with various procedural and substantive issues in the first decade of the 21st century.

Baxter v. Ontario (Superintendent of Financial Services)

Baxter v. Ontario (Superintendent of Financial Services), FST Decision No. P0154-2001-1 (the *Baxter* FST decision), is a matter where the FST considered two pension plans of an employer (NSC), which dealt with both salaried and hourly employees, respectively, and the request of NSC to the Superintendent under subsection 89(4) of the *PBA* to consent to a merger of the plans due to deficiencies in one of them. The Superintendent consented to the transfer of one plan to a merger of both plans and the employees who were part of the transferred plan made application to the FST questioning the Superintendent's giving consent to the transfer. The FST identified the issues involved as follows:

1. Does the FST have jurisdiction under section 89 of the *PBA* to hear this matter?
2. If the FST has jurisdiction, should the Superintendent's consent to transfer under section 81 of the *PBA* be set aside or reviewed?

A majority of the FST held that the *PBA* did not give it jurisdiction to hear the application, but the FST unanimously held that the Superintendent's consent should not be set aside. The majority held that the specific wording of the provisions of section 89 did not give the employees status to make application for the FST to hear the case; only the employer under section 89(4) had the right to make application to have the FST hear the matter and only if the Superintendent refused to consent. Even though the majority said the FST did not have to deal with issue #2, it did, and all three members held that the Superintendent was right to consent to the transfer. The FST reasoned that there were no grounds under subsection 81(5) to refuse consent as it did not fail to protect pension benefits or any of the members' benefits. The majority reviewed the 1994 SCC case of *Schmidt v. Air Products of Canada*, which considered the "benefit" of a contingent surplus as not really a benefit, and looked at other case law to reach its final conclusion reproduced as follows:

> There is nothing inherently objectionable about a merger of a pension plan that is in a surplus position with one that is not, even if the assets of the former plan are subject to a trust for the benefit of the members; see *Re Heilig and Dominion Securities Pitfield Ltd.* (1989), 67 O.R. (2d) 577, at p. 582 (Ont. C.A.). We were referred to the decision of the Divisional Court in *Retirement Income Plan for Salaried Employees of Weavexx Corp. v. Ontario (Superintendent of Pensions)* (2000), 133 O.A.C. 375, as authority for the proposition that on a transfer of assets the Superintendent is required, under subsection (5) of section 81 of the *PBA*, to protect a notional claim to surplus. However, the court's decision to set aside a consent of the Superintendent given under that subsection was based entirely on deficiencies in the process through which the Superintendent dealt with the application for consent to the transfer of assets and with objections to it. That is how the Court of Appeal, in an unreported decision dated February 14, 2002 (docket C35896 & C35919), characterized the decision in affirming it on appeal (with a modification to the form of remedy afforded by the Divisional Court). In the present case, the Applicants did not allege that there were any deficiencies in the procedure the Superintendent followed in dealing with NSC's application for consent.

The appellate case, *Baxter v. Ontario (Superintendent of Financial Services)*, [2004] O.J. No. 4909, 192 O.A.C. 293, 43 C.C.P.B. 1, 135 A.C.W.S. (3d) 502, 2004 Carswell, Ont 5062 (the *Baxter* Div. Ct. case), is a 2004 Div. Ct. case of the appeal of the *Baxter* FST decision. The court identified three issues before it:

1. Did the FST have jurisdiction to review the decision of the Superintendent?
2. What is the proper standard of review of the FST's decision?
3. Did the Superintendent/FST err in concluding that the transfer complied with subsection 81(5) of the *PBA*?

With respect to the first issue, the court held that "[as] the legislature intended equal protection for employer and employee on reviews of decisions by the Superintendent, ... the denial of a right of one party to be heard, while protecting the right of the other party, when both parties have substantial interests at stake, would require considerably clearer and less ambiguous legislative language". The court then used the 2004 SCC case of *Monsanto Canada Inc. v. Superintendent of Financial Services et al.*, [2004] S.C.C. 54, [2004] S.C.J. No. 51 (the *Monsanto* case), to help it interpret the provisions of the *PBA*. After looking at the case law, the court held that the need for a fair process would give the FST jurisdiction to hear an employer's application as well as an application by the employees in a pension plan where the Superintendent consents to the transfer.

The court then turned to the second issue of the standard of review for an FST decision and it stated the following:

> The determination of the appropriate standard of review of the decision of an administrative tribunal now requires the application of the pragmatic and functional approach as described in *Pushpanathan v. Canada (Minister of Citizenship and Immigration)*, [1998] 1 S.C.R. 982.
>
> The first of the four factors is the presence or absence of a privative clause. [The court noted that the there is no privative clause in the *PBA* and therefore suggests a less deferential standard of review.]
>
> The second and most important factor is the relative expertise of the Tribunal. [The court noted that the issue was a pure question of law and therefore pointed to a lower degree of deference to the decision.]
>
> The third factor is the purpose of the Act as a whole and in particular the provision under consideration. ... [The court found that] s. 81(5) does grant the Tribunal broad discretionary powers that involve the balancing of multiple sets of interests of competing constituencies. ... This points to a higher or more deferential standard of review. The question of whether the asset transfer complied with s. 81(5) is a question that lies at the heart or core of the Tribunal's regulatory mandate and expertise and the interpretation of that provision is squarely within the Tribunal's jurisdiction.
>
> The fourth and final factor is the nature of the problem under review, which in this case falls within the specialized administrative expertise of the Tribunal.

After examining all four factors, the court stated the following with respect to the standard of review:

> Taking into consideration all four factors, the Tribunal's decision on the merits must be accorded some deference and the appropriate standard of review is reasonableness *simpliciter*. To subject the Tribunal's decision to the strict scrutiny of the correctness standard would represent a failure to recognize the expertise and mandate of the Tribunal.

With the standard of review established, the court examined the FST decision to see if there was an error by the Superintendent giving consent. The court held that there was no error as the surplus was not a benefit and there was no trust in the original pension plan that prevented the merger.

FST Decision No. U0205-2002-1

This decision is a financial hardship decision of the FST, found on the FST website. In this case the FST heard the application related to the Superintendent's Notice of Proposal to Refuse to Consent, denying the applicant access to funds associated with a locked-in account. The applicant made the request to access funds in a locked-in account under subsection 67(5) of the *PBA*, under which access to funds is allowed if there is the existence of such circumstances of financial hardship as may be prescribed. One of the circumstances prescribed is low income; however, subsections 89(4) and (5) of O. Reg. 909, as amended, prevents more than one successful application in each 12-month period. The FST found that there were two applications made in the 12-month period. Although compelling evidence was given as to why the applicant did not draw sufficient funds in the first application, the FST "has no authority to allow an application that does not meet the requirements of the Regulation". The FST did note, however, that the applicant can bring another application within the 12-month period "**if such application could be put on the basis of one of the other criteria of financial hardship (i.e., other than low income as prescribed by the Regulation.)**" (The boldface was part of the decision.)

FST Decision No. U0216-2003-1

In this FST financial hardship decision, found also on the FST website, the FST heard a different application related to the Superintendent's Notice of Proposal to Refuse to Consent, denying the applicant access to funds associated with a locked-in account. The refusal was again based on the application being made within the 12-month period of a prior successful application on the ground of low income. Although the evidence showed serious hardship, such as unpaid utility bills and rent, it did not constitute a different criterion than low income and would not support a second application within the 12-month period.

Crosbie v. Superintendent of Financial Services of Ontario

Crosbie v. Superintendent of Financial Services of Ontario, FST Decision No. R0251-2005-1 (the *Crosbie* FST decision) dealt with FSCO-regulated persons carrying on business as statutory accident benefit representatives, a problem that no longer exists since the SABS incidents involving paralegals are no longer under the authority of FSCO or the FST as of May 1, 2008. In this situation, the superintendent issued two cease and desist orders against the applicants and any agents and representatives from carrying on the SABS representative business. Under the *Insurance Act*, as amended, and its appropriate regulations, a person can make claims against automobile insurers for benefits provided by O. Reg. 403/96, as amended, through a SABS representative. However under section 398 of the *Insurance Act*, any person who was not a lawyer, until the amendment to section 18 of the Regulation 664, effective May 1, 2008, was prohibited from acting as a public adjuster with respect to the SABS. Section 18 of Regulation 664 prior to May 1, 2008, exempted paralegals from the prohibition of section 398 if certain prerequisites, such as errors and omission, liability insurance coverage and filing a declaration with the Superintendent were done. Under the amended section 18, anyone licensed by the LSUC is exempt of the prohibition of section 398, and the LSUC will now police the situation.

However, a review of this *Crosbie* decision and the somewhat associated *Spiegel* decision, discussed below on page 286, is still valuable in that they show how the FST had decided matters in the past and to show the reader what the situation used to be for paralegals in Ontario in this area.

In the *Crosbie* FST decision, the FST looked at the matter in terms of "an unfair or deceptive act or practice" under sections 438 and 439 of the *Insurance Act*. The FST looked at what it called "operational misconduct" and "regulatory accountability misconduct" and examined the various claims by the Superintendent in situations, such as *Spiegel*, that such agents were acting as non-exempted paralegals. The FST determined that the situations did not show unfair or deceptive acts or practices under sections 438 and 439 of the *Insurance Act*. The FST then looked at regulatory accountability misconduct. In reviewing the investigation of the applicants, the FST held that delay in providing information requested by the investigator of FSCO was an unfair or deceptive act or practice, but it recognized there may have been a justification for the act of delay. The FST then looked at the fact that the applicants did not follow the first cease and desist order and held that such activities constituted the commission of acts prohibited by the *Insurance Act* and consequently unfair and deceptive acts and practices, which were characterized as regulatory accountability misconduct. However, the FST called for a lesser penalty. The FST ordered the applicants, for a period of one year, to cease and desist carrying on business as SABS representatives providing any service to anyone related in any way for statutory accident benefits, and holding out to the public for such services.

The applicants sought judicial review of the *Crosbie* FST decision in *Crosbie v. Ontario (Superintendent of Financial Services)*, [2006] O.J. No. 4298 to the Divisional Court (the *Crosbie* case). The full panel of the Divisional Court dismissed the application for judicial review on the basis that the decision was reasonable and correct in law. In reaching that the decision, the court stated that in order to "determine the standard of review, we must apply the pragmatic and functional approach (*Monsanto Canada Inc. v. Ontario (Superintendent of Financial Services)* (2004), 242 D.L.R. (4th) 193 (S.C.C.)". In determining whether the issues before the FST were questions of law and mixed fact and law, the court found the following:

> The Act contains a privative clause in s. 20(2), and there is no right of appeal from the Tribunal. Moreover, the Tribunal is an integral part of the regulatory scheme regarding insurance, although its primary role is adjudicative. However, it has no broad policy role.

The test applicable here, according to the court, is as follows:

> In this case, given the factors discussed above, we are satisfied that the Tribunal must be correct on pure questions of law. However, on questions of mixed fact and law, some deference is required to the Tribunal. On such questions, the standard is one of reasonableness.

As to the argument that the investigation lacked procedural fairness, the court held that it did not come into play.

Shrivastava v. Superintendent of Financial Services

Shrivastava v. Superintendent of Financial Services (2006), FST Decision No. I0281-2006-1 (the *Shrivastava* decision), dealt with the revocation of a life insurance agent's licence. The FST heard a stay application of an order by FSCO to revoke the Level II life insurance agent's licence held by the applicant while awaiting the hearing of the appeal of the revocation order. In determining whether to grant the stay, the FST enumerated the three-pronged test set out in the FST decision of *Rendall* (FST Decision No. 10087-1999-1). All of the three prongs must be answered in the affirmative for deciding to grant a stay of an order under appeal:

1. Is there a serious (as opposed to a frivolous or vexatious) question to be tried on appeal?
2. Would the appellant suffer irreparable harm if the request for a stay were to be denied?
3. Is this risk of harm to the appellant if the request were to be denied greater than the risk of harm to the public if the request were to be granted?

Although for an appeal from an order under the *Insurance Act* when there has been a hearing before an advisory board, the FST would normally not hear new evidence; the FST would on an application for a stay, as new evidence can be adduced and the matter is different than that under appeal. The FST looked at the reasons given by the advisory board to revoke the applicant's insurance agent licence and determined that the applicant was driven by greed and not the reasons he gave of supporting children, as indicated by the new evidence. As to the first and second prongs of the test, the FST stated that the applicant's submission of a conspiracy against him and irreparable harm are irrelevant as the third prong of the test is not satisfied. The acts of misconduct found by the advisory board were so serious that the risk of harm to the public was greater than the risk of harm to the applicant, and the stay was denied.

FST Decision No. U0295-2007-1

This FST decision dealt with a financial hardship where the FST heard an application related to the Superintendent's Notice of Proposal to Refuse to Consent, denying the applicant access to funds associated with a locked-in account. The facts showed that the applicant made two successive applications for funds in a locked-in account: one based in part on medical expenses, and the second, solely on medical expenses. Both grounds were prescribed by subsection 87(1) of O. Reg. 909, as amended. The first application was dated February 14, 2007, and was consented to on February 27, 2007. The second was dated February 27, 2007. The refusal of the second application was based on the application being made within the 12-month period of a prior successful application on the same ground of low income. The Superintendent had no authority to grant the second application because it was made during the same 12-month period and was not entitled to consider the merits of the second application.

Lomas v. Rio Algom Ltd.

Lomas v. Rio Algom Ltd., [2006] O.J. No. 5122, 57 C.C.P.B. 315, 154 A.C.W.S. (3d) 213, 2006 CarswellOnt 8291 (the *Lomas* case) is a 2006 case before the Superior Court of Justice. Although this case does not relate to a decision of the FST, as it deals with a motion to strike allegations in a application, it does give a good overview of the statutory scheme regulating pensions in Ontario:

> The statutory scheme regulating pensions in Ontario is contained in the *Financial Services Commission of Ontario Act, 1997*, S.O. 1997, c. 28 (the "*FSCOA*") and the *Pensions Benefits Act*, R.S.O. 1990, c. P.8 (the "*PBA*"). The *PBA* is intended to protect present and former members of pension plans.
>
> Section 2 of the *FSCOA* establishes the Financial Services Commission ("Commission") to regulate in the public interest, *inter alia*, pension plans. The Superintendent of Financial Services (the "Superintendent") administers and enforces the *FSCOA* and *PBA*, including the provisions relating to pension plans (s. 5(2) of the *FSCOA*).
>
> Section 20 of the *FSCOA* provides that the Financial Services Tribunal (the "Tribunal") has exclusive jurisdiction to exercise the powers conferred upon it under the *FSCOA* and the *PBA*. This includes the hearing of appeals from a partial or full wind up order by the Superintendent (ss. 89(8)–(11) of the *PBA*).
>
> Subsection 68(1) of the *PBA* allows an employer or administrator in its discretion to wind up in whole or in part a pension plan.
>
> Section 69 of the *PBA* affords the Superintendent the discretion to require the wind up of a pension plan in whole or in part if one or more of specified statutory conditions are met. If the Superintendent proposes to make an order requiring the wind up of a pension plan or declaring a pension plan wound-up, the Superintendent is required to serve notice of the proposal, together with written reasons therefore, upon the administrator and the employer stating that they are entitled to a hearing by the Tribunal if either so requires (ss. 89(5)–(6) of the *PBA*).
>
> The Tribunal is empowered to direct the Superintendent to take such action as the Tribunal considers the Superintendent ought to take in accordance with the *PBA* and may substitute its opinion for that of the Superintendent (s. 89(9) of the *PBA*). A party to a proceeding before the Tribunal may appeal to the Divisional Court from the decision or order of the Tribunal (s. 91 of the *PBA*). See generally *Chase v. Nortel Networks Ltd.* (2004), 70 O.R. (3d) 494 at 498 (Super. Ct.).
>
> Given the purposes of the *PBA*, the public policy ramifications in its administration and regulation of a complex and specialized, esoteric field of activity, and the experience and expertise of its elaborate administrating mechanisms, considerable deference is given

by the courts to the decision-making by those statutory bodies. See *Gencorp Canada Inc. v. Ontario (Superintendent of Pensions)* (1998), 39 O.R. (3d) 38 at 43–4 (C.A.).

If deference is to be paid to the actual decision of a tribunal, then deference should also be paid to the jurisdiction of the tribunal to make that decision. See *Ontario Hydro v. Kelly* (1998), 39 O.R. (3d) 107 at 115 (Gen. Div.).

In *Burshau v. Rogers Communications Inc.*, [2006] S.C.J. No. 28 [*Burshau*], although the Supreme Court of Canada split 4:3 on the issue of whether the Superintendent under the *Pension Benefits Standards Act* (Can.) has statutory authority to terminate a pension plan and trust, the entire Court agreed that the issue of whether to terminate and/or wind up a pension plan because there is no legitimate purpose seen in keeping the pension plan, called for a ruling by the Superintendent.

Spiegel v. Superintendent of Financial Services

Spiegel v. Superintendent of Financial Services, FST Decision No. R0301-2007-1 (the *Spiegel* decision) dealt with many of the same matters as the *Crosbie* FST decision, which is not surprising because Spiegel "worked for" Crosbie when his cease and desist order was given. The *Spiegel* FST decision related specifically to motions made at a pre-hearing conference that the FST ruled upon in this decision. The questions raised, which were answered, were as follows:

1. Whether Mr. Spiegel is engaged in a business activity that is subject to regulation under the *Insurance Act*?
2. What impact, if any, does the FST's decision in the *Crosbie* FST decision have on the current proceedings?
3. Whether the equitable doctrine of *laches* constitutes a bar to these proceedings?

In order to answer the first question, the FST looked at the evidence of Spiegel's activities, especially the pith and substance of seven letters signed by him. None of the letters looks at the benefits from a "health, medical, or rehabilitation perspective" as would be expected from a "health care provider" as Spiegel classifies himself. The letters, however, do support a finding that he "was also engaged in the business of insurance within the meaning of [s.] 31(1) of the *Insurance Act*". Also, the letters "are predominantly written from the perspective of a legal advocate" as argued by the FST, in looking at the language of those letters in detail. The FST then stated that "the question before the [FST] is not whether, or to what extent, Mr. Spiegel provides health care services to his clients. Moreover, the question is not whether health care providers are, as a general rule, subject to the authority of the Superintendent under the *Insurance Act* and its regulations. ... Simply stated, the question is whether the past business activities of Mr. Spiegel, as disclosed by the evidence before the [FST], are sufficient to trigger the duty to furnish information imposed by [s.] 31(1) of the *Insurance Act*". The FST said the evidence did trigger the duty.

With respect to the effect on these proceedings of the *Crosbie* FST decision, the FST stated that some sentences in the prior decision about the activities of Spiegel have to be read in context, and when done so those sentences are really nothing more than *obiter dicta* and not binding findings on Spiegel's activities.

On the question regarding *laches* (or undue delay), the FST noted the delays in the investigation and the issuance of the cease and desist order could be more than two years. But it then said there was no *laches* here for three reasons:

1. There was nothing inherently unfair about the lapse of time in this matter.
2. There is a reasonable explanation for both delays.
3. There is no evidence that Mr. Spiegel relied on the Superintendent's alleged inaction to his detriment.

Hydro One Inc. v. Ontario (Superintendent of Financial Services)

In *Hydro One Inc. v. Ontario (Superintendent of Financial Services)*, [2008] O.J. No. 1436 to the Divisional Court (the *Hydro One* case), the appellant sought an appeal of an FST decision partially winding up a pension plan. The order under appeal was made under subsection 89(9) of the *PBA*, directing the Superintendent of Financial Services (1) to refrain from carrying out a Notice of Proposal dated July 14, 2005, issued by the Deputy Superintendent of Financial Services, Pension Division, which proposed to refuse to make an order pursuant to subsection 69(1)(d) in respect of the Hydro One Pension Plan; and (2) to order a partial windup of the Hydro One Pension Plan (Pension Plan) with respect to Management Compensation Plan (MCP) members whose employment was terminated effective as of a date between September 1, 2002, and December 31, 2002 (the so-called "MCP 2002 initiative").

The first issue, as determined by the FST in its decision, was whether a significant number of members of the Pension Plan had ceased to be employed by Hydro One within the meaning of subsection 69(1)(d) of the *PBA*. The second issue for the FST was whether section 69 can properly be interpreted to permit one particular group, i.e., the employees in the MCP 2002 initiative, to be notionally segregated from other plan members so that a determination of whether the number of terminated members of that group resulting from a reorganization represents a "significant number of members of the pension plan" could be made.

The FST held, after looking at the case law and interpreting the legislation, that there were a "significant number of employees" affected and ordered the partial windup.

The court held that the key issue in the appeal is the statutory interpretation of the provisions by the FST. It then held that the standard of review of the FST order was based on the four factors discussed in the *Baxter* Div. Ct. case examined earlier:

> There are four factors comprising the pragmatic and functional approach to determine the appropriate level of deference. First, there is no privative clause in the *PBA*. Second, the primary issue is a pure question of law, i.e. the interpretation of the meaning of the statutory words "a significant number of members of the pension plan" under s. 69(1)(d). The interpretation is informed by its language, the scheme of the *PBA* as a whole and the purpose of the provisions. Third, the Tribunal does not have specific expertise in statutory interpretation.
>
> Fourth, the purposes of the *PBA* and s. 69(1)(d) are to be considered. The public policy underlying the *PBA* is to set forth minimum standards for the provision of pension benefits and funding by employers. Section 69 protects the members of the plan in certain extraordinary situations. Section 69(1)(d) protects the rights of a vulnerable group of involuntarily terminated employees through a corporate reorganization when the statutory conditions for a partial wind up are satisfied.
>
> In our view, the standard of review in this regard is one of correctness. The issue is: was the [FST] correct in law in the interpretation given to s. 69(1)(d)?

After the court looked at various ways to interpret the statutory provision of "significant" based upon how various cases have suggested it should be done, the court held as follows:

> From these cases we conclude the following. The number of terminated employees can be significant as an absolute number. It is not necessary to introduce proportions to the analysis, although it is sometimes done. When proportions are considered, the numerator might be the number of terminated employees and the denominator might be the total number of active members in the plan; or the numerator might be the number of terminated employees in a subset and the denominator might be the total number of members in that subset. Those examples are not exhaustive.
>
> Based on the decisions in those cases, on the ordinary and grammatical sense of the words, on the legislative history and the scheme and purpose of the Act, we do not agree with Hydro One's assertion that the words "significant number" must be determined by comparing the number of affected Pension Plan members against the total active plan membership (i.e., 73/3913). The jurisprudence has moved from this historical

approach to finding that the threshold of s. 69(1)(d) can be met simply by considering the absolute number of terminated employees without looking to the ratio. Indeed, the numerator may be the number of terminated employees in a subset and the denominator may be the total number of members in that subset in appropriate circumstances.

Based upon this interpretation of the statutory provision, the court dismissed the appeal, confirming "[the FST's] interpretation of section 69 is correct in law. It is consistent with the context in which section 69 appears, the language employed by the Legislature, and the scheme and purpose of the *PBA*. Furthermore, the approach taken by the Tribunal in the application of the statute to the facts was reasonable".

REVIEW QUESTIONS

1. What is the enabling legislation for the FST?
2. Where would you find the practices and procedures of the FST?
3. How does the *SPPA* apply to the FST?
4. What does the privative clause in the enabling legislation related to the FST prevent and allow and under what circumstances?
5. What Rule(s) gives discretion and flexibility to the FST in applying the FST Rules?
6. What Rules deal with Form 1, Form 2, and Form 4?
7. What Rule(s) deal with disclosure, and what is the result of insufficient disclosure?
8. What Rule(s) deal with motions and what is the appropriate procedure to have a motion dealt with by the FST?
9. What jurisdiction is the FST given to reconsider a decision under the various procedures and practices of the FST?
10. How do the various procedures and practices of the FST deal with the ability to appear on behalf of a party before the FST?
11. How do the various procedures and practices of the FST deal with giving access to persons before the FST and dealing with their needs?

EXERCISE

Based upon the facts of the FST Decision No. U0205-2002-1 in the chapter, fill out form(s) to institute this matter currently before the FST.

Appendix 7.1
Overview of Procedural Stages of a Matter Before the FST

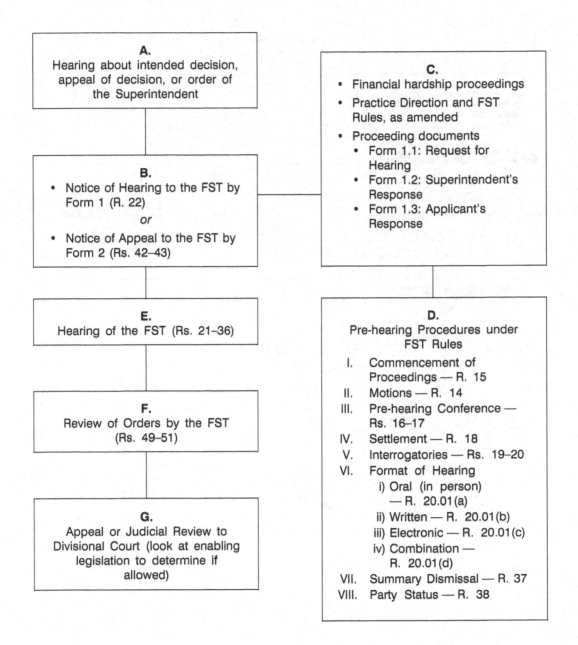

A.
Hearing about intended decision, appeal of decision, or order of the Superintendent

B.
- Notice of Hearing to the FST by Form 1 (R. 22)
  or
- Notice of Appeal to the FST by Form 2 (Rs. 42–43)

C.
- Financial hardship proceedings
- Practice Direction and FST Rules, as amended
- Proceeding documents
  - Form 1.1: Request for Hearing
  - Form 1.2: Superintendent's Response
  - Form 1.3: Applicant's Response

E.
Hearing of the FST (Rs. 21–36)

F.
Review of Orders by the FST (Rs. 49–51)

G.
Appeal or Judicial Review to Divisional Court (look at enabling legislation to determine if allowed)

D.
Pre-hearing Procedures under FST Rules

I. Commencement of Proceedings — R. 15
II. Motions — R. 14
III. Pre-hearing Conference — Rs. 16–17
IV. Settlement — R. 18
V. Interrogatories — Rs. 19–20
VI. Format of Hearing
   i) Oral (in person) — R. 20.01(a)
   ii) Written — R. 20.01(b)
   iii) Electronic — R. 20.01(c)
   iv) Combination — R. 20.01(d)
VII. Summary Dismissal — R. 37
VIII. Party Status — R. 38

Appendix 7.2
Form 1: Request for FST Hearings[1]

Request for Hearing
(for hearings before the Financial Services Tribunal)
(Form 1)

Financial
Services
Tribunal

To request a hearing in respect of a proposed or intended decision of the Superintendent of Financial Services, a person must complete and file this form with the Registrar, Financial Services Tribunal, 5160 Yonge Street, Box 85, 14th Floor, Toronto, ON M2N 6L9, or by fax to (416) 226-7750.

Personal information requested is collected under the authority of the *Financial Services Commission of Ontario Act*, 1997. This information will be used for the purposes of the proceeding and will be available to all parties to the proceeding and will become part of the public record. All questions about this collection may be directed to the Registrar, Financial Services Tribunal.

Applicant's Name and Address

Mr. ☐ Mrs. ☐ Ms. ☐   Last Name   First Name

Name of Company or Organization

Street Addrsess

City   Province   Postal Code   Phone No.

E-mail   Fax No.

Applicant's Representative (if any)

Mr. ☐ Mrs. ☐ Ms ☐   Last Name   First Name

Firm

Street Address

City   Province   Postal Code   Phone No.

E-mail   Fax No.

Section and Statute

☐ Additional sheets attached.

Superintendent's Proposed or Intended Decision

☐ Additional sheets attached.

Date of Proposal or Intention of the Superintendent of Financial Services

5-tr-00o-e2-Form 1 (August 1, 2004)
Page 1 of 2

---

[1] Source: FST website <http://www.fstontario.ca>

Relief Sought

Order of Relief Sought

☐ Additional sheets attached.

Other Interested Persons

Other Persons who may have an interest in the matter

☐ Additional sheets attached.

Documents

I am relying on the following documents for the application:

☐ Copies of documents are attached.

Signature

Name (Please Print)		Title
Applicant ☐	Representative ☐	Date
Signature		

Appendix 7.3
Form 2: Notice of Appeal for FST Hearings[2]

Ontario

Notice of Appeal
(for hearings before the Financial Services Tribunal)
(Form 2)

**Financial
Services
Tribunal**

To appeal a decision or order of the Superintendent of Financial Services, a person must complete and file this form with the Registrar, Financial Services Tribunal, 5160 Yonge Street, Box 85, 14th Floor, North York, ON M2N 6L9 or by fax to (416) 226-7750.

Personal information requested is collected under the authority of the *Financial Services Commission of Ontario Act, 1997*. This information will be used for the purposes of the proceeding and will be available to all parties to the proceeding and will become part of the public record. All questions about this collection may be directed to the Registrar, Financial Services Tribunal.

Applicant's Name and Address

Mr. ☐ Mrs. ☐ Ms. ☐   Last Name   First Name

Street Address

City   Province   Postal Code   Phone No.

E-mail   Fax No.

Applicant's Representative (if any)

Mr. ☐ Mrs ☐ Ms. ☐   Last Name   First Name

Street Address

City   Province   Postal Code   Phone No.

E-mail   Fax No.

Section and Statute

Section and Statute under which appeal is brought.

☐ Additional sheets attached.

Superintendent's Decision or Order

☐ Additional sheets attached.

Date of Decision or Order of the Superintendent of Financial Services

6-tr-00o-e2-Form 2 (August 1, 2004)
Page 1 of 3

---

2 Source: FST website <http://www.fstontario.ca>

Grounds for Appeal

☐ Additional sheets attached.

Relief Sought

Order of Relief Sought

☐ Additional sheets attached.

Parties Before the Superintendent

Parties before the Superintendent of Financial Services

☐ Additional sheets attached.

Other Interested Persons

Other Persons who may have an interest in the appeal

☐ Additional sheets attached.

Documents

I am relying on the following documents for the application:

☐ Copies of documents are attached.

Signature

Name (Please Print)		Title
Applicant ☐	Representative ☐	Date
Signature		

Appendix 7.4
Form 4: Request for Party Status for FST Hearings[3]

Application for Party Status
(for hearings before the Financial Services Tribunal)
(Form 4)

Ontario

Financial
Services
Tribunal

A person who is interested in actively participating as a party in a proceeding before the Tribunal must complete and file this form with the Registrar, Financial Services Tribunal, 5160 Yonge Street, Box 85, 14th Floor, Toronto, Ontario M2N 6L9 or by fax to (416) 226-7750. The Tribunal will then decide whether party status will be granted, either unconditionally or subject to some limitations on participation in the proceeding. The factors that the Tribunal may consider in deciding whether to grant party status are set out in Rule 38.04 of the *Rules of Practice and Procedure for Proceedings Before the Financial Services Tribunal*.

Personal information requested is collected under the authority of the *Financial Services Commission of Ontario Act, 1997*. This information will be used for the purposes of the proceeding and will be available to all parties to the proceeding and will become part of the public record. All questions about this collection may be directed to the Registrar, Financial Services Tribunal.

Matter | Tribunal File No.

Applicant for Party Status - Name and Address

Mr. ☐ Mrs. ☐ Ms. ☐ | Last Name | First Name

Name of Company or Organization

Street Address

City | Province | Postal Code | Phone No.

E-Mail: | Fax No.

Applicant's Representative (if any)

Mr. ☐ Mrs. ☐ Ms. ☐ | Last Name | First Name

Firm

Street Address

City | Province | Postal Code | Phone No.

E-Mail: | Fax No.

7-tr-00o-e2-Form 4 (August 1, 2004)
Page 1 of 3

---

[3] Source: FST website <http://www.fstontario.ca>

Interest in Proceeding

State your interest in the proceeding and indicate in what respects you intend to support the position of the party who initiated the proceeding and in what respects you intend to support the responding party or parties in the proceeding.

☐ Additional sheets attached.

Nature of Party Status Sought

Indicate whether full or limited party status is sought and indicate the level and nature of your proposed participation in the proceeding.

☐ Additional sheets attached.

Relief Sought

Indicate the nature of any relief you are seeking in the proceeding.

☐ Additional sheets attached.

Submissions

Indicate the reasons why you think you should be granted party status in the proceeding.

☐ Additional sheets attached.

Documents

List any documents you are relying on for this application.

☐ Additional sheets attached.

Signature

Name (Please Print):   Title:

Applicant ☐   Representative ☐   Date:

Signature:

Appendix 7.5
Instructions Regarding Financial Hardship Proceedings[4]

Ontario

Request for Hearing
Financial Hardship Proceeding
(before the Financial Services Tribunal)
(Form 1.1 Instructions)

Financial
Services
Tribunal

HOW TO REQUEST A HEARING

Use the attached **Form 1.1** to request a hearing before the Financial Services Tribunal about a proposed decision of the Superintendent of Financial Services if:

- you have applied to the Superintendent for consent to withdraw money from your Ontario locked-in retirement account, life income fund or locked-in retirement income fund **based on financial hardship,**
- the Superintendent has sent you a Notice of Proposal to Refuse to Consent to your application, and
- you want a hearing before the Financial Services Tribunal about the Superintendent's Notice of Proposal.

Complete the form and send it with any additional documents to the Registrar of the Financial Services Tribunal. The Registrar must receive the completed form **within 30 calendar days** after you receive the Superintendent's Notice of Proposal (see page 3 of these instructions for more information about calculating time). Send the completed form **by mail or fax** to:

The Registrar
Financial Services Tribunal
5160 Yonge Street
Box 85, 14th Floor
Toronto ON M2N 6L9
fax: (416) 226-7750

For more information about requesting a hearing or if you have any questions about your hearing, please contact the Registrar at (416) 226-7752 or toll free at 1-800-668-0128 ext. 7752.

MANNER OF HEARING

Your hearing will be conducted as a written hearing unless you request and the Tribunal agrees, or the Tribunal orders, that your hearing be conducted in a different format.

Send all documents related to your hearing to the Registrar of the Financial Services Tribunal at the address above. The Registrar will send you copies of any documents related to your hearing that are sent to the Registrar by the Superintendent of Financial Services. **Do not send any documents to the Superintendent directly.**

At any time, the Financial Services Tribunal may require that you provide further information or documents in order to understand your hearing.

FST Form 1.1 Instructions (08/2004)

Page 1 of 3

---

[4] Source: FST website <http://www.fstontario.ca>

SUPERINTENDENT'S RESPONSE TO YOUR REQUEST FOR A HEARING

After receiving your request for a hearing, the Registrar will send a copy of it to the Superintendent. The Superintendent will respond to your request by completing a written Superintendent's Response (Form 1.2) and sending it to the Registrar within 14 calendar days after receiving your request.

APPLICANT'S REPLY TO THE SUPERINTENDENT'S RESPONSE

The Registrar will send you a copy of the Superintendent's Response and you may reply in writing to any of the matters or information set out in the Superintendent's Response. You do not have to reply in order for your hearing to proceed.

To reply to the Superintendent's Response, complete an Applicant's Reply (Form 1.3) and send it to the Registrar at the address on page 1 of these instructions. The Registrar must receive your Applicant's Reply **within 14 calendar days** after you receive the Superintendent's Response (see page 3 of these instructions for more information about calculating time).

The Registrar will include a blank Applicant's Reply with the Superintendent's Response sent to you. If you do not wish to reply to the Superintendent's Response, you can either do nothing about it or complete the Applicant's Reply (be sure to check the circle that says "I do not wish to reply to the Superintendent's Response" on page 2 of the Applicant's Reply) and send it to the Registrar. Please note that if you do nothing about the Superintendent's Response, the Financial Services Tribunal must wait 14 calendar days from the date you were deemed to have received the Superintendent's Response before proceeding with your hearing (see page 3 of these instructions for more information about calculating time).

The Registrar will send a copy of any Applicant's Reply that you make to the Superintendent.

WITHDRAWAL OF A REQUEST FOR A HEARING

You can withdraw your request for a hearing at any time before the Financial Services Tribunal makes a decision and order by sending a letter requesting the withdrawal signed by you or your representative.

ORDER OF THE FINANCIAL SERVICES TRIBUNAL

After the Financial Services Tribunal has received all of the documents related to your hearing or the time has expired for receipt of those documents, the Financial Services Tribunal will consider your case and make an order.

The order will be published by the Financial Services Tribunal and contain the relevant Financial Services Tribunal file number, but will not identify you by name or provide any other information by which you could be readily identified.

CONFIDENTIALITY OF INFORMATION

Any personal or financial information contained in the forms or other documents sent to or by the Registrar must be held in confidence by you, your representative, the Superintendent and the Financial Services Tribunal.

CALCULATING TIME

If the day that the Registrar is due to receive a document falls on a Saturday, Sunday or holiday, the due date for receipt of the document becomes the next day that is not a Saturday, Sunday or holiday.

If a document is received by the Registrar after 4:45 p.m., it will be deemed to have been received by the Registrar on the following day.

If a document is sent by first class mail, the person to whom the document is addressed will be deemed to have received the document on the seventh calendar day after the document is mailed.

SENDING DOCUMENTS BY FAX

If you send any document to the Registrar by fax, the fax **should** include a cover page indicating:
- the name, address and phone number of the sender,
- that the fax is being sent to the Registrar,
- the date and time the document is transmitted,
- the total number of pages transmitted including the cover page,
- the fax number from which the document is transmitted, and
- the name and phone number of a person to contact if problems arise with the transmission of the fax.

FOR MORE INFORMATION

For more information about requesting a hearing or if you have any questions about your hearing, please contact the Registrar of the Financial Services Tribunal at (416) 226-7752 or toll free at 1-800-668-0128 ext. 7752.

8

The FSCO Dispute Resolution Group

LEARNING OBJECTIVES

After reading this chapter, the reader should be able to:

- understand how to research the Dispute Resolution Group (DRG) of the Financial Services Commission of Ontario (FSCO) by exploring its website to find the important information needed to understand the DRG's practices and procedures and how a paralegal would properly represent a client before the procedures available in the FSCO
- document the background of the DRG
- detail and explain the provisions of the enabling legislation relevant to the DRG
- state whether any regulations made under the enabling legislation are relevant to the DRG and if so, to discuss such provisions
- compare and prioritize the various sources of practice and procedure of the DRG
- identify the specific rules and procedures for the DRG and how they would be applied in a proceeding before, during, and after a hearing within the DRG
- review and explain the procedures and practices of the DRG by way of a flow chart and key forms and documents available on the DRG as part of the FSCO website
- assess whether the relevant provisions of the *Statutory Powers Procedure Act* apply to the DRG
- outline the various explanatory literature available on the FSCO website to assist the paralegal to understand the DRG and better represent the client
- appreciate the need to find decisions and/or cases in order to understand and argue the law before the services provided by the DRG
- illustrate and discuss principles that flow from the various cases and decisions as they relate to the services provided by the DRG

INTRODUCTION

As mentioned in Chapter 7, one of the areas the Financial Services Commission of Ontario (FSCO) deals with involves resolving disputes between claimants and insurance companies in respect of claims for personal injuries without going to court. Although not specifically related to hearings before administrative bodies as discussed in most of the other chapters in this book, this area is important for licensed paralegals. There are opportunities for paralegals to represent clients in this area; therefore, it is important for this book to examine the practices and procedures of those mechanisms created for FSCO to obviate the need for the court system in these matters. The materials examined below, including the quotes, are largely taken from the FSCO website, www.fsco.gov.on.ca, and specifically the discussion, the forms, brochures, and other materials found on the main Web page called "Dispute Resolution Services" under Insurance.

OVERVIEW AND BACKGROUND

Among the various tasks given to FSCO is the responsibility to deal with claims for personal injuries arising from a motor vehicle accident. As discussed below, the branch of FSCO that deals with disputes regarding the entitlement and amount of benefits payable for personal injuries is the Dispute Resolution Group (DRG). The mandate of the DRG is to "provide timely, cost-effective and fair dispute resolution services for claimants and insurance companies". Its services include the following:

- mediation
- neutral evaluation
- arbitration
- appeal
- variation and revocation

Each specific service set out above shall be examined below to give the reader a clear understanding of the forms and rules to follow in each service.

ENABLING LEGISLATION

There is no legislation that creates the DRG. However, sections of the *Insurance Act* give rise to the need for such mechanism.

The *Insurance Act*

Statutory Accident Benefits

Motor vehicle liability policy owners are entitled to statutory accident benefits under s. 268(1) of the *Insurance Act*:

> Every contract evidenced by a motor vehicle liability policy, including every such contract in force when the *Statutory Accident Benefits Schedule* is made or amended, shall be deemed to provide for the statutory accident benefits set out in the *Schedule* and any amendments to the *Schedule*, subject to the terms, conditions, provisions, exclusions and limits set out in that *Schedule*.

The insurer is liable to pay under the *Statutory Accident Benefits Schedule* (SABS) (s. 268(3)). Subsection 268(2) sets out the rules in determining, in various situations, who is liable to pay statutory accident benefits to both occupants and non-occupants connected to the motor vehicle accident. In most situations, one of the insurance companies involved, as determined by the rules, will be liable; however, the Motor Vehicle Accident Claims Fund can be liable as a last resort. The rules dealing with recourse to more than one insurer are set out in subsections 268(4–5.2).

If a dispute arises that needs to be resolved, remember subsection 268(8), which ensures that the claimant is receiving the benefits required by the SABS, notwithstanding the dispute:

> Where the *Statutory Accident Benefits Schedule* provides that the insurer will pay a particular statutory accident benefit pending resolution of any dispute between the insurer and an insured, the insurer shall pay the benefit until the dispute is resolved.

Section 268.3 requires that guidelines made in respect of the SABS, including subsection 268.3(1), which states that the "[s]uperintendent may issue guidelines on the interpretation and operation of the *Statutory Accident Benefits Schedule* or any provision of that *Schedule*", shall be considered in any determination involving the interpretation of the SABS.

Claims for Benefits

Section 273(1) states a claimant's obligation to inform:

> Where any person makes a claim for damages in respect of bodily injury or death sustained by the person or any other person while driving or being carried in or upon or entering or getting onto or alighting from or as a result of being struck by an automobile, the claimant shall furnish the person against whom the claim is made full particulars of all insurance available to the claimant under contracts falling within the scope of section 268.

The claimant shall also include the details required by subsection 273(2).

Dispute Resolution in Respect of Statutory Accident Benefits

The various services available through the DRG are set out in sections 279–288 of the *Insurance Act*. Disputes arising from a person's entitlement to statutory accident benefits give a party the "right to mediate, litigate, appeal or apply to vary an order as provided in sections 280 to 284" (s. 279(2)) and are resolved by those sections and by the SABS; they cannot be opted out of, except as detailed in the SABS. Note that for the purposes of sections 279–284, an "insured person" includes a person making a claim for death benefits or funeral expenses under the SABS. Both orders and interim orders can be made by the Director of Arbitrations or arbitrators appointed by the Director (ss. 279(3–4)). The representative of a party to any of the dispute resolution services must have the authority to bind his or her party, or else the service may be adjourned, with or without conditions (s. 279(5)).

Mediation

Under subsection 280(1), either the insured person or the insurer may refer to a mediator (appointed by the Director promptly (s. 280(3))) any issue regarding entitlement or the amount under the SABS (s. 280(1)) by filing with FSCO an application for the appointment of a mediator (s. 280(2)). There is a time limit for the matters in dispute to be settled by the mediator (s. 280(4)), which is prescribed in O. Reg. 403/96, section 51, as being within two years of the date of refusal by the insurer to pay the amounts claimed (s. 51(1)). In the event that mediation fails, a court proceeding "may be commenced within 90 days after the mediator reports to the parties under subsection 280(8) of the Act or within 30 days after the person performing the evaluation provides a report to the parties under section 280.1 of the Act, whichever is later." The time limit to complete the mediation can be extended by agreement of the parties (s. 280(5)). The mediator must notify the parties forthwith if the mediator believes that the mediation will fail (s. 280(6)). The mediation is also considered to have failed, in addition to the notice given by the mediator, if the agreed time for mediation has expired and no settlement is reached (s. 280(7)). If the mediation fails, the mediator must prepare and give the parties a report containing the following items as set out in subsection 280(8):

(a) the insurer's last offer and a description of the remaining issues in dispute
(b) a list of outstanding materials, requested but not yet provided, that are necessary for a settlement discussion
(c) a recommendation as to whether the issues should be referred for an evaluation under section 280.1

Under subsection 280(9), the mediator's report may also be given to a person performing a neutral evaluation under section 280.1 or to an arbitrator conducting an arbitration under section 282.

Neutral Evaluation

A neutral evaluation of the probable outcome of a court proceeding or an arbitration under section 282 can be requested by the parties jointly or by the mediator, as stated in subsection 280.1(1):

> If mediation fails, the parties jointly or the mediator who conducted the mediation may, for the purpose of assisting in the resolution of the issues in dispute, refer the issues in dispute to a person appointed by the Director for an evaluation of the probable outcome of a proceeding in court or an arbitration under section 282.

Such evaluator shall be appointed promptly by the Director (s. 280.1(2)) and shall be provided, by the parties, all the information requested (s. 280.1(3)). Such evaluator shall provide to the parties an oral opinion and a written report in accordance with subsection 280.1(4). The evaluator may give the written report to an arbitrator conducting an arbitration under section 282 (s. 280.1(5)).

Alternatives If Mediation Fails

Under subsection 281(1), the insured person may either "bring a proceeding in a court of competent jurisdiction" or refer the matter to an arbitrator appointed by the Director or a private arbitrator appointed by both parties to resolve the matter, provided that the steps in sections 280 and 280.1 have taken place first (s. 281(2)). Pursuant to section 281.1, a similar time limit as set out in subsection 280(4) is applicable to the commencement of the alternatives under subsection 280(1).

Arbitration

The *Arbitrations Act, 1991*, does not apply to arbitrations under section 282 pursuant to subsection 282(16). An insured person seeking arbitration under section 282 shall file an application for the appointment of an arbitrator with FSCO (s. 282(1)), and the Director shall ensure the appointment of such arbitrator promptly (s. 282(2)).

Whether the issues are raised by the insured person or the insurer, all issues in dispute shall be determined by the arbitrator (s. 282(3)). The arbitrator shall conduct the arbitration following the procedures and within the time limits set out in the regulations (s. 282(4)). If the arbitrator finds that the insurer unreasonably delayed or withheld payments that are to be made in accordance with the SABS, he or she can make a special award to the insured in accordance with subsection 282(10). In addition, under certain criteria set out in the regulations, the arbitrator can award the insured person or the insurer all or part of the expenses incurred in respect of an arbitration proceeding as prescribed in the regulations (s. 282(11)). The arbitrator can also make an interim award of expenses any time during the arbitration (s. 282(11.1)).

The arbitrator can award expenses required to be paid by a party and direct that the representative of such party be personally responsible to pay any or all of such expenses if (i) the arbitrator is satisfied that any of the three criteria set out in this subsection occurred (s. 282(11.2)), and (ii) the representative has been given reasonable opportunity to make representations to the arbitrator (s. 282(11.4)). Note that subsection 282(11.2) does not apply to a lawyer: "Clause (11.2)(a) does not apply to a barrister or solicitor acting in the usual course of the practice of law" (s. 282(11.3)).

Under subsection 282(12), if a party believes the arbitrator is biased, he or she may apply to the Director for a new arbitrator, but it will be the Director who determines the issue.

Immediately after making a decision, the arbitrator shall deliver to the parties and the Director a copy of the decision and the reasons (s. 282(13)).

Appeal Against Arbitration Order

According to subsection 283(1), a party to an arbitration under section 282 may appeal the arbitrator's order on a question of law. A written appeal shall be made to the Director and shall be delivered to FSCO within 30 days after the date of the arbitrator's order (s. 283(2)). However, the Director, under subsection 283(3), can extend the time to request an appeal if he or she is satisfied that there are reasonable grounds for granting the extension.

The nature of the appeal and the powers of the Director on such appeal are set out in subsections 283(4) and (5), respectively. The appeal does not stay the order of the arbitrator unless the Director declares otherwise (s. 283(6)). **Also note subsection 283(7), which states that subsections 282(10) to (11.2) shall apply with necessary modifications to appeals before the Director.** Furthermore, the Director can, under subsection 283(8), allow intervenors to make submissions on issues of law arising in an appeal.

Application for Variation of Director's or Arbitrator's Order

Any party under subsection 284(1) may apply to the Director to vary or revoke an order made by the Director or by an arbitrator appointed by the Director. The Director may decide the matter or he or she may return the matter to the same arbitrator or assign it to some other arbitrator (s. 284(2)). The variation requested under this section may be granted under the following circumstances (s. 284(3)):

(i)   if the person doing so considers it advisable to do so;
(ii)   if there is a material change in the circumstance of the insured;
(iii)   if there is new evidence available;
(iv)   if there is an error in the order.

The order of variation can be prospective or retroactive under subsection 284(4). **Also note subsection 284(5), which states that subsections 282(11) to (11.2) apply, with necessary modifications, to applications under this section.**

Representation of Parties

Under subsection 284.1(1), a party to a proceeding under sections 279–284 shall not be represented by a "person for compensation except in accordance with the regulations and subject to such terms and conditions as may be specified in the regulations". But such restriction does not apply to lawyers: "[Section 284.1] does not apply to a barrister or solicitor acting in the usual course of the practice of law." The regulation, R.R.O. 1990, Reg. 664, as amended in section 18, also exempts, for the purposes of subsection 398(1) of the *Insurance Act*, anyone licensed by the Law Society of Upper Canada to be a representative of a person making a claim under the SABS. Further, O. Reg. 7/00, as amended, in subsection 3(4)(b), exempts persons licensed by the Law Society of Upper Canada for the purposes of subsection 438(1) of the *Insurance Act* to be a representative of a person making a claim under the SABS.

Stated Case and Other Matters

Under section 285, the Director "may state a case in writing for the opinion of the Divisional Court upon any question that, in his or her opinion, is a question of law" which the Divisional Court shall hear.

Miscellaneous Provisions

A Director-appointed arbitrator of an order that is under appeal cannot revoke or vary that order or make a new order to replace that order (s. 286).

Insurers cannot unilaterally reduce benefits in any circumstances after an order is issued by the Director or by a Director-appointed arbitrator, as stated in section 287:

> An insurer shall not, after an order of the Director or of an arbitrator appointed by the Director, reduce benefits to an insured person on the basis of an alleged change of circumstances, alleged new evidence or an alleged error, unless the insured person agrees or unless the Director or an arbitrator so orders in a variation or appeal proceeding under section 283 or 284.

If the Director detects unfair or deceptive business practices of an insurer in the arbitration orders review process, the Director can recommend an investigation of such insurer to the Superintendent:

> **s. 288** The Director shall review arbitration orders and may recommend to the Superintendent that the Superintendent investigate the business practices of an insurer if the Director is of the opinion that any one or more arbitrations or appeals from arbitrations reveal unfair or deceptive business practices.

Prohibition against Public Adjusters of Motor Accident Claims

Section 398(1), by way of the regulations, previously exempted SABS representatives, who were licensed by FSCO, but it now states:

> ... no person shall, on the person's own behalf or on behalf of another person, directly or indirectly,
> (a) solicit the right to negotiate, or negotiate or attempt to negotiate, for compensation, the settlement of a claim for loss or damage arising out of a motor vehicle accident resulting from bodily injury to or death of any person or damage to property on behalf of a claimant; or
> (b) hold himself, herself or itself out as an adjuster, investigator, consultant or otherwise as an adviser, on behalf of any person having a claim against an insured or an insurer for which indemnity is provided by a motor vehicle liability policy, including a claim for Statutory Accident Benefits.

Note that the SABS can be handled by a licensed paralegal. For supervised staff at law firms, they also require a licence from the LSUC to represent claimants in the dispute resolution process at FSCO.

Unfair Deceptive Acts and Practices in the Business of Insurance

Part XVIII of the *Insurance Act* deals with unfair or deceptive acts or practices contrary to the statute (ss. 438–439) as prescribed in the regulations including as described in O. Reg. 7/00, as amended. As noted in that regulation, persons licensed by the Law Society of Upper Canada are, as of May 1, 2008, not in breach of such provision merely based on representing a person for compensation.

RELEVANT REGULATIONS

Regulatory Provisions under the *Insurance Act* Relevant to the SABS and Representatives of Persons Making Claims

The previous SABS, O. Reg. 403/96, details benefits available as follows:

- Income replacement benefit — Part II
- Non-earner benefit — Part III
- Caregiver benefit — Part IV
- Medical, rehabilitation, and attendant care benefits and case manager services — Part V
- Payment of other expenses — Part VI
- Death and funeral benefit — Part VII
- Optional benefits — Part VIII

The procedures for claiming benefits are detailed in Part X of the regulation. The current SABS (effective September 1, 2010), O. Reg. 34/10 came into force, replacing O. Reg. 403/96 for any matters arising from and after such date. The O. Reg. 34/10 has many of the same provisions as the previous SABS, including to following:

- Income replacement, non-earner and caregiver benefits — Part II
- Medical, rehabilitation, and attendant care benefits (which include case manager services) — Part III
- Payment of other expenses — Part IV
- Death and funeral benefits — Part V
- Optional benefits — Part VI

The procedures for claiming benefits are detailed in Part VII of the regulation. (Note: To determine the current law, the reader should closely examine such regulation.)

Also note the Automobile Insurance Regulation, R.R.O. 1990, O. Reg. 664, which states as follows:

> A person who is authorized to provide legal services in Ontario pursuant to the *Law Society Act* is exempt from subsection 398(1) of the *Insurance Act* in respect of a claim for benefits under the Statutory Accident Benefits Schedule.

O. Reg. 7/00, as amended, in subsection 3(4)(b) deals with unfair or deceptive acts or practices and exempts persons licensed by the Law Society of Upper Canada for the purposes of subsection 438(1) of the *Insurance Act* to be a representative of a person making a claim under the SABS.

As stated above, a person involved in a motor vehicle accident in Ontario is entitled to make a claim for benefits under the SABS to one's own insurance company (on a no-fault basis). If the claimant or the insurance company disagrees about the entitlement or the amount of the benefits, either may apply to FSCO's branch, called DRS, except for the following circumstances:

- Claims for damages due to pain and suffering
- Claims for damages to the claimant's automobile or other property
- Decisions on who was at fault in the accident
- Resolutions of disputes between insurers about which company is responsible for the claimant's claim

PROCEDURES

Dispute Resolution Practice Code

The Dispute Resolution Practice Code (DRPC), last updated in October 2003 contains the following clauses:

- Preamble
- Section A — Rules of Procedure
  - Part 1 — General Rules for Dispute Resolution
  - Part 2 — Mediation
  - Part 3 — Arbitration and Neutral Evaluation at FSCO
  - Part 4 — Appeal of Arbitration Order
  - Part 5 — Variation or Revocation of an Order
  - Part 6 — General Procedures for Hearings
- Section B — Guidelines
- Section C — Practice Notes
- Section D — Fees and Assessments
- Section E — Settlement Regulation
- Section F — Expense Regulation
- Section G — Forms

Below is a discussion of the key provisions of the DRPC so that the reader can have a clearer idea of the rules, procedures, and forms used in various services that exist under the DRG of FSCO.

Preamble

The DRPC is a user's guide published by the DRG to help consumers and insurers resolve disputes involving statutory accident benefits claims under the *Insurance Act* and the SABS. It creates rules for timely, cost-effective, and fair dispute resolution services provided through the DRG.

The first step in the process is mediation, which in Ontario is mandatory and must be conducted through FSCO before any other steps can be taken. When mediation cannot resolve a dispute, the insured person has several options:

> If the dispute remains unresolved after mediation at the [FSCO], the insured person has a number of choices. He or she can continue to negotiate directly with the insurance company. Alternatively, the insured person can opt for arbitration at the [FSCO], private arbitration, private neutral evaluation or a court action. Each option has its own rules, and the insured person may not be able to switch from one system to another.

The preamble notes that different legislative provisions apply, depending on if the accident occurred between June 22, 1990, and 1993; between 1994 and October 31, 1996; between November 1, 1996 and August 31, 2010, and after September 1, 2010. If a provision of the DRPC is found to be contrary to the *Insurance Act* or any other law, the law will prevail. The preamble provides a discussion of the contents of the DRPC and includes an FAQs section that gives general information on each service available. Locations where copies of the DRPC and DRG forms can be obtained, as well as sources for decisions of the various DRG services, are also given.

In the preamble, the various timelines for services available through the DRG are summarized as follows:

1. An insured person or an insurer may apply for mediation of a dispute about an insured person's entitlement to accident benefits where a claim has been denied by the insurer or the time period for the insurer to respond to the claim has elapsed (Rule 12.1).
2. An *Application for Mediation* in FORM A must be filed with the Dispute Resolution Group no later than **2 years** from the date the insurer provided written notice of a refusal to pay the amount claimed (Rule 11).
3. An *Application for Mediation* in FORM A, completed in accordance with the requirements of Rule 12.2, will be registered and assigned to a mediator within 3 weeks of its receipt.
4. Mediation will be concluded within **60 days** of the registration of the completed *Application for Mediation* (Rule 19).
5. A *Report of Mediator* (Rule 22) will be issued within **7 business days** of the conclusion of mediation.
6. An *Application for Arbitration* in FORM C must be filed with the Dispute Resolution Group no later than **2 years** from the date the insurer provided written notice of a refusal to pay an amount claimed. However, an insured person may file a completed *Application for Arbitration* within **90 days** after the mediator reports to the parties in the *Report of Mediator* (Rule 11).
7. An *Application for Arbitration* in FORM C will be registered and assigned to an arbitration case administrator within **5 business days** of receipt of an Application completed in accordance with Rule 25.1.
8. Dates for holding an arbitration pre-hearing discussion (Rule 33) will be available to the parties within **6 to 8 weeks** from the registration of a completed *Application for Arbitration*.
9. Dates for holding an oral arbitration hearing will be available to the parties within **4 to 6 months** from the conclusion of the pre-hearing discussion.
10. An oral arbitration hearing is generally concluded within **3 days**.
11. An arbitration order from an oral hearing will be issued within **60 to 85 days** from the conclusion of the oral hearing.
12. A written arbitration hearing is generally concluded within a **60 day** period (Rule 38).
13. An arbitration order from a written hearing will be issued on the later of:
    (a) **60 days** after the last day on which the insured person is entitled to file a *Reply by the Applicant for Arbitration;*
    (b) 30 days after the last day on which the parties are required to file additional materials or written submissions (Rule 38).
14. A *Notice of Appeal* in FORM I on a question of law, must be filed within **30 days** of the date of the arbitration order being appealed (Rule 52).
15. A decision in the appeal will be issued within **60 to 85 days** from the conclusion of the oral or written appeal hearing.
16. A request for an *Assessment of Expenses* must be made within **30 days** from the date the order of the arbitrator was issued (Rule 79).
17. An order on an *Assessment of Expenses* will be issued within **60 to 85 days** from the conclusion of the oral or written hearing on expenses.

Section A — Rules of Procedure

PART 1 — GENERAL RULES FOR DISPUTE RESOLUTION

Rule 1 — Interpretation: The sub-rules of Rule 1 deal with interpretation, as stated in R. 1.1, "[The Rules] will be broadly interpreted to produce the most just, quickest and least expensive resolution of the dispute", and the Director may change the Rules (R. 1.5).

Rule 2 — Guidelines: The Guidelines, which are contained in Section B of the DRPC, are intended for the interpretation and operation of the SABS.

Rule 3 — Practice Notes: Practice notes are issued from time to time by the DRG on its policies and administrative procedures and are located in Section C of the DRPC (R. 3.1). Practice notes, as stated in R. 3.2, "are designed to guide users in the dispute resolution process at [FSCO]"; however, "they are not binding and do not affect the duty of the adjudicator to make decisions based on the circumstances and merits of each case".

Rule 4 — Definitions: Currently, there are 23 definitions of words and phrases that are used throughout the DRPC.

Rule 5 — Dispute Resolution Services and Documents: Rules 5.1–5.5 deal with the language for the provision of services by the DRG and the use of interpretation services. Under R. 5.6, the DRG "may issue letters of direction, notices and other documents signed by the Director". When a document is deemed delivered by the DRG is detailed in R. 5.7.

Rule 6 — Filing: Any document required to be filed by the rules must be delivered to the DRG by one of the methods and in the time frames set out in R. 7.

Rule 7 — Service of Documents: A document to be served under the rules must be served pursuant to one of the seven methods set out in R. 7.1, two of which are facsimile and electronic transmission. If either of these two methods is used, a cover page containing information required by R. 7.2 must be included. The time frames where service is deemed, depending on the method of service, are set out in R. 7.3.

Rule 8 — Calculation of Time: Rule 8.1 details various situations and how time is calculated under the rules or an order.

Rule 9 — Representation: Under R. 9.1, a party can self-represent or appoint another person as a representative, but certain information about the party and the representative, as set out in the rule, must be provided to the DRG. Further, a representative who is neither a lawyer nor a law firm employee directly supervised by a lawyer must meet FSCO's filing requirements before he or she can provide representation for compensation. **(As of May 1, 2008, such person is required to be licensed by the Law Society of Upper Canada.)** Rule 9.2 requires that a party must give his or her representative full authorization to discuss, negotiate, and enter into an agreement or settlement of any and all issues in dispute, and the DRG may require written confirmation from the party that such authority has been given. If such requisite authority does not exist, the mediator, neutral evaluator, or adjudicator can adjourn the service being provided in accordance with R. 9.4. Notifications of a change of a representative are detailed in Rules 9.5–9.6 and the details of withdrawal by a representative are dealt with in Rules 9.7–9.8. Rule 9.9 states that an adjudicator can exclude anyone who acts as a representative or agent on behalf of a party or as an advisor to a witness, except a duly qualified lawyer, from a proceeding if the adjudicator finds such person (i) not competent to properly represent or to advise the party or witness, or (ii) not able to understand and comply with the Rules and the duties and responsibilities of a representative, agent, or advisor. **(It is not clear if this R. 9.9 would apply to a paralegal licensed by the LSUC.)**

Rule 10 — Party under a Disability: Rules 10.1–10.7 deal with various situations involving parties with disabilities and how such persons are to conduct proceedings as well as adults declared mentally incapable and how proceedings are to be carried out in those circumstances.

Rule 11 — Time Limits for Mediation, Neutral Evaluation, or Arbitration: Under R.11.1, the time limit for filing for any of the services set out in the Rules is two years from the date the insurer issued a written notice of refusal to pay the claimed amount. However, according to

R. 11.2, an insured person can still file a completed Application for Arbitration under two situations: (i) within **90 days** after the mediator provided the *Report of Mediator* to the parties, or (ii) within **30 days** after the neutral evaluator, appointed by the Director, issued the *Report of Neutral Evaluator* to the parties, whichever is later.

PART 2 — MEDIATION

Rule 12 — Application for Mediation: Rule 12.1 states that where a dispute arises because a claim has been denied or the prescribed time for the claim to be made has elapsed and the claim relates to an insured person's entitlement to accident benefits or the amount of those benefits, either the insured person or the insurer can apply for mediation. The party who seeks mediation must file, in duplicate, an Application for Mediation (Form A) containing the information set out in R. 12.2. If Form A appears to have jurisdictional concerns or deficiencies set out in R. 12.3, the DRG shall issue a written notice of those issues to the applicant and representative and shall suspend the application for 20 days, starting from the delivery of the notice. If the applicant does not address the concerns set out in the notice within the 20-day period, the DRG may reject the application (R. 12.4). Rule 12.5 restricts any party to re-apply for mediation of a dispute that has been mediated but not resolved as concluded in the *Report of Mediator*.

Rule 13 — Appointment of a Mediator: Pursuant to R. 13.1, upon receipt of a completed application for mediation, the DRG will deliver to the other party the application and Form B and will promptly appoint a mediator.

Rule 14 — Response to Application to Mediation: The party responding to Form A must, within 10 days of receipt, file a completed Form B containing the information detailed in R. 14.1. The DRG can reject an incomplete Form B under R. 14.2. Under R. 14.3, the responding party must also deliver the completed Form B to every party in the dispute.

Rule 15 — Combining Applications and Adding New Issues: The alternatives given to the DRG to deal with two or more applications for mediation involving the same parties or the same accident are laid out in Rule 15.1. The mechanisms to adding any additional issues to a mediation are set out in R. 15.2.

Rule 16 — The Mediation Process: Mediation can be done in a variety of formats and is decided by the mediator, as stated in R. 16.1. Parties of the dispute must exchange key documents required to discuss the settlement of the issues in the dispute, and those documents must also be provided to the mediator at least 10 days before the scheduled mediation (R. 16.2). The mediator, pursuant to R. 16.3, will look at all issues in dispute identified in Forms A and B and any new issues added under R 15.2 and will help the parties settle as many issues as possible.

Rule 17 — Participation in Mediation: Rule 17.1 requires all parties and their representatives to participate in good faith in the mediation process and provide all relevant documents as set out in the Rules. Appointment of a representative does not relieve a party of the obligations set out in R. 17.2; and if a party does not comply with R. 17.1 or 17.2, the mediator may adjourn the mediation or report to the parties that the mediation did not take place (R. 17.3).

Rule 18 — Confidentiality during Mediation: Specific concerns involving confidentiality during the mediation process (in order to allow for the best opportunity to settle without concern of possibly prejudicial information getting out) are dealt with under R. 18. Disclosure of statements and offers to settle other than what is set out in the *Report of Mediator* is restricted to avoid prejudicing a party in a subsequent proceeding (R. 18.1). A mediator is non-compellable as a witness as to what happened in the mediation process (R. 18.2). Any information or documents provided to the mediator in confidence cannot be disclosed or form part of the file by the mediator except with permission (Rs. 18.3–18.4). The DRG will not provide any part of the mediation file, other than the *Report of Mediator*, to a neutral evaluator or arbitrator (R. 18.5).

Rule 19 — Time Limits for Mediation: The time limit for concluding a mediation, as stated in R. 19.1, is 60 days after the filing of a completed Form A. Pursuant to R. 19.2, an extension is possible if it is agreed to by all parties and the parties have consulted with the mediator and provide the mediator with written confirmation of the extended dates they agreed on (R. 19.3).

Rule 20 — Settlement of an Issue: According to R. 20.1, the parties will advise the mediator of any issues they settled on their own during the mediation process, and such settlement is subject to the legal requirements detailed in R. 20.2.

Rule 21 — Failure of Mediation: Under R. 21.1, mediation on an issue is considered failed if (i) the mediator informs the parties that he or she believes the mediation will fail, or (ii) the time limit (including extension) is up and no settlement is made on the issue. Upon failure of the mediation, the insurer, under R. 21.2, will provide to the mediator its last offer relating to the outstanding issue or issues. No other proceeding in court or through an arbitrator, appointed privately or by the DRG, can be commenced unless mediation was sought and has failed (R. 21.3).

Rule 22 — Report of Mediator: Rule 22.1 lists the six items that must be included in the mediator's report. The DRG will deliver the report to the parties, to the Director-appointed neutral evaluator, and to the arbitrator (R. 22.2).

Rule 23 — Amendment of Mediator's Report: Under R. 23.1, a party who believes that the *Report of Mediator* is not accurate must notify the mediator and the other parties in writing and with reasons within **10 days** of receiving the report. The mediator, after reviewing the reasons and comments of the parties, can amend the report as he or she considers appropriate (R. 23.2). The DRG will deliver the amendment to the report to those who received the report under R. 22.2 (R. 23.3).

Rule 24 — Referral to Neutral Evaluation: As set out in R. 24.1, if mediation on any of the issues in dispute fails, the parties jointly or the mediator can ask for an evaluation of the probable outcome of a proceeding in court or arbitration by an evaluator appointed by the Director. Rule 24.2 lists the two options of neutral evaluation: (i) a jointly retained private neutral evaluator appointed by the Director, and (ii) a neutral evaluator at FSCO. Rule 24.3 details the procedures needed to appoint a privately retained neutral evaluator. Once neutral evaluation is elected, proceeding to court or arbitration must wait until the *Report of the Neutral Evaluator* has been given to the parties (R. 24.4).

PART 3 — ARBITRATION AND NEUTRAL EVALUATION AT THE COMMISSION

Rule 25 — Application for Arbitration: An insured person applying for arbitration must file a completed Form C, Application for Arbitration, containing the six items detailed in R. 25.1. A copy of the *Report of Mediator* and, if a private neutral evaluation has occurred, the *Report of the Neutral Evaluator* or a confirmation that the parties have received it must also be filed (R. 25.2). Under R. 25.3, if there was no private neutral evaluation, the insured can request in Form C a neutral evaluator at FSCO. If Form C appears to have any of the jurisdictional concerns or deficiencies set out in R. 25.4, the DRG will deliver a written notice of such issues to the applicant and representative and suspend the application for 20 days starting from the day of the delivery of the notice. Under R. 25.5, the DRG can reject the application if the applicant fails to resolve the concerns set out in the notice within the 20-day period. The DRG must deliver a copy of the completed Form C to the other parties, pursuant to R. 25.6.

Rule 26 — Options Available to an Insurer, Including Neutral Evaluation at the Commission: The insurer, within 20 days of receipt of the completed Form C, must respond by filing Forms E (Response by Insurer) and F (Statement of Service) or Form D (Agreement to Neutral Evaluation) as set out in R. 26.1. Under R. 26.2, where the parties jointly choose neutral evaluation at FSCO by Form D, it shall be done in accordance with Rs. 44–49.

Rule 27 — Response of the Insurer: Where the parties do not choose neutral evaluation, Form E is used and must contain the six items set out in R. 27.1. If Form E is found to have any of the jurisdictional concerns or deficiencies set out in R. 27.2, the DRG will deliver a written notice of those issues to the insurer and representative and suspend the application for 20 days starting from the day of the delivery of the notice. If the insurer fails to alleviate the concerns set out in the notice within the 20-day period, the arbitrator may reject the *Response* and proceed with the arbitration on an uncontested basis.

Rule 28 — Appointment of an Arbitrator: If there is no appointment of a neutral evaluator (privately retained or at FSCO), the Director can proceed to appoint an arbitrator. The Director can also appoint an arbitrator to conduct a pre-hearing or other interim proceeding.

Rule 29 — Reply by the Applicant for Arbitration: Within 10 days of being served with a Form E, the applicant must reply to any new issues raised by serving a Form G (Reply by the Applicant for Arbitration) accompanied by a Form F (R. 29.1). If the applicant finds no new issues brought up in Form E, Form G is not required (R. 29.2).

Rule 30 — Combining Applications: Where two or more Applications for Arbitrations show a common issue or question of law, fact, or policy, or where combining applications will result in the most just, quickest, and least expensive way to deal with those applications, the DRG can choose to proceed in one of the four options listed in R. 30.1. The DRG, according to the same rule, must issue a written notice of such intention to all parties involved. A party who objects to such notice must promptly notify in writing to the DRG and the other parties of his or her objection (R. 30.2). The arbitrator will consider the objection and make an order (R. 30.3).

Rule 31 — Severing Issues: An Application for Arbitration (Form C) can be divided into distinct issues to be heard separately if (i) the arbitrator considers it appropriate, or (ii) the parties agree and the arbitrator approves. If such a division is decided or agreed upon, the DRG will give written notification to the parties in accordance with R. 31.1. A party who objects to such notice must promptly notify in writing to the DRG and the other parties of the objection (R. 31.3), and the arbitrator will consider the objection and make an order (R. 31.4). Note that R. 31.2 states that each of the orders made in an arbitration application will stand on its own for the purposes of an appeal or a variation/revocation proceeding.

Rule 32 — Exchange of Documents before Pre-hearing: At least 10 days before the pre-hearing discussion, each party must fulfill the four requirements with regard to exchanging documents set out in R. 32.1. Pursuant to R. 32.2 but subject to timelines set out in Rule 39, the parties have an ongoing responsibility to ensure prompt and complete exchange of documents as necessary and the arbitrator may order production of documents under R. 32.3.

Rule 33 — Pre-hearing Discussion: Rule 33.1 listed eight types of assistance in preparing arbitration that an arbitrator may provide to parties during the pre-hearing discussions held before the arbitrator. The pre-hearing arbitrator will attempt to resolve the dispute while preparing the parties for arbitration. The formats for the pre-hearing discussion are listed in R. 33.2, and the DRG must give reasonable notice to the parties of the date and manner of the pre-hearing discussion, as stated in R. 33.3. The pre-hearing arbitrator will confirm in writing to the parties the results of the pre-hearing discussions (R. 33.4). According to R. 33.5, an arbitrator who presides at a pre-hearing discussion where there is an attempt to settle will not preside at the hearing unless the parties consent.

Rule 34 — Failure to Comply: An arbitrator may take any of the five actions listed in R. 34.1 if a party who fails to comply with a time requirement established by the Rules or by order or agreement, or fails to produce documents in compliance with an order or agreement. Under R. 34.2, either party may make a written request for the resumption of the pre-hearing discussion, which is suspended because a party fails to comply with the established time line or to produce required documents. The DRG, under R. 34.3, will attempt to accommodate such request for resumption.

Rule 35 — Settlement Conference Prior to Scheduled Hearing Date: Pursuant to R. 35.1, either party may ask the DRG for a settlement conference, and R. 35.2 requires the party who makes the request to provide proof of consent to settlement conference from all other parties as well as the agreed upon conference dates and times. R. 35.3 states that the DRG will attempt to accommodate the consented request for a settlement conference and may assign a mediator or facilitator to assist. In addition, the DRG or an arbitrator may also initiate a settlement conference if the parties consent (R. 35.4). Note that an arbitrator who facilitates at a settlement conference prior to a scheduled hearing cannot preside at the hearing unless the parties consent (R. 35.5).

Rule 36 — Confidentiality during Settlement Negotiations: Rule 36.1 states that statements made for the purpose of settlement or offers to settle made in pre-hearing discussions or a settlement conference cannot be used against any position the parties may take in subsequent proceedings. Further, the settlement facilitator of an issue in dispute before the DRG cannot be compelled to give information received as a facilitator in a private arbitration or in the courts in accordance with R. 36.2.

Rule 37 — Hearings: The possible formats of a hearing held by the arbitrator are set out in R. 37.1. The arbitrator will not hold a written hearing if there is a good reason for not doing so (R. 37.2) nor will the arbitrator hold an electronic hearing if it will significantly prejudice a party (R. 37.3). Such rules do not apply if the hearing is limited to deal with procedural matters (R. 37.4). In accordance with R. 37.5, parties to an arbitration must be given reasonable notice of the hearing, including the format and the right to object, if it is a written or electronic hearing of non-procedural matters. According to R. 37.6, the arbitrator will determine all issues in dispute and any other issues agreed by the parties through mediation. Where a party has been sent notice but fails to attend or participate in a hearing, the arbitrator is allowed to proceed with the hearing without the party's presence or participation, as stated in R. 37.7.

Rule 38 — Time Lines for Written Hearings: Pursuant to R. 38.1, the arbitrator in a written hearing can ask for additional materials or written submissions within 30 days of the last day that the insured is entitled to file a Form E. If the DRG has delivered such request and the party fails to provide the requested information, the arbitrator can proceed to determine issues and make an order based on existing materials and submissions. Such order must be issued within the time lines established in 38.1(d).

Rule 39 — Evidence: All documents, reports, and assessments to be introduced at the hearing by either party must be served on the other party at least 30 days before the first day of the hearing (R. 39.1). Subject to extraordinary circumstances, the arbitrator may give permission for service less than 30 days, as allowed in R. 39.2. The hearing arbitrator will determine the relevance, materiality, and admissibility of evidence submitted at the hearing. Any evidence that falls into one of the three categories set out in R. 39.3 will not be admitted: (i) inadmissible in a court for being a privilege under the law of evidence; (ii) inadmissible under the *Insurance Act*; or (iii) not served on the opposing parties as required in Rs. 39.1 and 39.2 (except under extraordinary circumstances accepted by the arbitrator).

Rule 40 — Surveillance Evidence: If a party intends to rely on any portion of surveillance or investigative evidence, the party must ensure conditions set out in R. 40.1 are met at least 30 days before the hearing.

Rule 41 — Witnesses: The parties are to exchange the names of witnesses that are to be called and provide the names of persons that are required to attend for cross-examination on a report at least 30 days before the first day of hearing (R. 41.1). Each party must also notify a potential witness of him or her being called to give evidence (R. 41.2) at least 30 days before the first day of the hearing. Pursuant to R. 41.3, an arbitrator may excuse a witness from attending if the witness was not identified under R. 33 or notified in accordance with R. 40.1, or the arbitrator considers it is just to do so. An arbitrator can summons a witness under R. 41.4, and a party can command the attendance of a witness by serving a Summons to Witness (Form N), as stated in R. 41.5.

Rule 42 — Expert Witnesses: Under R. 42.1, the full name and qualifications of the expert who prepared the report must accompany the report if it is to be introduced into the proceeding. If a party intends to call an expert witness, the party must serve and file a document providing the information required in R. 42.2 within the time lines and requirements set out under Rules 39 and 41. Such witnesses may be excluded for two reasons, as stated in R. 42.3: (i) requirements of R. 42 are not met; or (ii) the arbitrator considers it just to make an order to exclude. Note that R. 42.4 restricts the number of expert witnesses to give opinion evidence at a hearing to two for each party, unless the arbitrator orders otherwise.

Rule 43 — Reopening of Hearing: This rule allows the arbitrator to reopen a hearing at any time before a final order disposing of the hearing has been made. Rules 37 to 42 apply with arbitrator modifications allowed.

Rule 44 — Neutral Evaluation at FSCO: As stated in R. 44.1, upon receipt of a completed Agreement to Neutral Evaluation at the Commission (Form D) and confirmation of the consent of the parties, the Director will suspend the appointment of an arbitrator and appoint a neutral evaluator, whose appointment must be confirmed by the parties. The parties are given 30 days, from receiving the Director's notice of the appointment of the neutral evaluator, to file a Joint Statement for Neutral Evaluation at the Commission (Form H) containing the information required in R. 44.2. If it appears that Form H is incomplete in accordance with R. 44.2 or that the dispute is unsuitable for neutral evaluation (a determination made with regard to considerations set out in Practice Note 6 (R. 44.5)), the Director will deliver a written notice of identified concerns or deficiencies and suspend the evaluation for 10 days immediately following the delivery of the notice, pursuant to R. 44.3. If the party fails to address the deficiencies or concerns within the 10-day period, the Director can terminate the neutral evaluation and promptly appoint an arbitrator (R. 44.4). The Director must, upon receipt of a completed Form H, promptly select one of the two dates provided in the form for the neutral evaluation and notify the parties of the date, time, and location of the evaluation (R. 44.6).

Rule 45 — Case Summary for Neutral Evaluation: At least 10 days prior to the date of the neutral evaluation, each party must exchange and file a case summary containing the two items detailed in R. 45.1: (i) submission summary on issues to be evaluated, and (ii) copies of key documents required for each issue to be evaluated. The parties shall promptly provide any additional information requested by the neutral evaluator (R. 45.2).

Rule 46 — Termination of Neutral Evaluation: A party withdrawing from a neutral evaluation must give written notification to the other parties and the DRG (R. 46.1). The Director may terminate the neutral evaluation in one of the three circumstances set out in R. 46.2: (i) a party withdraws; (ii) a party fails to comply with Rs. 44 and 45; or (iii) a party fails to attend or participate in neutral evaluation. When a neutral evaluation is terminated, the Director must promptly appoint an arbitrator by written notice to the parties (R. 46.3). Arbitration hearing conducted after a termination of neutral evaluation pursuant to this rule must proceed in accordance with Rule 33 and following.

Rule 47 — Opinion of the Neutral Evaluator: If the evaluation proceeds, the neutral evaluator will give the parties his or her evaluation on the probable outcome of a proceeding in court or an arbitration verbally (R. 47.1), and such evaluation is confidential (R. 47.2). Further, the neutral evaluator is not compellable to disclose any information obtained in, or derived from, the evaluation process in any subsequent proceeding (R. 47.3).

Rule 48 — Report of the Neutral Evaluator: The neutral evaluator will promptly provide a *Report of the Neutral Evaluator* containing information required by R. 48.1: issues evaluated and settled; issues that remain in dispute and the insurer's last offer on those issues; and a list of outstanding materials requested by the evaluator. The neutral evaluator's opinion of the probable outcome of a proceeding, which is given verbally, shall not be part of the report (R. 48.2).

Rule 49 — Referral to Arbitration after Neutral Evaluation: Rule 49.1 states that the Director shall refer issues that remain in dispute after the evaluation to arbitration **two business days** after delivery to the parties of the *Report of the Neutral Evaluator*. An arbitrator shall be promptly appointed (R. 49.2), and all rules starting with Rule 37 apply to the post-evaluation arbitration proceeding (R. 49.4). Note that the neutral evaluator will not preside at the arbitration hearing (R. 49.3).

PART 4 — APPEAL OF THE ARBITRATION ORDER

Rule 50 — Appeal: As stated in R. 50.1, an appeal of an arbitration order to the Director can be made only on a question of law. No appeal of an interim or preliminary order is allowed until all issues in the dispute have been finally decided (R. 50.2), and an appeal does not stop an arbitration order from taking effect (R. 50.3). However, both Rs. 50.2 and 50.3 have made an exception for a Director's order.

Rule 51 — Starting an Appeal: To appeal an arbitration order, the appellant must comply with the provision of Rule 51.1 especially completing, serving, and filing with fee a Notice of Appeal (Form I), and the Director will promptly acknowledge the appeal (R. 51.4). An appeal may be rejected if the appeal falls within the five categories listed in R. 51.2. The Director, upon deciding the appeal is rejected under R. 51.2, will notify the parties and their representative of the rejection (R. 51.3).

Rule 52 — Time for Appeal: The appellant must file Form I within 30 days of the date of the arbitration order (R. 52.1). An extension can be granted by the Director if he or she is satisfied that there are reasonable grounds for the extension (R. 52.2).

Rule 53 — Response to Appeal: Within **20 days** of receiving the Director's acknowledgment of the Form I as required in R. 51.4, the respondent must complete and serve a Response to Appeal (Form J) on the appellant or the appellant's representative. This rule also requires the respondent to file a copy of Form J along with a Statement of Service (Form F).

Rule 54 — Written Submissions: Within 30 days of the date that Form J by the respondent is due, the appellant must serve and file submissions and must also file a Form F, unless the Director orders otherwise (R. 54.1). The 30-day time limit can be extended if a transcript is ordered, and the extension is limited to 30 days from the date the transcript is received (R. 54.2). According to R. 54.3, within 20 days of receiving the appellant's written submissions, the respondent must serve the written submissions and file the submissions with a Form F.

Rule 55 — Appeal by Respondent (Cross-appeal): If the respondent intends to appeal the arbitration order, he or she must complete a separate Notice of Appeal within the time periods for appeal set out in the rules above.

Rule 56 — The Appeal Process: Under R. 56.1, the Director can appoint a person, who will be given the same powers and duties of the Director, to conduct the appeal. Any order made in such capacity by such person is considered an order of the Director (R. 56.2). Unless otherwise ordered by the Director, the appeal will deal only with issues in the arbitration or in the arbitration order that is being appealed (R. 56.3). What should be included in the appeal record are set out in R. 56.4. The Director may decide the appeal on the record or by holding an oral or electronic hearing, as well as any format the Director considers appropriate (R. 56.5). If the Director decides to schedule an electronic or oral hearing, a notice of hearing will be delivered to the parties and their representatives (R. 56.6).

Rule 57 — Preliminary Conference: Under R. 57.1, the Director may require the parties to participate in one or more preliminary conferences; if so, Rule 33 applies (R. 57.2).

Rule 58 — Non-participation: Rule 58.1 states that the Director can proceed with an appeal despite the failure of a party to file a document required by the Rules. Where a notice of hearing has been delivered to a party, the Director can proceed with the appeal in the absence of such party, all in accordance with R. 58.2.

Rule 59 — Interventions: Under R. 59.1, persons who are not parties to an appeal may be asked by the Director to make submissions on an issue of law arising in an appeal, and their participation will be such terms as the Director considers appropriate. A person not a party to an appeal can also apply to make submissions on an issue of law arising in an appeal (R. 59.2) by completing and serving an Application for Intervention (Form K) as well as filing it with a Form F, in accordance with R. 59.3. A Form K without the reasons of wishing to participate and a summary of submissions on the issues of law can be rejected (R. 59.4), and the Director will notify the applicant, as well as the parties and their representatives to the appeal, of the rejection (R. 59.5). According to R. 59.6, all parties to the appeal are given 10 days, starting from the day of receiving Form K, to indicate support or objection of the application by filing his or comments and sending those comments to the applicant (R. 59.6).

Rule 60 — The Intervention Process: This rule states that Rules 56–58 apply to the intervention process with necessary changes.

PART 5 — VARIATION OR REVOCATION OF AN ORDER

Rule 61 — Application for Variation/Revocation: Both the insurer and the insured can apply to the Director to vary or revoke an arbitration order or an appeal order on any of the three grounds set out in R. 61.1. Unless the Director orders otherwise, application to vary or revoke a preliminary or interim order is disallowed until all the issues in dispute in the proceeding have been finally decided (R. 61.2). In applying for a variation or revocation of an order, a party must complete, serve, and file an Application for Variation/Revocation (Form L) in accordance with R. 61.3. The Director, according to R. 61.6, shall acknowledge the application upon receipt of a completed From L, Form F, and the filing fee. Form L can be rejected under four situations set out in R. 61.4: (i) the application relates to a preliminary order or interim order with unresolved issues in dispute; (ii) the Form is incomplete or missing detail for other parties to respond; (iii) the application relates to an order that is under appeal; or (iv) the applicant fails to pay the filing fee. The Director will inform the parties and their representatives if such rejection is made (R. 61.5).

Rule 62 — Response to the Application for Variation/Revocation: Within 20 days of the receipt of the Director's acknowledgement of Form L, the respondent must complete and serve a Response to Application for Variation/Revocation (Form M), and file in accordance with the rule.

Rule 63 — The Variation/Revocation Process: The Director can choose to decide application of variation/revocation by (i) himself or herself, (ii) a delegate who is given the Director's power, (iii) the adjudicator who made the original order; or (iv) another adjudicator. Rules 57–58 apply to the process with necessary changes (R. 63.2).

PART 6 — GENERAL PROCEDURES FOR HEARINGS

Rule 64 — Applicability: R. 64.1 states that Part 6 applies to all arbitrations, appeals, interventions, and variation/revocation proceedings.

Rule 65 — Orders: An adjudicator will determine the issues in dispute and make an order as he or she considers just (R. 65.1). The adjudicator may make an order with reasons orally under R. 65.2, which requires the adjudicator to confirm the oral order in writing if asked. Written supporting reasons will be given for an order that finally decides the issues in dispute (R. 65.3). Rule 65.4 states that the DRG will deliver a copy of the order as well as the adjudicator's written reasons, if any, to the parties. An adjudicator may, at any time, correct an error in his or her decision or order (R. 65.5), make clarification (R. 65.6), or make an order or give such directions necessary to prevent an abuse of process (R. 65.7).

Rule 66 — Court Enforcement of Orders: The Director will provide a party with a certified copy of an order upon receipt of a written request (R. 66.1). If a certified copy of the order is filed in the Ontario Superior Court of Justice, the order can be enforced as an order of the court (R. 66.2), and the Director should be notified of such filing within 10 days of the filing (R. 66.3).

Rule 67 — Orders within Proceeding: Motions: Within a proceeding, an adjudicator can make preliminary or interim orders (R. 67.1) and a party may request such order (R. 67.2) until a final order is made. Requests for preliminary or interim orders must be in writing and made in accordance with R. 67.3: (i) details of the order (description, grounds, and supporting documents); (ii) time, date, and format of the motion; and (iii) materials in (i) and (ii) must be served and filed. Rule 67.4 details what is required of a party seeking an order for production from a third party who, within 10 days of being served, being the responding party, must serve and file a written response and documents under R. 67.5. The adjudicator may determine the request on the basis of the materials filed or other procedures he or she considers appropriate (R. 67.6). The adjudicator may make an order for the production of documents against a third party if he or she is satisfied that the four conditions set out in R. 67.7 are met. An oral request for an interim order or an order for a preliminary issue can be made in various stages of the process, and the adjudicator can deal with the request in the format he or she considers appropriate (R. 67.8).

Rule 68 — Dismissal of Proceeding without Hearing: Pursuant to R. 68.1, an adjudicator can dismiss a proceeding without a hearing if he or she considers the proceeding frivolous, vexatious, or is commenced in bad faith, but the adjudicator must first deliver a written notice to all parties of his or her intention to dismiss (R. 68.2). A party objecting to the dismissal or seeking to make written submissions about the dismissal must comply with R. 68.3, and the adjudicator shall consider any written objection or submissions in accordance with R. 68.4.

Rule 69 — Settlement: As stated in R. 69.1, the parties can settle any or all issues in dispute at any time on condition that (i) at least one year has passed since the date of the accident, or (ii) a pre-hearing conference has been completed. Upon receiving the written confirmation of a dispute settlement, the DRG will close the file on the dispute, 20 days after it issued a notice of intention to close the file (R. 69.2). A party who objects to the closure of the DRG's file must, in writing, notify the DRG and the other parties and give reasons for the objection (R. 69.3). Either party may request the adjudicator to issue an order dismissing the proceeding on the consent of the parties upon filing the documents required by R. 69.4.

Rule 70 — Withdrawal: According to R. 70.1, a party can seek permission to withdraw all or part of a dispute in two ways: (i) serve a request to withdraw on all parties and file it with a Form F, or (ii) make an oral request to withdraw during a neutral evaluation, pre-hearing discussion, settlement discussion, preliminary conference, or at a hearing. An adjudicator may permit such withdrawal if all the parties agree (R. 70.2). If a party disagrees, the adjudicator has two options: (i) grant withdrawal on terms he or she considers just, or (ii) award expenses to either party in accordance with R. 75 and the rest (R. 70.3).

Rule 71 — Inability of an Adjudicator to Complete: If an adjudicator becomes unable to complete a proceeding for any reason, the matter may be reheard by a new adjudicator appointed by the Director per R. 71.1. If the incomplete hearing has kept a transcript, the Director may notify the parties of his or her intention to provide the transcript to the new adjudicator as well as the parties (R. 71.2). If a party objects to the use of the transcript, such party must provide promptly a written notice, including reasons for the objection to the Director and the other parties (R. 71.3).

Rule 72 — Adjournments: A request to adjourn a pre-hearing discussion or an arbitration proceeding must be made to the DRG, and a request to adjourn an appeal or variation/revocation proceeding must be made to the Director or to the delegate who is given the capacity to act as the Director. The request must be in writing and contains the reasons for the adjournment, an indication of a all-party consent, and dates that are accepted by all parties (R. 72.1). The request must be served and filed in accordance with R. 72.2. The adjudicator shall refer to the adjournments policy discussed in Practice Note 9 when deciding if an adjournment is appropriate (R. 72.3). The adjudicator may adjourn a proceeding on his or her own initiative or at the request of a party (R. 72.4) and may require the parties, who have consented to the adjournment, to attend in person to argue the adjournment (R. 72.5).

Rule 73 — Summons to Witnesses: An adjudicator has the same power to summons as a Superior Court judge by using a Summons to Witness (Form N) to require a person's attendance or participation in a hearing to give evidence and to require the person to produce documents as evidence (R. 73.1). If such person does not comply with the adjudicator's summons, a Superior Court judge may issue an arrest warrant or treat the non-compliance as a contempt of court and order punishment accordingly (R. 73.2). A summons must be prepared in Form N (R. 73.4), and the party requesting it must follow the requirements set out in R. 73.4. A witness can be excused from the obligation to attend or participate in a hearing by the adjudicator if the witness has not been provided notice under Rules 33, 41, and 73.3.

Rule 74 — Transcripts: Although the DRG does not supply reporting services for a hearing, a hearing can be recorded by a court reporter who has taken a proper oath and whose attendance and service are arranged and paid by the parties who want the record of the hearing (R. 74.1). When a party hires a reporting service to record the proceedings, the party must notify the other parties and the adjudicator, in addition to arranging and paying for the service (R. 74.2). If a party orders all or part of a transcript, the party is responsible to pay for the transcript. The party is also required to inform the other parties and the adjudicator and provide them a copy of the transcript (R. 74.3).

Rule 75 — Award of Expenses: Under R. 75.1, an adjudicator may award expenses for items and amounts as detailed in R. 78 and the schedule in Section F — Expense Regulation of the DRPC — if the adjudicator is satisfied that the award is justified, having considered the five criteria listed in Section F of the DRPC and repeated in R. 75.2.

Rule 76 — Offer to Settle: An adjudicator will consider an Offer to Settle relating to an award of expenses only if it is a written offer that complies with the conditions set out in R. 76.1. A Response to an Offer to Settle will be considered if it was in writing, specifying the related offer and was served on the other parties before the hearing concluded (R. 76.2). Either the offer or the response can be withdrawn at any time before it is accepted by serving written notice on the party who was the recipient of the document (R. 76.3). Under R. 76.4, the offer or the response expires on the earlier of the expiry date stated within the document or at the conclusion of the hearing. Written acceptance of the offer or the response must be served on the party who initiated it, before its expiry or withdrawal (R. 76.5).

Rule 77 — Communication of an Offer to Settle or Response to an Offer to Settle: The parties can jointly inform the adjudicator at the conclusion of the hearing whether any party seeks a consideration by the adjudicator on an Offer to Settle or a Response to an Offer to Settle in connection with an award of expenses (R. 77.1 and R. 77.2, respectively). If a request to consider is made, the adjudicator will determine the issues in dispute, except expenses, and issue an order accordingly (R. 77.3). Under R. 77.4, the DRG will deliver to the parties a copy of the expenses-excluded order and its written reasons, if any. Within 10 days of the delivery of such order, either party may file the relevant offer or response for consideration by the adjudicator in respect of expenses (R. 77.5). Alternatively, either party can request an appointment before an adjudicator for an award of expenses or an assessment of expenses in accordance with Rule 79 (R. 77.6).

Rule 78 — Expenses of Representatives (also look at Expense Regulation): The hourly rates used to calculate the maximum amount that may be awarded to an insured person or an insurer for legal fees are stated under R. 78.1. The rule also allows the adjudicator to award a higher hourly rate, up to $150, if he or she considers it just. The statute that governs the maximum amount that can be awarded for agents' fees is provided in R. 78.2.

Rule 79 — Assessment of Expenses: Where the parties cannot agree on the entitlement to or amount of the expenses, either party can ask the adjudicator to determine the expenses. Request must be made within 30 days of the adjudicator's issuing of his or her order that determines all issues except expenses (R. 79.1). In the case where the adjudicator's order includes awarding expenses, the request must be made in accordance with the five conditions set out in R. 79.2.

Rule 80 — Constitutional Question and/or Charter Issue: R. 80.1 states that the *Courts of Justice Act* may require a party who intends to raise a constitutional question (as defined by R. 80.4) to serve notice of the constitutional question on the other parties and on the Attorney General of Canada and the Attorney General of Ontario at least **15 days** before the day the adjudicator would hear the question. The notice must include supporting reasons and evidence that the party uses to initiate the proceeding (R. 80.2). The Attorneys General of Canada and Ontario may intervene in the proceeding (R. 80.3).

Rule 81 — Waiver of Procedural Requirements: Rule 81.1, subject to the requirements of the *Insurance Act* and the *SPPA*, allows the adjudicator to waive rules and/or procedural requirements on such terms as he or she considers just. To set aside procedural requirements of the *Insurance Act* and the *SPPA*, the parties and the adjudicator must agree (R. 81.2).

Rule 82 — Testimony and Civil Proceedings: Under R. 82.1, an adjudicator is not compellable to give testimony "respecting information obtained in the discharge of his or her duties".

Section B — Guidelines

1. **Guideline for Identifying Self-employed Individuals**

   Under the SABS, self-employment income is treated differently than employment income; therefore, this guideline sets out indicators of self-employment in traditional self-employment situations and in contract of service situations.

2. **Guideline for Statutory Accident Benefits Applications, the Claims Process, and the Mediation Process (Bill 59)**

   Applicable to accidents occurring on or after November 1, 1996, this guideline is intended to help insurers and claimants understand their rights and responsibilities when dealing with statutory accident benefit claims. A detailed list of insurer's and claimant's responsibilities in the claim and mediation process is included. Both insurers and insured persons (referred to as "claimants" in this guideline) are obligated to act fairly with each other when making an application for benefits and when processing claims.

3. **Guideline for Statutory Accident Benefits Applications, the Claims Process and the Mediation Process**

   This guideline is similar to #2 except there is no date limitation as to when it applies.

4. **Guideline on Designated Assessment Centre Selection Process**

   "Regulation 313/03, which comes into effect on October 1, 2003, changes the process under section 53 of the [SABS] for selecting a Designated Assessment Centre (DAC) to conduct a designated assessment. Effective October 1, 2003, the SABS no longer requires a claimant to be assessed at the DAC closest to his or her residence."

   This guideline details the process by which the Superintendent will select a DAC under section 53 of the SABS.

5. **Guideline for Identifying Students Who Qualify for the Student Non-Earner Benefit (Bill 59)**

   Applicable to accidents occurring on or after November 1, 1996, this guideline describes when an insured person would be qualified for the non-earner benefit as a student or as someone who has recently completed his or her education at the time of the accident.

6. **Guideline for Identifying Individuals Who Qualify for Education Disability Benefits**

   This guideline describes when an insured person would be qualified for education disability benefits.

7. **Guideline on the Management of Claims Involving Whiplash-Associated Disorders**
Applicable to all accidents occurring on or after January 1, 1994, including accidents on or after November 1, 1996, these guidelines are intended to help insurers, claimants, and providers understand what a reasonable medical and rehabilitation expense is for a person who sustained a whiplash injury in an auto accident. The SABS requires that insurers pay for all reasonable and necessary medical and rehabilitation expenses incurred by or on behalf of a claimant who suffers an impairment as a result of an auto accident. This guideline also describes three WAD case management tools developed by the Québec Task Force on WAD: (1) Québec Classification of Whiplash-Associated Disorders, (2) WAD Case Management Guide, and (3) Treatment Guide for Wad.

8. **Optional Indexation Benefit Guidelines**
The *Optional Indexation Benefit Guidelines* set out the procedures and formulas for indexation as referred to in section 29 of the *Statutory Accident Benefits Schedule — Accidents on or After November 1, 1996.* "These guidelines apply to named insured persons who have purchased the optional indexation benefit, their spouse, dependants and persons specified as drivers under the policy."

9. **Transportation Expense Guidelines**
This was replaced by #10, below, as of March 31, 2001.

10. **Transportation Expense Guidelines (Effective March 31, 2001)**
The *Transportation Expense Guidelines* provide a framework for insurers and insured persons to determine the circumstances under which an insurer must pay an insured person the transportation expenses he or she incurred to and from treatment sessions. The guidelines also list the authorized transportation expenses and applicable rates for the purpose of subsections 14(5), 15(11), and 24(3) of the *Statutory Accident Benefits Schedule — Accidents on or After November 1, 1996.*

11. **Guideline Respecting Conflict of Interest in the Provision of Medical and Rehabilitation Services**
Here, the disclosure provision identifies situations where referrals for profit are likely to exist and where a party could influence the course of treatment for their own monetary advantage. Although interests of the insured person might not always be paramount where a conflict of interests exists, the party having the conflict must disclose it. Some typical situations are included as guidance in this guideline.

Section C — Practice Notes

- **Practice Note 1: Using Medical Evidence to Support Your Claim for Accident Benefits**
This was being revised at the time of writing.

- **Practice Note 2: Reaching a Settlement within the Dispute Resolution Process**
This was being revised at the time of writing.

- **Practice Note 3: Participation and Representation at Dispute Resolution (Authority to Bind)**
For disputes over accident benefits, representatives of an insurance company or an insured person at a mediation, neutral evaluation, or arbitration must have the authority to discuss and negotiate agreements and settlements. It is, therefore, important that benefits claimants participate in mediation, neutral evaluation, or arbitration to hear and discuss settlement offers and give instructions to their representatives. The necessity of giving authority to rep-

resentatives and what happens when representatives do not have authority are discussed in this practice note.

- **Practice Note 4: Exchange of Documents**
  This note outlines the role and the need for early disclosure of supporting documents in various stages of the Commission's dispute resolution process. Types of documents required and when the documents should be gathered and exchanged vary in mediation, neutral evaluation, and arbitration. There are also cases where documents relating to a period more than one year prior to the accident are relevant and, therefore, required for disclosure. Parties involved in the process can find general guidelines regarding document disclosures in this practice note.

- **Practice Note 5: Mediator Referral to Private Neutral Evaluation — FSCO**
  As stated in this note, neutral evaluation is "a process designed to encourage the settlement of disputes in certain types of cases". It can be obtained privately or at the Commission (as part of the Commission's arbitration process). If parties involved choose private neutral evaluation (under the *Insurance Act*), they must agree on their choice of the neutral evaluator, the fee, and who will pay, and the evaluator must be appointed by the Commission's Director of Arbitrations. This note also discusses the appointment process of the neutral evaluator and how and why mediators make referrals to neutral evaluators.

- **Practice Note 6: Neutral Evaluation at the FSCO**
  After discussing what neutral evaluation is, this practice note reviews what cases are appropriate for neutral evaluation, how to obtain neutral evaluation at FSCO, preparation for the neutral evaluation, the need to attend and what happens in the session, and what happens if the matter does not settle at the neutral evaluation.

- **Practice Note 7: The Arbitration Pre-Hearing Discussion**
  "Parties to an arbitration are usually required to participate in one or more pre-hearing discussions of their case before the actual arbitration hearing. This discussion generally takes place within 6 to 8 weeks after the applicant receives the insurance company's *Response by Insurer*." This note discussed the various reasons to have a pre-hearing discussion, the various hearing formats for the discussion, what to bring to it, and the setting of the hearing date.

- **Practice Note 8: Attendance of a Witness to an Arbitration Hearing by Summons**
  This practice note details the four steps to be followed when a witness is required to attend a hearing:

    Step 1: Notice of intention to call witness to attend the arbitration
    Step 2: Getting the proper forms
    Step 3: Filling out the form
    Step 4: Delivering the form

  Also reviewed in this note is the calculation of the witness fee, the importance of keeping "copies of the summons and of the money order or cheque that goes to the witness for fees and expenses", and the requirement to get an affidavit of service. Finally, what to do if a witness does not show up is explored.

- **Practice Note 9: Adjournments**
  Pre-hearing and hearing dates are agreed upon and set well in advance; and because the Commission has an obligation to conduct arbitrations efficiently and speedily, adjournments are rarely granted once dates have been set. This note discusses specifically when adjournments will be granted and refused, the notice requirements for an adjournment request, the obtaining of a new hearing date, and the need of a written confirmation of the adjournment from FSCO.

- **Practice Note 10: Process for Settling Disputes between Auto Insurance Companies**
  This note is to advise claimants and insurers of the provisions of Regulation 283/95, *Disputes Between Insurers* (the Regulation). The Regulation ensures that claimants will have access to statutory accident benefits even where there is a dispute among insurers as to who has the responsibility to pay accident benefits. The Regulation also requires that disputes between insurers over the responsibility to pay accident benefits be referred to private arbitration under the *Arbitration Act, 1991*; the dispute resolution process at the Commission no longer deals with such disputes between insurers.

- **Practice Note 11: Jurisdictional Issues Arising in Mediation**
  This note advises claimants and insurers of the Commission's policy on jurisdictional issues that frequently arise during the mediation process. Discussion includes what the mediation cannot do; the expiry of certain limitation periods; disputes between insurers; a full and final release situation unless certain circumstances occur; and an application of a non-earner benefit in a specific circumstance.

- **Practice Note 12: What Claimants Need to Know About Designated Assessment Centres (DAC)**
  Discussed here are the five types of DACs, factors used to determine which DAC to use, joint selection of a DAC, and what happens if there is no joint selection and other issues involving DACs.

Section D — Fees and Assessments

1. **Fees**
   The application filing fee (for arbitration, which can be filed only by an insured, for appeal or a variation/revocation proceeding) is set out in 1.1. Other fees are listed in 1.2–1.5.

2. **Insurer Assessment**
   "An assessment is charged to an insurer that is a named party to an arbitration, an appeal or a variation/revocation proceeding." Various fees assessed to insurers in various situations are detailed in 2.1–2.8.

3. **Payment of Fees — By the Insured Person**
   When fees are payable (3.1), how to pay fees (3.2, 3.3), and what fees cannot be waived (3.4), deferred (3.5) or refunded of fees (3.6) are detailed here.

4. **Payment of Fees and Insurer Assessment — By the Insurer**
   These provisions deal with the invoicing of insurers for fees (4.1) to be combined in the regular assessment of the insurers (4.2).

Section E — Settlement Regulation
Excerpt from R.R.O. 1990, Reg. 664, as amended by O. Reg. 275/03
Excerpt from R.R.O. 1990, Reg. 664, as amended by O. Reg. 780/93

Section F — Expense Regulation
Excerpt from Regulation 664, R.R.O. 1990, Made Under the *Insurance Act*, as amended to O. Reg. 275/03 (Criteria for Awarding Expenses)
Schedule from Regulation 664, R.R.O. 1990, as amended.

Section G — Forms

Form A — Application for Mediation: This form is in the Appendix and is used to commence the mediation process. Also included is a guide to filling out Form A, which is included in the Appendix.

Form B — Response to an Application for Mediation

Form C — Application for Arbitration: This form is in the Appendix and is used to commence the arbitration process. Also included is a guide to filling out Form C, which is included in the Appendix.

Form D — Agreement to Neutral Evaluation at the Commission

Form E — Response by Insurer to an Application for Arbitration

Form F — Statement of Service

Form G — Reply by the Applicant for Arbitration

Form H — Joint Statement for Neutral Evaluation at the Commission

Form I — Notice of Appeal: This form is in the Appendix and is used to commence the appeal process. Also included is a guide to filling out Form I, which is included in the Appendix.

Form J — Response to Appeal: This form is in the Appendix and is used to answer the notice of appeal. Also included is a guide to filling out Form J, which is included in the Appendix.

Form K — Application for Intervention

Form L — Application for Variation/Revocation: This form is in the Appendix and is used to commence the variation/revocation process. Also included is a guide to filling out Form L, which is included in the Appendix.

Form M — Response to Application for Variation/Revocation: This form is in the Appendix and is used to answer the variation/revocation process. Also included is a guide to filling out Form M, which is included in the Appendix.

Form N — Summons to Witness

Form O — Affidavit of Service for a Summons to Witness

Form P — Representing Minors and Mentally Incapable Persons

EXPLANATORY LITERATURE OF THE BOARD

Brochures

There are two brochures relevant to making claims under the SABS and dispute resolution procedures available under FSCO:

1. "After an Auto Accident: Understanding the Claims Process"
2. "FSCO's Disputes Resolution Services: A Real Alternative"

These brochures explain the procedures, in lay terms, in those situations as noted in their titles and are both found on the FSCO website, under "Dispute Resolution Resources".

DRS Papers and Publications

Also on the FSCO website, under "Dispute Resolution Resources" in the "Educational Outreach" section are, at the time of writing, six papers that discuss practical procedure issues as well as recent case law and decisions in the area.

Dispute Resolution Services — Arbitration and Appeal Decisions

On the Web page noted in the title above, there is a service that can be accessed with a valid ID and password, which provides decisions and a search function for the decisions of arbitrations and appeals.

RELEVANT CASES AND/OR DECISIONS

You will find cases and decisions reviewed by members of the DRG on the "DRS Papers and Publications" Web page. You can also access arbitration and appeal decisions in the service mentioned in the preceding paragraph.

In addition to the eight appeal/judicial review cases, arbitration decisions, and appeal orders discussed in Chapter 2 — *Statutory Powers Procedure Act* — set out following are three further recent matters that have gone through various phases of the DRG. These will give the reader a sense of how matters are dealt with in the system.

Driver v. Traders General Insurance Company

The *Driver v. Traders General Insurance Company* (2003), Appeal P03-00004 (the *Driver* decision), conducted under the auspices of the FSCO is an appeal order of the appeal and the cross-appeal by the parties from the arbitrator's decision regarding certain expenses, such as "Vistasp therapy" and Tai Chi programs, and a special award claimed by the applicant. Prior to dealing with the substance of the appeal, the Director's Delegate dealt with a preliminary issue as follows:

> Traders' counsel raised a procedural issue at the outset of the appeal hearing. He complained that while Ms. Driver's *Notice of Appeal* mentioned only s. 14 of the *SABS-1996* (medical benefits), her written submissions were framed entirely in terms of s. 15 (rehabilitation benefits). He submitted that Ms. Driver should not be permitted to proceed on the s. 15 argument, at least not without an adjournment in order to move to amend the *Notice of Appeal*. He submitted that the motion is governed by Rule 52.2 of the *Dispute Resolution Practice Code* ("the *Code*"), which gives me discretion to extend the time for filing a *Notice of Appeal* if I am satisfied there are "reasonable grounds for granting the extension." He argued that the explanations offered by Ms. Driver's counsel (an oversight, a reassessment of her position) did not provide reasonable grounds. He stated he was not prepared to argue the appeal with respect to s. 15 and was prejudiced by Ms. Driver's non-compliance with the rules.
>
> I dismissed the objection. I agree with the approach taken by Director's Delegate McMahon in *Welsh and Economical Mutual Insurance Company* (Appeal P02-00024, April 23, 2003), another decision dealing with a motion to amend pleadings. Delegate McMahon concluded:
>
>> In my view, because Mr. Welsh met the initial requirement of filing his *Notice of Appeal* within 30 days, he does not have to rely on Rule 52.2. This case involves an amendment to an existing appeal, not the filing of a new appeal. However, Rule 52 is a useful starting point because, if the Director has a broad discretion to grant an extension of the time to file an initial *Notice of Appeal*, it follows that he has at least as broad a discretion to allow a party to amend an existing appeal, even if it involves a fresh challenge. The real question is — what factors should be considered in exercising this discretion?

The arbitrator then looked at the *Rules of Civil Procedure* to understand the factors to be used:

> The *Rules of Civil Procedure* may also provide procedural guidance where the *Code* is silent, although the adjudicative context is somewhat different in that FSCO arbitrations

and appeals are meant to be faster, cheaper and less formal than civil proceedings. However, the *Rules of Civil Procedure* represent a great deal of accumulated wisdom about fair and efficient process, and provide at least a good starting point for discussion when new procedural issues arise.

Delegate McMahon found that prejudice is the major factor considered under the civil *Rules* for amending pleadings; less important factors include the length of the delay, the reason for the delay, and the substance of the proposed amendment." On this basis, the director's delegate dismissed the preliminary issue.

As to the claim for the expenses of the Vistasp therapy, the finding was as follows: "The Arbitrator's finding that Vistasp therapy was not a service 'of a medical nature' for which s. 14 benefits were available, did not imply it was a rehabilitative measure under s. 15. Reimbursement for any treatment, including palliative treatment, must be found in s. 14 (medical benefits). I do not accept that the legislature intended claimants to have recourse under s. 15(5)(l) for any treatment that cannot be claimed as a medical benefit because it fails to satisfy the requirements of s. 14."

In respect of the special award, the Director's Delegate stated the following:

> For these reasons, I find it was not reasonable for Traders to rely on the Med Rehab DAC report to support its position that no further treatment was reasonable or necessary. The next step would have been to address the flaws in the report by requesting clarification, or, if necessary, a second opinion. (pp. 35–36).
>
> The Arbitrator's rejection of the DAC assessors' "objective, 'one-size-fits-all' standard of treatment" is consistent with a long line of arbitral authority requiring insurers to consider the individual treatment needs of insured persons, including treatment for chronic pain. [See note 38 below.] However, the Arbitrator failed to consider the effect of s. 38(14)(b), and her reasons indicate she treated the DAC like an insurer examination report, to which no pay-pending-dispute obligations apply. This was an error of law. Further, nothing in her reasons suggests that the deficiencies of the DAC report were sufficiently fundamental to pre-empt Traders' right to rely on the report pending resolution of the dispute. The Arbitrator's rejection of the report was within her adjudicative authority. Her failure to give effect to s. 38(14)(b) was not. For that reason, the special award cannot stand. Given the amounts at issue, it would not be cost-effective to refer the issue back to the Arbitrator. The special award is revoked.

Toor v. State Farm Mutual Assurance Insurance Company

The *Toor v. State Farm Mutual Assurance Insurance Company* (2009), FSCO A07-002320 (the *Toor* decision) is an arbitration decision under the FSCO's auspices. It involved whether the applicant was entitled to weekly caregiver and housekeeping benefits where the insurer terminated them. The arbitrator based his decision on the evidence and the interpretation of sections 13 and 22 of the SABS. The arbitrator stated the evidence did not support the applicant's position that she was the primary caregiver of her child under section 13 or that she did the housekeeping as required by section 22 prior to the accident and, therefore, neither benefits were payable.

Troubitsine v. TTC Insurance Company Limited

The *Troubitsine v. TTC Insurance Company Limited* (2009), FSCO A08-000681 (the *Troubitsine* decision) is the most recent matter set out here and it involved an arbitrator's decisions on various motions. The motions made by the insurer arose from the non-attendance of the applicant at numerous insurer physical examinations or scheduled examinations under oath without reasonable explanations. After hearing and then stating the evidence, the arbitrator looked at sections 33 and 42 of the SABS and made the following statement:

For all of the reasons above, I find that Mr. Troubitsine did not attend the examinations scheduled for January 4, 2007, January 22, 2007 and June 15, 2007 as required of him by TTC pursuant to section 33(1.1) of the *Schedule*. I find that, other than for the period of his incarceration from March to approximately October 2007, he has provided no reasonable explanation for his non-attendance.

He then said the following:

Accordingly, TTC is entitled to rely upon section 33(2) and is not liable to pay a benefit from January 22, 2007 to June 15, 2007 and then ongoing from November 1, 2007 to such time as Mr. Troubitsine attends for an examination under oath. The fact that TTC has not scheduled any examinations since that date is not an issue in this case. After each of the examinations that Mr. Troubitsine did not attend, TTC made it clear that if he should change his mind and wish to discuss scheduling an examination under oath, that he should contact TTC. At this point the obligation was on Mr. Troubitsine to advise TTC of his availability and intention to attend an examination.

As to the motion seeking an order to compel the applicant to attend an examination under oath, the arbitrator stated the following:

I agree that where a legislative provision provides for an express remedy, a statutory decision maker has limited jurisdiction to fashion other remedies. ... However, where the available remedy is not adequate in addressing issues of significant unfairness, then an arbitrator has a duty to prevent an abuse of the process. The *Statutory Powers Procedure Act* ("*SPPA*") provides arbitrators with the authority to control the hearing process.

After looking at three previous matters of somewhat similar situations, the arbitrator found the following:

Although arbitrators have stepped outside of the prescribed remedies in the case of non-compliance with section 42 assessments and ordered a stay of the arbitration proceedings, they have not gone so far as to compel attendance at a medical assessment. An examination under oath, however, serves a very different role in the arbitration process than a medical assessment. Most importantly, an examination under oath does not raise the obvious invasion of privacy concerns that compelling someone to undergo a medical exam would raise. Attending an examination under oath is part of the more general disclosure obligations placed on a claimant making a claim for benefits. For cases in which there are potential allegations of fraud, an examination under oath is an important investigative tool. It can assist in assessing credibility as well as identifying potential witnesses and relevant documents.

In conclusion, the arbitrator decided the following:

Although I agree with TTC that the available remedy under section 33(2) of the *Schedule* is not adequate to address the fairness issues and potential prejudice in this case, I do not agree that an order compelling Mr. Troubitsine to attend at an examination under oath is the most appropriate remedy. I find that ordering a stay of the proceedings until the Applicant attends for an examination under oath is a more appropriate remedy in this case.

REVIEW QUESTIONS

1. What is the enabling legislation for the DRG?
2. Where would you find the practices and procedures of the DRG?

3. What are the purposes of the DRG, and what mechanisms are used to achieve such purposes?
4. How does the *SPPA* apply to the services of the DRG?
5. What rule(s) gives discretion and flexibility to the persons with authority under the DRG in applying the DRPC?
6. What forms are relevant to arbitration under the auspices of the DRG?
7. What is a neutral evaluation, what is the authority for it, and what forms are relevant to it?
8. How does an arbitration order get appealed, to whom, and what forms are used in such situation?
9. What are Practice Notes, and how are they used?
10. How are guidelines relevant to the DRG process?
11. List the forms set out in the DRPC, and briefly discuss how each are used.

EXERCISE

Based upon the facts of the *Driver* decision briefed in the chapter, summarize the likely steps this matter took on its way to the appeal set out in the decision, listing the forms likely to have been used and each procedural step along the way.

Appendix 8.1
Overview of an FSCO Proceeding Related to the DRG

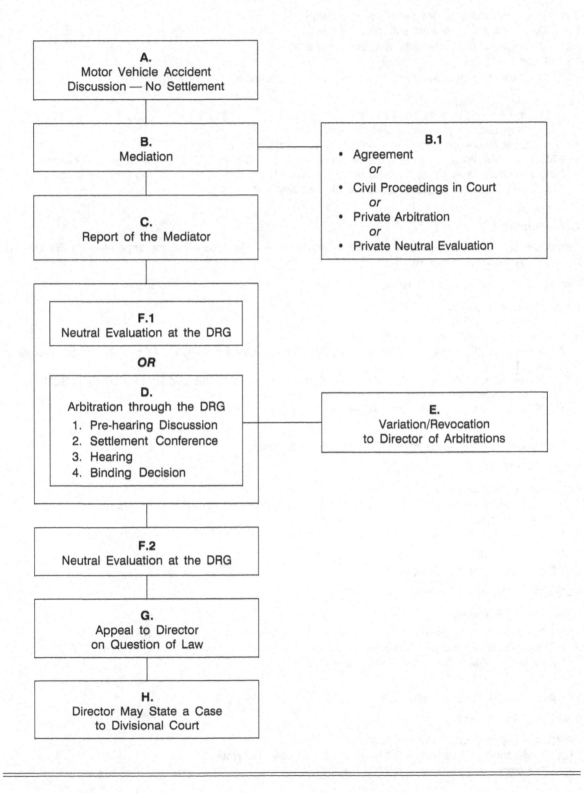

A.
Motor Vehicle Accident
Discussion — No Settlement

B.
Mediation

B.1
- Agreement
  or
- Civil Proceedings in Court
  or
- Private Arbitration
  or
- Private Neutral Evaluation

C.
Report of the Mediator

F.1
Neutral Evaluation at the DRG

OR

D.
Arbitration through the DRG
1. Pre-hearing Discussion
2. Settlement Conference
3. Hearing
4. Binding Decision

E.
Variation/Revocation
to Director of Arbitrations

F.2
Neutral Evaluation at the DRG

G.
Appeal to Director
on Question of Law

H.
Director May State a Case
to Divisional Court

SUMMARY

A. Discussions — No Settlement

Negotiations based on the SABS fail — Disagreement on the entitlement to the SABS or the amount

The DRG procedure is not used for the following:
1. Damages for pain and suffering
2. Damage to motor vehicle or other property
3. Fault
4. Disputes between insurers — which insurer responsible

Look at the following:
- *Insurance Act*, ss. 268, 268.3, 273, 279, 257.6
- *SABS Regulation* — O. Reg. 403/96, as amended
- *Automobile Insurance Regulation* — O. Reg. 664, as amended
- FSCO website, Web page, "Dispute Resolution Practice Code ('DRPC')" — Section B — Guidelines
- FSCO website, Web page, "After an Auto Accident: Understanding the Claims Process" and brochure
- FSCO website, Web page, "Dispute Resolution Services"

B. Mediation

Insurance Act, s. 280(1) — Either insured or insurer may refer to a mediator appointed by the Director by Form A and response by Form B

Timelines — 2 years and 90 days

Look at the following:
- *Insurance Act*, s. 280
- Forms A and B on "Forms" Web Page
- FSCO website, Web page, "Dispute Resolution Practice Code ('DRPC')" — Rs. 1–23; Practice Notes 3, 4 and 11
- FSCO website, Web page, "Dispute Resolution Resources" and the following brochure, "FSCO's Disputes Resolution Services: A Real Alternative"
- FSCO website, Web page, "Dispute Resolution Services"

B.1 Alternatives outside of DRG if Mediation Fails

Insurance Act, s. 281

Look at the following:
- FSCO website, Web page, "Dispute Resolution Resources" and the following brochure, "FSCO's Disputes Resolution Services: A Real Alternative"
- FSCO website, Web page, "Dispute Resolution Practice Code ('DRPC')" — Practice Note 5

C. Report of the Mediator

Insurance Act, ss. 280(6–8)

Look at the Following:
- FSCO website, Web page, "Dispute Resolution Practice Code ('DRPC')" — Rs. 22–23
- FSCO website, Web page, "Dispute Resolution Resources" and the following brochure, "FSCO's Disputes Resolution Services: A Real Alternative"

D. Arbitration through the DRG

Insurance Act, s. 282

DRPC — Parts 3 and 6; Forms C, E, and G
1. Pre-hearing discussion — DRPC, Rs. 33–34; Practice Note 7
2. Settlement Conference — DRPC, Rs. 35–36

3. Hearing — DRPC, Rs. 37–43; Practice Notes 4, 8, and 9
4. Binding Decision

Look at the following:

- FSCO website, Web page, "Dispute Resolution Resources" and the following brochure, "FSCO's Disputes Resolution Services: A Real Alternative"

E. Variation/Revocation to Director of Arbitrations

Insurance Act, s. 284

DRPC — Part 5; Forms L and M

Look at the following:

- FSCO website, Web page, "Dispute Resolution Resources" and the following brochure, "FSCO's Disputes Resolution Services: A Real Alternative"

F.1 & F.2 Neutral Evaluation at DRG

Insurance Act, s. 280.1

DRPC — Rs. 44–49; Practice Note 6; Forms D and H

Look at the following:

- FSCO website, Web page, "Dispute Resolution Resources" and the following brochure, "FSCO's Disputes Resolution Services: A Real Alternative"

G. Appeal to the Director

Insurance Act, s. 283

DRPC — Part 4; Forms I and J

Look at the following:

- FSCO website, Web page, "Dispute Resolution Resources" and the following brochure, "FSCO's Disputes Resolution Services: A Real Alternative"

H. The Director May State a Case

Insurance Act, s. 285

Look at the following:

- FSCO website, Web page, "Dispute Resolution Resources" and the following brochure, "FSCO's Disputes Resolution Services: A Real Alternative"

Appendix 8.2
FSCO's Dispute Resolution Services: Real Alternatives[1]

---

[1] Source: FSCO Website <www.fsco.gov.on.ca>

If you are injured in an automobile accident, you may be entitled to statutory accident benefits (also known as no-fault benefits), whether or not the accident was your fault.

Generally, accident benefits are paid by your own insurance company. Even if you do not have an automobile insurance policy, you can apply for benefits from the company that insures the automobile in which you were an occupant, or which hit you.

If you and the insurance company disagree about your entitlement to accident benefits, or the amount, the Financial Services Commission of Ontario's (FSCO) Dispute Resolution Services offers a dispute resolution process that is fair and cost-effective – a real alternative to court. FSCO's Dispute Resolution Services are available in English and French, and include:

- mediation,
- neutral evaluation,
- arbitration,
- appeal, and
- variation/revocation.

A Real Alternative

If you have been injured in an automobile accident, there are several things you should know.

1. An automobile insurance policy provides several different types of accident benefits. The list below provides a general summary of the benefits that are available:

- **Income replacement benefits** help replace lost income if you become disabled and can no longer work.
- **Caregiver benefits** pay certain childcare or caregiver expenses if you are a caregiver, and are unable to care for a child or other person in need of care.
- **Non-earner benefits** are paid if you are not working and are unable to engage in all of your pre-accident activities.
- **Medical and rehabilitation benefits** pay for the medical and rehabilitation expenses that are not covered by OHIP or your disability insurance plan.
- **Attendant care benefits** pay for an aide or attendant to look after you, if you have been seriously injured.
- **Funeral expenses and death benefits** are paid if you die as a result of the accident.

Depending on your circumstances, you may also be entitled to other benefits. Examples include: benefits to pay for lost education expenses, housekeeping assistance, visitors' expenses, repair or replacement of eyeglasses or clothing damaged in the accident, or case management services.

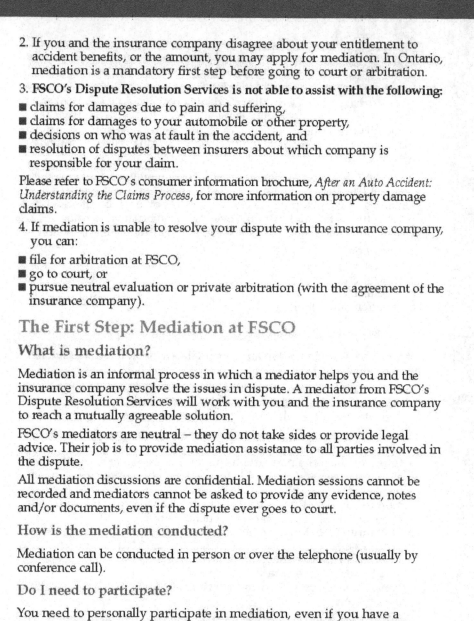

2. If you and the insurance company disagree about your entitlement to accident benefits, or the amount, you may apply for mediation. In Ontario, mediation is a mandatory first step before going to court or arbitration.

3. **FSCO's Dispute Resolution Services is not able to assist with the following:**
- claims for damages due to pain and suffering,
- claims for damages to your automobile or other property,
- decisions on who was at fault in the accident, and
- resolution of disputes between insurers about which company is responsible for your claim.

Please refer to FSCO's consumer information brochure, *After an Auto Accident: Understanding the Claims Process,* for more information on property damage claims.

4. If mediation is unable to resolve your dispute with the insurance company, you can:
- file for arbitration at FSCO,
- go to court, or
- pursue neutral evaluation or private arbitration (with the agreement of the insurance company).

The First Step: Mediation at FSCO

What is mediation?

Mediation is an informal process in which a mediator helps you and the insurance company resolve the issues in dispute. A mediator from FSCO's Dispute Resolution Services will work with you and the insurance company to reach a mutually agreeable solution.

FSCO's mediators are neutral – they do not take sides or provide legal advice. Their job is to provide mediation assistance to all parties involved in the dispute.

All mediation discussions are confidential. Mediation sessions cannot be recorded and mediators cannot be asked to provide any evidence, notes and/or documents, even if the dispute ever goes to court.

How is the mediation conducted?

Mediation can be conducted in person or over the telephone (usually by conference call).

Do I need to participate?

You need to personally participate in mediation, even if you have a representative. If you cannot participate for some extraordinary reason, your representative must have full authority to enter into a settlement agreement on your behalf. Your mediation may be delayed if your representative does not have this authority.

What is the time limit for applying for mediation?

You must apply for mediation within TWO YEARS after the insurance company refuses to pay the accident benefits claimed. This time limit is important. If you do not apply on time, you may not qualify for mediation.

How much does mediation cost?

As an insured person, there is no cost to you for mediation. However, you must pay for any personal expenses, such as lawyer's fees, travel costs, accounting services, and any additional medical reports you might need.

How long will the mediation process take?

FSCO will work with you to ensure that the application for mediation is complete. Once the application is finalized and assigned to a mediator, the mediation will be completed within 60 days. In special cases, this limit can be extended on written consent of all the parties.

At the end of the mediation process, the mediator will issue a written report called a Report of Mediator. This report will identify the issues that have been settled, the issues that remain unresolved, and the next steps to take.

What are My Options After Mediation?

If the Report of Mediator states there are issues remaining in dispute, you can proceed with one of the following options:

- You can apply for arbitration by a FSCO arbitrator.
- You can start a civil proceeding (law suit) in court.
- If you and the insurance company agree, you can pursue neutral evaluation, or have the dispute decided by a private arbitrator not employed by FSCO.

Arbitration at FSCO

If your dispute is not settled through FSCO's mediation services, you can apply for arbitration by a FSCO arbitrator.

You must apply for arbitration within TWO YEARS after the insurance company refuses to pay the accident benefits claimed, or within 90 days after the mediator issues the Report of Mediator, whichever is later.

Arbitration pre-hearing conferences

FSCO's Dispute Resolution Services will schedule a pre-hearing conference, either in person at FSCO, or by telephone conference. The pre-hearing arbitrator will schedule a hearing date and make sure all parties are ready for the hearing. The arbitrator will also try to help you and the insurance company settle the dispute.

Arbitration hearings

Arbitration hearings take place at FSCO's offices in Toronto or at other locations across Ontario. They are similar to hearings in court, but are quicker, less expensive and less formal. During the arbitration hearing, the arbitrator will hear evidence from you and the insurance company. The arbitrator will then provide a written decision, determining the issues in dispute.

The arbitrator's decision is binding on all parties. It has the same authority as an order of a judge in the Ontario Superior Court of Justice, and can be enforced by the court.

How much does arbitration cost?

There is a $100 filing fee for arbitration. You are also likely to incur some costs in preparing and presenting your case at arbitration. Examples of these costs include: witness fees, travel costs, legal expenses, as well as fees for reports prepared by doctors or other experts.

After deciding your case, the arbitrator has the power to:

- order you to pay all or part of the insurance company's arbitration expenses,
- order the insurance company to pay all or part of your arbitration expenses, or
- order each party to pay its own expenses.

The arbitrator's decision about expenses is based on:

- each party's degree of success in the outcome of the arbitration,
- any written offers to settle,
- whether any important legal issues were raised,
- the conduct of the parties and their representatives,
- whether any aspect of the proceeding was improper, or considered unnecessary, and
- whether the applicant refused or failed to attend an independent examination.

Refer to Ontario Regulation 664 (Criteria for Awarding Expenses), for rules on awarding expenses. This information is available on FSCO's website at www.fsco.gov.on.ca on the *Dispute Resolution Services* web page.

How long does arbitration take?

The length of the arbitration process will vary, depending on the nature and complexity of the case. The average length of an oral hearing at FSCO is between two and three days. Generally, arbitration decisions are issued within 85 days after the conclusion of the hearing.

What are My Options After Arbitration?

After the arbitration process is complete, there are two possible additional processes:

1. Appeal
2. Variation/revocation

Appeal

You or the insurance company can appeal an arbitrator's order within 30 days of the arbitration decision, but only on a question of law.

An appeal is decided by FSCO's Director of Arbitrations or a Director's Delegate, and is usually heard through written submissions and a short oral hearing. As a general rule, no new evidence can be presented in the appeal. Once the appeal process is completed, the Director of Arbitrations or Director's Delegate will issue a written decision with reasons. The appeal decision is final and cannot be appealed.

The only way you may be able to challenge an appeal decision is through a judicial review in the courts.

Variation/Revocation

You or the insurance company can apply to the Director of Arbitrations for variation/revocation of the arbitration or appeal order.

You can apply for variation/revocation if:

- there is a material change in your circumstances,
- new evidence becomes available after the arbitration or appeal has occurred, or
- there is an error in the arbitration or appeal order (for example, the order does not correspond to the reasons for the decision).

How Do I Apply for Dispute Resolution Services?

- To apply for **mediation**, you must send FSCO two completed copies (one original and one copy) of the *Application for Mediation - Form A*. There is no cost to you for mediation services.

- To apply for **arbitration**, you must send FSCO two completed copies (one original and one copy) of each of the following forms:

  1. *Application for Arbitration - Form C*
  2. *The Report of Mediator* you received.

  You will also need to send FSCO a cheque or money order for $100, made payable to the Minister of Finance.

- To start an **appeal**, you must send FSCO and the insurance company a completed *Notice of Appeal - Form I* within 30 days of the date of the arbitration decision. You also need to complete and send FSCO a *Statement of Service – Form F*, along with a cheque or money order for $250, made payable to the Minister of Finance.

- To apply for **variation/revocation**, you must send FSCO and the insurance company a completed *Application for Variation/Revocation - Form L*. You also need to send FSCO a *Statement of Service – Form F*, along with a cheque or money order for $250, made payable to the Minister of Finance.

Completed forms should be sent to the following address:

Financial Services Commission of Ontario
Dispute Resolution Services
5160 Yonge Street, 14th Floor
P.O. Box 85
Toronto, ON M2N 6L9

Do I Need a Lawyer?

You can choose to represent yourself. However, as disputes can become complicated and most insurance companies have lawyers representing them at arbitration and appeal, you should consider consulting a lawyer or licensed paralegal.

If you need help finding a representative, the Law Society of Upper Canada offers a referral service. For more information, visit their website at www.lsuc.on.ca, or call 1-900-565-4577. (There is a small fee for this referral service).

For More Information

Visit FSCO's website at www.fsco.gov.on.ca to:

- learn more about FSCO's Dispute Resolution Services,
- access a complete copy of the Dispute Resolution Practice Code,
- download dispute resolution forms, and
- access valuable consumer information on automobile insurance.

For general Dispute Resolution Services inquiries:

- Call (416) 250-6714 if you live in the Greater Toronto Area, or
- Call toll free: 1-800-517-2332.

To learn more about mediation, arbitration and appeals:

Mediation Hotline

- Call (416) 590-7210 if you live in the Greater Toronto Area, or
- Call toll free: 1-800-517-2332 (dial extension 7210).

Arbitration Hotline

- Call (416) 590-7202 if you live in the Greater Toronto Area, or
- Call toll free: 1-800-517-2332 (dial extension 7202).

Appeal Hotline

- Call (416) 590-7222 if you live in the Greater Toronto Area, or
- Call toll free: 1-800-517-2332 (dial extension 7222).

About FSCO

FSCO is an arm's-length agency of Ontario's Ministry of Finance. In addition to insurance, FSCO regulates pension plans, credit unions, caisses populaires, mortgage brokers, loan and trust companies, and co-operatives.

FSCO works with consumers, industry stakeholders and investors to enhance public confidence in, and access to, a fair and efficient financial services industry in Ontario.

For more information on any of these sectors, visit our website at www.fsco.gov.on.ca, or call our Contact Centre at: (416) 250-7250, Toll-free: 1-800-668-0128, TTY toll-free: 1-800-387-0584.

Remember to visit FSCO's website at www.fsco.gov.on.ca for more information on:

- insurance,
- how to file a complaint against your insurance company,
- FSCO's dispute resolution services,
- pensions,
- applying for special access to money in locked-in retirement savings accounts, and
- important consumer tips.

Financial Services Commission of Ontario
5160 Yonge Street, Box 85
Toronto, Ontario
M2N 6L9

Telephone: (416) 250-7250
Toll-free: 1-800-668-0128
TTY (416) 590-7108, 1-800-387-0584

FSCO website: www.fsco.gov.on.ca

Ce feuillet de renseignement est également disponible en français

Financial Services
Commission
of Ontario

ISBN 978-1-4249-6250-1
©Queen's Printer for Ontario, 2008.

Appendix 8.3
Application for Mediation (Form A: Guide and Form)[2]

Financial Services Commission of Ontario
5160 Yonge Street
Box 85
Toronto ON M2N 6L9

Dispute Resolution Services

Guide For Completing Dispute Resolution Services (DRS) Forms

Application for Mediation - Form A

What is mediation at the Financial Services Commission of Ontario (FSCO)?

- Mediation is an informal and confidential process in which a neutral third party (the mediator) helps resolve accident benefit disputes between insurance companies and claimants.

What accident benefits can be mediated at FSCO?

You can claim accident benefits (also known as statutory accident benefits or no-fault benefits) from the insurance company if you have been injured in an automobile accident. If you qualify, you may receive several kinds of accident benefits. Available accident benefits include:

- Income replacement benefits help replace lost income if an employed or self-employed claimant is disabled.
- Caregiver benefits pay certain childcare or other caregiver expenses if a stay-at-home parent or other caregiver is unable to care for a child or other person in need of care.
- Non-earner benefits are paid if a claimant who is not employed or self-employed is unable to carry on his or her normal pre-accident activities.
- Medical and rehabilitation benefits pay for treatment and rehabilitation assistance that is not covered by OHIP or another disability insurance plan.
- Attendant care benefits to pay for someone to look after a seriously injured claimant.
- Funeral expenses and death benefits are paid if an insured person dies as a result of the accident.
- Depending on the circumstances, the claimant may also be entitled to other benefits - for example, benefits to pay for housekeeping assistance, visitors' expenses, repair or replacement of eyeglasses or clothing damaged in the accident, or case manager services.

When to use the Application for Mediation - Form A?

- After a motor vehicle accident, when a dispute arises about whether you qualify for accident benefits and/or how much these benefits should be.

---

[2] Source: FSCO Website <www.fsco.gov.on.ca>

Before filing an Application for Mediation

- The parties should contact each other to identify the issues in dispute, clarify the facts, exchange documents relevant to the dispute and discuss settlement.

How to complete the Application - Answer all questions relevant to your dispute.

Section 1   Complete all parts in this section as follows:

- **General Information**
- **Claimant** - is the person making the claim for statutory accident benefits under an automobile insurance policy. The claimant is not necessarily the policyholder.
- **Claimant's Representative** - complete only if applicable
- **Insurance Company** - include full name of the insurance company, insurance company contact, name of the policy holder, policy number and claim number.
- **Insurance Company Representative** - for insurer applications only.

Section 2   Provide a **full** description of the accident benefits that are in dispute.

Section 3   Complete the **entire** section.

- **Document List** - list key documents (such as medical reports, tax returns) in your possession to which you will refer in the mediation.

    - also list key documents not in your possession, which you intend to get from other sources for use in the mediation.

    - include any documents requested from the other party which have not yet been provided.

- **Signature and Certification** - ensure that you read the declaration before signing.

    The claimant (unless a minor or mentally incapable) and/or their representative must provide an original signature and current date at the bottom of Section 3.

Language Preference

- Mediation services are provided in either English or French.
- Claimants who require interpretation services in languages other than English or French must arrange and pay the cost of any interpretation services that are required.

<u>**Once the Application for Mediation is completed, what happens next?**</u>

- Provide **the original and one copy** of the completed application to Mediation Services at the address noted below. Keep an additional copy of the completed application for yourself. **Incomplete applications may be rejected.**

- Include a copy of any relevant documentation (for example - insurance company's written explanation of why they denied the claimed benefit, medical reports, etc.).

- Mediation Services will review your application for completeness and timeliness and will contact you if additional information or clarification is required.

- Once your application has been accepted, a mediator will be appointed, your application will be forwarded to the other party and a mediation meeting will be scheduled.

- The claimant and insurance company representative are obliged to participate personally in the mediation process, even if they have a representative.

- The mediator issues a Report of Mediator describing what the parties agreed on and the issues that remain in dispute, which completes the mediation process.

<u>**What does mediation cost?**</u>

- There is no cost to an insured person for mediation.

- The claimant and insurance company must pay for their own expenses, for example, travelling expenses, accounting services, additional medical reports, interpreter expenses and any legal fees.

<u>**For additional information concerning this application or the mediation process, please refer to the Dispute Resolution Practice Code and FSCO's website at www.fsco.gov.on.ca or contact:**</u>

Mediation Services
Dispute Resolution Services
Financial Services Commission of Ontario
5160 Yonge Street, 14th Floor, Box 85
Toronto, ON M2N 6L9

Mediation Hotline   **In Toronto at: 416-590-7210 or Toll Free: 1-800-517-2332, ext. 7210**   **Fax: 416-590-7077**

Financial Dispute Services Resolution Commission Services Of Ontario Ontario	**Application for Mediation** **FORM A**	Mediation file number

Section 1 GENERAL INFORMATION   This section MUST be completed.

1. What was the date of the motor vehicle accident? Year Month Day	2. Who is making this application? ☐ Claimant ☐ Claimant's representative ☐ Insurance company ☐ Insurance company's representative

3. Have you applied for mediation before?

☐ No ☐ Yes

4. Language preferred ☐ English ☐ French ☐ Other, specify ▶	5. Do you want the mediation to be conducted in French? ☐ No ☐ Yes

Do you want an in-person meeting with the other party? Please note that it is within the mediator's discretion to conduct the mediation in person or by telephone conference.

☐ No ☐ Yes

CLAIMANT

☐ ☐ ☐ Last name Mr. Mrs. Ms.	First name	Middle name

Street address		Apt./Unit

City	Province/State	Postal Code/Zip	Country

Home phone number ( )	Work phone number Ext. ( )	Fax number ( )	Birth date Year Month Day

1. What is the best way to reach you? ☐ phone ☐ mail ☐ fax ☐ through my representative	2. Where is the best place to reach you? ☐ home ☐ work ☐ other, specify ▶

3. When is the best time to reach you? Specify days of the week and time.

4. Is the Claimant under 18 years old? ☐ No ☐ Yes   Or mentally incapable? ☐ No ☐ Yes If Yes, the person filing the application on behalf of the claimant

must also complete *Form P – Representing Minors and Mentally Incapable Persons* – and sign this application form. Form P is available on the Commission website: www.fsco.gov.on.ca or by calling the Mediation Hotline in Toronto at (416) 590-7210 or Toll-Free at 1-800-517-2332, ext. 7210.

CLAIMANT'S REPRESENTATIVE

☐ ☐ ☐ Last name Mr. Mrs. Ms.	First name	File reference number

Title	Firm Name

Street address	Apt./Unit

City	Province/State	Postal Code/Zip	Country

Work phone number Ext. ( )	Fax number ( )	Electronic mail address

The representative is:

☐ Lawyer   Law Society licence number _____

☐ Licensed paralegal   Law Society licence number _____

☐ Not required to be licensed

Specify the type of exemption from the list of exemptions
recognized in the Law Society 's by-laws   _____

Section 1 continued

INSURANCE COMPANY

Company name

Claim representative name	Claim number
Policyholder name	Policy number

INSURANCE COMPANY'S REPRESENTATIVE

☐ ☐ ☐ Last name	First name	File reference number
Mr. Mrs Ms.		

Title	Firm name

Street address	Apt./Unit

City	Province/State	Postal Code/Zip	Country

Work phone number Ext.	Fax number	Electronic mail address
( )	( )	

Section 2 ISSUES IN DISPUTE

Provide a **full** description of the accident benefits that are in dispute.   (Attach extra sheets if necessary)

Does this claim involve catastrophic impairment? ☐ No ☐ Yes | Does the Claimant have optional benefits? ☐ No ☐ Yes

☐ WEEKLY BENEFITS

	Year Month Day	Year Month Day
Which weekly benefit are you disputing?	Date submitted to insurer:	Date denied:

☐ income replacement
☐ non-earner

What are you disputing?
☐ initial entitlement to benefits
☐ length of time benefits were paid
☐ amount of weekly benefits
☐ entitlement to benefits past 104 weeks
☐ other, specify ▼

If the Claimant received income benefits, state weekly amount and duration of payments.

$ _____

From: To:

Is the insurance company claiming a repayment of benefits?

☐ No   ☐ Yes   If yes, amount ▼

$

☐ CAREGIVER BENEFITS

	Year Month Day	Year Month Day
Weekly amount in dispute?	Date submitted to insurer:	Date denied:
$ _____	Name of service provider(s):	
From: To:		

What are you disputing?
☐ initial entitlement to benefits
☐ length of time benefits were paid
☐ amount of benefits
☐ entitlement to benefits past 104 weeks
☐ other, specify ▼

Section 2 continued

☐ ATTENDANT CARE BENEFITS		Year	Month	Day		Year	Month	Day
Monthly amount in dispute?	Date submitted to insurer:				Date denied:			
$	Name of service provider(s):							
	Time period in dispute from:				to:			

☐ MEDICAL BENEFITS 1		Year	Month	Day		Year	Month	Day
Amount in dispute?	Date submitted to insurer:				Date denied:			
$	Name of service provider(s):							
	Type of service(s):							
	Time period in dispute from:				to:			

☐ MEDICAL BENEFITS 2		Year	Month	Day		Year	Month	Day
Amount in dispute?	Date submitted to insurer:				Date denied:			
$	Name of service provider(s):							
	Type of service(s):							
	Time period in dispute from:				to:			

☐ MEDICAL BENEFITS 3		Year	Month	Day		Year	Month	Day
Amount in dispute?	Date submitted to insurer:				Date denied:			
$	Name of service provider(s):							
	Type of service(s):							
	Time period in dispute from:				to:			

☐ MEDICAL BENEFITS 4		Year	Month	Day		Year	Month	Day
Amount in dispute?	Date submitted to insurer:				Date denied:			
$	Name of service provider(s):							
	Type of service(s):							
	Time period in dispute from:				to:			

☐ REHABILITATION BENEFITS 1		Year	Month	Day		Year	Month	Day
Amount in dispute?	Date submitted to insurer:				Date denied:			
$	Name of service provider(s):							
	Type of service(s):							
	Time period in dispute from:				to:			

☐ REHABILITATION BENEFITS 2		Year	Month	Day		Year	Month	Day
Amount in dispute?	Date submitted to insurer:				Date denied:			
$	Name of service provider(s):							
	Type of service(s):							
	Time period in dispute from:				to:			

☐ REHABILITATION BENEFITS 3		Year	Month	Day		Year	Month	Day
Amount in dispute?	Date submitted to insurer:				Date denied:			
$	Name of service provider(s):							
	Type of service(s):							
	Time period in dispute from:				to:			

☐ CASE MANAGER SERVICES BENEFITS		Year	Month	Day		Year	Month	Day
Amount in dispute?	Date submitted to insurer:				Date denied:			
$	Name of service provider(s):							
	Time period in dispute from:				to:			

Section 2 continued

☐ OTHER EXPENSES

A ☐ lost educational expenses		Year	Month	Day		Year	Month	Day
Amount in dispute?	A Date submitted to insurer:				Date denied:			
$	Detail of expenses:							
	Time period in dispute from:				to:			

B ☐ expenses of visitors		Year	Month	Day		Year	Month	Day
Amount in dispute?	B Date submitted to insurer:				Date denied:			
$	Detail of expenses:							
	Time period in dispute from:				to:			

C ☐ damage to clothing, glasses, etc		Year	Month	Day		Year	Month	Day
Amount in dispute?	C Date submitted to insurer:				Date denied:			
$	Detail of expenses:							
	Date of replacement expenses:							

D ☐ housekeeping and home maintenance		Year	Month	Day		Year	Month	Day
Amount in dispute?	D Date submitted to insurer:				Date denied:			
$	Name of service provider(s):							
	Time period in dispute from:				to:			

E ☐ cost of examinations		Year	Month	Day		Year	Month	Day
Amount in dispute?	E Date submitted to insurer:				Date denied:			
$	Date of examination or report:							
	Type of examination(s):							
	Examination(s) provided by:							

E ☐ cost of examinations		Year	Month	Day		Year	Month	Day
Amount in dispute?	E Date submitted to insurer:				Date denied:			
$	Date of examination or report:							
	Type of examination(s):							
	Examination(s) provided by:							

E ☐ cost of examinations		Year	Month	Day		Year	Month	Day
Amount in dispute?	E Date submitted to insurer:				Date denied:			
$	Date of examination or report:							
	Type of examination(s):							
	Examination(s) provided by:							

☐ DEATH BENEFITS		Year	Month	Day		Year	Month	Day
Amount in dispute?	Date submitted to insurer:				Date denied:			
$	Name of deceased:							
	Relationship of deceased to claimant:							

☐ FUNERAL EXPENSES		Year	Month	Day		Year	Month	Day
Amount in dispute?	Date submitted to insurer:				Date denied:			
$	Name of deceased:							
	Relationship of deceased to claimant:							

☐ OTHER DISPUTES		Year	Month	Day		Year	Month	Day
Amount in dispute?	Date submitted to insurer:				Date denied:			
$	Detail of expenses:							
	Time period in dispute from:				to:			

☐ INTEREST

Amount in dispute? Set out calculations.	
$	

Section 3 Document List	This section MUST be completed	(Attach extra sheets if necessary)

It is expected that both parties have exchanged key documents prior to filing this Application for Mediation.

Documents -1. List key documents in your possession which you will refer to in the mediation.

Extra sheets attached ☐

Documents -2. List key documents not currently in your possession which you intend to get from other sources.

Extra sheets attached ☐

Personal information requested on this form is collected under the authority of the Insurance Act, R.S.O. 1990, c.1.8 as amended. This information, including documents submitted with this application, will be used in the dispute resolution process for accident benefits.

Signature and Certification

I certify that all information in this Application and attachments is true and complete. I authorize the insurance company to release all medical reports and information relating to the issues in dispute to Mediation Services, Dispute Resolution Services, Financial Services Commission of Ontario. I realize that information filed with this Application may be given to the other party in this dispute.

Claimant name (please print)	Claimant Signature	Date	Year	Month	Day
Representative name (please print)	Representative Signature	Date	Year	Month	Day

Send the **original and one copy** of the **completed** application to Mediation Services at the address noted below. Keep an additional copy of the completed application for yourself.

Mediation Services
Dispute Resolution Services
Financial Services Commission of Ontario
5160 Yonge Street, 14th Floor, Box 85
Toronto, ON M2N 6L9

If you have any questions about this application, or want more information, contact:

Mediation Hotline In Toronto at: 416-590-7210 or Toll Free: 1-800-517-2332, ext. 7210   Fax: 416-590-7077

FSCO website: www.fsco.gov.on.ca

Appendix 8.4
Application for Arbitration (Form C: Guide and Form)[3]

Financial Services
Commission
of Ontario
5160 Yonge Street
Box 85
Toronto ON M2N 6L9

Dispute
Resolution
Services

Guide For Completing Dispute Resolution Services (DRS) Forms

Application for Arbitration - Form C

Arbitration at the Financial Services Commission of Ontario (FSCO)

- Arbitration is a decision-making process for accident benefit disputes. It is similar to a court proceeding but is less formal, shorter, and costs less. An arbitrator will hear witnesses called by the insured person and the insurance company, review all the evidence filed at the hearing and issue a written decision based on the evidence and the law that is binding on both parties.

- You may apply for arbitration only if the issues in dispute between you and the insurance company have been mediated at FSCO, and mediation failed.

- Insurance companies cannot apply for arbitration, but may raise additional issues in response if an insured person applies for arbitration, as long as these issues have been mediated.

Applying for arbitration

- Complete this application form, sign and date it, and send to Arbitration Services at FSCO as follows:

  - the **original and one copy** of the application
  - a copy of the Report of Mediator, if available
  - copies of any other documents that are relevant to your dispute (keep the originals for yourself)
  - the $100 filing fee, payable to the Minister of Finance

How to complete the Application - Answer all questions relevant to your dispute.

Section 1   Complete **all** parts of this section. Be sure to indicate whether you want an oral hearing and whether you want the hearing to be conducted in English or French. If you require interpretation services in a language other than English or French, FSCO will provide an interpreter for the hearing. If you need other special services (such as sign language or wheelchair access), please give details in this section.

        If the Applicant is less than 18 years old or is mentally incapable, an authorized person must sign the Application for Arbitration and complete and file **Form P - Representing Minors or Mentally Incapable Persons**, which is available on the FSCO website or by calling Arbitration Services.

Section 2   Provide a **detailed** description of the accident benefits that have been mediated and that are still in dispute, including, where possible, the amount and duration of each type of benefit in dispute, and, for medical and rehabilitation benefits, the date and service provider for the treatment in dispute.

---

[3] Source: FSCO Website <www.fsco.gov.on.ca>

Section 3

<u>Document List</u> -list key documents (such as medical reports, tax returns etc.) in your possession to which you will refer in the arbitration

-also list key documents not in your possession that you intend to get from other sources for use in the arbitration. Include any documents you are requesting from the other party (such as surveillance evidence, a summary of benefits paid, etc.) which have not yet been provided to you.

<u>Signature and Certification</u> - ensure that you read the declaration before signing.

The applicant (unless a minor or mentally incapable) and/or their representative must provide an original signature and current date at the bottom of Section 3.

<u>Once the Application for Application is completed, what happens next?</u>

- Arbitration Services will review your application and contact you if additional information or clarification is required.

- Once your application has been accepted, Arbitration Services will forward it to the insurance company. The insurance company must file a *Response by Insurer to an Application for Arbitration* (Form E) within 20 days of receiving your *Application for Arbitration*. You will get a copy of the insurance company's *Response*. The *Response* will set out the company's position on the dispute and may raise further issues that were not resolved at mediation.

- If you wish to reply to the issues raised in the insurance company's *Response*, you may file a *Reply by the Applicant for Arbitration* (Form G) within 10 days of receiving the insurer's *Response*. This step is optional, but if you decide to file a *Reply*, you must provide a copy of your *Reply* to both the insurance company and FSCO.

- In most cases FSCO will schedule a pre-hearing discussion with an arbitrator before you have a hearing. You are required to exchange all relevant documents and reports with the insurer **before** the pre-hearing discussion. At the pre-hearing discussion, you and the insurance company will discuss the issues with an arbitrator, who will assist you to settle the matter or, failing that, will make arrangements for the hearing. You and the insurance company representative are obliged to participate personally in the pre-hearing, even if represented.

- If you do not settle the dispute at the pre-hearing discussion, a hearing will be scheduled. After the hearing, the written decision of the arbitrator, which is binding on both parties, will be sent to you and the insurance company.

<u>For additional information concerning this application or the arbitration process, please refer to the Dispute Resolution Practice Code and FSCO's website at www.fsco.gov.on.ca or contact:</u>

Arbitration Services
Dispute Resolution Services
Financial Services Commission of Ontario
5160 Yonge Street, 14th Floor, Box 85
Toronto, ON M2N 6L9

In Toronto at: 416-590-7202 or Toll Free: 1-800-517-2332, ext. 7202   **Fax: 416-590-8462**

FSCO website: www.fsco.gov.on.ca

Financial Services Commission Of Ontario	Dispute Resolution Services	**Application for Arbitration** **FORM C**	Arbitration file number

Section 1 GENERAL INFORMATION

1. What was the date of the motor vehicle accident?	2. Provide mediation number and attach Report of Mediator
Year Month Day	M- Report of Mediator attached ☐ No ☐ Yes

3. Do you have issues in dispute currently in arbitration?

☐ No ☐ Yes   If Yes, provide arbitration file numbers ▶ A-

4. Language preferred

☐ English ☐ French ☐ Other, specify ▶

APPLICANT

☐ ☐ ☐ Last name	First name	Middle name
Mr. Mrs. Ms.		

Street address		Apt./Unit

City	Province/State	Postal Code/Zip	Country

Home phone number ( )	Work phone number ( ) Ext.	Fax number ( )	Birth date Year Month Day

1. What is the best way to reach you? ☐ phone ☐ mail ☐ fax ☐ through my representative	2. Where is the best place to reach you? ☐ home ☐ work ☐ other, specify ▶

3. When is the best time to reach you? Specify days of the week and time.

4. Is the Claimant under 18 years old? ☐ No   Or mentally incapable? ☐ No
☐ Yes   ☐ Yes   If Yes, the person filing the application on behalf of the applicant

must also complete *Form P – Representing Minors and Mentally Incapable Persons* – and sign this application form. Form P is available on the Commission website: www.fsco.gov.on.ca or by calling the Arbitration Hotline in Toronto at (416) 590-7202 or Toll-Free at 1-800-517-2332, ext. 7202.

APPLICANT'S REPRESENTATIVE

☐ ☐ ☐ Last name	First name	File reference number
Mr. Mrs. Ms.		

Title	Firm Name

Street address		Apt./Unit

City	Province/State	Postal Code/Zip	Country

Work phone number Ext. ( )	Fax number ( )	Electronic mail address

The representative is:

☐ Lawyer   Law Society licence number   _____

☐ Licensed paralegal   Law Society licence number   _____

☐ Not required to be licensed

     Specify the type of exemption from the list of exemptions recognized in the Law Society 's by-laws   _____

Section 1 continued

INSURANCE COMPANY

Company name

Claim representative name	Claim number
Policyholder name	Policy number

NEUTRAL EVALUATION

Do you want Neutral Evaluation through the Commission?

☐ No ☐ Yes If Yes, 1. do you have the consent of the insurance company? ☐ No ☐ Yes

2. do you certify that all documents or reports listed in the Report of Mediator have been exchanged and that no other documents are required for the purpose of evaluating the issues in dispute? ▼

☐ Yes **Signature ▶**

ARBITRATION HEARING

1. Do you want to have an oral arbitration hearing? ☐ No ☐ Yes

2. Do you want the arbitration hearing to be conducted in French? ☐ No ☐ Yes	3. Will you require the services of an interpreter at the arbitration hearing? ☐ No ☐ Yes If Yes, what language? ▶

4. Do you require other special services such as wheelchair access or sign language interpreter?
☐ No ☐ Yes If Yes, describe? ▶

5. Do you want the hearing to be outside the Greater Metropolitan Toronto Area?
☐ No ☐ Yes If Yes, where? ▶

Section 2 ISSUES IN DISPUTE

Check the benefits that were not resolved in mediation and which you now want arbitrated.
You cannot add new issues at this stage until they have been mediated.
For each benefit claimed, briefly explain the details, adding extra sheets or a Schedule if necessary.

☐ WEEKLY BENEFITS

Which weekly benefit are you disputing?	From:	Year	Month	Day	To:	Year	Month	Day
☐ income replacement ☐ non-earner ☐ amount								

☐ CAREGIVER BENEFITS

Weekly amount in dispute?	From:	Year	Month	Day	To:	Year	Month	Day
$								

☐ ATTENDANT CARE BENEFITS

Weekly amount in dispute?	From:	Year	Month	Day	To:	Year	Month	Day
$								

Section 2 continued

☐ MEDICAL BENEFITS	1			
		Year	Month	Day

Amount	Date of Treatment Plan:
$	Name of service provider(s):
Does this claim involve catastrophic impairment? ☐ No ☐ Yes	Type of service(s) provided:

☐ MEDICAL BENEFITS	2			
		Year	Month	Day

Amount in dispute?	Date of Treatment Plan:
$	Name of service provider(s):
	Type of service(s) provided:

☐ MEDICAL BENEFITS	3			
		Year	Month	Day

Amount in dispute?	Date of Treatment Plan:
$	Name of service provider(s):
	Type of service(s) provided:

☐ MEDICAL BENEFITS	4			
		Year	Month	Day

Amount in dispute?	Date of Treatment Plan:
$	Name of service provider(s):
	Type of service(s) provided:

☐ REHABILITATION BENEFITS	1			
		Year	Month	Day

Amount in dispute?	Date of Treatment Plan:
$	Name of service provider(s):
	Type of service(s) provided:

☐ REHABILITATION BENEFITS	2			
		Year	Month	Day

Amount in dispute?	Date of Treatment Plan:
$	Name of service provider(s):
	Type of service(s) provided:

☐ REHABILITATION BENEFITS	3			
		Year	Month	Day

Amount in dispute?	Date of Treatment Plan:
$	Name of service provider(s):
	Type of service(s) provided:

☐ CASE MANAGER SERVICES BENEFITS	
Amount in dispute?	Name of service provider(s):
$	
from : to:	Year Month Day Year Month Day
	Service(s) provided from: to:

Section 2 continued

For each benefit claimed, briefly explain the details. *(Attach extra sheets if necessary.)* ▼

☐ **OTHER EXPENSES**

What is being disputed?

☐ lost educational expenses
☐ expenses of visitors
☐ damage to clothing, glasses, etc.

Amount in dispute?

$ _____

☐ housekeeping and home maintenance

Total Amount in dispute?

$

Weekly amount in dispute:

	Year	Month	Day		Year	Month	Day

Service(s) provided from: to:

Name of service provider(s):

☐ cost of examinations

Amount in dispute?

$

	Year	Month	Day

Date of examination or report:

Type of examination(s):

Examination(s) provided by:

Amount in dispute?

$

	Year	Month	Day

Date of examination or report:

Type of examination(s):

Examination(s) provided by:

Amount in dispute?

$

	Year	Month	Day

Date of examination or report:

Type of examination(s):

Examination(s) provided by:

☐ **DEATH BENEFITS**

Amount claimed?

$

☐ **FUNERAL EXPENSES**

Amount claimed?

$

☐ **OTHER DISPUTES**

Amount claimed?

$

☐ **INTEREST**

☐ **EXPENSES OF THE HEARING**

☐ **SPECIAL AWARD -PROVIDE PARTICULARS**

| Section 3 Document List | This section MUST be completed | (Attach extra sheets if necessary) |

It is expected that the Applicant and the Insurer have exchanged key documents prior to the filing of an Application for Arbitration.

Documents -1. List key documents in your possession to which you will refer in the arbitration.
Identify the type of document (letter, medical report, tax return), the name of the writer or issuing institution and the date of the document.

Extra sheets attached ☐

Documents -2. List key documents not currently in your possession, which you intend to get from other sources (such as employers, doctors, Revenue Canada) for use in the arbitration. You should also include any documents requested from the other party (such as surveillance evidence, a summary of benefits paid) which have not yet been provided. *Wherever possible, identify the type of document (letter, medical report, tax return), the name of the writer or issuing institution and the date of the document.*

Extra sheets attached ☐

Personal information requested on this form is collected under the authority of the Insurance Act, R.S.O. 1990, c.1.8 as amended. This information, including documents submitted with this application, will be used in the dispute resolution process for accident benefits.

Signature and Certification

I certify that all information in this Application and attachments is true and complete. I authorize the insurance company to release all medical reports and information relating to the issues in dispute to Arbitration Services, Dispute Resolution Services, Financial Services Commission of Ontario. I realize that information filed with this Application may be given to the other party in this dispute.

Applicant name (please print)	Applicant Signature	Date	Year	Month	Day
Representative name (please print)	Representative Signature	Date	Year	Month	Day

Send the **original and one copy** of the **completed** application to Arbitration Services at the address noted below. Keep an additional copy of the completed application for yourself.

Arbitration Services
Dispute Resolution Services
Financial Services Commission of Ontario
5160 Yonge Street, 14ᵗʰ Floor, Box 85
Toronto, ON M2N 6L9

If you have any questions about this application, or want more information, contact:

Arbitration Hotline   In Toronto at: 416-590-7202 or Toll Free: 1-800-517-2332, ext. 7202   Fax: 416-590-8462

FSCO website: www.fsco.gov.on.ca

Appendix 8.5
Notice to Appeal (Form I: Guide and Form)[4]

**Financial Services
Commission
of Ontario**
5160 Yonge Street
Box 85
Toronto ON M2N 6L9

Dispute
Resolution
Services

Notice of Appeal
Form I

Guide For Completing Dispute Resolution Services (DRS) Forms

Use this form to appeal an Arbitration decision. **Appeals are only allowed on questions of law.**

You must file your completed *Notice of Appeal* with the Financial Services Commission of Ontario (the "Commission") at the address below, **within 30 days of** the date of the arbitration order you wish to appeal. The Director of Arbitrations may extend the time based on the reasons for the delay and the apparent strength of the appeal. The steps you must take are set out in this form.

Personal information requested on this form is collected under the authority of the *Insurance Act*, R.S.O. 1990, c.I.8, as amended. This information, including documents submitted with this application, will be used in the dispute resolution process for accident benefits. This information will be available to all parties to the proceeding. Any questions about this collection of information may be directed to the Director of Arbitrations, Dispute Resolution Services, at the address below.

If you have any questions or want more information, contact:

Appeals Unit
Dispute Resolution Services
Financial Services Commission of Ontario
5160 Yonge Street, 15th Floor, Box 85
Toronto ON M2N 6L9

In Toronto: (416) 590-7222

Toll Free: 1-800-517-2332, extension 7222

Fax: (416) 590-7077

Commission website: www.fsco.gov.on.ca

---

[4] Source: FSCO Website <www.fsco.gov.on.ca>

Appealing an Arbitration Decision

For a complete set of the rules for appeals, see the *Dispute Resolution Practice Code.*

Step 1

Complete this *Notice of Appeal* form within **30 days** of the date of the Arbitration order. If the *Notice of Appeal* is incomplete, it may be rejected. After completing the form, you must serve a copy on the respondent (the other party). If the respondent was represented at the arbitration hearing by a lawyer, you should serve the *Notice of Appeal* on the lawyer. If not, serve the respondent.

Service may be done by personal delivery, courier, fax, regular mail, registered mail or any other method allowed by the *Dispute Resolution Practice Code.*

Then file the following with the Commission:
- Completed *Notice of Appeal*
- Original *Statement of Service* form stating when and how you served the respondent with the *Notice of Appeal*
- The fee

Step 2

Upon receiving a properly completed *Notice of Appeal, Statement of Service* and the application fee, the Commission will promptly acknowledge the appeal.

Step 3

To oppose your appeal, the respondent must file a *Response to Appeal* within **20 days** of receiving acknowledgement of the appeal from the Commission. You will get a copy of the *Response to Appeal* from the respondent.

Step 4

Unless the Director of Arbitrations or an adjudicator delegated by the Director (known as Director's Delegate) advises you differently, your written submissions must be served on the respondent and filed with the Commission within **30 days** of the date the *Response to Appeal* was due. If a transcript is ordered, this time limit is extended to **30 days** from receipt of the transcript.

Step 5

The Director or Director's Delegate may decide the appeal with or without a hearing.

How to Complete the Notice of Appeal

PLEASE PRINT

Arbitration Decision Details

This information can be found in the arbitration decision.

Applicant's Name and Address

Fill in completely. Provide any alternative addresses, phone numbers, fax numbers or electronic mail addresses that will make it easier for us to contact you.

Appellant's Representative

You may choose to have someone represent you. Although many people are represented by a lawyer in an appeal, a lawyer is not required. If you have a representative, fill in the name, address and phone number of your representative. If it is a firm, please give the name of the firm in the box provided. **A minor (a person under the age of 18) or a person who has been declared mentally incapable, must have a representative.**

Reasons for the Appeal

Appeals are only available on questions of law. If your appeal does not involve a question of law, it may be rejected.

Briefly state what part(s) of the Arbitration order you are appealing and the error(s) of law you claim the arbitrator made. Attach extra sheets if necessary. Your *Notice of Appeal* must be sufficiently detailed to allow the other party to respond. It is not necessary, however, for you to file your complete written submissions until later.

Action Sought

Briefly state the remedy or outcome you are seeking in your appeal.

Transcript

Indicate if the Arbitration hearing was recorded by a reporting service. If it was recorded, indicate if you have ordered a transcript of the hearing. If you do not intend to order a transcript, you must state why a transcript is not needed for the appeal.

Stay

The usual rule is that an appeal does not stop the Arbitration order from taking effect. If you are asking that the Arbitration order not go into effect, you must explain why the usual rule should not apply.

It is likely that the stay will be decided without further submissions, so your reasons should be as complete as possible.

Appeal from a Preliminary or Interim Order

The usual rule is that a party may not appeal a preliminary or interim order of an arbitrator until all of the issues in the arbitration dispute have been finally decided. If you are seeking to appeal a preliminary or interim order, you must explain why the usual rule should not apply.

It is likely that this issue will be decided without further submissions so your reasons should be as complete as possible.

Evidence

Appeals are usually decided based on the evidence presented at the arbitration hearing. The Director's Delegate will have access to the arbitration exhibits and, therefore, it is not necessary to refile them.

If you want to rely on any additional or new evidence – documents or witnesses – you must explain what the evidence is and why it should be allowed in the appeal.

This issue may be decided without further submissions so your explanation should be as detailed as possible.

Signature

Sign the form and return it to the Appeals Unit at the Commission.

Fee

If you are an insured person, be sure to enclose the filing fee of $250 by cheque or money order made out to the **MINISTER OF FINANCE. The application will be rejected if the filing fee is not enclosed.**

If you are an insurer, the Commission will invoice your company for the filing fee ($250) and the insurer assessment ($500).

Note: You may settle your dispute with the respondent directly at any time during the appeal process.

**Financial Services
Commission
of Ontario**
5160 Yonge Street
Box 85
Toronto ON M2N 6L9
Ontario

Dispute
Resolution
Services

**Notice of Appeal
Form I**

Commission file number
P-

*Complete ALL sections.
Attach extra sheets if necessary.*

ARBITRATION DECISION DETAILS

Applicant	Insurer(s)

Date of Arbitration decision (yyyy/mm/dd) Arbitrator	Arbitration file number
	A

APPELLANT

☐ Mr. ☐ Mrs. ☐ Ms. Company name **OR** Last name	First name	Middle name

Street address	Apt./Unit

City	Province/State	Postal Code/Zip	Country

Home phone number	Work phone number	Ext.	Fax number	Email address
( )	( )		( )	

APPELLANT'S REPRESENTATIVE

☐ Mr. ☐ Mrs. ☐ Ms. Last name	First name	File reference number

Title	Firm name

Street address	Apt./Unit

City	Province/State	Postal Code/Zip	Country

Phone number	Ext.	Fax number	Email address
( )		( )	

The representative is:

☐ Lawyer   Law Society licence number   _____

☐ Licensed paralegal   Law Society licence number   _____

☐ Not required to be licensed

Specify the type of exemption from the list of exemptions recognized
in the Law Society 's by-laws   _____

REASONS FOR THE APPEAL

Briefly explain the reasons for your appeal (questions of law only).

☐ Extra sheets attached

ACTIONS SOUGHT FROM THE APPEAL

Briefly explain what outcome or result you are looking for in the Appeal.

☐ Extra sheets attached

TRANSCRIPTS

Was the Arbitration recorded?
☐ No
☐ Yes

Are you ordering a transcript of the hearing?
☐ No
☐ Yes

If **Yes**, you must inform the other party and arrange for a transcript copy to be provided to him/her and the Director's Delegate. State when you expect to receive the transcript. ▼

If **No**, briefly explain why a transcript is not needed for the Appeal. ▼

☐ Extra sheets attached

STAY OF THE ARBITRATION ORDER

Are you asking for a Stay of the Arbitration Order?
☐ No
☐ Yes

If **Yes**, briefly explain why you are asking for a Stay. Your reasons should be as complete as possible. ▼

☐ Extra sheets attached

APPEAL FROM A PRELIMINARY OR INTERIM ORDER

Are you asking for an Appeal of a Preliminary or Interim Order?
☐ No
☐ Yes

If **Yes**, briefly explain why you should be permitted to appeal a preliminary or interim order. Your reasons should be as complete as possible. ▼

☐ Extra sheets attached

EVIDENCE

List any evidence that you intend to rely on that was not part of the Arbitration hearing. Explain why this evidence is necessary. Your explanation should be as complete as possible.

☐ Extra sheets attached

SIGNATURE AND CERTIFICATION

I certify that all information in this Notice of Appeal and attachments is true and complete. I realize that copies of all information filed with this Notice of Appeal will be given to the other party in this dispute.

☐ Appellant
☐ Representative

Name (please print)

Title

Signature	Date (yyyy/mm/dd)	☐ Cheque or money order enclosed	Total number of extra sheets attached ▼

Appendix 8.6
Application for Variation/Revocation (Form L: Guide and Form)[5]

**Financial Services
Commission
of Ontario**
5160 Yonge Street
Box 85
Toronto ON M2N 6L9

Dispute
Resolution
Services

Application for
Variation/Revocation
Form L

**Guide For Completing Dispute Resolution
Services (DRS) Forms**

Use this form to apply for a Variation or Revocation of an
Arbitration or an Appeal decision.

An Application for *Variation/Revocation*, instead of a
Notice of Appeal, is appropriate if the circumstances of the
insured person have changed significantly since the
hearing, new evidence not available at the arbitration
hearing or the appeal, has become available, or there is
some clear error in the order (for example, the order does
not correspond to the reasons for the decision).

After completing your *Application for Variation/Revocation*
form, you must file one copy with the Financial Services
Commission of Ontario (the "Commission") at the address
below. The steps you must take are set out in this form.

Personal information requested on this form is collected
under the authority of the *Insurance Act*, R.S.O. 1990,
c.l.8, as amended. This information, including documents
submitted with this application, will be used in the dispute
resolution process for accident benefits. This information
will be available to all parties to the proceeding. Any
questions about this collection of information may be
directed to the Director of Arbitrations, Dispute Resolution
Services, at the address below.

**If you have any questions or want more information,
contact:**

Appeals Unit
Dispute Resolution Services
Financial Services Commission of Ontario
5160 Yonge Street, 15th Floor, Box 85
Toronto ON M2N 6L9

In Toronto: (416) 590-7222

Toll Free: 1-800-517-2332, extension 7222

Fax: (416) 590-7077

Commission website: www.fsco.gov.on.ca

Dispute Resolution Services – Guide for Form L (2008/05/01)
Page 1 of 2

---

[5] Source: FSCO Website <www.fsco.gov.on.ca>

Applying for Variation or Revocation of an Arbitration order or an order of an Appeal Decision

For a complete set of the rules for variations/revocations, see the *Dispute Resolution Practice Code.*

Step 1

Complete this *Application for Variation/Revocation* form. If it is incomplete, it may be rejected. After completing the form, you must serve a copy on the respondent (the other party). If the respondent was represented by a lawyer, you should serve the *Application for Variation/Revocation* on the lawyer. If not, serve the respondent.

Service may be done by personal delivery, courier, fax, regular mail, registered mail or any other method allowed by the *Dispute Resolution Practice Code.*

Then file the following with the Commission:
- Completed *Application for Variation/Revocation*
- Original Statement of Service form stating when and how you served the respondent with the *Application for Variation/Revocation*
- The fee

Step 2

Upon receiving a properly completed *Application for Variation/Revocation, Statement of Service* and the application filing fee, the Commission will promptly acknowledge the Application.

Step 3

To oppose your Application, the respondent must file a *Response to Application for Variation/Revocation* within **20 days** of receiving acknowledgement of the *Application for Variation/Revocation* from the Commission. You will get a copy of the *Response to Variation/Revocation* from the respondent.

Step 4

Unless the Director of Arbitrations or an adjudicator delegated by the Director (known as Director's Delegate) advises you differently, your written submissions must be served on the respondent and filed with the Commission within **30 days** of the date the *Response to Variation/Revocation* was due. If a transcript is ordered, this time limit is extended to **30 days** from receipt of **the transcript.**

Step 5

The Director or Director's Delegate may decide the Variation/Revocation with or without a hearing.

How to Complete the Application for Variation/Revocation

PLEASE PRINT

Decision Details

This information can be found in the arbitration or appeal decision.

Applicant's Name and Address

Fill your name and address as the person or insurance company making this *Application for Variation or Revocation.* Provide any alternative addresses, phone numbers, fax numbers or electronic mail addresses that will make it easier for us to contact you.

Applicant's Representative

You may choose to have someone represent you. Although many people are represented by a lawyer in these proceedings, a lawyer is not required. If you have a representative, fill in the name, address and phone number of your representative. If it is a firm, please give the name of the firm in the box provided. **A minor (a person under the age of 18) or a person who has been declared mentally incapable, must have a representative.**

Reasons for the Application

Briefly state what part(s) of the Arbitration or Appeal decision you want varied or revoked and the reasons for your request. Attach extra sheets if necessary. Your *Application for Variation/Revocation* must be sufficiently detailed to allow the other party to respond. It is not necessary, however, for you to file your complete written submissions until later.

Action Sought

Briefly state the remedy or outcome you are seeking in your *Application for Variation/Revocation.*

Transcript

Indicate if the hearing was recorded by a reporting service. If it was recorded, indicate if you have ordered a transcript of the hearing. If you do not intend to order a transcript, you must state why a transcript is not needed for the Application.

Evidence

If you want to rely on any additional or new evidence in your Application for Variation or Revocation, you must identify the new evidence and explain why it should be allowed. This should include whether the evidence could have been presented at the hearing and whether it would have led the adjudicator to a different decision.

The Director's Delegate will have access to the Arbitration exhibits and, therefore, it is not necessary to refile them.

This issue may be decided without further submissions so your explanation should be as detailed as possible.

Preliminary or Interim Order of an Adjudicator

The usual rule is that a party may not apply to vary or revoke a preliminary or interim order of an adjudicator. If you are seeking to vary or revoke an interim or preliminary order, you must explain why the usual rule should not apply.

It is likely that this issue will be decided without further submissions, so your reasons should be as complete as possible.

Signature

Sign the form and return it to the Appeals Unit at the Commission.

Fee

If you are an insured person, be sure to enclose the filing fee of $250 by cheque or money order made out to the **MINISTER OF FINANCE. The Application will be rejected if the filing fee is not enclosed.**

If you are an insurer, the Commission will invoice your company for the filing fee (**$250**) and the insurer assessment (**$500**).

Note: You may settle your dispute with the respondent directly at any time during the appeal process.

**Financial Services
Commission
of Ontario**
5160 Yonge Street
Box 85
Toronto ON M2N 6L9
Ontario

Dispute
Resolution
Services

Application for
Variation/Revocation
Form L

Commission file number

Complete ALL sections.
Attach extra sheets if necessary.

DECISION DETAILS

Applicant		Insurer(s)

Date of Decision (yyyy/mm/dd)	Adjudicator	Arbitration or appeal file number
		A

APPLICANT

☐ Mr.
☐ Mrs.
☐ Ms.

Company name **OR** Last name	First name	Middle name

Street address	Apt./Unit

City	Province/State	Postal Code/Zip	Country

Home phone number	Work phone number	Ext.	Fax number	Email address
( )	( )		( )	

APPLICANT'S REPRESENTATIVE

☐ Mr.
☐ Mrs.
☐ Ms.

Last name	First name	File reference number

Title	Firm name

Street address	Apt./Unit

City	Province/State	Postal Code/Zip	Country

Work phone number	Ext.	Fax number	Email address
( )		( )	

The representative is:

☐ Lawyer   Law Society licence number _____

☐ Licensed paralegal   Law Society licence number _____

☐ Not required to be licensed

   Specify the type of exemption from the list of exemptions recognized
   in the Law Society 's by-laws   _____

REASONS FOR THE APPLICATION FOR VARIATION/ REVOCATION

Briefly explain the reasons for your Application.

Extra sheets attached ☐

ACTIONS SOUGHT FROM THE VARIATION/ REVOCATION

Briefly explain what outcome or result you are looking for in the Application.

Extra sheets attached ☐

TRANSCRIPTS

Was the hearing recorded?
☐ No
☐ Yes

| Are you ordering a transcript of the hearing?
☐ No
☐ Yes | If **Yes**, you must inform the other party and arrange for a transcript copy to be provided to him/her and the Director's Delegate. State when you expect to receive the transcript. ▼ |
| | If **No**, briefly explain why a transcript is not needed for the Variation/Revocation. ▼ |

Extra sheets attached ☐

PRELIMINARY OR INTERIM ORDER OF AN ADJUDICATOR

Are you asking for a Variation/Revocation of a Preliminary or Interim Order of an Adjudicator?

☐ No
☐ Yes

If **Yes**, briefly explain why you should be permitted to vary or revoke a preliminary or interim order. Your reasons should be as complete as possible. ▼

Extra sheets attached ☐

EVIDENCE

List any evidence that you intend to rely on that was not part of the hearing. Explain why this evidence is necessary. Your explanation should be as complete as possible.

Extra sheets attached ☐

SIGNATURE AND CERTIFICATION

I certify that all information in this Application for Variation/Revocation and attachments is true and complete. I realize that copies of all information filed with this Application for Variation/Revocation will be given to the other party in this dispute.

☐ Applicant
☐ Representative

Name (please print)

Title

Signature	Date (yyyy/mm/dd)	☐ Cheque or money order enclosed	Total number of extra sheets attached ▼

Appendix 8.7
Response to Application for Variation/Revocation
(Form M: Guide and Form)[6]

**Financial Services
Commission
of Ontario**
5160 Yonge Street
Box 85
Toronto ON M2N 6L9

Dispute
Resolution
Services

Response to Application for Variation/Revocation
Form M

Guide For Completing Dispute Resolution Services (DRS) Forms

Use this form if you want to oppose an *Application for Variation/Revocation* filed by the other party to the arbitration or appeal.

You must file this *Response to Application for Variation/Revocation* form with the Commission (address below) **within 20 days** of receiving confirmation of the *Application for Variation/Revocation* from the Commission. The Director of Arbitrations may extend the time limit based on the reasons for the delay and the apparent strength of the Response. The steps you must take are set out in this form.

Personal information requested on this form is collected under the authority of the *Insurance Act*, R.S.O. 1990, c.I.8, as amended. This information, including documents submitted with this application, will be used in the dispute resolution process for accident benefits. This information will be available to all parties to the proceeding. Any questions about this collection of information may be directed to the Director of Arbitrations, Dispute Resolution Services, at the address below.

If you have any questions or want more information, contact:

Appeals Unit
Dispute Resolution Services
Financial Services Commission of Ontario
5160 Yonge Street, 15th Floor, Box 85
Toronto ON M2N 6L9

In Toronto: (416) 590-7222

Toll Free: 1-800-517-2332, extension 7222

Fax: (416) 590-7077

Commission website: www.fsco.gov.on.ca

Dispute Resolution Services – Guide for Form M (2008/05/01)
Page 1 of 2

---

[6] Source: FSCO Website <www.fsco.gov.on.ca>

Responding to an Application for Variation/Revocation

For a complete set of the rules for variations/revocations, see the *Dispute Resolution Practice Code.*

Upon receiving a properly completed *Application for Variation/Revocation*, the Commission will promptly acknowledge the application by sending letters to all parties to the original arbitration or appeal.

If you want to oppose the variation/revocation, you must respond within **20 days** of receiving confirmation of the application from the Commission. The Director of Arbitrations can extend the time limit based on the reasons for the delay and the apparent strength of the Response.

Step 1

Complete this Response to *Application for Variation/Revocation* form.

After completing the form, you must serve a copy on the applicant. If the *Application for Variation/Revocation* shows that the applicant is represented, you must also serve the representative.

Service may be done by personal delivery, courier, fax, regular mail, registered mail or any other method allowed by the *Dispute Resolution Practice Code.*

Then file the following with the Commission:
- Completed Response to Application for Variation/Revocation.
- Original *Statement of Service* form stating when and how you served the applicant with the *Response to Application for Variation/Revocation.*

Fee

If you are an insured person, there is no fee for filing a *Response to Application for Variation/Revocation.*

If you are an insurer, the Commission will invoice your company the insurer assessment (**$500**).

Step 2

When you receive the applicant's written submissions, your written submissions must then be served on the applicant and filed with the Commission within **20 days**.

Step 3

The Director of Arbitrations or adjudicator delegated or appointed by the Director (known as Director' Delegate), may decide the *Application for Variation/Revocation* with or without a hearing.

How to Complete the *Response to Application for Variation/Revocation*

PLEASE PRINT

Applicant for Variation/Revocation

This information can be found in the *Application for Variation/Revocation.*

Respondent's Name and Address

Fill in completely. Provide any alternative addresses, phone numbers or fax numbers that will make it easier for us to contact you.

Respondent's Representative

You may choose to have someone represent you. Although many people are represented by a lawyer in these proceedings, a lawyer is not required. If you have a representative, fill in the name, address and phone number of your representative. If it is a firm, please state the name of the firm. **A minor (a person under the age of 18) or a person who has been declared mentally incapable, must have a representative.**

Response to Application for Variation/Revocation

Briefly state your response to the reasons for variation/revocation set out in the *Application for Variation/Revocation.* Attach extra sheets if necessary. Although you should state your position, it is not necessary for you to file your complete written submissions until later.

Response to Preliminary Matters

Provide your response to the preliminary matters raised in the *Application for Variation/Revocation* (transcript, preliminary or interim order, new evidence). The Director or Director's Delegate may decide the preliminary matters without further submissions, so your response should be set out in detail. Attach extra sheets if necessary.

Transcript

If the applicant does not intend to order a transcript, you may state whether you think a transcript is needed for the Response.

Preliminary or Interim Order

The usual rule is that a party may not vary or revoke a preliminary or interim order of an adjudicator. If you object to the Variation/Revocation of a preliminary or interim order, you must explain your objection.

Evidence

The Director or Director's Delegate will have access to the arbitration exhibits and therefore, it is not necessary to refile them.

If you want to rely on any additional or new evidence – documents or witnesses – you must explain what the evidence is and why it should be allowed.

If you object to the introduction of new evidence, you should explain why you object.

This issue may be decided without further submissions so your explanation should be as detailed as possible.

Signature

Sign the form and return it to the Appeals Unit at the Commission.

Note: You may settle your dispute with the applicant directly at any time during the arbitration process.

**Financial Services
Commission
of Ontario**
5160 Yonge Street
Box 85
Toronto ON M2N 6L9

Ontario

Dispute
Resolution
Services

Response to Application
Variation/Revocation
Form M

Variation/Revocation file number
P-

Complete ALL sections.
Attach extra sheets if necessary.

APPLICANT FOR VARIATION/REVOCATION

☐ Mr. ☐ Mrs. ☐ Ms.	Company name **OR** Last name	First name	Middle name

RESPONDENT'S NAME AND ADDRESS

☐ Mr. ☐ Mrs. ☐ Ms.	Company name **OR** Last name	First name	Middle name

Street address		Apt./Unit

City	Province/State	Postal Code/Zip	Country

Phone number	Ext.	Fax number	Email address
( )		( )	

RESPONDENT'S REPRESENTATIVE

☐ Mr. ☐ Mrs. ☐ Ms.	Last name	First name	File reference number

Title	Firm name

Street address	Apt./Unit

City	Province/State	Postal Code/Zip	Country

Phone number	Ext.	Fax number	Email address
( )		( )	

The representative is:

☐ Lawyer   Law Society licence number _____

☐ Licensed paralegal   Law Society licence number _____

☐ Not required to be licensed

Specify the type of exemption from the list of exemptions recognized
in the Law Society's by-laws   _____

RESPONSE TO APPLICATION FOR VARIATION/REVOCATION

Briefly explain your response to the Applicant's reasons for variation/revocation.

Extra sheets attached ☐

RESPONSE TO PRELIMINARY MATTERS

Set out your response to the preliminary matters raised in the **Application for Variation/Revocation** (transcript, preliminary or interim order, new evidence). *See instruction sheet for details.* **Your response should be as complete as possible.**

Extra sheets attached ☐

SIGNATURE AND CERTIFICATION

I certify that all information in this Response to Variation/Revocation and attachments is true and complete. I realize that copies of all information filed with this Response to Variation/Revocation will be given to the other party in this dispute.

☐ Respondant
☐ Representative

Name (please print)

Title

| Signature | Date (yyyy/mm/dd) | Total number of extra sheets attached ▼ |

Part III

Selected Federal Agencies

How to Deal with Selected Federal Tribunal

This part discusses selected federal tribunals under the following topics:

- Overview and Background
- Enabling Legislation, including statute(s) and any appropriate regulation(s)
- Relevant Regulation(s), if any (in addition to those discussed in Enabling Legislation)
- Tribunal Procedures:
  - Rules
  - Practice Directions
  - Forms
- Policies
- Explanatory Literature of the Tribunal
- Relevant Cases and/or Decisions

The selected tribunal shall be discussed as applicable to paralegals representing clients at those agencies.

The material being discussed will primarily be from the tribunal itself as posted on its own website, which shall be referenced extensively, as well as from the websites of the appropriate government departments dealing with the tribunal. **Note that the Ontario statute, the *Statutory Powers Procedure Act* (*SPPA*), does not apply to federal agencies.** The "Relevant Cases and/or Decisions" contains cases and decisions that can be found on the tribunal website and/or from research online or at most law libraries. Paralegals are not lawyers, but to be a good advocate and to best represent a client, paralegals need to find, understand, and use cases and/or decisions in their work. Further research over and above what is found in this book must always be done by the paralegal in preparing to appear before any tribunal.

The websites reviewed and the research done for this edition occurred in the summer of 2010. As the law constantly changes, it is important that paralegals review the tribunal's website and research the matter that they are involved in. All selected tribunal websites are reviewed systematically here. This systematic review approach can be applied to other tribunals that are not explored here.

In respect of federal agencies, there is no statute of general application such as the Ontario *SPPA*. The rules and procedures imposed on these agencies arise from the following sources:

- What is set out in their enabling legislation
- The rules and practice directions (or notes) of each agency
- The rules of natural justice (or procedural fairness) derived from case law and the *Charter*, as discussed in the opening chapter of this book as applied by decision and case law
- Other relevant statutes

One federal statute relevant to all federal agencies, unless specifically excluded under its enabling legislation, is the *Federal Courts Act*, R.S.C., 1985, c. F-7, as amended (*FCA*). This statute allows for judicial review to the Federal Court — Trial Division or the Federal Court of Appeal.

The sections of the *FCA* that are relevant to the jurisdiction of the Federal Court — Trial Division to hear applications for judicial review of a federal agency are as follows:

EXTRAORDINARY REMEDIES, FEDERAL TRIBUNALS

18.(1) Subject to section 28, the Federal Court has exclusive original jurisdiction

(a) to issue an injunction, writ of *certiorari*, writ of prohibition, writ of *mandamus* or writ of *quo warranto*, or grant declaratory relief, against any federal board, commission or other tribunal; and

(b) to hear and determine any application or other proceeding for relief in the nature of relief contemplated by paragraph (a), including any proceeding brought against the Attorney General of Canada, to obtain relief against a federal board, commission or other tribunal.

Extraordinary remedies, members of Canadian Forces

(2) The Federal Court has exclusive original jurisdiction to hear and determine every application for a writ of *habeas corpus ad subjiciendum*, writ of *certiorari*, writ of prohibition or writ of *mandamus* in relation to any member of the Canadian Forces serving outside Canada.

Remedies to be obtained on application

(3) The remedies provided for in subsections (1) and (2) may be obtained only on an application for judicial review made under section 18.1.

APPLICATION FOR JUDICIAL REVIEW

18.1(1) An application for judicial review may be made by the Attorney General of Canada or by anyone directly affected by the matter in respect of which relief is sought.

Time limitation

(2) An application for judicial review in respect of a decision or an order of a federal board, commission or other tribunal shall be made within 30 days after the time the decision or order was first communicated by the federal board, commission or other tribunal to the office of the Deputy Attorney General of Canada or to the party directly affected by it, or within any further time that a judge of the Federal Court may fix or allow before or after the end of those 30 days.

Powers of Federal Court

(3) On an application for judicial review, the Federal Court may

(a) order a federal board, commission or other tribunal to do any act or thing it has unlawfully failed or refused to do or has unreasonably delayed in doing; or

(b) declare invalid or unlawful, or quash, set aside or set aside and refer back for determination in accordance with such directions as it considers to be appropriate, prohibit or restrain, a decision, order, act or proceeding of a federal board, commission or other tribunal.

Grounds of review

(4) The Federal Court may grant relief under subsection (3) if it is satisfied that the federal board, commission or other tribunal

(a) acted without jurisdiction, acted beyond its jurisdiction or refused to exercise its jurisdiction;

(b) failed to observe a principle of natural justice, procedural fairness or other procedure that it was required by law to observe;

(c) erred in law in making a decision or an order, whether or not the error appears on the face of the record;

(d) based its decision or order on an erroneous finding of fact that it made in a perverse or capricious manner or without regard for the material before it;

(e) acted, or failed to act, by reason of fraud or perjured evidence; or

(f) acted in any other way that was contrary to law.

Defect in form or technical irregularity

(5) If the sole ground for relief established on an application for judicial review is a defect in form or a technical irregularity, the Federal Court may

(a) refuse the relief if it finds that no substantial wrong or miscarriage of justice has occurred; and

(b) in the case of a defect in form or a technical irregularity in a decision or an order, make an order validating the decision or order, to have effect from any time and on any terms that it considers appropriate.

INTERIM ORDERS

18.2 On an application for judicial review, the Federal Court may make any interim orders that it considers appropriate pending the final disposition of the application.

REFERENCE BY FEDERAL TRIBUNAL

18.3(1) A federal board, commission or other tribunal may at any stage of its proceedings refer any question or issue of law, of jurisdiction or of practice and procedure to the Federal Court for hearing and determination.

Reference by Attorney General of Canada

(2) The Attorney General of Canada may, at any stage of the proceedings of a federal board, commission or other tribunal, other than a service tribunal within the meaning of the *National Defence Act*, refer any question or issue of the constitutional validity, applicability or operability of an Act of Parliament or of regulations made under an Act of Parliament to the Federal Court for hearing and determination.

HEARINGS IN SUMMARY WAY

18.4(1) Subject to subsection (2), an application or reference to the Federal Court under any of sections 18.1 to 18.3 shall be heard and determined without delay and in a summary way.

Exception

(2) The Federal Court may, if it considers it appropriate, direct that an application for judicial review be treated and proceeded with as an action.

EXCEPTION TO SECTIONS 18 AND 18.1

18.5 Despite sections 18 and 18.1, if an Act of Parliament expressly provides for an appeal to the Federal Court, the Federal Court of Appeal, the Supreme Court of Canada, the Court Martial Appeal Court, the Tax Court of Canada, the Governor in Council or the Treasury Board from a decision or an order of a federal board, commission or other tribunal made by or in the course of proceedings before that board, commission or tribunal, that decision or order is not, to the extent that it may be so appealed, subject to review or to be restrained, prohibited, removed, set aside or otherwise dealt with, except in accordance with that Act.

In summary, an application for judicial review for a prerogative writ or other remedies, as discussed in the first chapter of the book, can be made in accordance with the provisions of sections 18 and 18.1–18.4, provided that if legislation allows for an appeal, then such matter is not subject to judicial review except as detailed in such legislation.

The jurisdiction of the Federal Court — Trial Division to hear an application for judicial review is also affected by section 28 of the *FCA*, which gives sole jurisdiction to the Federal Court of Appeal to hear an application for judicial review in the following circumstances:

JUDICIAL REVIEW

28.(1) The Federal Court of Appeal has jurisdiction to hear and determine applications for judicial review made in respect of any of the following federal boards, commissions or other tribunals:

(a) the Board of Arbitration established by the *Canada Agricultural Products Act*;

(b) the Review Tribunal established by the *Canada Agricultural Products Act*;

(b.1) the Conflict of Interest and Ethics Commissioner appointed under section 81 of the *Parliament of Canada Act*;

(c) the Canadian Radio-television and Telecommunications Commission established by the *Canadian Radio-television and Telecommunications Commission Act*;

(d) the Pension Appeals Board established by the *Canada Pension Plan*;

(e) the Canadian International Trade Tribunal established by the *Canadian International Trade Tribunal Act*;

(f) the National Energy Board established by the *National Energy Board Act*;

(g) [Repealed, 1992, c. 49, s. 128]

(h) the Canada Industrial Relations Board established by the *Canada Labour Code*;

(i) the Public Service Labour Relations Board established by the *Public Service Labour Relations Act*;

(j) the Copyright Board established by the *Copyright Act*;

(k) the Canadian Transportation Agency established by the *Canada Transportation Act*;

(l) [Repealed, 2002, c. 8, s. 35]

(m) umpires appointed under the *Employment Insurance Act*;

(n) the Competition Tribunal established by the *Competition Tribunal Act*;

(o) assessors appointed under the *Canada Deposit Insurance Corporation Act*;

(p) the Canadian Artists and Producers Professional Relations Tribunal established by subsection 10(1) of the *Status of the Artist Act*;

(q) the Public Servants Disclosure Protection Tribunal established by the *Public Servants Disclosure Protection Act*; and

(r) the Specific Claims Tribunal established by the *Specific Claims Tribunal Act*.

Sections apply

(2) Sections 18 to 18.5, except subsection 18.4(2), apply, with any modifications that the circumstances require, in respect of any matter within the jurisdiction of the Federal Court of Appeal under subsection (1) and, when they apply, a reference to the Federal Court shall be read as a reference to the Federal Court of Appeal.

Federal Court deprived of jurisdiction

(3) If the Federal Court of Appeal has jurisdiction to hear and determine a matter, the Federal Court has no jurisdiction to entertain any proceeding in respect of that matter.

9

Canadian Human Rights Tribunal

LEARNING OBJECTIVES

After reading this chapter, the reader should be able to:

- understand how to research any federal agency by exploring its website to find the important information needed to understand the agency's practices and procedures and how a paralegal would properly represent a client before such agency by doing so with the Canadian Human Rights Tribunal (CHRT)
- document the background of the CHRT
- detail and explain the provisions of the enabling legislation relevant to the CHRT
- elaborate on various concepts of public policy relevant to the CHRT and the relevant sections of the *Federal Courts Act* (*FCA*)
- state whether any regulations made under the enabling legislation are relevant to the CHRT and, if so, discuss such provisions
- compare and prioritize the various sources of practice and procedure of the CHRT
- identify the specific rules and procedures for the CHRT and how they would be applied in a proceeding before, during, and after a hearing of the CHRT
- review and explain the procedures and practices of the CHRT by way of a flow chart and key forms and documents available on the CHRT website
- assess how the relevant provisions invoked by the duty to act fairly apply to the CHRT
- outline the various explanatory literature available on the CHRT website to assist the paralegal to understand the CHRT and better represent the client
- appreciate the need to find decisions and/or cases in order to understand and argue the law before the CHRT
- illustrate and discuss principles that flow from the various cases and decisions as they relate to the CHRT

INTRODUCTION

The Canadian Human Rights Tribunal (the CHRT or Tribunal) is an independent, adjudicative body. It hears matters referred to it by the Canadian Human Rights Commission (the CHRC or Commission) on issues arising "through the fair-minded and equitable interpretation and enforcement of the *Canadian Human Rights Act* and the *Employment Equity Act*", as stated on the CHRT website, <www.chrt-tcdp.gc.ca>, to help ensure an environment free from discrimination. The Tribunal was originally created by the federal Parliament in 1977 to "apply the *Canadian Human Rights Act* [(the "*CHRA*")] based on the evidence presented and on the case law". The *CHRA* confers jurisdiction on the CHRT only to deal with federally regulated matters, as set out on its "FAQ" Web page:

> The Tribunal's jurisdiction covers matters within the legislative authority of the Parliament of Canada which includes federal government departments and agencies, Crown corporations, banks, airlines, and other federally regulated employers and service providers. Provincial and territorial human rights commissions also operate under provincial/territorial human rights codes and jurisdictions.

In 1996, the *Employment Equity Act* (*EEA*) was proclaimed, and the Tribunal was given the responsibilities to adjudicate complaints under the Act, which regulates employers with more than 100 employees. The *EEA* also stipulates that the CHRT operate as Employment Equity Review Tribunals, which are assembled as needed from members of the CHRT. The Employment Equity Review Tribunal will be briefly discussed in the "Enabling Legislation" section, but the focus of this chapter shall be on the practices and procedures of the CHRT.

OVERVIEW AND BACKGROUND

As of June 1998, the CHRT officially became a separate agency from the CHRC. However, the process still starts with the CHRC's receiving and investigating complaints and then referring matters to the CHRT, as described on the Web page, "About the CHRT", on the CHRT website:

> If [the Commission] believes that further inquiry is warranted, and a resolution between the parties cannot be reached, it refers the case to the Tribunal for formal hearing. At this stage, the Commission will take one of three positions:
> 1) It may act like a crown attorney and fully participate at the hearing in the public interest by leading evidence to prove a case of discrimination;
> 2) It may participate as above, but in a limited capacity by addressing specific issues or legal questions, but will not [be] present during the whole hearing; or
> 3) It may choose not to participate in the hearing process at all.
>   In the last two scenarios, the complainant, through a lawyer or on their own, will be required to lead the evidence necessary to prove their case to the Tribunal. The Tribunal's role in all situations is comparable to that of a judge, deciding the case fairly and impartially by weighing all the evidence ·introduced by all parties and deciding if discrimination under the Act has occurred. If yes, the Tribunal will determine an appropriate remedy.

Once a matter is referred, the CHRT will hold a public hearing to inquire about the complaints of discrimination. The Chairperson will assign one or three members, selected among the Chairperson, Vice-Chairperson, and 13 other full- or part-time members, to hear each case. The panel (containing one or three members) will decide whether discrimination has occurred, based on the evidence presented and on the law. If the panel hearing the case concludes that discrimination has occurred, it will decide on the appropriate remedy and how to prevent similar cases of discrimination in the future.

The administrative functions of the CHRT are carried out by the Registry staff. The Registrar and staff of the Tribunal plan, organize, and direct the Tribunal's operations, but their activities are entirely separate from the decision-making process. The staff plan and arrange hearings, provide administrative support to members to carry out their duties, and act as a liaison between the parties and the members of a hearing.

For each hearing, there is a Registry Officer assigned to it, and the officer is deemed an "officer of the court" responsible to the Tribunal. Under the direction of the Tribunal, the officers manage the logistical support services necessary for the hearings they are assigned. Officers can also provide advice and guidance to the members, counsel, and parties on Tribunal practices, such as media coverage, scheduling of witnesses, and future hearing dates. During a hearing, the Registry Officer also receives and files documents on behalf of the Tribunal, administers the oath, records a brief summary of the proceedings, and drafts orders under the specific direction of the Tribunal. Not only a liaison between the members and the parties in a case, the officer also serves as a liaison between the public and media.

ENABLING LEGISLATION

Although the jurisdiction and authority of the CHRT are defined by the *CHRA*, which creates the CHRT and sets out a few procedural rules, the *Federal Courts Act* (*FCA*), as a statute of general application, deals with appeals and judicial review from the decisions of the CHRT and ties the CHRT Rules that have been published into the process. (The relevant sections of *FCA* on the CHRT operation are discussed in the introduction to this part). Below is a discussion of the *CHRA*. In matters before the CHRT, other sections of the relevant enabling legislation and a quick review of the *EEA* may be discussed and possibly interpreted; however, such sections are outside the purview of this book and are discussed only in the decisions and cases.

The *CHRA*

A quick overview of the *CHRA* related to prohibited grounds of discrimination can be found in the FAQ section under "About the CHRT" in the CHRT website. In summary, as set out in section 3, the *CHRA* prohibits discrimination on the following grounds:

1. race
2. national or ethnic origin
3. colour
4. religion
5. age
6. sex (e.g., pay equity, harassment, which also applies to all other grounds, pregnancy, and childbirth)
7. marital status
8. family status
9. sexual orientation
10. disability (e.g., mental/physical disability, disfigurement, past or present, alcohol or drug dependence)
11. conviction that has been pardoned

If one or more of these prohibited grounds of discrimination occur, resulting in a denial of goods, services, facilities, accommodation, employment, membership in an employee organization, or receipt of equal wages, a complaint about a "discriminatory practice" can be made. Subject to certain exceptions, complaints can also be filed against communication of hate messages or the infliction of harassment or retaliation.

The complaint process generally involves a complaint to the Commission, which appoints a person to investigate. The person would provide a report and the matter would be dismissed or a conciliator might be appointed to try to settle. If settlement is not achieved or if the Commission decides to directly refer the matter to the CHRT, a hearing will be held and a decision shall be made, all in accordance with the CHRT Rules. An appeal or an application for judicial review of the Tribunal's decision can be made to the Federal Court.

Keeping the overview set out above in mind, we shall look at specific provisions of the *CHRA*, especially those provisions relevant to the CHRT.

Purpose

Section 2 states "all individuals should have an opportunity equal with other individuals to make for themselves the lives that they are able and wish to have and to have their needs accommodated, consistent with their duties and obligations as members of society, without being hindered in or prevented from doing so by discriminatory practices". The *CHRA* is the mechanism used to achieve such public policy and within federal authority.

Part I — Proscribed Discrimination

PROHIBITED GROUNDS OF DISCRIMINATION AND DISCRIMINATORY PRACTICES

Stated in section 3 are the prohibited grounds of discrimination, which are shown above in the overview. A discriminatory practice may include a practice based on one or more prohibited grounds of discrimination (s. 3.1) or on the effect of a combination of the prohibited grounds. If the results of such discriminatory practice fall in the description of sections 5–14.1, the practice may be the subject of a complaint under Part III (s. 4).

DENIAL OF GOOD, SERVICE, FACILITY, OR ACCOMMODATION

Pursuant to section 5, it is a discriminatory practice to deny or deny access to or "to differentiate adversely in relation to any individual" to any good, service, facility, or accommodation customarily available to the general public on a prohibited ground of discrimination.

DENIAL OF COMMERCIAL PREMISES OR RESIDENTIAL ACCOMMODATION

Under section 6, it is a discriminatory practice to deny or deny access to or "to differentiate adversely in relation to any individual" in the provision of residential accommodation or commercial premises on a prohibited ground of discrimination.

EMPLOYMENT

Section 7 states that it is a discriminatory practice, whether directly or indirectly, "(a) to refuse to employ or continue to employ any individual, or (b) in the course of employment, to differentiate adversely in relation to an employee, on a prohibited ground of discrimination". Under section 8, an employment application or advertisement or any inquiry "that expresses or implies any limitation, specification or preference based on a prohibited ground of discrimination" is a discriminatory practice.

EMPLOYEE ORGANIZATIONS

Pursuant to section 9, it is a discriminatory practice to exclude an individual from full membership in an employee organization or do anything that adversely affects the status of the individual's membership in such organization. A company practice or policy "that deprives or tends to deprive an individual or class of individuals of any employment opportunities on a prohibited ground of discrimination" is a discriminatory practice under section 10.

EQUAL WAGES
Setting or keeping differences in wages between male and female employees doing work of equal value in the same establishment is a discriminatory practice, as detailed in section 11.

PUBLICATION OF DISCRIMINATORY NOTICES
Displaying or publishing materials that express or imply discrimination, or that intend to discriminate, or that incite or intend to incite discrimination are deemed discriminatory practices. This concept is addressed in section 12.

HATE MESSAGES
It is a discriminatory practice under section 13 for a person or persons to communicate by telephone or electronically "any matter that is likely to expose a person or persons to hatred or contempt by reason of the fact that that person or those persons are identifiable on the basis of a prohibited ground of discrimination".

HARASSMENT (INCLUDING SEXUAL HARASSMENT)
In providing the services set out in sections 5–7, it is a discriminatory practice per section 14 to harass (including sexually harass) an individual on a prohibited ground of discrimination.

RETALIATION
Under section 14.1, retaliation against a complainant of discriminatory practice is itself a discriminatory practice.

DEFENCES
Various exceptions and defences defining actions that are considered not discriminatory practices are detailed in section 15, and specific programs designed to prevent discrimination or lessen disadvantages suffered by a group by favouring such group are not a discriminatory practice as stated in section 16.

Part II — Canadian Human Rights Commission
POWERS, DUTIES AND FUNCTIONS OF THE CHRC
The broad duties of the CHRC, in addition to dealing with complaints of discriminatory practices under Part III, are set out pursuant to section 27.

Part III — Discriminatory Practices and General Provisions
COMPLAINTS
Under subsection 40(1), but subject to subsections (5) and (7), an individual or a group who under reasonable grounds believes that a person is engaging in or has engaged in a discriminatory practice can file a complaint with the Commission. The complaint must be in a form that is acceptable to the Commission. The Commission can initiate a complaint under subsection 40(3) if it believes someone is engaged in a discriminatory practice.

COMMISSION TO DEAL WITH COMPLAINTS

The CHRC is to deal with any complaint filed with it under section 40 except complaints that fall within the five situations set out in subsection 41(1).

NOTICE

Under subsection 42(1), if the CHRC decides not to proceed with a complaint, the CHRC must notify the complainant, in writing, of its decision and provide the reason behind its decision.

INVESTIGATOR

Section 43(1) states that the CHRC may designate an "investigator" to investigate a complaint. Various powers are given to the investigator, which are detailed in subsections 43(2.1)–43(3).

REPORT

As soon as possible after the conclusion of the investigation, the investigator shall submit to the CHRC a report of the investigation's findings (s. 44(1)). Upon receipt of the report, the CHRC can take one of the following actions:

(a) Refer the complainant to the proper authority if the CHRC is satisfied that the complaint fits within subsection 44(2).
(b) Refer the complaint to the Chairperson of the CHRT to institute an inquiry if the CHRC is satisfied that the complaint fits within subsection 44(3)(a)
(c) Dismiss the complaint if the CHRC is satisfied that the complaint fits within subsection 44(3)(b).

Once the CHRC decides on its course of action, it must notify the complainant and any other person pursuant to subsection 44(4) of its action.

CONCILIATOR

The CHRC may, in accordance with section 47, appoint a conciliator to try bring about a settlement of the complaint.

REFERRAL OF A SETTLEMENT TO THE CHRC

Under subsection 48(1), settlement made between the parties after a complaint has been filed with the CHRC but before a CHRT hearing must be referred to the CHRC for approval.

ESTABLISHMENT OF THE CHRT

Under section 48.1, the CHRT is established and the qualifications, appointment, and make-up of the Tribunal are set out.

TERM OF OFFICE

Section 48.2 deals with the term of office and reappointment of the members of the CHRT.

CONDUCT OF PROCEEDINGS

The CHRT shall conduct proceedings before it "as informally and expeditiously as the requirements of natural justice and the rules of procedure allow" (s. 48.9(1)). The Chairperson of the CHRT may make rules of procedure governing the practice and procedure before the CHRT, which include the following:

(a)   the giving of notices to parties;
(b)   the addition of parties and interested persons to the proceedings;
(c)   the summoning of witnesses;
(d)   the production and service of documents;
(e)   discovery proceedings;
(f)   pre-hearing conferences;
(g)   the introduction of evidence;
(h)   time limits within which hearings must be held and decisions must be made;
(i)   awards of interest.

REQUEST FOR INQUIRY

Section 49(1) states that, any time after the filing of a complaint, the Commission can request the Chairperson of the Tribunal to institute an inquiry into the complaint if the Commission deems an inquiry is warranted. In accordance with subsection 49(2), the Chairperson may assign one member or a panel of three members to hear the inquiry. A copy of the rules of procedure shall be made available to the parties involved, pursuant to subsection 49(4).

CONDUCT OF THE INQUIRY

After notice of an inquiry is given to the Commission and the parties involved in the complaint, the hearing member or panel shall inquire into the complaint. All parties should be given sufficient time and opportunity to appear at the inquiry and present evidence and make representation.

> **50**(1) After due notice to the Commission, the complainant, the person against whom the complaint was made and, at the discretion of the member or panel conducting the inquiry, any other interested party, the member or panel shall inquire into the complaint and shall give all parties to whom notice has been given a full and ample opportunity, in person or through counsel, to appear at the inquiry, present evidence and make representations.

Sections 50(2)–(3) grant various powers to the member or panel appointed to hear the inquiry, including the power to determine all questions of law and fact (s. 50(2)). However, the power is also limited: "[s. 50(4)] The member or panel may not admit or accept as evidence anything that would be inadmissible in a court by reason of any privilege under the law of evidence."

DUTY OF THE CHRC ON APPEARING

If the CHRC decides to participate at a hearing, it must take a position of representing the public interest (s. 51): "In appearing at a hearing, presenting evidence and making representations, the Commission shall adopt such position as, in its opinion, is in the public interest having regard to the nature of the complaint."

HEARINGS TO BE PUBLIC EXCEPTION

An inquiry by the CHRT is to be public, but the member or panel conducting the inquiry may, on application, make an order to ensure the confidentiality of the inquiry. The measure not to hold a public inquiry can be taken only if the member or panel anticipates that one of the four risks set out in subsection 52(1) may occur.

COMPLAINT DISMISSED

If the complaint is concluded to be not substantiated by the inquiry, the member or the panel must dismiss the complaint (s. 53(1)).

COMPLAINT SUBSTANTIATED

If the inquiry concludes that the complaint is substantiated, the member or panel may make an order against the person found guilty of discriminatory practice using any of the actions listed in subsection 53(2) that are considered appropriate (refer to the provisions of section 54 if the complaint related to hate messages):

(a) that the person cease the discriminatory practice and take measures, in consultation with the Commission on the general purposes of the measures, to redress the practice or to prevent the same or a similar practice from occurring in future, including
   (i) the adoption of a special program, plan or arrangement referred to in subsection 16(1), or
   (ii) making an application for approval and implementing a plan under section 17;
(b) that the person make available to the victim of the discriminatory practice, on the first reasonable occasion, the rights, opportunities or privileges that are being or were denied the victim as a result of the practice;
(c) that the person compensate the victim for any or all of the wages that the victim was deprived of and for any expenses incurred by the victim as a result of the discriminatory practice;
(d) that the person compensate the victim for any or all additional costs of obtaining alternative goods, services, facilities or accommodation and for any expenses incurred by the victim as a result of the discriminatory practice; and
(e) that the person compensate the victim, by an amount not exceeding twenty thousand dollars, for any pain and suffering that the victim experienced as a result of the discriminatory practice.

The member or panel, under subsection 53(3), can also award special compensation of an amount not to exceed $20,000 to the victim if the discriminatory practice was committed wilfully or recklessly. An award for compensation may, subject to the Rules of the CHRT, include an award for interest at a rate and for a period considered appropriate.

ORDERS RELATED TO HATE MESSAGES

Three specific orders, set out in subsection 54(1), can be made if a complaint under section 13 is substantiated. The factors used to determine if a person shall pay the penalty are set out in subsection 54(1.1).

INTIMIDATION OR DISCRIMINATION

Section 59 states that "[n]o person shall threaten, intimidate or discriminate against an individual because that individual has made a complaint or given evidence or assisted in any way in respect of the initiation or prosecution of a complaint or other proceeding under this Part, or because that individual proposes to do so".

The *EEA*

As stated in section 2, this legislation was enacted "to achieve equality in the workplace so that no person shall be denied employment opportunities or benefits for reasons unrelated to ability and, in the fulfilment of that goal, to correct the conditions of disadvantage in employment experienced by women, aboriginal peoples, persons with disabilities and members of visible minorities by giving effect to the principle that employment equity means more than treating persons in the same way but also requires special measures and the accommodation of differences." The CHRC is given a large role in determining if inequality exists and in making orders to correct such inequality. If an inquiry is required under the *EEA*, the Employment Equity Review Tribunal (the EERT) shall be established to hear the matter. The members of the EERT are appointed from the CHRT.

It is unlikely that paralegals will appear before the EERT, so this chapter shall not discuss the agency further. For further information, the reader should examine the *EEA* in greater detail.

RELEVANT REGULATIONS

The *Human Rights Tribunal Appeal Regulations*, SOR/80-394, is the only regulation in force at the time of writing that is relevant to the CHRT and deals with notice and the forms to be used to appeal a decision or order of the CHRT.

Procedures of Tribunal

The Canadian Human Rights Tribunal Rules of Procedure (the CHRT Rules) can be found, in both html and pdf formats, on the CHRT website, under "About the CHRT — Tribunal Rules and Procedures". The rules of procedures were made under the authority given by section 48.9 of the *CHRA*: "the authority to make rules to govern its practices and procedures". The Rules contain nine main rules and some transitional provisions. **The CHRT Rules and amendments and other similar provisions such as the "Mediation Procedures" are discussed in a summary fashion and in varying detail. The reader, therefore, should rely only on her/his own reading and interpretation of both the rules and the forms.** Keep in mind that the procedures in the enabling legislation and other relevant legislation, such as the *FCA*, also applicable.

RULES

Purpose, Interpretation (R. 1)

The three main purposes of the CHRT Rules are stated in R. 1(1):

    (a) all parties to an inquiry have the full and ample opportunity to be heard;
    (b) arguments and evidence be disclosed and presented in a timely and efficient manner; and
    (c) all proceedings before the Tribunal be conducted as informally and expeditiously as possible.

Both Rs. 1(2) and (4) give much flexibility to the panel in charge of the matter to apply the CHRT Rules liberally or even to dispense with the compliance of any rule to advance the purposes of the rules.

Service, Filing (R. 2)

R. 2(1) states that "[u]nless otherwise stipulated, all written communications made under the Rules shall be served on all parties and filed with the Registry". Methods of service and proof of each type of service are set out in Rs. 2(2) and (3), respectively, and the method of filing to the Registry is laid out in R. 2(4). The language of all documents filed and served is detailed in R. 2(5).

Motions, Adjournments (R. 3)

All motions, including those for adjournments, are to be made by Notice of Motion in accordance with R. 3(1). Upon receipt of the Notice of Motion, the panel shall and/or may take the following action under R. 3(2):

    (a) shall ensure that the other parties are granted an opportunity to respond;
    (b) may direct the time, manner and form of any response;
    (c) may direct the making of argument and the presentation of evidence by all parties, including the time, manner and form thereof;
    (d) shall dispose of the motion as it sees fit.

Administrative Information (R. 4)

Rule 4(1) sets out the requirements of Form 1, to be prepared by the CHRC based on its current knowledge or belief and to accompany a request by the CHRC to the CHRT to institute an inquiry. As it is a form to be prepared by the CHRC, there is no Form 1 on the CHRT website. Under R. 4(2), the Registrar of the CHRT may request further information from a party by questionnaire, which must be completed and filed as directed.

Case Conferences (R. 5)

Pursuant to R. 5(1), a case conference held either in person or by telephone may be scheduled "to resolve matters of an administrative or procedural nature in respect of the inquiry". Any matters or motions to be raised will be by Notice of Motion per R. 5(2). Six obligations or powers given to the panel at the case conference are detailed in R. 5(3).

Statement of Particulars, Disclosure, Production (R. 6)

Rule 6(1) requires the service and filing, within a time fixed by the panel, a Statement of Particulars detailing key information about the case:

- the material facts
- the position on the legal issues
- the relief sought
- two lists of documents in the party's possession where privilege is (list #1) and is not (list #2) claimed related to the case
- a list of all witnesses, together with a summary of the anticipated testimony

A reply to the respondent's Statement of Particulars shall be prepared, served, and filed by the complainant and the CHRC in the two situations set out in R. 6(2). Within the time fixed by the panel, each party shall serve and file a report in respect of any expert witnesses such party intends to call, containing the information set out in R. 6(3). Under R. 6(4), each party shall provide other parties a copy of the documents for which privilege is not claimed, as set out in the party's Statement of Particulars. Such documents shall not be filed with the CHRT. Each party shall provide additional disclosure and production as is necessary for either of the two reasons set out in R. 6(5).

Book of Authorities (R. 7)

Under R. 7, a party may serve and file a book of authorities containing copies of the statutory provisions, case law, and other legal authorities (with the relevant provisions highlighted) that a party intends to refer to, provided that if a case or decision referred to is included in the CHRT Book of Jurisprudence, only the excerpt relied upon has to be included.

Addition of Parties and Interested Parties (R. 8)

Rule 8 allows for the addition of parties and for the recognition of interested parties by motion as detailed in the sub-rules of such rule.

Hearing, Evidence (R. 9)

The usual hours of the hearing, unless otherwise directed by the panel, are stated in R. 9(1). Under R. 9(2), a party that requires special arrangements or an interpreter for the hearing shall notify the Registrar as soon as possible. **Except by leave of the panel or the need to lead evidence in reply, items, such as issue, witness, relief, document or report, not disclosed in the Statement of Particulars and/or produced as required, all as detailed in R. 6, shall not be raised, called, or introduced, as stated in R. 9(3).** A party can, under R. 9(5), bring a motion for an order to examine a person, who is unable to attend a hearing, as directed by the panel under R. 9(6). A party intending to challenge the constitutional validity, applicability, or operability of a legislation before the panel must serve notice in accordance with section 57 of the *FCA* and Form 69 of the *Federal Court Rules* pursuant to R. 9(7). As per R. 9(8), the hearing may proceed even though a party fails to appear before the panel, provided the panel is satisfied that such party received proper notice of the hearing. The panel, under R. 9(9), may order the exclusion of witnesses except in the situations set out in R. 9(10), and there shall be no communication with the excluded witness as detailed in R. 9(11). Unless the panel orders otherwise, the rate and accrual of any interest awarded shall be in accordance with R. 9(12).

MEDIATION PROCEDURES

The CHRT published document, "Mediation Procedures", effective January 27, 2006, can be found, in both html and pdf formats, on the CHRT website, under "About the CHRT — Tribunal Rules and Procedures". Mediation is optional to the parties to a CHRT proceeding. The Mediation Procedures document is meant to explain the mediation process so that the parties involved can decide if mediation would help and, if so, to help them to prepare for it.

The document first explains that mediation is a process to help the parties explore settlement possibilities and then details how the mediation process works in the CHRT. The mediators are members of the CHRT who are trained in mediation. Once mediating a matter that proceeds to a hearing, that mediating member will not be an adjudicator on that case nor can he or she divulge to the adjudicator(s) any information learned in the mediation.

A mediation will occur as soon as it is practical after the matter is referred to the CHRT, and it tends to be a short, confidential, and voluntary process. After discussing what information should be provided to the mediator, the document indicates that persons who can make decisions to settle should attend the session. Special needs will be accommodated with best efforts during the mediation. Even if settlement is not reached in the mediation, efforts should be made to resolve or narrow issues and to agree upon facts to hopefully shorten the hearing time. A sample "Terms and Conditions of the Settlement" form is attached as an appendix to the document.

Book of Jurisprudence

This document, referred to in R. 7(3) of the Tribunal Rules, effective March 13, 2001, can be found, in pdf format, on the CHRT website, under "About the CHRT — Tribunal Rules and Procedures". The document consists of a list of 39 cases with citation. This list is sorted by case name. These are important cases in matters before the CHRT.

PRACTICE NOTES

Practice notes may be issued by the CHRT, and as of the summer of 2010, there are three practice notes, which can be found, in html and/or pdf formats as listed, on the CHRT website, under "About the CHRT — Tribunal Rules and Procedures" under the following names: "Canadian Human Rights Tribunal Practice Note No. 1 — Timeliness of Hearings and Decisions"; "Canadian Human Rights Tribunal Practice Note No. 2 — Representation of Parties by Non-Lawyers"; and Canadian Human Rights Tribunal Practice Note No. 3 — Case Management".

Practice Note No. 1

This practice note is dated October 22, 2007. There are two reasons for this practice note:

1. Section 48.9(1) of the CHRA requires that proceedings before the CHRT shall be conducted as expeditiously as the rules of procedure allow.

2. Five key observations were made by the court in *Nova Scotia Construction Safety Association v. Nova Scotia Human Rights Commission*, 2006 NSCA 63, in particular, the fifth observation: "that there is a public interest in having complaints of discrimination dealt with expeditiously", which was also stated in the case of *Bell Canada v. C.E.P.* (1997), 31 C.H.R.R. D/65.

For these two reasons, the practice note states "all participants in *CHRA* inquiries are reminded of their obligation to assist in the timely completion of the hearing and deliberation process" and the intent of the CHRT "to release decisions as often as possible within a four month time frame".

Practice Note No. 2

Due to the importance of this practice note to the readers, the practice note will be reproduced in full as Appendix 9.3.

Practice Note No. 3

This practice note sets out time periods to the pre-hearing case management process from the Initial Letter from the CHRT to First Case Management Conference Call, to Commission File, to Statement of Particulars, to Disclosure of Documents, to Second Case Management Conference Call, to Identification and Anticipated Testimony of Proposed Witnesses, to Expert Witness Reports. Refer to the practice note for specific details.

FORMS

There are no mandated forms on the CHRT website.

POLICIES

There are no policies on the CHRT website.

EXPLANATORY LITERATURE OF THE TRIBUNAL

Other than the documents already discussed, on the CHRT website, under "About the CHRT — Tribunal Rules and Procedures", there are two downloadable guides that explain the mechanisms of the procedures before the CHRT: "What Happens Next? A Guide to the Tribunal Process" and "Guide to the Operations of the Employment Equity Review Tribunal". Included in the appendix to this chapter is an edited version of the guide to the CHRT process, which gives great details of the usual processes of the CHRT. The second guide, which deals with the EERT process and is outside the scope of this chapter, is neither discussed nor excerpted here. However, the reader who wants further information about EERT procedures should review but not rely on this guide.

On the Web page "Reports and Disclosures" are links to the Annual Reports of the CHRT, Departmental Performance Reports, and Reports on Plans and Priorities, the last of which, as of the time of writing, are 2007, 2006–2007, and 2008–2009, respectively.

On the CHRT website, there is direct access to decisions of the CHRT by title, using the search engine.

RELEVANT CASES AND/OR DECISIONS

The cases and decisions discussed below are not meant to be exhaustive and are only those found as of the summer of 2010. The discussion reflects only the author's viewpoint and should not be regarded as legal opinion. Readers should continue to update and research on new cases and decisions, and briefing must be done in any event.

Fourteen matters, including cases before the Federal Court (Fed. Ct.), the Federal Court of Appeal (the Fed. C.A.), and before the Supreme Court of Canada (SCC), as well as decisions of the CHRT, shall be discussed in chronological order, with the oldest one first (unless the case is one in a series, which will be discussed starting with the lowest court) so as to give the reader a sampling of how these cases and decisions have been decided and their relevance to the CHRT. Not every case discussed is a ground-setting decision; however, the review should give the reader some idea of how the CHRT and the courts have dealt with various procedural and substantive issues in the first decade of the 21st century.

Thompson v. Rivtow Marine Limited

Thompson v. Rivtow Marine Limited 2001 CanLII 25844, (2001), 43 C.H.R.R. 502 (the *Thompson* decision) involved a motion requesting the CHRT to decline to deal with a complaint of alleged discrimination due to the complainant not being allowed to come back to work after a medical leave of absence. The motion was made because the complainant's union filed a grievance on his behalf citing the respondent's failure to rehire the complainant. The respondent argued that the CHRT should therefore defer to the grievance arbitration process. If the CHRT did not decline, the respondent requested that the CHRT be bound by the ruling of the arbitration process pursuant to a legal concept known as "issue estoppel".

On the question of deference, the CHRT stated the following:

> There is no doubt that workplace disputes at the Federal level give rise to numerous potential avenues of redress. It is by no means uncommon for matters underlying a human rights complaint to also be the subject of a grievance arbitration, or proceedings under statutes such as the Canada Labour Code, Worker's Compensation legislation or the Employment Insurance Act. These multiple avenues of redress are the source of much concern, and have been the subject of comment in several recent studies.
>
> A review of the Canadian Human Rights Act discloses that Parliament was alive to this concern. Indeed, the Act specifically contemplates consideration of whether a matter

might best be dealt with in another forum at two different points in the complaints process. In each case, however, the determination of whether the matter should be referred elsewhere is a decision for the Canadian Human Rights Commission, and not for the Tribunal.

Once a complaint is referred to the Tribunal, Section 49(2) of the Act provides that the Chairperson of the Tribunal shall institute an inquiry.... According to Section 50(1) of the Act, upon due notice being given to the parties, the member or members assigned to the case shall inquire into the complaint. In light of the mandatory nature of this language, and having regard to the structure of the legislative scheme as a whole, I do not think that it is open to the Tribunal to simply decline to deal with a complaint on the basis that, in the Tribunal's view, the matter might better be dealt with elsewhere.

While the Tribunal may not have any jurisdiction to refuse to hear a case altogether, as master of its own procedure, it clearly has the power to determine when the hearing will take place. The issue of whether this hearing should be adjourned in light of the pending arbitration will be dealt with further on in this ruling.

In respect of "issue estoppel", the CHRT first set out the three elements necessary to give rise to "issue estoppel":

i) The same question is being decided in each proceeding;
ii) The decision which raises the issue estoppel is a final decision; and
iii) The parties to the two proceedings are the same parties or their privies.

After reviewing the first two elements, the CHRT concluded that the parties are not the same in both hearings:

A review of the Canadian Human Rights Act makes it clear that both the Commission and Mr. Thompson are parties to the complaint under the Act. The Commission does not represent Mr. Thompson; rather, the responsibility of the Commission is to represent the public interest. This is reflective of the quasi-constitutional nature of the rights guaranteed by the Act. In my view, a finding that the Commission is a privy of a complainant would be contrary to the policy considerations underlying the Act. Such a conclusion would result in the ability of the Canadian Human Rights Commission to take positions that it believes are in the public interest being inhibited by findings made in the context of other proceedings, proceedings of which the Commission would likely have had no notice and no opportunity to participate in.

Finally, on the request of an adjournment of the CHRT hearing pending the grievance arbitration, the CHRT held that since complaints of discrimination should be held expeditiously, no adjournment would be granted.

Hujdic v. Air Canada

In *Hujdic v. Air Canada*, 2001 CanLII 25845 (the *Hujdic* decision), the respondent made a motion for a stay of the proceedings due to the possible appeal of a case to determine if there was a reasonable apprehension of institutional bias of the CHRT. The case in question was *Bell Canada v. CTEA, Femmes Action and Canadian Human Rights Commission* (Bell Canada) before the Trial Division of the Federal Court. In *Bell Canada*, Madam Justice Tremblay-Lamer found that the CHRT was not an institutionally independent and impartial body due to the fact that the CHRC has the power to issue guidelines binding upon the Tribunal. Tremblay-Lamer J. also concluded that the independence of the Tribunal was compromised by requiring the Tribunal Chairperson's approval for members of the Tribunal to complete cases after the expiry of their appointments. As a consequence, Tremblay-Lamer J. ordered that there be no further proceedings in the Bell Canada matter until such time as the problems that she identified with the statutory regime were corrected. That case was overturned by the Federal Court of Appeal, and the Bell Canada's application for leave to appeal to the Supreme Court of Canada was pending at the time of that decision. The CHRT held that the Federal Court of Appeal decision was binding and therefore should be applied. As to the respondent's request for a stay to await a possible appeal, the CHRT stated that there was no evidence of irreparable harm if the matter proceeded, and therefore the motion was dismissed.

Desormeaux v. Ottawa–Carleton Regional Transit

The decision of *Desormeaux v. Ottawa–Carleton Regional Transit*, 2003 CHRT 2, (2003), 46 C.H.R.R. 1 (the *Desormeaux* decision) reached the Supreme Court of Canada through an application for judicial review and subsequent appeals. In the original hearing, the complainant claimed discrimination due to disability by the employer because of the termination for chronic innocent absenteeism arising from medical issues. The CHRT found that there was a *prima facie* case of discrimination on the basis of a disability based on the evidence of her doctor regarding migraines and that she was terminated due to her medical condition. The *prima facie* case shift the onus on the respondent "to establish that attending work on a regular and reliable basis is a *bona fide* occupational requirement for a bus operator". The CHRT held that there was a duty on the employer to accommodate, and after reviewing the facts and the case law the CHRT stated the reason for its decision as follows:

> The law regarding the duties of employer and employee in relation to accommodation is clear: it is the responsibility of the disabled employee to bring the facts relating to the discrimination to her employer's attention. Through the efforts of Mr. Vye, Ms. Desormeaux did this. It is not up to the employee to originate a solution — that is the responsibility of the employer. In these circumstances, I am satisfied that Ms. Desormeaux fulfilled her duty to facilitate the search for accommodation.

Based on the findings, the CHRT found that the respondent had to comply with a number of orders to grant the complainant relief.

There was an application for judicial review of the *Desormeaux* decision to the Federal Court, and a judgment was reached, in conjunction with a similar matter against the same employer, in *City of Ottawa v. Canada (Human Rights Commission)*, [2004] F.C.J. No. 2172, [2004] A.C.F. no. 2172, 2004 FC 1778, 2004 CF 1778, 267 F.T.R. 216, [2005] CLLC para. 230-019, 136 A.C.W.S. (3d) 338 (the *Desormeaux* Fed. Ct. case). After reviewing the evidence and the parties' submissions, the judge first addressed the standard of review by stating the following:

> Applying the guidance provided by the Supreme Court in *Pushpanathan*, [1998] 1 S.C.R. 982, and more recently in *Baker v. Canada (Minister of Citizenship and Immigration)*, [1999] 2 S.C.R. 817, I am satisfied that the standard of review of decisions of the Tribunal in this matter is correctness in respect of questions of law, reasonableness simpliciter in respect of questions of mixed law and fact, and patent unreasonableness in respect of "fact-finding and adjudication in a human rights context". On the facts of this matter, I find the standard of review of questions of law and questions of fact-finding and adjudication in a human rights context by the Tribunal not to have been modified by recent decisions of the Supreme Court of Canada or of the Federal Court Trial Division regarding the pragmatic and functional approach to the determination of standard of review. [**Author's Note: The case law currently states that there are only two standards of review being correctness and reasonableness, not three. See *Dunsmuir v. New Brunswick*, [2008] 1 S.C.R. 190, 2008 SCC 9 (the *Dunsmuir* case), where the majority stated that there are only two standards of review by the courts judicially reviewing a decision of an agency: correctness and reasonableness.**]

In respect of the raised issue of issue estoppel, the court did not have to address the matter as the court determined that the judicial review on this matter should have been within 30 days after the decision of the CHRT on a preliminary motion and not the final motion; therefore, it was made too late.

The judge then examined whether the CHRT erred on the issue of whether the *prima facie* discrimination was proven. After examining some possible problems with the findings of the CHRT, the judge found as follows:

> In the case of Ms. Desormeaux, I conclude that the Tribunal's finding that she suffered from a disability was unreasonable based upon the evidence. Dr. Meehan was qualified as an expert in family medicine, not as a neurologist. Accordingly, I find that the Tribunal's reliance on her evidence was in error to the extent that her evidence exceeded the legitimate purpose for which her expert testimony was receivable: see *R. v. Reid* (2003), 65 O.R. (3d) 723 at 736. I conclude that there is no prima facie case for the employer to answer as I am not satisfied that there is properly admissible evidence to support a finding of disability. The application for judicial review will be allowed in respect to Ms. Desormeaux.

Desormeaux appealed this judgment to the Federal Court of Appeal: *Desormeaux v. Ottawa (City)*, 2005 FCA 311, (2005), 54 C.H.R.R. 462 (the *Desormeaux* Fed. C.A. case). After reviewing the history of the matter, the court first held that the issue estoppel argument was not time barred and could be raised in the appeal. The Federal Court of Appeal, however, found the CHRT's consideration of the matter legally unimpeachable, "in that two of the three elements required for issue estoppel — that is, same question and same parties — had not been established (following the test set out in *Danyluk v. Ainsworth Technologies Inc.*, 2001 SCC 44 (CanLII), [2001] 2 S.C.R. 460 at para. 25, citing *Angle v. Canada (Minister of National Revenue)*, 1974 CanLII 168 (S.C.C.), [1975] 2 S.C.R. 248 at 254, per Dickson, J)". As a result, the court further concluded there was no need to consider the scope of the residuary discretion residing in the Tribunal on the estoppel issue.

The court then addressed the matter of whether the *prima facie* discrimination was proven. The court disagreed with the judge in the *Desormeaux* Fed. Ct. case where it was found that there was proof of *prima facie* discrimination and stated as follows:

> [T]his conclusion was incorrect. Whether the standard of review for this mixed question of law and fact was reasonableness or patent unreasonableness, the Tribunal's decision on this issue was clearly one that deserved considerable deference. As the Supreme Court established in *Granovsky v. Canada*, 2000 SCC 28 (CanLII), [2000] 1 S.C.R. 703 at para. 34 and in *City of Montreal, supra*, at para. 71, disability in a legal sense consists of a physical or mental impairment, which results in a functional limitation or is associated with a perception of impairment. In light of this test, there was evidence before the Tribunal upon which it could reasonably find that there was a disability because of the headaches, whether they were migraine headaches, migraine/tension headaches or some other type of severe headache condition. The Report of Dr. Rabinovitch did not really conflict with the evidence of Dr. Meehan; it may have been less forceful and more tentative, but, in any event, the Tribunal was persuaded on all of the evidence that there was disability on the basis of the headaches. The Tribunal's conclusion was certainly a reasonable one based on all the evidence and should not have been upset on judicial review.
>
> On the matter of the comparator group, the Applications Judge found that the wrong comparator group was identified by the Tribunal; in any event, however, the error furnished no basis for judicial intervention, since the standard of review was reasonableness. On appeal, Counsel correctly devoted very little attention to this issue. Whichever comparator group was chosen, the conclusion that there was differentiation established in the treatment of the complainant would not be affected.
>
> Hence, *prima facie* discrimination being established, it was necessary to determine whether OC Transpo's standard of reasonable and regular attendance was a *bona fide* occupational requirement (BFOR). As the Tribunal correctly stated, the applicable three-stage test was set out in *British Columbia (Public Service Employee Relations Com-*

mission) v. BCGSEU, 1999 CanLII 652 (S.C.C.), [1999] 3 S.C.R. 3 at para. 54 ["*Meiorin*"]. To qualify as a BFOR, the employer must show that the standard was (1) adopted for a purpose rationally connected to the performance of the job; (2) adopted pursuant to an honest and good-faith belief; and (3) is reasonably necessary to the accomplishment of the legitimate work-related purpose. A standard is considered "reasonably necessary" if the employer can demonstrate that it is impossible to accommodate individual employees sharing the characteristics of the claimant without imposing undue hardship on the employer.

The court agreed with the CHRT, holding that the BFOR test was not met as there was no reasonable necessity found and that the employer should have accommodated the employee, but did not. [Note: The Fed. Ct. case did not address this issue as it stopped once it concluded there was no *prima facie* discrimination.] Although the employer advanced the argument that the employee did not specially request that her disability be accommodated, the court found the following:

> The Tribunal correctly stated (at para. 110) the law on this question: the employee has a duty to bring to the attention of the employer the facts relating to discrimination, and to facilitate the search for accommodation, but the duty to originate a solution remains with the employer (*Central Okanagan School District No. 23 v. Renaud*, 1992 CanLII 81 (S.C.C.), [1992] 2 S.C.R. 970 at 994–95). The Tribunal found that there was sufficient discussion with the employer on this issue to fulfill Ms. Desormeaux's duty of notification and facilitation with respect to accommodation (see Tribunal's findings at paras. 29 and 109–110). I am not persuaded that there was any error made by the Tribunal on this issue, let alone an unreasonable or patently unreasonable error.

Based on the foregoing, the court allowed the appeal and reinstated the CHRT decision.

There was one final attempt to appeal to the Supreme Court of Canada, but the application for leave to appeal was dismissed: [2005] S.C.C.A. No. 534 (the *Desormeaux* SCC case).

Brown v. Royal Canadian Mounted Police

Brown v. Royal Canadian Mounted Police, [2005] F.C.J. No. 2124, [2005] A.C.F. no 2124, 2005 FC 1683, 2005 CF 1683, 284 F.T.R. 291, 144 A.C.W.S. (3d) 922, 58 C.H.R.R. D/482 (the *Brown* Fed. Ct. case), was an application for judicial review to set aside a decision of the CHRT. The complainant was represented at the CHRT hearing by a non-lawyer, and after the complaint of discrimination was found substantiated, the CHRT awarded legal costs to the complainant's representative. The key parts of the decision were summarized by the Federal Court as follows:

> Regarding the Tribunal's jurisdiction to award costs, the Tribunal concluded that the power to award costs cannot be found in the Act. The Tribunal held that its jurisdiction derives more from its broad and quasi-constitutional mandate under the Act than from the literal wording of the Act. The Tribunal found that the Act's mandate gives the Tribunal all the incidental powers to protect the viability of the remedies under the Act. The Tribunal also found that the cumulative effect of subsection 53(2) in relation to personal remedies is Parliament's express intention to make a victim of discrimination whole. Therefore, the Tribunal has the power to order the payment of costs in order to preserve the damages awarded and, as a result, allow a victim of discrimination to an effective remedy. The Tribunal concluded that the Respondent was entitled to reasonable costs but was not entitled to claim the entirety of her legal costs because the principle of *restitutio in integrum* applies only to damages and not to costs.
>
> With respect to the Applicant's arguments based on subsection 50(1) of the Act that Mr. Finding was not entitled to represent the Respondent, the Tribunal observed that Mr. Finding represented the Respondent throughout the hearing with the full

knowledge of the Applicant who did not object to his participation until the final submissions. The Tribunal also noted the position taken by the Applicant that Mr. Finding had contravened the *British Columbia Legal Profession Act*, R.S.B.C. 1998, c. 9 in doing so. The Tribunal commented that whether subsection 50(1) of the Act permits non-lawyers to represent complainants at Tribunal hearings is a live issue for the Tribunal but it should be resolved in a case where it has been properly addressed. Similarly, the question of whether a non-lawyer representative appearing before the Tribunal is practising law contrary to the governing provincial legislation should be dealt with in a case where the matter is properly raised at the outset of the process.

On the question of whether the fees of a lay representative are recoverable, the Tribunal simply noted the parties' positions on the matter. The Applicant argued that there is no authority under the Act to award costs for the services of a lay representative. The Respondent argued that there was no reason to distinguish between representatives who are lawyers and those who are not, and suggested that the Tribunal should follow the approach of the British Columbia Labour Relations Board in *Graham (Re)*, [2000] B.C.L.R.B.D. No. 1, in which the Board recognized that the fees of non-lawyer representatives should be recoverable.

The court stated that the issue to be determined was "whether the Tribunal erred in law and in fact in awarding costs to the Respondent for 'legal and representation fees' of a non-lawyer". The court first look at the standard of review of the CHRT decision and found that since "the determinative issue raises a question of mixed fact and law, the decision will be reviewed on a standard of reasonableness". The court held that subsection 50(1) of the CHRA in the English version uses the word "counsel" but in the French version uses the word "advocat" and the court stated as follows:

> In *R. v. Mac*, [2002] 1 S.C.R. 856 at 857, Justice Bastarache held that where the words of one version of bilingual legislation may give rise to an ambiguity, the Court should first look at the other version to ascertain whether its meaning is plain and unequivocal. Where the ambiguity in one version is resolved by the clear and unambiguous language of the other version, there is no need to consider other rules of statutory interpretation.
>
> In the present case, the French text is clear and unambiguous. Accordingly, I conclude that the term "counsel" in the English version means "lawyer" and excludes non-lawyers. However, this does not end the matter.

The next submission on the matter examined was the SCC case of *Law Society of British Columbia v. Mangat*, [2001] 3 S.C.R. 113, where the court found that the case stands for the following authority:

> The Supreme Court of Canada concluded that there was a conflict between the two statutes. Sections 30 and 69(1) of the *Immigration Act* expressly authorized non-lawyers to appear before the tribunal for a fee but the *Legal Profession Act* prohibited non-lawyers from engaging in the practice of law for a fee. The Court found that it was impossible to comply with both statutes without frustrating Parliament's purpose. The Court concluded that where there is a conflict between two statutes the principle of paramountcy applies and, in that case, the *Immigration Act* prevailed over the *Legal Profession Act*.

The court distinguished the case because it stated that there was no conflict here.

> Unlike the *Immigration Act*, the Act does not contain a statutory provision authorizing non-lawyers to appear for a fee before the Tribunal or a provision in relation to expenses for such representation. Again without deciding the issue, even if the Tribunal has the implied jurisdiction to award costs to a successful complainant under the Act, Parliament has not expressly authorized non-lawyers to appear for a fee before the Tribunal in the legislation. On the other hand, the *Legal Profession Act* clearly prohibits

non-lawyers from appearing as counsel or advocate for a fee. In this case, the *Legal Profession Act* prevails.

The finding was therefore that the CHRT did err in awarding fees and costs and that part of the decision was set aside. [**Author's Note: Does the amendment to the *Legal Profession Act* to licence paralegals change how this case would be decided?**]

Goodwin v. Birkett

The CHRT decision of *Goodwin v. Birkett* [2004] C.H.R.D. No. 17, [2004] D.C.D.P. No 17, 2004 CHRT 29, 2004 TCDP 29 (the *Goodwin* decision) led to judicial review and then an appeal in the Federal Court, all from a complaint of sexual harassment. In recounting the facts, the CHRT found that the complainant's evidence of the sexual harassment was credible over the respondent's testimony after noting what sexual harassment is as follows:

> Sexual harassment is broadly defined as unwelcome conduct of a sexual nature that detrimentally affects the work environment or leads to adverse job-related consequences for the victims of harassment. Sexual harassment in the workplace attacks the dignity and self-respect of the victim, both as an employee and as a human being. (*Janzen v. Platy Enterprises Inc.*, [1989] 1 S.C.R. 1252)

Based upon the evidence and the definition set out above, the CHRT found as follows:

> I am also satisfied that his behaviour that night constituted sexual harassment. His conduct was unwelcome, of a sexual nature and detrimentally affected her work environment. She was no longer comfortable working at the same workplace with the Respondent, which was one of the factors in her decision to resign from PMCL. While the incident occurred during a single evening, the Respondent's conduct was severe enough to create a hostile working environment by the measure of any reasonable person (See *Canada (HRC) v. Canada (Armed Forces) and Franke* (1999), 34 C.H.R.R. D/140 at paras. 29–50 (F.C.T.D.)).
>
> I therefore find that the Respondent discriminated against the Complainant by sexually harassing her. The complaint is substantiated.

In so finding, the CHRT then determined what relief should be granted to the complainant and stated the following:

> Taking these circumstances into account, and considering the prevailing case law with respect to non-pecuniary damages involving harassment (see e.g., *Bushey v. Sharma*, 2003 CHRT 21; *Woiden v. Lynn (No.2)* (2002), 43 C.H.R.R. D/296 (C.H.R.T.)), I am satisfied that both of the Complainant's claims are more than justified. The Respondent is ordered to pay the Complainant the sum of $2,500 in compensation for her pain and suffering (s. 53(2)e)), and the sum of $2,500 in special compensation (s. 53(3)). Simple interest shall be payable on both of the monetary awards, to be calculated on a yearly basis, at a rate equivalent to the Bank Rate (Monthly series) set by the Bank of Canada. The interest will run from August 29, 1999.
>
> The Complainant has also requested that the Respondent be ordered to provide her with a letter of apology. In *Canada (Attorney-General) v. Stevenson*, 2003 FCT 341, the Federal Court found that the Act does not empower Tribunals to make such orders. The Complainant's request for a letter of apology is therefore denied.

The respondent made an application for judicial review to the Federal Court: *Birkett v. Canada (Human Rights Commission)*, 2007 FC 428, (2007), 312 F.T.R. 71 (the *Goodwin* Fed. Ct. case). The respondent submitted that there was no evidence for the CHRT to make its findings and that there were a number of breaches of the rules of natural justice and procedural fairness, including a claim of a reasonable apprehension of bias at the hearing. The court first looked at the standard of review and stated the following:

> As always, a prime issue is the degree of deference the Court owes the Tribunal. As noted by Mr. Justice Gibson in *International Longshore & Warehouse Union (Marine Section), Local 400 v. Oster (T.D.)*, 2001 FCT 1115 (CanLII), 2001 FCT 1115, 2001 FCT 1115 (CanLII), [2002] 2 F.C. 430, and the cases cited therein, the Canadian Human Rights Tribunal has superior expertise when it comes to fact finding and adjudication in a human rights context. He concluded that the standard of review in respect of questions of law was correctness, reasonableness *simpliciter* in respect of questions of mixed law and fact, and patent unreasonableness in respect of fact finding. There is nothing in the subsequent decisions of the Supreme Court in *Dr. Q. v. College of Physicians and Surgeons of British Columbia*, 2003 SCC 19 (CanLII), [2003] 1 S.C.R. 226 and *Law Society of New Brunswick v. Ryan*, 2003 SCC 20 (CanLII), [2003] 1 S.C.R. 247, to put the *Oster* decision into question when it comes to the pragmatic and functional approach to judicial review in this context. However, natural justice and procedural fairness are another matter all together. The Court owes the Tribunal no deference (*C.U.P.E. v. Ontario (Minister of Labour)*, 2003 SCC 29 (CanLII), 2003 SCC 29, 2003 SCC 29 (CanLII), [2003] 1 S.C.R. 539 and *Canada (Attorney General) v. Sketchley*, 2005 FCA 404 (CanLII), 2005 FCA 404).

The court then looked at the transcript, which existed for the whole two-day hearing and stated that "the Chair was scrupulously fair and helpful to both parties". After looking at specific situations in the hearing, the court found that the hearing was fair, and then it looked to the evidence:

> What it comes down to then is credibility. One point seized upon by the Chair was that Ms. Goodwin testified clearly that there had been two beds in the room and that she had removed her suitcase and clothing from one so that Mr. Birkett could sit on it. Mr. Birkett's memory was vague. He suggested at first that there was only one bed and then allowed that he might be wrong. Findings of fact are not to be disturbed unless patently unreasonable.
>
> As noted by Mr. Justice Evans in *Cepeda-Gutierrez et al. v. Canada (Minister of Citizenship and Immigration)* 1998 CanLII 8667 (F.C.), (1998), 157 F.T.R. 35 at paragraph 14:
>
>> It is well established that s. 18.1(4)(d) of the **Federal Court Act** does not authorize the court to substitute its view of the facts for that of the Board, which has the benefit not only of seeing and hearing the witnesses, but also of the expertise of its members in assessing evidence relating to facts that are within their area of specialized expertise. In addition, and more generally, considerations of the efficient allocation of decision-making resources between administrative agencies and the courts strongly indicate that the role to be played in fact-finding by the court on an application for judicial review should be merely residual. Thus, in order to attract judicial intervention under s. 18.1(4)(d), the applicant must satisfy the court, not only that the Board made a palpably erroneous finding of material fact, but also that the finding was made "without regard to the evidence" ...

In dismissing the application for judicial review, the court found as follows:

> In my opinion, the application of the Tribunal's findings of fact to the law was a mixed question. The Tribunal was entitled to deference on a reasonableness *simpliciter* standard. It was not unreasonable for the Tribunal to conclude that Mr. Birkett's conduct was unwelcome, of a sexual nature and detrimentally affected Ms. Goodwin's work environment. She was no longer comfortable working at the same workplace as him which was one of the factors leading to her resignation.

Finally on the question of double jeopardy, which the respondent characterizes as issue estoppel, Ms. Goodwin was entitled in law to avail herself of the *Canadian Human Rights Act* regardless of whether Mr. Birkett's employer conducted an inquiry into the issue or not (see *Tweten v. RTL Robinson Enterprises Ltd.*, [2004] C.H.R.D. No. 14 (QL)).

The matter was then appealed to the Federal Court of Appeal: *Birkett v. Canada (Human Rights Commission)*, [2008] F.C.J. No. 537, 2008 FCA 127, 165 A.C.W.S. (3d) 504 (the *Goodwin* Fed. C.A. case). As noted by the appellate court, the appeal from the Fed. Ct. decision "was limited to the issue of procedural fairness as the finding as to the characterization of the conduct giving rise to the complaint was not appealed". One of the matters examined was the fact that the CHRT did not allow the respondent to call and question the complainant's ex-husband.

The appellate court held as follows:

> The appellant now says that he was not allowed to call the complainant's ex-husband and that in addition to the evidence already described, the latter would have testified as to her general character. The application judge noted that the Tribunal had found that the complainant had not put her character in issue: see paragraph 24 of his reasons. Leaving aside that the decision not to call the complainant's ex-husband was made with the appellant's apparent consent, the fact remains that, since the complainant did not put her character in issue, it would have been improper to allow evidence of general character in any event: see *R. v. Beland*, [1987] 2 S.C.R. 398. While administrative tribunals are not bound by the strict rules of evidence, they ought, nonetheless, to be especially careful when an attempt is made to refute an allegation of a sexual misconduct by evidence of the victim's character. We find no error in the application judge's disposition of this question. As for the issue of the complainant's willingness to call the police, the relevant facts were admitted and the appellant was free to make what he could of them.

In conclusion, the appellate court found no errors were made and dismissed the appeal.

Yarinder Brar and the Royal Canadian Mounted Police

This is a group of cases involved Yarinder Brar and the Royal Canadian Mounted Police (RCMP) with the CHRT interim decision, *Brar v. R.C.M.P.*, 2007 CHRT 12 (the *Brar* decision), related to a joint motion made by the parties in which the CHRT ordered, *inter alia*, the following:

> [1] The Respondent's motion to clarify the nature and scope of the complaint which will be the subject matter of the inquiry before the Tribunal is disposed of on the basis that the Complainant will be allowed to make the allegations as set out in paragraphs 33–52, but excluding paragraphs 51(b), (f) and (h), of his Statement of Particulars dated June 23, 2006 and call evidence relating to those allegations, without precluding the Respondent from objecting to any of these allegations, or any of the witnesses coming forward to support these allegations on the basis of prejudice or other objections.

> [2] The Respondent's motion for an order prohibiting the Complainant from calling certain witnesses is dismissed, without prejudice to the Respondent to argue the relevance of the evidence, the timeliness of the evidence, any prejudice of the evidence, or the fact that the evidence should be subject to immunity, in context of the hearing.

> [3] The Respondent's motion for an order limiting the ambit of the testimony to be given by certain other witnesses is dismissed, without prejudice to object at the time of the hearing when these witnesses appear.

The respondent made application to judicially review the interlocutory orders to the Federal Court, *Canada (A.G.) v. Brar*, [2007] F.C.J. No. 1629, 2007 FC 1268, 162 A.C.W.S. (3d) 643 (the *Brar* Fed. Ct. case). The court looked at the CHRT's orders and stated the following:

> In his oral decision, the Tribunal Chairperson explained the basis for his decision, observing that:
>
> > [T]he reason I made this decision is because it is my view that there is a link between the allegations that I am allowing the Complainant to pursue and the complaint. Having come to this conclusion, this is not to preclude, once the hearing has started, and in the context, and more fulsome evidence — this does not preclude the Respondent from objecting to any of these allegations going forward, or any of the witnesses coming forward to support these allegations on the basis of relevance, or on the basis of prejudice, or whatever other objection the Respondent may seek to put forward at the time of the hearing.
> >
> > As I said, I am reluctant to eliminate allegations in a Statement of Particulars or put into a Statement of Claim, unless it is apparent that there is no relevance, or that they have absolutely nothing to do with the facts alleged in the complaint.
>
> While a number of matters were dealt with at the case management conference, this application is restricted to challenging the Tribunal's refusal to limit the ambit of Sgt. Brar's complaint. At this point in time, the RCMP does not take issue with the Tribunal's decision not to limit the list of witnesses, their testimony, or the RCMP's disclosure obligations.
>
> While the Attorney General has raised several issues, I am satisfied that the question of prematurity is dispositive of the matter.

The court then looked at the matter of the judicial review of interlocutory orders:

> As a general rule, in the absence of special circumstances, interlocutory rulings made by administrative tribunals should not be challenged until the tribunal has rendered its final decision: see, for example, *Sherman v. Canada (Customs and Revenue Agency)*, [2006] F.C.J. No. 912, 2006 FC 715 at para. 39, *Zündel v. Canada (Human Rights Commission)*, [2000] 4 F.C. 255, 256 N.R. 125 (C.A.), at para. 10 and *Szczecka v. Canada (Minister of Employment and Immigration)*, [1993] F.C.J. No. 934, 116 D.L.R. (4th) 333 at 335.
>
> There are a number of reasons why this is so, including the fact that the application may be rendered moot by the ultimate outcome of the case, and the risk of the fragmentation of the process, with the accompanying costs and delays. Also of concern is the absence of a full record at the preliminary stage, with the resultant inability to see how the ruling actually played out in the ultimate determination of the case. There is also the possibility that the tribunal may end up modifying its original ruling as the hearing unfolds.
>
> The fact that an issue may arguably relate to the tribunal's jurisdiction does not automatically justify immediate judicial review: see *Air Canada v. Lorenz*, [2000] 1 F.C. 494 para. 13. See also Brown and Evans, *Judicial Review of Administrative Action in Canada* (Toronto: Canvasback Publishing, 1998), at 3: 4100.
>
> Many of the underlying policy concerns which support the principle that interlocutory decisions of inferior tribunals should not ordinarily be subject to immediate judicial review arise in this case.
>
> In particular, it is clear that the ruling of the Tribunal Chairperson did not finally determine the scope of the hearing to be held before the Canadian Human Rights Tribunal. Indeed, the Chairperson was very careful to reserve the final decision in this regard to the Tribunal member ultimately dealing with the merits of Sgt. Brar's complaint.
>
> That is, the Chairperson specifically preserved the right of the RCMP to object to particular post-complaint allegations being advanced by Sgt. Brar on whatever basis it deemed appropriate, deferring the final determination of the scope of the hearing to the hearing on the merits.

In dismissing the application for judicial review, the court found the following:

> The fact that the hearing into Sgt. Brar's complaint may be shortened by an immediate ruling from this Court is not determinative. In this regard, I note that in the *Lorenz* case, Justice Evans declined to entertain an application to judicially review a decision regarding an allegation of bias, preferring to wait until the Board had rendered its final decision. This notwithstanding the fact that there were several weeks of hearing left to go, which would have been invalidated, had the allegations of bias ultimately been sustained.
>
> Moreover, as was the case in *Lorenz*, I am of the view that the possibility of waste in this case is mitigated by the fact that it is not plain and obvious that the Tribunal is without jurisdiction to entertain the allegations in issue.

Powell v. United Parcel Service Canada Ltd.

In *Powell v. United Parcel Service Canada Ltd.*, 2008 CHRT 43 (the *Powell* decision), the respondent made a motion to confirm an "alleged" settlement of the complainant's human rights complaint and bring the matter before the CHRT to a close. The respondent claims that a settlement was reached by the parties after the matter was referred to the CHRT by the Commission, but then the complainant, after changing counsel, refused to sign either the proposed minutes of settlement or the release. The respondent therefore brought the motion to confirm settlement upon which the CHRT ruled in this matter. It was first noted that according "to section 48 of the *Act*, settlements of any complaints that are reached before the commencement of a hearing must be referred to the Commission for approval or rejection". As to the meaning of section 48 and what occurred in this matter, the CHRT stated the following:

> Prior to the commencement of the hearing, no complaint can be settled without Commission approval. The Federal Court pointed out in *Loyer v. Air Canada*, 2006 FC 1172 (CanLII), 2006 FC 1172 at para. 87, that:
>
>> There has been little judicial consideration of section 48 of the *Canadian Human Rights Act*. However, when the section is read in context, consistent with the aims of the Act as a whole, and <u>in light of the public interest mandate of the Canadian Human Rights Commission, it is clear that the section is there to ensure that the Commissioners themselves have input into settlements</u>, so as to ensure that the remedial goals of the Act are adequately addressed in the resolution of individual complaints. [emphasis added]
>
>> Under s. 48, there is no option made available to the parties to choose whether or not to submit the settlement to the Commission. In the English rendering of the section, it is stated that the settlement "shall be referred to the Commission". In the French rendering, the parties "present" the terms of the settlement for approval by the Commission. This requirement is consistent with the finding in *Loyer* that the section exists to ensure that the Commissioners have an input into settlements to make certain that the remedial goals of the *Act* are adequately addressed in the resolution of the individual complaints. Without such input, there can be no settlement.
>
>> There is no indication that the Commission has either explicitly or tacitly approved the alleged settlement between Ms. Powell and UPS. Absent such approval, it cannot be said that there exists a settlement bringing about an end to the Tribunal's inquiry into the complaint.

The respondent then argued that there was no need for the Commission to approve the settlement as the matter was not prior to the commencement of the hearing; steps such as the case management process and the motion being heard indicated that the CHRT had embarked on the hearing process. The CHRT found the following in respect of that position:

While the *Act* refers to a "hearing" and an "inquiry", there is no mention made anywhere of a "hearing process". The Federal Court considered these two terms ("hearing" and "inquiry") in *Canada (Canadian Human Rights Commission) v. Canada Post Corp.*, 2004 FC 81 (CanLII), 2004 FC 81 at para. 17. The Court pointed out that s. 50 of the *Act* makes reference to each of these expressions separately, and treats them as distinct notions. The Court was sitting in review of a ruling by the Tribunal on a preliminary motion that the respondent had filed seeking the dismissal of the complaint prior to the start of the hearing into the merits of the complaint. The Commission had argued that the Tribunal was required to conduct the hearing before dismissing the complaint and that the motion was therefore premature. The Court disagreed. It concluded that although, according to s. 50, a Tribunal must conduct an "inquiry" into every complaint referred to it, there is no requirement that there be a "hearing" in every case. The motion to dismiss was thus not premature.

I take it, therefore, from the Court's finding, that the meaning to be assigned to the term "hearing" is the conduct of the actual hearing into the merits of the complaint itself. It does not encompass any preceding activity, including preliminary motions that the Tribunal may entertain in order to "clear the procedural underbrush" (*Canada Post* at para. 14), such as the motion to dismiss that had been brought in that case.

The motion was therefore dismissed.

Zhou v. National Research Council et al.

In *Zhou v. National Research Council et al.*, 2009 CHRT 11 (the *Zhou* decision), the complainant made an application to adjourn a scheduled hearing due to newly retained counsel needing time to prepare. The request was for three months, but the CHRT granted a two-week adjournment with the following reasons:

> [The] Tribunal must weigh the goal of resolving human rights complaints in a timely manner against the requirement to be fair to all parties and to provide them with a full and ample opportunity to present their case (*Leger v. Canadian National Railway Company*, Interim Ruling, November 26, 1999 (CHRT); stay application dismissed [2000] F.C.J. 243 (T.D.)).
>
> A two week adjournment in the present case will give counsel 5 weeks to prepare. There is, therefore, enough time to prepare so that the Complainant's right to a fair hearing is not compromised.
>
> Moreover, it must be noted that on October 3, 2008, all of the parties agreed to set down four weeks for a hearing in April and May of the following year. Dr. Zhou had ample time to seek counsel or the assistance of his bargaining agent. However, it was not until March 18, 2009, a month before the commencement of the hearing, that the Tribunal was informed that counsel had been retained to represent Dr. Zhou.
>
> Translation services for the hearing have been booked and confirmed. The hearing rooms have been reserved. Staffing resources have been allocated. Other cases that could have been set for hearing during this time period were not set down for that time.
>
> The Tribunal must run an efficient hearing system in order to achieve its legislative mandate to hear and resolve complaints expeditiously (s. 48.9(1) of the CHRA; *Canada Post Corporation v. PSAC and the CHRC*, 2008 FC 223 at para. 274; *Nova Scotia Construction Safety Association, Collins and Kelly v. Nova Scotia Human Rights Commission and Davison*, 2006 NSCA 63 at para. 76). A hearing requires the dedication of considerable financial and human resources. Those resources cannot be reallocated without significant disruption to the whole system, especially at this stage in the process. Such disruptions have an impact on the timeliness not only of the present case, but also of other cases in the system. For those reasons, an adjournment is granted only in cases where proceeding will clearly have an impact on the fairness of the hearing.

REVIEW QUESTIONS

1. What is the enabling legislation for the CHRT?
2. Where would you find the practices and procedures of the CHRT?
3. List five grounds (or groups) protected under the *Human Rights Act* from being discriminated against or harassed.
4. Pursuant to the *CHRA*, how does the duty to act fairly apply to the CHRT?
5. What does the privative clause of the *FCA* related to the CHRT prevent and allow, and under what circumstances?
6. What rule(s) gives discretion and flexibility to the CHRT in applying the CHRT Rules?
7. What rule(s) deal with disclosure, and what is the result of insufficient disclosure?
8. What rule(s) deal with motions, and what is the appropriate procedure to have a motion dealt with by the CHRT?
9. What jurisdiction is the CHRT given to reconsider a decision under the various procedures and practices of the CHRT?
10. How do the various procedures and practices of the CHRT deal with mediation before the CHRT?
11. How do the various procedures and practices of the CHRT deal with giving access to persons before the CHRT and dealing with their needs?

EXERCISE

Based upon the facts of the *Desormeaux* decision briefed in the chapter, summarize the steps this matter took before the CHRT to its decision and then briefly discuss how it got to the court system.

Appendix 9.1
Overview of Procedural Stages of a Complaint under the *CHRA*

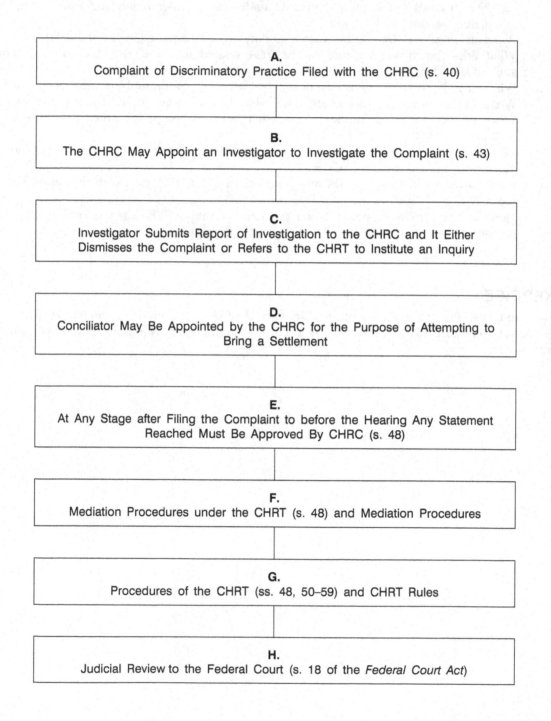

A.
Complaint of Discriminatory Practice Filed with the CHRC (s. 40)

B.
The CHRC May Appoint an Investigator to Investigate the Complaint (s. 43)

C.
Investigator Submits Report of Investigation to the CHRC and It Either Dismisses the Complaint or Refers to the CHRT to Institute an Inquiry

D.
Conciliator May Be Appointed by the CHRC for the Purpose of Attempting to Bring a Settlement

E.
At Any Stage after Filing the Complaint to before the Hearing Any Statement Reached Must Be Approved By CHRC (s. 48)

F.
Mediation Procedures under the CHRT (s. 48) and Mediation Procedures

G.
Procedures of the CHRT (ss. 48, 50–59) and CHRT Rules

H.
Judicial Review to the Federal Court (s. 18 of the *Federal Court Act*)

Appendix 9.2
Excerpts from the CHRT's Guide to the Tribunal Process[1]

OVERVIEW

This booklet consists of five parts.

- Part 1 describes the roles of the Canadian Human Rights Commission and the Canadian Human Rights Tribunal and explains who should use the guide and why.

- Part 2 explains how a typical case unfolds once it has been referred to the Tribunal.

- Part 3 sets out the steps that parties must take once a case has been referred to the Tribunal.

- Part 4 explains the terms and concepts that appear in Parts 1, 2 and 3.

- Part 5 consists of samples of some of the documents you are likely to encounter.

HOW TO READ THIS GUIDE

If you are involved in a case that has been referred to the Tribunal, you will find it helpful to familiarize yourself with the Tribunal process that is about to unfold by reading this guide. Part 2 gives you a general, overall view of the process and time lines. Part 3 describes the steps you will follow as the process unfolds. (If a lawyer will be acting on your behalf, most of the steps described in Part 3 will be conducted by your lawyer.) Throughout the guide, specialized terms appear in bold blue type. Terms identified in this manner are explained in alphabetical order in Part 4. Sample documents can be found in Part 5.

A WORD ABOUT ICONS
The icons below are used in the margins to help you navigate through the guide.

Points to remember

Important actions to be taken

Sample documents to be found in Part 5. The number inside the icon indicates which document number it is in Part 5. The name of the document is underlined in the text.

5

---

[1] Source: CHRT Website <www.chrt-tcdp.gc.ca>

From referral to decision: the big picture

This part (and the timeline that follows it) describes the chain of events that unfolds from the moment a case is referred to the Tribunal until the Tribunal issues its decision. The entire process can take a year or more.

BEFORE THE HEARING

Shortly after receiving a referral from the **Canadian Human Rights Commission**, the Tribunal **Registry** sends a letter to each of the parties:

* the **complainant(s)**
* the **respondent(s)**
* the Commission

The letter asks you to advise, within 21 days (three weeks), whether you agree to participate in a one-day **mediation** of the complaint by a Tribunal member. The letter will include a copy of the Tribunal's mediation procedures to assist you in making this decision. If all parties agree to mediation, the Tribunal **Registry Officer** will contact the parties to determine a date for mediation within the next few weeks.

7

What happens next? A guide to the Tribunal process

If the mediation succeeds in resolving the complaint, the Tribunal's file is closed after the minutes of settlement have been signed by the parties and approved by the Commission in accordance with the *Canadian Human Rights Act*.

If mediation does not resolve the complaint, or if the parties do not agree to mediation, the Registry Officer will contact the parties to determine their availability to participate in the first of three to four case management conference calls with a Tribunal member. This case-planning phase assists the Tribunal in understanding:

- whether the parties will be represented by a lawyer and, if so, the name and address of the lawyer(s)
- how many witnesses (including expert witnesses) each party plans to call at the hearing
- how many days each party will take to present their side of the story
- whether there are any preliminary matters you would like to raise
- what remedy you are seeking (complainant and Commission only)
- dates for parties to file a statement of particulars surrounding the complaint
- dates for parties to complete disclosure of witnesses and documents
- whether it will be possible to jointly submit an agreed statement of facts
- when, where and in what language you would like the hearing to take place
- other matters, such as whether you, or your witnesses, require any special services (for example, sign language interpretation or a sound system)
- dates when parties can be available for a next case management conference call

If either of the parties wants a particular issue dealt with before the hearing, he or she should raise the matter with the Tribunal at the first case management conference. However, some pre-hearing issues need to be resolved by a more formal process. For example, when a respondent feels that the Tribunal does not have the authority to decide the case, he or she must file a motion with the Tribunal requesting a ruling on the matter. A motion can be filed at any time before or during the hearing, but should generally be brought as soon as the party becomes aware of the need for a ruling from the Tribunal on an issue.

The Tribunal will outline a process for dealing with the motion. In some cases, the Tribunal will decide the motion right away. In other circumstances, the Tribunal may reserve its decision until a later point in the hearing process.

During the pre-hearing stage, the parties will gather all the documents they intend to put forward as evidence at the hearing, including summaries of the testimony that their witnesses will give and the written reports of expert witnesses. The complainant will also decide what remedy to ask for. These documents, as well as all other documents that are relevant to the case, even if they will not be relied on at the hearing, are then copied and exchanged among the parties in a process called disclosure. The parties also exchange lists of documents that are relevant to the case but that they don't plan to disclose because they consider these documents privileged. In preparing for the hearing, the parties will also develop their arguments. This involves developing a line of argument to explain why the Tribunal should reach a particular conclusion in this case and may include reference to earlier decisions of human rights tribunals or the courts. Finally, it means being prepared to explain why the arguments put forward by the other side are not applicable to the facts of your case.

1/ Once the hearing is scheduled, you will receive from the Registry Officer an official Notice of Hearing, usually well in advance of the hearing date.

Approximately one month before the hearing, the Tribunal sends a letter to all parties telling them how many copies of each document they'll need to bring with them to the hearing.

> **NOTE:**
> *At any point in the process, the parties may reach a settlement instead of seeking a decision from the Tribunal.*

AT THE HEARING

Hearings are most often conducted in the town or city where the alleged discrimination took place. The location is often a hotel or conference centre. In larger cities, it is not uncommon for hearings to be held in a federal courthouse.

9

What happens next? A guide to the Tribunal process

On average, a hearing lasts 10 days. Present at the hearing are the complainant, the respondent, their respective lawyers, the lawyer for the Canadian Human Rights Commission (unless the Commission decides not to participate in the hearing), the various witnesses who will be testifying on behalf of the parties, the court reporter, a Registry Officer and the member or members of the Tribunal who will be hearing the case. The media, members of the general public and interested parties may also attend the hearing.

As the hearing begins, each party is asked to introduce herself or himself. The Tribunal then invites the Commission (if appearing) and complainant to make an opening statement, which summarizes what they intend to prove during the hearing. The respondent may then deliver an opening statement or choose to do so when presenting his or her case.

Then the Commission and the complainant present evidence intended to demonstrate that discrimination occurred. The evidence generally consists of documents and testimony from witnesses. (The process of questioning one's own witness to elicit testimony is called direct examination.) In addition to proving that the respondent's actions constituted discrimination, the Commission and the complainant may also attempt to prove that the complainant sustained damages as a result of the respondent's actions. The respondent is entitled to question the witnesses who testify on behalf of the Commission and the complainant. This cross-examination may be intended to cast doubt on the version of the facts put forward by the witnesses. Once the respondent has had a chance to cross-examine the witnesses, the Commission and the complainant may re-examine their witnesses to clarify, or to elaborate, on new issues raised during cross-examination. The members of the Tribunal may also ask questions of the witnesses to more fully understand their evidence.

It is not uncommon for a witness to spend a few hours giving testimony. If the Commission is a party to the case, the witnesses called by the complainant should not repeat the case put forward by the Commission's witnesses; however, the complainant can call witnesses to amplify or supplement (or even contradict) the case put forward by the Commission.

The Tribunal then invites the respondent to respond to the allegations (and the evidence called in support of them) by calling his or her own witnesses and documentary evidence. During this portion of the hearing, the respondent may present evidence that is intended to contradict, or cast doubt on, the case presented by the Commission and the complainant. Both the Commission and the complainant are entitled to cross-examine the respondent's witnesses. The respondent can re-examine his or her witnesses in regard to new issues raised during cross-examination. Finally, the Commission and the complainant may, if allowed by the Tribunal, be entitled to present reply evidence (also subject to cross-examination by the respondent). The members of the Tribunal may ask questions of any reply witnesses.

When either side wishes the Tribunal to admit into evidence a witness statement without calling the witness to testify, that testimony may be admitted into evidence, with the Tribunal's permission, through the use of a sworn document called an affidavit. This statement then becomes part of the official public record as if the witness had testified at the hearing.

On the other hand, one of the parties may wish to have a document or a witness statement admitted into evidence, but the other party may disagree. The Tribunal will then hear arguments about why a particular piece of evidence should or shouldn't be admitted and will rule on its admissibility.

The Tribunal considers the documents and the statements of all the witnesses and decides how credible they are and how much weight to give to the evidence presented by each side in the case.

After the witnesses have finished being examined, the Commission and the complainant are each given the opportunity to link all the evidence together into a narrative that summarizes what the respondent did to the complainant and why those actions should be considered discrimination within the meaning of the *Canadian Human Rights Act*. This segment of the proceedings is called the final argument. At this point, the Commission and the complainant explain why the evidence proves that discrimination occurred within the meaning of the Act. The respondent then presents his or her own final argument with reasons why the evidence does not support the conclusion that discrimination occurred or, if the respondent acknowledges that his or her actions were discriminatory, why the discrimination was justified. The Commission and the complainant are then given the opportunity to respond to new points raised by the respondent. This is called reply argument.

After the hearing

When the Tribunal has heard all the arguments, it adjourns the case and reserves its decision. The Tribunal strives to complete its decision within four months of the close of the hearing.

If a party is dissatisfied with the decision, he or she may seek judicial review of the Tribunal's decision by filing an application in the Federal Court within 30 days of the date the Tribunal's decision was first communicated to him or her. If the Court disagrees with the Tribunal's ruling, the case is generally referred back to the original one- or three-member Tribunal, which will reconsider certain aspects of the inquiry based on the directions of the Court. However, in certain circumstances, the Federal Court may direct that the entire process begin anew before a Tribunal made up of a different member, or members. Finally, it is possible for the Court to simply set aside the Tribunal's decision.

Part 3

What you'll need to do

As a complainant or a respondent in a case before the Tribunal, you will be given the chance to present your side of the story. This part details what you'll need to do to prepare for and participate in your hearing. If you are represented by counsel, your lawyer will normally do this for you.

BEFORE THE HEARING

Mediation

Shortly after receiving notification that the **Canadian Human Rights Commission** has referred your complaint for inquiry, you'll receive a letter from the Tribunal **Registry** asking you to advise, within 21 days (three weeks), whether you agree to participate in a one-day **mediation** facilitated by a Tribunal **member**. The letter will include a copy of the Tribunal's mediation procedures.

If all parties agree to mediation, the Tribunal **Registry Officer** will contact you to determine a date for mediation within the next few weeks.

If the mediation succeeds in resolving the complaint, the Tribunal file will be closed once the **minutes of settlement** are signed by the parties and approved by the Commission, in accordance with the *Canadian Human Rights Act*.

15

What happens next? A guide to the Tribunal process

Case management

If mediation does not resolve the complaint, or a party declines mediation, the Registry Officer will contact you to determine your availability to participate in the first of three to four case management conference calls with a Tribunal member. A letter from the Tribunal Registry will confirm the date and time of the first conference call.

Included with the letter, you will find:

* a copy of this guide
* a copy of the Tribunal's **Rules of Procedure**
* a copy of the *Canadian Human Rights Act*

The first conference call will occur shortly after mediation has either been declined or was unsuccessful in resolving the complaint.

On the first conference call, the member will ask you to indicate:

* whether the parties will be represented by a lawyer and, if so, the name and address of the lawyer(s)
* how many witnesses (including expert witnesses) each party plans to call at the hearing
* how many days each party will take to present their side of the story
* whether there are any preliminary matters you would like to raise
* what remedy you are seeking (complainant and Commission only)
* dates by which the parties can file a statement of particulars surrounding the complaint
* dates by which the parties can complete their disclosure of witnesses and documents
* whether it will be possible to jointly submit an agreed statement of facts
* when, where and in what language you would like the hearing to take place
* other matters, such as whether you, or your witnesses, require any special services (for example, sign language interpretation or a sound system)
* dates when parties can be available for a next case management conference call

Following the first conference call, a summary of the discussion that took place and the directions that were given by the member will be confirmed by the Registry Officer in a letter to you. The letter will also confirm the deadlines fixed by the member for the exchange of certain kinds of information among the parties, a process called **disclosure**. Specifically, disclosure involves **serving** the other parties with:

- a list of all documents in your possession that are relevant to the case, whether or not you intend to rely on them during the hearing, *including* documents you don't plan to disclose because you consider them **privileged**

  ➤ with this list, include copies of all documents in your possession that are relevant to the case, whether or not you intend to rely on them during the hearing, *excluding* the documents you consider privileged

- a brief written summary of the topics you plan to address during the hearing, the facts you intend to prove and the **arguments** you plan to present; the **complainant** and the Commission must also explain the remedy they're seeking

- a statement of particulars

- a list of the witnesses you plan to call and a summary of the **testimony** they will give (see **will-say statement**)

- written reports prepared by expert witnesses.

All of the items above (except for actual copies of your relevant document disclosure) must also be **filed** with (delivered to) the Tribunal. There are rules about how a document can be served or filed, and about the proof you'll need that a document was served. See the glossary (under serving and filing) for more information.

The date of the hearing is not fixed until after the second case management conference call, which normally occurs when disclosure is completed. Disclosure deadlines for the complainant and the respondent may be different, but give all the parties about a month to produce the required documents. The complainant and the Commission are expected to disclose their documents, statement of particulars (including remedies sought), witness lists/will-say statements and expert witness reports to the respondent, and the respondent provides similar information to the complainant and the Commission. The

17

complainant and the Commission are usually given a further two to three weeks to provide additional disclosure in response to matters arising from the respondent's disclosure. However, depending on the circumstances of each case, the timelines for disclosure may change.

If you fail to disclose a document, you may not be allowed to introduce it into evidence at the hearing. Similarly, you may not be permitted to examine witnesses or raise legal issues (including remedy sought) that you have failed to identify in advance. The Tribunal will allow a party to rely on evidence not disclosed before the hearing only in exceptional circumstances. You also have an ongoing duty to disclose any new relevant document as soon as it comes into your possession and any new witness or legal issue as soon as it comes to your attention.

On the second case management conference call, which normally occurs following completion of disclosure, the member will ask you to:

- identify any concerns regarding, for example, an apparent failure to make full disclosure of documents and/or witnesses
- confirm the length of time you will require at the hearing
- confirm your dates of availability for the hearing
- identify your availability for the next case management conference call

Again, following the conference call, a summary of the discussion that took place and the directions that were given by the member will be confirmed by the Registry Officer in a letter to you. The letter will also confirm the dates and place fixed for the hearing. Later, but well in advance of the start of the hearing, the Registry Officer assigned to your case will send you an official Notice of Hearing.

A third conference call normally occurs halfway between the time of the second conference call and the first day set for the hearing. At this conference, the member will discuss with you any issues that need to be resolved in order for the hearing to proceed on the dates fixed.

A fourth case management conference call may be convened by the member to deal with any problems that you may be having in preparing for the hearing.

18

Preparing for the hearing

The information you provide to the other side outlines the evidence and arguments you plan to present at the hearing. Before you can forward this information, you must figure out the best way to tell your side of the story. If you are the complainant, you must prove what you say the respondent did and show why the actions constitute discrimination under the *Canadian Human Rights Act*. If you are seeking a specific remedy, you need to present evidence of the damage you suffered as a result of the respondent's actions. If you are the respondent, you should decide what evidence you can use to challenge the allegations against you.

Whether you are the complainant or the respondent, your presentation to the Tribunal will be made up of evidence and legal submissions or arguments. Evidence generally consists of documents and witness testimony that attest to the truth of what you are presenting as the facts of the case. For example, if you are claiming damages from a discriminatory dismissal, you might use an income tax return to prove that you had reduced earnings that year, or a personnel file to prove that you were about to be promoted before you lost your job.

In preparing your case, you may plan to use witnesses, including expert witnesses. It is possible that a witness you plan to examine at the hearing does not wish to appear before the Tribunal. If you feel that your presentation will be less effective in the absence of the witness, you can compel a witness to attend the hearing by serving her or him with a subpoena. You can request a subpoena from the Tribunal by writing to the Registry Officer assigned to your case and explaining why that person must be called as a witness. If you require the witness to bring to the hearing any documents or items that he or she has control over and that relate to the complaint, you will need to request a subpoena *duces tecum*. If the Tribunal grants your request to subpoena a witness, the Registry will provide you with a signed subpoena, which you must then arrange to have served on the witness.

Once you have gathered and copied every document you intend to file as evidence in the case, compiled a list of all relevant documents, prepared a list of the witnesses you plan to call at the hearing and summarized what they will say, and obtained more detailed reports of the testimony of your expert

19

What happens next? A guide to the Tribunal process

witnesses, you must deliver copies of all these documents to the other side. You must also deliver copies of your statement of particulars. The statement of particulars should list the topics you plan to address, set out the facts you intend to prove and state the conclusions you plan to draw from the evidence (complainants must also set out the remedy sought). File all the above items (except for actual copies of your documentary disclosure) with your Registry Officer.

> ✔ DISCLOSURE CHECKLIST
>
> *Served on the other parties and filed with the Tribunal Registry by the disclosure deadline:*
> - ❑ *document list*
> - ❑ *witness list*
> - ❑ *will-say statements for every witness*
> - ❑ *expert witness reports*
> - ❑ *statement of particulars*
>
> *Served on the other parties by the disclosure deadline (but not filed with the Tribunal Registry):*
> - ❑ *copies of all relevant documents, including affidavits, except privileged documents*
>
> *Filed with the Tribunal Registry by the disclosure deadline:*
> - ❑ *letter to the Tribunal Registry confirming that you have met the disclosure deadline*

Developing your presentation

If you are the complainant, proving that you were discriminated against may require more than simply proving what was done to you. If you are the respondent, countering the complaint may require more than simply refuting the facts alleged by the complainant. It is not uncommon for the complainant and the respondent to agree about the facts but disagree about whether they actually add up to discrimination within the meaning of the *Canadian Human Rights Act*. For example, a respondent may admit that the reason that an individual was not hired was because of a disability. However, the respondent may also believe that the individual, because of his or her disability, is not capable of performing the essential duties of the job, even with reasonable accommodation. The Tribunal, based on the evidence, will decide whether there is a justifiable reason for not hiring the individual.

If you are the complainant, you must explain how your evidence supports the conclusion that discrimination occurred. You may wish to use past human rights cases decided by the Tribunal or the courts.

If you are the respondent, you can counter the complainant's argument by:

- explaining why the case law relied on by the complainant is not applicable to the facts in your case

- citing case law that dismissed a complaint made in a similar situation

Final preparations for the hearing

About four weeks before the hearing, you will receive a letter from the Tribunal Registry explaining the Tribunal's procedures on the filing of exhibits and case law. The letter will ask that you prepare a set number of copies of all the documents and other exhibits you plan to file with the Tribunal, as well as the case law that you plan to rely on during the hearing (see book of authorities).

You will be expected to prepare a copy of each document for: the Tribunal Chairperson, two additional Tribunal members (unless the case is being heard by only one member), the official record, the court reporter, witnesses and all other parties to the case.

Since many of the cases you may be relying on at the hearing will already be familiar to the Tribunal, you need not copy all these cases in their entirety. Your Registry Officer will send you an alphabetical index of human rights decisions most often cited. If a case you plan to refer to is listed in this Book of Jurisprudence, you need only copy the pages of the case that you plan to refer to during the hearing.

Assemble all your documentary evidence. Exhibits should be submitted in three-ring binders (maximum width: 2 inches), indexed, divided with tabs and pages numbered. Documents should be placed in the binder in the order in which they will be filed as exhibits. For example, tab 1 will be the first exhibit filed.

Make copies (as instructed by your Registry Officer) to file with the Tribunal. Select the legal cases that you plan to rely on during your final

21

What happens next? A guide to the Tribunal process

argument. Photocopy in their entirety the cases that are not contained in the Tribunal's Book of Jurisprudence and the relevant excerpts of those that are. Assemble all the cases and excerpts in alphabetical order. Prepare an index. Make the required number of copies. Bind the authorities and insert a tab at the start of each case. Also, find out what type of oath or affirmation each of your witnesses will wish to take when they are sworn in. This information will be requested by your Registry Officer at the hearing.

> **NOTE:**
> *Either party can file a motion at any time before or during the hearing, asking the Tribunal to rule on a particular matter. The Tribunal, however, may not always rule on the matter at the time the motion is brought.*

AT THE HEARING

The objective of the hearing is to allow the Tribunal to hear all the relevant evidence and arguments of the case so it can decide whether discrimination occurred. If you are the complainant, the hearing is your chance to explain how you were discriminated against and what remedy you are entitled to. If you are the respondent, the hearing is your chance to refute the allegations and the claim for remedy.

Unlike in a criminal case, where the Crown must prove the existence of the alleged facts beyond a reasonable doubt, the standard of proof in a human rights case is less stringent. The threshold for substantiating a complaint is that, based on the facts, it is more likely than not that discrimination occurred. In other words, the complainant needs to tip the scales of probability by only a small margin. If the complainant succeeds in establishing a *prima facie* case, then the respondent must justify his or her actions, explaining why acts that may appear to be discriminatory were not.

Hearing day

3/ When you arrive at your hearing, the Registry Officer will ask you to complete a <u>**Record of Appearance**</u>. This form requires the name of every witness you plan to call over the course of the hearing (you can be a witness on your own behalf) and the type of **oath** or affirmation that each of your witnesses wishes to take when they are sworn in. You should come to your hearing with this information. The Registry Officer will have a bible available. You and your witnesses may also bring your own holy books.

Several people may be present at the hearing. They include the complainant, the respondent, their respective lawyers, the lawyer for the **Canadian Human Rights Commission** (if the Commission decides to participate at the hearing), the witnesses that will be testifying on behalf of the **parties**, the Registry Officer responsible for the case, the court reporter, and the member or members of the Tribunal who will hear the case. **Interested parties**, journalists and members of the public may also be present in the hearing room. The hearing is a public proceeding, unless otherwise ordered by the Tribunal, and anything said in the hearing room usually becomes part of the public record.

Once all the parties have filled in and returned their Record of Appearance forms, the Registry Officer will call the hearing to order, introduce the Chair and any other members of the Tribunal — a Tribunal always consists of either one or three members — and can call for appearances of, or on behalf of, the parties. The normal order for introductions is: the Commission, the complainant, the respondent and any interested parties. The parties and their lawyers each take turns standing up and introducing themselves.

During the hearing, the custom is to address the Chairperson as "Mr./Madam Chairperson" and the other members of the panel as "Member or Mr./Mrs./Ms. (*Surname*)."

The Tribunal Chair will then invite each party to make an **opening statement**. When invited to make your opening statement, you should briefly summarize the main points that you plan to establish before the Tribunal during your presentation.

23

What happens next? A guide to the Tribunal process

A Typical Hearing Room

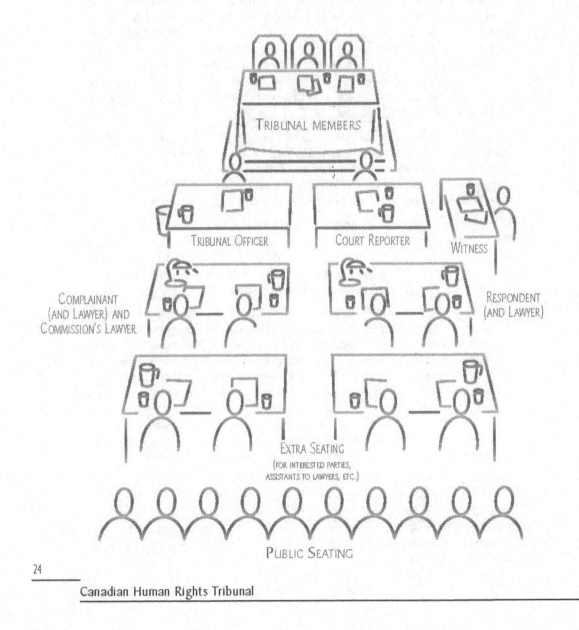

When opening statements are completed, the Tribunal Chair will invite the Commission, if it is a participant, to call its first witness. The Commission will usually call the complainant as its first witness. If the Commission is not participating in the hearing, the complainant will be asked to call the first witness. (As the complainant, you may wish to take the stand and state the facts as you understand them.) The complainant and the Commission call their witnesses before the respondent is invited to call his or her witnesses. When the Commission or the complainant is finished questioning each witness (also called **direct examination** of a witness), the respondent is invited to **cross-examine** that witness.

After the respondent has cross-examined a witness, the Commission or the complainant is offered the opportunity to **re-examine** the witness. The purpose of this re-examination is to clarify or explain new issues that arose during cross-examination. No other topics may be introduced at this stage. The Tribunal **member(s)** may also ask questions of the witnesses.

It is not uncommon for a witness to spend a few hours giving testimony. If the Commission is a party to the case, the witnesses called by the complainant should not duplicate the case put forward by the Commission's witnesses. However, the complainant can call witnesses to amplify or supplement (or even contradict) the case put forward by the Commission.

Once all of the witnesses appearing on behalf of the Commission and the complainant have given their evidence, the Tribunal will invite the respondent to call his or her witnesses. (Respondents may also take the stand and testify on their own behalf.) During this portion of the hearing, the respondent calls and examines witnesses with a view to presenting evidence that supports his or her case. Both the Commission and the complainant are entitled to cross-examine the respondent's witnesses. After the Commission or the complainant cross-examines each of the witnesses, the respondent may re-examine them to address any new matters arising from the cross-examination. The members of the Tribunal may also ask questions of the respondent's witnesses.

When any party wants to present as evidence the statement of a witness who is unable to appear at the hearing, this statement can be admitted into evidence at the hearing in the form of an **affidavit**, an agreed statement of facts or an unsworn statement. Any of these documents, if accepted by the Tribunal, becomes part of the official public record as if the witness had testified at the hearing.

25

What happens next? A guide to the Tribunal process

During the portion of the hearing dedicated to the presentation of evidence, it is important that you stick to the facts. You'll have an opportunity later in the hearing to draw conclusions from those facts.

An exception to this rule arises if there is a matter, other than the merits of the complaint, that needs to be decided in the course of the hearing. For example, perhaps one party objects to another party calling a particular witness or filing a particular document into evidence. In that case, the Tribunal will invite both parties to make a submission about why a particular witness's testimony or piece of documentary evidence should or shouldn't be admitted. After hearing submissions, the Tribunal will often render a ruling on the objection (dismissing or upholding it), but sometimes it will defer ruling on the matter until later in the hearing process.

After the respondent's witnesses have been examined, cross-examined and re-examined, the Commission and complainant may be given an opportunity to reply to new facts or issues introduced by the respondent that were not covered during the complainant's or Commission's direct evidence. Reply evidence can relate only to new matters arising out of the respondent's evidence.

When all of the evidence has been presented, the Commission and the complainant are each given the opportunity to explain in narrative form how the evidence supports their factual assertions regarding what the respondent did to the complainant and why, based on the case law, the respondent's actions should be considered discrimination within the meaning of the *Canadian Human Rights Act*. This segment of the proceedings is called the final argument. The respondent will then be given the opportunity to present his or her final argument. As the respondent, your argument should demonstrate why the evidence presented by the parties, together with the case law, does not support a finding of discrimination or, if it does, why your actions were justified in the circumstances. This portion of the hearing allows each party to draw together all the threads of evidence in his or her favour and to link them to the conclusions he or she would like the Tribunal to reach.

The Tribunal's job is ultimately to consider all the documents and witness testimony, determine how much weight to give to the evidence presented by each side in the case, and assess the arguments presented by each party.

AFTER THE HEARING

When the Tribunal has heard all the arguments, it usually adjourns the case and reserves its decision, rather than rendering its decision immediately at the conclusion of the hearing. The Tribunal strives to render its decision within four months of the close of the hearing. A copy of the decision will be sent to you by courier and e-mail (if possible) the same day it is released.

If you are dissatisfied with the Tribunal's decision and wish to have that decision reviewed by a higher court, you must file an application for judicial review in the Federal Court within 30 days of the date the Tribunal's decision was first communicated to you.

27

What happens next? A guide to the Tribunal process

Appendix 9.3
The CHRT's Practice Note No. 2[2]

PRACTICE NOTE

CANADIAN HUMAN RIGHTS TRIBUNAL PRACTICE NOTE No. 2

12 June 2009

RE: Representation of Parties by Non-Lawyers

1. On occasion, parties to the inquiry process are represented by non-lawyers.

2. The Tribunal expects non-lawyer representatives to accept the obligations of participating in the inquiry process by:
    a. treating the Members and staff of the Tribunal, as well as the other participants in the inquiry process, with courtesy and respect;
    b. obtaining a clear written authorization from the party they are representing which sets out the terms and conditions of their mandate;
    c. being well informed of the case and the position of the party they are representing;
    d. being available for conference calls, hearings and other events scheduled by the presiding Member;
    e. complying with any time limits set by the Tribunal, as well as any other directions or orders given by the Tribunal;
    f. complying with the Tribunal's Rules of Procedure, except where the rules require the services of a lawyer;
    g. fulfilling any undertakings given to the Tribunal or to another party, including confidentiality undertakings;
    h. refraining from any activity that would undermine the proper administration of justice, such as knowingly presenting false or misleading evidence, failing to disclose the existence of relevant documents or dissuading a witness from giving evidence.

3. Non-lawyer representatives do not have the same representative responsibilities and rights as lawyers in the Tribunal inquiry process. In some instances, the law, or the Tribunal rules, authorize only lawyers to accomplish certain acts, (such as proof of service by a solicitor's certificate under rule 2(3)). Non-lawyers who choose to represent parties before the Tribunal must do so in full knowledge and acceptance of these limitations.

4. Finally, it should be noted that the Tribunal Member presiding over the inquiry retains the authority to limit or exclude the participation of non-lawyer representatives where the Member has formed the opinion that such participation, for example, is likely to hinder, rather than facilitate, the inquiry process.

---

[2] Source: CHRT Website <www.chrt-tcdp.gc.ca>